Aging

CONCEPTS AND CONTROVERSIES

third edition

TITLES OF RELATED INTEREST FROM PINE FORGE PRESS

Critical Thinking for Social Workers: A Workbook, Revised Edition by Leonard Gibbs and Eileen Gambrill

Exploring Social Issues Using SPSS for Windows, Second Edition by Joseph F. Healey, John Boli, Earl Babbie, and Fred Halley

Dimensions of Human Behavior by Elizabeth Hutchison

The Social Work-Out Book: Strength Building Exercises for the Pre-Professional by Alice Lieberman

Social Work Practice by Kimberly Strom-Gottfried

Aging: The Social Context by Leslie Morgan and Suzanne Kunkel

Aging: Social Inequality and Public Policy by Fred C. Pampel

Worlds of Difference: Inequality in the Aging Experience, Third Edition by Eleanor Palo Stoller and Rose Campbell Gibson

Community Resources for Older Adults; Programs and Services in an Era of Change by Robbyn R. Wacker, Karen A. Roberto, and Linda E. Piper

Aging

CONCEPTS AND CONTROVERSIES

Third Edition

Harry R. Moody

National Program Director,
Faith in Action Program,
Robert Wood Johnson Foundation

PINE FORGE PRESS
Thousand Oaks, California
London • New Delhi

For information, address:

Pine Forge Press
A Sage Publications Company
2455 Teller Road
Thousand Oaks, California 91320
(805) 499-4224
E-mail: sales@pfp.sagepub.com

Sage Publications Ltd.
6 Bonhill Street
London EC2A 4PU
United Kingdon

Sage Publications India Pvt. Ltd.
M-32 Market
Greater Kailash I
New Delhi 110 048 India

Publisher: Stephen D. Rutter
Assistant to the Publisher: Ann Makarias
Production Editor: Diana E. Axelsen
Production Assistant: Cindy Bear
Typesetter/Designer: Rebecca Evans/Lynn Miyata
Cover Designer: Ravi Balasuriya

Printed in the United States of America

00 01 02 03 04 05 06 7 6 5 4 3 2 1

Library of Congress Cataloging-in-Publication Data

Moody, Harry R.
      Aging: Concepts and controversies / by Harry R. Moody. — 3rd ed.
          p.   cm.
      Includes bibliographical references and index.
      ISBN 0-7619-8680-4 (pbk.: alk. paper)
      1. Gerontology—United States.   2. Aging—United States.
I. Title
      HQ1064.U5M665   2000
      305.26′0973—dc21   00-008038

ABOUT THE AUTHOR

Harry R. Moody is a graduate of Yale University and received his Ph.D. in philosophy from Columbia University. He has taught philosophy at Columbia University, Hunter College, New York University, and the University of California at Santa Cruz. For more than 20 years, he was at the Brookdale Center on Aging of Hunter College, where he was Executive Director. Currently, he serves as National Program Director for the Faith in Action Program of the Robert Wood Johnson Foundation. He is author of over 75 articles and three books: *Abundance of Life: Human Development Policies for an Aging Society* (1988); *Ethics in an Aging Soceity* (1992); and most recently, *The Five Stages of the Soul* (1997), a study of spiritual growth in the second half of life. He is known for his work in older adult education, and he currently serves as Vice Chairman on the board of Elderhostel. He has also been active in the field of biomedical ethics and is an Adjunct Associate of the Hastings Center, Garrison, New York.

ABOUT THE PUBLISHER

Pine Forge Press is an educational publisher, dedicated to publishing innovative books and software throughout the social sciences. On this and any other of our publications, we welcome your comments and suggestions. Please call or write us at

> **Pine Forge Press**
> A Sage Publications Company
> 31 St. James Avenue, Suite 510
> Boston, MA 02116
> (617) 753-7512
> E-mail: sdr@pfp.sagepub.com

Visit our World Wide Web site, your direct link to a multitude of online resources: www.pineforge.com

Brief Contents

BASIC CONCEPTS I AGING, HEALTH CARE, AND SOCIETY / 1

How do we respond to the rising cost of health care in an aging society? Some have urged that health care costs should be rationed on the basis of age; that is, priority should be given to quality of life rather than extending survival for those who have lived a full life span. But critics argue that such a plan is deeply misguided and that better alternatives are needed.

Family members already provide care at home for the frail elderly. But if it is necessary for an elder to enter a nursing home, should affluent families be able to use the Medicaid program to protect their inheritance? Should families be required to impoverish themselves to pay for long-term care?

If an older person who is mentally competent engages in risky behavior or makes risky investments, does the family have a right to interfere? When is it right to intervene in other people's actions if those actions constitute a danger to themselves? When does such behavior become self-neglect? What happens when others are involved who may be the cause of abuse?

Detailed Contents

APPENDIXES

Preface

This third edition of *Aging: Concepts and Controversies* is published at the start of a new century. Given current demographic trends, tens of thousands of Americans born in 2000, the year of its publication, will live to see the dawn of yet another entirely new century, the 22nd. Readers of this book will also spend the greatest part of their lives experiencing dramatic changes already evident in such fields as telecommunications, biotechnology, and genetics. This phenomenon of ever-accelerating change will produce even more debate and controversy as to how we are to live, individually as well as collectively, in an aging society and in this new century.

This volume responds to this remarkable set of social conditions with the same unique approach that inspired earlier versions of the book. Like other texts, it presents key ideas and content from the field of gerontology. But, more important, it aims to strengthen each student's capacity for critical thinking about issues in the study of aging. As we move into this new century as an increasingly age-conscious society, we all have a stake in developing a better understanding of the subject. This book consciously focuses on issues of interest to all of us as citizens and as educated human beings, not just as potential gerontologists or professional service providers. It takes a similarly broad view toward what aging is all about. From the opening chapter, students are encouraged to see aging not as a fixed period of life but as a process beginning at birth and extending over the entire life course. This open-ended quality of human aging is a theme woven throughout the book: from biological experiments on extending the life span to difficult choices about allocation of health care resources.

The multiple possibilities for how we might age both as individuals and as a society create complex concerns that are important for all of us. New thinking is needed if we are to grasp the central issues at stake. That is why the pedagogical design of this book focuses on controversies and questions rather than on assimilating facts or coming up with a single "correct" view about aging or older people. The readings are selected to accentuate contrast and conflict and to stimulate students to think more deeply about what is at stake in the debates presented here. In contrast to other textbooks, this volume directs the student's attention toward original sources and encourages teachers to provide the tools to appraise claims made in those texts. This strategy is nothing more, or less, than liberal education for gerontology.

The point is not to find the "right answer" to questions raised in the debates in this book. Rather, as students become engaged in the debates, they will appreciate the need for having the factual background necessary to make responsible judgments and interpretations. That is the purpose of the three major essays around which the book's controversies are organized. The data and conceptual frameworks offered in these essays will help students make sense of the controversies, understand their origin, engage in critical thinking, and, finally, develop their own views. The introductions preceding each controversy and the questions that follow reinforce the essential link between factual knowledge and interpretation that is at the heart of this book. This book, then, can best be seen as a textbook constructed to provide drama and compelling interest for the reader. It is structured so as to encourage a style of teaching and learning that is more than conveying facts and methods.

Other, more specific features of the book reinforce this pedagogical approach: The "Focus on Practice" sections demonstrate the relevance of the controversies to care and human services work in our society. The "Focus on the Future" sections make us ever mindful of the accelerating pace of change in our society and its implications. The Appendix offers guidance for researching and writing term papers on aging, and the online resources open up access to tools for tapping the World Wide Web. Whether students reading this book go on to specialized professional work or whether they never take another course in gerontology, my aim is directed squarely at issues of compelling human importance, now and in the future. By returning again and again to those questions of perennial human interest, it is my hope that both teachers and students will find new excitement in questions that properly concern us all at any age.

What is New to This Edition?

The close link between "Concepts" and "Controversies" in each of the three broad domains of human aging—health care, socioeconomic trends, and the life course—proved to be so teachable from the first edition that this organization has been reinstated. Thanks to excellent help from Maria Schmeeckle at the Ethel Percy Andrus Center for Gerontology at the University of Southern California, I have also completely updated and augmented the figures and graphics in the book, bringing them as up-to-date as possible, using an effective illustration wherever appropriate. I also am indebted to Bob Vernon and his student colleagues at the University of Indianapolis for providing a wonderful online appendix of Web-based resources for use in pursuing the issues and controversies addressed by my book. To access this appendix, simply go to the Web site for my book at my publisher's address: www.pineforge.com. I am also grateful to James Peacock at University of

North Carolina, Charlotte, for developing a vastly improved *Instructor's Manual,* available from the publisher upon adoption, that includes an entirely new set of suggested test materials as well as other new resources.

Acknowledgments

In preparing this *Third Edition,* I have also been helped enormously by the many professors around the country who have used earlier editions and have thoughtfully offered ideas on how to improve the book, and I am indebted to them even though some of them may not be named here. It is impossible for me to give adequate acknowledgement to my colleagues at the Brookdale Center on Aging of Hunter College who have helped me over many years to refine the ideas found in these pages. I am especially grateful to Rose Dobrof, Sam Sadin, and Pat Gilberto, who have been friends and colleagues for more than two decades at the Brookdale Center. Many other reviewers have contributed to improve the third edition of the book, including the following:

Jacqueline Angel, University of Texas at Austin

Spencer Blakeslee, Framingham State College

Jane A. Brown, Baldwin-Wallace College

Susan Calvano, Gannon University

Deborah D. Dougherty, Syracuse University

David Hall, Wipissing University, Canada

Sharon King, Michigan State University

Catherine Marrone, State University of New York at Stony Brook

Kathleen L. McKenna, Bunker Hill Community College

James Peacock, University of North Carolina, Charlotte

Ellen Watkins, Illinois College

Scott D. Wright, University of Utah

Finally, I want to pay tribute to Steve Rutter, Publisher of Pine Forge Press, who provided the original stimulus for this book. Above all, I thank my wife Elizabeth, patient reader and thoughtful commentator, and my children, who have made all the difference in my life.

Prologue: America as an Aging Society

It is no secret that the number of people over age 65 in the United States is growing rapidly, a phenomenon recognized as the "graying of America." The numbers are staggering. There has been a 30-fold increase in older people in the United States since 1870: from 1 million up to nearly 32 million in 1990—a number now larger than the entire population of Canada. During recent decades, the 65+ age group has been increasing twice as fast as the rest of the population.

As a result, the U.S. population looks different from what it did early in the 20th century. Life expectancy at birth was 47 in 1900, but at the end of the 20th century it was 76. A hundred years ago, only 4% of the population was over the age of 65, but today, that figure has jumped to 13%. The pace of growth will continue in the first decades of the 21st century, when the huge **baby boom generation**—those born between 1946 and 1964—moves into the ranks of senior citizens. The proportion over age 65 will increase in the future to 20% by the year 2030. This rate of growth in the older population is unprecedented in human history. Within a few decades, one in five Americans will be eligible for Social Security and Medicare, contrasted with one in eight today.

We usually think of aging as strictly an individual matter. But we can also describe an entire population as "aging" or growing older, though to speak that way is a metaphor. In literal terms, only organisms, not populations, grow older. Still, metaphorical or not, there is no doubt about a key trend in contemporary society: The average age of the population is increasing and the proportion of the population made up of people over age 65 is rising. This change in the demographic structure of the population is referred to as **population aging** (Redburn, 1998).

Population aging results more from a drop in the numbers of children than from people living longer. In 1900, America was a relatively "young" population: The percentage of children and teenagers in the population was 40%. By 1990, that proportion of youths had dropped to 24%. By contrast, seniors increased from 4% in 1900 to 13% in 1990, with larger increases still to come. During the next several decades, overall population growth in the United States will be concentrated among middle-aged and older Americans.

The United States is not the only country undergoing population aging. Life expectancy at birth in Japan, for example, is 81 years, the highest in the world. In Germany, Italy, and Japan, the population is aging and also actually shrinking in total size because of low birthrates. Think of the state of Florida today as a model for population aging, that is, a population where nearly one out of five people is over the age of 65. We can ask: How long will it take various nations to reach "Florida-ization"? The answer is that Italy will look like Florida today by the year 2003, Japan by 2005, and Germany by 2006. France and Great Britain will resemble Florida a decade later and the United States will not reach Florida-ization until 2023.

Population aging also shows up as an increase in the **median age** of the entire population, that is, the age for which half the population is older and half the population is younger. The median age of the U.S. population in 1820 was only 17 years; by 1900 it had risen to 23 and by 1990, to 33 years. In the first years of the 21st century, the median age of the American population is estimated to be 36; by 2030 it will rise to 42 years. This shift, too, is another measure of the dramatic impact of population aging.

It is clear, then, that populations "age" for reasons different from how individuals do, and the reasons have to do with demographic trends. In the first place, population aging occur because birthrates decline. With a smaller proportion of children in the population, the average age of the population will go up. Population aging can also come about because of improvements in life expectancy: people living longer on average. Finally, the process of population aging can be influenced for a time because of birth **cohorts.** This term refers to groups of people who are born at particular times and who thereby experience common **life events** during the same historical periods. The cohort born just before World War II, for example, was relatively small and thus has had minimal impact on the average age of the population. Quite the opposite is true of the large baby boom generation coming after them. At least for a time, baby boomers will dramatically hasten the aging of the U.S. population.

In short, then, trends in birthrates, death rates, and the flow of cohorts all contribute to what we see as population aging. What makes matters confusing is that all three trends can be happening simultaneously, as they have been in America in recent decades. Population aging, then, is more complex than it seems. Casual observers sometimes suggest that the American population is aging mainly because people are living longer. But that impression isn't quite accurate because it fails to take into account multiple trends defined by demographic factors of fertility, mortality, and the flow of cohorts.

A demographic description does not explain the reason these trends happen in the first place. One logical question is this: Why has this process of population aging occurred? The rising proportion of older people in the population can be explained by **demographic transition theory,** which points

Exhibit 1. Percentage Increase by State of the Elderly (age 65+) and Oldest-Old (age 85+) Populations: 1995-2020

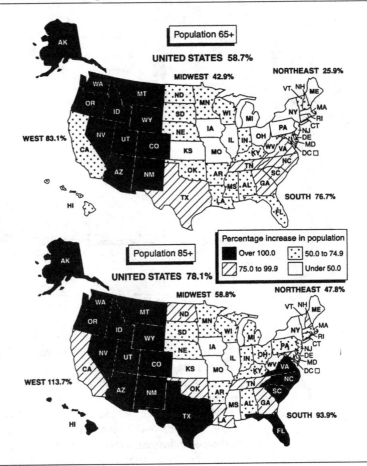

SOURCE: U.S. Bureau of the Census (1997).

to the connection between population growth and the economic process of industrialization. In preindustrial societies, there is a generally stable population because both birthrates and death rates remain high. With industrialization, death rates tend to fall while birthrates remain high for a period, and thus the population grows. But at a certain point, at least in advanced industrial societies, birthrates begin to fall in line with death rates. Eventually, when the rate of fertility is exactly balanced by the rate of mortality, we have a condition of stability known as zero population growth (Chu, 1997).

The industrial revolution of the 19th century brought improved agricultural production, improved standards of living, and therefore an increase in population size. At the same time, there came a shift in the age structure of the population, known to demographers as the demographic transition. This

Exhibit 2. Actual and Projected Increases in the Elderly (65+) and Oldest-Old (85+) Populations

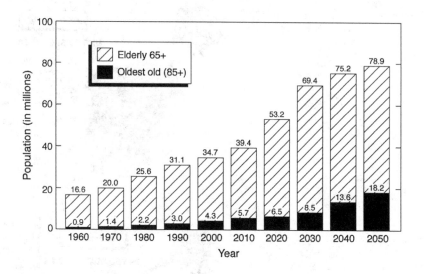

SOURCE: U.S. Bureau of the Census (1997).

was a shift away from a population with high fertility and high mortality to one having low fertility and low mortality. That population pattern is what we see today in America, Europe, and Japan. The result in all industrialized societies has been population aging: a change in the age distribution of the population.

Most developing countries in the Third World—in Africa, Asia, and Latin America—still have fertility rates and death rates much higher than advanced industrialized countries. For the United States in 1800, as for most Third World countries today, that population distribution can be represented as a population pyramid: many births (high fertility) and relatively few people surviving to old age (high mortality). For countries that are approaching zero population growth, that pyramid becomes replaced by a cylinder: Each cohort becomes approximately the same in size.

As we have seen, the increased number of older people is only part of the cause of population aging. It is important to remember that overall population aging has actually been brought about much more by declines in fertility than by reductions in mortality. The trend toward declining fertility in America can be traced back to the early 19th century, and the process of population aging has causes that date back a long time. To complete the demographic picture, we need to point to other factors that influence population size and composition, such as improvements in the chance of survival of people at different ages, or the impact of immigration into the United States, largely by younger people. But one conclusion is inescapable. Today's in-

Exhibit 3. Elderly as a Percentage of Total Population and Distribution of Elderly by Age and Sex, Selected Years, 1940-2025

Age and Demographic Group	Year							
	1940	1950	1960	1970	1980	1990	2000	2025
Population age 65 and older (in thousands)	9,556	12,752	17,250	20,919	26,148	31,978	35,407	61,395
Population age 65 and older as a percentage of total population	6.8	8.0	9.1	9.7	11.1	12.3	12.4	18.2
Population age 75 and older as a percentage of total population	2.0	2.5	3.1	3.8	4.4	5.2	5.9	7.6
Population age 85 and older as a percentage of total population	0.3	0.4	0.5	0.7	1.0	1.3	1.5	1.9
Certain age and sex groupings as a percentage of population age 65 and older								
Men 65 and older	48.4	46.8	44.5	41.5	40.3	40.6	41.6	44.7
Men 65-74	34.8	32.6	30.2	26.8	26.2	25.8	23.9	27.9
Men 75-84	11.9	12.2	12.2	12.3	11.3	12.0	14.1	13.5
Men 85 and older	1.7	2.0	2.2	2.4	2.7	2.9	3.6	3.4
Women 65 and older	51.6	53.2	55.5	58.5	59.7	59.4	58.4	55.3
Women 65-74	35.8	35.7	35.7	33.9	31.9	28.4	30.7	
Women 75-84	13.4	14.7	16.3	19.1	19.3	20.0	21.1	17.6
Women 85 and older	2.3	2.8	3.5	4.7	6.5	7.5	8.9	7.0
Total age 65 and older	100.0	100.0	100.0	100.0	100.0	100.0	100.0	100.0

SOURCE: U.S. House of Representatives (1998), and Office of the Chief Actuary, Social Security Administration, 1997.
NOTE: Projections are based on intermediate assumptions.

creased proportion of people over age 65 springs from causes that are deeply rooted in American society. Population aging is a long-range trend that will characterize our society into the 21st century. It is a force we all will cope with for the rest of our lives.

But how is American society coping with population aging? And how are the major institutions of society—government, the economy, the family— responding to the aging of a large number of individuals? The answer, in simplified terms, is rooted in a basic difference between individual and population aging. As human beings, we are all quite familiar with individual aging. It is therefore not surprising that, as a society, we have devised many policies and practices to take into account changes that predictably occur in the later years, for example, retirement pensions, medical interventions for chronic illness, and familiar government programs such as Social Security and Medicare.

Whether it involves changes in biological functioning or changes in work roles, individual aging is tangible and undeniable: a pattern we observe well enough in our parents and family members, not to mention in ourselves. But population aging is more subtle and less easily observed. We have many institutional policies and programs to deal with individual aging. But our society is just beginning to wrestle with the controversies generated by the population aging trends now emerging, with the prospect of even more dramatic debate and change in the decades ahead. The fact that these demographic changes are so significant and are stimulating so much ferment in our society's fundamental institutions is one important reason why this book is organized by controversies along with the facts and basic concepts that lie behind them.

Our society's response to population aging can best be summed up in the aphorism that generals prepare for the "next" war by fighting the "old" one over again. That is to say, in our individual and our social planning, we tend to look back to past experience to guide our thinking about the future. Thus, when the railroad was first introduced, it was dubbed "the iron horse." But it wasn't a horse at all, and the changes that rail transport brought to society were revolutionary, beyond anything that could be expected by looking to the past.

The same holds true for population aging. We cannot anticipate the changes that will be brought about by population aging by looking backward. Population aging is historically unprecedented among the world's societies. Moreover, we should not confuse population aging with the process of individual aging. An aging society, after all, is not like an individual with a fixed life span. Why is it that people are so often fearful when they begin to think about America's future as an aging society? Part of the reason is surely that many of us are locked into images of decline that are based on prejudice or on outdated impressions of what individual aging entails. Because our social institutions have responded to aging as a problem, we tend to see only losses and to overlook opportunities in the process of aging.

An important point to remember is that the solutions to yesterday's problems may not prove adequate for the challenges we face today. Social Security, for example, has proved to be a vital program that protects older Americans from the threat of poverty in old age. But Social Security was never designed to help promote second careers or new forms of productivity among older people. We may need to think in new ways about pensions and retirement in the future. Similarly, Medicare has proved to be an important, though expensive, means of guaranteeing access to medical care for older people. But it was never designed to address the problem of long-term care for elderly people who need help to remain in their own homes. Finally, as the sheer number of people over age 65 increases, America as a society will need to consider what institutions and policies are best able to provide for the needs of this growing population.

Social gerontologist Matilda Riley has pointed out that our failure to think deeply about population aging is a weakness in gerontology as a discipline. Gerontologists know more about individual aging than about opportunity structures over the whole life course. A good example is the way the life course itself has been shaped, with transitions from education to work to retirement. These transitions do not seem to prepare us well for an aging society in the future. In effect, we have a "cultural lag" in facing the future. We know that in the 20th century the age of leaving the workforce to retire had been gradually going down, while the age for leaving schooling has been going up. Riley points out that if we were to project these trends into the future, sometime in the 21st century people would leave college at age 38 and immediately enter retirement! This scenario, of course, is not serious. But it does make a serious point. We must not take current trends and simply project them into the future.

Part of the problem is that we have less knowledge than we ought to have about the interaction between individual lives and the wider society. During the 20th century, nearly three decades were added to human life expectancy. Now more than a third of adult life is spent in retirement. People over age 65 are healthier and better educated than ever before. Yet opportunity structures are lacking to integrate this older population into major institutions of society such as education or the workplace. We have yet to design a blueprint for what an aging society of the future might look like. Today, we grow old very differently from the way grandparents did, so it does little good to look backward as we anticipate the 21st century (Krain, 1995).

The challenge is to change our way of anticipating the future by thinking critically about our underlying assumptions. This task of critical thinking may actually be more difficult in gerontology than in other fields, because of the familiarity of aging itself. Revolutionary changes took place in the 20th century, but most of us tend to assume that aging and the human life course have remained the same. In spite of our commonsense perceptions, however, history and social science tell us that the process of aging is not something fixed but is both changeable and subject to interpretation.

Taking a more critical and thoughtful stance, we know that "stages of life" have been viewed very differently by different societies. Even in our own society, the experience of growing older is not uniform, but means very different things to individuals depending on their gender, race, or ethnicity. From this perspective, a familiar practice like retirement turns out to be less than a century old and now is in the process of being reexamined and redefined. Even in the biology of aging, scientists are engaged in serious debate about whether it is possible to extend the maximum human life span from what we have known in the past.

In short, wherever we look—in biology, economics, the social and behavioral sciences, or public policy—we see that "aging," despite its familiarity, cannot be taken as a fixed fact about human life. Both individual aging and population aging are socially and historically constructed, subject to interpretation, and therefore open to controversy, debate, and change. What aging will mean for us now that the 21st century has begun is not something we can predict merely by extrapolating from the present and the past. Still less can the study of aging consist of an accumulation of facts to be assimilated, as if knowing these facts could somehow prepare us for the future. The changes are too far-reaching for such an approach.

What we need most of all is to see facts about individual and population aging in a wider context: to understand that facts and theories are all subject to interpretation and revision. That is the second major reason why the study of aging in this book is presented in the form of controversy and debate, offering all of us an opportunity to reflect on and construct an old age worthy of "our future selves."

Aging, Health Care, and Society

F ive hundred years ago, the Spanish explorer Ponce de León embarked on a journey to the new world in search of the fountain of youth. He never found it. Instead, he discovered what is today Florida, the state with the largest percentage of elderly people. Ponce de León might have smiled at the irony of how his discovery turned out. But discoveries often have a way of turning out differently than expected. When we think about medical advances in our time, things also have turned out unexpectedly. For instance, people are living longer today, but is the prolongation of life into old age always a benefit? Or have recent gains in human **life expectancy** instead been a prolongation of decrepitude and frailty? Will further medical advances only make matters worse? This question was raised nearly three centuries ago by Jonathan Swift in his satirical novel *Gulliver's Travels*.

The Challenge of Longevity

The Case of the Struldbruggs

Swift describes a voyage to the fictional country of Luggnagg, where his hero, Lemuel Gulliver, meets a strange group of beings, the "Struldbruggs," who are a race condemned to immortality. It turns out that, for the Struldbruggs, unlimited life span has not proved the blessing it promised to be. Longevity has come but without good health. Their existence is a dismal prolongation of senescence and decay, a nightmare-like unlimited existence in a nursing home, as Swift describes them:

> They were the most mortifying sight I ever beheld. . . . Besides the usual deformities in extreme old age, they acquired an additional ghastliness in proportion to their number of years, which is not to be described.
>
> The diseases they were subject to still continue without increasing or diminishing. In talking they forget the common appellation of things, and the

names of persons, even of those who are their nearest friends and relations. . . . The least miserable among them appear to be those who turn to dotage, and entirely lose their memories.

In describing the Struldbruggs, Swift raises a question that is still of compelling interest:

> The question therefore [is] not whether a man would choose to be always in the prime of youth, attended with prosperity and health, but how he would pass a perpetual life under all the usual disadvantages which old age brings along with it.

No doubt Swift exaggerates to make his point. To speak of the usual disadvantages of old age misses the positive aspects of aging. Today, we see countless examples of older people who are not debilitated or dependent but, rather, maintain health and vigor into their later years. Yet Swift's vision does raise profound questions about our values: Are the old less valued than the young? Where will we find the resources to take care of the frail elderly? Could medical breakthroughs have unforeseen consequences for society, either for good or for ill? These questions have no easy answers. Indeed, they are at the center of the controversies examined in this book.

As a beginning, however, we will examine several major challenges that people face as they grow older. The first is the challenge of coping with an aging body. Medical advances that help people live longer may seem beneficial, but a longer period of physical and mental decline has implications for individuals and for society. The second challenge is that of maintaining a valued place in society while aging. Older people are often stereotyped as marginal members of society. However, as the average age in the United States steadily increases, we are beginning to confront questions of when people cross from capable old age to dependency. Finally, as individuals grow older, they do so in the wider context of an entire society that is undergoing a shift to population aging.

Biomedical advances. There are those who believe that biology will save us from the problem. They argue that biomedical researchers can meet the challenge of longevity by developing techniques for delaying the onset of debilitating conditions in old age. In effect, they hope to postpone sickness until a final, brief period of life and so eliminate prolonged dependency. Other biologists believe that we can make good on Ponce de León's dream and discover a fountain of youth by altering the fundamental biological mechanism that makes us grow old. Whether by delaying illness or by actually preventing biological aging, the scientific optimists believe the "Struldbrugg problem" can eventually be solved.

Rationing health care. Their optimism is not shared by all. Others believe that hard choices are called for, and they doubt that biology will save us from making those choices. We do better, it is said, to acknowledge the biological limits rather than hope for a technological fix for the problems that often come with aging. In this spirit, ethicist Daniel Callahan wants to reject high-tech medical care used to prolong life for the very old (see Reading 1). Instead, he believes, we do better to ration health care on the basis of age. He recommends forgoing life-extending treatment once elderly people have lived out a full and natural life span.

Providing long-term care. If more and more of the population live into advanced old age, we will see growing numbers of frail, chronically ill elderly in need of long-term care, at home or in institutions. Without unexpected biomedical advances, growing numbers will suffer from joint diseases, dementia, and other chronic disorders that keep them from living independently. In that case, long-term care will loom even larger in the future than it does today. Opinions differ about who should bear the cost of that care, but paying the bill for longevity is already a serious challenge to society.

Self-determined death. Neither prolonged debilitation nor rationing of health care is popular with most Americans. But growing numbers today do feel that decline and a diminished quality of life might be sufficient reasons for ending one's own life. Those who hold this view usually reject the idea of society setting limits but would instead leave the choice about dying up to the individual. Advocates of this idea believe that deliberate termination of treatment must be more openly recognized by law and should be actively supported by health care services.

So here we have four different answers to the Struldbrugg dilemma: hoping for a medical breakthrough, making tough cost-cutting decisions, providing long-term care, or permitting individuals to end life. All are ways of coping with the prospect of a prolonged period of frailty and dependency at the end of life.

The biology of longevity, the economics of health care, and the right to die are all related. By appreciating some key facts about biology, economics, and death and dying, we can better approach the debates surrounding these critical issues. A difficulty arises from the fact that contemporary medical practice in the United States is based on a strategy of curing disease, not promoting health. This familiar strategy has led to the conquest of many killer diseases, such as smallpox and polio, thus permitting a greater portion of the population to reach old age. Since the 1960s, death rates from cardiovascular disease, on an age-adjusted basis, have dropped by 50% (National Center for Health Statistics, 1995). The net effect of all these interventions has been to raise average life expectancy in America from 47 years in 1900 to 76 years today.

But gains in life expectancy are not the same as raising maximum life span. Life expectancy, or expected years of life from birth, has risen, but **life span,** which is defined as the maximum possible length of life, has evidently not changed at all. The causes of maximum life span and of aging itself still remain unknown. Biological evidence suggests that maximum life span is genetically determined, and therefore fixed, for each species.

Normal Aging

In a broad sense, one might say that aging begins at birth, but we normally identify aging with changes that come after maturity. Gerontologists often use the term **normal aging** to describe this underlying irreversible process characteristic of each species. Aging can be defined as a time-dependent series of cumulative, progressive, intrinsic, and harmful changes that begin to manifest themselves at reproductive maturity and eventually end in death (Arking, 1998). Primary aging would describe those changes that occur over time independent of any specific disease or trauma to the body, while secondary aging would describe disabilities resulting from forces such as disease.

Normal aging is not a disease but eventually leads to functional declines and involves increased susceptibility to death from specific diseases. For example, decline in short-term memory, wrinkled skin, and gray hair are signs of normal aging. But they are not symptoms of disease and need not result in greater susceptibility to death. On the other hand, a weakening of the immune system does increase susceptibility to death.

The idea of normal aging is important because health care professionals see mainly sick people; as a result it is easy to develop negative stereotypes about older people. One common stereotype depicts older people as frail and sick. But in fact, more than three-quarters of people over age 65 are healthy enough to engage in most **activities of daily living,** such as bathing, dressing, or preparing meals. More than four out of five report no limitations on such everyday activities of life.

Longevity and Disease

Steps toward health promotion, such as improved diet or increased exercise, can reduce the likelihood of illness and thus increase life expectancy. These steps may also reduce morbidity in later life, but not invariably so. It is clear that declines in the mortality rate need not be matched by decline in morbidity or sickness. Data drawn from the National Health Interview Survey between 1969 and 1986 indicated that there was little significant improvement in self-reported health among the American population. Whether morbidity will be diminished remains an open question (Crimmins and Ingegneri, 1993). A patient with a strong cardiovascular system who has Alzheimer's disease can live for many years in a dismal state resembling the Struldbruggs. Thus hopes for delaying disease by health promotion strategies alone may not be convincing. The rising curve of survival into old age does nothing to alter maximum life span, the "natural death" that the Struldbruggs longed for.

Basic research on the biology of aging has been pursued by scientists in the hope of avoiding the Struldbrugg problem, namely, having enormous numbers of frail, sick, and dependent elderly people whose lives are prolonged in a desperate condition. But do we really need to understand the biology of aging itself? Couldn't we simply concentrate research attention on eliminating the big "killer diseases" that prevent people from living out a full life span? For example, if the most prevalent diseases of later life, the big killers such as stroke, heart disease, and cancer, were eliminated, wouldn't we all live to be over 100? Unfortunately, the answer is no. Curing all these diseases would give us, on average, only a decade or so more years before some other disease would kill us.

And what if we could eliminate all diseases? Would immortality then be at hand? Alas, the answer is no. Time and chance take their toll in the form of accidents. Unless we turn our attention to the underlying vulnerability, we may change life expectancy but not maximum life span. Still worse, we might succeed in creating more and more long-living "Struldbruggs." It is quite possible that future declines in death rates will actually have a small effect on average life expectancy but create much larger numbers of very sick old people. The fear, then, according to critics, would be a Struldbrugg scenario: an expansion of morbidity.

This trend will take place, pessimists believe, because medical technology is improving survival prospects for patients with disabling conditions associated with fatal disease—Alzheimer's would be a good example. But the basic progression of the disease itself remains unchanged. The length of life lived with disability for this part of the population would increase. A second reason for expansion of morbidity is the increasing role of nonfatal diseases of aging, such as arthritis and some forms of stroke (Olshansky et al., 1991).

But optimists take a different view. Analysis of data from the National Long Term Care Survey by Kenneth Manton and colleagues showed a significant decline in chronic disability in the elderly population between 1982 and 1989. The proportion of nondisabled persons who were disabled actually became *lower* in this period, reflecting improved treatments and lifestyle modifications. For instance, the number of those over age 65 with high blood pressure dropped from 46% in 1982 to 39% in 1989; the percentage with emphysema went down from 8.9% to 6.4%. The research team concluded that there is reason to expect further progress in the future as successive generations of older people show gains in income and education. But on the negative side, they pointed to conditions requiring special attention, such as musculoskeletal problems (e.g., arthritis) and dementia (Manton, Corder, and Stallard, 1997).

Basic research may find answers to the common diseases of old age. But beyond curing specific diseases, researchers are also looking at interventions that could delay or actually reverse the process of aging. Here we confront very far-reaching questions about the impact of research on the biology of aging. Are we talking about moving the average life expectancy closer to the upper limit of the maximum life span—say, closer to age 120? Or are we talking about pushing that upper limit itself—say, up to age 150 or 200? In either event, successful antiaging interventions would have large consequences for human society. But until such research yields practical results, society will have to cope with the consequences of having more long-living individuals, and one of those consequences is vulnerability to disability and disease.

Exhibit 4. Death Rates for 10 Leading Causes of Death Among Older People, by Age: 1995 (rates per 100,000 population in age group)

Cause of Death	65+	65 to 74	75 to 84	85+
All causes	5,069.0	5,263.5	5,851.8	15,469.5
Cardiovascular (heart) disease	1,842.5	799.9	2,064.7	6,484.1
Malignant neoplasms	1,136.2	868.2	1,364.8	1,823.8
Cerebrovascular diseases (e.g., stroke)	414.9	137.2	481.4	1,636.5
Chronic obstructive pulmonary diseases	269.3	160.6	351.8	527.8
Pneumonia and influenza	223.7	57.2	233.2	1,035.7
Diabetes mellitus	132.6	86.5	162.7	278.0
Accidents	85.1	44.8	98.4	268.2
Nephritis	60.6	24.5	72.5	207.1
Alzheimer's disease	59.8	11.1	73.4	274.7
Septicemia	50.8	21.2	59.5	173.1

SOURCE: Adapted from the National Center for Health Statistics (1996).

Epidemiology of Aging

While aging is not in itself a disease, it tends to increase susceptibility to disease. The diseases of later life are the subject of **geriatrics,** or the medical specialty of old age. Much has been learned about the major diseases of later life, and this subject is important for debates about aging, health care, and society (Blumenthal, 1983).

The discipline of **epidemiology** originally acquired its name from the scientific study of epidemics. Today, epidemiology is more broadly understood as the use of statistical techniques to study the distribution of diseases in human populations. A basic goal for the epidemiology of aging is to understand what diseases are most common among older people and to assess their impact (White et al., 1986). An example of how epidemiological data are organized is given in Exhibit 4, indicating the 10 leading causes of death among older people.

Major Diseases in Old Age

Today, three-quarters of all deaths of persons over age 65 come from just three diseases: heart disease, cancer, or stroke. Death rates for heart disease and stroke have declined in recent decades, but they still remain the leading causes of death. If heart disease were completely eliminated as a cause of death, the average life expectancy for someone 65 years old would increase 7 years, ignoring the likelihood of death from one of the other leading causes. Though often not listed separately as a cause of death in vital statistics, Alz-

Exhibit 5. Top 10 Major Chronic Health Conditions for Elderly Americans: 1992

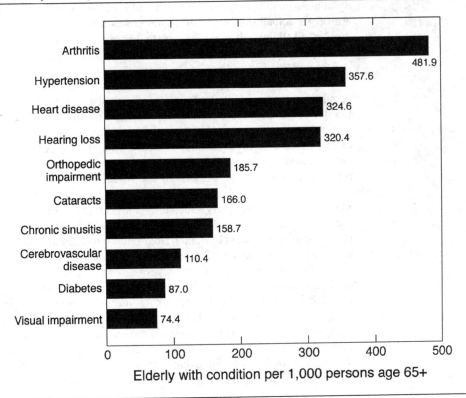

Elderly with condition per 1,000 persons age 65+

Arthritis	481.9
Hypertension	357.6
Heart disease	324.6
Hearing loss	320.4
Orthopedic impairment	185.7
Cataracts	166.0
Chronic sinusitis	158.7
Cerebrovascular disease	110.4
Diabetes	87.0
Visual impairment	74.4

SOURCE: Treas (1995) and National Center for Health Statistics (1994).

NOTE: Rates apply to the noninstitutionalized population. People may have multiple chronic conditions.

heimer's disease is probably the fourth leading cause of death, chiefly afflicting people over age 65.

Along with diseases causing death, we also need to consider **chronic conditions** that persist for a long period, whether or not they cause death. Chronic illness is much more common among the old than among the young. Rates of chronic illness are 46% for those over age 65 compared with only 12% for those younger than that age. Four out of five older people have one or more chronic conditions, such as arthritis (National Center for Health Statistics, 1982). Exhibit 5 shows the top 10 chronic conditions for people over age 65. It is important to note that some conditions such as cataracts and hearing impairment can be limiting but not life threatening. Other conditions, such as hypertension (high blood pressure) and heart disease, can lead to fatal disorders.

Arthritis. Arthritis is the most familiar and most prevalent chronic disease of later life; it afflicts nearly half of all persons over age 65. Arthritis is basically an inflammation of the joints, also commonly known as rheumatism, and it is the most important cause of physical disability in the United States. Symptoms include red, swollen joints and muscles, and pain. Like cancer, arthritis is actually the name of a group of as many as 100 different syndromes, all slightly different. Rheumatoid arthritis can occur at any age, but osteoarthritis is distinctly related to old age and is aggravated by degeneration caused by wear and tear of the joints.

Degenerative joint disease in some variety is almost certain to occur in people over the age of 70. But the effect of such disease on activities of daily living varies tremendously, and most people live full and active lives with it. The cause of arthritis is not known and there is no cure, but treatment of the disease to reduce symptoms can be effective. Painkilling drugs are not costly, but for the very serious cases, joint surgery—for example, for hip replacement—can be expensive (Moskowitz and Haug, 1985).

Osteoporosis. Osteoporosis is a condition involving deterioration or disappearance of bone tissue leading to loss of strength and, often, a fracture. The disease is most prevalent in women (four times more common than in men), especially beyond the age of menopause. About one in four white women over the age of 65 will develop osteoporosis. When weakened by osteoporosis, bones are more likely to break, with serious consequences. It is estimated that 1.5 million fractures occur each year as a result of osteoporosis. A hip fracture, often related to a fall, is one of the most common events precipitating admission to a nursing home. About half of those who survive fractures will require some form of long-term care. It is estimated that more than 12 million people in the United States have osteoporosis, and the annual cost of fractures resulting from the disorder is in the range of $7 to $10 billion.

Parkinson's disease. Parkinson's disease is a degenerative neurological disorder characterized by a loss of control over bodily movement. It afflicts about half a million people in the United States, chiefly older people. Symptoms include tremors or shaking of the head and hands, leading to progressive loss of muscle control and the ability to walk unaided. Parkinson's disease is an age-related syndrome, and its incidence increases steadily after middle life. For reasons not clear, dementia is quite prevalent among persons with Parkinson's and depression is common as well. Parkinson's appears to be caused by lack of dopamine production in brain cells, but there is no treatment that slows the progression of the disorder. Drug treatment, however, such as L-Dopa, can relieve symptoms of the disease (Mcgoon, 1990).

Cancer. Recent research has focused on aging and changes in the immune system of the body. The strength of the immune function begins to decline after puberty, and with advanced age comes a propensity to autoimmune disorders, such as arthritis, as well as higher rates of cancer. In fact, cancer is overwhelmingly a disease of old age, with half of all cancers occurring in people over age 65. The incidence of malignant disease rises progressively with age, so that cancer today is the second leading cause of death for Americans over age 65, accounting for 21% of deaths among older people (London and Morgan, 1995).

Different forms of cancer seem related to age but actually may be the result of longer exposure to cancer-causing chemical substances known as carcinogens, for example, asbestos or tobacco. Because of successful medical interventions, older people who have cancer are living much longer than in the past, so that cancer can often become a chronic disease. A person diagnosed with slow-growing or controllable forms of cancer may live many years, thus increasing the cost of medical care over a longer period of time. But it is also possible to prolong the period of dying for those with incurable cancer, raising questions not only about the ethics of termination of treatment but also about the cost of life prolongation.

Cardiovascular disease. The leading cause of death for people over age 65 remains cardiovascular disease, which includes stroke and heart disease (Kaiser, Morley, and Coe, 1997). Heart disease alone accounts for 43% of all deaths, while stroke accounts for another 9% of those deaths. In the past two decades, there has been a decline of almost 30% in deaths from heart disease, and the cardiovascular condition of older people shows wide variations. For example, according to a study by the National Institute of Aging, the heart of a healthy 80-year-old man performs about as well as that of a man in his 20s. But unfortunately, about two-thirds of men in their 70s have clear evidence of coronary heart disease, so death rates remain high. The economic cost of heart disease is staggering: more than $120 billion a year, according to figures from the American Heart Association.

Stroke refers to a neurological deficit in the brain arising from a sudden disturbance in the blood supply. A stroke often results in some degree of paralysis, often on one side of the body, or loss of other functions, such as speech, and it can result in coma or death. While one stroke in three leads to immediate death, another one in three also causes permanent disability, such as paralysis or loss of speech (Gorelick, 1994). It is estimated that there are 3 million stroke survivors and 150,000 deaths resulting from stroke each year in the United States. The costs for caring for impaired stroke victims are estimated at $30 billion, and the loss of quality of life can be substantial for the patient and family (Locke, 1983).

Dementia and Alzheimer's disease. Dementia is an organic mental disorder involving progressive loss of the capacity to think and remember. The disease is characterized by confusion and memory impairment and may manifest itself in a wide range of symptoms, such as wandering or losing things. But Alzheimer's patients may also retain social skills and conceal their impairment to some degree. Alzheimer's disease is often hard to diagnose and separate from other cognitive impairments, such as multi-infarct dementia, a condition caused by a series of small strokes affecting the brain.

Senile dementia of the Alzheimer's type (SDAT), or Alzheimer's disease, is the most common cause of irreversible dementia of old age, accounting for two-thirds of all dementing conditions. The proportion of people with Alzheimer's disease rises dramatically each decade over age 65, doubling every five years. It strikes 1 out of 12 persons beyond age 65, but the figure rises to 1 out of 3 among those over age 80. Between 2 and 4 million Americans may now be afflicted with the disease. About half the residents of nursing homes have some form of dementia, usually Alzheimer's but sometimes multi-infarct dementia that comes from accumulated damage to blood vessels in the brain.

Alzheimer's is a disease caused by deterioration of brain cells with characteristic plaques and tangles. The disorder typically progresses through stages from mild memory loss, through significant cognitive impairment, to very serious confusion and the loss of ability to handle dressing, bathing, or other activities of daily living (Reisberg, 1983). By the end stage of the disease, there may be incontinence, loss of speech, and inability to walk. A definitive diagnosis of Alzheimer's is difficult, and confirmation usually can be made only upon autopsy. But a mental status examination, such as the Folstein Mini-Mental Status Exam, can assess functional cognitive losses produced by the disease (Folstein, Folstein, and McHugh, 1975).

Alzheimer's disease is irreversible and generally foreseeable in its course. In advanced stages, taking care of patients at home usually becomes impossible. The result is often placement in a skilled nursing home, sometime lasting many years. Even when a patient's quality of life has severely declined, it is feasible to use modern medical techniques to cure physical illness, such as pneumonia or kidney failure, and thus prolong the lives of patients with dementia, resulting in great expense.

In terms of the health care rationing debate, it is worth noting that acute care medical intervention can actually be less costly than long-term care over a period of many years for Alzheimer's patients (Cassel, Rudberg, and Olshansky, 1992). The National Institute on Aging projects that, unless a cure for Alzheimer's is found, by the middle of the next century there could be 14 million people with the disorder, costing billions of dollars each year to maintain.

Alzheimer's appears to be one of the most common diseases of late adulthood, and genetic factors clearly contribute to Alzheimer's disease with early onset. One indication of genetic influence is the association between Down's syndrome and Alzheimer's. Genes found on chromosomes 21 and 14 are known to cause early-onset Alzheimer's while another gene on chromosome 19 seems linked to late-onset Alzheimer's. The lifetime incidence among relatives of patients with Alzheimer's is estimated at around 20%, or three to four times the risk among comparable groups. But if Alzheimer's were purely a genetic disease, then it would be expected that identical twins would always come down with the disease. But they do not, thus proving that environmental factors must also play a role in expression of the disease.

While Alzheimer's disease is a major problem, its prevalence among older people should not be exaggerated. Most people over age 65 *do not* suffer from memory defects or dementia. Among all those over 65 there are significant numbers—perhaps one in five—who have a mild or moderate mental impairment. But this means the overwhelming majority of older people have no mental impairment at all. Memory defects are quite limited among the large majority of older people, and the capacity for learning and growth in later life remains impressive.

Responses to the Geriatric Diseases

Interventions to eliminate specific diseases, such as cancer or stroke, can increase life expectancy but they do not raise the maximum life span of individuals. Furthermore, curing a life-threatening illness does not prevent other nonfatal diseases that may bring chronic disability. One of the big questions about aging, health, and society is whether our health care system is capable of dealing with a growing elderly population. Many critics charge that it is not. Medicine in the United States has often neglected the dimensions of caring for and coping with people who have illnesses that cannot be cured, such as Parkinson's or Alzheimer's. That neglect is a matter of special concern for geriatric medicine.

The approach of clinical medicine in most advanced countries, and certainly in the United States, focuses almost entirely on discrete causes of disease and their cures. Intrinsic causes within the organism—in other words, vulnerabilities of aging—are not well understood and are not the focus of attention. The paradox here is that, because survivorship has been increasing, aged adults have become an increasing proportion of society and the remaining fatal diseases, whether cancer or Alzheimer's, are themselves linked to the process of aging itself.

Will a breakthrough in understanding the biology of aging solve this problem? There are reasons for doubt. For example, there is a whole class of age-related changes not likely to be affected by improved DNA repair, a favored mechanism for explaining biological aging. Many physical changes of old age are in the wear-and-tear category and include the decalcification of bones, uric acid incrustation in cartilage of joints, and cholesterol accumulation in blood vessels. It might be possible for geriatric medicine to develop strategies to control causes at this tissue level and to introduce rehabilitative methods that improve the clinical picture. The problem is that many of today's dramatic techniques of medicine—such as kidney transplants or bypass surgery—do nothing to affect the underlying process of aging. We can keep patients alive but do little to improve their quality of life.

An overview of geriatric epidemiology gives a concrete picture of what the Struldbrugg problem might look like in the future. Success in curing some forms of cancer or heart disease could raise life expectancy but leave larger numbers of people living with the burden of chronic diseases such as stroke, arthritis, or osteoporosis. A pragmatic approach to geriatric medicine might favor interventions designed to reduce the burden of age-related diseases on individuals as well as society.

Advances in medical technology and adoption of health promotion measures could bring average life expectancy closer to the theoretical upper limit of the maximum life span. But would we then be inadvertently multiplying the Struldbrugg problem? Those in favor of age-based health care rationing would cut funding from expensive life-sustaining interventions for the very old and redirect those resources toward quality of life interventions for age-related diseases. But there are serious questions about whether paying for extended long-term care is actually cheaper than any alternative we can imagine. Those questions involve the economics of health care.

Economics of Health Care

The emergence of the Struldbrugg problem in America has had an important public consequence: rising health care expenditures for the very old. The elderly, comprising 12% of the population, consume more than 36% of total health care expenditures: more than four times what is spent on younger people. This increase has taken place against a background of escalating costs for health care in general. The proportion of gross national product for health care today is twice what it was in 1965 when Medicare was first enacted, and Medicare remains at the center of the economics of health care for aging.

As a nation, the United States has gone from spending approximately 9% of its gross national product on health care in 1980 to spending 14% today, which is more than a trillion dollars a year. Health care is now the second-biggest item in the federal budget, consuming 20 cents of every dollar spent. Health care spending is growing faster than the general rate of overall inflation, and it remains a concern for the future.

Reimbursement Systems

Medicare is the chief federal government program that pays for health care for 34 million Americans over age 65 and another 5 million disabled people of all ages. Medicare has serious limitations. It doesn't pay for the first day of hospitalization and doesn't cover hearing aids, prescription drugs, eyeglasses, or dental care. It excludes long-term care coverage, except for limited periods after hospital discharge. Like most insurance plans, Medicare has deductibles and copayments and covers only 80% of physician expenses. Medicare is available primarily on the basis of age, in contrast to **Medicaid,** a health program funded by both the states and the federal government, which is available to those below the poverty line and pays for a substantial portion of nursing home care. Both Medicare and Medicaid are administered by the **Health Care Financing Administration,** a federal government agency.

Medicare was created in 1965 as part of the Social Security Act. Before its inception, half of people over age 65 were without health insurance, while today almost all are covered. Much has changed in the Medicare population in more than three decades. Since 1965, life expectancy has risen from 70 to 76, and the 65+ population grew from 9% to 13% of the total U.S. population. Medicare has had a major impact on the health of the elderly popula-

Exhibit 6. Where the Medicare Dollar for the Elderly Goes: 1995

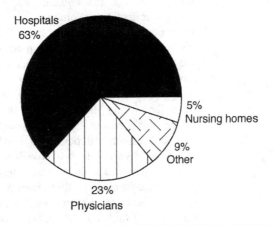

SOURCE: U.S. Health Care Financing Administration, Bureau of Management and Strategy; data from the Office of Health Care Information Systems.

NOTE: Total exceeds 100% due to rounding.

tion: Since 1965, half as many Americans die of heart attacks and a third as many die of strokes, a tremendous accomplishment.

Like Social Security, Medicare is funded from payroll taxes with additional funding from general revenues and premiums from beneficiaries. But unlike Social Security, whose problems will surface decades into the future, Medicare faces short-term financing problems. Overall, Medicare spending has risen much faster than the cost of living, and thus it presents government policymakers with a serious problem of cost control.

Medicare actually comprises two distinct programs: Part A, or hospital insurance, and Part B, supplementary medical insurance, covering non-hospital care, which primarily includes physicians' services along with limited home and outpatient services. Medicare Part A is financed by a compulsory payroll tax administered as part of the Social Security tax levied on all wages up to a specified limit. Part B covers 80% of doctors' bills as long as Medicare beneficiaries pay a $50 monthly premium, deducted from their Social Security checks. Exhibit 6 shows where money from Medicare goes.

In 1965, when it was first enacted, Medicare spent just over $3 billion. Today, it spends nearly $200 billion each year. Nearly two-thirds of that total goes to hospitals, where acute care and often high-technology care are provided. If health care rationing on the grounds of age were ever to be introduced, it would probably take place in the Medicare program and would show up in the large sector of Medicare concentrated on hospitals (Inlander and MacKay, 1991).

Although Medicare expenditures have climbed dramatically, Medicare still covers only about half of the **out-of-pocket medical expenses** of older people. These amount to approximately $1,500 per beneficiary per year—roughly the same percentage as when the Medicare program was first enacted in 1965. Part of the reason is that Medicare Part B reimburses 80% of physician's "reasonable charges." In fact, the amount reimbursed may or may not reflect actual charges in a specific geographic area. In practice, many physicians in the past have charged much more than the officially allowed Medicare rate, with the patient paying the difference. But that practice has now begun to change. Since 1993, physicians participating in Medicare are limited by law to charging no more than 15% above the rate set for Medicare reimbursement. That law was passed because fewer than half of physicians were willing to accept the official Medicare reimbursement as full payment because the reimbursement rate was too low. Because of limits on what Medicare will pay, around 30% of Medicare beneficiaries also have private **Medigap** policies to cover the remainder of their medical bills.

Our experience so far with both the Medicare and the Medicaid programs gives cause for concern about what might happen if cost-containment measures cut down on physician reimbursement from government insurance programs. Officials of the American Medical Association have rejected the idea of the government setting limits on the fees of doctors, and they have argued that such fee limits will inevitably bring about de facto "rationing" of health care.

Similar fears erupted after 1983 when Congress passed a law limiting payments to hospitals under Medicare. In 1983, Congress responded to the high hospital costs of Medicare Part A by introducing a **prospective payment system**: a new way of reimbursing hospitals for the cost of treating Medicare patients. Under prospective payment, hospitals receive a fixed amount for a specific diagnosis given to a patient, no matter how long the hospital stay or the type of service required. Over the past decade, the new prospective payment system has held down hospital costs below what they would have been without these cost controls. But critics charge that the system resulted in higher outpatient costs and in displacing costs onto families of patients who were discharged "quicker and sicker."

The system created hundreds of diagnostic categories, or **diagnosis related groups** (DRGs), that determined how much a hospital would be reimbursed for patient care. The system in effect gives an incentive to hospitals to keep their costs down and discharge patients as early as medically feasible. Despite protests and concerns about the new reimbursement system, DRGs have become an accepted fact of life in American hospitals.

In the 1980s, it was widely feared, and sometimes charged, that these cost-containment measures would lead to "patient dumping" by hospitals along with widespread deterioration of patient care. Such widespread deterioration did not occur, but the 1983 law did have its intended effect in holding down Medicare Part A spending from where it would have been otherwise. Cost containment for hospital spending proved effective, but during the 1980s Medicare Part B spending for physicians tripled in size, and outpatient costs—for example, home health care spending—has increased dramatically in recent years.

In part because of the success of DRGs, Congress acted to try to control costs under Medicare Part B. In 1989, Congress passed another law revising the Medicare reimbursement formula for physicians in different medical specialties. The new legislation introduced a so-called Resource Based Relative Value Scale (RBRVS) in the national Medicare program. Since its introduction, the RBRVS has meant that primary care health providers, such as internists, geriatricians, and family practitioners, are paid somewhat more for their services, while other specialists, such as surgeons, are paid less than before.

This reimbursement scheme is an effort to give more incentive to medical specialties involving prevention, health promotion, and quality of life, in contrast to the expensive technologies of life prolongation. Doctors who spend more time with patients but do not use "high-tech" procedures are to be paid more than previously. The aim of the new measures is to provide a more equitable system of payments reflecting skill, time, and intensity of work.

Despite the ongoing debate about the particulars of Medicare, it commands strong public support as a universal public insurance program for physical illness. By contrast, no consensus has been mobilized to make Medicare a universal public program for long-term care, mental health treatment, or early detection of illness, which might be beneficial in the long run. Medicare will not pay for regular physical examinations or for dental care. The elderly make use of mental health services at only about half the rate of younger people, partly because of lower rates of mental illness but also because today's older generation is likely to be more resistant to using formal services.

Despite recent changes in Medicare, preventive care and health promotion still remain low priorities. Critics of this bias note that a great deal of money is spent on acute conditions such as heart disease and cataracts. An expensive procedure like coronary bypass surgery remains fully covered by Medicare, but a physical exam to detect hypertension or recommend a preventive diet or medication is not. Medicare reflects the same priorities favored by the health care system for the younger population. The emphasis on technology is in some ways perplexing. Contrary to popular belief, it was not medical technology but largely social interventions—such as improved sanitation, diet, and public health measures—that accounted for the big drop in mortality in the 20th century. Perhaps further efforts to make lifestyles healthier could help control health care expenditures for our aging population.

Prospects for the Future

The escalating cost of health care has become a major problem for the elderly and for other groups in society. Will biomedical technology help solve the problem or only make it worse? Since World War II, the federal government has subsidized research and development in biomedical science to an extraordinary degree: up from $3 million to more than $11 billion today. Yet, unlike in private industry, where investment in research and development leads to lower costs, advances in medical technology have led to higher costs for health care. With each new technique for life prolongation, the lives of those who are very sick and very old can be extended, but at greater and greater cost.

In the future, this picture seems likely to grow worse, for two reasons: First, health care costs, even after adjusting for inflation, have continued to rise faster than inflation; and second, the aging of America's population will add to these expenses because incidence of illness and disability is higher among the old. Those over age 65 spend about four times as much money on health care as do people below that age. In terms of overall spending for health care, expenditures for those above age 65 now amount to a third of all health care spending, while comprising only about 12% of the total population.

It is difficult to predict future levels of use of health care by an aging population. In the past, there were gross underestimates of expenses. In 1965, planners projected the cost of supplemental medical insurance under Medicare. But in 1970, only five years later, there had been a fivefold increase in the cost of that program. Between 1967 and 1975, the rate of use in both parts of Medicare had gone up from 367 per 1,000 enrollees to 528 per 1,000. Recently, Medicare has been growing at a rate three times the rate of inflation.

In light of these huge and rising costs, it is not surprising that there is widespread concern about the prospect of an aging population in the future. Based on U.S. Census Bureau middle-range population forecasts, it is estimated that the Medicare costs for the **oldest-old** (age 85+) could increase sixfold by the year 2040 (Schneider and Guralnik, 1990).

Long-Term Care

Dramatic end-of-life decisions often attract public attention in debates about the economics of health care. But a far more widespread phenomenon is taking place away from the hospital intensive care ward, in nursing homes, where growing numbers of older people spend years receiving costly care for chronic health problems. *Long-term care* refers to the support given to individuals suffering from chronic illnesses or disability that limit their ability to live independently.

How will we provide these needed services? The problem cannot be left for the future. Growing numbers of frail, chronically ill elderly are already in need of long-term care, at home or in institutions. Instead of expecting old people to die early or hoping to find the biomedical fountain of youth, we face the practical problem of how to pay for long-term care, whether furnished by families or in institutions. Opinions differ about who should bear the cost of that care.

Consider the hypothetical case of George and Martha Walton. They never expected to live into their 80s, but they're glad to be alive and glad still to be in their own home in Middletown, USA. Maintaining their home, however, has gotten harder since George had his first stroke. Martha finds herself exhausted, and her arthritis prevents her from getting around the way she used to. They can't afford to hire help to come into their home. They've looked into alternative housing arrangements. But the one thing George fears most of all is that his condition will deteriorate and that he'll end up in a nursing home. They wonder, where will they turn next?

Housing for the Elderly

George and Martha Walton are struggling with long-term care issues, whether or not they use the term *long-term care*. They like living in their own home and don't want to go into an unfamiliar residential facility. Their situation, which is typical, shows why the distinction between long-term care services and housing for the aging is not so clear-cut. Housing for the elderly was long conceived as primarily a bricks-and-mortar affair; that is, it was mainly a matter of financing or subsidizing shelter dedicated to the elderly. But increasingly, it is recognized that social as well as physical concerns must be taken into account in planning for housing for the aging population (Newcomer, Lawton, and Byerts, 1986).

Today, around 90% of the older population in the United States live in conventional housing, mostly single-family houses or apartments. Only 5% of the population over age 65 are in nursing homes, while another 5% reside in some form of housing that provides congregate facilities or services. Even among the oldest-old, only about a quarter of the population live in specialized or supportive housing. But health care for an aging population inevitably brings consideration of housing needs as well.

Housing in the early 21st century of an aging U.S. population may produce greater demand for low-cost housing and coordination of services. Building affordable housing for an aging population is a challenge as funding from the federal government for senior housing continues to shrink. Community-based services, such as home health and adult day care, are likely to be important in the future as cost containment pushes providers to look for alternatives to expensive, medicalized facilities like the nursing home. At the same time, interest in new approaches to senior housing is also growing (Gamzon, 1995).

Today, many public and private sector strategies for planned senior housing are being discussed, including a wide range of options: naturally occurring urban and rural, leisure-oriented, and continuing care retirement communities; board-and-care homes; adult day care and respite services; and homesharing, assisted living, and medical care in residential settings.

What are the alternative housing arrangements that George and Martha Walton might want to look into? In the past, a home for the aging might have been an option. A home for the aging is a facility typically sponsored by a church or fraternal organization and dedicated to helping the impoverished or dependent elderly. These residential facilities are less common today, but commercially developed retirement communities have been attractive to the more affluent elderly (Hunt et al., 1983).

Also to be noted is a newer type of facility that has recently been growing rapidly: the **continuing care retirement community** (CCRC) (Sherwood et al., 1997). These offer a combination of housing and health care and typically provide a level of social support for those who find it difficult to live on their own. Originally known as "life care communities," CCRCs promise residents the opportunity to "age in place" by combining different levels of health care with housing, nutrition, social supports, and physical security. CCRCs integrate these services under a comprehensive insurance contract, which may involve a form of managed care.

Some analysts believe that, at their best, CCRCs can offer a nearly ideal model of health care for the elderly because of the guaranteed commitment and integrated approach to housing and long-term care needs (Somers and Spears, 1992). But there are drawbacks. CCRCs are often expensive: George and Martha probably would not qualify. A distinguishing feature of the life care community is that residents are committed to remain there for the rest of their lives: They pay a large entry fee, which can be above $100,000, in return for guaranteed support as they grow older and more frail.

If CCRCs represent the high-income end of the housing continuum, it is also important to note the prevalence of **domiciliary care facilities** and **board-and-care homes** at the lower end (Morgan, Eckert, and Lyon, 1995). These are homes that provide mainly custodial or personal care for elderly and disabled people who don't need the intensive medical supervision of a nursing home but do need help with activities of daily living.

Another approach is shown by **assisted-living facilities** that offer residents and their families a homelike environment with personal but very limited supportive care (Fisher, 1995). The atmosphere of assisted living promotes a maximum degree of autonomy, independence, and privacy. But assisted-living complexes can also cover the entire continuum of care: from those that provide only minimal help with activities of daily living to those that allow residents complete nursing care. Assisted living is much more attractive than a nursing home. As hospitals have been pressured to discharge patients earlier, and as nursing homes have become facilities for very sick people, assisted living has grown rapidly.

A great advantage of assisted living is that, in contrast to separate retirement communities, assisted-living providers expect to integrate themselves into a surrounding service network, including adult day care, meals on wheels, or other social services. Payment for assisted living today is mostly private out-of-pocket, but insurance and public financing seem likely to grow in the future. Already, 1.2 million people are living in approximately 50,000 assisted-living facilities around the United States, and it is one of the fastest growing businesses in the country. Still, some questions about assisted living remain unanswered, for instance, what happens when residents begin to get sick or seriously impaired? In contrast to skilled nursing facilities, state regulation of assisted living is not consistent.

The federal government subsidizes rental housing through the **Section 202** and **Section 8 housing programs** for low-income elderly (Lawton, 1980). But housing programs have often looked only at "bricks and mortar" and have often failed to take into account the social support needs of older people, which tend to increase with advancing age. Those needs are better taken into account through **congregate housing**: a residential facility providing nutrition, housekeeping, and supportive services for the marginally independent elderly (Chellis et al., 1982). Along the same lines, there has been interest in **shared housing,** an alternative housing arrangement involving either group residence with shared common areas or a homeowner who rents out unused rooms (McConnell and Usher, 1980). These options, including subsidized housing, have mostly been targeted at low-income elderly.

On the other hand, for those who can afford it, middle-class and more affluent groups will want to consider leisure-oriented retirement communities, which are different from CCRCs and other supportive living arrangements because they lack a formalized network of social support services. Residents are mostly on their own and are expected to live quite independently. Leisure-oriented communities have a prominent focus on recreational activities: by both image and reality, they cater to a healthy, **young-old** (ages 65-74) population who aim at enjoying the positive lifestyle offered by such communities.

A question for the future is whether these leisure communities can maintain their recreational identity as the population begins "aging in" and a demand for increasingly intensive support services develops (Folts and Streib, 1994). Still another question, discussed in later chapters of this book, is whether it is socially desirable for housing for the elderly to be segregated from younger generations.

All of these options are important, but they probably won't help George and Martha Walton, who just want to remain in their own home. Much of the effort at improved housing for the aging has been planned housing initiated either by government or by the private marketplace. But the overwhelming majority of older Americans live in unplanned housing, typically in the same home and neighborhood they had lived in before, just like George and Martha.

Chronic Care in Old Age

An explosion in demand for long-term care is found in all advanced industrialized countries as a larger and larger proportion of the population survive into old age. Compared with the general population, older people on average show twice as many days in which activities are restricted because of chronic conditions. The most important of these conditions are arthritis, rheumatism, and heart conditions. But there are sharp differences in the impact of such conditions among the population over age 65. Apart from people in nursing homes, the young-old have only a very small proportion—5.7%—who say they need help with everyday tasks such as household chores, dressing, or going shopping. By contrast, among the oldest-old, the percentage of those needing help jumps to 40%.

Long-term care is fundamentally different from acute health care. Acute care is appropriate for conditions that result from a single cause that can be treated by medical intervention. By contrast, the chronic conditions requiring long-term care last a long time and may have varied causes. Examples of such disorders are Alzheimer's disease or other dementias and stroke leading to permanent disability. The result is an inability to perform activities of daily living (Katz et al., 1963).

What does this mean in concrete terms? Consider the case of George Walton, who has reached this point. A series of small strokes has affected him profoundly. His condition has deteriorated to the point where he needs help getting to the bathroom and even feeding himself. Martha has done the best she can, but their children, Carol and Robert, have now convinced them that the only alternative is for George to go into the local Middletown nursing home, where he can get the round-the-clock care he needs now. George and Martha are afraid to do it; they don't like the idea at all.

Nursing home can refer to any residential facility giving some degree of nursing care (Johnson and Grant, 1986). In the United States, about 80% of these facilities are proprietary, that is, operated as commercial, for-profit organizations. Most of the rest are voluntary or nonprofit, with a few run by municipal governments. Among these facilities, it is useful to identify the *skilled nursing facility,* which is an institution offering medical care, such as a hospital, as well as everyday personal care services to elderly or disabled people. An *intermediate care facility,* on the other hand, gives health-related care to patients needing a lower level of support. An *extended care facility* offers short-term convalescent help to patients coming from hospitals for an extended period of time.

In light of George Walton's deterioration, he will probably enter a skilled nursing facility. As shown in Exhibit 7, 1.7 million older Americans live in nursing homes, more than all those in hospitals at any one time but still less than 5% of the elderly population. The growth of today's nursing home population is partly a tribute to medical technology and the success of the longevity revolution. But it may also reflect the fact that American society has failed to provide accessible alternatives to living in a nursing home, namely, long-term care based in the home or community. A sizable number of people in nursing homes don't need to be there and could probably live in community settings if appropriate services were available. Estimates of the proportion of the nursing home population in this situation range from 10% to as high as 40%.

Why are George and Martha so fearful about entering a nursing home? Are they right to be afraid? The nursing home has been called a *total institution,* a term used to describe organizations such as prisons, mental hospitals, or boarding schools, that is, facilities that treat people like inmates rather

Exhibit 7. People Age 65+ in Need of Long-Term Care: 1980-2040

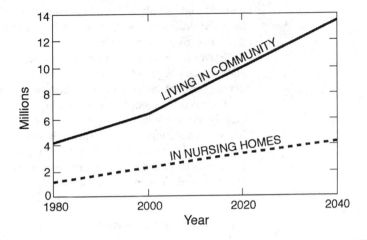

SOURCE: Manton and Soldo (1985).

than as individuals (Goffman, 1961). In a nursing home, the daily regimen is carefully organized and scheduled, so residents may lose any sense of control over their environment and easily become depressed.

A lot of criticism of nursing homes finds support in careful observational studies of life in these facilities (Gubrium, 1975), and there have been devastating journalistic stories that expose poor conditions in some institutions. Responsible studies have shown how the poor quality of nursing homes arose out of repeated failures in public policy to guarantee good-quality long-term care (Vladeck, 1980). In light of these facts, it is understandable that so many older people today fear institutionalization.

On the other hand, it is important to remember that, just as with schools or hospitals, the quality of nursing homes varies widely. The stereotyped view that "all nursing homes are bad" is mistaken and does a disservice not only to those who must place their loved ones who actually need skilled nursing care in a nursing home, but also to the untold numbers of devoted nursing home employees. Government monitoring and regulation have meant that nursing homes today are much better than in the past, and improvements continue (Kane and Kane, 1987). Moreover, there is a common misconception that, once someone is admitted to a nursing home, residence there is inevitably a life sentence. In fact, 32% of those in nursing homes stay less than a month; many return home.

How likely is it for older people to anticipate entering a nursing home? Among all people over 65, only about 4% to 5% (1.6 million people) are in nursing homes at any given time. In other words, it is a mistake to imagine that most or even many older people are in nursing homes. But this low 4%-5% figure may understate the importance of nursing homes in the lives of the very old. It turns out that the percentage of those who will spend some time in a nursing home before they die is much larger: up to 40% of people age 65. The lower 4%-5% figure that comes from citing the percentage of people in a nursing home only at a single point in time is called the **four percent fallacy** (Kastenbaum and Candy, 1973). Note that this difference between these two figures—5% in a nursing home at a single point in time versus 40% over the course of a lifetime—shows the dramatic difference in how statistics can be presented. These two figures correspond, respectively, to a **cross-sectional** versus a **longitudinal** view of nursing home residence.

The need for chronic care varies significantly among subgroups of the elderly. For those between ages 65 and 74, the chance of entering a nursing home is small: only 1 in 100. But for those over age 85, the chance goes up to nearly 1 in 5. Specific risk factors that increase the chances for nursing home placement include mental impairment, chronic disability, advanced age, and spending time in a hospital or other health facility.

Functional Assessment

A key step in determining what kind of help people need is professional long-term care assessment. This determination often serves a "gatekeeping" role in deciding what services will be provided. A **multidimensional functional assessment** takes place when a geriatric professional, such as a doctor or nurse, conducts a full examination of an elderly person's physical, mental, and social conditions. This test is more than a physical examination because it covers activities of daily living as well as physical and mental health. Among the most important of these activities are feeding, toileting, transferring out of a bed or chair, dressing, and bathing (Katz and Akpom, 1976). A comprehensive functional assessment also looks at social and economic resources as well as elements such as the physical environment and even strain on caregivers. All these elements play a part in determining the kind of service an elderly person may need.

Does a failing score on an assessment test mean that it's time to enter a nursing home? Not necessarily. The key to interpreting an assessment lies in the functional emphasis, that is, asking how an impairment actually affects performance of daily tasks such as shopping, doing housework, handling personal finances, and preparing meals. A comprehensive approach to functional assessment is important because someone with, for instance, mild memory impairment or limited physical mobility may be able to live quite satisfactorily alone in an apartment as long as the environment remains safe and a neighbor or relative comes by regularly to help out. For the same reason, a physical assessment not only looks at biological organ systems but also medications being taken and the impact of sensory impairment on activities of everyday life.

Gerontologists have developed specialized instruments or questionnaires designed to carry out functional assessments (Kane and Kane, 1981; Gresham and Labi, 1984). A classic example is the Older American Resources and Services (OARS) questionnaire, one of several widely used assessment instruments in the United States today (Duke University, Center for the Study of Aging and Human Development, 1978). The OARS questionnaire gathers information on topics such as mental status, self-assessed well-being, social contact, and help from family. A second part of the instrument looks at the use of services ranging from physical therapy and meal preparation to employment training or transportation. By carefully assessing activities of daily living in this way, professionals can identify the exact type of help a client needs, for example, a walker device for people at risk of falling, a homemaker-home health aide for someone who can't prepare meals, and other kinds of help that might enable people to remain safely in their own homes.

The Continuum of Care

A 65-year-old today can expect to live, on average, for 17 more years. During those years, it is likely that health status and service needs for any individual will change, so provision for long-term care will have to reflect changes over time. Why shouldn't long-term care services take into account those changes? The idea of a **continuum of care** is based on the goal of offering a range of options responsive to changing individual needs, whether from less intense to more intense, whether at home or in an institution (Brickner et al., 1987).

The ideal of a continuum of care expresses the aim of keeping elderly people as long as possible out of nursing homes—the most expensive and service-intensive setting. The aim instead is to maintain people in the home, in independent living, or in the least restrictive alternative. If we were to take seriously the ideal of a continuum of care, it would mean spending more money to enlarge the availability of community-based long-term care services. Such a goal, however, would serve the purpose of promoting maximum independence and personal control and might also help minimize public expense (Koff, 1982; Eustis, Grenberg, and Patten, 1984). The reasons for promoting a continuum of care include both choice and economics, but it is rare to find a full continuum of care in most communities in America. There are many gaps, and the long-term care service system remains fragmented and confusing.

Health care is important, but we should not forget the importance of social care and social contact for people like George and Martha. What happens to Martha when she is left all alone after George has entered the nursing home? Who will watch out for her and her needs? If George and Martha were lucky, Middletown, USA, would have a full range of services to help them out, as a few communities already do. The kinds of formal support services delivered to the home that are shown in Exhibit 8 can play a key role in enabling frail elderly people to remain in their homes as long as possible (Quinn et al., 1982).

All these formal support systems provide a degree of companionship, monitoring, and concrete services for frail, isolated elderly. They also can

Exhibit 8. Support Systems Across the Continuum of Care

Senior centers and congregate housing	Senior citizens centers offer social and recreational opportunities. Lunches provided for elderly at neighborhood sites, such as senior centers and churches.
Telephone reassurance	Usually performed by peer volunteers. Daily phone calls, typically shortly after wake-up time, to provide support and monitor status. If telephone is not answered, someone goes to the home to check on the client.
Friendly visitor	Volunteer visits, talks with or reads to a frail homebound elder.
Chore service or handyman	Visiting person performs outdoor tasks, such as lawn care or snow removal, for the elder; also may make small repairs and perform minor maintenance.
Homemaker	Visiting person performs light housekeeping (cleaning, washing dishes, vacuuming, laundry, meal preparation, etc.) and food shopping. Services are performed in the home, but do not include services that involve touching the client.
Meals-on-wheels	Home delivery of meals supported under the Older Americans Act.
Personal care	Visiting person performs trained but not professional work for the elder, such as bathing, dressing, assistance with grooming. Services include touching the client but not health care services.
Home health care	Performed by a trained professional, such as a registered nurse or licensed practical nurse. Administration of medications, measurement of blood pressure, changing of dressings, and so on.
Mental health services	Provision of counseling, psychotherapy, and psychological support services. Practitioners may be psychiatrists, psychologists, nurses, and social workers.
Outpatient medical care	Provision of a range of services, from checkups and diagnostic monitoring through therapeutic procedures short of hospital admission.
Adult day care	Supervision of dependent elderly by professionals or paraprofessionals, offering respite to family caregivers.
Board and care	Residential placement. Meals are provided, housekeeping is performed, and medication reminders are available.
Intermediate care nursing home	Placement in a facility with (less than 24 hour) supervision and nursing care provided.
Skilled nursing facility	Placement in a nursing home with 24-hour services provided by registered nurses.
Inpatient hospital care	Admission as an inpatient to an acute care facility.

SOURCE: Krain (1995).

shore up the social network of family, friends, and neighbors, that is, the totality of informal helping relationships that maintain integrity and well-being. Gerontologists have documented the crucial role that these natural support systems play in providing social care and their enormous role in the lives of the elderly (Cantor, 1980).

If George Walton had not needed round-the-clock care, there might have been alternatives for him other than going into a nursing home. For instance, why not provide some nursing home services on a daytime basis while he still remains at home? That, in essence, is the strategy of adult day care, which is usually offered five days a week. Patients are transported to a health facility, where they are given needed services as a group during the day and then returned to their homes at the end of the day.

Another alternative is home health care in which home care aides provide health-related tasks such as rehabilitation exercises or toileting and transferring patients who are bed-bound (Ginzberg, Balinsky, and Ostow, 1984; Portnow, 1987). Visiting nurses who can dispense medication and perform skilled nursing functions also play a critical role. Home health services have expanded dramatically in recent years, as an alternative to institutionalization and as a means of ensuring speedier discharge from hospitals.

These forms of community-based long-term care can sometimes be more cost-effective than a residential nursing home because housing costs are not involved. Most important, they offer an opportunity for those who can to remain relatively independent. The experience of other countries, such as Canada and Great Britain, suggests that adult day care, along with other varieties of community-based long-term care, will have to play a larger role in the United States than it has in the past (Kane and Kane, 1985).

Paying for Long-Term Care: An American Dilemma

The costs of long-term care are going up fast (see Exhibit 9). In the past 10 years, the annual growth rate for nursing home care has been more than 12%. Expenditures now stand at over $40 billion and are still climbing. Few individuals can afford to pay the complete cost of long-term care in a nursing home. Usually, Medicaid pays part of the bill. Future projections of long-term care expenditures suggest that private (out-of-pocket) and Medicaid sources will continue to be the biggest source of payment for nursing homes.

Advocates for home care or other community-based care believe that staying at home costs less than entering a nursing home, just as George and Martha want. But home care is not always cheaper than institutional care. Cost estimates for home care typically fail to include the real value of housing or the value of unpaid family caregiving. Moreover, there is sharp debate about whether we ought to pay family caregivers to do what is normally done by family members for one another.

The experience of Medicaid payment for nursing home care suggests that some frail elderly people may end up being placed in nursing homes because institutional care, not community care, is the only form of long-term care paid for under the American system. When advocates for the elderly propose large increases in long-term care, the question arises of who will pay for the expansion (Rivlin and Wiener, 1988).

Should families provide for their own or should the cost of expanded long-term care be covered by government? Paying for long-term care remains an American dilemma.

Exhibit 9. Projected Nursing Home Expenditures for People Age 65+ by Source of Payment: 1990-2020

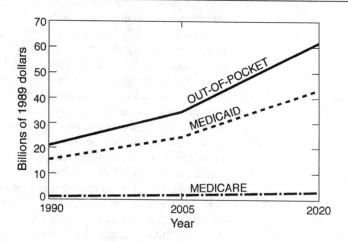

SOURCE: Brookings/ICF (1990).

Self-Determined Death

Our society so far has not been prepared to explicitly ration health care on the grounds of age. Nor do we seem willing to face up to the public policy problem of paying for long-term care. But at some point, decisions become unavoidable, and therefore we turn to our last option: self-determined death. Modern biomedical technology not only enables larger numbers of people to survive into old age, it has also forced care providers to make explicit decisions about the end of life. The result has been a continuing debate about the so-called right to die, which involves choices from forgoing life-sustaining treatment all the way to assisted suicide (Glick, 1992). In this debate, the elderly occupy a central place.

Today, this debate is taking new forms as the cost of health care rises and the oldest-old population increases in numbers. In the future, termination of treatment decisions may unavoidably become intertwined with cost-containment pressures. Instead of individuals claiming a "right to die," we may even see health care providers or policymakers suggesting that some people have a "duty to die" to stop "futile" medical treatment that uses up scarce resources.

This prospect is not just hypothetical. A case in point is the story of Helga Wanglie, who at age 86 broke her hip and was admitted to a nursing home. As a result of complications, Mrs. Wanglie ended up on a respirator and suffered brain damage. The hospital staff felt that, due to her medical condition and advanced age, Mrs. Wanglie should not receive further life support. Her family, however, insisted that treatment be maintained, so the case wound up in court, which agreed with the family. In many other cases, providers have taken a different view and insisted on treating patients, while the family asked to end medical treatment.

Another case in which financial considerations became mixed up with termination of treatment was the 1989 case of *Grace Plaza of Great Neck, Inc. v. Elbaum* (1993). In this instance, Mrs. Jean Elbaum was in a persistent vegetative state (coma) and was being kept alive by tube feeding. Mrs. Elbaum had made it clear that she would not want to be kept alive under such circumstances. But the nursing home refused to honor the family's wishes. Instead, the facility provided treatment and then sued the family for payment of care provided against their wishes.

Over the past 20 years in the United States, discussion about the right to die has developed along legal and ethical lines focused entirely on individual rights and decisions; it has not focused on resource allocation issues. But both the *Elbaum* and the *Wanglie* cases, in different ways, show how end-of-life decisions may now become entangled in considerations about who will pay the bill and whether institutions should expend resources on care that is "medically futile."

The question of medical futility will involve values and will depend on the different treatments involved. A 1987 study looked at several different kinds of treatment that might be withheld from the elderly and explored the differences among them (U.S. Office of Technology Assessment, 1987). Antibiotics, respirators, cardiopulmonary resuscitation, and kidney dialysis are all very different forms of medical technology. A patient's personal decision about one kind of intervention may not hold for another kind. Similarly, a decision may be made in one way at home and differently in a nursing home or in a hospital. The setting could make a big difference in how health care personnel act and what families can expect. Perhaps the most important new developments in the right-to-die debate will center on the question of whether the American health care system can devise practices and forms of treatment that are both respectful of patients' wishes and attentive to the uncertainties involved in end-of-life decisions.

The question arises of whether it is actually in the best interest of depressed or debilitated patients to have life-sustaining care terminated because of poor quality of life. The topic is controversial because the patient's best interest may or may not coincide with the interest of the family or health care providers. When subjective well-being declines and patients want to end their lives, should geriatric health care professionals treat this as a matter of self-determination or as a case of suicide prevention?

Most people are uncomfortable when economic considerations become involved with end-of-life decisions. But increasing pressure for cost containment in health care may make it difficult to keep the two matters separate. In 1990, Congress passed the Patient Self-Determination Act to uphold patients' rights. But analysts quickly noted that the law is expected to decrease costs for health care by ending unwanted care. As financial concerns become intertwined with right-to-die considerations, we may wonder whether "backdoor" rationing of health care could make it more difficult for elderly patients to assert their rights. It is always cheaper to say no to treatment than to say yes.

Debates about costs and self-determination take place against a background of hopes and fears centered on end-of-life decisions. Our hopes are symbolized by the wonderful one-horse shay, or carriage, which lasted "a hundred years and a day" and then fell apart all at once (see Controversy 8). Our common hope, in other words, is to live a long life and "fall apart" all at once without decay. But our fears are symbolized by the horrifying image of Gulliver's Struldbruggs, the same people who today might be wandering in dementia or hooked up to feeding tubes. For increasing numbers of older Americans, self-determined death seems a way to resolve this struggle between hope and fear at the end of life.

Late-Life Suicide

Self-determined death can mean many different things, ranging from termination of treatment to active euthanasia or assisted suicide. Those who favor self-determination for end-of-life decisions generally assume that it is possible to make a rational decision to end one's life, for example, to refuse further treatment and simply permit death to occur. That, at least, is the premise involved in the court decisions that uphold the right to self-determination.

But are these decisions always rational? And if they aren't, does that fact mean that end-of-life decisions cannot be left to individual choice? The question is a difficult one. It is not possible to consider the arguments about end-of-life decisions for older people without taking into account mental health issues: specifically, depression, which is a primary cause of old-age suicide. Suicide is now one of the leading causes of death among the old. The suicide rate for the general population is 12 per 100,000, while the suicide rate for those over age 65 is 17 per 100,000: nearly 50% higher.

How can we understand old-age suicide and its causes? The first great sociological investigator of suicide, Émile Durkheim, distinguished several different types of suicide. He described altruistic suicide, or self-sacrifice for the sake of the group or society (Durkheim, 1897/1951). A soldier giving up his life on the battlefield to save comrades would be an example of such self-sacrifice. This pattern could describe the voluntary death of some elderly persons in preindustrial societies facing conditions of economic scarcity. The same pattern might also apply to end-of-life decisions among elderly people today who fear becoming a burden on their families.

Durkheim also described a form he called anomic suicide, derived from his sociological concept of anomie, or a condition where individuals feel hopeless and cut off from any sense of meaning in life. This condition is relevant to thinking about the position of old age in contemporary society. Today, elderly people commonly experience **role loss** when they give up previous roles upon retirement, the death of a spouse, or the loss of other social positions. Rosow described old age itself in contemporary society as a roleless role, that is, a status with no clearly defined purpose or rules of

Exhibit 10. Suicide Rates for People Age 65+

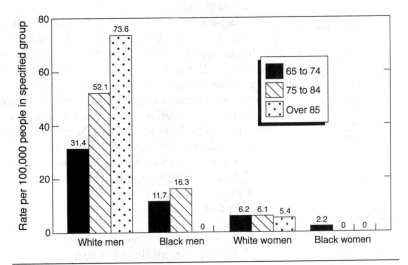

SOURCE: National Center for Health Statistics (1993, 1994).

behavior (Rosow, 1974; Blau, 1981). A final type of suicide described by Durkheim is egoistic suicide, where an individual may not be closely integrated into wider society—for example, among the oldest-old, who have outlived most close relatives. In such cases, it might seem perfectly rational for people to end their lives.

As a general rule, the rate of suicide tends to go up with age and to hit a peak after age 65 in America as in other advanced industrialized countries. Estimates of suicide remain uncertain because there are 100 suicide attempts for every completed suicide. Among the elderly, however, 80% who threaten suicide actually follow through. Furthermore, among the ill elderly, there is no way to estimate those who end their lives by noncompliance with medical treatment or other forms of self-neglect.

There are pronounced differences in suicide rates among subgroups of the elderly, as Exhibit 10 indicates. Among ethnic groups, blacks have a suicide rate only about 60% of the average for whites, and unlike whites, the rate does not increase in old age. For all age groups, men are much more likely to commit suicide than women, and the difference between the sexes widens with advancing age. For example, according to 1980 data, there were 66 completed suicides per 100,000 white males above the age of 85 in comparison to a rate of only 5 for white females. In fact, the highest rate of suicide in the United States occurs among older white men.

Characteristic conditions preceding late-life suicides include loneliness, social isolation, diminished economic resources, the presence of illness or disability, and above all, depression (McIntosh et al., 1994). Depression is an important public health problem for the elderly and must therefore be taken very seriously by clinicians and others who work with older people.

Early identification and treatment for depression remain a key measure for suicide prevention.

In considering depression and suicide in old age, it is important to maintain a balanced perspective. Most older people in fact enjoy good mental health and a positive attitude. A 1987 Louis Harris survey found that 72% of those over age 65 report feeling satisfied with their lives. Even when exposed to stress, older people often show a remarkable capacity for adaptation, for instance, in coping positively with bereavement or chronic illness in later life. Adaptation reflects the capacity of the individual to cope with environmental demands and maintain subjective well-being. But when stress exceeds the capacity for coping, psychotherapy and other mental health interventions may play an important role in maintaining the capacity of those in the last stage of life to make rational decisions about the end of life (Butler and Lewis, 1982).

End-of-life choices must also take into consideration what has been learned about the process of death and dying itself. Glaser and Strauss (1965) described the dying trajectory by which a person passes from good health to progressively worse health to the point of death. In her popular book *On Death and Dying,* Elisabeth Kubler-Ross (1969) developed a stage theory of dying in which the terminally ill individual moves through stages from denial to acceptance. With respect to end-of-life decisions, it seems clear that elderly people who are experiencing a stage of denial or a condition of depression might make different kinds of "rational" decisions about terminating treatment. It would therefore be unwise simply to accept a patient's "spoken choice" at face value. On the other side, clinicians might well have a less positive view of initiating aggressive medical treatment if they were aware that an elderly patient was in a period of terminal decline and facing imminent death.

Conclusion

The overall picture of aging and health care today is a mixed one. On the one hand, some optimists hope for a "compression of morbidity" in which disease is postponed and good health continues until late in life. On the other hand, larger numbers of elderly with physical or mental frailties are now surviving into old age. The need to make choices about treatment and life prolongation is becoming unavoidable.

The root cause of the problem is that contemporary geriatric medicine is largely symptomatic: Health care responds only after people are sick. Responding to symptoms this way is expensive and frustrating. It proceeds the same way that treatment of polio might have gone if specialists had worked to create ever more complex and refined versions of the iron lung instead of finding a vaccine to prevent the disease in the first place. In the same way, the "iron lung" approach to geriatric care is bound to be expensive and frustrating.

The American health care system, including geriatric care, spends a great deal of money on acute care conditions such as heart disease and cataracts. In that respect, Medicare simply reflects the same priorities that are favored in health care for the broader population. An expensive procedure, like a coronary bypass operation, is fully covered by Medicare, but a physical exam to detect hypertension or recommend preventive diet change is not. Such imbalanced emphasis on technology is in some ways perplexing. Contrary to popular belief, it was not medical technology, but largely social interventions—such as sanitation, improved diet, and public health measures—that accounted for the big drop in mortality in infancy and before middle age that occurred at the beginning of the 20th century.

As a universal public insurance program for physical illness, Medicare commands strong public support. By contrast, it has not proved possible to mobilize a consensus behind a universal public program for long-term care or for mental health treatment or for such activities as early detection that might be beneficial in the long run. Medicare will not pay for regular physical examinations or for dental care. Preventive care and health promotion also remain low priorities.

Changing these priorities will be difficult, and solutions to the problems of health care and aging remain elusive. Research on the basic biology of aging will continue, and no one can exclude a dramatic breakthrough that might reshape the conditions of health and sickness in later life. As costs continue to rise, there will be pressure for tough decisions, perhaps even for rationing (Mechanic, 1985). It is unlikely that overt age-based rationing will be adopted in this country, but some form of "backdoor rationing" could come as a result of cost-containment efforts. It seems likely that efforts to liberalize end-of-life decisions will also continue, but we have no way of knowing how many older people or families will decide deliberately to terminate life or where such decisions may lead us as a society. Debates about aging, health care, and society are sure to continue throughout the 21st century.

Should We Ration Health Care for Older People?

> To every thing there is a season, and a time to every purpose under the heaven. A time to be born, and a time to die . . .
>
> —*Ecclesiastes 3:1-2*

It is no secret that we're spending a lot of money on health care for the elderly: Americans over age 65 now account for one-third of all national health care expenditures, more than $200 billion on Medicare alone each year, and that figure is growing. Health care expenditures for the older population have outpaced general economic growth by up to 4.0% in recent years, even though Medicare itself covers less than half of older adults' expenses for health care (Fuchs, 1999).

As America's population grows older, it seems inevitable that we must spend even more. But what are we getting for all that money? Can we really afford so much health care for an aging population, or are we heading toward a health care crisis in the 21st century (Wolfe, 1993)? These questions would have been unthinkable a few years ago. But today, more and more people are asking such questions. Some have even urged that we cut off expensive health care services for the very old.

Rationing health care on grounds of age is troubling to most Americans. How are we to think about the justice, or the wisdom, of spending vast amounts of money prolonging the lives of the elderly? Prolonging life seems desirable, but it isn't cheap. With rising costs and new advances in expensive medical technology, decisions about life prolongation are no longer questions just for medical practitioners. The decisions quickly become questions of economics and social justice: Who will get access to expensive health care resources?

Answers to these questions are not easy to find. Some answers that have been given are disturbing and controversial. One of the most controversial is the idea that someday, perhaps soon, we are going to have to "ration" health care to people above a certain age; in effect, we will be telling older people: "You've lived long enough." Philosopher Daniel Callahan proposes something akin to the sentiment of Ecclesiastes—there is "a time to be born, and a time to die"—in short, a "natural" human life cycle, which people should accept.

Callahan, in his 1987 book *Setting Limits,* provoked enormous debate with a serious proposal to ration health care on grounds of age. But Callahan has not been alone. Others have agreed that age can be a legitimate factor in distributing scarce resources, and some public figures, such as former Colorado Governor Richard Lamm, have called for rationing health care on grounds of age (Daniels, 1988; Lamm, 1993). Callahan has argued that using age as a way of limiting health care access is unavoidable, and he points to European countries, including England, Switzerland, and some Scandinavian countries, that already engage in rationing.

Callahan's questions are basically these: How much medical progress can Americans afford, and how much money do we want to pay to keep an aging population alive longer and longer? How much should younger generations be prepared to pay for health care of the elderly as a group?

Precedents for Health Care Rationing

An important question in the health care rationing debate is a practical one: Has it ever been done before? How is rationing based on age likely to be introduced in America? A few examples are suggestive here.

Denial of kidney dialysis in Britain. In Britain, for many years, kidney dialysis has routinely been withheld from people above a certain age—usually 55 (Aaron and Schwartz, 1984). Doctors in Britain's National Health Service simply didn't refer such patients to clinics that offered dialysis treatment, and the patients died. In addition, despite official denials, it is estimated that in Britain 19% of coronary care units have upper-age limits for admission and 40% have an upper limit for clot-dissolving cardiac therapy (Evans, 1993). CT scans, feeding tubes, hip replacements, and cancer chemotherapy are administered at lower rates than in America. In short, British health care authorities use a variety of mechanisms, including deterring people from seeking health care, delaying services, dilution of quality, or outright denial (Harrison and Hunter, 1994).

British primary care physicians have been forced to serve as gatekeepers for the system; they are responsible for denial of lifesaving care or for imposing an age cutoff. Some officials defended the policy on the grounds that, with limited resources, it made more sense to provide funding to improve quality of life, for example, offering ample home health care for elderly people. But as the covert practice of withholding some treatment for older people became known, public defense of the practice was abandoned (Halper, 1989).

Waiting lines in Canada. In Canada, medical care is provided by a national health insurance system, a plan urged by many for the United States. But during the American debate over national health reform in 1994, there were conflicting views about the Canadian system (Marmor, 1995). Under the Canadian system, virtually no one is deprived of health care because of inability to pay. However, for some forms of care, such as certain surgical procedures that are not needed to save life, it may be necessary to wait long periods. In effect, the waiting list has replaced a market system for allocating some types of medical care (Naylor, 1991).

Life-and-death decisions in Seattle. During the 1960s when kidney dialysis first became available, there were not enough kidney machines in Seattle to take care of all the patients who could benefit. For a period, hospitals set up special committees to decide who would have access to dialysis. The committees wrestled with life-and-death decisions and took into account such factors as severity of illness, age, compliance with medical regimen, and social contribution. Decisions by such committees were criticized, and eventually, Medicare reimbursement for kidney dialysis made it unnecessary to ration treatment.

A rationing plan in Oregon. The Oregon state legislature in 1990 passed legislation putting into effect a computer-based ranking of health care problems covered under the state's Medicaid program. According to this ranking system, funding would be made available and services would be rationed not according to individual cases but according to a consensus reached by democratic means. The state finally obtained federal government approval for the new rationing scheme, but Oregon's proposal received approval over objections that the plan would discriminate against people with disabilities (Brown, 1991).

These examples show how hard it is to get public agreement on when or how to ration scarce health care resources. Rationing policies are sometimes put into effect when a clear-cut, unavoidable scarcity exists; organ transplants would be a good example. But if all that is needed is more funding, then rationing health care seems especially open to public criticism. There is evidence that other European countries along with Great Britain have practiced age-based rationing. But virtually none has ever come out publicly and acknowledged this or defended it.

The Justification for Age-Based Rationing

Would age-based rationing be acceptable in the United States? Public opinion surveys tend to show that Americans are concerned about high costs of health care but are not likely to attribute these costs to overuse by the elderly. A majority of the American public seems willing to withhold life-prolonging medical care for critically ill older persons near the point of death, yet few people would withhold care on the basis of age alone (Zweibel, Cassel, and Karrison, 1993).

Some interesting light is shed on age-based rationing through an opinion survey that asked a British sample: Which of two individuals should be treated if only their ages were different and it was not possible to treat both? Respondents favored treating a 5-year-old over a 70-year-old by a ratio of 84 to 1 and a 35-year-old over a 60-year-old by 14 to 1 (Lewis and Charny, 1989). In short, while rejecting proposals for age-based rationing, people tend to favor choosing younger over older patients for treatment (Kuder and Roeder, 1995).

There are a variety of ways to ration health care besides age. These include ability to pay; anticipated clinical effectiveness; waiting lists, or first-come first-served; and productivity to society or social worth. In contrast to these approaches, Callahan believes that chronological age is the best criterion to use because, in his view, each of us has a "natural" life span of 80-85 years. When people have completed this natural life span, it is time to "move over" and give others their fair share.

Some good reasons can be given in favor of age-based rationing: It would be relatively efficient to administer; from a utilitarian viewpoint, older people are less productive in the economy; from an efficiency standpoint, the likelihood of benefit and years of survival derived from medical care would be less for older than for younger people. Perhaps most important, all people theoretically are members of every age group at some point over a full life course.

But there are powerful reasons against age-based rationing. One major argument against age-based rationing is the fact that the elderly as a group are highly heterogeneous. Chronological age by itself isn't a good predictor of outcome for medical treatments. Once we control for confounding explanations such as disease or functional status, age largely disappears as an explanatory variable.

Age-based rationing is criticized by people on different sides of the political spectrum. Those who are more conservative feel that government rationing is morally objectionable and instead favor a market approach, where each consumer buys insurance coverage appropriate to individually defined need—for example, "medical savings accounts" that work somewhat like individual-retirement accounts. By contrast, those who are more liberal believe that, instead of the marketplace, we should eliminate the profit motive altogether from health care. They favor access on a more egalitarian basis, perhaps on the pattern of European welfare states.

As we look to the future, U.S. health care spending is likely to rise from around 14% today to an estimated 16.6% by the year 2007. Medicare currently enrolls just under 15% of the U.S. population, but is expected to rise to 20% by 2025 and to go even higher after that. Of all factors, mortality rates have the most powerful influence on Medicare's future, because the death rate determines the number of people who survive to become eligible for Medicare and expenditures depend on how long they will live. Would delaying the age of eligibility save Medicare? Apparently not. Even if we raised the age of eligibility from 65 to 70—a dramatic increase—this change would save less than 15% of total Medicare costs. If Medicare faces financial problems, more far-reaching changes may have to be considered (McKusick, 1999).

Others look to strategies like means testing, using income-related premiums, or seeking alternative sources of revenue beyond the payroll tax for Medicare. Finally, there are those, like economist Uwe Reinhardt (Altman, Reinhardt, and Shactman, 1999), who believe some form of rationing is required to improve the efficiency of the system but do not necessarily favor age-based rationing.

Still another strategy is "backdoor rationing," where implicit or indirect methods limit access to the health care system. For example, when reimbursement rules such as diagnosis related groups (DRGs) require a patient to leave the hospital for home care, backdoor rationing may be involved. Faced with reimbursement limits, staff carry out screening procedures that can lead to denial of services. These "gatekeeping" practices have become a familiar part of the practice of hospital discharge planning and case management in geriatric health care. In fact, efficiency and cost control have been motives for adopting case management in many localities (Capitman, 1988).

Rationing as a Cost-Saving Plan

One problem with age-based rationing is knowing just how much money it would save. Most of the money spent on health care for older people doesn't go for "high-tech" care in a hospital setting. A substantial share goes for prescription drugs, nursing home care, and home health services. The cost of these last two categories—long-term care for the elderly—is increasing rapidly as more and more people survive to advanced ages. Callahan himself favors spending more on long-term care instead of high-technology medicine.

But the rapid rise in health care costs is not chiefly attributable to longevity alone. Several other forces are also responsible: increases in intensity of services, rate of utilization; introduction of new medical technologies; the rise in real wages of health care personnel; general price inflation; and fraud, waste, and abuse, including excessive or futile medical treatment (Smith et al., 1998). Various strategies that have been put forward to contain costs, including regulatory cost controls, enhanced competition, and managed care, all seem to have had some impact. But will they enable us to pay for the health care costs of an aging society? Pessimists believe that controlling costs by eliminating unnecessary care, as managed care tries to do, will provide only temporary relief because we have already gotten most of the cost savings from managed care. In the long run, population aging and technological innovation may make rationing a necessity (Schwartz, 1987).

Technology is a major driving force behind the long-term rise of health care spending. Along with medical technology come expensive treatments for life-threatening diseases such as AIDS, heart disease, and cancer.

Singling out aging alone seems to miss this larger picture. Even if aggressive, high-cost interventions for older patients likely to die within a year were eliminated, the impact on total U.S. health expenditures would be negligible. Callahan's proposals, even if fully implemented, would save only $5 billion a year—not a large amount in a nearly $1 trillion annual health care budget (Binstock, 1994).

Others have questioned Callahan's assumption that high-technology care for the elderly is inappropriate or wasteful. For instance, coronary artery bypass grafting and angioplasty offer important benefits to older heart patients. Some studies show that older patients can emerge healthy from an intensive hospital stay, proving that age alone is not a good predictor of long-term survival or quality of life among critically ill older patients (Burke, 1993).

Still others have replied to Callahan's proposal by insisting that rationing of health care isn't necessary in the first place (Relman, 1990). They point out that the current health care system is riddled with waste and inefficiency. For example, by comparing statistics with other countries, some analysts have argued that up to half of all the cardiac bypass operations in the United States may not be needed. A 1992 study by the U.S. General Accounting Office (GAO) found that the present health care system permits unscrupulous providers of services to defraud insurance companies at a staggering rate. It is estimated that 10%, or $90 billion, is lost to fraud and abuse every year.

No doubt medical expenses do rise toward the end of life, but costs vary quite dramatically among people over age 65. For example, the healthiest 90% of the population over 65 incurred bills of only $1,430 for Medicare in 1993, excluding a comparable amount of out-of-pocket expenses. But in that same year the sickest 10% had annual costs of $28,000, or nearly 20 times as much as the larger, healthy group. Are we confronting the principle of diminishing returns? Advancing age brings greater health care expenses, and health care spending is greatest for the oldest-old (85+): Overall personal health care spending for this group is well over $9,000 a year per person, or 2½ times greater than for persons ages 65 to 69. For nursing home care alone, the ratio is 23 times greater. Yet Callahan is not in favor of cutting off care for people who live in nursing homes, even though the annual cost might run up to $50,000 or more.

Behind Callahan's argument is a common image of frail, elderly patients subjected to high-technology procedures before being allowed to die. Callahan is concerned that prolonging the lives of these patients is wasteful if the same resources could be used to improve the quality of life of other old people or people of other ages. Overtreatment does occur, of course, partly because of reimbursement incentives and a humanly understandable desire to "do everything possible." However, aggressive treatment of the elderly actually seems to decrease as the level of impairment rises. Those with poor quality of life—for example, late-stage dementia patients—are not treated as aggressively as others. A study of heart patients over the age of 75 found that these older patients were more than 12 times *less* likely to receive therapy to dissolve blood clots and 8 times *less* likely to undergo coronary diagnostic procedures compared with patients under 65 years of age (Rosenthal and Fortinsky, 1994). In sum, frail, totally impaired patients seldom receive expensive, high-technology care; instead, they receive supportive care (Smith, 1993).

Callahan's proposal for age-based rationing assumes that care for elderly patients in their last year of life is expensive because of high-technology, life-sustaining medical treatment. But the proportional cost for Medicare beneficiaries in their last month of life remained unchanged between 1976 and 1988, suggesting that expensive high-technology care was not being administered to growing numbers of dying elderly patients. In 1990, 6.6% of Medicare beneficiaries who died accounted for 22% of Medicare expenditures. These figures seem to support Callahan's argument. But it turns out that patients who are near death are not the biggest cause of large Medicare payments. Instead, the high-cost beneficiaries tended to be survivors. Medicare expenditures for people who died actually *went down* with advancing age. These facts suggest that it may be difficult to develop a policy limiting expenditures for people in the last year of life without also curtailing health care for sick Medicare beneficiaries who have the potential to survive (Garber, MaCurdy, and McClellan, 1998).

Perhaps by voluntarily avoiding unneeded care or treatment that prolongs dying, we could avoid rationing health care. The problem here, though, is that it is not so easy to predict how long a given patient will live. Medical costs in the last year of life amount to approximately 18% of total lifetime medical costs and nearly 30% of the entire Medicare budget (Lubitz and Prihoda, 1984). But we only know that we've spent money on the "last year of life" when that life is over, that is, in retrospect. Clinical studies of medical care at the end of life confirm what doctors have admitted for a long time: Medical science lacks any realistic way of determining who would have died if they hadn't gotten the care they received. In a careful study of Medicare expenditures, among the 1% of beneficiaries who had the highest costs, a majority survived, and of the 5% with the highest costs, nearly two-thirds survived. Those in favor of rationing health care on grounds of age cannot claim any special new power of prediction.

There are many myths about the cost of care in the last year of life (Alliance for Aging Research, 1997). One study of the last year of life found that the elderly who got expensive, high-technology care were those with good functional status ages 65-79. By contrast, frail patients with poor functional status tend to receive mainly supportive care in their final year. In other words, despite difficulty of predicting when death will occur, and despite lack of explicit rationing criteria, it may be that high-cost medical services are already being provided to the older people with age and functional status being taken into account. Moreover, high technology is not the only factor responsible for high expenses. The frail and debilitated "older old" are likely to have high expenses even without high-technology care. In short, the biggest factor in high costs at the end of life may not be inappropriate high technology after all (Scitovsky, 1988).

The real solution, some critics argue, would be a system of national health care combined with careful cost controls to ensure that appropriate care, but not overtreatment, is provided to people at all levels throughout the health care system, not simply in the last year of life. A variety of proposals for providing more health care in a cost-effective manner have been put into practice in recent years. These include new forms of managed care (see Focus on Practice in this chapter), popular with private industry, and case management, practiced by community-based health service programs. Both are methods for deciding how much care to provide individuals, based on some verified assessment of individual need.

The Impetus for Rationing

Will more efficient management of health care distribution solve the problems of access and allocation in an aging society? The answer we give involves some forecast about the health status and needs of the aging population in decades to come. For example, what is the likely impact of health promotion, such as reductions in smoking, or the probability of a breakthrough in understanding the biology of aging or the causes of specific diseases?

A prime factor in the rationing debate is economics, which can be defined as the science of scarcity. It is only when scarcity is at hand, when the wolf is at the door, that rationing is seriously considered. In times past, some societies have deprived older people of resources, sometimes even life itself, to make way for the young. One example often cited is the Aleut (Eskimo) tribes who at the point of starvation were sometimes forced to put an elderly person out on an ice floe to die in order to have enough food for the remainder of the group. Similarly, in Leningrad during World War II, hundreds of thousands of people, including the very old, died of starvation in order that young children might survive.

These life-threatening conditions that prompted rationing have become rare as economic conditions have improved. Today, we face a different kind of scarcity created by the fact that medical technology can save and extend the lives of the very sick and old. Even when the technology is cheap, caring for elderly people with chronic diseases like stroke or Alzheimer's disease can be very expensive. As new medical technologies enable us to prolong the lives of the chronically ill, the expense continues to rise.

Exhibit 11 shows a large actual and projected increase in the population 85 years and older. This group, age 85+, sometimes called the oldest-old, also has the greatest number of health problems and costs the most. If expensive health care resources were rationed on grounds of age, as Callahan proposes, then this group would probably be the group denied care.

Exhibit 11. Actual and Projected Increase in the Age 85+ Population: 1900-2050

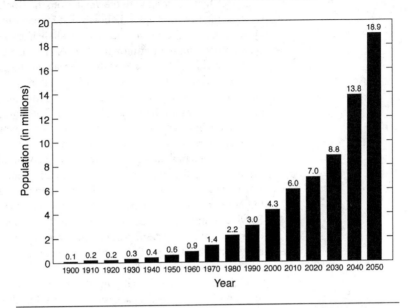

SOURCE: U.S. Bureau of the Census (1996).

Cost Versus Age

As medical technology advances, Callahan fears that life-extending technology will run up against the law of diminishing returns. We end up spending more and more to achieve limited incremental gains, often with very poor quality of life, while other social needs go unmet. But is this assumption about the cost of technology correct? Some life-extending technology, such as a penicillin shot, is actually quite inexpensive. On the other hand, keeping a patient alive and cared for in a low-technology environment such as a nursing can be very expensive: $50,000 or $60,000 a year, or more. If we really want to cut down on the expense created by too many old people, why wouldn't we also withhold cheap life-extending technologies? As long as we look exclusively at the economic aspect of health and aging, it is hard to avoid thinking of choices in terms of cost-benefit or cost-effectiveness standards (Avorn, 1984). But once we adopt those standards, don't we tend to downgrade the value of life in old age? Callahan himself believes that society owes the elderly a decent minimum of health care, at least up to a certain age.

The high cost of more health care for the elderly is part of the problem. But cost alone is not the whole story for Callahan, because he would accept paying for certain expensive procedures for younger people. The basic principle that Callahan wants us to consider is chronological age. In the end, Daniel Callahan, along with the verse from the Book of Ecclesiastes cited at the opening of this chapter, believes that human life has a natural rhythm or cycle: a time to live and a time to die. Callahan argues that this "natural" life span comprising the traditional 70 years and then 10 years, or maybe a bit more, should be the basis for thinking about the goals of health care. He believes we should do what we can to enable people to live out a full life span, however defined, but nothing more. After that, we should not expend scarce resources on the very old. Instead, we should let them die.

Pushing this argument further, some have even urged a "duty to die cheaply." If preserving a life of diminished quality in old age is less of a benefit to the aged patient than the resources saved for others, then it would be in the mutual self-interest of all to have death come more quickly (Menzel, 1990). This idea of solidarity and altruism makes sense in some situations, but not in others. For instance, rationing within the British National Health Service is more easily justified than in the United States because Britain operates a closed system, providing universal access to care under a regionally centralized budget. Denial of a treatment for one patient means money is available for treatments for other patients.

Callahan's goal is initially idealistic: He wants to guarantee the elderly, along with everyone else, access to universal health care and help everyone avoid an early, premature death. He proposes to reform the health care system by achieving a better balance of caring and curing, specifically, by improving long-term care and home care. Only after accomplishing these goals, he insists, would it be time to introduce an age-based cutoff of life-extending technologies under Medicare (Callahan, 1994).

Critics of Callahan argue that age-based rationing actually affects only those who depend on government-run health programs—elderly people who can't afford private care. Thus proposals for rationing health care actually amount to a rationale for spending less for the neediest in society. Age-based rationing would tend to perpetuate or make worse the problem of access according to ability to pay.

But Callahan and others who favor age-based rationing reply that invisible forms of rationing already take place for the 40 million Americans who lack health insurance. They believe that adopting an explicit rationing policy would force everyone to face up to the allocation decisions already in effect but kept invisible. The result of this honesty would be greater fairness for all. Indeed, Oregon's rationing plan for Medicaid was put into effect with this idea in mind.

Alternative Approaches to Rationing

A variety of other approaches to rationing have been put forward by health economists and others concerned with improving the efficiency of the health care system (Jones and Higgs, 1992). One approach is to limit medical procedures based on effectiveness as measured by health outcomes research. For example, angioplasty, an otherwise useful procedure, does not produce any medical benefit when performed on a person already experiencing an acute heart attack. Many procedures of doubtful benefit are employed with the Medicare population. A study by the Commonwealth Fund estimated that more than a third of all procedures reimbursed under Medicare were performed for equivocal or inappropriate reasons. Some procedures are used because doctors are familiar with them and reimbursement is available, whether inappropriate or not.

Other approaches to rationing include **cost-benefit analysis,** in which we ask how much a treatment costs in comparison to the total benefit that will be created if the patient lives. For example, we might measure the patient's future economic productivity. Obviously, a cost-benefit approach would discourage high-cost treatments for elderly people. Still another approach is known as **cost-effectiveness analysis.** Here, we look at which treatment provides desired the same outcome for the least cost. But again, depending on the outcome measure used, the lives of the young may be favored over the lives of people who are older (Welch, 1991).

One interesting approach in health care economics is known as **quality-adjusted life years** (QALYs). The idea behind QALYs is the commonsense view that 10 years of life with disability may not have the same value as 10 years of good health. People with more disabilities have a poorer quality of life. If functional assessment determines that some people have poor QALYs, then they should be denied health care. But who decides what counts as "quality of life"? Economists use exercises where a patient's own priorities and preferences are used to construct an index for comparative purposes. Then different forms of treatment with alternative outcomes can be ranked according to cost. But again, QALYs may result in resources being channeled away from the elderly or chronically ill (Evans, 1993).

The "Notch" Problem

Callahan calls for changes in public expenditure programs to carry out his plan for age-based rationing. How would this work in practice under the Medicare program? In practice, it might create a troublesome "notch" problem for people as they come near the age for cutting off health care resources. The situation could be comparable to what we now have under Medicare. If you're very sick and need care but you're only 64, you can't qualify for Medicare. As soon as you pass the magic age of 65, you become qualified. Under Callahan's plan, once you passed over another notch, you would no longer be qualified for life-extending treatment.

Why is the notch problem troubling? Imagine being in line at a movie theater when the people in front of you are admitted but the line is halted just when it's your turn. Somehow it seems unfair; it seems like an arbitrary cutoff. Imagine the quandary for a doctor with a patient just above the cutoff age (85 or whatever) when lifesaving health care is no longer permitted under Callahan's proposal.

The notch problem arises when we try to clearly define when aging begins. In fact, Callahan takes for granted that old age is a distinct stage of life, perhaps comparable to adolescence, with certain boundaries and distinctive characteristics. But we might wonder whether aging fits that picture anymore. Some gerontologists, such as Bernice Neugarten (1983), argue that America today is now more of an "age-irrelevant" society, that people of advanced ages—those over 70 or 80—should not be stereotyped with any set of fixed characteristics. If America is becoming the kind of society where chronological age makes less and less difference, then Callahan's proposal would seem to face some problems in being accepted.

Euthanasia and Suicide

Callahan is against deliberately killing people or having doctors collaborate with patients who want help in ending their lives. His rationing proposal calls for holding back treatment, not directly killing people, say, by an injection. But other critics have wondered if Callahan's argument isn't self-contradictory. Why is it acceptable to hold back treatment, when that holding back will predictably result in a patient's death, but not acceptable to cooperate with a patient who voluntarily asks for help in ending life?

It seems as if Callahan is calling for involuntary death for people above a fixed age, but at the same time he wants to prohibit acts, such as voluntary euthanasia, that people might adopt as a matter of personal choice. Is it possible that his own proposal could make more headway if he also supported voluntary withdrawal of treatment for people of advanced age (Battin, 1987)? And if we moved to a voluntary system, rather than the involuntary one urged by Callahan, what might be the likely consequences for society? For health professionals like doctors and nurses? For older people themselves?

Debate Over Age-Based Rationing

The questions continue, and the debate goes on. Callahan himself has repeatedly maintained his original call for age-based rationing. But he has gone further in calling for wider reform of health care. He makes it clear that, in his view, not only must health care for the elderly be rationed, but other hard choices will have to be made to have a just system for all (Callahan, 1994). Whether he is right remains the subject of vigorous debate.

In the readings that follow, we see this debate unfold along different lines. Nat Hentoff in his article vigorously criticizes Callahan and asks what kind of society would we become if Callahan's proposal were adopted. Terrie Wetle and Richard Besdine also reject the proposal, worrying about the danger of a negative view of older people. Daniel Perry and Robert Butler take a different approach. They, too, worry about rising health care costs in an aging society, but they urge medical research to improve health and thereby reduce the expense of old-age illnesses. William Schwartz and Henry Aaron, like Callahan, recognize the need to face up to tough choices, but they doubt that age-based rationing will be the answer.

Daniel Callahan is serious about his proposal, and this fact has shocked many people. Critics have responded to his proposals by calling them ageist and discriminatory and dangerous. Callahan denies that he is urging age discrimination. Instead, he wants to guarantee the elderly, along with everyone else, access to universal health care and thereby help everyone avoid a premature death. To accomplish this goal, he believes, means we need to get a better balance between caring and curing in our health care system. As a practical matter, he wants a trade-off: between improving long-term care and cutting off life-extending technologies to be paid for under Medicare. Setting an age limit is tragic, but it is the best we can do, believes Callahan.

Is Daniel Callahan cruel and hard-hearted, or is he instead courageous and far-sighted in willing to advocate a controversial idea? His own words, and the response of his critics, must be the basis for what the fair-minded reader will conclude.

READING 1

Why We Must Set Limits

Daniel Callahan

In October 1986 Dr. Thomas Starzl of Presbyterian University Hospital in Pittsburgh successfully transplanted a liver into a seventy-six-year-old woman, thereby extending to the elderly patient one of the most technologically sophisticated and expensive kinds of medical treatment available (the typical cost of such an operation is more than $200,000). Not long after that, Congress brought organ transplants under Medicare coverage, thus guaranteeing an even greater range of this form of lifesaving care for older age groups.

That is, on its face, the kind of medical progress we usually hail: a triumph of medical technology and a newfound benefit provided by an established health-care program. But at the same time those events were taking place, a government campaign for cost containment was under way, with a special focus on Medicare. It is not hard to understand why.

In 1980 people over age sixty-five—11 percent of the population—accounted for 29 percent of the total American health-care expenditures of $219.4 billion. By 1986 the elderly accounted for 31 percent of the total expenditures of $450 billion. Annual Medicare costs are projected to rise

Source: "Setting Limits," by Daniel Callahan, in *A Good Old Age? The Paradox of Setting Limits* (pp. 23-35), edited by P. Homer and M. Holstein. New York: Simon & Schuster, 1990. Copyright © 1987 by Daniel Callahan. Reprinted by permission.

from $75 billion in 1986 to $114 billion by the year 2000, and that is in current, not inflated, dollars.

Is it sensible, in the face of rapidly increasing health-care costs for the elderly, to press forward with new and expensive ways of extending their lives? Is it possible to hope to control costs while simultaneously supporting innovative and costly research? Those are now unavoidable questions. Medicare costs are rising at an extraordinary pace, fueled by an increasing number and proportion of the elderly. The fastest-growing age group in the United States is comprised of those over age eighty-five, increasing at a rate of about 10 percent every two years. By the year 2040, it has been projected, the elderly will represent 21 percent of the population and consume 45 percent of all health-care expenditures. How can costs of that magnitude be borne?

Yet there is another powerful reality to consider that moves in a different direction: Medicare and Medicaid are grossly inadequate in meeting the real and full needs of the elderly. The system fails most notably in providing decent long-term care and home care. Members of minority groups, and single or widowed women, are particularly disadvantaged. How will it be possible, then, to provide the growing number of elderly with even present levels of care, and also rid the system of its inadequacies and inequities, and yet at the same time add expensive new technologies?

The straight answer is that it will be impossible to do all those things and, worse still, it may be harmful even to try. The economic burdens that combination would impose on younger age groups, and the skewing of national social priorities too heavily toward health care, would themselves be good reasons to hesitate.

Beyond Economics: What Is Good for the Elderly?

My concern, however, extends beyond the crisis in health-care costs. "I want to lay the foundation for a more austere thesis: that even with relatively ample resources, there will be better ways in the future to spend our money than on indefinitely extending the life of the elderly. That is neither a wise social goal nor one that the aged themselves should want, however compellingly it will attract them. . . . Our affluence and refusal to accept limits have led and allowed us to evade some deeper truths about the living of a good life and the place of aging and death in that life" (*SL*, 53, 116).[1]

The coming economic crisis provides a much-needed opportunity to ask some fundamental questions. Just what is it that we want medicine to do for us as we age? Other cultures have believed that aging should be accepted and that it should be in part a time of preparation for death. Our culture seems increasingly to dispute that view, preferring instead, it often seems, to think of aging as hardly more than another disease, to be fought and rejected. Why does our culture have such difficulty with this question?

Let me start by saying that "the place of the elderly in a good society is a communal, not only an individual, question. It goes unexplored in a culture that does not easily speak the language of community and mutual responsibility. The demands of our interest-group political life constitute another obstacle. . . . It is most at home using the language of individual rights as part of its campaigns, and can rarely afford the luxury of publicly recognizing the competing needs of other groups. Yet the greatest obstacle may be our almost utter inability to find a meaningful place in public discourse for suffering and decline in life. They are recognized only as enemies to be fought: with science, with social programs, and with a supreme optimism that with sufficient energy and imagination they can be overcome. We have created a way of life that can only leave serious questions of limits, finitude, the proper ends of human life, of evil and suffering, in the realm of the private self or of religion; they are thus treated as incorrigibly subjective or merely pietistic" (*SL*, 220).

In its long-standing ambition to forestall death, medicine has reached its last frontier in the care of the aged. Of course children and young adults still die of maladies that are open to potential cure, but the highest proportion of the dying (70 percent) are over sixty-five. If death is ever to be humbled, that is where endless work remains to be done. This defiant battle against death and decline is not limited to medicine. Our culture has worked hard to redefine old age as a time of liberation, but not decline, a time of travel, of new ventures in education and self-discovery, of the ever-accessible tennis court or golf course, and of delightfully periodic but thankfully brief visits from well-behaved grandchildren. That is, to be sure, an idealized picture, but it arouses hopes that spur medicine to wage an aggressive war against the infirmities of old age.

As we have seen, the costs of such a war would be prohibitive. No matter how much is spent, the ultimate problem will still remain: People will grow old and die. Worse still, by pretending that old age can be turned into a kind of endless middle age, we rob it of any meaning.

The Meaning and Significance of Old Age

There are various sources of meaning and significance available for the aged, but it is the elderly's particular obligation to the future that I believe is essential. "Not only is it the most neglected perspective on the elderly, but it is the most pertinent as we try to understand the problem of their health care. The young—children and young adults—most justly and appropriately spend their time preparing for future roles and developing a self pertinent to them. The mature adult has the responsibility to procreate and rear the next generation and to manage the present society. What can the elderly most appropriately do? It should be the special role of the elderly to be the moral conservators of that which has been and the most active proponents of that which will be after they are no longer here. Their indispensable role as conservators is what generates what I believe ought to be the *primary* aspiration of the old, which is to serve the young and the future. Just as they were once the heirs of a society built by others, who passed on to them what they needed to know to keep going, so are they likewise obliged to do the same for those who will follow them.

"Only the old—who alone have seen in their long lives first a future on the horizon and then its actual arrival—can know what it means to go from past through present to future. That is valuable and unique knowledge. If the young are to flourish, then the old should step aside in an active way, working until the very end to do what they can to leave behind them a world hopeful for the young and worthy of bequest. The acceptance of their aging and death will be the principal stimulus to doing this. It is this seemingly paradoxical combination of withdrawal to prepare for death and an active, helpful leave-taking oriented toward the young which provides the possibility for meaning and significance in a contemporary context. Meaning is provided because there is a purpose in that kind of aging, combining an identity for the self with the serving of a critical function in the lives of others—that of linking the past, present, and future—something which, even if they are unaware of it, they cannot do without. Significance is provided because society, in recognizing and encouraging the aged in their duties toward the young, gives them a clear and important role, one that both is necessary for the common good and that *only* they can play" (*SL,* 43).

It is important to underscore that while the elderly have an obligation to serve the young, the young and society have a duty to assist the elderly. Before any limits are imposed, policies and programs must be in place to help the elderly live out a "natural life span," and beyond that to provide the means to relieve suffering.

A "Natural Life Span" and a "Tolerable Death"

Earlier generations accepted the idea that there was a "natural life span"—the biblical norm of threescore and ten captures that notion. It is an idea well worth reconsidering and would provide us with a meaningful and realizable goal. Modern medicine and biology have insinuated the belief that the average life span is not a natural fact at all, but instead one that is strictly dependent on the state of medical knowledge and skill. And there is much to that belief as a statistical fact:

Average life expectancy continues to increase, with no end in sight.

There are, moreover, other strong obstacles to the development of a notion of a "natural life span." This notion "requires a number of conditions we seem reluctant to agree to: (1) that life has relatively fixed stages—a notion rejected on the ground that we are free to make of our different stages of chronological age whatever we want; biology presents no unalterable philosophical and moral constraints or any clear pointers; (2) that death may present an 'absolute limit' to life—an idea repudiated because of the ability of medicine to constantly push back the boundary line between life and death; life is an open-ended possibility, not a closed circle; (3) that old age is of necessity marked by decline and thus requires a unique set of meanings to take account of that fact—a viewpoint that must be rejected as part of the political struggle against ageism, which would make of the old a deviant, marginal, and burdensome group; and (4) that 'our civilization' would be better off if it shared some common view of 'the whole of life'—rejected as a politically hazardous notion, more congenial to authoritarian and collectivist cultures than to those marked by moral and religious pluralism and individualism" (*SL*, 40-41).

I want to argue that we can have and must have a notion of a "natural life span" that is based on some deeper understanding of human needs and possibilities, not on the state of medical technology. I offer a definition of the "natural life span" as "one in which life's possibilities have on the whole been achieved and after which death may be understood as a sad, but nonetheless relatively acceptable event.

"Each part of that definition requires some explanation. What do I mean when I say that 'one's life possibilities have on the whole been accomplished'? I mean something very simple: that most of those opportunities which life affords people will have been achieved by that point. Life affords us a number of opportunities. These include work, love, the procreating and raising of a family, life with others, the pursuit of moral and other ideals, the experience of beauty, travel, and knowledge, among others. By old age—and here I mean even by the age of 65—most of us will have had a chance to experience those goods, and will certainly experience them by our late 70s or early 80s. It is not that life will cease, after those ages, to offer us some new opportunities; we might do something we have never done but always sought to do. Nor is it that life will necessarily cease to offer us opportunities to continue experiencing its earlier benefits. Ordinarily it will not. But what we have accomplished by old age is the having of the opportunities themselves, and to some relatively full degree. Many people, sadly, fail to have all the opportunities they might have: they may never have found love, may not have had the income to travel, may not have gained much knowledge through lack of education, and so on. More old age is not likely to make up for those deficiencies, however; the pattern of such lives, including their deprivations, is not likely to change significantly in old age, much less open up radically new opportunities hitherto missing" (*SL*, 66-67).

A longer life does not guarantee a better life. No matter how long medicine enables people to live, death at any time—at age 90 or 100 or 110—would frustrate some possibility, some as-yet-unrealized goal. The easily preventable death of a young child is an outrage. Death from an incurable disease of someone in the prime of young adulthood is a tragedy. But death at an old age, after a long and full life, is simply sad, a part of life itself, what I would call a "tolerable death."

This notion of a "tolerable death" helps illumine the concept of a "natural life span," and together these two notions set the foundation for an appropriate goal for medicine in its approach to aging. "My definition of a 'tolerable death' is this: the individual event of death at that stage in a life span when (a) one's life possibilities have on the whole been accomplished; (b) one's moral obligations to those for whom one has had responsibility have been discharged; and (c) one's death will not seem to others an offense to sense or sensibility, or tempt others to despair and rage at the finitude of human existence. Note the most obvious feature of this definition: it is a biographical, not a biological, definition" (*SL,* 66).

The Principles and Priorities of a Plan

How might we devise a plan to limit the costs of health care for the aged under public entitlement programs that is fair, humane, and sensitive to their special requirements and dignity? Let me suggest three principles to undergird a quest for limits:

"1. Government has a duty, based on our collective social obligations, to help people live out a natural life span, but not actively to help extend life medically beyond that point. By life-extending treatment, I will mean any medical intervention, technology, procedure, or medication whose ordinary effect is to forestall the moment of death, whether or not the treatment affects the underlying life-threatening disease or biological process.

"2. Government is obliged to develop, employ, and pay for only that kind and degree of life-extending technology necessary for medicine to achieve and serve the end of a natural life span; the question is not whether a technology is available that can save a life, but whether there is an obligation to use the technology.

"3. Beyond the point of a natural life span, government should provide only the means necessary for the relief of suffering, not life-extending technology" (*SL,* 137-38).

What would the actual policy look like? "A full policy plan would include detailed directions, for example, for determining priorities within basic biological research, within health-care delivery, and between research and delivery. That I will not try to provide. I can only sketch a possible trajectory—or, to switch metaphors, a kind of likely general story. But if that at least can be done in a coherent fashion, avoiding the most flagrant contradictions, it might represent some useful movement" (*SL,* 141-42).

Three elements of health policy emerge from my position: "The first is the need for an antidote to the major cause of a mistaken moral emphasis in the care of the elderly and a likely source of growing high costs of their care in the years ahead. That cause is constant innovation in high-technology medicine relentlessly applied to life-extending care of the elderly; it is a blessing that too often turns into a curse. . . . No technology should be developed or applied to the elderly that does not promise great and inexpensive improvement in the quality of their lives, no matter how promising for life extension. Incremental gains, achieved at high cost, should be considered unacceptable. Forthright government declarations that Medicare reimbursement will not be available for technologies that do not achieve a high, very high, standard of efficacy would discourage development of marginally beneficial items" (*SL,* 142, 143).

"The second element is a need to focus on those subgroups of the elderly—particularly women, the poor, and minorities—who have as yet not been well served, for whom a strong claim can be entered for more help from the young and society more generally. . . . The elderly (both poor and middle-class) can have no decent sense of security unless there is a full reform of the system of health care. It may well be that reforms of the sweeping kind implied in these widely voiced criticisms could more than consume in the short run any savings generated by inhibitions of the kind I am proposing in the development and use of medical technology. But they would address a problem that technological development does nothing to meet. They would also reassure the old that there will be a floor of security under their old age and that ill health will not ruin them financially, destroy their freedom, or leave them dependent upon their children (to the detriment of both)" (*SL,* 142, 147).

"The third is a set of high-priority health and welfare needs—nursing and long-term care, prevention—which would have to be met in pursuit of the goals I have proposed. . . . Beyond avoiding a premature death, what do the elderly need from medicine to complete their lives in an acceptable way? They need to be as independent as possible, freed from excess worry about the financial or familial burdens of ill health, and physically and emotionally positioned to seek whatever meaning and significance can be found in old age. Medicine can only try to maintain the health which facilitates that latter quest, not guarantee its success. That facilitation is enhanced by physical mobility, mental alertness, and emotional stability. Chronic illness, pain, and suffering are all major impediments and of course appropriate targets for medical research and improved health-care delivery. Major research priorities should be those chronic illnesses which so burden the later years and which have accompanied the increase in longevity" (*SL,* 142, 149).

Euthanasia and Assisted Suicide

Some might view my position as an endorsement of euthanasia and assisted suicide. My position "is exactly the opposite: a sanctioning of mercy killing and assisted suicide for the elderly would offer them little practical help and would serve as a threatening symbol of devaluation of old age. . . . Were euthanasia and assisted suicide to be legalized, would there be a large and hitherto restrained group of elderly eager to take advantage of the new opportunity? There is no evidence to suggest that there would be, in either this country or in any other. But even if there might be some, what larger significance might the elderly in general draw from the new situation? It would be perfectly plausible for them to interpret it as the granting of a new freedom. It would be no less plausible for them to interpret it as a societal concession to the view that old age can have no meaning and significance if accompanied by decline, pain, and despair. It would be to come close to saying officially that old age can be empty and pointless and that society must give up on elderly people. For the young it could convey the message that pain is not to be endured, that community cannot be found for many of the old, and that a life not marked by good health, by hope and vitality, is not a life worth living. . . .

"What do we as a society want to say about the elderly and their lives? If one believes that the old should not be rejected, that old age is worthy of respect, that the old have as valid a social place as any other age group, and that the old are as diverse in their temperaments and outlooks as any other age group, an endorsement of a special need for euthanasia for the old seems to belie all those commitments. It would be a way of legitimizing the view that old age is a special time of lost hopes, empty futures, and personal pointlessness. Alternatively, if it is believed that old age can have a special value, that it can—with the right cultural, economic, and political support—be a time of meaning and significance, then one will not embrace euthanasia as a special solution for the problem of old age, either for the aged as individuals or for the aged as a group. It would convey precisely the wrong symbolism. To sanction euthanasia as a special benefit for the aged would signal a direct contradiction to an effort to give meaning and significance to old age" (*SL,* 194, 196, 197). We as a society should instead guarantee elderly persons greater control over their own dying—and particularly an enforceable right to refuse aggressive life-extending treatment.

Conclusion

The system I propose would not immediately bring down the cost of care of the elderly; it would add cost. But it would set in place the beginning of a new understanding of old age, one that would admit of eventual stabilization and limits. The elderly will not be served by a belief that only a lack of resources, better financing mechanisms, or political power stands between them and the limitations of their bodies. The good of younger age groups will not be served by inspiring in them a desire to live to an old age that maintains the vitality of youth indefinitely, as if old age were nothing but a sign that medicine has failed its mission. The future of our society will not be served by allowing expenditures on health care for the elderly to escalate endlessly and uncontrollably, fueled by the false altruistic belief that anything less is to deny the elderly their dignity. Nor will it be aided by the pervasive kind of self-serving argument that urges the young to support such a crusade because they will eventually benefit from it.

We require instead an understanding of the process of aging and death that looks to our obligation to the young and to the future, that recognizes the necessity of limits and the acceptance of decline and death, and that values the old for their age and not for their continuing youthful vitality. In the name of accepting the elderly and repudiating discrimination against them, we have succeeded mainly in pretending that with enough will and money the unpleasant part of old age can be abolished. In the name of medical progress we have carried out a relentless war against death and decline, failing to ask in any probing way if that will give us a better society for all.

"There is little danger that the views I advance here will elicit such instant acclaim (or any ac-claim, for that matter) that the present generation of the elderly will feel much of their effect. That could take two or three decades if there is any merit in what I say, and what I am looking for is not any quick change but the beginning of a long-term discussion, one that will perhaps lead people to change their thinking, and most important, their expectations, about old age and death" (*SL*, 10).

Note

1. Daniel Callahan, *Setting Limits: Medical Goals in an Aging Society* (New York: Simon & Schuster, 1987). References to this volume appear in text here with the notation "*SL*."

The Pied Piper Returns for the Old Folks

Nat Hentoff

I expect that the sardonic Dean of Dublin's Saint Patrick's Cathedral, Jonathan Swift, would appreciate Daniel Callahan's *Setting Limits*—though not in the way he would be supposed to. Swift, you will recall, at a time of terrible poverty and hunger in Ireland, wrote *A Modest Proposal*. Rather than having the children of the poor continue to be such a burden to their parents and their nation, why not persuade the poor to raise their children to be slaughtered at the right, succulent time and sold to the rich as delicacies for dining?

What could be more humane? The children would be spared a life of poverty, their parents would be saved from starvation, and the overall economy of Ireland would be in better shape.

So, I thought, Callahan, wanting to dramatize the parlous and poignant state of America's elderly, has created his modern version of *A Modest Proposal*.

I was wrong. He's not jiving. . . .

Callahan sees "a natural life span" as being ready to say goodbye in one's late seventies or early eighties. He hasn't fixed on an exact age yet. Don't lose your birth certificate.

If people persist in living beyond the time that Callahan, if not God, has allotted them, the government will move in. Congress will require that

Source: "The Pied Piper Returns for the Old Folks," by Nat Hentoff, *The Village Voice*, April 26, 1988. Reprinted by permission.

anybody past that age must be denied Medicare payments for such procedures as certain forms of open heart surgery, certain extended stays in an intensive care unit, and who knows what else.

Moreover, as an index of how human the spirit of *Setting Limits* is, if an old person is diagnosed as being in a chronic vegetative state (some physicians screw up this diagnosis), the Callahan plan mandates that the feeding tube be denied or removed. (No one is certain whether someone actually in a persistent vegetative state can *feel* what's going on while being starved to death. If there is a sensation, there is no more horrible way to die.)

What about the elderly who don't have to depend on Medicare? Millions of the poor and middle class have no other choice than to go to the government, but there are some old folks with money. They, of course, do not have to pay any attention to Daniel Callahan at all. Like the well-to-do from time immemorial, they will get any degree of medical care they want.

So, *Setting Limits* is class-biased in the most fundamental way. People without resources in need of certain kinds of care will die sooner than old folks who do not have to depend on the government and Daniel Callahan. . . .

Callahan reveals that once we start going down the slippery slope of utilitarianism, we slide by—faster and faster—a lot of old-timey ethical norms. Like the declaration of the Catholic bishops of America that medical care is "indispensable to the protection of human dignity." The bishops didn't say that dignity is only for people who can afford it. They know that if you're 84, and only Medicare can pay your bills but says it won't pay for treatment that will extend your life, then your "human dignity" is shot to hell. . . .

It must be pointed out that Daniel Callahan does not expect or intend his design for natural dying to be implemented soon. First of all, the public will have to be brought around. But that shouldn't be too difficult in the long run. I am aware of few organized protests against the court decisions in a number of states that feeding tubes can be removed from patients—many of them elderly—who are not terminally ill and are not in intractable pain. And some of these people may

not be in a persistently vegetative state. (For instance, Nancy Ellen Jobes in New Jersey.)

So, the way the Zeitgeist is going, I think public opinion could eventually be won over to Callahan's modest proposal. But he has another reason to want to wait. He doesn't want his vision of "setting limits" to go into effect until society has assured the elderly access to decent long-term home care or nursing home care as well as better coverage for drugs, eyeglasses, and the like.

Even if all that were to happen, there still would be profound ethical and constitutional problems. What kind of society will we have become if we tuck in the elderly in nursing homes and then refuse them medical treatment that would prolong their lives?

And what of the physicians who will find it abhorrent to limit the care they give solely on the basis of age? As a presumably penitent former Nazi doctor said, "Either one is a doctor or one is not."

On the other hand, if the Callahan plan is not to begin for a while, new kinds of doctors can be trained who will take a utilitarian rather than a Hippocratic oath. ("I will never forget that my dedication is to the society as a whole rather to any individual patient.") Already, I have been told by a physician who heads a large teaching institution that a growing number of doctors are spending less time and attention on the elderly. There are similar reports from other such places.

Meanwhile, nobody I've read or heard on the Callahan proposal has mentioned the Fourteenth Amendment and its insistence that all of us must have "equal protection of the laws." What Callahan aims to do is take an entire class of people—on the basis only of their age—and deny them medical care that might prolong their lives. This is not quite *Dred Scott,* but even though the elderly are not yet at the level of close constitutional scrutiny given by the Supreme Court to blacks, other minorities, and women, the old can't be pushed into the grave just like that, can they?

Or can they? Some of the more influential luminaries in the nation—Joe Califano, George Will, and a fleet of bioethicists, among them—have heralded *Setting Limits* as the way to go.

Will you be ready?

Letting Individuals Decide

Terrie Wetle and Richard W. Besdine

Setting Limits is disturbing in several ways. First, there is the premise that we are justified in setting public policy that determines a "natural life span" for an entire cohort of the population. Referring to the Nazi concept of the *Untermensch,* Callahan notes the evils that result from the political determination that a life is dispensable, but he sets aside the concern far too easily that the elderly— or any other age group, for that matter—would interpret his "natural life span" policy as devaluation of life in old age.

A second concern is whether the program could be applied consistently and fairly. Noting that a policy to limit public payment for life-sustaining care on the basis of age would lead to a two-tiered system in which wealthy older people could still buy such care, Callahan still does not believe that "a society would be made morally intolerable by that kind of imbalance." It was just such an imbalance between those who could pay for care and those who could not that led to the enactment of Medicare and Medicaid 25 years ago.

Many distinctions on which the proposed program would depend are not made clearly or reliably. For example, the distinction between interventions that prolong life and those that relieve suffering is perhaps easy to make conceptually and in situations, but not at the bedside or in that vast middle ground where the majority of cases are found. An 80-year-old man with excruciating abdominal pain and fecal vomiting due to adhe-

sions obstructing his small bowel will have his suffering relieved quickly and best by surgery to release the obstruction. In the process, his life may also be saved. We wonder whether Callahan would urge morphine rather than surgery for such a patient.

Callahan uses the treatment of diabetes to define the rules of his game further. Considering insulin a life-prolonging rather than a symptom-relieving treatment, he states that a diabetic using insulin before the end of his policy-defined natural life span would be "grandfathered" into a continuation of that medication, whereas the person who acquires diabetes after the cutoff age would not be provided such treatment. Similarly, dialysis would be continued indefinitely if it was initiated before the cutoff date, but it would not be provided for late-onset renal disease. Thus, the patient whose diabetes or renal failure develops before the cutoff age and who begins treatment promptly is given preference over the person healthy at that age but in whom illness develops later. This is a peculiar logic.

Much of the book, it seems, is based on the premise that such a policy would save the taxpayer money and allow a reallocation of resources. It is not clear, nor is evidence provided, that the policy actually would accomplish these goals. In fact, it is possible that certain "life-prolonging" interventions also improve function, resulting in the decreased use of other expensive forms of care.

Certainly, the book is worth reading, but with a critical eye. Care must be taken to avoid facile applications of its arguments in support of negative views of older people. Although Callahan has warned against the tyranny of individualism throughout his career, perhaps aging and health care are one arena in which an acute focus on the individual is most appropriate. The decision to provide or withhold life-prolonging interventions may still be best left to the individual patient, family, and care provider.

Aim Not Just for Longer Life, but Expanded "Health Span"

Daniel Perry and Robert Butler

Most Americans instinctively recoil at the thought that their government would try to save money by pulling the plug on life-sustaining care when it is needed by older people. In this case, their instincts are correct.

To determine a person's access to medical care solely on the basis of that person's age is clearly unfair, unworkable, and unnecessary. It is wrong to blame the elderly for rising hospital expenses and physicians' fees that are driven principally by other factors or to require older Americans to pay for the failure of government and industry to find a more humane and workable policy to curb health care costs.

President Reagan signed into law the most sweeping Medicare expansion in that program's 22-year history, indicating the nation's strong commitment to providing health care to the elderly. The new catastrophic care program will cost about $31 billion over five years. Even that amount will seem small when compared to proposals for insuring Americans against the costs of long-term care, the next major health care issue to face Congress and the Bush presidency.

As the curtain rose on Congressional debate over long-term care, some came forward to argue that the United States could save billions by simply denying lifesaving medical interventions to people over a certain age—say 65 to 75. But there is a better way to control costs of providing health care to the elderly: work to eliminate the very afflictions of old age, which are costing billions in health care, long-term care, and lost productivity. By attacking diseases associated with aging—such as Alzheimer's disease, stroke, osteoporosis, arthritis, and others—the need for many costly medical procedures, lengthy hospital stays, and financially draining long-term care could be ended or reduced.

Why not start with a real commitment to scientific research that could extend the healthful middle years of life and compress the decline of aging into a very short time?

Why not redirect federal research efforts to aim for scientific and medical discoveries to reduce frailty, improve health status, and increase independence in older people? It's a far better goal—and more realistic—than rationing medical treatment.

At present, however, aging research is not where the U.S. government is placing its biggest bets. Most people don't believe much can be done to change aging. Therefore, research funds generally go elsewhere.

There is every reason to fear spiraling health costs if effective ways to lengthen healthy years

Source: "Aim Not Just for Longer Life, but Expanded 'Health Span,' " by Daniel Perry and Robert Butler, *The Washington Post,* December 20, 1988. Reprinted by permission of the authors.

and delay the onset of debilitating age are not found before the baby boomers become the biggest Medicare generation in history.

Americans already are paying billions because medical science lacks the ability to cure, prevent, or postpone many chronic maladies associated with aging. And national investment in research to avoid these costs is minuscule when compared to the billions spent for treatment.

Of the $167 billion a year spent on health care for people over age 65, far less than one half of 1 percent of that amount is reinvested in research that could lead to lower health care costs for chronic diseases and disabilities. That is a poor investment strategy for a nation soon to experience the largest senior boom in history.

Tinkering with changes in the health care delivery system can save some money, but these savings will not equal the long-term benefits of dramatic medical and scientific changes that alter the way people experience old age.

If scientists do not find a way to treat Alzheimer's, for instance, by the middle of the next century, there will be five times as many victims of this disease as there are now simply because of the demographic shift that is occurring. Incontinence, memory loss, and immobility are the main factors driving long-term care and high health costs to the elderly. If no advances occur in these and other conditions of aging, up to 6 million older Americans will be living in nursing homes, instead of the 1 million who are there today.

Unfortunately, there may be no way to prevent aging per se. However, there are conditions that occur only as a person ages. Many of these can be prevented. The risk of suffering a chronic disease such as arthritis or osteoporosis is very slight at middle age. But from the forties onward, that risk doubles exponentially about every five years until someone in the mid-eighties has about a one-in-three chance of having dementia, immobility, incontinence or other age-related disabilities.

If medicine could delay the beginning of decline by as few as five years, many conditions and the costs they incur could be cut in half. The ability to re-set biological clocks to forestall some of the decline of aging may be closer than anyone realizes, thanks to new knowledge in immunology and in the molecular genetics of aging.

Answers may be near. Help for immobility, osteoporosis, and incontinence can be achieved with only a modest extension of present technologies. If the U.S. doubles its present meager $30 million for osteoporosis research, by the year 2010 this condition could be eliminated as a major public health problem, which now affects 90 percent of all women over 75.

Learning how to postpone aging could help lower health care costs and improve the health of older Americans at the same time. The goal here is not just longer life span but extended "health span," with fewer problems caused by chronic disease.

A Tough Choice on Health Care Costs

William B. Schwartz and Henry Aaron

Daniel Callahan, an ethicist and author of the book *Setting Limits,* has stirred sharp debate over his proposal for slowing the rise in health care costs by eliminating life-extending care for most people over the age of 75.

Mr. Callahan's recommendation has attracted attention because other vaunted panaceas for soaring health care costs, such as health maintenance organizations and other competitive mechanisms, are having little effect.

But Mr. Callahan's proposal suffers from two major shortcomings. First, it almost certainly would not be acceptable to patients, health care providers, or, one suspects, anyone else. Second, it would do almost nothing to slow the rise in costs of medical care.

Mr. Callahan's idea is something less than thoroughly reasoned. He provides no analysis of current costs and offers no estimate of the savings he hopes to achieve. In fact, the impact on costs would be minimal.

In 1986, people aged 75 or older constituted less than 5 percent of the United States population. Because per capita medical costs for the very old run about three times the national average, such costs account for about 15 percent of annual health care spending. Abruptly eliminating half of the services used by this group—a Draconian cut, because even Mr. Callahan has not proposed denying routine care or ignoring life-threatening illness in the aged who are otherwise healthy—would reduce total spending by only about 7 percent.

In recent years, health care spending has risen by 5.5 to 6 percent annually after adjusting for inflation. Thus, a sudden cut in services to the elderly would reduce current outlays by no more than the costs typically grow in a little more than a year—a significant amount but not enough to materially slow the steady climb in health care costs.

Most of the growth in health care spending results from scientific advances—open heart surgery, organ transplants, magnetic resonance imaging, clot-dissolving agents to prevent heart attacks—that are applied to the general population, not just the few who are 75 or older.

Indeed, a simple calculation shows that even if all fruits of future medical progress were denied to the elderly, the nearly 5 percent annual growth rate in medical costs would be slowed by less than half a percentage point.

If cutting care to the elderly won't contain health care costs, what will? The United States is not the first developed country to face this question. The British health care system, which has rationed health care for years, shows that age is only one of many social, medical, and economic factors invoked to contain costs.

For example, visible suffering commands far more resources than private pain. The grotesque swollen joints and massive bleeding of hemophiliacs have caused the British to reject all restrictions on therapy. But because angina pectoris, or chest pain from coronary artery disease, causes silent and invisible suffering, Britain spends less than one-fifth as much as the United States does on coronary artery surgery.

Many other basic societal values also determine what services the British withhold. Services dependent on equipment allocated by bureaucrats located far from the point of treatment are rationed far more than are those dependent on resources readily available in hospitals. A case in point: many major British hospitals lack a CAT scanner, now widely acknowledged to be vital in modern diagnosis.

Simple fear also shapes rationing decisions. The dread of cancer has led the British not to stint on radiotherapy or chemotherapy even for cases in which the treatment is designed only to relieve pain rather than to prolong life.

Aggregate costs of therapy is a further key factor. Bone marrow transplants, averaging $50,000 to $100,000 a patient, are provided as often in Britain as in the United States, largely because only a few patients require them.

In contrast, some British patients must wait five years for hip replacements because the thousands of people with arthritic hips would impose burdensome costs on the health care system if all were treated.

One British expert, asked what would happen if a high-cost curative drug became available for a common form of metastatic cancer, responded, "I wake up screaming at such a prospect" and expressed the opinion that many people would go untreated.

If the American public ever gets serious about containing health care costs, rationing of treatment will likely proceed along lines similar to those in Britain, not simply on the basis of age. But Americans are unlikely to be as willing as the British to accept reduced quality of care. Americans, promptly informed by the media of each new medical advance, are quick to demand the new treatment.

How will we resolve the conflict in the basically incompatible goals of controlling costs while maintaining quality? Some real economies can be achieved by increased efficiency, but no matter what, a significant reduction in the growth of medical spending will require the sacrifice of beneficial services not by just the very old but by all of us.

FOCUS ON PRACTICE   MANAGED CARE

Something new in geriatric health care today is the rapid spread of managed care, such as Medicare health maintenance organizations (HMOs). By early 1998, 6 million Medicare beneficiaries—or 14% of the Medicare-eligible population—had enrolled in a managed care plan (Bonifazi, 1998). **Managed care** is a system combining insurance with health care providers and facilities in a unified network intended to provide cost-effective services. To qualify for Medicare reimbursement, these managed care plans must provide all the services Medicare covers and as a result they have proved attractive to many older people. A growing minority of older Americans are using managed care.

Managed care is already the dominant pattern in health care delivery in the United States today. A 1996 survey by KPMG Peat Marwick found that nearly three-quarters of all Americans who have health insurance through their employers are enrolled in some type of managed care plan, which is a dramatic rise from 29% in 1988. By 1995, a majority of health maintenance organizations offered some type of Medicare managed care plan.

There are both advantages and disadvantages for an individual to change from conventional Medicare fee-for-service to a managed care plan or Medicare HMO. On the positive side, managed care demands less paperwork. Doctors' visits, hospital bills, and lab tests are almost covered in full, with low copayments and without high deductibles. Medicare HMOs may also offer extra benefits such as low-cost prescription drugs or vision care. They also eliminate the need for private Medigap insurance, which is widespread in the Medicare population. Above all, the whole concept of "managed" care is intended to improve coordination of care and services. Finally, managed plans have a clear incentive to offer preventive health care such as checkups and immunizations. All these are positive points in favor of managed care.

On the negative side, managed care has the drawback of imposing limits. When people sign up, they must go through the Medicare HMO network to receive their health care. Patients can't choose their own doctors, hospitals, or other service providers. For elderly people, it may prove a hardship not to be able to continue using a doctor they've known for many years. For those who travel, the plan may limit coverage when outside the service area. Above all, the managed care plan will pay only for preapproved services.

Medicare beneficiaries have long had the option of switching from traditional fee-for-service coverage to HMOs. Since the mid-1990s, managed care providers have been successful in enrolling Medicare beneficiaries in large numbers. In 1999, the Medicare Plus Choice program has allowed beneficiaries to choose from eight standardized health plan categories, including HMOs, fee-for-service plans, and provider-sponsored organizations. Managed care plans remain attractive because they offer no deductibles, extremely low copayments, and almost no paperwork or claim forms. In many instances, they provide eye and ear exams or low-cost prescription drugs.

Enrollment in Medicare HMOs remains voluntary. The young-old who are healthy today may find managed care plans attractive but their attitude could change later, especially if they are denied coverage or face limited choice of doctors. In the new environment of managed care, physician-patient relationships are likely to take on importance for the elderly, because older people's expectations about medical encounters have developed over a lifetime under the traditional fee-for-service approach (Putnam, 1996). Elderly consumers will have to educate themselves in order to evaluate health marketing appeals and become capable of choosing the most appropriate managed care provider for themselves.

There is ongoing debate about whether encouraging more older Americans to enroll in managed care organizations will actually reduce Medicare costs. Some critics fear that managed care is just a means of "backdoor rationing." Yet surveys suggest that older patients enrolled in Medicare HMOs may actually be more satisfied with their coverage than those enrolled in traditional fee-for-service plans (Margolis, 1995).

Yet the issue of hidden or backdoor rationing persists because of reimbursement under managed care. Under a complex formula, the federal government pays a Medicare managed care plan a fixed sum of money on a per person basis, rather than per service basis. This reimbursement method is known more broadly as **capitation** (per head). What this means is that after receiving a fixed amount under capitation, a managed care plan then becomes responsible for each beneficiary's full health care costs. If a person stays healthy, the managed care group gets to keep the extra money. But if someone gets sick, even if treatment costs $100,000, then the plan is responsible for covering the cost, just as with any insurance plan. The profit motive, then, may introduce incentives for backdoor rationing in unexpected ways.

For example, Medicare managed care plans are motivated to avoid signing up those likely to incur large medical costs. This form of backdoor rationing can be accomplished indirectly by marketing techniques. But refusing to enroll frail elderly people is against federal law. Furthermore, even people who sign up while healthy are likely to get sick later on. Another approach is to cut costs by denying coverage to those who are very sick. Backdoor rationing may take the form of refusing treatments on grounds of "medical necessity." If a treatment fails that test, it doesn't qualify for coverage.

What happens if someone in a Medicare HMO is denied coverage? A study by the GAO (1995) found that appealing a denial of coverage is slow. It can take up to six months, and that is a significant time factor for someone 70 or 80 years old. Another federal study reported that a quarter of Medicare HMO members weren't even aware that they had the right to appeal a denial of coverage. When beneficiaries do appeal, patients win about 40% of the time, but many decide not to go through the process. Nor does the appeals process deal with the question of quality assurance. What happens if backdoor rationing takes the form of substandard care?

One problem here is that quality of care is not easy to measure. A study by the Mathematica policy analysis group found that, compared with a control group under conventional Medicare coverage, stroke patients in a Medicare HMO were discharged from hospitals "quicker and sicker" (Brown et al., 1993). The HMO saved money by getting them out of the hospital earlier, but patients faced serious problems because they ended up at home or in facilities that could not provide appropriate rehabilitation.

Denial of coverage can take place in many different kinds of services. In rehabilitative services, for example, Medicare requires "steady and meaningful improvement." Medicare HMOs may be inclined to interpret that requirement in very stringent terms. A patient who fails to make sufficient progress gets no more rehabilitation. In a class action suit against the federal government, *Grijalva v. Shalala* (1998), attorneys for a Medicare HMO patient claimed that the health plan repeatedly provided less coverage for a whole group of conditions, ranging from pneumonia to hip replacements.

The controversy over age-based rationing has shifted to new terrain with debates about how far companies can go in limiting health care services because of the bottom line. The ultimate threat is for managed care companies simply to drop Medicare coverage. In 1999, a GAO report found that more than 400,000 seniors had to look for new health plans when their managed care providers dropped Medicare contracts. Ethical principles—justice, rights, the greatest good for the greatest number—may not be easy to apply in these circumstances. Backdoor rationing under managed care presents a confusing picture. Or should we even speak about "rationing" when managed care groups control access through indirect requirements that create delays and appeals without any clear resolution? As more older people sign up for Medicare managed care plans, the public debate about gatekeeping will continue.

FOCUS ON THE FUTURE   SCENARIOS FOR RATIONING—
FICTION OR FORECAST?

Sometimes our most provocative images of the future come from science fiction, which has explored some of the issues involved in rationing health care resources in a society coping with burdens of an aging population.

Holy Fire is a science fiction novel by Bruce Sterling (1997), set in the year 2096. The book depicts a world after years of plague and natural disasters. Its heroine is a 94-year-old medical economist named Mia Zemann, who is a member of the gerontocracy, or ruling elite composed of the elderly. She has been able to afford the best technology has to offer for life extension.

As the story unfolds, Mia has undergone a technique known as Neo-Telomeric Dissipative Cellular Detoxification, or NTDCD, which is a revolutionary technique for reversing aging and promising virtual immortality. But one day Mia wakes up convinced she is another person and she explores a world in ways that call her basic identity into question. *Holy Fire* contains other messages worth pondering. The gerontocracy of the late 21st century is a society that has allocated extraordinary resources to keeping the elderly alive. But at what cost to other age groups? And at what cost even to the rejuvenated elderly themselves? These are questions that Daniel Callahan also posed in his proposal for age-based rationing of health care.

The feature film *Logan's Run* takes up the prospect of age-based extinction as a means of promoting the greater social good. This 1976 movie, starring Michael York and Peter Ustinov, portrays a futuristic world set in the year 2274. It is a society of unlimited pleasure followed by extinction at the age of 30: a macabre fulfillment of the 1960s slogan "Don't trust anyone over 30!" In this youth-worshiping society, young people don't know what awaits them on their 30th birthday. They believe that after participating in a ritual ceremony they will be "taken up" and transported into another state of being. In fact, they are to be killed to make room in a society threatened by overpopulation.

As the film unfolds, we discover that the entire society is located underground, a remnant left over after a nuclear holocaust has destroyed life on the surface of the earth. Forced to ration resources, this future world arranges for a limited life span, at a much lower age than Daniel Callahan ever anticipated in his rationing proposal.

Another film on the theme of overpopulation and planned death is *Soylent Green* (1973), starring Charlton Heston and Edward G. Robinson. The film is an adaptation of Harry Harrison's (1994) science fiction novel *Make Room! Make Room!* set in the year 2022. Just like in the film *Escape From New York,* Manhattan has become a crowded, nightmare world. Heston plays a police officer who investigates the murder of a prominent figure and stumbles onto a vast conspiracy. The government, it turns out, has plans for people to die and then arranges for their bodies to be taken away to be "recycled" and used as part of the food supply for a world gripped by shortages of everything.

Some of these science fiction images of the future could have been scripted by Thomas Malthus, an 18th-century clergyman and writer who warned of a race between overpopulation and dwindling natural resources. Malthus advocated population control but never urged killing as a solution. However, Jonathan Swift, writing a few decades earlier than Malthus, actually wrote down an extinction plan in his *Modest Proposal,* suggesting one way to solve the population problem in Ireland. In an elaborate joke, Swift asked his readers to consider the possibility of cannibalism carried out on infants killed in order to reduce the Irish population. But genocide in the 20th century proved to be no joke at all. Could science fiction scenarios of mass killing to reduce undesirable populations one day become a reality? It is a question worth pondering.

QUESTIONS FOR WRITING, REFLECTION, AND DEBATE

1   Is Callahan right in his suggestion that our modern American culture thinks of aging as "hardly more than another disease"? Does it make sense to talk about aging as a "disease" whose cause might be identified and then perhaps even "cured"? How do we decide whether something is a disease? Following Callahan's own argument, would it be a good idea to promote antiaging research if this might reduce the expenses of geriatric care?

2   Antibiotic therapies like erythromycin today are very inexpensive. According to Callahan's own argument, would they have to be withheld from the very old just because they are "life-extending"? Or is it only expensive therapies that should be withheld? What happens if a cheap therapy helps people to survive an illness but then it turns out to be very expensive to take care of them?

3   How do we know when "rationing" starts taking place? During World War II, everyone knew that butter, gasoline, and other commodities were being rationed. But some critics argue that rationing of health care is already going on in America. Is it possible for resources to be "rationed" without public knowledge of it? As a hypothetical exercise, assume that you are a journalist who has just discovered that a local hospital routinely makes decisions about health care based on the age of the patients. Write a short newspaper article bringing public attention to the practice.

4 Hentoff argues that Callahan's proposal is class biased—that is, it discriminates against the poor—because people with money can purchase any amount of medical care they want. Is this argument convincing? Is there any alternative to this arrangement? Does Hentoff's point, if valid, destroy Callahan's argument?

5 At the end of his article, Hentoff argues that the Callahan proposal deprives an entire class of people of the "equal protection of the laws" and he cites the *Dred Scott* case in which the U.S. Supreme Court approved slavery. Is age-based rationing a kind of discrimination like slavery? In what ways is age discrimination like, or unlike, race discrimination? Assume that you are a lawyer arguing this case before the U.S. Supreme Court. Write a brief (a summary of a client's case) based on Hentoff's general idea and offer your strongest possible arguments to convince the justices.

6 Wetle and Besdine, like Hentoff, cite the case of the Nazis and their program of killing off certain groups of people who were judged unworthy to live. Is it fair to judge Callahan's proposal by comparing it to what the Nazis did? Assume for a moment that you are Daniel Callahan and write a letter to the editor of a newspaper defending yourself against this charge of being like the Nazis.

7 Schwartz and Aaron offer economic calculations to suggest that Callahan's proposal, if adopted, won't really save much money as long as rationing is limited to people over age 75. If their figures are right, should Callahan be willing to lower his age limit to 70, or 65? Why or why not?

8 Managed care depends on some form of "gatekeeping" to decide who will get services. What are the ethical dilemmas involved in gatekeeping? What can be learned from considering the activities of gatekeepers in other domains—for example, college admissions officers or case workers in the welfare system? Imagine that you are a gatekeeper and that you're faced with a situation where it might not be possible to provide a questionable service needed by an elderly person. Write a memorandum to your boss giving arguments on why the service should be provided.

SUGGESTED READINGS

Barry, Robert L., and Bradley, Gerard V. (eds.), *Set No Limits: A Rebuttal to Daniel Callahan's Proposal for Limited Health Care for the Elderly,* Chicago: University of Illinois Press, 1991.

Binstock, Robert H., and Post, Stephen G. (eds.), *Too Old for Health Care? Controversies in Medicine, Law, Economics and Ethics,* Baltimore: Johns Hopkins University Press, 1991.

Hackler, Chris (ed.), *Health Care for an Aging Population,* Albany: SUNY Press, 1994.

Homer, Paul, and Holstein, M. (eds.), *A Good Old Age? The Paradox of Setting Limits,* New York: Simon & Schuster, 1990.

Smeeding, Timothy M. (ed.), *Should Medical Care Be Rationed by Age?* Totowa, NJ: Rowman & Littlefield, 1987.

Should Families Provide for Their Own?

W hen problems arise in old age, most people turn to their families for help. The vast bulk of care for the frail elderly, perhaps 80%, is furnished by families and other private individuals (Shanas, 1979). But the American family itself is changing at the same time that American society is witnessing changes in the proportion and character of the aging population (Burton, 1993; Cantor, 1992). Families are facing new challenges to give care and help as well as bearing the cost of long-term care for elderly members (Brubaker, 1987).

Aging and the American Family

Many older Americans have a rich and extended family life. For example, more than half of Americans above age 65 are married, and most of them have adult children. An equivalent proportion of them have at least one brother or sister, and three-quarters are grandparents. In 1994, more than two-thirds of older noninstitutionalized people lived in a family setting. These facts show that the popular image of old people as lonely and abandoned is inaccurate.

But advanced age frequently brings a need for caregiving. Indeed, caregiving responsibility for the elderly has already become a major and predictable part of the life cycle of Americans (Glick, 1977). Among married couples, the primary caregiver tends to be the healthy spouse (Stephens and Christianson, 1986). But a big problem for old-old couples is that, with advancing age, older spouses themselves are more and more likely to be impaired. In that event, older people typically turn for help to adult children, who are also the chief caregivers for older men or women who are no longer married (Brubaker, 1985).

Some patterns of caregiving over the life span are illuminated by the **exchange theory** of aging, which is based on the idea that interaction in

Exhibit 12. Caregivers and Their Relationship to Elderly Care Recipients

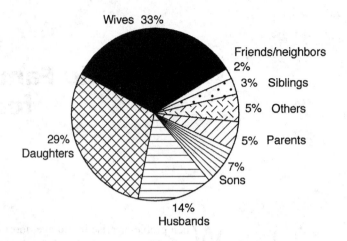

Wives 33%

Friends/neighbors 2%

3% Siblings

5% Others

5% Parents

7% Sons

14% Husbands

29% Daughters

SOURCE: California's Caregiving Resource Centers Assessment database, 1997-1998.

NOTE: Caregiver population includes primary and secondary caregivers who are caring for a brain-impaired adult.

social groups is based on reciprocal balance (Dowd, 1975). Thus parents care for children, and spouses care for one another because they are motivated both by moral obligation and by the knowledge that they can count on reciprocal help in time of difficulty (Dowd, 1984).

Many different kinds of family members can be involved in caregiving (Hays, 1984), but responsibilities still tend to be divided according to gender, as Exhibit 12 demonstrates. The overwhelming majority of care for aged relatives is still provided by women, typically wives, daughters, or daughters-in-law, who must balance the burden of care for the elderly with the demands of employment and their own families. The term **sandwich generation** describes the impact of such caregiving responsibilities on middle-aged women (Brody, 1985, 1990). But while multiple caregiving duties are real, some empirical studies question how widespread or severe the burden may be (Rosenthal, Matthews, and Marshall, 1989).

It has been estimated that the average American woman will spend more years with elderly parents than years spent caring for children under age 18 (Watkins, Menken, and Bongaarts, 1987). Of course, this generalization overlooks the fact that "caregiving" may entail very different levels of responsibility: For some, it is a weekly telephone call, for others, it is round-the-clock support for someone with Alzheimer's or for someone recovering from a stroke (AARP and National Alliance for Caregiving, 1997). Still, it remains true that for many women during the middle-aged years, that time will be spent with caregiving obligations. Among those 45 to 54 years of age, for example, 17% have some responsibility for a disabled older parent

(Stone and Kemper, 1989). Like child care, the issue of elder care has attracted interest from business (Work/Family Elder Directions, 1988).

In cases of extreme frailty or dependency, the burden on family members may prove exhausting, leading to burnout and perhaps even elder abuse or neglect (Stone, Cafferata, and Sangl, 1987). The burdens created by Alzheimer's disease or other varieties of dementia would be a case in point. As the disease progresses and the patient's behavior becomes more extreme, caregiving stress can become almost unbearable in a home setting (Springer and Brubaker, 1984; Corbin and Strauss, 1988). These conditions have led gerontologists to speak of family caregivers themselves as the "hidden victims" of the disease (Zarit, Orr, and Zarit, 1985).

The portrait of caregiver burden, however, should not be exaggerated. Many caregivers remain in their role for a long time and never burn out. There is a normalcy to family caregiving, especially between spouses, that makes it seem unextraordinary to those who render care.

Moreover, significant help for caregiver burden exists. Social supports, especially the informal support of family or friends, can prove helpful for caregivers under stress. In addition, caregivers may benefit from **respite care**: temporary care for dependent older people to allow the caregiver some time off (Klein, 1986). Such programs can relieve some of the strain involved in efforts to delay placing a relative who has dementia or who is severely ill in a nursing home (Montgomery, 1989). Mutual self-help groups, such as those sponsored by the Alzheimer's Association, have also proved very effective for caregivers (Mace and Rabins, 1981). In all these cases, formal support services complement what the family does, not to replace it but to support it (Litwak, 1985).

Abandonment or Independence?

The stereotype of elderly people abandoned by their children is mostly wrong. First of all, there is no evidence to support the widely heard "empty nest" idea that parents typically become depressed when the last child leaves home. Nearly half of seniors report that they presently live or expect to live in proximity to their children, two-thirds within 30 minutes of a child (Shanas, 1980). Significantly, more than 40% are in daily contact with their children, and three-fourths talk on the phone at least weekly with children. Older people whose families are spread out geographically do not necessarily consider their families broken up or believe that the young have abandoned the old.

Nonetheless, a clear trend toward independence in living arrangements among the elderly has been apparent for a long time. For instance, in 1960 only one-fifth lived alone; by 1984, the proportion had increased to one-third. Sharing a household in an extended family has also dropped significantly in recent years. In 1960, 40% of older people were residing with their adult children, but by 1984, the proportion had dropped to 22% (U.S. Congressional Budget Office, 1988).

The sentimental image of the family in the "good old days" is mistaken in several ways. In Europe and America, multigenerational living arrangements were never very common, even in agrarian societies centuries ago (Laslett, 1972). Idealizing the **extended family**—that is, several generations living under one roof—is part of the **"world-we-have-lost" myth** (Laslett, 1965/1971), in which we idealize the "golden age" of preindustrial society (Stearns, 1982). Yet Western societies have tended toward a separate residence for the **nuclear family**—only parents and children—for a long time.

There is also a common stereotype of elderly people as isolated from others. Yet a majority of older people live with others: around half with their spouse, another 14% with other relatives, and smaller numbers in other living situations. Less than 30% of the elderly are living alone. Even those alone are usually within close distance of relatives or only a phone call away. Fewer than 1 out of 20 are socially isolated, usually because they have lived that way most of their lives.

Families today typically remain in close and frequent contact. This pattern has been called **intimacy at a distance,** and it reflects a common desire by older people to live independently yet still remain close enough to have regular contact with grown children. When illness or need arises, a spouse, adult child, or other relatives are typically the first to help.

We do need to recognize that the living arrangements of older people today are different from those of a century ago. One reason for change is simply demographic. Today, unlike in the past, vastly larger numbers of older people survive into advanced age and thus require sustained help with activities of daily living. In cases of debilitating chronic illness, such as stroke or Alzheimer's disease, these elderly people may live many years in conditions of dependence that exceed the capacity of family caregivers. Other older people may have never been married or may simply outlive available family members. The result is that we must increasingly rely on government to provide what families are no longer in a position to give.

Family Responsibility

The development of social welfare programs for older people, such as Social Security and Medicare, has meant that health care and income support for the elderly have become a societal responsibility rather than a family obligation. But in the United States, unlike other advanced industrialized countries, long-term care has remained a family responsibility (Buchanan, 1984). Government has been reluctant to provide coverage for long-term care, so families remain an important source of both hands-on care and financial support. When it comes to long-term care needs, elderly people first rely on spouses; **spousal responsibility** is deeply embedded in our culture as a matter of both ethics and law. If a spouse is not available to provide care, then other family members such as children or siblings take responsibility.

In some cultures, such as the Chinese, Confucian teachings inculcate filial piety or strong reverence for parents, including the duty to support parents over one's own children (Cowgill, 1986). In the United States, **filial responsibility**—that is, responsibility for care of the elderly by adult children—is treated ambiguously as a matter of law, custom, and ethics (Schorr, 1961; Callahan, 1985; Post, 1989). In fact, half the states do have laws on the books that could compel children to give financial support to aged parents, but these laws have rarely been enforced (Garrett, 1980; Lammers and Klingman, 1986), partly because of deeply conflicting public attitudes toward filial responsibility (Seltzer and Troll, 1982). In contrast, in 1995 Singapore began enforcing stringent laws of compulsory filial responsibility that allow elderly people to sue their adult children for support.

In America, however, filial responsibility continues to be practiced not as a matter of law but as a matter of ethics or custom, and gerontologists have documented rich intergenerational ties in American families (Pfeifer and Sussman, 1991). The unresolved question is how government programs in the United States should interact with spousal and filial caregiving duties and financial responsibilities.

Medicaid and Long-Term Care

Under Medicare, the U.S. health care system provides near-universal coverage for acute diseases among the old. A majority of Medicare beneficiaries don't realize that in fact Medicare does not cover long-term care to any great extent. Financing of acute care and long-term care remains separate (Hellman and Hellman, 1991). About half the money spent on long-term care in nursing homes comes from some branch of government, chiefly Medicaid, and Medicaid is the primary payer for two-thirds of nursing home residents.

Medicaid, a joint government program supported by federal and state funds, was created in 1965 to provide health care for the poor. But over the years, it has become the primary government mechanism to pay for long-term care for the elderly and disabled (Spiegel, 1979). Medicare pays only 2% of those nursing home costs; Medicaid pays 36%. Medicaid is a large and expensive program, whose cost is growing rapidly. As the number of oldest-old in the 85+ population increases, long-term care expenses are likely to grow even greater.

Although created as a health care program for poor people, Medicaid has in fact become a key factor in nursing home coverage for middle-class elderly people. Three-fourths of Medicaid recipients are low-income parents with children, but these families receive only about a quarter of total Medicaid dollars. About two-thirds of all that Medicaid spends goes to institutional care for elderly, disabled, or mentally retarded people.

Financing Long-Term Care

Presumably, middle-class families rely on Medicaid for long-term care because they do not have the financial capacity to bear the cost of care

(Cohen et al., 1987). Long-term care already consumes a larger portion of the private health care dollar for the elderly than any other type of expenditure. The cost of a year in a nursing home today can range up to $75,000 or more. Few individuals or families can afford that cost on an extended basis. Of those who enter a nursing home as a "private-pay" patient, after only three months nearly 70% have reached the poverty level, and within a year 90% are impoverished.

In the likely event that long-term care costs exceed savings, those who face such costs have few options. One option is to qualify for Medicaid. But Medicaid is a means-tested entitlement program. That is, it makes use of eligibility rules based on income and assets to determine whether people qualify for Medicaid coverage. An unmarried applicant for Medicaid can keep nonexempt assets of only $2,000 or less, excluding the value of a home. Married couples, taking advantage of recent changes in the law, can keep up to $66,000 in such assets. Thus all but a limited portion of a spouse's assets are assumed to be available to pay for the partner's long-term care (Tilly and Brunner, 1987).

Many of those who do not qualify for Medicaid still do not have enough assets to pay for long-term care themselves. They face a cruel choice: Struggle to provide home-based care or do what is necessary to obtain Medicaid. To qualify for Medicaid, it is necessary to "spend down" lifetime accumulated assets to become impoverished and thereby eligible for assistance (Liu and Manton, 1991). Under regulations of the Medicaid law, spouses of those thus impoverished may obtain some protection, but children and grandchildren lose their share of accumulated life savings. One major problem with Medicaid financing of long-term care is that it introduces inequities across families, age groups, and social classes (Arling et al., 1991). For example, should people who become poor in old age be treated the same as those with a lifetime of poverty? Should families who contribute their own labor for caregiving have that contribution taken into account?

According to public opinion surveys, 82% of the general public recognizes that they cannot afford to pay the cost of long-term care either at home or in a nursing home. They also know that they cannot rely on the family alone: 86% want the government to help pay for long-term care instead of leaving it entirely up to the family. Significantly, in an era of strong sentiment against taxes, more than two-thirds say they would be willing to pay for a long-term care program with increased taxes (data from a Louis Harris Survey reported in Older American Reports, April 1, 1988).

But despite such clear public sentiment, a universal public insurance program for long-term care is still not available in America. On the contrary, Medicaid has become the public program of last resort to pay nursing home costs. In fact, Medicaid is the fastest-growing component of state budgets and is increasingly becoming an old-age program; nearly 40% of all Medicaid benefits go to the elderly, chiefly for nursing home care, as Exhibit 13 demonstrates.

The growing burden of Medicaid on the government has prompted a search for more affordable alternatives. For years, aging advocates have sold

Exhibit 13. Where the Medicaid Dollar for the Elderly Goes: 1996

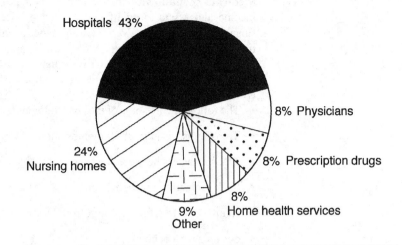

SOURCE: Health Care Financing Administration (1996).

the idea of home care to legislators and to the public with the argument that home care is more humane, in keeping with people's preferences to stay at home, and also more cost-effective. Unfortunately, the facts are not so clear. National demonstration projects and other studies have shown that home care may be more desirable but doesn't necessarily save money. One reason may be the so-called **woodwork effect,** or latent demand (Fama and Kennell, 1990). Government policymakers are afraid of people "coming out of the woodwork" to demand services that families would have provided otherwise or that weren't provided before (Arling and McAuley, 1983). Once the government is willing to pay, people may ask "someone else" to pick up the tab.

It is often said that older people should go into a nursing home only as a matter of their own choice, not for the convenience of the family. But when the bulk of hands-on care is given by family members, it is not so simple to say that the legitimate interests of the family are to be disregarded (Dill et al., 1987). The reality is that virtually no one enters a nursing home as a matter of choice. Government financing of nursing home care under Medicaid does introduce a certain financial incentive, but few would be inclined to take advantage of this incentive without some compulsion. People go into nursing homes, by and large, as an act of desperation, when everything else fails and when the family has no other alternative.

Medicaid Planning

As older people and their families have become more aware of the cost of long-term care, middle-class families have found ways of qualifying for

Medicaid. In doing so, families have tried to avoid the harsh requirements of **Medicaid spenddown**—that is, impoverishing themselves by spending all income and assets to qualify for Medicaid coverage. Both attorneys and financial planners urge a variety of strategies to enable middle-income families to qualify for Medicaid coverage of nursing home costs. The heart of these strategies comes down to **divestment planning**—that is, appearing to be poor by taking advantage of legal loopholes to "avoid the Medicaid trap" (Budish, 1989).

The following are some of the key strategies the specialists recommend:

- Transfer assets at least 30 months ahead of applying for Medicaid

- Transfer assets between husband and wife

- Seek protection through a court order

- Keep assets in a form exempt from Medicaid

- Set up a trust account

It is not known exactly how many middle-class older people presently take advantage of loopholes in the Medicaid law to appear impoverished and thus protect their family wealth. But the numbers are large enough to have sustained a rapidly growing body of **elderlaw** attorneys, who have now established their own association, the National Elderlaw Academy. As Medicaid divestment planning has become more widespread, the practice has attracted criticism. Some equate the practice with the deception used by some poor people to qualify for welfare payments and with schemes by rich people who dodge taxes through loopholes. In 1997, Congress enacted legislation making it a criminal offense to use professional consultation as a way of "spending down" to qualify for Medicaid coverage.

Regardless of whether middle-class spenddown is technically "legal," the critics argue that this form of Medicaid planning is socially immoral. This moral criticism is another way of insisting that taxpayers in general should not pay to protect the inheritance wealth of affluent families (Freedman et al., 1983). Indeed, it is not possible to understand what is at stake in the debate about Medicaid and family responsibility without seeing the importance of inheritance and the intergenerational transfer of assets (Dobris, 1989; Langbein, 1991).

It is easy enough to recognize that family abandonment of the elderly is a myth and to acknowledge that families are already taking care of their own by giving time and effort. But it is not easy to agree on whether families have an obligation to go further and make use of a portion of their assets to pay for long-term care costs, even if doing so eliminates inheritance.

Similarly, we know that informal supports enable frail elders to remain at home when the only alternative might be entering a nursing home. But people also disagree about whether families should be paid in cash by the government for giving the kind of hands-on care that they customarily give. Knowledge of the facts is essential for debating the issue. But because values and choices are involved, the debate will not be settled by facts alone (Stone, 1991).

In the readings that follow, strong opinions are expressed about whether people ought to take advantage of Medicaid eligibility laws and whether it's right for government to pay family members. On one side of the debate are Peter Strauss and Nancy Lederman, both elderlaw attorneys who believe that families should realistically plan ahead for nursing home costs and that this planning may involve Medicaid. Planning ahead to qualify for Medicaid, they believe, is not immoral or illegal. Don't make the mistake of thinking that Medicaid is only for the poor, they tell us.

On the other side of the debate, Andrew Bates finds transfer of assets to be a very troubling practice at the borderline of legality and social morality. Bates echoes a widely shared opinion. It seems wrong for some families to preserve an inheritance while others are forced to impoverish themselves to pay for long-term care.

In his article, Stephen Moses focuses directly on the phenomenon of impoverishment due to nursing home expenses. Moses moves the debate away from moralistic rhetoric and urges us instead to look carefully at the facts about paying for long-term care.

Finally, in the piece by Gunhild Hagestad, we hear a different perspective on the debate about family caregiving. Equity or fairness is also an issue regarding the role of women who assume the burden of caregiving. It's not just "families" who provide for their own but, overwhelmingly, women. The legal and financial debate about Medicaid spenddown must take into account this other form of inequity as we think about steps to provide better care for elderly people.

READING 6

Medicaid and Long-Term Care

Peter J. Strauss and Nancy M. Lederman

Medicaid is a public assistance grant program, the twin Great Society benefit signed into law along with Medicare by President Lyndon B. Johnson in 1965. Financed jointly by federal and state moneys, it provides health benefits to 35 million low-income people who are aged, blind, or disabled as well as those who are poor.

Although designed to serve low-income people of all ages, Medicaid has become a lifeline for the elderly, providing essential services that Medicare doesn't—home health care and long-term nursing home care.

Source: The Elder Law Handbook: A Legal and Financial Survival Guide for Caregivers and Seniors, by Peter J. Strauss and Nancy M. Lederman. Copyright © 1996 by Peter J. Strauss and Nancy M. Lederman. Reprinted with the permission of Facts on File, Inc.

Medicaid is the major payer of long-term care for those who can't afford the average yearly cost of $40,000 or more (more than double that amount in some areas). Medicaid covers the "nonskilled" but unbelievably expensive custodial care services that Medicare doesn't. Thousands of middle-income Americans have found themselves divesting themselves of their assets or "spending down" to eligibility levels in order to qualify for benefits under Medicaid. Medicaid pays for 42 percent of all nursing home costs nationwide. It covers over 60 percent of all nursing home patients.

Administered by the states, Medicaid represents the fastest-growing component of many state budgets. States pay approximately 45 percent and the federal government 55 percent of Medicaid costs. The federal share amounts to 6 percent of federal outlays. Nearly one-third of Medicaid spending goes to home health services and long-term nursing home care. Total costs for Medicaid reached $142 billion in 1994.

Medicaid rules must be understood in context. One target for budget cuts has been the benefits furnished to middle-income people who have made themselves eligible for Medicaid to avoid the astronomical costs of long-term care. Stricter eligibility rules have made qualifying for benefits harder than ever before, and service and program cuts have affected both home care and nursing home care as well as programs such as adult day care. Additional changes and restrictions are being contemplated by Congress and several states. These events make it more important than ever that you understand the rules and how Medicaid works.

Before learning how to qualify for Medicaid, you should understand what benefits you're trying to obtain. In general, Medicaid pays for doctors and hospital stays, like Medicare. It also provides coverage for long-term nursing home care not covered by Medicare. Nursing homes operate according to a Medicaid plan which requires doctor certification of the need to enter the facility and periodic review of the need for continued care.

Medicaid also covers home health care services, medical supplies, and equipment. It commonly pays for at-home services supplied under state plans for people who would otherwise be institutionalized, covering part-time skilled nursing, home-health, and homemaker services provided by certified home health agencies.

"Spending Down" for Medicaid

For millions of older Americans, Medicaid is the only means by which long-term custodial care can be supported. Each year half a million people "spend down" their assets in order to qualify for long-term care assistance available under Medicaid. Some actually pay for their care until their assets are used up. Others purchase "exempt" items or transfer their assets, all legitimate Medicaid-planning strategies to allow them to keep their independence and autonomy without sacrificing their life savings.

These strategies all follow one basic rule. *All* your income and assets above specified levels must be spent to pay for care before you will qualify for Medicaid. Various planning strategies using statutory exemptions, spousal protections, and asset transfers are described below.

Plan ahead! This is one area in which advance planning is critical. Depending on your circumstances, it may take time to spend down or otherwise divest yourself of your assets in order to meet eligibility levels—and the law imposes penalty periods after transfers before you can qualify for benefits. Last-minute action may not work.

Although financing long-term care in this manner is entirely legal, Medicaid planning has become a major political issue. So many people have been forced to try to qualify for Medicaid benefits that the various methods for achieving that goal are under continuous attack.

Applying for Medicaid

Applying for Medicaid entails verification of your financial resources as well as citizenship and residency requirements.

Financial requirements are strict. You will be asked for your bank statements, tax returns, and other financial records reflecting your income, assets, and expenses.

More and more older people seeking Medicaid for nursing home and home care services are enlisting professional help in obtaining Medicaid, using lawyers or social workers familiar with the process and its requirements. We recommend this approach highly. Regardless of whether you need to avail yourself of other Medicaid-planning strategies to protect assets, you want to ensure that you get the health care coverage you need.

As we've described, Medicaid is a *means*-tested program. In order to qualify, you must establish financial eligibility by meeting [an] income and assets test set by the states. Depending on where you live, you can qualify for Medicaid under one or more of these programs: Eligibility rules in the states are confusing even for experts. Many states distinguish between nursing home and other home- and community-based care in determining Medicaid eligibility for those services. In some states there is a "medically needy" option for nursing home care only but not for general services.

Don't make the mistake of thinking that Medicaid benefits are limited to the very poor. Medicaid is a complex, confusing, but important government program which has become the lifeline for many middle-income families who need help paying for long-term care in order to avoid impoverishment.

Originally intended for the poor, it has become the payer of last resort for persons of modest means. Spousal protections for resources and income clearly indicate Congressional intent that Medicaid continue as a program for middle-income Americans. Yet the use of Medicaid to finance long-term care, particularly nursing home costs, has had a profound impact on state budgets and resulted in attempts to restrict access to the program and limit benefits through calls for block grants.

Despite intended overhaul, with the federal government unlikely to increase Medicare benefits in the foreseeable future, Medicaid is likely to continue as the only government-funded program that deals with long-term care.

There may be any number of reasons not to apply for Medicaid, including personal, family, and psychological reasons; quality-of-care issues; and tax consequences. Nevertheless, it is an option that deserves serious consideration. While access to Medicaid is complicated and may not be available to or right for everyone, it is a possible source of financing for long-term care—even for those who may not now imagine they can take advantage of it.

Middle-Class Medicaid

Andrew Bates

Golden Girls

With the dramatic surge in the elderly population during the past couple of decades, it's not surprising that there's now a cottage industry of attorneys and financial planners specializing in "elder law." Sounds pretty innocuous, as does the specialty called "Medicaid estate planning." What this really means, however, is helping middle- and upper-income seniors shelter their assets—no matter how great—so they can qualify for Medicaid coverage. It's a practice—and a perfectly legal one—that puts extra pressure on the already financially strapped Medicaid program by squandering precious resources on those who should not have taxpayers financing their care.

Because Medicare covers only the cost of short-term, acute care, paying for long-term care has always been a problem for the elderly. But until the recent explosion of medical costs, old folks were typically able to pick up their own tabs, with the help of their children. In the past decade, however, the cost for nursing home care has soared; it now averages between $25,000 and $30,000 a year. The pressure for loopholes has thus intensified. More and more elderly patients are taking advantage of flaws in the Social Security Act, which enable them to avail themselves of government-subsidized care *and* save their assets for their heirs.

Several recent studies suggest that only 10 percent to 25 percent of nursing home patients have impoverished themselves on medical bills ("spent

Source: "Middle-Class Medicaid," by Andrew Bates, *The New Republic,* February 3, 1989, pp. 17-18. Reprinted by permission.

down," in health care vernacular) to qualify for Medicaid. Even these relatively low figures, which are based on the numbers of patients who start as private pay and end up on Medicaid, overestimate the extent of "spend down" by failing to account for the artificial "impoverishment" that's occurring.

The lawyers who exploit Medicaid loopholes are neither obscure nor shady. The American Bar Association sponsors seminars about where the loopholes are and how to exploit them. Senior citizens can even get advice on Medicaid estate planning from many state Medicaid offices. Boston attorney Harley Gordon, whose *How to Protect Your Life Savings From Catastrophic Illness and Nursing Homes* has sold over 200,000 copies and landed him appearances on talk shows throughout the country, is at least blunt about his agenda: "Every city in America has thousands of lawyers whose job it is to help wealthy people and corporations avoid as much tax as legally possible. What I do is the same thing. Only I help the little people." "Little people" in Gordon's mind means the same as in Leona Helmsley's: The typical recipient of his and others' advice are individuals with between $100,000 and $400,000 in liquid assets.

How does Medicaid planning work? In most states, a single individual cannot qualify for Medicaid until her "countable assets" have been reduced to about $2,000. (For married couples, the rules are more lenient: Depending on the state, the spouse can keep anywhere from about $13,000 to $66,000 in assets and from $1,000 to $1,600 a month for personal maintenance needs.) Since virtually all cash and securities have to go to pay nursing home bills, the theory is to convert countable liquid assets into exempt assets. The largest shelter in Medicaid estate planning is your home, so elder gurus advise you to pay off your mortgage, remodel your kitchen, or build on. If you don't own a home, buy one.

To spend the rest of your disposable income, pay off your debts, buy a car (the more expensive the better, of course, since it's all exempt), or, in most states, buy personal property—clothing, furniture, jewelry—of any value. Take a vacation. Or, as financial planners Ira Schneider and Ezra Huber advise in *Financial Planning for Long-Term Care,* "An applicant could spend all of his or her assets on something 'frivolous,' such as a ninetieth birthday celebration of Ziegfeld Follies proportion."

Not surprising, Medicaid officials say that Medicaid planning is being driven not by the elderly, but by heirs desperate to preserve their inheritance. In doing so, heirs face an ethical dilemma, since Medicaid recipients have more trouble getting into top-quality nursing homes than private-pay patients, and nursing homes with mostly private-pay patients provide much better care than those facilities dependent on Medicaid patients. To avoid having to choose between inheritance and consigning Mom and Dad to second-rate care in understaffed nursing homes, Medicaid-planning gurus often recommend that the patient retain enough money to pay privately for at least six months to get into a top-notch nursing home. The elderly patient then "spends down" to qualify for Medicaid, yet at the same time remains in the high-quality, well-regarded nursing home. It's the best of all worlds: Mom and Pop get top-notch care, the kids get the full inheritance, and taxpayers foot the bill.

Although there is little empirical data on the precise extent of asset sheltering by the elderly and their attorneys, Medicaid officials throughout the country say that the practice is widespread. For instance, Massachusetts Medicaid workers have reported that roughly 30 percent to 50 percent of Medicaid applications from affluent Boston suburbs involve the sheltering of assets.

The policy implications of this trend are enormous. Taxpayer dollars are being used to preserve the assets of the middle-class and fairly well-to-do elderly, while Medicaid dollars for poor women and children and the elderly poor are scarce. In addition, with the vast majority of their patients on Medicaid, many nursing homes are in desperate shape financially. Since Medicaid reimbursement covers only about 80 percent of the full cost of care, nursing homes have to charge more from private-pay patients—those middle- to upper-income elderly who, either misinformed or highly principled, aren't inclined to make the rest of us pay their medical bills. For those covered by private insurance, this cost is passed on in the form of higher premiums.

In an effort to crack down on such abuses, states such as New York and Connecticut are developing "public-private" solutions that would allow individuals to retain some of their assets and still qualify for Medicaid. Under the Connecticut venture, for example, an individual buys an experimental policy that pays nursing home bills up to a fixed amount, say, $100,000. Once the coverage runs out, Medicaid kicks in automatically. At first glance, these programs seem to be a palatable compromise. The problem is that unless the federal Medicaid eligibility requirements are tightened, there's little incentive to buy three years' worth of private insurance when one can qualify for Medicaid almost immediately.

What to do? The inspector general of the Department of Health and Human Services laid the groundwork for a feasible solution in two major studies released in 1988 and 1989. Congress should tighten many of the loopholes in the Social Security Act, strengthening the transfer of assets rules so that patients could not artificially impoverish themselves to qualify for Medicaid. Congress should also allow families to retain and manage property while their parents are on Medicaid. In return, as a condition of eligibility for such public assistance, the government would require a lien (which would equal the total amount of Medicaid benefits paid) be placed on the recipient's property and assets. But Congress hasn't followed through on these recommendations.

Recovery on estates should be made mandatory so that heirs cannot, in the words of one analyst, "reap the windfall of Medicaid subsidies." With the exception of Oregon, however, most states have proved reluctant to recover expenses from the estates of deceased Medicaid recipients. Recovery programs are politically unpopular but they save states money that can then be plowed back into Medicaid budgets. Congress could provide an incentive to states to build up effective recovery programs by reducing federal Medicaid payments to those that fail to do so.

If the elderly and their heirs don't like these tougher rules, that's too bad. If seniors want to avoid liens on assets and estate recovery after their death, they should purchase private long-term care insurance by using the equity built up in their homes (which can cover the average senior citizen's medical bills) or insisting that their heirs contribute to the cost of care. Like it or not, it is not the birthright of upper-income and middle-class Americans to have their medical bills paid by the rest of us. At least not yet.

The Fallacy of Impoverishment

Stephen Moses

The debate over how to solve the long-term care financing crisis has reached a new and perilous stage: stalemate. Big government solutions are out of favor, but private sector initiatives appear inadequate. When a problem seems intractable, wise counsel is to check your premises. Is there a

Source: "The Fallacy of Impoverishment," by Stephen Moses, *The Gerontologist,* vol. 30, no. 1, pp. 21-25, 1990. Copyright © The Gerontological Society of America. Reprinted by permission. This essay is based on research conducted by the Office of Inspector General of the Department of Health and Human Services and published in *Medicaid Estate Recoveries* (OAI-0986-00078), June 1988, and *Transfer of Assets in the Medicaid Program: A Case Study in Washington State* (OAI-09-8801340), May 1989. . . . The views expressed herein are those of the author. Neither the Office of Inspector General nor the Department of Health and Human Services reviewed the paper in draft and no endorsement by them should be inferred. [The author was] . . . project director for the studies cited above.

missing piece in the long-term care financing puzzle? Does a false assumption underlie the deadlock on this issue?

Conventional wisdom holds that eligibility for Medicaid, the nation's single largest financier of long-term care, requires the spenddown of assets and income to impoverishment. Federal and state laws, regulations, and policies seem to say that a person must spend down to the poverty level or below before qualifying. If this is true, elderly people and their heirs should seek private risk-sharing protection aggressively, but they do not. If it is false, private sector options such as long-term care insurance are severely handicapped—people only insure against real risks.

This [essay] describes research that casts doubt on the belief that Medicaid requires impoverishment. It also explores the broader social and policy ramifications of such a finding.

Background

Although originally intended to ensure access to mainstream health care for the poor, Medicaid has become the major payor of nursing home care for the middle class (Rymer, Burwell, Adler, & Madigan, 1984, p. 122). The program funds 44% of America's nursing home costs (Letsch, Levit, & Waldo, 1988) and is the principal payor for over 63% of patient days (Dean, personal communication, Oct. 20, 1989). Nevertheless, from the enactment of the Medicaid statute in 1965 until 1981, no federal rules existed against transferring assets to qualify for assistance. People who needed nursing home care could give away their property in order to qualify for Medicaid.

In 1981, Congress took the first step to limit this practice with the Boren-Long amendment. This statute allowed states to restrict asset transfers made for the purpose of qualifying for Medicaid. But Boren-Long did not apply to exempt property. Inasmuch as Medicaid exempts the home, and 70% of the net worth of the median elderly person is in a home (U.S. Bureau of the Census, 1986), Boren-Long excluded large amounts of property from the transfer restrictions.

Congress corrected this shortcoming and developed a more comprehensive approach in 1982 with the Tax Equity and Fiscal Responsibility Act (TEFRA). The TEFRA authorized states to (1) restrict asset transfers within 2 years of Medicaid nursing home eligibility, (2) place liens on the property of living recipients, and (3) recover from the estates of deceased recipients. Each of these procedures was optional for state Medicaid programs. Nevertheless, the expressed intent of Congress was "to assure that all of the resources available to an institutionalized individual, including equity in a home, which are not needed for the support of a spouse or dependent children will be used to defray the cost of supporting the individual in the institution" (U.S. Code, 1982, p. 814).

In 1985, a draft report of the Health Care Financing Administration revealed lax state enforcement of the TEFRA asset control authorities (Moses & Duncan, 1985). For example, transfer of assets rules were fraught with loopholes, only one state (Alabama) fully used the lien power, and although 18 states recovered from estates, most did so with very little success. Based only on telephone inquiries to state Medicaid programs and a valid random sample of cases in Idaho, this report speculated that estate recoveries could leap from $36 million nationally per year to $535 million if all states followed the asset control methodologies of Oregon's exemplary program. Although it remained unpublished, the report was released to the Office of Inspector General (OIG) of the Department of Health and Human Services and to the General Accounting Office (GAO). Both the OIG and the GAO began national studies of Medicaid estate recoveries in 1986.

OIG and GAO Medicaid Estate Recovery Studies

Office of Inspector General (1988)

The OIG sent a 17-page questionnaire to all 50 state Medicaid programs probing their policies and practices on transfer of assets, liens, and estate recoveries. The objective of the study was

> to find out exactly what States have done since 1982 to implement TEFRA's asset control authorities . . . to determine the extent and effectiveness of Medicaid estate recovery programs throughout the country . . . to report on "best practices" . . . [and] to examine State Medicaid eligibility policy with regard to transfer of assets and liens, because estate recoveries are obviously moot if no property is retained in recipients' possession that can be recovered after their deaths. (OIG, 1988, p. 2)

Both the Health Care Financing Administration and the Office of Management and Budget approved the OIG's survey instrument in advance. All 50 states and the District of Columbia responded. The study team did extensive telephone follow-up with Medicaid eligibility and estate recovery staff in three-fourths of the responding programs.

The OIG found very weak enforcement of asset transfer restrictions: "The States report that Medicaid eligibility rules permit knowledgeable individuals to transfer or shelter property from Medicaid resource limitations in a manner reminiscent of income tax avoidance" (p. ii). Three pages of quotations from Medicaid eligibility staff across the country supported this conclusion. For example: "People are starting to use a lot of fancy footwork to avoid losing the 'family fortune' " (Maryland). "Many, many, many attorneys call on a daily basis looking for 'loopholes.' There are lots of welfare specialists who help people avoid welfare resource limits" (Minnesota). "We recover from people who are not clever enough to transfer their property, and everyone else goes scot-free" (California).

Only two states had implemented TEFRA's lien provisions to secure property for estate recovery. Most states found the lien authority too restrictive to administer cost effectively. For example: "Liens are too difficult to administer because of Federal restrictions. Other property retention techniques, such as aggressive identification of assets, reversing illegal transfers, and challenging every possible resource shelter, are more effective under the circumstances" (Oregon, p. 20). Commenting on the ineffectuality of transfer of assets and lien rules, the OIG observed, "States cannot recover what is not there" (p. 23).

Twenty-three states and the District of Columbia recovered $42 million from the estates of Medicaid recipients in 1985, according to the OIG. But most states were very inefficient at recoveries. Even under the existing restrictive laws, regulations, and policies, the OIG concluded that "if all States recovered at the same rate as the most effective State (Oregon), national recoveries would be $589 million annually" (p. 46).

General Accounting Office (1989)

The GAO study sought to "assess the extent and effectiveness of state efforts to reduce program costs by using the estates of Medicaid nursing home recipients or their surviving spouses to recover all or part of the costs of care paid for by Medicaid" (GAO, 1989, p. 14). The agency reviewed 200 randomly selected nursing home cases in Oregon and seven other states. Oregon

was chosen "to identify the key elements of a successful estate recovery program because it reported annual recoveries per nursing home recipient more than twice those reported by any other state" (p. 14). It recovered "about $10 for every $1 spent administering the program . . . " (p. 3). Projections of potential estate recoveries in the other states were based on their use of Oregon's policies and procedures.

The GAO found that ". . . two-thirds of the amount spent for nursing home care for Medicaid recipients who owned a home could be recovered from their estates or the estates of their spouses. If implemented carefully, estate recovery programs can achieve savings, while treating the elderly equitably and humanely" (p. 3). The six states GAO studied that lacked recovery programs "could recover $85 million from recipients admitted to nursing homes in fiscal year 1985" (p. 4). Only "about 14 percent of the Medicaid nursing home residents in the eight states GAO reviewed owned a home . . . " (p. 4). The GAO did not account for the discrepancy between this percentage and the well-known statistic that three-quarters of elderly people own their homes (Rivlin & Wiener, 1988, p. 123). One presumes that people are either selling their homes and "spending down" before going on Medicaid or they are effectively transferring or sheltering the home's value.

Thus, both the OIG and the GAO studies confirmed that large amounts of private resources ($589 million nationally and $85 million in six states, respectively) pass to heirs each year instead of being used for long-term care costs or to reimburse Medicaid. Additionally, for reasons discussed in the next section, the OIG and GAO projections may be vastly underestimated.

Medicaid Asset Shelters

Assets that do not remain in an estate until the death of a Medicaid recipient are obviously not recoverable and would not show up in studies like the OIG's and GAO's. Therefore, the extensive anecdotal evidence of asset transfers and shelters discovered by the OIG in its estate recovery study raised another serious question. If people are jettisoning property before they apply for Medicaid nursing home care, how could we possibly know how much money is diverted from private to public long-term care costs? The OIG conducted further research that bears on this question (OIG, 1989). It found that people initially denied but subsequently approved for Medicaid nursing home benefits in Washington state for 1 year possessed $27.5 million in assets at the time of their denial. These assets had to be disposed of before they could qualify for assistance. Over 80% of the assets had been sheltered: 59% were transferred to a spouse, 11% were transferred to adult children, and 11% were retained as exempt. Only 8% were consumed for long-term care. The remainder was of uncertain disposition.

To account for the magnitude of these figures, the OIG interviewed 32 professional advisers on Medicaid eligibility. These people described a network of private "elder law" attorneys, publicly funded legal services attorneys, social workers, and even Medicaid staff who counsel families on how to qualify an infirm elder for Medicaid while preserving income and assets. The sheltering techniques recommended by such advisers included: interspousal and other legal transfers, trusts, purchase of exempt assets, "intent to return" to the home, life estates, joint tenancy with right of survivorship, gift and estate planning, durable power of attorney, guardianships, divorce, relocation, care contracts, and nonsupport suits. One attorney, whose bag of tricks is highlighted in the OIG report, guaranteed Medicaid eligibility within 30 days for a $950 fee. . . .

Finally, the OIG observed that "financial abuse of the elderly, according to study respondents, is 'commonplace,' 'bigger than anyone thinks,' 'rife.' We heard many stories about people forced onto Medicaid when their income or resources were taken" (OIG, 1989, p. 11).

Medicaid Asset Spenddown

A common understanding, often referenced in the literature, is that half or more of all nursing home patients on Medicaid were private pay until they spent down to poverty (Branch et al., 1988,

p. 649; Burwell, Adams, & Meiners, 1989, p. 2; Davis, 1984, p. 3; DHHS, 1987, p. 19; Dobris, 1989, p. 10; NAIC, 1987, p. 2). Tragically, many people actually do sell their homes and spend their life savings on nursing home care before they qualify for Medicaid. Evidence is mounting, however, that such draconian measures are both unnecessary and less common than previously supposed. Impoverishment is not the only path to Medicaid nursing home eligibility, according to the OIG work. Financially sophisticated people who are accustomed to dealing with attorneys, accountants, and financial planners can find ways to protect their assets and still qualify for Medicaid. Others, with less financial savvy, often lose what little they have before they learn how the system works (OIG, 1988, p. ii).

Very little is known about the magnitude of asset spenddown. For example, Branch reported how fast people would become impoverished if they spent down in nursing homes (Branch et al., 1988). He did not tell us how often or to what degree they actually do spend down. Several recent studies have found that spenddown is actually much smaller than previously believed (Burwell, Adams, & Meiners, 1989; Liu & Manton, 1989; Liu, Doty, & Manton, 1989; Spence & Wiener, 1989). Like the Branch study, however, these studies assume that people who had significant assets at one time, but ended up on Medicaid, must have had catastrophic care costs. None of them develop the possibility that assets were transferred or sheltered in order to qualify for nursing home assistance. Nevertheless, the techniques to transfer and shelter assets, and the counseling to learn them, are readily available, according to the OIG.

Spousal Impoverishment

Impoverishment of the spouse at home caused by institutionalization of a disabled husband or wife used to be a serious problem. Medicaid rules allowed only a few hundred dollars of income per month to be shifted from an institutionalized to a community spouse who had little or no separate income (Neuschler, 1987, pp. 48-49). The new community spouse "minimum monthly maintenance needs allowance" was designed to solve that problem at considerable public expense. We should keep in mind, however, that the same people whose income and resources will now be protected may live in homes they own free and clear. Their problem is not poverty per se, but rather cash flow.

Medicare Catastrophic Coverage Act

The Medicare Catastrophic Coverage Act of 1988 changed Medicaid long-term care eligibility in several ways that affect asset shelters and estate recovery potential. Some of the changes, such as more generous treatment of community spouse income and resources, will make Medicaid benefits easier to obtain. This could mean that more assets will remain to be recovered from estates or, alternatively, that people will have longer to find ways to protect the assets. Other changes, such as mandatory and lengthened transfer of assets restrictions, make eligibility somewhat more difficult. This could lead to liquidation of assets and greater spenddown or, alternatively, to wider use of better planning and qualifying techniques. Most of the methods used to shelter or transfer assets legally in the past are still intact. The basic condition remains unchanged: Families can preserve significant assets while qualifying elders for Medicaid nursing home care. Without estate recovery programs, these assets pass unencumbered to noncontributing heirs and Medicaid shoulders the full brunt (minus mandatory contributions to cost of care) of the long-term care costs.

Implications

Medicaid requires impoverishment. Few scholarly papers or popular articles on long-term care financing say otherwise or explain further. Yet, impoverishment is neither a sufficient nor a necessary cause of Medicaid eligibility. Two-thirds of the elderly poor in America are not covered by Medicaid (Holahan & Cohen, 1986, p. 99). On the other hand, people with median and even higher income and resources often qualify for the program's most expensive benefit (nursing home care) while preserving the bulk of their assets for heirs (Neuschler, 1987, p. 20; OIG, 1988; OIG, 1989).

Looming in the background of last year's "catastrophic" debate was the question: What shall we do about *long-term care* costs? That predicament is front and center now. Most of the work done by the federal government on this issue has encouraged the development of private risk-sharing solutions. Private sector answers, however, have been much slower to develop than anticipated. This is a puzzle, because most of the obstacles to market-based solutions do not seem insurmountable. Experts on long-term care financing have assumed that Medicaid is not a major impediment.

In light of the findings discussed here, however, consider that elderly people are often unclear about catastrophic long-term care risks. They deny their personal jeopardy and do not plan ahead to protect privately against financial catastrophe. They do not plan to rely on public assistance either, but once they get sick, welfare is their only option. Under today's system, they can avoid paying insurance premiums (often in excess of $100 per month) or risk-sharing membership fees, wait to see if they are stricken by a long-term debilitating illness, and still receive nursing home care paid for by Medicaid while preserving their assets for heirs. Because of the shame felt by families forced to qualify their elders for welfare, the negative aspects of Medicaid nursing home care—dependency, loss of income, access and quality problems, institutional bias, and stigma—often go uncommunicated to others.

Therefore, the elderly population perceives no urgent need to purchase insurance, join a Social/ Health Maintenance Organization or Continuing Care Community, convert the equity in their home, or save toward long-term care costs. Without a compelling need among consumers to buy (low demand), sellers of such services lack sufficient reason to invest in the necessary research, development, and marketing of private protection (low supply). This in itself could explain why the impact of private sector long-term care financing options has been disappointing.

Conclusion

A plan to eliminate this impasse between public and private long-term care financing options is quite simple conceptually: Give middle-class elderly people a clear choice between access to public funding of long-term care or preservation of their estates—not both. The rudiments of such a plan are evident in the OIG report's (1988) recommendations:

- Change Medicaid rules to permit families to retain and manage property while their elders receive long-term care.

- Strengthen the transfer of assets rules so that people cannot give away property to qualify for Medicaid.

- Require a legal instrument as a condition of Medicaid eligibility to secure property owned by applicants and recipients for later recovery.

- Increase estate recoveries as a nontax revenue source for the Medicaid program while steadfastly protecting the personal and property rights of recipients and their families. (p. ii)

Underlying these recommendations is the belief that we should eliminate the indignities and inequities associated with qualifying for nursing home assistance. We should not pressure people to divorce, impoverish their spouses, liquidate their property, or hire estate planners in order to qualify. Elderly people, financially independent all their lives, but stricken by catastrophic illness in their most vulnerable years, should not be compelled to rely on welfare because of temporary cash flow problems. To correct such deficiencies in the existing program, however, we would have to pay for the solution. We can do this by closing the loopholes in transfer of assets restrictions, requiring legal encumbrances on property as a condition of eligibility, and mandating cost-effective estate recoveries as a prerequisite for federal financial participation. Alternatively, we could offer middle-class seniors a line of credit secured by their estates with which to purchase home or nursing care and get them off welfare entirely.

If implemented, these recommendations would increase Medicaid estate recoveries substantially. But this new nontax revenue is not the most important aspect of the recommendations. We would also be sending a message to America's senior citizens and their families: If they do not or cannot protect themselves privately against the risk of catastrophic long-term care costs, their government will provide the necessary care. But, if they own property, they must understand that it will be recovered—when it is no longer needed for the livelihood of their immediate dependents—to pay for publicly funded care and ensure that the same benefits will be available for others. Only the remainder after reimbursement of costs will pass to their heir and beneficiaries. So if they do not want to encumber their estate, then they or their heir should purchase protection in the private market- place.

If we send this message, we can expect the demand for private risk-sharing products to increase. Greater demand means more suppliers, increased competition, better products, leaner pricing, thriving new industries, and, therefore, increased employment and tax revenues.

The last piece in the puzzle is to explain how seniors will pay for private risk sharing. The experts say older people lack the cash flow to purchase private long-term care protection (Rivlin & Wiener, 1988). Yet people over 65 possess more than $800 billion in home equity (Rivlin & Wiener, 1988, p. 131). Seniors are "house rich" and "cash poor." Home equity conversion experiments intended to solve this problem have failed. These experiments have failed, however, because Medicaid pays for nursing home care and exempts the home. Why encumber the house to buy insurance you may not need when the government will pay for your care if you need it and save the house anyway? When people know they can save the house or get Medicaid, but not both, they will be more likely to seek home equity conversion to provide the cash flow to purchase private protection. This change could make home equity conversion economically viable as private enterprise.

Finally, faced with the potential loss of their inheritances, adult children of elderly people will contribute voluntarily toward long-term care insurance premiums or other forms of financial protection for their parents. They have the cash flow and their aging parents have the assets. Both parties have an intense interest in preserving the estate, including the family home. Under the current system, the adult children of elderly people reap a windfall from Medicaid for ignoring the risk of catastrophic costs.

The proper role of government in this arena is to help those who cannot help themselves. It is not to transfer wealth from tax payers to indemnify heirs. If we make long-term care assistance more readily available than now, but require a payback from estates, middle-class elderly people will have better access to care and stronger reasons to seek nonwelfare protection. In time, they will be freed entirely from the indignity of legal maneuvering to qualify for public assistance.

References

Branch, L. G., Friedman, D., Cohen, M., Smith, N., & Socholitzky, E. (1988). Impoverishing the elderly: A case study of the financial risk of spenddown among Massachusetts elderly people. *The Gerontologist, 28,* 648-652.

Burwell, B., Adams, E., & Meiners, M. (1989). *Spenddown of assets prior to Medicaid eligibility among nursing home recipients in Michigan* (contract 500-86-0016). Washington, DC: SysteMetrics/McGraw-Hill for the Health Care Financing Administration.

Davis, C. (1984). *Long-term care financing and delivery systems: Exploring some alternatives* (conference proceedings). Washington, DC: Health Care Financing Administration.

Department of Health and Human Services (DHHS). (1987). *Report of the task force on long-term health care policies.* Washington, DC: U.S. Government Printing Office.

Dobris, J. C. (1989). Medicaid asset planning by the elderly: A policy view of expectations, entitlements, and inheritance. *Real Property, Probate and Trust Journal, 24,* 1-32.

General Accounting Office. (1989). *Medicaid. Recoveries from nursing home residents' estates could offset program costs* (GAO/HRD-89-56). Washington, DC: U.S. Government Printing Office.

Holahan, J. F., & Cohen, J. W. (1986). *Medicaid: The trade-off between cost containment and access to care.* Washington, DC: The Urban Institute.

Letsch, S. W., Levit, K. R., & Waldo, D. R. (1988). National health expenditures, 1987. *Health Care Financing Review, 10,* 109-122.

Liu, K., Doty, R., & Manton, K. (1989). *Medicaid spenddown of disabled elderly persons: In nursing homes or in the community?* (unpublished paper prepared under Cooperative Agreement No. 18-C-98641/4-02). Washington, DC: Health Care Financing Administration.

Liu, K., & Manton, K. (1989). The effect of nursing home use on Medicaid eligibility. *The Gerontologist, 29,* 59-66.

Moses, S. A., & Duncan, J. (1985). *The Medicaid estate recoveries study* (unpublished report). Seattle, WA: Health Care Financing Administration.

National Association of Insurance Commissioners (NAIC). (1987). *Long-term care insurance: An industry perspective on market development and consumer protection.*

Neuschler, E. (1987). *Medicaid eligibility for the elderly in need of long-term care.* Washington, DC: National Governors' Association.

Office of Inspector General. (1988). *Medicaid estate recoveries* (OAI-09-86-00078).

Office of Inspector General. (1989). *Transfer of assets in the Medicaid program: A case study in Washington State* (OAI09-88-01340).

Rivlin, A. M., & Wiener, J. M. (1988). *Caring for the disabled elderly: Who will pay?* Washington, DC: The Brookings Institution.

Rymer, M., Burwell, B., Adler, G., & Madigan, D. (1984). *Grants and contracts report, short-*

term evaluation of Medicaid. Selected issues (contract no. HHS-100-82-0038). Washington, DC: Health Care Financing Administration.

Spence, D. A., & Wiener, J. M. (1989). Medicaid spenddown in nursing homes: Estimates from the 1985 national nursing home survey (unpublished draft). Washington, DC: The Brookings Institution.

U.S. Bureau of the Census. (1986). Household wealth and asset ownership: 1984 (Current Population Reports Series P-70, No. 7). Washington, DC: Author.

U.S. Code. (1982). Congressional and Administrative News, 97th Congress—Second Session, Legislative History (Public Laws 97-146 to 97-248, Vol. 2). St. Paul, MN: West.

READING 9

The Family
Women and Grandparents as Kin-Keepers

Gunhild O. Hagestad

Concern is growing over the strain experienced by families who provide care for their ill or impaired elderly members. It is frequently argued that families in an aging society must be prepared to assume more of a care load than was the case for families in the past. We do not really have the historical data to judge if such statements are accurate, but it is important to keep in mind that before improved living conditions and medical advances produced rectangular survival curves, illness and death were encountered in all phases of family life—and at a time when there were far fewer outside institutional facilities and programs to alleviate their pressures. Families have always been expected to experience and absorb the shocks of illness and bereavement. The main difference between today's families and those of the past is not likely to be in the total *amount* of care and concern they expend, but the *focus* of them.

Infants and young children have always been regarded as vulnerable and dependent. But now, after childhood, these attributes are linked nearly exclusively with old age. Never before in human history has the experience of human frailty and the loss of a family member been so clearly linked to one group: the old. Perhaps part of the sense of burden associated with their care stems from the fact that the illness and loss are represented by parents—individuals who for decades were perceived as pillars of strength and support. . . .

Effects of "The Mortality Gap"

Women in the United States currently outlive men by about seven to eight years. The world of the very old is a world of women, both in society and within families. Men and women also spend the latter part of their lives in differing living arrangements and relationships. Most older women are widows living alone; most older men live with their wives. For example, among individuals over the age of seventy-five, two-thirds of the men are living with a spouse, while less then one-fifth of the women are.

These contrasts between older men and women have strong implications for the rest of their family members. First of all, the oldest members of a family are likely to be women. Women are also more likely to have great- and great-great-grandchildren. In societies where historical events have made sex ratios even more imbalanced than in this country, the three oldest generations may be populated only by women. For example, a German study found that many five-generation families contained three generations of widows.

Differences in widowhood and remarriage mean that men tend to maintain a significant horizontal, intragenerational relationship until the end of their lives; women do not. Consequently, women draw more on their intergenerational relationships for help and support in old age. At the time when men face serious impairment, they are likely to have a wife to care for them, while frail and ill older women are typically widows who turn to younger generations for help. This may be one reason why women, throughout their adulthood, invest more time and energy in intergenerational ties than men do. . . .

New Forms of Interdependence

. . . Over the last century, economic needs have given way to emotional needs as the main family "glue," especially in relationships among adults. Over the same time period, we have seen a shift in emphasis from the needs of the family as a group to the needs and wishes of individuals. Individual choices, such as the decisions about when to marry and leave the family, were once guided by the needs of the family unit as a whole. The twentieth century, with its pension and health-care plans, has "freed" generations from many of these economic interdependencies.[12] It is commonly argued that, as a result, family ties are seen as more *voluntary* in nature.[13] Kin connections are

seen as a latent potential, from which active and viable relationships may or may not develop.

Even though we have a good deal of cultural ambiguity regarding relationships between young and old in the family, members of our society still share some key values and norms about family responsibilities and interconnections.[14] Surveys that have compared the attitudes and expectations of parents and children have often found that children are more ready than parents to state that the younger generation should provide help to needy elderly parents. It has also been found that the old are the most receptive to formal, nonfamily services, while the young are those most in favor of family-provided help. Researchers attribute such contrasts to "youthful idealism" on the part of the young. The middle-aged and the old, on the other hand, are often responding on the basis of actual care-taking experiences. Recently, a number of writers have argued that with the growth of societal supports for the old, an increasingly important function of the family will be to serve as mediators between bureaucracies and the aged,[15] and the modern families not only meet needs, they identify needs, so that other institutions can address them.

While pension systems and health plans have lightened the economic pressures for most families, there is still a steady flow of intergenerational support, and the majority of the states have enacted so-called "family responsibility" laws, statutes that establish relatives' responsibility for family members who are indigent, needy, or dependent. But recent research and public debate indicate that enormous complexity still remains in sorting out rights and obligations among family members in an aging society.

Kin-Keeping and Its Costs

There is a rather extensive literature showing that women are kin-keepers, and that their preparation for this role starts early in life. Kin-keeping tasks include maintaining communication, facilitating contact and the exchange of goods and services, and monitoring family relationships. These functions are often performed for the husband's kin as well as for the women's own family line. Even when they are not the initiators and orchestrators of family get-togethers, old women may nevertheless facilitate family contact by serving as the "excuse" for bringing kin together. The mother-daughter connection has emerged as the pivotal link, both in the maintenance of family contact and in the flow of support.

Daughters have been found to be the linchpin of widows' support systems. When aging parents live with offspring, eight out of ten are mothers, and two-thirds of them are living with a daughter. It is estimated that when older family members are in need of constant care, 80 percent of such care is provided by kin, usually by wives and daughters.[17] It is interesting to note that the same clear trends, identifying women as carrying an extensive and complex load of family caring, have emerged in studies of welfare states. Although Norway eliminated family-responsibility laws following the introduction of a "law for comprehensive care" which covered the young as well as the old, the care provided by Norwegian women has been described as "the hidden welfare state."[18]

It has been common, especially in the popular press, to suggest that women's involvement in the world of work will make them spend less time and effort on kin-tending. There is little evidence to support such a claim. Indeed, there are indications that an opposite trend is occurring. A growing number of women may be adjusting their work plans and work schedules to accommodate the needs of elderly parents[19]—much as they formerly planned around the needs of their children. Recent research found that employment significantly reduced caregiving to aging parents among sons, but this was not a statistically significant trend for daughters.[20]

There seems to be good reason to worry about what Betty Friedan has called "the superwoman squeeze"—the overload experienced by middle-generation women who provide support for both children and parents, in addition to facing the demands of the workaday world.[21] A growing number of writers express concern that our current social expectations regarding family help to the elderly are unrealistic—even dysfunctional, given recent demographic and social change. One asks: "At what point does the expectation of filial responsibility become social irresponsibility?"[22]

It is quite possible that as a result of dramatic and rapid demographic change—particularly the enormous increase in the proportion of people who survive to advanced old age and face chronic health problems—we are finding that old attitudes and expectations about family care for impaired members simply do not work. The main casualties of this situation are likely to be middle-aged and young-old women, who face unmanageable burdens or strong feelings of guilt. It is important, however, to regard such conclusions cautiously; in devoting so much attention to the sick and the needy old, we may go too far in equating "old" with "needy." . . .

During recent decades, ideology has stressed equality between the sexes in their family roles. Yet, as we have seen, demographic and social changes have in many ways created very different family worlds for men and women. An increasing proportion of men have only precarious vertical ties, both up and down generational lines, while women's intergenerational ties are more varied, complex, and durable than ever before in human history.

Families are social arenas in which historical changes take on personal and shared meanings. They are also groups that meet critical human needs, and settings where biographies are written and rewritten as lives unfold, take on structure, and become interwoven. This [essay] has reviewed some of the recent demographic and social changes that have transformed family life. Siblings, parents and children, grandparents and grandchildren, now look forward to decades of shared biographies. Altered patterns of mortality have not only created relationships of unprecedented duration, but have also made the timing of family deaths more predictable. As the number of children per family has decreased, differences in life experiences among siblings have become reduced, and a greater proportion of family relationships are conducted across generational lines rather than with generational peers. Trends in fertility and mortality have resulted in increasingly "top-heavy" families, and family care-giving has become more and more focused on very old members. Multigenerational families have become more common, which means that a wider spectrum of kinship roles and relationships are open to family members.

Finally, many of these recent changes have affected men and women quite differently, in some ways creating sharper contrasts between their family and social worlds.

Notes

[Only the notes that are included in the excerpted material appear here.]

12. John Modell, Frank F. Furstenberg, Jr., and Theodore Hershberg, "Social Change and Transitions to Adulthood in Historical Perspective," *Journal of Family,* Winter 1976, pp. 7-32.

13. Matilda White Riley, "The Family in an Aging Society: A Matrix of Latent Relationships," *Journal of Family Issues,* Sept. 1983, pp. 439-54.

14. Lillian E. Troll, Sheila J. Miller, and Robert C. Atchley, *Families in Later Life* (Belmont, CA: Wadsworth Publishing Co., 1979).

15. [Ethel] Shanas and Marvin B. Sussman, eds., *Family, Bureaucracy, and the Elderly* (Durham, N.C.: Duke University Press, 1977).

17. Troll, et al., op. cit.

18. Kari Waerness, "The Invisible Welfare State: Women's Work at Home," *Acta Sociologica,* supplement 1978, pp. 193-207.

19. Elaine M. Brody, "Aged Parents and Aging Children," in P. K. Ragan, ed., *Aging Parents* (Los Angeles: University of Southern California Press, 1979), pp. 267-88.

20. Eleanor Palo Stoller, "Parental Caregiving by Adult Children," *Journal of Marriage and the Family,* Nov. 1983, pp. 851-58.

21. Betty Friedan, *The Second Stage* (New York: Summit Books, 1981).

22. Brody, op. cit.

FOCUS ON PRACTICE   LONG-TERM CARE INSURANCE

Many middle-income elderly people and their relatives have been following the debate over Medicaid coverage of long-term care with great interest. In recent years, there has been a dramatic growth in privately paid long-term care services, especially assisted living and home and community-based long-term care (Bonifazi, 1998). Those who don't have enough financial resources to pay for an extended stay in a nursing home or who have a strong desire to pass along an inheritance have had to face the dismaying prospect of bankrupting themselves to qualify for Medicaid. Today, however, families who want to plan ahead for long-term care costs have a new option: purchasing private long-term care insurance. More than 100 insurance companies now offer these policies, and interest in this type of insurance is growing (Sloane, 1992). It is estimated that more than 2.5 million policies are in force.

Private long-term care insurance covers nursing home care and sometimes other community-based services. The best of long-term care insurance pays for such medically necessary services for a period from one year up to a lifetime, but typically with a maximum period of coverage. At present, private long-term care insurance provides only 2% of total funding for long-term care in the United States. Good policies are guaranteed to be renewable and need not require a prior hospital stay, as Medicare does.

Long-term care insurance is bought mainly by people above age 55; half the current policyholders are in their 60s. The age when a policy is first purchased is important, because the premium paid, though it remains level once the policy is purchased, rises sharply with age at purchase. For example, the same policy that goes for $250 a year at age 50 would cost up to $2,000 a year at age 70. But as more employers include such insurance in benefit programs, it is likely that more younger people will participate, and group rates may bring costs down. Less than 4% of the older population are covered by such policies (U.S. General Accounting Office, 1991).

Because paying for long-term care is an expensive and widespread problem, one might wonder why more people do not buy private long-term care insurance. One answer is that older people and their families mistakenly believe that Medicare will cover such expenses. Another reason is that many policies are simply not affordable when purchased at an advanced age. The best estimates are that only a tiny proportion of the older population can afford to buy private long-term care insurance (Wiener, 1998). Furthermore, many consumers, as well as state governments, lack confidence in the products on the market.

Is long-term care insurance a good buy? Consumer advocacy organizations have raised doubts (*Consumer Reports*, 1997). Long-term care policies have many exclusions and limitations that complicate comparisons of competing products. For example, insurance companies generally will not write insurance for preexisting conditions—an exclusion that covers many chronic diseases. Still another problem is that long-term care policies generally pay a fixed dollar amount for each day of care covered in contrast to Medicare, which pays a percentage of customary or reasonable fees, regardless of inflation. Without inflation protection, a person buying long-term care coverage at age 60 may find the policy inadequate when it is needed, say, at age 80.

Private long-term care insurance is now regulated entirely by state governments, but states differ in the regulations they apply. Without some kind of federal regulation, many states appear unlikely to implement standards for long-term care insurance to protect vulnerable consumers, such as protection from forfeiture of the policy should a single payment be missed.

As long as government funding for long-term care is explicitly income based or means tested, as it is under Medicaid, middle-class elderly people will naturally look to private insurance to protect themselves. Government policies have begun to encourage private long-term care insurance. The Health Insurance Portability and Accountability Act of 1996 gives more favorable tax treatment to long-term care insurance (Guttchen and Pettigrew, 1998). Still another option might be to organize public long-term care coverage funded through some combination of tax revenues and individual contributions premiums. But until such insurance is available, older people and their families will need to be familiar with all practical options for covering long-term care costs, and private long-term care insurance is certainly one of those options.

FOCUS ON THE FUTURE   GENETIC SCREENING FOR ALZHEIMER'S DISEASE?

The year is 2008 and the time is 7 a.m. A voice on your home computer wakes you up. A blinking light on the screen indicates you have overnight e-mail: two messages. One is from your elderly Aunt Mabel. She's gotten back her genetic screening testing results for Alzheimer's disease, and the news is not good. They've told her the odds of her getting Alzheimer's are 90%, and she's pretty depressed by the news. She's decided that she doesn't want to live with that prospect ahead of her. Now she's having trouble finding a doctor who'll do assisted suicide for her. There are plenty of doctors who do it, of course, but she needs one who'll accept Medicare assignment for the procedure. Now she wants advice from you.

The other message is from your health maintenance organization (HMO): It's time to come in and have a blood test to determine your genetic susceptibility to hypertension and colorectal cancer. These new tests are now required by your HMO for everyone in its plan. The HMO assures you that the genetic test is not for purposes of discrimination: You're already enrolled in its plan, so you'll be covered. But by getting genetic information about you, the HMO insists it'll be able to tell you how to engage in preventive health practices to limit your risk of a heart attack or cancer. The e-mail message promises that the HMO has your best interests at heart. But if you don't comply, they warn, you'll be subject to penalties. Seems like they know everything about you. It's a good thing they have your best interests at heart, you tell yourself. Time to get on the phone to Aunt Mabel.

Questions to Ponder

Researchers have recently identified a link between Alzheimer's disease and a specific genetic pattern known as apolipoprotein or ApoE-4. This form of the gene, ApoE-4, appears in around half of those with Alzheimer's. However, the other half of those with Alzheimer's do not carry ApoE-4, so another factor besides the gene must also be at work. Nonetheless, 90% of people who have double copies of the ApoE-4 gene will develop Alzheimer's disease by the time they reach age 80. People with double copies of ApoE-4 are only 1% of the total population, but their chances of developing Alzheimer's are about 10 times what they are for people with a different distribution of ApoE genes.

It is important to remember that the presence of ApoE in any of its forms doesn't give absolute prediction of Alzheimer's. An official statement on genetic testing was issued by a working group of the American College of Medical Genetics warning that DNA tests for Alzheimer's should not be used for routine clinical diagnosis or for predictive testing (Wagner, 1996).

At present, then, the ApoE blood test doesn't give a definitive prediction of Alzheimer's, but it is possible, even likely, that a better genetic screening test will be developed in the future. However, the development of such a genetic test for Alzheimer's disease raises troubling questions:

- There is presently no cure for Alzheimer's. Are we justified in testing for diseases before any treatment is available?

- Who should be tested, and who will pay for testing? Who will have access to the results?

- How will insurance and health care systems be affected? Will legislative antidiscrimination safeguards be necessary?

The discovery of a new genetic screening test for Alzheimer's disease raises questions about an individual's right to know, and the right *not* to know, about a diagnosis. If there were a reliable test for predicting Alzheimer's, why shouldn't people have the right to know the results? But what if genetic test isn't as reliable as people believe? Consumers may not understand that the current test yields only a probability estimate. People may mistakenly believe that the test is like a pregnancy test or like screening for Huntington's disease, which yield definitive knowledge. There has already been controversy about using genetic tests for Alzheimer's disease.

The case of Alzheimer's testing seems different from, say, cholesterol or hypertension screening, where knowledge about genetic markers or other predictors can motivate patients to change behavior and reduce the likelihood of illness. In the case of genetic markers for colon cancer, genetic screening can lead to actions that might actually reduce the risk of disease, which is different from Alzheimer's disease, where preventive measures are limited. In the scenario presented above, Aunt Mabel believes that the genetic test has value for her. She has lived a full life and now prefers to end her life rather than face some likelihood of developing dementia. We might recall that the first patient who died at the hands of Dr. Jack Kevorkian's was Janet Adkins, a woman age 54 suspected of having Alzheimer's disease but no definitive symptoms.

The availability of a genetic predictor for Alzheimer's raises important questions for private long-term care insurance. In the scenario above, the HMO wants people to have genetic tests for hypertension and colorectal cancer. Private insurers someday might want applicants to undergo Alzheimer's genetic testing. We could pass laws prohibiting discrimination based on genetic tests. But is it fair to prohibit insurers from using genetic-risk data on

Alzheimer's while the test results remain available to individuals? In that case it seems likely that individuals who find they have a higher than average probability of developing Alzheimer's are likely to purchase long-term care insurance, which could overload insurers with big claims—a classic instance of a pattern called *adverse selection*.

Furthermore, once a genetic screening test for Alzheimer's becomes widely used, would there be pressure for using it with older people under consideration for prominent positions? For example, Bob Dole was 72 when he ran for president of the United States in 1996. Should he have been urged to have an Alzheimer's screening test? In asking that question, we cannot forget that Ronald Reagan was diagnosed with Alzheimer's soon after leaving office.

We are only at the beginning of debate over the implications of genetic testing for society, and Alzheimer's is one of many diseases that will be at the center of this debate. In the early years of the 21st century, the Human Genome Project will be nearing completion and scientists will then have detailed knowledge of the entire genetic code. But the genetic code is not the whole story about human health and well-being. As we have seen, a genetic screening test for Alzheimer's yields a prediction of probability alone—a message of chance, not of fate. We misunderstand the test if we see too much of our destiny in it. It has been said that it is a blessing that prevents us from seeing our future, especially our future suffering, because each of us can bear more suffering than we can presently imagine. But new knowledge of genetics is likely to enlarge our ability to see into the future in ways we've barely begun to consider.

QUESTIONS FOR WRITING, REFLECTION, AND DEBATE

1   Elderlaw attorneys often argue that transfer of assets is perfectly right because it is permitted by law. Is this argument a convincing one? Imagine that you are an elderlaw attorney who has suddenly been questioned about your practice by a reporter from a local newspaper. Write a detailed statement defending your practice to be distributed to the newspaper.

2   Elderlaw attorneys sometimes defend transfer of assets by arguing that Medicare treats physical illnesses differently from Alzheimer's disease or similar impairments. Is this argument a persuasive one? If Medicare were amended to provide full coverage for Alzheimer's and related disorders, would transfer of assets no longer be justified?

3   Critics like Andrew Bates have charged that for older people to deliberately transfer assets to qualify for Medicaid is a form of "middle-class

welfare." Is this charge a fair one? List each of the arguments in favor and against this charge. Then look over what you've written and produce a rebuttal for each argument.

4   Some who favor the idea of transfer of assets from aged parents to adult children to qualify for Medicaid argue that elderly people have a "right to leave an inheritance." Is this a "right" that ought to be encouraged or discouraged either by Medicaid or by the tax system? Who would benefit and who would be harmed if we were to expand that right? Who would benefit and who would be harmed if we were to limit it?

5   Many believe that frail elderly people should be able to select anyone, including a family member, to provide the services to which they are entitled and have the government pay for that care. Are there any valid reasons for prohibiting the hiring of family members to perform home care services? Draft a letter to your congressional representative suggesting why you think this practice should be permitted or why you believe such a practice is mistaken.

6   Assume you are an assistant to a U.S. senator responsible for drafting an expanded version of a national health care law to cover the whole range of long-term care, from community care to the nursing home. Write a bill describing the kinds of services that might be provided to the public under the new law, including the types of conditions covered. Then write an accompanying memorandum for the senator suggesting ways the new services could be paid for. What combination of taxes and fees would cover the full package of long-term care services?

7   Gunhild Hagestad points out what most families would immediately recognize—namely, women end up handling most caregiving for frail elderly people. Is this fact about gender differences something that government ought to be concerned about or is it an issue best left for families to work out for themselves? If we wanted to correct this apparent unfairness in the burden of caregiving, how could the government make things fairer?

8   Assume that you have a close family member who may need long-term care. Visit the following Web sites and identify the factors that seem most attractive about the services described on those sites: American Association of Homes and Services for the Aging (www.aahsa.org) and Assisted Living Federation of America (www.alfa.org). What questions *aren't* well addressed by the information you found at those Web sites?

SUGGESTED READINGS

Biegel, David E., and Blum, A., *Aging and Caregiving: Theory, Research, and Policy,* Newbury Park, CA: Sage, 1990.

Finch, Janet, *Family Obligations and Social Change,* Cambridge, MA: Basil Blackwell, 1989.

Kane, Rosalie, and Kane, Robert, *Long-Term Care: Principles, Programs, and Policies,* New York: Springer, 1987.

Linsk, Nathan, and Keigher, Sharon, *Wages for Caring: Compensating Family Care of the Elderly,* New York: Praeger, 1991.

Wiener, Joshua M., *Sharing the Burden: Strategies for Public and Private Long-Term Care Insurance,* Washington, DC: Brookings Institution, 1994.

Should Older People Be Protected From Bad Choices?

Uncle Bert's bad judgment. The trouble started when Bert, 79 years old and a widower for five years, arranged for a housekeeper to come in a few days each week to take care of the house. Lilly at first seemed very dedicated to her job, and gradually Bert began paying her extra money to do other jobs for him, such as reading to him when his eyes began to fail. Soon it seemed natural for her to help him with his checkbook. Before long, Lilly was staying overnight at the house, and it seemed like Bert was becoming her only job. But Bert brightened up whenever Lilly was in the house.

Several times, when Bert's nephews or niece dropped by early in the morning, they found Lilly in bed with Uncle Bert. Something was going on with the two of them, but no one knew exactly what it was. One of the nephews told another he was afraid Uncle Bert was becoming "a dirty old man."

Another factor in their concern was Lilly's brother, Shawn, who got involved in the household. Shawn runs a multilevel marketing program selling vitamins and health products door to door. Uncle Bert began taking megadoses of vitamins in the belief that they could reverse his diabetes. He also invested his substantial life savings in Shawn's business, which was soon being operated out of Uncle Bert's garage.

When Lilly wasn't around, Uncle Bert didn't stay at home. He had a lifelong habit of taking long walks through the city and sometimes he still walked after dark through dangerous neighborhoods. He frequently walked all the way across town to the dog track, where he would lose a lot of money gambling. Uncle Bert's nephews and niece are worried about all this and have told their elderly uncle about it.

But Uncle Bert dismissed their concerns. He said he had a right to spend his money the way he wanted, and he asked simply to be left alone. "I'm old enough to live as I please," he told everyone, "and the quality of my life has never been better."

Some questions about Uncle Bert's case. Bert's nephews and niece didn't like the way he was living. They thought he was acting in ways that were misguided, even dangerous. Specifically, Uncle Bert was acting in ways that put his health and maybe his life at risk. But what do "risk" and "danger" actually mean in this case? True, Bert was following unorthodox medical treatments and walking after dark in dangerous neighborhoods. But don't younger people act in risky ways, too? Does making bad choices or running a risk constitute some kind of self-neglect? Are we ever justified in interfering when someone acts that way? Does age make any difference in a case like this? The ill-defined relationship with Lilly makes one of the nephews ridicule their uncle as "a dirty old man." What can they do about any of this? When all is said and done, does Uncle Bert have a right to be left alone? Bert stoutly defends his own definition of "quality of life."

If these questions are troublesome, the problems only became worse as this case progressed.

Shawn's vitamin and health product business was apparently going well, but Bert's nephews and niece could not see any evidence that the vitamins were helping their uncle. On the contrary, one of them happened to see on the table a copy of Uncle Bert's income tax return—filled out by Lilly—and it indicated that all his savings had been depleted. The nephews and niece were dismayed in part because, ever since they were little, their father told them that his brother Bert, who was childless, planned to leave his fortune to his favorite nephews and niece, who are his only family.

Still worse, Bert had some small strokes and began using a walker to get around the house. He couldn't go out much anymore but still kept taking his vitamins, though not his blood pressure medication. Lilly started staying at the house all the time now. Whenever members of the family visited, they tried to ask how things were going but Uncle Bert seemed confused and also very fearful about answering questions. He would act uneasy whenever Lilly or Shawn were in the room. The nephews and niece noticed that his back and neck were bruised. When asked about the bruises, Lilly said Bert had fallen but hadn't seriously injured himself. It was nothing to worry about, she added.

Uncle Bert's nephews and niece decided to have Bert's doctor look at his bruises. In the course of the examination, Bert said things that made the doctor believe he might have been abused by Shawn and Lilly, so the doctor reported the case to the local Department of Social Welfare. Within a few days, a social worker came to the door and asked to interview Bert. But Uncle Bert, standing in the doorway with Shawn by his side, quietly told the social worker to go away—he didn't want any interference in his life.

The Vulnerabilities of Older People

The case of Uncle Bert presents a dilemma. He asserts his right to make his own choices, but the signs that he is being manipulated or abused are growing stronger and stronger. Bert might be subject to financial exploitation by people he trusted, perhaps foolishly, in an investment scheme. His money is rapidly being depleted, and there are bruises that may indicate physical abuse. Family members are concerned about his welfare, but they also have an interest in protecting their inheritance.

How has Bert's quality of life changed as events have unfolded? From Bert's point of view, his quality of life seemed to be strengthened by being able to do things he had always enjoyed, whether wandering through city neighborhoods or gambling at the dog track. His relationship with Lilly, from Bert's point of view, was also a favorable factor at first. But now his quality of life has been diminished because he is limited to staying at home. The relationship with Lilly and her brother seems to have introduced an element of fear into Bert's own home.

Other questions also need to be answered. Was the doctor right to have reported Bert's case to the Department of Social Welfare? Is Bert acting freely when he rejects outside interference in his life? What should we make of the fact that the family is concerned about preserving the money for their inheritance? What can be done in a case like this?

The decision is never easy, because aging does tend to make people more vulnerable physically, socially, and sometimes emotionally. At the same time, however, we know that individuals have different competencies, even as they age. And we are finding that some of our stereotypes about the vulnerabilities of the elderly are simply not accurate. Why should the old be protected from risky choices that may be important for their quality of life?

Interfering When People Make Bad Choices

The dilemmas in Uncle Bert's case boil down to a single question: When is it right to interfere with other people's actions if those actions constitute a danger to themselves? The law tells us that we are not permitted to curtail a person's liberty just because that person lacks the ability to carry out decisions without outside help; thus a quadriplegic, for example, would not be legally incompetent—just a person unable to carry out decisions made. But it could be proper to intervene if the individual is unable to make decisions at all, say, because of an incapacity to understand what's going on. That may happen, for instance, in a delusional state or in dementia where a person cannot understand or evaluate information.

As the case of Uncle Bert began, Bert seemed able to understand the risks he was taking by walking in dangerous neighborhoods or by taking vitamins to manage his diabetes. He simply evaluated matters differently from his family. There was no evidence at all that Uncle Bert was mentally incompetent. Sometimes competent people make bad choices, as we all do from time to time.

As the case unfolded, Bert continued to engage in risky behavior—for example, not taking his blood pressure medication. But there was evidence of other threats: first, the suggestion that his life savings was being depleted, and second, signs that Bert might be subject to physical abuse. Even more disturbing, he seemed fearful in the presence of Lilly and Shawn. But in the eyes of the law, Uncle Bert still remained a free and competent adult. If a person wants to put money at risk or remain in a dangerous living situation, he or she is free to do so and also free to reject help offered from outside.

One reason for intervening might be that he seemed confused. If indeed Uncle Bert were unable to understand his decisions, then that might be a sign of diminished mental capacity and could be grounds for intervening, whether Bert agrees or not. Note here that there is a difference in a case of potential elder abuse from a case of potential child abuse. An adult, unlike a child, is always presumed mentally competent until proven otherwise. Uncle Bert may be fearful, he may be in what seems like an intolerable condition of exploitation, but unless we have grounds for doubting his mental competence, we cannot override his liberty.

The case of Uncle Bert's bad judgment raises many questions and suggests the need for some basic concepts to understand the issues presented by this case:

- *Elder abuse and neglect.* Older people, like other adults, have a basic right to live in ways that others judge risky or ill advised. At what point does such behavior become categorized as "self-neglect" and justify intervention? What happens when others are involved who may be the cause of physical, psychological, or financial abuse? When harm is threatened, how do we assess a person's mental capacity for decision making?

- *Quality of life.* What is it that constitutes "quality of life"—in short, that makes life worth living? Could an elderly person make a judgment that quality of life is more important than quantity—even if it means running risks to health and safety or having relationships that others might regard as unorthodox?

- *Sexuality.* What patterns of sexual behavior are most prevalent in old age? What is the relationship between sexuality and mental health in later life?

- *Crime and safety of older people.* Are older people more likely than others to be crime victims? Do older people fear crime more than do people in other age groups? What is the impact of crime and the fear of crime on the quality of life of older Americans?

Elder Abuse and Neglect

Just how common is elder abuse? Reliable statistics are hard to obtain, but the evidence suggests that physical violence, chronic verbal aggression, and neglect do fester among a small segment of the elderly population. A comprehensive community study found that elder abuse was prevalent at a rate of 1.6% in the population of people over age 65 living outside institutions (Lachs et al., 1997). Nearly half of the perpetrators of mistreatment were adult children, and one-quarter of them were spouses. An earlier study found that two-thirds of elder abuse cases were physical while the remainder were verbal (Pillemer and Finkelhor, 1988).

Research on elder abuse suggests that this phenomenon is complex (Quinn and Tomita, 1987; Wolf and Pillemer, 1989). We must look carefully at victims and perpetrators, and at the different types of abuse. There is a series of known risk factors for elder abuse, including the presence of psychopathology, especially alcohol and substance abuse; family history of violence; a family member dependent on others for financial support; caregiving burdens; social isolation; and the recent occurrence of stressful life events (Bloom, Ansell, and Bloom, 1989). Lifelong patterns of domestic violence are often reversed when the parent or the formerly dominating spouse becomes less powerful and is now the victim instead of the abuser (Anetzberger, 1987).

Physicians and home care workers are often in a position to identify preliminary signs of potential elder abuse. The problem of reporting elder abuse has been addressed by lawmakers. All states now have formal reporting arrangements for suspected cases of elder abuse. Laws often require **mandatory reporting** whenever there is evidence of abuse. But some elder advocates have questioned the effectiveness of mandatory reporting. Reports do not necessarily lead to any follow-up action. Furthermore, as in Bert's case, not all instances of abuse are readily apparent. When we broaden the issue to include "self-neglect," it becomes even more difficult to draw clear lines, especially when an older person simply insists on living his or her own life independent of interference by outsiders.

When professionals come across cases of suspected abuse or neglect, they face a dilemma. If they report the matter to authorities, are they violating privacy or confidentiality? How serious do the signs have to be to prompt reporting people against their will? And what happens if accusations turn out to be false? Could reporting a case of potential abuse even make matters worse? These questions bring us to the heart of the controversy about whether older people should be protected from bad choices.

Perceptions of Quality of Life

In the case study of Uncle Bert's family, his doctor and a social worker questioned whether Bert was taking unreasonable risks—making bad investments, exposing himself to the danger of crime and abuse—in order to live independently. Bert believed that he alone had the right to define the quality of his life. At age 79, he may have felt he had lived long enough to make his own decisions about risks and benefits. With regard to money, there is an important relationship between subjective well-being and financial control of one's life. Quality of life in old age may be tied to an individual continuing to exercise control over money (Cutler, Gregg, and Lawton, 1992). But exercising control and making choices means running certain risks.

Debates about risky behavior and mental health in later life often come back to the ambiguous phrase, "quality of life." Defining quality of life and measuring well-being in old age are serious problems for gerontology (George, 1980). They have been the center of many research studies by gerontologists concerned with successful aging (Larson, 1978). Broadly speaking, **life satisfaction** can be defined as a person's attitude toward past and present life as a whole. In contrast, morale is a specific feeling, whether optimistic or pessimistic, about the future. These psychological concepts, along with happiness and mood, are obviously important. But notice that they address the issue of subjective well-being in later life, which is the older person's perception. Thus the concepts of life satisfaction and morale present serious difficulties in measurement and theoretical interpretation.

To measure subjective well-being, gerontologists make extensive use of an instrument called the Life Satisfaction Index, which considers items such as zest and apathy, self-blame, attainment of life goals, and mood. The Philadelphia Geriatric Center Morale Scale has also been used to measure subjective well-being. Chronological age by itself is only weakly correlated with subjective well-being; in other words, old age by itself is not necessarily a condition for poor morale or unhappiness. Physical health, however, especially self-rated health, is a strong predictor of subjective well-being. Health problems, of course, are more common in later life. But subjective rating of one's own health reflects individual coping style and not simply objective physiological function. We cannot ignore individual capacity for adaptation.

Relationships are another factor in subjective well-being. Is Uncle Bert's living situation—cuddling in bed with his housekeeper—a pattern of adaption that we could call "successful aging"? The mere existence of relationships does not prove that people are aging well; more important is the quality of those relationships (Adams and Blieszner, 1995). We can't simply analyze the numbers of social networks or kinship patterns to measure well-being. Older adults need to develop relationships with people who help them in ways they want to be helped, whether those people are family, friends, or others. No single pattern of personal relationships is optimal for all people as they age.

Sexuality

Uncle Bert's nephews and niece were uneasy about the possibility of their uncle having a sexual relationship with Lilly. To them it seemed inappropriate for a 79-year-old man to have sex with a much younger woman without being married. In all likelihood, Uncle Bert's nephews and niece had some misconceptions and stereotypes about late-life sexuality (Butler and Lewis, 1993). Sex among the elderly has long been a topic for humor, even in Roman comedy and the poetry of Chaucer. But of 106 traditional societies studied around the world, in only 3 did sexual behavior among the elderly violate social mores. In Western culture, however, the sexuality of older people is still considered unusual or a subject for humor (Kaye, 1993).

Each decade of age does bring some sexual decline, but aging itself is not the determining factor as much as marital status, general physical health, or the feelings of an older person about sexuality. Complete cessation of sexual activity is most often a result of a decline in the physical health of one or both partners.

In fact, studies by sex researchers Masters and Johnson (1966) have shown that female sexuality has no time limit and that male sexual capacity may extend into a man's 80s. However, sexual activity in late life is most

Exhibit 14. Imbalances in the Sex Ratio Among Older People

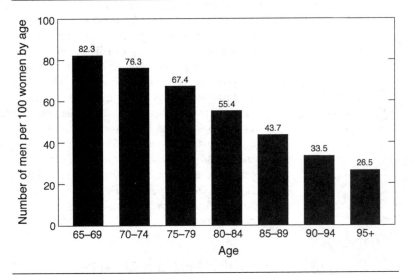

SOURCE: U.S. Bureau of the Census (1996).

clearly accounted for by the **continuity theory** of aging: The best predictor of sexual behavior in later life is earlier sexual behavior. The biggest limiting factor, especially for women, is the availability of a partner.

A key feature of late-life sexuality is its multidimensional character: Sensuality, intimacy, and touching are all at least as important as genital sexuality. Nevertheless, one Swedish population health study found that among 70-year-olds, 46% of the men and 16% of the women still found enjoyment in sexual intercourse.

The contrast between the figures for men and women mostly reflects the changing sex ratio in later life. Exhibit 14 shows the discrepancy in the numbers of elderly men and women. The reason for the imbalance is that women tend to outlive men by an average of seven years, and they tend to marry men two to three years older. With advancing age, therefore, widowhood takes its toll: Nearly half of all older women in 1994 were widows (47%); there are nearly five times as many widows as widowers, and older widowers are more likely than older widows to remarry quickly. In 1994, older men were nearly twice as likely to be married as older women.

Assuming the opportunity exists, most elderly men and women can have a sex life. Men can maintain fertility and generate sperm into their 80s, although men in their 70s are more likely to be worried about sexual function and sexual performance than men in middle age (Panser et al., 1995). Like women, men experience hormonal changes as they age, but men do not experience a distinct climacteric phase during which they completely lose reproductive capacity. Older men do experience a slowing down of the speed of sexual responsiveness, and they and their partners need to adapt to these changes. As continuity theory suggests, men's pattern of earlier sexuality is the best predictor of their sexuality in old age (Whitbourne, 1990).

A major difference between the sexes is that by the end of middle age women experience menopause and loss of fertility. This decline in hormones that causes menopause is usually gradual, and thus menopause need not be a traumatic event. With longer life expectancy, menopause can actually be an opportunity for a second adulthood. However, menopause does bring distinct physical changes. For example, decreased production of the hormone estrogen can increase the risk of osteoporosis (Peden and Newman, 1993). Traditional images of women's late-life sexuality have sometimes been quite negative (Covey, 1989). But hormone replacement, other therapies, and a positive outlook can minimize the negatives. Literature abounds with examples of vigorous postmenopausal female figures, like Penelope in Homer's *Odyssey,* Chaucer's Wife of Bath, and several heroines in Shakespeare. Modern writers like Toni Morrison and Alice Walker have picked up on these positive themes of late-life development (Banner, 1993).

Crime and the Elderly

In the case study that opened this chapter, Bert seemed unafraid of crime, while his nephews and niece thought his attitude proved his incompetence. Who is right about the risk of crime? Actually, well-established statistics show that Uncle Bert may be right. Perhaps his nephews and niece are fearful because the media give heightened attention to crime against the elderly. But the facts suggest a different picture. Annual figures from the National Crime Victimization Surveys show that people above age 65 have *lower* rates than other age groups for serious crimes like robbery, personal theft, assault, and rape (McCabe and Gregory, 1998). When all crimes are taken together, the victimization rate for the elderly is less than one-fourth the rate for the rest of the population. Is Uncle Bert safe when he walks in the dangerous parts of the city at night? Not necessarily. Crime against persons of any age may be more likely in certain neighborhoods. If an elderly person does become a crime victim, then the aftereffects—for example, from serious injury—can be more long-lasting than with a younger person.

Whatever the actual incidence of crime, fear of crime is widely believed to be more common among older people than among the young. Nonetheless, serious studies have failed to find a clear relationship between age and fear (Ferraro and LaGrange, 1992). The popular stereotype of older people becoming "prisoners in their own homes" because of fear of crime is exaggerated.

The biggest threats to older people may actually come from intimate relationships and patterns of financial exploitation. Older adults are vulnerable to investment scams perpetrated by con artists and unscrupulous advisers. A 1989 study of randomly selected older people in Canada found a much smaller proportion—only one-half of 1%—suffering physical abuse, but also a rate of 2.5% for financial exploitation, which may be the most common form of abuse. Another study found that individuals over age 65 make up approximately 30% of all scam victims, even though they comprise only 12% of the total population (Davis, 1993).

Because many seniors have nest eggs set aside for retirement, they are tempting targets for swindlers. Women, especially the newly widowed, are among the most vulnerable. Lonely and frightened, the new widow who has never been in the workforce, balanced a checkbook, or paid a bill sometimes trusts too quickly someone who offers to handle her finances. Scams may involve real estate, stocks, mutual funds, or business investments—like Bert's involvement in Shawn's vitamin business.

Strangers may perpetrate these scams, but opportunities for exploitation are also found closer to home. Defining exploitation is not always easy. For example, in many cultures older people share their financial assets with younger people in the family. But loved ones can exert emotional pressure that may be just as detrimental to the older person's interests as the deliberate manipulation of strangers and acquaintances. Since abusers are often dependent on their elderly victims for financial support, exploitation can be linked to verbal or physical abuse. We saw the "slippery slope" toward exploitation in Bert's case. But if a presumed "victim" doesn't report financial exploitation, then how can we prove a crime was committed? Are we justified in interfering for a person's own good?

Intervention in the Lives of the Vulnerable Elderly

How can society, and loved ones, intervene to protect an elderly person who seems incapable of functioning safely? The answer is that it is possible to restrict people's liberty for their own good through legal procedures intended for that purpose.

Civil commitment is a legal procedure whereby people can be placed in a psychiatric hospital against their will. The rationale for civil commitment is to diagnose or treat a mental disorder if there is reason to believe a person may be in danger of causing harm to self or others. Civil commitment is an extreme measure causing loss of personal liberty. In previous decades, disoriented elderly people were often sent against their will to mental hospitals, but today more guarantees are in place to protect against such actions. In earlier times, "old age" alone might be a sufficient reason for labeling someone incompetent to make decisions. But today, instead of relying on vague labels like "senility" we must undertake a formal court proceeding to declare someone mentally incompetent.

When a person is capable of some independence but is unable to manage money or make decisions, another approach is to appoint a guardian or conservator for the incapacitated person's affairs (Zimny and Grossberg, 1998). **Guardianship** can take two different forms: guardianship of the person, in which the guardian has the power to determine where the older person will live and what treatment or services he or she may receive, and guardianship of the estate, in which the guardian has power to manage property and take over financial affairs (Ritter, 1995). Appointing a guardian is less restrictive than committing someone to a mental hospital, but it still represents a restriction of liberty.

Guardianship is overwhelmingly a procedure applied to the elderly, compared with other age groups. One empirical study from Florida revealed an average age of individuals referred for guardianship of 73 years; nearly three quarters were over age 70 (Peters, Schmidt, and Miller, 1985). Two-thirds of those who received guardianship were females, and a comparable number lived in private homes. Wards, or those subject to guardianship, were moderately wealthy: Nearly half had estates greater than $50,000. Guardianship was very much a "family affair": Relatives were available and willing to serve as guardians in 70% of these cases. All petitions to declare a person incompetent were affirmed by the probate court, but in 90% of the cases, reports did not provide the specific behavioral information for the court that is required by law.

Despite the legal safeguards, both civil commitment and guardianship proceedings are viewed by many informed critics as a kind of "new paternalism" that can be oppressive to older people (Regan, 1981; Crystal, 1987). Moreover, some studies have shown that depicting patients in age-related terms is a common, even routine feature of civil commitment proceedings, and age depictions are rarely challenged. Specifically, behavior that is considered age inappropriate—for example, sexual activity—is frequently cited as grounds for viewing a range of behaviors as "symptoms" of mental illness (Holstein, 1990). For example, laws intended to "protect" older people have vague standards and weak accountability for those who are appointed as guardians or conservators. Civil commitment proceedings may fail to grant the elderly an opportunity for a fair hearing, and statutes may not require legal notice, the presence of the elderly individual at the hearing, or the right to counsel (Rein, 1992). The result is that programs intended to protect the old can end up disregarding their rights (Bell, Schmidt, and Miller, 1981).

Some of the worst failings of the guardianship system are its disregard for the rights of the elderly. The courtroom hearings for incompetency are too often one-sided and superficial, and vague laws permit a ruling of incompetency based on flimsy evidence. Moreover, follow-up supervision of guardians who are appointed by the courts remains minimal. Financial incentives make matters worse because guardians and conservators are paid out of the ward's assets. Appointments to conservatorship jobs may be awarded to politically well-connected lawyers. Once a guardian is appointed, guardianship is rarely revoked before the death of the ward. Efforts to reform the guardianship system have been frustrated, so advocates today tend to recommend guardianship only as a last resort.

In the readings that follow, we see some of the dilemmas and controversies that result from efforts to protect elderly people from vulnerability. The first reading, by Robert Brown, emphasizes the basic constitutional right to freedom from restraints. Writing from a civil liberties perspective, Brown raises the basic question: When is government ever justified in intervening in any of our lives?

The excerpt from Terrie Wetle and Terry Fulmer looks at the ethical dilemmas of how to balance the best interests of people with their right to autonomy. Instead of looking at this question in abstract or societal terms, Wetle and Fulmer stress the social context of families and health professionals who may be obliged to report suspected cases of elder abuse.

On one side we have the human service professions, but on the other side we have the legal system. Candace Heisler and Mary Joy Quinn describe the presuppositions of the legal system, in particular its adversarial nature. By defining ideas of "autonomy," "least restrictive autonomy," and "mental competency," the legal system sets the boundaries in which we debate when it is possible to intervene to protect people from their own bad choices.

Finally, Dorothy Fabian and Eloise Rathbone-McCuan examine the concept of elder self-neglect. In this instance, there may be no outside party engaged in abuse or exploitation. Instead, an elderly person may simply insist on living independently under conditions of danger that frustrate our ability to provide protection to people who are vulnerable.

READING 10

The Right to Freedom From Restraints

Robert N. Brown

We know that people, even those without mental or physical limitation, possess differing abilities and have differing needs. Sometimes physical or mental impairments leave people totally unable to manage their personal or financial affairs, as for example a person in a coma. Sometimes impairments affect only part of a person's ability to care for himself. A person with quadriplegia may be unable to care for himself physically but can

Source: "The Right to Freedom From Restraints," in *The American Civil Liberties Handbook: The Rights of Older Persons,* by Robert N. Brown, pp. 328-331. Copyright © 1989 by The American Civil Liberties Union, reprinted by permission of the publisher, Southern Illinois University Press.

direct others in providing care. Some impairments are temporary, such as the mental confusion that may occur as a side effect of medication, while some impairments seem to be permanent, such as the progressive physical and mental deterioration associated with Alzheimer's disease. Most impairments pose harm only to their victim, who will suffer the effects of not being able to provide for his needs. Some impairments, however, are alleged to pose a risk of harm to others, uch as a patient with schizophrenia whom psy - chiatrists may believe to be nearly certain to physically assault another. In short, there are a variety of physical and mental conditions which may affect, to varying degrees, for a limited or lasting amount of time, a person's ability to prevent harm to himself or to restrain himself from harming others.

When such conditions exist, and a person no longer can manage to prevent harm to herself or to others, the question is whether, and at what point, the legal system ought to intervene. The means by which legal intervention may be sought, broadly referred to as "protective proceedings," include such processes as guardianship, conservatorship, and civil commitment. These procedures seek to prevent harm from occurring to an impaired person by legally removing, to one extent or another, the impaired person's right to make decisions on her own behalf and appointing a surrogate to make decisions in her place. To appreciate the impact of this, some understanding of what "decision making" entails is needed.

Life presents each of us with a constant succession of choices requiring decisions. Most are minor, such as what to wear in the morning, what newspaper to read, or whether to order fish or fowl in a restaurant. Some are major, such as whether to marry, or whether, near the end of one's life, to move from one's home into a nursing home, or to undergo painful chemotherapy to fight a terminal cancer. All these decisions, for the purpose of understanding protective proceedings, can be placed into two categories: those that affect financial interests and all others. These latter decisions are considered personal decisions. Financial matters that may be acted on can range from buying a candy bar in a vending machine, to giving a gift to a favorite niece, to selling one's home to pay for medical care or a college education. Personal matters that may be acted on range from deciding what book to read or television show to watch to deciding where to live, with whom to associate, or whether to have an organ transplant.

When a person loses part or all of the ability to make decisions, it may become necessary for someone else to have the legal authority to act on his or her behalf. If the impaired person had, at an earlier time, entered into an arrangement (such as a power of attorney or a multiple-party bank account) that would allow another person to act on his behalf, further legal intervention may not be required. If not, however, a protective proceeding may need to be sought. The consequence of such an action is that the impaired person's right to make independent decisions is diminished or eliminated. The right to make decisions is turned over to the guardian or conservator.

Whether losing one's right to make decisions and having to abide by the decisions of another is unfair or unjust depends on the circumstances. It may not be a great loss to a person in a coma, who is unaware of any loss of control, to have his choices made by a guardian. It is a good deal less clear what the impact is of making a mentally ill person who makes "not very good" financial choices subject to a style of life dictated by the financial decisions of a court-appointed conservator, on the presumption that the conservator's decisions will better protect the person's assets. A person who is not mentally ill but who makes the same "not very good" financial decisions could not be subjected involuntarily to such control. Furthermore, the actual outcome of a decision is never certain. All decisions entail a certain amount of risk; well-thought-out plans often fail, and ill-advised schemes often succeed. There is, in addition, the question of values. What is best for an individual may not be the safest and most long-lasting life, but may include the chance to do what that individual believes is best and most important.

Guardians and conservators are often ignorant of, or fail to heed, the concerns and wishes of their wards. Protective proceedings often give little weight to these concerns. These proceedings seem unable to accommodate the differing natures and degrees of impairments and may not recognize that an impairment which affects one area of a person's ability to care for himself may not affect other areas. The result is that the law, in seeking to "help," sometimes takes away rights from those who are merely "different" and not disabled and often fails to respond appropriately to those who need some, but not complete, help.

What Is the Justification for Government Intervention Into Our Lives?

A general rule of our legal system is that people are allowed to exercise self-determination; people have both the right and responsibility to make their own decisions about how they will live, on what they will spend their money, and how they will spend their days. For the most part, people are free to think, speak, and do as they please without interference from our government. Yet there are limits. Laws limit our freedom by prohibiting us from injuring others or from harming their property. The legal authority for such laws is the "police power" of the state. This power authorizes the state to proscribe activities which are dangerous to others in order to protect society. A person convicted of violating such laws may, for the protection of society, be deprived of his or her freedom. The loss of liberty suffered by persons "civilly committed," or confined involuntarily in state mental hospitals, is justified in part by the police power, inasmuch as such persons are thought to be dangerous to others. Another limitation on individual freedom is the power of the state to protect individuals incapacitated by disease or other causes who consequently cannot care for themselves, their dependents, or their property. This power is called *parens patriae,* or "parentage of the state." Unlike police power, which is aimed at protecting others, this power focuses on the incapacitated individual and declares that the state has the responsibility of protecting those who cannot protect themselves. Under the *parens patriae* power, the state has the authority to determine when a person cannot care for him- or herself adequately and has the authority to appoint another person, usually called a guardian or conservator, to provide such care.

Because the exercise of police power entails a great loss of liberty (for example, confinement to a prison), procedural protections have long been established to ensure that a person involved in a criminal proceeding is not mistakenly imprisoned or penalized. Examples of these protections are rights to a lawyer, against self-incrimination, to trial by jury, and to cross-examination of witnesses. Unfortunately, not all of these procedural safeguards are provided to persons threatened with such protective proceedings as civil commitment, guardianship, or conservatorship. The reason is that protective proceedings are, for the most part, theoretically founded on the idea that the intervention will benefit the person, in effect "protect" him from himself. Such benevolent proceedings may be felt to pose no real loss of liberty or harm to a person unable to exercise such rights independently. However, in practice, these proceedings are often brought against persons at least partially if not fully able to exercise their rights and for reasons far from benevolent. The resulting genuine deprivations of liberty and property that occur, such as loss of control of one's finances or confinement in an institution such as a psychiatric facility or nursing home, suggest there is no justification for failing to offer procedural and substantive safeguards in protective proceedings. Lawmakers should ensure that the most appropriate and least restrictive processes available are used in seeking intervention in an individual's life.

Ethical Dilemmas in Elder Abuse

Terrie T. Wetle and Terry T. Fulmer

The application of values and ethical concepts to specific cases of elder mistreatment often engenders ethical dilemmas involving conflict among two or more values or concepts. Several such dilemmas are outlined below including the balancing of individual autonomy with beneficence and paternalism, concerns of confidentiality and legal reporting requirements, the impact of reporting on patient and professional relationships, and the issue of respect for autonomy for patients with diminishing cognitive capacity.

Balancing Patient Autonomy and the Best Interests of Patients

Perhaps the most difficult ethical dilemma for health professionals is the effort to respect the expressed wishes of the patient (autonomy) while protecting the patient from harm (beneficence) (Wetle et al., 1991). It is not uncommon for individuals to behave in ways that place themselves at risk or are personally injurious, or to choose to remain in risky or abusive circumstances. Respecting the autonomous wishes of such an individual may be in direct conflict with the professional's judgment of what is in the patient's best interest. On the one hand, the principle of respect for the autonomy of an individual would prevent the health professional from intervening with a service or action that is in opposition to the expressed wishes of a competent patient. On the other hand, health professionals are required, by law, to report cases of suspected elder mistreat-

Source: "A Medical Perspective," by Terrie T. Wetle and Terry T. Fulmer, *Journal of Elder Abuse and Neglect,* vol. 7, nos. 2/3, pp. 36-38, 1995. Copyright © 1995 by The Haworth Press. Reprinted by permission.

ment. Moreover, there is also an obligation to determine that the patient's refusal of assistance is an autonomous decision, free of coercion or undue duress. These cases are often complicated by questionable decisional capacity or cognitive impairment of the elder patient. Disagreement with a health professional's judgment or advice is not sufficient evidence to make a determination of decisional incapacity. Certainly, we have moral obligations to protect incompetent elders from incapacitated decision making, but we are also obligated to determine if they are truly incapacitated before intervening against their wishes. Such a determination requires a formal evaluation of decisional capacity. If the patient is determined to be competent, even if suspected mistreatment is confirmed, the competent patient has the right to refuse interventions.

Confidentiality and reporting requirements. Another aspect of patient autonomy is respect for confidentiality. Once again, the elder abuse reporting laws override the obligation for confidentiality under very specific circumstances. Nonetheless, this is not a blanket override, in that such reported information must be handled with extreme care, and information identified in subsequent investigations should be shared only on a "need to know" basis.

Impact of reporting on patient/professional relationship. Many professionals express justified concern that an elder abuse report and the subsequent investigation will have deleterious effects on their relationships with patients (and patients' families). Much progress has been made in improving the response system and investigating approaches used to determine whether or not mistreatment has occurred and in planning appropriate interventions. Nonetheless, even the most skilled response to such a report may damage the relationship between professional and patient. Several steps can be taken to reduce negative impacts, including informing the patient that such a report is to be made, describing the process, identifying potential positive outcomes of the process and suggested interventions, working with the family as a unit if possible, and recognizing the needs and concerns of all involved.

Ethical Issues Related to Families and Health Professionals

Family members are often intimately involved in the care of frail elders. Several ethical issues and conflicts relevant to elder mistreatment are faced as health professionals care for the individual patient in the context of family caregiving. These issues include questions regarding just who is the patient, caregiver burden and inadequate family supports, changing dependency relationships and longstanding patterns of family interaction, and ethical approaches to families. Many of these issues are discussed elsewhere in this volume in substantial detail, but are briefly discussed here from the perspective of the health professional.

Who is the patient? It is not uncommon for health professionals to become involved in the treatment of the family as a unit, as well as in care of an individual patient. The burden of caregiving can be substantial, and some cases of elder mistreatment occur when a well-intentioned primary caregiver becomes overwhelmed by caregiving tasks. The health professional faces a particularly thorny dilemma when treating two members of a family as patients and encounters evidence of mistreatment of one by the other (Fulmer, 1991). This raises the question of just who is the primary patient, and how are the professional's obligations to be balanced among various members of the family. Certainly, there is a first-level responsibility to the patient who appears to have been mistreated but successful approaches include offering information and services to all involved parties.

Dependency relationships in families change as one member becomes increasingly dependent on the family for care. The health professional may be unaware of longstanding patterns of interaction among family members. The stresses of family caregiving may exacerbate a relationship that has always been characterized by verbal and physical abuse. In some cases, changing dependency relationships may turn the tables, and the previously abused may become the abuser. Being aware of these patterns and the specific relationship history of caregiver and care receiver may help explain observed dynamics and provide crucial information for developing effective intervention strategies.

Caregiver burden and spousal and intergenerational responsibilities involve differing personal and societal expectations. Society remains unclear as to the reasonable level of caregiving to be expected from a spouse or adult child. It is not unusual for family caregivers to drain all physical and emotional resources before accepting help or assistance. One responsibility of health professionals is to assist caregivers in recognizing the limits of their own health and to promote their well-being by identifying supportive services and encouraging their use and by assisting in balancing caregiving among all available family members. This may in fact have a double protective effect. First, it may prevent the elder abuse or neglect that might have been triggered by caregiver over-burden and stress. Second, such interventions may protect the caregiver from the over-burdening that also could be considered a form of "caregiver mistreatment" or abuse.

References

Fulmer, T. (1991). "Elder Mistreatment: Progress in Community Detection and Intervention." *Family and Community Health,* 2, 26-34.
Wetle, T., Crabtree, B., Clemens, E., Dubitzky, D., Eslami, M., and Kerr, M. (1991). "Balancing Safety and Autonomy: Defining and Living With Acceptable Risk." *The Gerontologist,* 31(11), 237.

A Legal Perspective on Elder Abuse

Candace J. Heisler and Mary Joy Quinn

Most practitioners working with older adults have had limited experience with the American legal system. As a result, it is underutilized in the prevention and resolution of elder mistreatment. . . .

Goals of the Legal System

The civil and criminal legal systems approach the prevention and resolution of elder mistreatment matters with common *goals* and certain *rules* that govern their handling. The *goals* of the legal response to elder mistreatment are to: (1) Stop the unlawful, improper, or exploitive conduct that is being inflicted on the victim; (2) Protect the victim and society from the perpetrator and further inappropriate or illegal acts; (3) Hold the perpetrator accountable for the conduct and communicate a message that the behavior is unacceptable and exceeds societal norms; (4) Rehabilitate the offender, if possible; and (5) Make the victim whole by ordering restitution and/or the return of property as well as the payment of expenses incurred by the victim as a result of the perpetrator's conduct.[1] The two parts of the legal system also seek to act in ways that create the least disruption or invasion into the victim's life; that take into account that person's individual situation, competency, wishes, and desires; and that keep the situation from becoming worse. . . .

The legal system is adversarial in nature. In the clash between the parties in a search for the truth, the legal system mandates roles for the participants. On the civil side, the person who files the lawsuit is termed the plaintiff and that person must meet one of the two legal burdens previously described in order to prevail. Because the lawsuit generally concerns the interaction of two or more parties, the parties themselves retain control over the case. The plaintiff and the defendant can settle the case, come to agreements, and otherwise direct what takes place. Where guardianships are concerned, the person filing the case is typically termed the petitioner because traditionally, guardianship hearings have not been adversarial. Rather, there has been an assumption that the petitioner is acting on behalf of an older adult who needs help. Traditional views are giving way to many system reforms as it is realized that sometimes persons seeking guardianship are acting in their own interests rather than to assist an elder in need. The result is that guardianship proceedings are becoming more complex and, at times, adversarial in nature. Legal rights of proposed wards are protected to a greater degree than occurred previously. . . .

Ethical Issues

The ethical issues most apparent in legal proceedings with elder mistreatment are (1) promotion of autonomy and (2) least restrictive alternative. Ethical dilemmas arise when evaluating these issues in light of an older adult's mental competency.

Autonomy

American legal and ethical values place a high priority on autonomy. The issue is self-governance:

Source: "A Legal Perspective," by Candace J. Heisler and Mary Joy Quinn, *Journal of Elder Abuse and Neglect,* vol. 7, nos. 2/3, pp. 131–140, 1995. Copyright © 1995 by the Haworth Press. Reprinted by permission.

"being one's own person, without constraint either by another's action or by psychological or physical limitations." [7] The high value placed on autonomy is reflected in the Constitution and the professional ethical protocols of the medical, legal, and nursing professions.[8] Autonomy may be an idealized notion given the very real interdependence most elders have within their families and their communities and given the reality of high levels of impairment in old age.[9]

The issue of autonomy is always present whether the older adult is in the civil or the criminal justice system. In the criminal justice system, the issue of autonomy comes into play when the elder is informed and consulted about the various options available to keep him or her safe and when the sentencing of the offender is under consideration. It is not a victim's responsibility to determine if criminal charges will be brought against an offender and in many jurisdictions, victims are not asked to "press charges." The prosecuting attorney, as the state's representative, makes that decision in order to communicate the message that the conduct is criminal, not simply a "private matter," and to ensure that the victim is protected, rather than manipulated, exploited, or threatened.

In guardianship matters, autonomy is the main issue when an adult is thought to be incapable of managing his or her affairs, whether due to abuse or neglect by self or others. In guardianship, decision making is placed in the hands of surrogates. With changes in state laws and the dissemination of current gerontological thought, courts now carefully consider autonomy and the wishes of the elder as expressed in the past, the present, and for the future. Forward-looking courts seriously consider these expressions in their deliberations, regardless of the mental status of the older adult.

Ethical practice requires that practitioners are careful not to err on the side of failing to take action to protect an elder. Blind adherence to the concept of autonomy can lead to resolutions that fail to ask even the most basic questions and can result in the abandonment or death of a client who declines the first offer of help or who has an unpleasant personality or is "difficult."

Least Restrictive Alternative

The concept of the least restrictive alternative, a legal doctrine first articulated in the field of mental health, has gained wide acceptance among courts and service professionals. It creates an ethical duty for practitioners to fashion individualized solutions that are least intrusive upon their client's personal freedom. The concept applies to the personal and the environmental care of the elder and the handling of material resources. It recognizes that elders may have capacities in some areas and lack capacity in others. Ideally, the more restrictive the option, the greater the due process protections and the opportunities for the individual to object and state preferences.[10] The doctrine is primarily civil in nature, though on occasion it is applied in criminal matters, particularly in the placement of persons found to be criminally insane.[11]

In civil law, legal options begin with the client handling [his or her] own affairs and then move up the ladder to more restrictive options in the following manner: client signs name to checks but someone else fills out the checks, direct deposit to bank accounts, representative payee arrangements for certain checks, joint tenancy on bank accounts and/or real property, trusts, the various powers of attorney, protective orders (for placement or medical treatment), guardianship of estate, and, lastly, involuntary placement in a locked mental health facility.[12]

Legal alternatives to guardianship are used more frequently, especially since 1987 when the Associated Press conducted a nationwide investigation into the guardianship system and found it woefully lacking in protections for frail elders. In most cases, a neutral person never spoke to elders or advised them of their legal rights despite the fact that a guardianship often deprives them of many rights such as the rights to vote, to make a will, to select a physician, or to control finances. Following that investigation, most states amended their guardianship laws.[13] Also as a result of the investigation, practitioners began relying on less restrictive legal options, sometimes without fully considering their benefits and burdens. For instance, there has been heavy reliance on powers of attorney with little understanding that there is no bonding, no notice to other relatives, no monitoring by a third party, and no way to regain misappropriated or mishandled assets short of a civil law suit. There has also been reliance on trusts that may be beneficial financially in some situations but make no provisions for personal care or abusive trustees. Additionally, individuals who become trustees or attorneys-in-fact seldom understand what is required and as a result, they assume responsibilities that they are not prepared to handle. Ethical practice requires that practitioners in the position of recommending legal options have basic knowledge of the benefits and burdens of each legal option and mandates that practitioners fully discuss all available options with the client.

The concept of least restrictive alternative is not easily transported to the criminal justice system. It is not a guiding principle for the criminal system though most courts decide sentences by balancing what a perpetrator did with available sentencing alternatives while attempting to protect the public, hold the offender accountable, and protect the victim and society at large. The concept of least restrictive alternative can be seen in criminal matters that are relatively minor and may have elements which are both civil and criminal in nature. Interventions may begin in the civil arena and move to the criminal side if the offender does not comply. For instance, the offender may first be warned and urged to make changes, then officially admonished, then cited, and eventually arrested. This process is sometimes used in situations involving public nuisances or neighborhood disputes. Finally, the least restrictive alternative approach is applied in the criminal justice context with those found criminally insane. Persons are placed in facilities according to the amount of treatment and control they need and the degree of protection the community requires.

Competency

The issue of competence is critical in the legal context. It determines whether a witness will be allowed to testify in a criminal case, if a guardianship will be imposed, and if a lawsuit is "winnable" based on the allegations and evidence a victim produces. And yet, the term is as poorly understood in legal circles as it is in mental health and clinical gerontological settings. Marin et al. note . . . that there is growing recognition of the difference between *legal competence* and *clinical competence*. All adults are thought to be *legally competent* until a court of law rules otherwise. This means they can execute legal documents, make medical decisions, decide where to live, and in general, have full control of their lives. *Clinical competence* relies on observations of health and social services practitioners. It is task and time specific. It is interesting to note that recent guardianship reform laws have tended to incorporate concepts of clinical competence into the law.

Over the years, competency has been variously measured by old age, the quality of decision making, medical or psychiatric diagnosis, risk of impoverishment through heedless spending, and physical endangerment.[14] In truth, the search for a commonly accepted definition of competence can be likened to the search for the Holy Grail. The journey is ongoing but as yet there is no mutually agreed upon conclusion. Each discipline functions with its own definition. For instance, the legal profession focuses on what an elder is *incapable* of doing while psychology looks at what the elder is *capable* of doing.[15]

Many state laws provide that a guardianship can be imposed on an individual who is "subject to undue influence" but that concept does not appear in the medical or psychiatric reports upon which criminal prosecutors and civil attorneys must rely. It does not appear to be a concept that is familiar to practitioners outside the legal field. Undue influence situations can occur even when an elder is alert, oriented, and capable of carrying out activities of daily living. Undue influence has been defined as the substitution of one person's will for the true desires of another. It can be accompanied by fraud, duress, threats, or the application of various types of pressure on susceptible persons including frail elders.[16]

Current trends conceptualize "competency" in ways other than simply evaluating the quality of the elder's decision making. There is growing reliance on a constellation of factors to determine competency. There is more focus on what the older adult *actually does* to take care of the needs of daily living including the management of material assets. There is consideration of the elder's past decision making. For example, was the elder in the habit of giving large sums of money to perfect strangers or is this new behavior? Medical and psychiatric diagnoses offer valuable information as to conditions that impinge on mental functioning and are able, with some measure of accuracy, to predict the course of a given condition. There is recognition that mental and physical functioning is subject to a variety of factors such as nutritional status, the presence of mental illness such as clinical depression, the time of day, isolation, grief states, substance or medication intake, relationship status, and self-esteem. There is also recognition that "competence" is dependent on the types of personal and environmental support an older adult may be receiving.[17]

Given all these complexities, it is understandable that there is no single tool to determine competency. Nevertheless, practitioners working with frail older adults who are the victims of elder abuse and/or neglect must try to determine if their client is "competent," often in order to take decision making away for what are usually good and benevolent reasons.[18] In general, practitioners look for two elements when assessing competency: (1) Does the individual have the capacity to assimilate the relevant facts? and (2) Can the person appreciate or rationally understand his or her own situation as it relates to the facts at hand? Relevant questions include: Can the person make and express choices regarding his or her life? Are the outcomes of these choices "reasonable"? Are the choices based on "rational" reasons? Does the person understand the personal implication of the choices made?[19]

The reality is that dealing with competency is less about creating the perfect definition and more about working with the characteristics of the individual older adult.[20] Practitioners must deal with the definitions that are set forth in their respective laws and disciplines while understanding the everyday realities of "competence." For instance, the criminal prosecutor or civil attorney may realize that the elder victim is less cognitively clear in the afternoon and therefore will attempt to have him or her testify in the morning. Those working within civil and criminal courts may attempt to ensure that judges who hear elder mistreatment cases are familiar with their special dynamics. In the absence of valid tools to accurately measure the various features of competence, we must rely on a variety of pieces of knowledge about elders and the conditions that affect them. Ethical practice demands no less.

Notes

[Only the notes that are included in the excerpted material appear here.]

1. Modified from Carter, J., Heisler, C., Lemon, N. K., *Domestic Violence: The Crucial Role of the Judge in Criminal Court Cases.* Family Violence Prevention Fund, San Francisco (1991); Heisler, C., "The Role of the Criminal Justice System in Elder Abuse Cases," *Journal of Elder Abuse and Neglect* 3(1), pp. 5-33 (1991).

7. Beauchamp, T. L., Childress, J. F., *Principles of Biomedical Ethics,* 2nd ed., Oxford University Press, New York (1983).

8. American Nurses Association, *American Nurses Association Code for Nurses* (1950); Wood, E. F., "Statement of Recommended Judicial Practice," adopted by the National Conference of the Judiciary on Guardianship Proceedings for the Elderly, Commission on Legal Problems of the Elderly, American Bar Association and the National Judicial College (1986); American Medical Association, *American Medical Association Principles of Medical Ethics* (1980).

9. Caplan, A. L., "Let Wisdom Find a Way," *Generations* 10(2), 10-14 (1985); Moody, H. R., "Ethics and Aging," *Generations* 10(2), 5-9 (1985).

10. Quinn, M. J., "Elder Abuse and Neglect," *Generations* 10(2), 22-25 (1985); Quinn, M. J., Tomita, S. K., *Elder Abuse and Neglect: Causes, Diagnosis, and Intervention Strategies.* Springer Publishing, New York (1986).

11. See, e.g., Calif. Penal Code Sections 1026 et seq.

12. Quinn, M. J., Tomita, S. K., *Elder Abuse and Neglect: Causes, Diagnosis, and Intervention Strategies, supra.*

13. Keith, P. S., Wacker, R. R., "Guardianship Reform: Does Revised Legislation Make a Difference in Outcomes for Proposed Wards?" *Journal of Aging and Social Policy* 4(3/4), 139-155 (1992).

14. Quinn, M. J., "Everyday Competencies and Guardianship: Refinements and Realities," in Snyder, M. A., Kapp, M. B., Schaie, K. W. (Eds.), *Impact of the Law on Older Adults' Decision Making Capacity.* Springer Publishing, New York (in press).

15. Willis, S. L., "Assessing Everyday Competence in the Cognitively Challenged Elderly," in *Impact of the Law on Older Adults' Decision Making Capacity.* Ibid.

16. Grant, L. H., Quinn, M. J., "Guardianship and Abuse of Dependent Adults," in Zimny, G. H., Grossberg, G. T. (Eds.), *Guardianship of the Elderly: Medical and Judicial Aspects.* Springer Publishing, New York (in press).

17. Willis, S. L., *supra.*

18. Caplan, A. L., *supra.*

19. Kapp, M. B., *Geriatrics and the Law: Patient Rights and Professional Responsibilities,* 2nd ed., Springer Publishing, New York (1992); Gutheil, T. G., Applebaum, P. S., *Clinical Handbook of Psychiatry and the Law,* 2nd ed., Springer Publishing, New York (1991); Roth, L. H., Meisel, A., Lidz, C., "Tests of Competency to Consent to Treatment," *American Journal of Psychiatry,* 134, 279-283 (1977).

20. Moody, H. R., "Ethics and Aging," *Generations,* 10(2), 5-9 (1985).

READING 13

Elder Self-Neglect
A Blurred Concept

Dorothy R. Fabian and Eloise Rathbone-McCuan

Self-neglect has been emerging poignantly as one of the many troublesome problems that beset the elderly. It is a source of anxiety and frustration for practitioners, family members, and the community because self-neglecting elders may present themselves in antisocial and life-threatening situations. That is because self-neglect is frequently manifest by disregard of the needs of both the self and the environment. Usually, self-neglect results from physical and/or mental impairments that reduce the elder's ability to perform essential life

tasks. There may be no shame about the situation, and outside help may be refused or passively sabotaged. . . .

Self-Neglect in the Literature

Self-neglect is probably not a new phenomenon. Isolated, frequently unkempt, and often eccentric individuals such as hermits, witches, tramps, and recluses have long been depicted in the social history, literature, folklore, and opera of Western society. These were the early sources of cultural stereotypes depicting extreme examples of self-neglecters. Often arousing fear, discomfort, and disgust, some of these men and women were seen as mentally ill; some were expected to be able to call on fearful supernatural powers; some were thought to hoard treasure. All were considered strange and lived on the social, if not the physical, periphery of their communities. The local populace tended to subject such individuals to jeers, taunts, beatings, and ostracism. Imprisonment, banishment, or violent death at times followed attention by authorities.

The stereotyping of elderly self-neglecters continues through mass media efforts to keep the U.S. homeless population viable as a newsworthy phenomenon. An increasing amount of contemporary medical and psychiatric literature has addressed gross neglect as a manifestation of individual dysfunction even though it is not clear that the rate and severity of self-neglect in the aging population have increased. Clinical case studies and reports of small samples attempt to verify that self-neglecters become embroiled with the police, wander into emergency rooms, and plague social service agencies. Lurid published accounts lead the public to conclude that high-cost care to improve the condition of these persons provides no long-term benefits and that many of those who do receive community resources will eventually die in very deteriorated conditions.

In attempts to understand self-neglect, certain observers noted an age-related dimension. Macmillan and Shaw (1966) used the senile breakdown syndrome to describe persons failing to maintain levels of cleanliness that the community found acceptable:

> The usual picture is that of an old woman living alone, though men and married couples suffering from the condition are also found. She, her garments, her possessions, and her house are filthy. She may be verminous and there may be feces and pools of urine on the floor. These people are often tolerated for years by the neighbors, who may suddenly decide that they cannot stand this state of affairs any longer and report the case to various organizations, such as the police or the health department. (p. 1032)

Clark, Mankikar, and Gray (1975), referring to the fourth-century Greek philosopher Diogenes, who reportedly admired lack of shame, outspokenness, and contempt for social organization, suggested the phrase "Diogenes Syndrome" to characterize elderly patients who appeared filthy and unkempt, whose homes were dirty and untidy and usually full of hoarded rubbish, but who showed no shame for these circumstances. Although not necessarily poor or in substandard housing, these self-neglecting individuals were usually known to social service agencies, whose efforts were frequently resisted.

The term "Diogenes Syndrome" became a stereotype for self-neglecting elders perceived as grossly neglectful of their person and the environment, who displayed not only lack of shame but also contempt for, or at least lack of interest in, the recommendations of neighbors, family members, health providers, or the community at large. The Diogenes Syndrome is used to describe patients in at least one nursing care study (Cornwall, 1981) as well as in a paper on psychotic disturbances (Klosterkotter and Peters, 1985). It is also referred to in a study of the social breakdown syndrome in community-dwelling elderly (Radebaugh, Hooper, and Gruenberg, 1987). . . .

Conceptual Ambiguities

Insights into how to treat or resolve self-neglect among the elderly are subject to as much ambiguity as are the diverse explanations of causality. Cybulska and Rucinski (1986) comment:

> Regrettably, when one is faced with a clinical decision whether to intervene or not, the scanty research, medical textbooks, and professional training offer little help. If a crisis occurs in the community, it is often difficult to determine whether the neglect was a result of a consciously determined free choice, some deeply rooted unconscious factors, helplessness, or mental or physical illness. (p. 25)

This ambiguity and the contradictions that surround the problem of self-neglect among elderly persons result in decisions regarding intervention that may become mired in a morass of ethical dilemmas. The desire to guarantee a client's personal safety is often pitted against that client's right to self-determination. The struggle to provide some responsible intervention may be experienced at several levels. The first is between the practitioner and the would-be client who is not amenable to assistance but is in rapid decline or dangerous circumstances that can be attributed to self-neglect. Also, the practitioner's effort to obtain access to what the client needs may be frustrated because agencies and organizations controlling resources have not responded in accordance with client need. A third issue may involve matters of jurisdiction over a client, the resources needed by the client, or a combination of the two.

Important ethical questions seem to surface at almost every turn when practitioners are attempting to work with self-neglect problems. Debates about lifestyle and judgments made by others do not entitle society to develop a general polity of pitchforking people into institutional tidiness (Roe, 1987). Even the mentally ill have an increasing amount of protection from those who would help out of concern and from others who would act out of a blatant or subtle desire to control behavior that is considered unacceptable by some sector of the community.

The field of aging needs to consider what guidelines are appropriate to direct intervention around matters of elder self-neglect. Part of that process will involve helping clinicians to gain the expertise to engage the self-neglecting elderly in a process that respects client autonomy to make a choice even if that choice is counter to clinical opinion, that engages clients in a process of decision making rather than mere debate over the decision, that helps clients accomplish steps toward health and well-being, and that facilitates the best outcomes of those decisions, once made and implemented. . . .

Is There a "Typical" Case of Self-Neglect?

In the image that comes to mind when health professionals think of self-neglect, both person and environment are consistently and persistently neglected, and help from the community is either refused or passively sabotaged by noncompliant behaviors. The individual shows no shame regarding this situation and does not, therefore, understand the concerns of the community. Usually, no clear-cut psychopathology is apparent that explains the behavior. Finally, the behavior often places the elder in severe and life-threatening risk, if not immediate, then relatively imminent. However, the pure case rarely exists.

Although a situation is sometimes discovered that exemplifies all these characteristics, most cases involve many causes with many possible directions for solutions. Sometimes organic brain impairment is involved. Strong intervention may be required although the individual's rights need to be protected. Additionally, mental illness may be diverting the elder's attention from the lacks of cleanliness and adequate nutrition. Lifestyle plays a part in the situation. Alcohol and drug abuse may also contribute to, or form the central core of, the problem in some cases. Thus, the stereotypic or "typical" case is actually exceptional. In order to understand the nature of the entire phenomenon of elder self-neglect, we must examine all of its possible causal factors and the socio-medico-legal conditions that currently affect its clinical deposition. We need to resist the impulse to accept stereotypic and simplistic solutions to complex and multicausal problems if we are to make an impact on the issue of self-neglect, which has remained so impervious to current intervention approaches.

References

Clark, A. N. G., Mankikar, G. D., and Gray, I. (1975). Diogenes Syndrome: A clinical study of gross neglect in old age. *The Lancet 1* (790): 366-68.

Cornwall, J. A. (1981). Filth, squalor, and lice. *Nursing Mirror 153* (10): 48-49.

Cybulska, E., and Rucinski, J. (1986). Gross self-neglect in old age. *British Journal of Hospital Medicine 36* (12): 21-25.

Klosterkotter, J., and Peters, U. H. (1985). Das diogenes-syndrome. *Fortschr. Neurol. Psychiat.* *53* (1): 427-34.

Macmillan, D., and Shaw, P. (1966). Senile breakdown in standards of personal and environmental cleanliness. *British Medical Journal 2* (5521): 1032-37.

Radebaugh, T. S., Hooper, F. J., and Gruenberg, E. M. (1987). The social breakdown syndrome in the elderly population living in the community: The helping study. *British Journal of Psychiatry 151:* 341-46.

Roe, P. F. (1987). A letter. *British Journal of Hospital Medicine 37* (1): 83-84.

FOCUS ON PRACTICE   ADULT PROTECTIVE SERVICES

We have seen, in Uncle Bert's case, that an elderly person's poor judgment raises a difficult problem: How do we respect an older person's right to make personal decisions while safeguarding that person from situations of abuse, exploitation, and neglect? There are no easy answers to that question, but practitioners who work with the elderly have come up with some practical strategies that deserve attention. One of these is **adult protective services,** a service program that attempts to balance individual rights with concern for safety and welfare (Byers and Hendricks, 1993).

The vast majority of states now have special legislation and social service programs aimed at protecting people like Uncle Bert—that is, people who seem vulnerable to physical or financial abuse and who may be impaired and unable to protect themselves. Laws that protect these vulnerable adults are administered by local departments of aging or social welfare.

Adult protective services workers begin a case by trying to define exactly what they are facing:

- Is it *abuse*? Is someone else in a position to harm a vulnerable adult either physically or psychologically?

- Is it *exploitation*? Is financial abuse, which involves misappropriating another person's money, a possibility?

- Is it *neglect*? Has a caregiver or someone responsible for a frail elder's welfare failed to provide minimal support?

Another possibility is *self-neglect* or *endangerment:* An individual, entirely independently, may have fallen into a life-threatening situation—for example, wandering around outside in cold weather without adequate clothing or failing to take essential medication. Bert's case shows how difficult it is to classify a situation as abuse, exploitation, neglect, or endangerment.

What usually happens is that someone in a position to know—a physician, a home care worker, a neighbor, or a friend—reports to authorities that an elderly person appears to be abused or neglected. Adult protective services then begins a prompt investigation, usually by visiting the home and talking with the people who are involved.

Following this preliminary investigation, adult protective services would prepare a report and decide what to do next. Further fact-finding may be required. For example, it may be necessary to look at financial records or to test an individual's mental status or competency to make decisions. If the facts warrant doing so, the agency will intervene in the case.

Intervention can take a variety of forms, some more aggressive than others. For example, a social worker might try to arrange home health care or work with the caregivers to make sure that services are delivered smoothly. In cases like Bert's, adult protective services would want to make sure that his bruises weren't the result of harm inflicted by the people who were supposed to care for him. Adult protective services would also look at Bert's own actions that seem to endanger his welfare, like wandering in dangerous neighborhoods and taking unorthodox medication.

This review would try to strike a balance between ensuring the client's safety and welfare while taking serious account of individual autonomy and quality of life. Striking such a balance is not easy, and adult protective services faces a challenging professional task. The agency has to weigh competing interests of family members, elderly persons, and the values of society as a whole.

In more extreme situations, adult protective services can bring in the police or go to court to obtain a formal order of conservatorship or guardianship. But such serious measures involve risks, which are usually justified only if clear harm is threatened and if a person seems mentally incapable of making decisions about harm and risk. Many cases are borderline, and some individuals simply lead an eccentric lifestyle. In such cases, adult protective services workers need great skill and judgment to find a good solution. But the availability of adult protective services gives hope that cases like Uncle Bert's can be resolved.

FOCUS ON THE FUTURE INHERITANCE IN AN AGING SOCIETY

How important to American families is the transfer of wealth from one generation to another? The question is not just one for individual families; it is part of a broader issue about the role of inheritance in society. In previous times, inheritance was of interest mainly to the wealthy, but inheritance now commands attention from more and more middle-class people. A rise in real estate values of homes bought in the 1950s or 1960s combined with high stock market values in the 1990s makes many elderly parents more wealthy than they, or their children, ever imagined they would be.

Inheritance can permit adult children of today's retirees to put their own children through college, to start a business, or to prepare for their own retirement. Laws curbing Medicaid spenddown and the growth of private long-term care insurance are two signs of concern around inheritance issues. Much of the practice of elderlaw attorneys is concerned with inheritance in one way or another.

Inheritance plays a large role in late-life financial planning, and it has a major impact on family wealth, which is partly why guardianship law came into being. It is estimated that transfers of assets account for at least 20% of total family net worth (Gale and Scholz, 1994). In the first decades of the 21st century, an enormous amount of wealth is likely to be transferred to baby boomers through inheritance over the next two decades—an estimated $8 trillion or more (Fix, 1994).

Although a majority of Americans do not have wills, those who do are most likely to be older: About 70% of Americans over the age of 70 do, and the proportion that have wills rises with household income and assets as well as educational background (O'Conner, 1996). In these wills, 89% provide for family members apart from the spouse, mostly leaving property to children.

Gerontologists have recently identified how important it is to older people to leave some kind of legacy to their children, but they note that the meaning of legacy has been changing in recent years (Kane, 1996). In fact, some analysts point to what they call an "inheritance revolution." Parents transfer wealth to their children by paying for their education rather than transferring property, such as the family farm. As a result, their children may not expect to receive an inheritance upon their parents' death. In addition, with people living longer, more of their assets may be consumed—for example, by long-term care expenditures. Other elders may take the view that surviving generations do not have a valid claim on assets in the first place; a popular bumper sticker reads "I'm spending my children's inheritance." Still others take the view of wealthy financier Warren Buffett, who has limited what his own children will receive because he feels that inheritance can have a negative influence.

Questions about inheritance are always related to the distribution of wealth and income across the broader population. In general, wealth is very unequally distributed in the United States, and the inequality has increased in recent years. More than half of all wealth is held by those in the top tenth of income distribution, and most of this wealth is held by the very richest 1%. Estate taxes, which would tend to even the score, amount to less than 1% of federal tax receipts. More than half of the states have some form of estate or inheritance tax, but many exempt transfers to surviving spouses. The federal estate tax has a $600,000 exemption ($1.2 million for couples) for the federal estate tax, and as a result only around 2% of estates are susceptible to federal taxation (Mieskiel, 1996). Recent efforts to raise this exemption threshold even higher make it likely that inheritance and intergenerational transfers will become an even more important part of family life in years to come.

QUESTIONS FOR WRITING, REFLECTION, AND DEBATE

1 List the things that define "quality of life"—what makes life worth living for you personally. Then rank the terms on your list, with the most important first. Now try to imagine yourself as the elderly man introduced before the readings (Uncle Bert, 79 years old). List the things that would constitute "quality of life" for you at that age. Is your second list the same as the first one, or is it different? What conclusions do you draw from that fact?

2 When it comes to deciding on matters of personal liberty, the law is supposed to treat adults alike, regardless of age: There are no exceptions based on age or personal circumstance. The only basis for civil commitment is the combination of danger plus mental incapacity. Do you think the law should be rewritten to make an exception for frail elderly people who are vulnerable to mistreatment? Write a newspaper editorial to make your case one way or the other.

3 Suppose that one of Uncle Bert's nephews or his niece was spending many hours each week doing errands for him and taking care of him. Should such caregiving be a basis for expecting some share of an inheritance? Defend your opinion.

4 Imagine that you are the social worker from the Department of Welfare who knocked on Uncle Bert's door and was turned away. Write a memorandum to your supervisor stating what you believe should be done next, using all the facts you know about issues of elder abuse. What is the biggest risk you can think of if your boss agrees and you do what you've recommended?

5 Imagine you are a local police precinct captain in a city that has recently had some much-publicized crimes against elderly people. You are getting ready to give a speech to the local Kiwanis Club about the Police Department's plans for responding to the situation. What facts about crime and the elderly would you cite in preparing your speech?

6 Make a visit to the Web site for the National Center on Elder Abuse at http://www.gwjapan.com/NCEA/index.html. How would you assess the reliability of the statistics cited on this Web site? Give some reasons why the number of victims of elder abuse in the United States could be much *smaller* than the statistics cited here. Can you think of reasons why the number of victims of elder abuse could be much *larger* than the statistic cited here?

7 Financial exploitation of elders is becoming a much bigger problem today. Make a visit to the Web site for the Internet Fraud Watch at www.fraud.org. What frauds and scams are most likely to target elders in the future as the older population becomes more familiar with computers?

SUGGESTED READINGS

Bennett, Gerald, and Kingston, Paul, *Elder Abuse: Concepts, Theories and Interventions,* New York: Chapman and Hall, 1993.

Butler, Robert N., and Lewis, Myrna I., *Love and Sex After 60,* New York: Ballantine, 1993.

Dejowski, Edmund (ed.), *Protecting Judgment-Impaired Adults,* New York: Haworth, 1990.

Fattah, E. A., and Sacco, V. F., *Crime and Victimization of the Elderly,* New York: Springer-Verlag, 1989.

Kane, Rosalie (guest editor), Special issue, "Legacy," *Generations,* 20:3 (Fall, 1996).

Simmons, J. L., *67 Ways to Protect Seniors From Crime,* New York: Henry Holt, 1993.

Smyer, Michael, Schaier, K. Warner, and Kapp, Marshall B. (eds.), *Older Adult Decision-Making and the Law,* New York: Springer, 1996.

Should People Have the Choice to End Their Lives?

It is just as neurotic in old age not to focus upon the goal of death as it is in youth to repress fantasies which have to do with the future.

—*Carl Jung,* The Soul and Death

The play *Whose Life Is It Anyway?* (Clark, 1978) tells the story of a patient (played by Mary Tyler Moore on Broadway, and later, in a film, by Richard Dreyfuss) who is paralyzed and confined to bed. In the play, the patient engages in a spirited debate with her doctor, asking for help in ending her life. She is no longer able to live as the kind of person she has always known herself to be, and so the drama of the play centers on the question: What to do?

Increasingly, this kind of question is being asked not about people like the character in the play but about their grandparents. Over two-thirds of all deaths in the United States occur among people over age 65. More and more, the timing of death is not an event that happens according to nature but is a decision made by human beings.

End-of-life decisions are rapidly becoming our choice to make, whether we want to make them or not. Medical advances force us to make decisions unforeseen just a few decades ago. For example, in times past a person who was unable to breathe without help would die within minutes. Today, mechanically assisted respiration or artificial nutrition and hydration (tube feeding) can sometimes sustain life for years. But medical technology that is a benefit to some can become a burden to others. The decision, in any event, is not easily avoided.

How we understand the decisions to be made will help shape the kind of decisions we make. Consider the moral problem of *euthanasia,* a term that originally came from ancient Greek, meaning simply a "good death." The question put by the play *Whose Life Is It Anyway?* is whether a doctor should help the patient end her life. Will the doctor, in other words, engage in *active euthanasia*—sometimes called "mercy killing"? The term active euthanasia is used here to denote some deliberate intervention to end the patient's life, such as giving a fatal dose of painkilling medication. *Passive euthanasia,* by contrast, means not doing something, such as withdrawing life-supporting therapy, with the result that the patient dies (Rachels, 1986). Finally, there is the option of *assisted suicide,* in which a doctor or family member actively provides the means or carries out the instructions required for an individual to end his or her life (Wennberg, 1989).

People interpret the morality of these acts or omissions in very different ways. Some answers depend on how we ask the question and the terms that we use. Most people sharply condemn involuntary euthanasia—that is, killing someone without his or her consent because one believes that person would be better off dead. But there is much more controversy about voluntary euthanasia (Kohl, 1975). Moreover, some critics wonder if there really is a valid ethical distinction between active versus passive euthanasia. Others ask, is there any difference between direct killing and assisting someone who takes his or her own life?

These questions are not abstract or hypothetical at the moment when it is time to terminate life-sustaining treatment (Hastings Center, 1988). Does it make any difference if we withhold a treatment from the beginning or withdraw that treatment once it has already started—for example, "pulling the plug" in the case of a mechanical respirator? Then again, what really counts as "treatment" anyway? For instance, would providing food and water be considered a "treatment" in the same way as administering antibiotics is a treatment?

These are some of the ethical issues involved in end-of-life decisions. As the timing of death has been displaced more and more in later life, older people obviously have a vital interest in this debate. On one side are those who argue that the right to self-determination means patients should have the means to end their lives at a time of their own choosing. On the other side are those who warn that the right to suicide or euthanasia runs grave moral risks. For example, should we encourage depressed elderly people to end their lives instead of changing the conditions that gave rise to the problem?

Depression and Suicide

Psychologists have identified a number of common predictors of suicide: intolerable psychological pain and frustration, psychological needs, a feeling of hopelessness or helplessness, and communicating the intent to kill oneself (Osgood, 1992). Old age is not a time of happiness for everyone. A 1986 Harris survey found that 48% of persons over age 65 felt depressed at least occasionally. But what exactly does "depression" mean? Clinical depression is different from the "down" state that is a common response to setbacks but is usually temporary. Depression following bereavement and depression among residents of nursing homes may be a reaction to the fact that it is difficult to "start over" in later life.

Clinical depression remains the most important cause of suicide among the old (Blazer, 1993). But depression is rarely the result of social isolation or withdrawal alone. In fact, most elderly suicide victims either live with family or are in contact with family and friends. Nearly three-quarters of older people who commit suicide have had a recent visit to their primary care provider. But rarely has any elderly person who committed suicide received mental health services, specifically, treatment for depression.

Of all age groups, older people are most at risk of suicide. Suicide rates do not rise with increasing age for women, but they do go up with advancing age for men. Older people make up around 13% of the U.S. population, but account for 20% of suicides. Epidemiological studies estimate the rate of major depression at under 1% in the population over age 65. But at least a quarter of elderly people living in the community show significant depressive symptoms that have a functional impact on their lives. For older people who are isolated, however, lack of social support can make it difficult for them to cope with depression and overcome it.

Depression is not always diagnosed because it can manifest itself in a variety of symptoms. Insomnia, fatigue, inability to concentrate, anxiety, and other physical or emotional discomforts may be reported by older patients. Depression is also hard to diagnose among the elderly because its expressions are transient or it appears along with other problems, such as dementia. In addition, some symptoms of depression can be confused with changes associated with normal aging, such as withdrawal from activities. Finally, late-onset depression may differ from depressive disorders that begin earlier in adulthood.

Psychiatrists use the term **clinical depression** to describe the presence of five or more symptoms, such as loss of appetite, sleep disturbance, and so on. But late-life depression might better be viewed along a continuum, with an individual's place determined by the number of symptoms experienced during a defined period of time (George, 1993). Older adults report higher levels of depressive symptoms than do younger adults, but are less likely to meet all the criteria for diagnosis of clinical depression. Age by itself is not necessarily a risk factor for depression, and depression is not necessarily more common among the elderly than among younger adults (Blazer, 1991).

The majority of older people do not feel sad or unhappy most of the time. A national Harris Survey conducted in 1981 found that only a quarter of respondents said, "This is the dreariest time of my life," while around half reported being just as happy as they had been when younger. Contrary to stereotype, a third of respondents said old age was the *happiest* period of their life. In short, while people differ, the stereotype of old-age misery is wrong.

The psychological problem is that multiple losses and the expectation of further losses can be damaging to self-esteem and can weaken healthy psychological defense mechanisms (Vaillant, 1977). Denial may no longer be possible when an elderly person faces deterioration and dependency in the course of illness (Busse and Blazer, 1980). In such cases, it is not easy to say whether an elderly patient's rejection of lifesaving treatment, for instance, represents an informed choice to be respected, or instead is a sign that the patient needs help for a depressive disorder.

Depressed elderly patients do not differ from nondepressed elders in the number and types of medical interventions they want when their overall outlook is poor. However, depressed patients are more likely to refuse procedures in situations where the medical prognosis is actually good. The factor that explains most of the difference may not be clinical depression but broader quality of life, which may not be captured by a diagnosis of clinical depression (Lee and Ganzini, 1992).

A serious ethical dilemma arises for elderly people and their families. Many doctors are intensely committed to keeping patients alive and may therefore doubt that anyone who rejects a life-sustaining treatment can be fully rational. The mere fact of deciding not to continue living becomes "proof" of irrationality. But this attitude of "treatment at all costs" fails to take seriously the possibility that some people in the last stage of life may decide that they simply have lived long enough. Should we therefore fail to respect their decision?

The dilemma was clear in the case of Theresa Leguerrier, a resident in the Good Samaritan Nursing Home in upstate New York. The patient was in her 80s but not suffering from any serious medical problems. One day, she began to refuse food and water, expressing a wish to die of starvation. Staff in the nursing home were divided in their opinion about what to do. The nursing home administration claimed that by refusing food a resident might make the home vulnerable to legal penalty for assisting suicide. Against this view, a physician and social worker involved in the case maintained that Theresa Leguerrier was rational and competent to make her own decision in the matter. The nursing home petitioned a court to institute artificial feeding, but the court eventually agreed with the patient's right to refuse treatment in this case.

Some patients who reject a treatment or behave in another way that puts life at risk, such as refusing food, may be suffering from a treatable depressive disorder. They may simply lack enough "tender loving care." The 1985 National Nursing Home Survey, for example, discovered that 25% of residents in nursing homes had a major depression, and this figure does not include the majority of nursing home residents who suffered some degree of mental impairment. To adopt a laissez-faire attitude—"Well, it's their choice to make"—fails to take seriously the way depressive disorders can impair judgment. Failing to diagnose and treat late-life depression could consign untold numbers of older people to self-imposed death by neglect under the label of "self-determination." But regarding anyone who refuses treatment as suffering from mental illness is disrespectful of the patient's autonomy.

The "Right to Die"

Widespread public discussion of the ethics of death and dying began during the late 1960s (Filene, 1998). The first great stimulus to this debate was the problem of brain death, a condition in which a critical part of the brain loses its ability to function. When mechanical respirators were developed that could be used to keep patients in this condition alive, states passed laws defining when "death" could be said to have occurred under these conditions. But defining the moment of death was not as vexing a problem as resolving the ethical dilemmas around end-of-life choices.

The first major "right to die" case was that of Karen Ann Quinlan, in New Jersey (*In re Quinlan,* 1976). The patient, 21 years old at the time, was in a coma. Her family asked the court's permission to discontinue the use of a mechanical respirator, which they termed an "extraordinary means" of sustaining life. Upon appeal, the New Jersey Supreme Court ruled that there was a constitutional "right to privacy" to permit withholding or withdrawing life-sustaining treatment. Karen Ann Quinlan was then removed from the ventilator and brought to a nursing home, where she remained for nine years, sustained by feeding tubes and antibiotics until her death in 1985.

The *Quinlan* case was not an isolated incident but stimulated new legislation. The first important "right to die" law passed was the California Natural Death Act (1976). Since then, other states have been the scene of both legislation and court decisions that pushed far beyond the California law (Glick, 1992).

Under widely recognized principles of common law in the United States, people have a basic right to accept or reject medical treatment and therefore a right to refuse treatment. Many state courts, along with the U.S. Supreme Court, have found that a constitutional right to refuse treatment can be exercised by another person on behalf of someone who has become legally incompetent. Where no family member is present, courts have relied on a *guardian at litem:* a designated spokesperson who represents the interests of the incapacitated person and reports to the court.

Courts have relied on two different kinds of standards to determine when it is proper to withhold or withdraw life-sustaining treatment from incompetent patients: the standard of **substituted judgment** (What would this patient have wanted under these conditions?), and the **best interest** standard (What is the balance of benefits and burdens that a "reasonable person" might want under these conditions?).

The American Medical Association (AMA) in 1986 issued a statement approving, in appropriate cases, the removal or withholding of life-prolonging medical treatment. The AMA stated that discontinuing all means of life-prolonging treatment was "not unethical" even if the patient's condition was not terminal but the patient was instead in an irreversible coma. This view echoed the finding of some courts.

Typical of a whole range of end-of-life decisions among the very old was the case of Claire Conroy, age 84 and a nursing home resident (*In re Conroy,* 1985). Her nephew, appointed as her guardian, asked a New Jersey court for permission to remove a nasogastric tube. The trial court first granted permission on the grounds that life for the patient had become too great a burden. But the New Jersey Supreme Court, reviewing the *Conroy* case, rejected that reasoning and instead defined a range of procedures incorporating tests of substituted judgment and patient's best interest. Another case of this kind was that of Earle Spring, 77 years old and suffering from both dementia and kidney failure. The Supreme Judicial Court in Massachusetts ruled that court approval is not necessarily required before withholding treatment from an incompetent patient (*In re Earle Spring*, 1980).

But decisions in one state court may not be consistent with those in other states. In the *O'Conner* case (1988), New York's appellate court adopted a very strict interpretation of the idea of substituted judgment. In this case, the court insisted that there is a duty to preserve life in all cases, unless there is "clear and convincing evidence" that the patient intended to refuse treatment under a particular circumstance. The New York court was fearful that, without a strict standard of proof, the vulnerable elderly could be abused by family members interested in inheriting property or by caregivers exhausted by the burden of care. Their concern was gerontocide, or the killing of the old, a practice prevalent in some primitive societies facing conditions of extreme scarcity (Simmons, 1945).

In an attempt to guarantee that their wishes regarding life-sustaining treatment will be carried out, some people write **living wills.** However, a living will does not answer all questions that can arise in end-of-life decisions. Consider the case of Estelle Browning of Florida, who suffered a massive stroke at age 86 (*In re Guardianship of Estelle M. Browning*, 1990). In a previously written living will, Mrs. Browning had stated that she wanted medical treatment, including artificial nutrition, withheld or withdrawn in the event that her condition was terminal and death was imminent. But did these provisions of her living will apply to the present condition? Mrs. Browning was not in a coma, but damage from the stroke was extensive and irreversible. But is "irreversible" the same as "terminal"? The court eventually agreed to permit withdrawal of Mrs. Browning's feeding tube on grounds of a right to privacy and in recognition of the substituted judgment rendered by a proxy decision maker.

One of the most important cases was that of Nancy Beth Cruzan, a young woman who suffered brain damage following an accident and was kept alive with artificial nutrition and hydration (*Cruzan v. Director of Missouri Department of Health*, 1990). A Missouri court denied her parents' request to discontinue treatment, maintaining that clear and convincing evidence of Nancy's wishes was not available. In 1990, this Missouri decision was upheld, by a 5-4 vote, by the U.S. Supreme Court. But by an 8-1 vote, the Supreme Court endorsed "the principle that a competent person has a constitutionally protected 'liberty interest' in refusing unwanted medical treatment." At the same time, the Court ruled that there were legitimate state interests in preserving life and preventing potential abuse in terminating treatment. For this reason, the Court judged it proper to permit states to impose a high standard of evidence in determining whether an action by a surrogate decision maker (for example, Nancy Cruzan's parents) actually reflects the wishes of the patient.

The *Cruzan* case was the first time the U.S. Supreme Court had rendered a verdict on right-to-die cases. In its decision, it upheld the right to refuse life-sustaining care, including artificial nutrition as a medical treatment. A majority of the Court found that an appointed proxy or surrogate decision maker, just like a competent patient, would be legally entitled to refuse treatment. Significantly, the Court finally endorsed the use of **advance directives** (King, 1996), such as the living will and the **durable power of attorney for health care.** But the Court also left procedural requirements to the states, ensuring that both legislation and litigation will continue for years to come.

In many ways, the recent evolution of right-to-die laws and court cases is a continuation of long-held cultural ideals: above all, the idea of self-determination and protection of rights by due process of law. For a competent adult, the right to refuse medical treatment, even at risk of death, has been widely recognized in U.S. common law tradition. The *Natanson v. Kline* case (1960) expressed the ideal of self-determination in these words: "Each man is considered to be master of his own body, and he may, if he be of sound mind, expressly prohibit the performance of life-saving surgery, or other medical treatment." But these developments do not confer on anyone a right to have active euthanasia performed, nor do they confer a right to involve other people in assisting with suicide. The right to die in all cases under law has involved some variety of passive euthanasia.

Should the right to die be extended further? Where to draw the line between a passive right to die and more active forms of assisted suicide or active euthanasia remains an unresolved issue. An early case, *Perlmutter* (1978), illustrates the point. A 73-year-old man was terminally ill but fully competent and sought to have his respirator disconnected. The Florida state attorney argued that anyone helping to disconnect the respirator could be criminally charged with assisting a suicide, an argument that was firmly rejected by the Florida Supreme Court.

Today, very few people would regard withdrawing treatment from the terminally ill as equivalent to suicide. Courts have repeatedly concluded that termination of life-sustaining treatment is not homicide, suicide, or assisted suicide. At the same time, assisting a suicide does remain a crime in most jurisdictions of the United States. This fact is important in weighing the actions of Dr. Jack Kevorkian, who developed an infamous "suicide machine" that delivers a lethal dose of drugs to patients requesting it. The so-called suicide manual titled *Final Exit* (Humphry, 1992) remains popular among the elderly. Although a jury finally convicted Dr. Kevorkian, public opinion polls showed substantial support for him.

In 1997, Oregon became the first and only state to permit physician-assisted suicide. In the first years after the law was passed, few people took advantage of the Death With Dignity Act, which permits doctors to prescribe lethal medications for patients with a terminal illness who want to end their lives. The average age of those making use of the law to date has been over 70, so the law has implications for an aging population. One interesting side effect of the new law has been vastly greater interest in Oregon in use of pain medications as well as hospice. The Oregon assisted-suicide law remains controversial, and no other state has followed Oregon's lead.

In 1997, in the *Washington v. Glucksberg* case, the Supreme Court ruled that terminally ill individuals do not have a constitutional right to assisted suicide. The result of this decision is that states may make their own regulations in this area, as Oregon has done.

Whatever the outcome of public debate over assisted suicide, many elderly people are taking matters into their own hands. Suicide rates increase with advancing age among Americans age 65 and reach a peak for those over age 75 (McIntosh et al., 1994). Elderly men are more likely to commit suicide than those in any other age group in the United States, most often by guns. But old-age suicide is a complex phenomenon (Leenaars et al., 1992). For instance, there are dramatic differences in the elderly suicide rate among different ethnic groups. White males are the group most likely to kill themselves in old age; black females are the least likely to die by their own hands (Baker, 1994).

Despite wide public discussion, Americans lack a clear consensus about exactly how "dying well" might be defined (Kearl, 1996). At a minimum, dying well would mean having the right to know one's medical condition and the choice to accept or reject life-prolonging treatment. At the same time, there is growing public approval for the right of the terminally ill to have the options of euthanasia or assisted suicide. Some surveys suggest that two-thirds of Americans favor legalizing physician-assisted suicide. One factor pushing public opinion in this direction is the loss of control that terminally ill patients experience in hospitals: Even completing an advance directive does not guarantee that it will be honored in practice.

What is distinctive about the current debate is that some critics are coming to view suicide in old age not as a problem but perhaps as a rational choice in a desperate situation. The Hemlock Society argues that suicide and assisted suicide in the face of a terminal illness that causes unbearable suffering should be ethically and legally acceptable. The Netherlands has gone furthest in legalizing euthanasia and physician-assisted suicide. But some observers see the experience of the Netherlands as proof of the inability to effectively regulate euthanasia and suicide (Gomez, 1991; Muller et al., 1994). One study of the practice showed that for more than half the patients in the Netherlands who had legal euthanasia, the procedure was performed without their full consent (Butler, 1996). Critics have argued that the real focus should be on *palliative care,* such as hospice and pain medication. Some opinion polls showing a majority of Americans favor legalizing assisted suicide give different results if respondents are given a choice of better palliative care at the end of life (Shelanski, 1998).

Outlook for the Future

By the time Karen Ann Quinlan finally died in 1985, public opinion in the United States had undergone a substantial change that paralleled dramatic developments in the legal sphere. Withdrawal or withholding of heroic measures such as artificial respiration or cardiopulmonary resuscitation (CPR) has become more acceptable to a majority of Americans, at least in cases of terminal illness. But most health care professionals and vocal elements of the public still disapprove of active euthanasia.

Other issues remain controversial. For example, is artificial nutrition or hydration to be considered in the same category as other medical treatments? The AMA has claimed that there is no ethically significant difference between withdrawing food and water and using other life-supporting measures. Most medical ethicists and courts have agreed. But many laypeople and professionals remain unconvinced (Solomon et al., 1993).

In a similar way, ethicists have argued that withholding life-supporting treatment is no different morally from withdrawing treatment once it has already begun. But, again, most families and health care practitioners remain persuaded that there is an important psychological difference: It is easier not to start a treatment than to withdraw it once already begun. Clearly, the social and interpersonal context of a decision continues to make a difference to those who are involved in end-of-life decisions.

A major step in the process of resolving these issues came with the enactment of the Patient Self-Determination Act (PSDA), which went into effect in 1991. This law requires hospitals, nursing homes, and other health care facilities to advise all patients at the point of admission about their right to accept or refuse medical treatment. The PSDA in effect creates new requirements for hospitals, but it does not create new rights for patients. Under the law, patients are specifically to be told about their right to determine in advance whether they wish life-sustaining treatment if they become ill without hope of recovery. The staff of health facilities are required to document and implement policies that respect the wishes of patients (LaPuma, Orentlicher, and Moss, 1991).

Despite this law, however, relatively few patients actually complete an advance directive of any kind. Public opinion polls have revealed that close to 90% of American adults would not want to be maintained on life-support systems without prospect of recovery. Yet a survey by the AMA revealed that not even 15% of the general public had actually completed a living will, and a low proportion holds true for persons over age 65.

Why is the proportion so low? It appears that physicians in general favor the idea of advance directives, but they remain reluctant to open a discussion with patients on the topic. But some empirical studies of attitudes held by older people suggest that a majority actually want the doctor to begin a discussion. This communication problem between doctors and patients means that the PSDA by itself is unlikely to be the final answer to helping patients make end-of-life decisions. In 1997, the U.S. Supreme Court (*Vaco v. Quill et al.*) issued a landmark decision that assisted suicide is not a constitutional right, thus leaving the matter up to individual state legislatures. Neither court decisions nor legislative action will put an end to the ethical debate about right-to-die issues, which is certain to continue for many years to come.

In the readings that follow, we hear impassioned voices in the debate over the right to die. Martin Tolchin's article describes the desperation leading more and more elderly people to take their own lives. Lilian Stevens gives voice to those people for whom suicide would be a welcome relief, not a symptom of mental illness. Sidney Hook, a distinguished philosopher, argues along much the same lines in favor of voluntary euthanasia.

In his article "A Time to Die," we hear from a practicing physician, Charles McKhann, who argues in favor of physician-assisted suicide under some circumstances. On the other hand, Leon Kass decisively rejects the idea of assisted suicide. Kass offers strong arguments for why doctors must never kill and why physician-assisted suicide is morally wrong. Kass's arguments force us to think carefully about a basic question arising in end-of-life decisions. To what extent is the decision to end one's life a purely individual matter and to what extent does it involve other people? For example, does the ending of one's life become a different matter because physicians, family members, or others participate or assist in the act of suicide?

As individuals and society debate the issue in years to come, we will be preoccupied with the question of how individual choices are connected to wider values such as the cost of health care or the condition of old age in our society.

READING 14

When Long Life Is Too Much
Suicide Rises Among Elderly

Martin Tolchin

Reversing a half-century trend, the suicide rate among elderly Americans steadily increased in the 1980s, according to government records.

The 25 percent increase from 1981 to 1986, the last year for which the government has records, brought the suicide rate among those 65 and older to 21.6 per 100,000 people, as against an overall national rate of 12.8. The trend per-

Source: "When Long Life Is Too Much: Suicide Rises Among Elderly," by Martin Tolchin, *The New York Times,* July 19, 1989. Copyright © 1989 by The New York Times Co. Reprinted by permission.

plexes health care experts, who note that the elderly are generally more financially secure and healthier, and they live longer than their forebears.

"There's no other group showing that kind of an increase," said Dr. John L. McIntosh, associate professor of psychology at Indiana University. "Teenage suicide peaked in 1977 and is going down."

But some experts speculate that the technological advances extending the lives of the elderly sometimes bring a quality of life that they cannot accept.

Life at What Cost?

Dr. McIntosh, who with Dr. Nancy J. Osgood wrote "Suicide and the Elderly," a 1986 review of literature in the field, said the increase in suicides among the elderly suggested that "medical technology may have created physically longer lives, but it also has created new concerns."

"People say, 'I'm going to live longer, but is that going to be the kind of life I want to live?' " Dr. McIntosh added.

Dr. Robert Butler, chairman of the department of geriatrics at the Mount Sinai School of Medicine in New York, said, "There's a much greater awareness of Alzheimer's disease and other incurable diseases, and people know they're going to become helpless and the costs are going to be great."

Dr. Osgood, associate professor of gerontology at the Medical College of Virginia, said the increase in the suicide rate reflected society's changing attitude toward suicide by the elderly.

"There's been more of an attitude that suicide is an acceptable solution to life's problems, especially those of the elderly," Dr. Osgood said.

The suicide rate of those 65 and older, long the highest of any single group, steadily declined from 1933, during the height of the Depression, to 1981, according to statistics compiled by the National Center for Health Statistics, an agency of the Department of Health and Human Services.

In 1933, the first year in which the agency collected data from all the states, the suicide rate among the elderly was 45.3 per 100,000, as against a national average of 15.9. In 1981, it was 17.1 per 100,000, as against a national average of 12.0. But from then until 1986, it steadily increased.

The suicide rate of those 15 to 24 was 13.1 in 1986, and the rate of those 25 to 44 was 15.5. Those 45 to 64 had a suicide rate of 16.7 per 100,000.

Statistics May Mislead

Of the elderly, those 65 to 74 had a suicide rate of 19.7, those 75 to 84 had a rate of 25.2, and those 85 and over had a rate of 20.8.

The government statistics are based on death certificates that list suicide as the cause of death. But the number of elderly suicides is believed to be underestimated because older people sometimes end their lives surreptitiously, by starving themselves or not taking medication, and their deaths are seldom reported as suicides.

"An awful lot of suicide in old age doesn't get reported as suicide," Dr. Butler said.

Dr. McIntosh said, "We think older people are supposed to die, so we're not as concerned about knowing the circumstances as we are with younger people." What of other countries? Dr. McIntosh says that long-term declines in the suicide rate among the elderly had been noted in most Western countries, but that he is unaware of any published material to indicate a reversal in this trend, like the reversal that has occurred in the United States.

Some health experts note the growing acceptance of the concept of "rational suicide," by which older people calmly examine their lives and decide whether they are worth living.

"The concept of rational suicide is gaining credence," said Dr. Seymour Perlin, professor of psychiatry at the George Washington University School of Medicine and [the second president of] the American Association of Suicidology.

But Dr. Perlin says "rational suicide" often masks the complicity of grown children, who tacitly agree with an ailing elderly parent, aware that his medical treatment is draining the family resources, that "you would be better off without me."

Children May Play Role

By not protesting, children encourage the parent to commit suicide, Dr. Perlin said.

"Often the neutral stance in favor of rational suicide is actually collusion, because the parent is really reaching out to the child for affirmation of a desire to live," said Dr. Perlin, who is the editor of the "Handbook for the Study of Suicide." "The concept of rational suicide thus creates an expectation of suicide."

A new study of elderly suicide by the American Association of Retired Persons notes that white males 65 and over have the highest suicide rate, 43.2 per 100,000, or nearly four times the national average. The ratio of male to female suicides in the age range of 65 to 69 is 4 to 1 but gradually increases to 12 to 1 by the age of 85.

"It's an accumulation of losses that just keeps getting worse," said Dr. Susan O. Mercer, professor of social work at the University of Arkansas, who prepared the A.A.R.P. report. "It's loss of spouse, friends, health, status, and a meaningful role in society."

"More older people are committing suicide, not out of depression, but because they just don't want to go on living," Dr. Mercer said. "They are projecting what's ahead, and just don't want to go through it. They're living longer, but the quality of life is not that great."

Decision Ends in Death

The A.A.R.P. study said that when older persons decided to commit suicide, they were likely to succeed. "The elderly can more easily commit 'covert' suicide by starving themselves, terminating life-sustaining medications, or overdosing on prescribed medications," the report said. "Such suicides may also be disguised as fatal accidents." The study also found that men are more likely than women to use firearms.

The increased suicide rate of older Americans comes as their economic security has been enhanced by such government programs as Medicare and Social Security. The percentage of those 65 and over living below the poverty level has declined to 12.2 percent in 1987, from 35.2 percent in 1959. The current poverty level is defined by the federal government as $5,671 for an individual 65 or older, and $6,152 for those under 65.

At the same time, medical technology has brought steady increases in longevity, from an expected life span of 62.9 years for those born in 1940 to 74.7 years for those born in 1985.

READING 15

For an Ill Widow, 83, Suicide Is Welcome

Lilian Stevens

A close friend, an 83-year-old widow in rapidly declining health, plans to commit suicide within a couple of months.

She finds travel difficult but made the effort to come from another city to tell me. Blocked arter-

Source: "For an Ill Widow, 83, Suicide Is Welcome," by Lilian Stevens, *The New York Times,* August 4, 1989. Copyright © 1989 by The New York Times Co. Reprinted by permission.

ies have left her vulnerable to a stroke that, unless fatal, would doom her to the horror of vegetating in a nursing home.

When I suggested that surgery might prolong her active life, she replied that, even if successful, it would leave her too weakened to make continued activity possible.

Still suffering from the aftereffects of surgery two years ago, she said: "I think people at this advanced age should review their prospects very carefully before accepting major surgery, as I should have done. I simply forgot that one's recuperative powers at this stage of life aren't what they were 10 or 20 years ago."

She sees no justification for becoming a burden to herself, her friends, and society. She wishes only to leave the scene as quietly as possible.

In contemplating her own death, she recalls her father's declining years. He was a highly intelligent man who survived a major stroke and spent four years paralyzed and speechless.

Tragically, he retained enough sensibility to realize his condition and to beg, by emphatic gestures, for release. He repeatedly pointed to a drawer of a cabinet that her mother opened to find a gun. She bitterly regrets that neither she nor her mother could summon the courage to grant him this gift. His last three years in a nursing home were agony for them all. Her mother died senile, also in a nursing home.

Haunted by those memories and those of close friends who have suffered the humiliation of complete helplessness, she feels quite unable to face a similar fate.

She says she has known for years that she would end her life when it became insupportable. She considered suicide when her husband died 14 years ago, but out of an old-fashioned sense of duty decided that she should continue her volunteer activities, using her knowledge and long experience.

One of her chief interests was the serious threat to her local environment. She wishes now that she had included an effort toward legislation that would permit a decent suicide in situations such as hers.

Following her visit, after considerable thought, I wrote her, expressing my deep concern and asking reassurance.

I asked: "What about society's condemnation of suicide? Have you really considered that?"

She replied: "Oh yes. I realize that many people can't accept the taking of life under any circumstances, either from religious scruples or reverence for tradition. But I think the Almighty will forgive our attempts to solve the mysteries of the universe and to determine our role in it. I'm sure everyone who really knows me will understand my viewpoint.

"Eventually society will come to terms with situations like mine, not only for humanitarian reasons but out of economic necessity. There have been repeated warnings that the alarming increase in our numbers versus the declining birthrate will soon force severe cutbacks in government support of radical surgery and extended care. Those costs are already an unjustifiable burden upon the younger generations and those to come.

"Many doctors agree with me, and their number is increasing. Some act out of mercy, but until the law becomes similarly enlightened and sensitive, they're at great risk.

"My fondest hope is that everyone who realizes the urgency of the situation—and particularly those with families—will exert pressure for legislation that will enable physicians to comply with their patients' wishes. In a civilized era, a gentle, peaceful death could be accomplished by a simple injection.

"In all other ways a law-abiding citizen, I am now obeying what I consider to be a higher law. The alternative would be unendurable. I simply haven't the courage to spend years dying by inches in a nursing home. I've earned the rest that only 'turning out the light' will give."

She hopes to find a sure, quick, painless method of release. For her sake, I hope that she will have been able to accomplish it in a humane manner.

In Defense of Voluntary Euthanasia

Sidney Hook

A few short years ago, I lay at the point of death. A congestive heart failure was treated for diagnostic purposes by an angiogram that triggered a stroke. Violent and painful hiccups, uninterrupted for several days and nights, prevented the ingestion of food. My left side and one of my vocal cords became paralyzed. Some form of pleurisy set in, and I felt I was drowning in a sea of slime. At one point, my heart stopped beating; just as I lost consciousness, it was thumped back into action again. In one of my lucid intervals during those days of agony, I asked my physician to discontinue all life-supporting services or show me how to do it. He refused and predicted that someday I would appreciate the unwisdom of my request.

A month later, I was discharged from the hospital. In six months, I regained the use of my limbs, and although my voice still lacks its old resonance and carrying power I no longer croak like a frog. There remain some minor disabilities and I am restricted to a rigorous, low-sodium diet. I have resumed my writing and research.

My experience can be and has been cited as an argument against honoring requests of stricken patients to be gently eased out of their pain and life. I cannot agree. There are two main reasons. As an octogenarian, there is a reasonable likelihood that I may suffer another "cardiovascular accident" or worse. I may not even be in a position to ask for the surcease of pain. It seems to me that I have already paid my dues to death—indeed, although time has softened my memories

they are vivid enough to justify my saying that I suffered enough to warrant dying several times over. Why run the risk of more?

Secondly, I dread imposing on my family and friends another grim round of misery similar to the one my first attack occasioned.

My wife and children endured enough for one lifetime. I know that for them the long days and nights of waiting, the disruption of their professional duties and their own familial responsibilities counted for nothing in their anxiety for me. In their joy at my recovery they have been forgotten. Nonetheless, to visit another prolonged spell of helpless suffering on them as my life ebbs away, or even worse, if I linger on into a comatose senility, seems altogether gratuitous.

But what, it may be asked, of the joy and satisfaction of living, of basking in the sunshine, listening to music, watching one's grandchildren growing into adolescence, following the news about the fate of freedom in a troubled world, playing with ideas, writing one's testament of wisdom and folly for posterity? Is not all that one endured, together with the risk of its recurrence, an acceptable price for the multiple satisfactions that are still open even to a person of advanced years?

Apparently those who cling to life no matter what, think so. I do not.

The zest and intensity of these experiences are no longer what they used to be. I am not vain enough to delude myself that I can in the few remaining years make an important discovery useful for mankind or can lead a social movement or do anything that will be historically eventful, no less event-making. My autobiography, which describes a record of intellectual and political experiences of some historical value, already much too long, could be posthumously published. I have had my fill of joys and sorrows and am not greedy for more life. I have always thought that a test of whether one had found happiness in one's life is whether one would be willing to relive it—whether, if it were possible, one would accept the opportunity to be born again.

Having lived a full and relatively happy life, I would cheerfully accept the chance to be reborn, but certainly not to be reborn again as an infirm octogenarian. To some extent, my views reflect what I have seen happen to the aged and stricken who have been so unfortunate as to survive crippling paralysis. They suffer, and impose suffering on others, unable even to make a request that their torment be ended.

I am mindful too of the burdens placed upon the community, with its rapidly diminishing resources, to provide the adequate and costly services necessary to sustain the lives of those whose days and nights are spent on mattress graves of pain. A better use could be made of these resources to increase the opportunities and qualities of life for the young. I am not denying the moral obligation the community has to look after its disabled and aged. There are times, however, when an individual may find it pointless to insist on the fulfillment of a legal and moral right.

What is required is no great revolution in morals but an enlargement of imagination and an intelligent evaluation of alternative uses of community resources.

Long ago, Seneca observed that "the wise man will live as long as he ought, not as long as he can." One can envisage hypothetical circumstances in which one has a duty to prolong one's life despite its costs for the sake of others, but such circumstances are far removed from the ordinary prospects we are considering. If wisdom is rooted in knowledge of the alternatives of choice, it must be reliably informed of the state one is in and its likely outcome. Scientific medicine is not infallible, but it is the best we have. No rational person would forgo relief from prolonged agony merely on the chance he thought a miraculous cure might presently be at hand. Each one should be permitted to make his own choice—especially when no one else is harmed by it.

The responsibility for the decision, whether deemed wise or foolish, must be with the chooser.

A Time to Die
The Place for Physician Assistance

Charles F. McKhann

My interest in physician-assisted dying and the earliest impetus to write this book grew out of my father's death in one of the best hospitals in the country. A physician himself, he died in 1988, at the age of eighty-nine, with widespread intra-abdominal cancer. In the process, he was kept alive for more than a month when his outlook was clearly hopeless. At one point he asked whether I thought he was on his deathbed. When I said that he probably was, he replied, "That's what I think, too, and I wish they would just let me go." He complained to us on several occasions that too much was being done, that he just wanted to be left alone. In truth, we don't know what he said directly to his doctors, but we passed his concerns on to them, along with our own. We were assured that they were "doing everything possible" for our father. Everything possible included palliative surgery, blood transfusions, and intravenous feedings. Even his two physician sons, one of whom is on the staff of the same hospital, were unable, or too timid and conflicted, to influence the decision making so that he might be *allowed* to die sooner.

It seems unfair that people who manage their own affairs successfully in life should be required to turn over so much of their death and dying to others. We direct the disposition of our belongings through wills and trusts, but except for the limited protection provided by "living wills," we have no such control over the conditions of our

death, and the physicians who have this responsibility may be deaf to our entreaties and those of our families. Behind them stand tradition, a conservative profession, and the law. Regardless of a physician's personal compassion, helping people to die is risky in today's atmosphere. This atmosphere is changing, though, and one can already distinguish between the conservative views of medical societies—representing "the profession"—and those of practicing physicians who are concerned about the suffering of their patients. Many physicians have helped people to die, and many more would be willing to do so if it were legal.

Given a choice, most of us would like to live to old age, satisfied that we have accomplished what we could, and then to die peacefully, perhaps with enough warning to say our good-byes, but without undue suffering from prolonged illness. Old age, however, can be marred by severe disability, and death may not be kind or peaceful. Acute infections that killed swiftly and relatively painlessly fifty years ago have been replaced by organ failures and chronic diseases that take their victims slowly and sometimes very painfully. Through the passing of friends and relatives we have learned that there are good deaths and bad deaths, even horrible deaths. What term then is best applied to the person who wishes to die and asks for help? The death is intended and expected, both by the person dying and by the person providing the help. Both also anticipate that the death will be accomplished in a gentle and humane fashion, not a violent one. The assistance is a compassionate response to an individual's considered wishes. The term that I will use is physician-assisted dying, rather than assisted suicide. *Dying* is a much more appropriate term than *suicide* for people who are already terminally ill. More accurately, assisted dying includes both assisted suicide, in which the patient must bring about his own death with materials provided by a physician, and euthanasia, in which the physician directly causes the death. Morally, they are quite similar activities, and eventually I think that both should be made legal. But there are also important differences, and in the immediate future the public, the medical profession, and our legal processes will be looking only at assisted suicide. Any consideration of assisted dying, however, requires acceptance of the concept of rational suicide—namely, that there are circumstances when death is clearly preferable to continued suffering. The question of whether suicide is ever morally acceptable is really the heart of the controversy.

The current movement for assisted dying began in direct response to the requests of individual patients and has expanded to the level of public demand. Society's concern about unnecessary suffering at the end of life is reflected in recent polls, which show that about 65 percent of people in the United States favor legislation that would permit physician-assisted dying. Many feel that their own needs should be placed above those of their physicians or the medical profession. They feel that even the promise of help would increase their confidence in their physicians and would allow them to better enjoy their remaining days.

Public concerns about assisted dying include the roles of various financial interests in prolonging or shortening life, the possibility of medical error, the potential for abuse, and the chance of a misstep onto a "slippery slope" leading to irreversible moral decay of our society. Abuse could come at the hands of family, custodians, or even physicians. The slippery slope could be a devaluation of life by individual physicians, the medical profession, even society as a whole. As a result, euthanasia could be legally extended beyond the limits of voluntary subjects to incompetents, and then still further to a spectrum of disadvantaged people: the poor, racial minorities, and the handicapped. These important concerns, which have become the cornerstones of most of the opposition to assisted dying, must be analyzed, understood, and addressed.

The differing views on assisted dying must eventually be assimilated into constructive laws that meet the needs of those immediately affected while protecting all others.

Oregon was the first state to pass a law permitting physician-assisted dying. For such laws to succeed they must include appropriate safeguards, but not so many restrictions as to make them unworkable. Several models are evolving through legislative attempts in different states. Some will succeed.

A rational decision or action is one that is well thought out by a competent individual, for reasons that are understood and can be explained to others. To wish to die in order to be spared unendurable pain from illness is seen by many as perfectly rational.

Quality of life to the last and control over the circumstances of dying are issues that touch everyone, and assisted dying will become legal and accepted when the public wants it to be. It is essential that the issues be understood, recognizing that today's needs are not necessarily met by yesterday's laws, that reason can counteract dogma, and that hypothetical fears of tomorrow's abuse and the slippery slope can be tested against today's reality in our own society. Assisted dying is destined gradually to be accepted as an end-of-life option. The trend will begin with assisted suicide in a few states, then spread to other states as voters and legislators see that it is desirable and socially safe. After it becomes acceptable in many states, the courts may step back in to provide similar protection for people residing in more conservative parts of the country. Eventually, assisted dying should be extended to include euthanasia for some people, and the range of underlying disorders should be extended to include neurological diseases that entail severe suffering but are not necessarily fatal, dementia, and even severe debility from old age. Assisted dying must be an option that can be requested by those who have lived with dignity and are determined to die the same way.

Neither for Love nor Money

Why Doctors Must Not Kill

Leon Kass

Contemporary Ethical Approaches

The question about physicians killing is a special case of—but not thereby identical to—this general question: May or ought one kill people who ask to be killed? Among those who answer this general question in the affirmative, two reasons are usually given. Because these reasons also reflect the two leading approaches to medical ethics today, they are especially worth noting. First is the reason of *freedom* or *autonomy*. Each person has a right to control his or her body and his or her life, including the end of it; some go so far as to assert a right to die, a strange claim in a liberal society, founded on the need to secure and defend the unalienable right to life. But strange or not, for patients with waning powers too weak to oppose potent life-prolonging technologies wielded by aggressive physicians, the claim based on choice, autonomy, and self-determination is certainly understandable. On this view, physicians (or others) are bound to acquiesce in demands not only for termination of treatment but also for intentional killing through poison, because the right to choose—freedom—must be respected, even more than life itself, and even when the physician would never recommend or concur in the choices made. When persons exercise their right to choose against their continuance as embodied beings, doctors must not only cease their ministra-

tions to the body; as keepers of the vials of life and death, they are also morally bound actively to dispatch the embodied person, out of deference to the autonomous personal choice that is, in this view, most emphatically the patient to be served.

The second reason for killing the patient who asks for death has little to do with choice. Instead, death is to be directly and swiftly given because the patient's life is deemed no longer worth living, according to some substantive or "objective" measure. Unusually great pain or a terminal condition or an irreversible coma or advanced senility or extreme degradation is the disqualifying quality of life that pleads—choice or no choice—for merciful termination. Choice may enter indirectly to confirm the judgment: If the patient does not speak up, the doctor (or the relatives or some other proxy) may be asked to affirm that he would not himself choose—or that his patient, were he *able* to choose, *would* not choose—to remain alive with one or more of these stigmata. It is not his autonomy but rather the miserable and pitiable condition of his body or mind that justifies doing the patient in. Absent such substantial degradations, requests for assisted death would not be honored. Here the body itself offends and must be plucked out, from compassion or mercy, to be sure. Not the autonomous will of the patient, but the doctor's benevolent and compassionate love for suffering humanity justifies the humane act of mercy killing.

As I have indicated, these two reasons advanced to justify the killing of patients correspond to the two approaches to medical ethics most prominent in the literature today: the school of autonomy and the school of general benevolence and compassion (or love). Despite their differences, they are united in their opposition to the belief that medicine is intrinsically a moral profession, with its own immanent principles and standards of conduct that set limits on what physicians may properly do. Each seeks to remedy the ethical defect of a profession seen to be in itself amoral, technically competent but morally neutral.

For the first ethical school, morally neutral technique is morally used only when it is used according to the wishes of the patient as client or consumer. The implicit (and sometimes explicit) model of the doctor-patient relationship is one of *contract:* The physician—a highly competent hired syringe, as it were—sells his services on demand, restrained only by the law (though he is free to refuse his services if the patient is unwilling or unable to meet his fee). Here's the deal: for the patient, autonomy and service; for the doctor, money, graced by the pleasure of giving the patient what he wants. If a patient wants to fix her nose or change his gender, determine the sex of unborn children, or take euphoriant drugs just for kicks, the physician can and will go to work—provided that the price is right and that the contract is explicit about what happens if the customer isn't satisfied.[2]

For the second ethical school, morally neutral technique is morally used only when it is used under the guidance of general benevolence or loving charity. Not the will of the patient, but the humane and compassionate motive of the physician—not as physician but as *human being*—makes the doctor's actions ethical. Here, too, there can be strange requests and stranger deeds, but if they are done from love, nothing can be wrong—again, providing the law is silent. All acts—including killing the patient—done lovingly are licit, even praiseworthy. Good and humane intentions can sanctify any deed.

In my opinion, each of these approaches should be rejected as a basis for medical ethics. For one thing, neither can make sense of some specific duties and restraints long thought absolutely inviolate under the traditional medical ethic—e.g., the proscription against having sex with patients. Must we now say that sex with patients is permissible if the patient wants it and the price is right, or, alternatively, if the doctor is gentle and loving and has a good bedside manner? Or do we glimpse in this absolute prohibition a deeper understanding of the medical vocation, which the prohibition both embodies and protects? Indeed, as I will now try to show, using the taboo against doctors killing patients, the medical profession has its own intrinsic ethic, which a physician true to his calling will not violate, either for love or for money. . . .

Assessing the Consequences

Although the bulk of my argument will turn on my understanding of the special meaning of professing the art of healing, I begin with a more familiar mode of ethical analysis: assessing needs and benefits versus dangers and harms. To do this properly is a massive task. Here, I can do little more than raise a few of the relevant considerations. Still the best discussion of this topic is a now-classic essay by Yale Kamisar, written thirty years ago.[4] Kamisar makes vivid the difficulties in assuring that the choice for death will be *freely* made and adequately *informed,* the problems of physician error and abuse, the troubles for human relationships within families and between doctors and patients, the difficulty of preserving the boundary between voluntary and involuntary euthanasia, and the risks to the whole social order from weakening the absolute prohibition against taking innocent life. These considerations are, in my view, alone sufficient to rebut any attempt to weaken the taboo against medical killing; their relative importance for determining public policy far exceeds their relative importance in this essay. But here they serve also to point us to more profound reasons why doctors must not kill.

There is no question that fortune deals many people a very bad hand, not least at the end of life. All of us, I am sure, know or have known individuals whose last weeks, months, or even years were racked with pain and discomfort, degraded by dependency or loss of self-control, isolation or insensibility, or who lived in such reduced humanity that it cast a deep shadow over their entire lives, especially as remembered by the survivors. All who love them would wish to spare them such an end, and there is no doubt that an earlier death could do it. Against such a clear benefit, attested to by many a poignant and heartrending true story, it is difficult to argue, especially when the arguments are necessarily general and seemingly abstract. Still, in the aggregate, the adverse consequences—including real suffering—of being governed solely by mercy and compassion may far outweigh the aggregate benefits of relieving agonal or terminal distress.

The "Need" for Mercy Killing

The first difficulty emerges when we try to gauge the so-called "need" or demand for medically assisted killing. This question, to be sure, is in part empirical. But evidence can be gathered only if the relevant categories of "euthanizable" people are clearly defined. Such definition is notoriously hard to accomplish—and it is not always honestly attempted. On careful inspection, we discover that if the category is precisely defined, the need for mercy killing seems greatly exaggerated, and if the category is loosely defined, the poisoners will be working overtime.

The category always mentioned first to justify mercy killing is the group of persons suffering from incurable and fatal illnesses, with intractable pain and with little time left to live but still fully aware, who freely request a release from their distress—e.g., people rapidly dying from disseminated cancer with bony metastases, unresponsive to chemotherapy. But as experts in pain control tell us, the number of such people with truly intractable and untreatable pain is in fact rather low. Adequate analgesia is apparently possible in the vast majority of cases, provided that the physician and patient are willing to use strong enough medicines in adequate doses and with proper timing.[5]

But, it will be pointed out, full analgesia induces drowsiness and blunts or distorts awareness. How can that be a desired outcome of treatment? Fair enough. But then the rationale for requesting death begins to shift from relieving experienced suffering to ending a life no longer valued by its bearer or, let us be frank, by the onlookers. If this becomes a sufficient basis to warrant mercy killing, now the category of euthanizable people cannot be limited to individuals with incurable or fatal painful illnesses with little time to live. Now persons in all sorts of greatly reduced and degraded conditions—from persistent vegetative state to quadriplegia, from severe depression to the condition that now most horrifies, Alzheimer's disease—might have equal claim to have their suffering mercifully halted. The trouble, of course, is that most of these people can no longer request for themselves the dose of poison. Moreover, it will be difficult—if not impossible—to develop the requisite calculus of degradation or to define the threshold necessary for ending life.

From Voluntary to Involuntary

Since it is so hard to describe precisely and "objectively" what kind and degree of pain, suffering, or bodily or mental impairment, and what degree of incurability or length of anticipated remaining life, could justify mercy killing, advocates repair (at least for the time being) to the principle of volition: The request for assistance in death is to be honored because it is freely made by the one whose life it is, and who, for one reason or another, cannot commit suicide alone. But this too is fraught with difficulty: How free or informed is a choice made under debilitated conditions? Can consent long in advance be sufficiently informed about all the particular circumstances that it is meant prospectively to cover? And, in any case, are not such choices easily and subtly manipulated, especially in the vulnerable? Kamisar is very perceptive on this subject:

> Is this the kind of choice, assuming that it can be made in a fixed and rational manner, that we want to offer a gravely ill person? Will we not sweep up, in the process, some who are not really tired of life, but think others are tired of them; some who do not really want to die, but

who feel they should not live on, because to do so when there looms the legal alternative of euthanasia is to do a selfish or a cowardly act? Will not some feel an obligation to have themselves "eliminated" in order that funds allocated for their terminal care might be better used by their families or, financial worries aside, in order to relieve their families of the emotional strain involved?

Even were these problems soluble, the insistence on voluntariness as the justifying principle cannot be sustained. The enactment of a law legalizing mercy killing on voluntary request will certainly be challenged in the courts under the equal-protection clause of the Fourteenth Amendment. The law, after all, will not legalize assistance to suicides in general, but only mercy killing. The change will almost certainly occur not as an exception to the criminal law proscribing homicide but as a new "treatment option," as part of a right to "A Humane and Dignified Death."[6] Why, it will be argued, should the comatose or the demented be denied such a right or such a "treatment," just because they cannot claim it for themselves? This line of reasoning has already led courts to allow substituted judgment and proxy consent in termination-of-treatment cases since *Quinlan,* the case that, Kamisar rightly says, first "badly smudged, if it did not erase, the distinction between the right to choose one's own death and the right to choose someone else's." When proxies give their consent, they will do so on the basis not of autonomy but of a substantive judgment—namely, that for these or those reasons, the life in question is not worth living. Precisely because most of the cases that are candidates for mercy killing are of this sort, the line between voluntary and involuntary euthanasia cannot hold, and will be effaced by the intermediate case of the mentally impaired or comatose who are declared no longer willing to live because someone else wills that result for them. In fact, the more honest advocates of euthanasia openly admit that it is these nonvoluntary cases that they especially hope to dispatch, and that their plea for *voluntary* euthanasia is just a first step. It is easy to see the trains of abuses that are

likely to follow the most innocent cases, especially because the innocent cases cannot be precisely and neatly separated from the rest.

Damaging the Doctor-Patient Relationship

Abuses and conflicts aside, legalized mercy killing by doctors will almost certainly damage the doctor-patient relationship. The patient's trust in the doctor's wholehearted devotion to the patient's best interests will be hard to sustain once doctors are licensed to kill. Imagine the scene: You are old, poor, in failing health, and alone in the world; you are brought to the city hospital with fractured ribs and pneumonia. The nurse or intern enters late at night with a syringe full of yellow stuff for your intravenous drip. How soundly will you sleep? It will not matter that your doctor has never yet put anyone to death; that he is legally entitled to do so—even if only in some well-circumscribed areas—will make a world of difference.

And it will make a world of psychic difference too for conscientious physicians. How easily will they be able to care wholeheartedly for patients when it is always possible to think of killing them as a "therapeutic option"? Shall it be penicillin and a respirator one more time, or perhaps just an overdose of morphine this time? Physicians get tired of treating patients who are hard to cure, who resist their best efforts, who are on their way down—"gorks," "gomers," and "vegetables" are only some of the less than affectionate names they receive from the house officers. Won't it be tempting to think that death is the best treatment for the little old lady "dumped" again on the emergency room by the nearby nursing home?

Even the most humane and conscientious physician psychologically needs protection against himself and his weaknesses, if he is to care fully for those who entrust themselves to him. A physician friend who worked many years in a hospice caring for dying patients explained it to me most convincingly: "Only because I knew that I could not and would not kill my patients was I able to enter most fully and intimately into caring for them as they lay dying." The psychological burden of the license to kill (not to speak of the brutalization of the physician-killers) could very well be an intolerably high price to pay for physician-assisted euthanasia, especially if it also leads to greater remoteness, aloofness, and indifference as defenses against the guilt associated with harming those we care for.

The point, however, is not merely psychological and consequentialist: It is also moral and essential. My friend's horror at the thought that he might be tempted to kill his patients, were he not enjoined from doing so, embodies a deep understanding of the medical ethic and its intrinsic limits. We move from assessing the consequences to looking at medicine itself. . . .

The Essence of Medicine

Healing is the central core of medicine: to heal, to make whole, is the doctor's primary business. The sick, the ill, the unwell present themselves to the physician in the hope that he can help them become well—or, rather, as well as they can become, some degree of well-ness being possible always, this side of death. The physician shares that goal; his training has been devoted to making it possible for him to serve it. Despite enormous changes in medical technique and institutional practice, despite enormous changes in nosology and therapeutics, the center of medicine has not changed: it is true today as it was in the days of Hippocrates that the ill desire to be whole; that wholeness means a certain well-working of the enlivened body and its unimpaired powers to sense, think, feel, desire, move, and maintain itself; and that the relationship between the healer and the ill is constituted, essentially even if only tacitly, around the desire of both to promote the wholeness of the one who is ailing.

Can wholeness and healing ever be compatible with intentionally killing the patient? Can one benefit the patient as a whole by making him dead? There is, of course, a logical difficulty: how can any good exist for a being that is not? "Better off dead" is logical nonsense—unless, of course, death is not death at all but instead a gateway to a new and better life beyond. But the error is more than logical: to intend and to act for someone's good requires his continued existence to receive the benefit.

Certain attempts to benefit may in fact turn out, unintentionally, to be lethal. Giving adequate morphine to relieve the pain of the living presupposes that the living still live to be relieved. This must be the starting point in discussing all medical benefits: no benefit without a beneficiary.

To say it plainly, to bring nothingness is incompatible with serving wholeness: one cannot heal—or comfort—by making nil. The healer cannot annihilate if he is truly to heal. The boundary condition, "No deadly drugs," flows directly from the center, "Make whole."

But there is a difficulty. The central goal of medicine—health—is, in each case, a perishable good: Inevitably, patients get irreversibly sick, patients degenerate, patients die. Unlike—at least on first glance—teaching or rearing the young, healing the sick is *in principle* a project that must at some point fail. And here is where all the trouble begins: How does one deal with "medical failure"? What does one seek when restoration of wholeness—or "much" wholeness—is by and large out of the question? . . .

Although I am mindful of the dangers and aware of the impossibility of writing explicit rules for ceasing treatment—hence the need for prudence—considerations of the individual's health, activity, and state of mind must enter into decisions of *whether* and *how vigorously* to treat if the decision is indeed to be for the patient's good. Ceasing treatment and allowing death to occur when (and if) it will seem to be quite compatible with the respect that life commands for itself

Ceasing medical intervention, allowing nature to take its course, differs fundamentally from mercy killing. For one thing, death does not necessarily follow the discontinuance of treatment; Karen Ann Quinlan lived more than ten years after the court allowed the "life-sustaining" respirator to be removed. Not the physician, but the underlying fatal illness becomes the true cause of death. More important morally, in ceasing treatment the physician need not *intend* the death of the patient, even when the death follows as a result of his omission. His intention should be to avoid useless and degrading medical *additions* to the already sad end of a life. In contrast, in active, direct mercy killing the physician must, necessarily and indubitably, intend *primarily* that the patient be made dead. And he must knowingly and indubitably cast himself in the role of the agent of death. . . .

The enormous successes of medicine these past fifty years have made both doctors and laymen less prepared than ever to accept the fact of finitude. Doctors behave, not without some reason, as if they have godlike powers to revive the moribund; laymen expect an endless string of medical miracles. It is against this background that terminal illness or incurable disease appears as medical failure, an affront to medical pride. Physicians today are not likely to be agents of encouragement once their technique begins to fail.

It is, of course, partly for these reasons that doctors will be pressed to kill—and many of them will, alas, be willing. Having adopted a largely technical approach to healing, having medicalized so much of the end of life, doctors are being asked—often with thinly veiled anger—to provide a final technical solution for the evil of human finitude and for their own technical failure: If you cannot cure me, kill me. The last gasp of autonomy or cry for dignity is asserted against a medicalization and institutionalization of the end of life that robs the old and the incurable of most of their autonomy and dignity: Intubated and electrified, with bizarre mechanical companions, helpless and regimented, once proud and independent people find themselves cast in the roles of passive, obedient, highly disciplined children. People who care for autonomy and dignity should try to reverse this dehumanization of the last stages of life, instead of giving dehumanization its final triumph by welcoming the desperate goodbye-to-all-that contained in one final plea for poison.

Notes

[Only the notes that are included in the excerpted material appear here.]

2. Of course, any physician with personal scruples against one or another of these practices may "write" the relevant exclusions into the service contract he offers his customers.

4. Yale Kamisar, "Some Non-Religious Views Against Proposed 'Mercy-Killing' Legislation," *Minnesota Law Review* 42: 969-1042 (May, 1958). Reprinted, with a new preface by Professor Kamisar, in "The Slide Toward Mercy Killing," *Child and Family Reprint Booklet Series,* 1987.

5. The inexplicable failure of many physicians to provide the proper—and available—relief of pain is surely part of the reason why some people now insist that physicians (instead) should give them death.

6. This was the title of the recently proposed California voter initiative that barely failed to gather enough signatures to appear on the November 1988 ballot. It will almost certainly be back.

FOCUS ON PRACTICE   ADVANCE DIRECTIVES

The ethical dilemmas of end-of-life decisions have increasingly led to demands for a greater measure of control in how those decisions are made. One practical response has been the spread of so-called advance directives, or written statements prepared well before a serious illness arrives in which an individual can state the choice to be made when a decision is necessary.

Under the law, everyone already has the right to refuse all or any part of medical treatment if it isn't desired. But sometimes, because of diminished medical capacity, people are unable to let others know whether or not they would want a specific treatment. An advance directive solves this problem by giving specific directions or by designating someone else in case an individual is not able to express a wish about medical treatment.

There are two general types of advance directives, both intended to give guidance and retain validity even after the person who executed the document has lost mental capacity. These are the *living will* and the *durable power of attorney for health care*. A living will is a written statement expressing an individual's wish for what should be done in a life-threatening situation. A living will permits physicians to stop undesired medical treatment, even if stopping treatment might result in death. If a clear living will has been drafted beforehand, everyone can know that the patient would want life-sustaining treatment withdrawn.

A second legal instrument naming a specific person to make health care decisions is the durable power of attorney for health care. This instrument permits an incapacitated person to designate, in advance, another person who is trusted to make health care decisions for the patient.

A living will permits an adult of sound mind to stipulate the kind of life-prolonging treatment to be provided in the event of an emergency when the patient cannot indicate a choice—for example, "I desire food and fluids but no cardiopulmonary resuscitation." A living will is a legal document and should be prepared on a standard form, although a simple written declaration of preference may also suffice. Different states have different legal requirements about witnesses and other rules for writing a living will.

A durable power of attorney is also a witnessed legal document. But an individual need not specify all the details about treatment to be given or withheld. Instead, the individual designates someone else—called a proxy or a health care agent—to make those decisions in the event the patient is incapacitated. This proxy could be a family member, a close friend, or any trusted person. As with living wills, different states have varying rules and regulations applying to power of attorney documents and their acceptability for health care decision making.

Federal law now requires hospitals, nursing homes, and other health providers covered by either Medicare or Medicaid to give people information about advance directives. No one is required to fill out an advance directive, but organizations are required by law to let patients know that they have the right to do so.

If you have an advance directive, this legal tool goes into effect only if you are unable to speak on your own behalf. An advance directive doesn't prevent you from changing your mind at a later date if you are conscious and able to act on your own behalf. An advance directive can be changed or canceled by the person who wrote it at any time.

People sometimes ask, Which is better, a living will or a durable power of attorney? Living wills were the first type of advance directive to become popular, but health care powers of attorney have turned out to be more flexible. The exact kind of document required depends on state laws, which have become a critical factor in light of the *Cruzan* decision. Such variations in law from state to state can, of course, be a problem because it is unclear whether one state will always honor a directive from another state.

When end-of-life decisions must be made in the absence of a written directive, the decision about discontinuing treatment is typically made by the family and health care providers in consultation. It is rare for such decisions to end up being made by a court, which is a cumbersome way to proceed. Written advance directives can be helpful in keeping such cases out of the legal system and in the hands of those closest to patients.

At this point, only a small proportion of Americans—fewer than one in five—has actually prepared any kind of written advance directive. Why don't more older people use advance directives? Studies of educational interventions promoting advance directives have turned up some answers. One careful demonstration project achieved success by combining a moderate level of information along with practical help completing the documents (High, 1993). Over the four-month period, the completion rate for the living will increased from 25% to 50%, and the completion rate for the health care proxy rose from 14% to 30%. These results suggest that older people don't simply lack information or need encouragement. They need better help in achieving communication with family and health professionals.

Advance directives in any case may not be the total solution for end-of-life decisions. For example, in a study of patients on kidney dialysis, 61% said they wanted the doctor or proxy decision maker to have "leeway" to disregard the patient's own previously expressed preferences. Instead of simply following a living will, decision makers were supposed to take into account circumstances and the patient's best interest.

Some critics have argued that the move toward advance directives may end up making decisions to refuse treatment easier only for those who have filled out the necessary "paperwork." Those who have not completed the proper legal documents—for instance, persons without the necessary information or education—may find themselves lacking rights theoretically granted to them by law.

Still other critics argue against advance directives because people often change their minds about end-of-life decisions. It is common for older people to say, "I would never want to live in an old-age home." Yet, after living for a time in a retirement residence or nursing home, the same people often discover that life is quite satisfactory there. That same point could hold true for living with chronic illness. People fear they would be unable to go on living under an extreme disability, yet adaptation to loss and living with disability does take place.

These problems of uncertainty, however, do not make advance directives a bad idea. Instead, they suggest a need to improve the way advance directives are used in practice. For example, we should strengthen communication between health care professionals and patients and not simply treat written directives as another form of paperwork. The need for better communication also suggests that advance directives can be an occasion for family members to share with one another their own values and expectations. Used in this way, advance directives can help older people and their families better approach end-of-life decisions.

FOCUS ON THE FUTURE   NEIGHBORHOOD SUICIDE CLINICS?

Imagine that it's the year 2010. Assume that you're having a conversation with your cousin Michael, who has spent the past three years in a remote rural village in Central Africa, working on village agriculture projects for the Agency for International Development. He's just gotten back to the United States, and on the way from the airport, he asks you about something new he's noticed—signs for local "Suicide Clinics."

"What are these places, anyway?" asks Michael in shock.

"I guess you've been a little out of touch," you reply. "These clinics offer assisted suicide or euthanasia on demand. They provide a public service."

Michael is astonished. "How is that possible? When did they get started?"

"You remember that a long time ago the courts ruled that everyone has a constitutional right to assisted suicide? Later rulings expanded on that idea and opened up federal funding for life termination. Soon entrepreneurs moved in to fill the need. There are over 50,000 suicides each year now. It's a growing market, and funded by Medicaid."

"I thought that sort of thing happened in hospitals, in intensive care units?"

"Oh, it still does, lots of times, and in nursing homes, too. Many of those people are better off dead. But what about people who aren't institutionalized? The idea is that everyone should have a right to death with dignity and have access to professional suicide services. People who are unhappy nowadays find these clinics a godsend. You know, if you don't have good alternatives, ending your life can be the best thing. Anyway, everybody has a right to decide for themselves."

"Why doesn't the regular health care system handle this new service?"

"Well, some doctors do it, and insurance companies naturally pay for it because it keeps their costs down. But the medical establishment has never been keen on euthanasia—it looks bad for business. So a specialist group has taken up end-of-life practice. Remember back in the 1990s when Dr. Jack Kevorkian was hooking people up to his 'suicide machine'? He's the one who had the original idea: specialists in end-of-life practice."

"There are enough people who want to kill themselves to justify a new medical specialty like that?"

"Oh, you'd be surprised, especially when you include executions. Thousands of people every year are being executed by lethal injection since the new Omnibus Capital Punishment Law went into effect. Most physicians didn't want to have anything to do with executions or killing patients, so a specialty group started up. Those doctors got in early as investors with the

Thanatos Corporation, which franchises most of the suicide clinics. Those early investors made a killing, so to speak."

"But what about people who really shouldn't be ending their lives?"

"Well, it's 'buyer beware' in the marketplace, you know. Nobody forces anyone to go. Anyway, people would rather make these decisions instead of letting the government decide for them."

"What about people who are mentally ill?"

"Oh, the clinics don't discriminate against them. Discrimination against the mentally ill is against the law. There was a big court case on that issue two years ago. If you're mentally ill, you have the same right to use suicide services as anyone else. Well, welcome back to America, Michael."

QUESTIONS FOR WRITING, REFLECTION, AND DEBATE

1 In the early 1980s, when Sidney Hook was close to death, he asked the doctor to discontinue life support, but the doctor refused. Hook recovered and went on to publish his autobiography as well as other writings before he finally died in 1989. Are these examples of Hook's later productivity enough to justify the doctor's refusal to honor Hook's request? If not, is there any other reason to justify the doctor's refusal?

2 A main point in Sidney Hook's argument for voluntary euthanasia is that he dreads imposing a burden on his family. Is this a convincing reason for encouraging infirm older people to end their lives? Imagine that you are Sidney Hook's son or daughter and then proceed to write a detailed letter to your father explaining why you agree, or disagree, with Hook's fear about becoming a burden on the family.

3 Are Dr. McKhann's reasons for a physician to help a terminally ill patient to die convincing? Would exactly the same reasons apply if the patient were not terminally ill but instead suffering from a chronic condition—for example, the aftereffects of a stroke—that diminished the quality of life?

4 Advocates for physician-assisted suicide generally believe that, if a person is depressed and not rational, others should not help to end that person's life. Is it possible for someone to be deeply gloomy about life yet still be rational and therefore decide to commit suicide? Imagine that you have just received a letter from an elderly friend expressing such gloomy thoughts in favor of suicide. Write a detailed response giving your reasons for agreeing or disagreeing with the conclusions reached.

5 Is there really a difference between a doctor going along with a request to terminate treatment that will result in a patient's death and a doctor intentionally giving a deadly drug? What about the case of withdrawing artificial nutrition or hydration from a patient?

6 Leon Kass offers a "slippery slope" argument against allowing doctors to engage in mercy killing. That is, Kass believes that, once we set a precedent and get used to the idea of deliberate killing, we will have no way to stop the practice from expanding. Is Kass's fear of the danger realistic, or is it exaggerated? What steps could be taken to avoid the dangers?

7 Assume that you have been asked by your employer, the chief of a nursing home, to draft a statement of policy expressing what the nursing home should do in cases where a resident says he or she no longer wants to go on living. In developing your policy statement, be sure to give guidance to doctors, nurses, and social workers on how they should act when they come in contact with such a situation.

8 Visit the Web site for Choice in Dying at www.choices.org. If you were most worried about the suicide rate among older people, could you find anything to criticize in the material available on this site?

9 Visit the Web site for the International Anti-Euthanasia Task Force at www.death.net. What claims made on this site seem most doubtful for a person who subscribes to a "right to die" philosophy favoring rational suicide?

10 Visit a Web site that calculates your personal life expectancy, such as the "Living to 100 Life Expectancy Calculator" at http://www.beeson. org/Livingto100/default.htm. Or try "The Longevity Game" at http:// www.northwesternmutual.com/games/longevity/main.html.

SUGGESTED READINGS

Annas, George J., *The Rights of Patients: The Basic ACLU Guide to Patients' Rights,* Totowa, NJ: Humana Press, 1992.

Cohn, Felicia, Forlini, Janet Heald, and Lynn, Joanne, *Advocate's Guide to Better End-of-life Care: Physician-Assisted Suicide and Other Important Issues,* Washington, DC: Americans for Better Care of the Dying, 1997.

Kapp, Marshall B., *Ethical Aspects of Health Care for the Elderly: An Annotated Bibliography,* Westport, CT: Greenwood, 1992.

Moody, Harry R., *Ethics in an Aging Society,* Baltimore: Johns Hopkins University Press, 1992.

Woodman, Sue, *Last Rights: The Struggle Over the Right to Die,* New York: Plenum, 1998.

Social and Economic Outlook for an Aging Society

In centuries past, when few people survived to old age, it wasn't essential for society to give much thought to planning for old age. Traditional societies throughout history had only a small proportion of people who were old. But today, larger numbers of people are living longer, and population aging raises new questions about roles and responsibilities in an aging society. Because government has assumed a role in providing older people with income, health care, and social services, more resources are now going to the older generation than in the past. That fact prompts unavoidable questions. How has government expenditure affected the condition of older people? What about resources needed by other age groups? What has been the effect of age-based political advocacy in shaping government response to aging in America?

No doubt Social Security, Medicare, and private pensions encouraged by tax policy have decisively improved the economic well-being of older Americans. But we cannot make a generalization that all older people today are comfortably retired, traveling and playing golf, while the rest of society supports them. Generalizations overlook dramatic differences within the elderly population. Those called "old" are divided by social class, minority status, and gender. How should we take into account those differences? How can government best target resources to the most vulnerable or least advantaged groups among the elderly?

With increased life expectancy, more people spend a larger part of their lives in old age, and retirement income therefore becomes a major consideration. How will individuals plan and provide for retirement? Within the next few decades, as baby boomers enter their retirement years, we will see a very rapid aging of the American population. To cope with this huge demographic shift, we have already begun to rethink some major institutions of our society. For instance, the age of eligibility for retirement under Social Security will gradually rise slightly over the next two decades.

As a rapidly aging society, we face many questions that we have never had to face before. There are still disputes about whether Social Security fairly treats subgroups among the elderly. But there is no dispute that Social Security, along with private pensions, has given older people more freedom to retire at earlier ages. Will this freedom endure, or will we someday look back on the late 20th century as the "golden age of the golden years" (Weinstein, 1988)?

With larger numbers of older people eligible for Social Security and Medicare, these programs already claim a major share of the federal budget. Questions have therefore been raised about whether age or need should be the basis for entitlement. It is not surprising that these questions provoke intense controversy.

Other issues of an aging society are also claiming our attention, such as the meaning of work and leisure in the later years. Why do we encourage older people to withdraw from productive roles after a certain age? The fact that retirement is common, indeed nearly universal, today should not make us take the practice for granted.

These issues about the diversity of the aging population, the role of government, and the future of work and retirement all provoke vigorous debate. An understanding of basic concepts of aging in society can help us ask the right questions and be familiar with the key facts involved in the debates. Understanding the facts and clarifying our values can be vital in shaping what the aging society of the future will be like for all of us.

Varieties of the Aging Experience

People often speak about "aging" as if it were a universal human experience. But describing broad trends and discussing older people as a group may obscure marked differences. Stereotypes suggest that age itself is a great leveler; as a result, elders are commonly thought to be much alike. In fact, just the opposite is true. As people grow older they tend to become less and less similar. Heterogeneity increases with age, and this tendency is in keeping with accumulated advantage or disadvantage from earlier in life.

We are all, as members of U.S. society, experiencing population aging. As we move through the adult life course, we also experience small, telltale signs of aging, such as gray hairs or limited visual capacity. Those who have reached age 65 will likely begin to experience what it means to grow old in a more pronounced way. With advancing age there may be gains, such as retirement leisure, but also losses, such as increasing threat of chronic illness. The balance of gains and losses is hard to judge from the outside. For instance, two individuals with the same objective indicators for health status may interpret and even experience their own health in completely different ways, as we know from surveys that ask for self-reporting on subjective health status. Aging remains very much an individual affair, manifesting itself in subtle ways, so that we may fail to recognize systematic ways in which society itself gives structure to the variations we see.

In a sense, old age in contemporary society is well described as a roleless role, a status with no clearly defined purpose or rules of behavior (Rosow, 1974; Blau, 1981). Some individuals find that freedom exhilarating. Others interpret it as a matter of role loss, as social scientists would label it. In fact, role losses are real. Leaving a valued position in the workforce, losing parental authority as children leave home, experiencing bereavement with the death of family or friends—these losses can create problems for those who are unable to establish new sources of morale and satisfaction.

A big problem in reestablishing connection comes from attitudes about aging, attitudes held by other people and often shared by older people themselves. Telltale signs of aging after middle age need not signify decline. But older people are often the victims of **ageism,** or stereotyping and discrimination based on age. The typical stereotypes of ageism suggest that people over age 65 are all sick and frail or worse: impoverished, impotent, senile, and unhappy (Palmore, 1999).

One important step toward overcoming stereotyping is to recognize the varieties of the aging experience and to see how these variations are tied to structures of social class, gender, and ethnicity. Another step is to see today's elders in longer historical terms. When looking at an old face, for example, try to imagine the life experience that led up to conditions encountered by that person today. Last, all generalizations, including understanding conveyed by gerontology, should be balanced by acknowledgment of individual differences. By combining understanding of social structure with history and individuality, we can better appreciate the experiences of aging in a diverse society.

Objectively, it may not make much sense to speak of the elderly as a homogeneous group. People often speak about aging as if it were a universal human experience. But describing broad trends and discussing those who have reached later life as a group may obscure marked differences among individuals. It may make more sense to distinguish between at least two broad groups in the 65+ population: the "ill-derly" and the "well-derly." The first group of older people tends to be poor and subject to chronic illness. The second group tends to be well-off, both physically and financially (Cook and Kramek, 1986). These two groups have been described as the two worlds of aging (Crystal, 1986).

Issues of social class, race and ethnicity, and gender create further distinctions. Old men and old women are treated differently in our society, as are the elderly of various races and ethnic backgrounds (Ruiz, 1995). Some elderly individuals are more socioeconomically disadvantaged than others, and some may be both privileged and disadvantaged at the same time. A good example is the elderly white widow played by Jessica Tandy in the film *Driving Miss Daisy,* who continued to enjoy advantages, in comparison to her African American chauffeur, by virtue of her race and wealth. At the same time, she faced a certain measure of discrimination as a Jew and as a woman. Finally, as Miss Daisy became very old and frail, she maintained the advantages of social class but encountered other problems based on stereo-typed images of old age. What we see in any concrete case, such as the story of Miss Daisy, is that age, gender, race, and social class interact in complex ways to define individual experiences (Dressel, 1988).

Moreover, socioeconomic disadvantage alone is not a good way to determine whether an older person is socially well-off. Many disadvantaged older people are still able to cope, to find meaning in life, and to be productive. For example, aged African Americans often draw self-esteem and a sense of well-being from their involvement in the Black church, which historically has provided a critical informal support system (Walls and Zarit, 1991). And many women today experience old age as a time of independence and self-affirmation, a time when they can come into their own at last (Martz, 1987; Thone, 1992). A full account of the aging experience must acknowledge the adaptive strength of many disadvantaged older people.

In years to come, the aged population will reflect the increasing diversity of U.S. society, and disadvantages related to social class and gender will be an important issue. Another will be our ability to accommodate equitably the millions of immigrants who came to this country in the 1990s, most of whom are Asian or Hispanic. As these immigrants age, they will make the older population far more diverse than it is today. Increasing ethnic diversity and a growing population of the elderly will present a challenge for decades to come and will demand thoughtful attention to the aging experience for all members of our society (Rogers and Raymer, 1999).

Social Class

Social class is a key factor influencing the experience of old age in all societies. The concept of social class involves unequal shares of wealth, status, and power in a society. In adulthood, social class tends to be related to employment, but in old age, the impact of social class is largely a matter of accumulated advantage or disadvantage built up over a lifetime.

Four elements influence the class position a person inhabits in old age: occupation, income, property, and education (Streib, 1985). It is easy to see how economic factors such as savings, a home, and a private pension can determine an individual's experience of later life. But less tangible factors can also be linked to social class; educational attainment and family support networks, for instance, can influence the resources available to elderly people. A good example is occupational status. A retired governor or judge may still command prestige even if his or her available income is reduced, and such a person might get better access to health care or other special treatment not available to less favored people who lack connections.

Yet old age does not simply reproduce the pattern of social class that holds in earlier years. Consider what happens when a person of high social class, such as a physician or a prominent writer, becomes ill or impoverished to the point where his or her living conditions are seriously degraded. Such downward mobility is not unusual among elderly people who outlive their economic resources, as when widowhood or serious illness causes a drastic depletion of assets. As a general rule, after the point of retirement, income tends to decline. Thus the oldest-old (85+) are also likely to be the poorest old.

It is a mistake, however, to equate old age with poverty and economic vulnerability. Until quite recently, elderly people in most societies have formed a large segment of the poor. At the same time, however, the richest people have also been more likely to be old, with net worth tending to rise with chronological age, at least until the 70s. The greatest concentration of wealth tends to be among people in their 50s and 60s. Significantly, about half the millionaires in the United States are women, perhaps reflecting the role of inheritance and the fact that women typically outlive men. One clear conclusion is that social class has a complex influence on the experience of aging.

Race and Ethnicity

In the United States today, 85% of people over age 65 belong to the non-Hispanic white majority. However, the minority aging population, especially Hispanic and Asian elderly, is growing faster proportionally than the white population. By the middle of the 21st century, non-Hispanic whites are expected to constitute only about 67% of the elderly population; in California, nearly 40% of the elderly are expected to be minority group members (Torres-Gil and Hyde, 1990). These population changes will greatly affect services for the aging, such as those provided under the **Older Americans Act** (OAA), which were developed with a white, middle-class population in mind (Jacobson, 1982). Increasingly, service providers need to take into account differences in language and ethnic customs (Gelfand, 1994).

Any discussion of race and ethnicity as it applies to the aging population presents some definitional problems. For one thing, not every distinctive ethnic group is thought of as a minority group requiring special consideration. Consider the Irish Americans of today, for example. Nor is a minority group necessarily limited to one definable ethnic or racial group; for example, among Hispanics there are many nationality subgroups, all of which have distinctive customs and dialects. The term *minority group,* which emphasizes social disadvantage or discrimination, may therefore be more useful than the term *ethnic group* in a discussion of how different subgroups experience aging.

The *Harvard Encyclopedia of American Ethnic Groups* lists literally hundreds of distinct ethnic subgroups deserving of consideration (Thernstrom, 1980). In this discussion, we focus on four groups that have been studied extensively because of their history of disadvantage in the United States.

African Americans. African Americans constitute the largest minority group among the elderly, comprising 9% of all Americans over age 65. By 2025, it is estimated that 14% of the older population will be African American. In comparison with whites, they generally face a lower life expectancy at birth and in most decades of life. Older African Americans also tend to experience more functional impairment from chronic illness, yet they are far less likely than whites to be admitted to nursing homes. Is this disparity attributable to the **crossover phenomenon** (whites are likely to live longer than blacks until their 70s, at which time blacks are likely to live longer than whites), to discrimination in long-term care facilities, or to some other factor, such as family caregiving patterns (Stoller and Gibson, 1994)? This last possibility points to a source of strength among many black families, namely, extensive informal support networks (Dilworth-Anderson, 1992).

Although African Americans face many disadvantages (Jackson, 1988), all are not disadvantaged to the same degree. For instance, some are quite well-off at retirement, especially those who have had college educations and professional careers. Out of every 10 older African Americans, 9 now receive Social Security, a proportion comparable to the rest of the older population. But 25% receive Supplemental Security Income, reflecting a higher poverty rate.

Hispanics. The Spanish-speaking elderly represent 4% of the older population of the United States, but their numbers are growing rapidly (Applewhite, 1988). In 1990, nearly half of these elderly were of Mexican origin, with 15% Cuban, 12% Puerto Rican, and the remainder largely from other countries in Central and South America. In terms of religion, Hispanic or Latino elderly are overwhelmingly Catholic, but they show great diversity on other dimensions, such as immigrant status, poverty, and educational level. Generalizing can therefore be dangerous, although some tendencies seem clear. For instance, traditional Latino cultures tend to encourage respect for older persons, and women fulfill key caregiving roles (Coles, 1974). However, compared with the older population as a whole, elderly Hispanics are more likely to be poor and in need of long-term care.

In short, the elderly Hispanic population is quite definitely a group at risk (Lopez and Aguilera, 1991). Like African Americans, Hispanics are more likely to rely on informal supports than on formally organized services. This tendency may give rise to an assumption by service providers that Hispanics, and other minorities, simply "take care of their own" (Gratton, 1987). But we should not forget that elderly Hispanics face significant barriers to information and services, such as poor- quality health care, lack of transportation, and lack of materials available in Spanish (Aleman, 1997).

Asian Americans. Like Hispanics, Asian Americans come from many different countries of origin, and thus have many differences in languages and customs. The largest subgroups are those of Chinese origin (24%), Japanese (24%), Filipino (8%), and Korean (5%). Older Asian Americans, like other minority group members in the United States, have faced discrimination over the course of their lives (Fujii, 1976). In addition, elderly Asian immigrants face difficulties in reconciling their cultural heritage with the American values adopted by their children and grandchildren (Cheung, 1989). In East Asian societies influenced by Confucian religion, the obligation to honor one's parents in old age is still taken seriously, despite modernization and industrialization (Palmore, 1975; Kim, Kim, and Hurh, 1991). But American attitudes toward filial piety are likely to be very different. Today's older Asian immigrants must therefore cope with the erosion of the status and traditional roles of the elderly (Yee, 1992). As a result, they commonly experience family strains (Koh and Bell, 1987; Kao and Lam, 1997).

Native Americans. Native Americans, or American Indians, make up a relatively small proportion of the total aged population in the United States. Members of this group have their origins in more than 500 distinct tribes in North America (Kunitz and Levy, 1991); therefore, it is difficult to generalize about them. It is common, however, for elderly Native Americans, especially those who remain on isolated reservations, to suffer from major economic disadvantages. These problems are sometimes partly offset by family support and a strong degree of social integration (John, 1995). In addition, tribal elders may take the role of cultural conservators, gaining respect for their memories of old ways (Johnson, 1994). This role not only enhances their prestige but also helps the next generation to achieve a better future (Weibel-Orlando, 1990).

Although today's minority elderly are better off than they once would have been, they still carry the accumulated disadvantages of a lifetime spent in a harsher environment. For example, the civil rights movement began to produce school desegregation and equal employment opportunity only after the 1950s and 1960s. Thus today's older blacks carry with them the effects, including poverty and poor health status, of prejudice that limited their life chances many decades ago. In addition, immigrants of all ethnic groups were once encouraged to assimilate into the dominant culture and to discard their old customs.

Today, we have come to celebrate ethnic differences more readily, but minority elderly still carry with them the impacts of earlier policies. For instance, in the past, Native American children were often sent away from the reservations to boarding schools, where they were discouraged from maintaining traditional languages or tribal ways (Stoller and Gibson, 1994). The results included disruptive changes in the relationships between the generations.

Gender and Aging

The role of gender in aging deserves special consideration, not least because so many more women survive into old age than men (Coyle, 1997). In all parts of the world, women comprise the majority of the older population (Gist and Velkoff, 1997). Indeed, the sex ratio, or proportion of men to women in the population, shifts dramatically each decade after age 65. In the United States today, there are 84 men per 100 women between ages 65 and 69, but only 39 per 100 among those over age 85. The typical fate is for men to die earlier and for women to survive with chronic diseases.

Exhibit 15. Percentage of Older Men and Women Widowed, by Age and Ethnicity

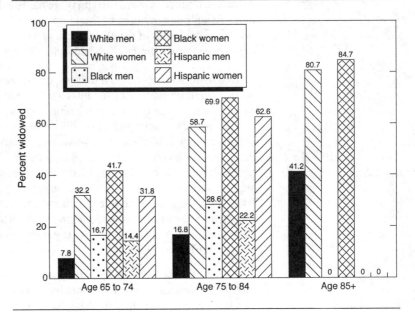

SOURCE: Saluter (1995).

The experience of growing old is different for men and women in our society in some obvious ways, others less obvious. For instance, physical signs of aging bring more severe consequences for women than for men (Bell, 1989). Media images celebrate youth and sexuality in younger women, so that older women become virtually invisible in general society. In the family division of labor, older women typically play a vital role of kin-keeping through social networks and caregiving (Rosenthal, 1985). However, the family caregiving role taken on by women often has the consequence of removing them from the paid labor force, so that they accumulate lower pension benefits than men do.

In gender roles, we can see a pattern similar to that noted among minority groups; namely, cumulative disadvantage means diminished economic security in retirement. Retirement income for older women is on average only about 55% of what it is for comparable men. The feminization of poverty in old age in fact has many causes, including sex discrimination, patterns of economic dependency, and widowhood (Smolensky, Danziger, and Gottschalk, 1988).

Longevity and living arrangements have significant impacts on older women's quality of life. Statistically, women tend to marry men who are older than they are, and women's longevity is greater. Thus women are much more likely than men to be widowed and to live alone in old age. Among Americans ages 65 to 75, up to 80% of men are married and living with their

Exhibit 16. Percentage of Elderly Men and Women Living Alone: 1970, 1980, and 1995

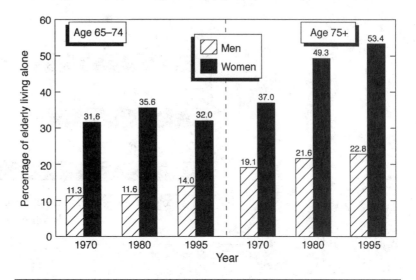

SOURCE: U.S. Bureau of the Census (1997).

spouses; for women in this group, the figure is only 52%. For women, how-ever, the number of those over 75 who are living with their spouses drops sharply, to 24% (U.S. Bureau of the Census, 1988). Thus, whereas most older men are married, nearly half of all women over age 65 are widowed. Furthermore, there are differences according to age and ethnicity, as Exhibit 15 indicates. Of all seniors living alone, two out of three are women (see Exhibit 16).

Divorce is also becoming an increasingly significant influence on older women's living arrangements. Divorced older persons constituted only 6% of those over age 65 in 1994, but in the 1990s the proportion of older people who are divorced increased four times as fast as the growth of the older pop-ulation overall. Divorced women usually experience a sudden reduction in their financial circumstances, and they are less likely than older men to remarry. Thus the dramatic increase in the number of older divorced women today could mean serious socioeconomic problems in the decades ahead (Uhlenberg, Cooney, and Boyd, 1990).

Older women's problems remain unresolved, but some positive steps have been taken. For example, mutual self-help groups for widows have shown great effectiveness in helping isolated older women. The Widow-to-Widow Program is one outstanding example of this kind of group (Silver-man, 1986). Another step toward improving the lives of older women takes the form of organized advocacy, such as that demonstrated by the Older Women's League (OWL), founded in 1980 to address issues faced by

Exhibit 17. Median Income of Elderly Men and Women, by Ethnicity

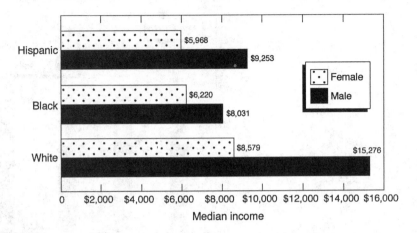

SOURCE: U.S. Bureau of the Census (1996).

middle-aged and older women. Finally, although in earlier phases the feminist movement focused on issues more relevant to younger groups, such as abortion and day care (Lewis and Butler, 1972), in recent years feminists have paid more attention to the physical and mental health concerns of older women and to the problems of divorced older women.

Multiple Jeopardy

Patterns of inequality involving social class, race or ethnicity, and gender reinforce one another. An older person who is simultaneously a member of two (or more) disadvantaged groups faces what has been called **double jeopardy** (Dowd and Bengtson, 1978; Minkler and Stone, 1985) or multiple jeopardy. The consequences of multiple jeopardy are understandable in terms of cumulative disadvantage. If women earn less than men and if minority group members are subject to prejudice over their lifetimes, it is not surprising that older minority women suffer multiple problems in the areas of health status, income, housing, and so on. Exhibit 17 shows the cumulative disadvantage of being old, black or Hispanic, and female.

Empirical proof of the effects of multiple jeopardy has not been convincing to all. Some point out that old age, instead of widening disadvantage, may perhaps serve as a leveling influence; in other words, the elderly become more alike in their economic and social circumstances than younger people are. Moreover, not all minority groups are alike. African American and Native American elderly tend to have serious health problems, but Hispanic and Asian-Pacific Islander elderly are usually better off in this area. Perhaps the older Asians and Hispanics who immigrated to this country in

Exhibit 18. Percentage of Elderly Below Poverty Level, by Selected Characteristics: 1995

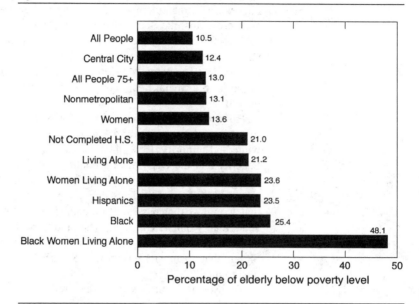

SOURCE: U.S. Bureau of the Census (1996) and unpublished data from the Current Population Survey (March 1990).

their earlier years had to be relatively healthy to undertake such traumatic change. Clearly, more research is needed to clarify just how the multiple disadvantages of aging, gender, and minority status shape later life. Just as clearly, differential disadvantage among subgroups of the elderly remains a potent challenge for public policy in an aging society (Markides and Black, 1996).

Economic Well-Being

The poverty rate is one important yardstick for financial status. For aged persons, the poverty rate is higher than for any other adult age group but is still below the poverty rate for children. As Exhibit 18 reveals, the rate of poverty among the elderly varies dramatically according to different characteristics. We see here, for example, that the poverty rate for women living alone is more than twice the average rate for all people. The poverty rate for older black women living alone is 48%—more than four times the average.

Regardless of age, the poverty rate among minorities is more than twice as high as among whites (Wu Ke Bin, 1997). It is not surprising, then, that higher poverty rates are found among older women, minorities, and those with chronic illnesses: all groups that could be candidates for those who are least advantaged.

The differences in economic well-being among subgroups of the elderly are important to keep in mind when we debate age versus need in distributing benefits and entitlements. For example, the great strength of social insurance programs like Social Security or Medicare has been universality and egalitarianism. Everyone is treated alike. Growing old is seen as part of a universal human experience, like birth and death, a great leveler. The elderly are thought of as being "our future selves," and Americans are not reluctant to pay into a Social Security system from which we all hope one day to benefit.

However, when we focus on heterogeneity and diversity, a different reality comes into view. There are sharp differences between male and female, white and minority. How, then, should universal programs, such as Social Security and the OAA, take account of such differences? For example, if average life expectancy for blacks is lower than whites, does that mean the age of eligibility for Social Security should be reduced for blacks? If we did that, would we then have to do the same for men, who live, on average, fewer years than women? But then, what about the fact that women on average have lower earnings and income in retirement, or a higher poverty rate? Should that mean we revise Social Security to give more to women in contrast to men?

The Social Security system does redistribute income, in modest ways, toward lower-income people, regardless of gender or ethnicity. But the redistributive function in Social Security is balanced by other elements in the system. Much more controversial is the question of how to take account of women's experience in family roles and how those characteristic gender differences should influence Social Security.

Aging in a Diverse Society

In years to come, America's aged population will reflect the diversity of American society. An important issue at the beginning of the 21st century is our ability to equitably accommodate an influx of immigrants, most of whom are Asian or Hispanic. The 8 million immigrants who came to America during the 1980s is a figure comparable to the number who came to these shores early in the 20th century. Most of those in this immigrant group are young, but as they age in decades to come, they will make the older population far more diverse than it is today.

Finally, there are unresolved questions about the meaning of ethnicity in relation to citizenship and national identity. In the last decade of the 20th century, we saw the breakup of large multiethnic nation states, most notably the former Soviet Union and the former Yugoslavia. The question is whether different racial and ethnic groups can live together in the United States without disintegrating tensions. Can we do better than other societies? The verdict is not yet in. But America's history has been one of a society produced by successive waves of immigrants and guided by a political ideal of equal treatment under law. Increasing ethnic diversity and a growing population of the elderly will present a challenge for the future and will demand thoughtful attention to the varieties of the aging experience.

The Economic Status of Older Americans

Economic circumstances, we know, vary sharply among different sub-groups of older Americans, but along with variation we now need to address a basic question: How has the economic condition of older people as a group fared in recent decades? Since the early 1980s, the income of older people in the United States has grown faster than the income of younger people (Radner, 1987; Smolensky et al., 1988). The rate of poverty among the elderly has been drastically cut, and the soaring value of some assets, like homes purchased 20 or 30 years ago, has brought dramatic rises in net worth.

But here we should distinguish between two very different economic concepts: income and wealth. Income denotes available money or its equivalent in purchasing power; wealth denotes all economic assets of value, whether they produce cash or not. A person's wealth and income are not necessarily related. For example, an elderly person might continue to live in a home that has substantially increased in market value but not be able to maintain it on a modest fixed income. Older people do tend to have more wealth than younger people, and they receive more in government benefits than other age groups. On average, however, older people have lower incomes than other adults in the United States, as demonstrated in Exhibit 19.

The issue is further complicated by enormous diversity in the financial status of older people. Both their assets and their income have a much wider range than is seen in other age groups; that is, more extremes of wealth and poverty exist among the old (Quinn, 1987). Most studies look only at average or mean measures, and means are skewed by extreme values (very rich or very poor). To get a truer picture of the status of a typical individual, we should look at median figures (half the cases are above the median and half are below). Median cash income is highest for middle-aged families and lowest for the very young and for those age 85 and over. When noncash income (such as Medicare benefits) or wealth is considered, the median financial status of the elderly as a group looks better (Radner, 1992).

Sources of Retirement Income

Retirement income policy in the United States has often been described as a three-legged stool. The three components are Social Security, private pensions, and individual savings and other assets that yield income. Some older people also have earnings from employment, but in the past three decades, the contribution of earnings to the income of older people has clearly declined. Thus this discussion focuses on Social Security, pensions, and assets. Exhibit 20 indicates the relative importance of these different income sources for households headed by someone over age 65.

Exhibit 19. Median Income of People in 1997

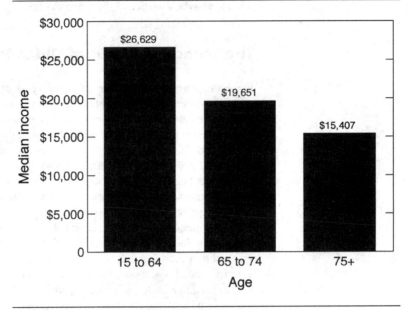

SOURCE: U.S. Bureau of the Census (1997).

Note the trends in sources of income. As Social Security has grown to become a larger portion of income for older people, earnings from employment have sharply diminished. For instance, in the late 1960s, earnings were still the leading income source for married couples over age 65, but by 1976, earnings had been surpassed by Social Security. Another trend has been the rising importance of assets and private pensions. Between 1978 and 1984, income from assets, such as savings accounts, increased dramatically, from 18% to 27% of elderly income, while pensions grew modestly, from 14% to 16%. Sources of income for unmarried older people followed similar trends, except that for them Social Security was even more important.

Overall, retirement income has increased significantly. Between 1947 and 1995, the median income for those over age 65 rose more than 170%, compared with a rise of only 49% in the median income of the general population (Bandon, 1997). Most of the increase has been attributed to increases in Social Security benefits.

However, older people have not shared equally in the increase in retirement income. Disadvantaged people—those who are poorly educated, minorities, and women—have not had the jobs that allow them to collect maximum Social Security benefits or private pensions or to accumulate much wealth. The concept of accumulated disadvantage helps explain the disparity in income among different subgroups of the aging population. For instance, Gibson (1983) found that older African American women typically had disadvantaged work lives in which opportunity was constricted by

Exhibit 20. Income Sources by Units Age 65+: 1994

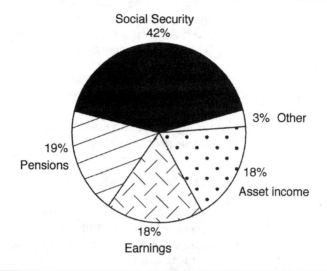

SOURCE: U.S. Social Security Administration (1994).

prejudice. In previous decades, black women too often ended up confined to the secondary labor market, where a job such as household maid would pay low wages with negligible fringe benefits and poor job security. By contrast, a white male would be much more likely to find employment in the primary labor market: in a managerial or unionized position offering job security and the opportunity to accumulate pension benefits or other assets for old age (Crystal and Shea, 1990).

The situation of older women can be particularly troublesome, because often their financial well-being changes drastically when they lose their husbands. For instance, most women are likely to become widows at some point. Although widows receive Social Security benefits at age 60 based on their husband's earnings record (O'Grady-LeShane, 1990), spousal benefits under private pensions are typically less generous. Only 3% of American women receive a benefit from their deceased husband's pension. Widowhood therefore generally means a drop in income (Lopata, 1979; Holden, Burkhauser, and Myers, 1986): Two-thirds of older widows live in poverty (U.S. Bureau of the Census, 1986).

Older divorced women, even those who were long married, are worse off. One consequence of no-fault divorce is that they receive little or no compensation in the form of alimony for years of investment in a marriage (Weitzman, 1985). Nor do today's older women who become "displaced homemakers," divorced after spending their prime adult years maintaining the home and raising the kids, have much paid work history to exploit in finding a job. Typically, they receive nothing from their ex-husband's pension either. They can therefore easily be plunged into poverty.

Gender differences in employment also produce inequities for older women. Among people over age 65, more than twice as many men as women receive private pensions. With more women in the labor market accumulating pension rights on their own, the economic position of women could improve in the future. However, women frequently leave the workforce to take care of small children or elderly relatives; today, 72% of those caring for frail elderly are female (Stone, Cafferata, and Sangl, 1987). When they leave the workforce for caregiving, they reduce their opportunity to increase income with experience or to guarantee eligibility for a pension. Finally, women reap the cumulative disadvantage of persistent patterns of pay inequity. In that regard, they are like other disadvantaged groups.

Social Security. Today, Social Security is the biggest source of income for people over age 65 in the United States. Nine out of 10 older households rely on Social Security for some portion of income; 3 out of 10 older households depend on it for four-fifths or more of their total income; 13% get all their income from Social Security. Social Security is vital for the poorest elderly.

At present, approximately 95% of the American workforce is covered by Social Security, and the trend has been toward universal coverage. Social Security payments go to 29 million retirees (age 62 and over) along with 7 million survivors (widows and children) and 4.6 million disabled workers of all ages. In effect, 16% of the U.S. population comprising the retired elderly, the disabled, and family dependents receive payments from Social Security.

To be eligible for full retirement benefits under Social Security, a person must be 65 years old (or 62, for partial benefits under an early retirement option) and must have a wage-earning history in a job covered by Social Security or be married to a spouse with such a history. In other words, both chronological age and a record of earnings are necessary to qualify.

The principle of individual **equity** would insist that people get back an amount in Social Security income proportional to whatever they contributed. Conversely, the principle of social **adequacy** would give lower-income retirees a larger replacement proportion to compensate for the fact that they are much less likely than wealthier people to have adequate assets or private pensions in retirement. Social Security, as it has evolved over time, incorporates principles of both equity and adequacy and tries to achieve a compromise between the two. Many debates about the fairness of Social Security have come about because of this compromise between two opposing values. (See Controversy 6, "What Is the Future for Social Security?")

Pensions. A pension is a contractual plan by an employer to provide regular income payments to employees after they have left employment, typically at retirement. Pensions are thus a form of deferred compensation. This fringe benefit became widespread only in the years after World War II. Over the years, the proportion of private sector workers covered by private pension plans grew from 25% in 1950 to a peak of 50% in the mid-1980s. By contrast, 90% of state and local government employees are covered by civil service pensions. But pensions are far from universal among older Americans: Today, only 45% of households over age 65 have private pension income and that proportion is declining, a worrisome trend for the future well-being of an aging population.

Two different types of pension plans are available today. One is the **defined-benefit plan,** which promises a specific or defined amount of pension income for the remainder of life. The company then is responsible for setting aside funds to cover the benefits promised. Another type of pension is the **defined-contribution plan.** In this plan, employers, employees, or both contribute money, but the amount of pension income depends on how much is contributed to the fund over the years and also on how successfully it is invested. In the past, most workers eligible for pensions, chiefly employees of large companies, were mainly enrolled in defined-benefit plans. The current trend is to offer only a defined-contribution plan, which means that retirees in the future could face less economic security than retirees enjoy today. Still another approach is the **cash balance plan,** which combines elements of both defined-benefit and defined-contribution types (Gordon, Mitchell, and Twinney, 1997). Today, cash balance plans may erode the value of defined-benefit promises for many older workers.

Employers in the United States are not required to offer a pension plan to employees, but if they do they must satisfy certain legal requirements. A major step in protecting workers and retirees came with passage in 1974 of the **Employee Retirement Income Security Act,** known as **ERISA.** ERISA regulates private pension plans in the United States and provides protection against loss of benefits to retired workers. Protection is not absolute, however. A pension plan can be terminated if a company goes out of business or is merged with another company. In addition, employers with pension plans aren't required to include those who work fewer than 20 hours a week, a crucial omission in light of the tremendous growth of part-time employment in the United States in recent years.

Equally ominous is the financial outlook for the Pension Benefit Guaranty Corporation (PBGC), a federal agency established to protect pensions when companies cannot meet their obligations. The PBGC has a deficit of $2.3 billion and will confront up to $50 billion in underfunded obligations in the future for bankrupt or financially ailing companies. This hidden deficit could be a major problem for future generations.

A key point to understand about pensions is **vesting** rights, or the period an employee must meet the employer's requirements to become eligible to collect the pension. If an employee leaves a job before being vested in the plan, then the worker is not entitled to receive benefits. Until recently, most pension plans required at least 10 years of employment for full vesting. But legislation following adoption of ERISA reduces this period to only five years, a move likely to help workers in our increasingly mobile society. Critics have urged a system of pension portability as well, so workers can transfer their pension rights from one employer to another after changing jobs. Such portability, it is argued, would not only improve equity but would also promote flexibility and better use of middle-aged or older workers, who might be more inclined to move to new opportunities if they wouldn't lose their pension rights in the process.

An increasingly important feature of private pension income is the option for **early retirement benefits,** that is, pension eligibility at age 55 or 60. A 1986 study by Hewitt Associates, a benefits research company, found that 32% of companies of all sizes offered some form of early retirement plan. But early retirement may be a growing trend. When pressure builds for lay-offs and downsizing the workforce, early retirement benefits may be enriched to give older workers an inducement to leave, thereby saving jobs for those who remain. This trade-off between early retirement and jobs for younger workers is not always fully voluntary, however, and it also poses significant hidden risks that may need to be considered carefully. For example, employees who have opted for early retirement may face a reduction in employer-sponsored retiree health benefits at a later date.

Private pension coverage is often designed to be coordinated with Social Security coverage, sometimes in ways that present retirees with an unpleasant surprise. For instance, some private pension plans unilaterally reduce the amount of the pension by whatever Social Security benefits a retiree gets, a practice that in the future may be limited to a loss of up to half the total pension promised.

Social Security benefits are indexed for inflation, meaning that income automatically increases when the cost of living does, but private pensions usually have not been fully indexed. As a result, pension income may be quite sufficient early in retirement but become inadequate as inflation diminishes its real value over time.

Individuals whose employers do not provide pension benefits and those who are self-employed can set aside savings to provide pensions for themselves. One vehicle for retirement savings that has been around for a long time is the **annuity,** an investment vehicle sold by life insurance companies permitting one to defer taxes on accumulated earnings. Congress has also created a number of tax incentives for people to save for their own retirement. One is the **individual retirement account,** or **IRA,** in which a person can accumulate money until retirement, subject to certain limitations but on a tax-deductible and tax-deferred basis. The Tax Reform Act of 1986 tightened eligibility for IRA contributions, which are now limited to taxpayers with incomes below $25,000 ($40,000 for couples). The so-called Keogh plan and the 401(k) plan have the same basic purpose, but they are not limited to people below a certain income.

Assets and savings. People accumulate assets over a lifetime; here again, a person's circumstances over an entire life course have consequences for financial status in old age. Some assets are tangible, like a home; others are financial, like shares of stock. Assets are second only to Social Security as a source of income for older people: Around one-fourth of retirement income is based on assets. As a group, older households own many more assets and have more accumulated wealth than nonelderly households, at least until household members are roughly 80 years old.

Exhibit 21. Median Net Worth, by Age Group: 1993

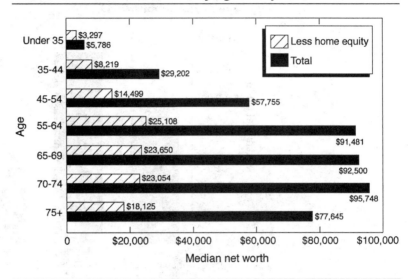

SOURCE: U.S. Bureau of the Census (1995).

The net worth of an individual or family consists of the total value of all assets—including real estate, savings, and personal property—minus the debts. Exhibit 21 shows the median net worth of households based on the age of the householder. Half of all householders under age 35 have a net worth of $5,786 or higher, but among people in their late 60s, half have a net worth of $92,500 or higher. Among households headed by someone over age 65, the median net worth in 1988 was $73,471, compared with a median net worth of $35,752 for all households.

From Exhibit 21, it is clear that the overwhelming majority of assets for those over age 35 are in the form of home equity: the market value of a home, exclusive of mortgage debt. The value of home equity is even more important for older people. Approximately 75% of people over age 65 are home-owners, and the vast majority of those have paid off the mortgage. Two-fifths of the assets of elderly households are in the form of home equity, which amounts to a staggering total of $1.1 trillion, or 30% of the total U.S. home equity. In 1993, the median value of homes owned by people over age 65 was $76,200. Typically, older homeowners bought a home years ago and thus have seen a dramatic appreciation in its market value.

Because so much wealth is represented by elderly home ownership, there has been repeated interest in enabling older people to convert the accumulated value of a home into a regular monthly income (Scholen and Chen, 1980). One approach to home equity conversion is the **reverse mortgage,** through which a bank guarantees a monthly income to a homeowner for the remainder of life but claims ownership of the home upon death (Vitt, 1998). To date, very few older people have participated in reverse mortgages, so

Exhibit 22. Median Net Worth for Elderly (65+) Households, by Type of Household: 1993

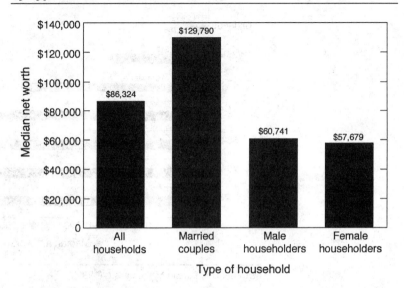

SOURCE: U.S. Bureau of the Census (1995).

home ownership remains an important contributor to assets but not to income for older people.

The importance of home equity distorts the net worth of elderly households in average statistics. About 70% of elderly people's assets are represented by home ownership. When home equity is left out of the reckoning, median net worth of all households over age 65 is only $23,856 (1988 data). These assets are chiefly in the form of interest-bearing savings and checking accounts, with much smaller amounts in stocks and bonds or other real estate.

Just as general well-being differs dramatically according to social class, gender, and ethnicity, so too does the distribution of assets. Exhibit 22 illustrates the dramatic difference between the averages for married couples and for all households, more testimony to the importance of marriage for financial well-being in later life.

Changing Financial Outlook

The financial picture for today's older people, at least on average, may look pretty good. They enjoy historically high Social Security and pension income and have a comparatively high net worth. Why, then, do so many older people feel financially insecure?

The poorest elderly have reason to feel insecure; they are by no means living comfortably. Other questions here revolve around the economic status of the baby boom generation, who will be nearing retirement age in the first decade of the 21st century. A 1995 survey by the Merrill Lynch brokerage firm revealed that two-thirds of workers age 45 and over were concerned about the adequacy of their retirement income. The Merrill Lynch Baby Boom Retirement Index estimates that baby boom households are saving at only a third of the rate needed to provide them with a secure retirement at age 65. But this index may underestimate the importance of home equity as a form of savings. If housing wealth is taken into account, baby boomers are actually saving at a full 84% of the rate needed to maintain current living standards.

Despite gloom about the future, baby boomers in overall terms may be better off than their parents. Their median household income and wealth is already higher than that of their parents at comparable ages. But will this be enough to ensure adequate retirement income? The **life cycle model of savings** predicts that as baby boomers reach their 40s, they begin to put more money into savings when retirement looms on the horizon. Whether this is happening, of course, depends on other factors besides age: Cohort and period effects also influence savings behavior.

Other unanswered questions also demand attention. Will housing prices remain high so that home equity values are not lost? What will happen to market values in the early decades of the 21st century if large numbers of retiring baby boomers try to convert mutual fund assets into cash? The problem for both home equity values and mutual funds is that a marketplace requires both buyers and sellers. Real estate, like the stock market, tends to go through cycles—what goes up may also come down. Again, there are no easy ways to avoid risk. As individuals take on more responsibility for retirement investment decisions, each of us will have to prepare for a future certainly different from the past.

Perhaps the biggest source of financial uncertainty for older people is how their expenditures will change as the years go by. The turbulent American economy of the past two decades has had important effects on the well-being of America's elderly. Older people, who live disproportionately on fixed incomes from pensions and annuities, are affected more severely by inflation than other groups. Fortunately, government policies and economic trends have reduced the erosion of buying power through inflation. For example, 86 federal programs increase their benefits for the old based on some index for inflation (Clark et al., 1984). The largest of these programs is Social Security, indexed for inflation since the early 1970s. On the economic front, although the United States is currently experiencing a low inflation rate, it is accompanied by historically low interest rates, which have sharply diminished the income of the elderly, who rely on interest from savings more than do other groups.

Nevertheless, the overall economic position of older Americans has improved substantially in the past two decades. Improvements in pension coverage and indexing of Social Security are the main reasons for this improvement in income, while rising home equity is the main reason for the gain in assets. Income from earnings has declined as more older Americans have left the labor force for retirement.

Despite the good news, the stereotype that most older people are affluent is mistaken. When we look behind the average figures, we see two things: first, enormous variation among subgroups of the aging with respect to economic circumstance, and second, a large group of older people who have been brought above the poverty line but are still near-poor. The insidious feature of old-age poverty is that it lasts longer and is more likely to be permanent than poverty among younger people. The elderly poor have fewer chances for remarriage or finding better jobs. For all these reasons, income and services for elderly who are poor have enormous importance, and so has the question of how to target those benefits to those who are least advantaged.

The change in the economic circumstances of older Americans can be both a source of pride in the success of government programs, chiefly Social Security, and also a challenge for the future of those programs. These matters have become items of broad public controversy and are likely to continue to provoke vigorous debate.

We have seen that the rise in home equity is the reason for increases in wealth of most elderly. But a home is much more than a financial asset in the lives of older people. Until they reach a condition of needing daily care, the overwhelming majority of older people prefer to live in their own homes, in the same neighborhood they have always lived in. If the neighborhood is stable, and few homes are sold over the years to younger families, eventually the neighborhood will be dominated by long-term, older residents.

In the early 21st century, as the baby boom generation begins to retire, the demand for housing may jump dramatically. But building affordable senior housing will be a major challenge, because many baby boomers will have inadequate retirement assets and because federal funding for senior housing has shrunk and is not likely to increase if the current budget-cutting climate continues. Thus many new public and private sector strategies for senior housing are being discussed.

Public Policy on Aging

When we look at income programs, housing subsidies, and health and long-term care, it is clear that government action has had a decisive effect on the well-being of today's generation of elderly. That fact in itself marks an important historical change. When today's older Americans were born—mainly before 1935—the U.S. government gave no special attention at all to issues of old age. Yet by the 1970s, a prominent political scientist took note of the "graying of the federal budget." Trends since then have amply confirmed his point (Hudson, 1978). Today, more than 30% of the total federal budget is spent on the elderly, and the percentage is rising each year.

Action by both state and federal government on behalf of older people has a long history in the United States, but for the most part early government action was limited to paying pensions for war veterans or their widows (Achenbaum, 1978). Until the 20th century, the aged population was small,

Exhibit 23. Federal Outlays Benefiting the Elderly

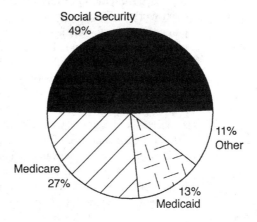

SOURCE: U.S. Congressional Budget Office baseline and Chambers and Associates estimates (1989).

and the role of government was quite limited. The big change came during the Great Depression of the 1930s, with the passage of the Social Security Act (1935). It remains the cornerstone of U.S. policy on aging. The expansion of Social Security to families (1939) and the provision of early retirement benefits (1956) were important changes in the law. After World War II, Social Security coverage slowly but steadily expanded. Revisions of Social Security in 1977 and 1983 helped put the program on a more secure financial foundation.

Like the 1930s, the decade of the 1960s was one of social upheaval and pressure for political change. The Great Society legislation of the 1960s included such steps as the federalization of old-age assistance and such landmark laws as Medicare and Medicaid (1965). But during the 1970s and 1980s, federal commitments to all social programs were scaled back (Estes, 1989). Cost-containment measures for Medicare were enacted in 1983, and efforts to expand Medicare were repealed. Still, the bulk of federal funding for the elderly goes for Social Security and Medicare, as Exhibit 23 indicates.

Another area of concern in federal legislation has been retirement. Today, more than 40 million private sector workers in the United States participate in 800,000 pension plans. Those plans represent retirement security for millions of workers, and for this reason the safety of pension funds is critical. Steps to protect pensions culminated in passage and adoption of ERISA, which was strengthened in 1986. Retirement benefits came under further federal protection in 1984 and 1990. In addition, the federal government is directly involved in providing pension income through civil service retirement, military retirement, and the railroad retirement system.

Federal legislation has been responsive to older workers as well as retired persons. The general trend has been to protect the rights of older workers against arbitrary dismissal on grounds of age. The key breakthrough was the Age Discrimination in Employment Act of 1967, which gave protection to older workers; it was significantly expanded in 1978. By 1986, a long campaign to eliminate mandatory retirement was finally successful in prohibiting age discrimination in hiring and retention of employees.

Still another area of federal government activity on behalf of older people has been the direct provision of social services. The 1978 Congregate Housing Act brought housing and social services for the elderly together, an important step for long-term care policy. The enactment of comprehensive social service programs was made possible by the OAA in 1965. Funding for OAA programs has been inadequate, just as it has been inadequate for comprehensive social services under Title XX of the Social Security Act. Still, the OAA has provided a strong stimulus for planning and advocacy on behalf of the aged population. Exhibit 24 summarizes the high points of 20th-century federal legislation on aging.

The Aging Network

One component of government was specifically created to serve older people and advocate on their behalf. The OAA, first passed in 1965 and amended in 1973, created a national **aging network** of services for older people, such as nutrition programs, senior citizen centers, and information and referral services (Gelfand, 1999). A key element of the aging network is local Area Agencies on Aging, generally based in city or county government and responsible for planning and organizing services to older people in that region. Each state also has a State Agency on Aging that plans and disburses federal funds under the OAA. At the federal level, the U.S. Administration on Aging coordinates OAA programs and provides a focal point for advocacy.

Among the key service programs under the OAA are senior centers, which have grown from the first, founded in 1943, to more than 10,000 today (Krout, 1989). Despite that growth, OAA programs reach only a tiny proportion of Americans over 65, at most, 5% to 10%. Yet the professionalized aging network provides a vehicle for planning and advocacy at all levels of government that would otherwise be lacking.

Those who criticize the professionalized aging network do so from contrasting perspectives. Analysts on the political left argue that human service programs, such as those created by the OAA, provide a meager response to "social problems" faced by older people that doesn't do anything about the underlying causes of the problems (Olson, 1982; Minkler and Estes, 1984). These analysts favor an approach that attacks the discrimination, unemployment, and oppression that they believe are inherent in capitalist society. By contrast, analysts on the conservative right tend to see the current system of services for the aging as wasteful social spending by the welfare state (Rabushka and Jacobs, 1980). Still others believe older Americans are being helped at the expense of young people (Peterson and Howe, 1988) and reject arguments made by advocates for the elderly.

Exhibit 24. Key Federal Legislation on Aging

Social Security Act	1935
Expansion of Social Security benefits (for spouses and children)	1939
Early retirement benefits under Social Security (men added in 1961)	1956
Medicare and Medicaid	1965
Older Americans Act, or OAA	1965
Age Discrimination in Employment Act	1967
Older Americans Act amendments (creating a national aging network)	1973
Employee Retirement Income Security Act, or ERISA (amended 1986)	1974
Congregate Housing Services Act	1978
Social Security amendments	1983
Medicare prospective payment system	1983
Retirement Equity Act	1984
Abolition of mandatory retirement	1986
Medicare Catastrophic Coverage Act (repealed 1989)	1988
Older Workers Benefit Protection Act	1990

Aging Interest Groups

Indisputably, the role of the federal government in helping older people has expanded remarkably. The federal government went from paying virtually no attention to aging in 1930 to spending more than $3 out of every $10 on older Americans. This increase in the budget has come about primarily for two reasons: population aging, meaning a growing proportion of older people in the population, and the enactment of programs that protect income and provide health care to the elderly. But why did government respond as it did? To understand what happened, we need to appreciate the influence of aging-based interest groups (Van Tassel and Meyer, 1992).

From the beginning, the United States has thought of itself as a "young" country, and old age did not attract much government interest. The Great Depression, however, made Americans willing to think in new ways about the role of government. During the early years of the Great Depression, Social Security did not exist, and older people were among the poorest in America. It is not surprising that older Americans banded together while government was expanding social welfare programs to advocate for their own interests.

One of the first groups established was the Townsend Movement, founded in 1934 to eliminate old-age poverty and stimulate the economy (Holtzman, 1963). Some scholars believe that the Townsend Movement was influential in passage of the Social Security Act in 1935, which marked the birth of a federal government policy on aging. A similar group was the colorfully named "Ham and Eggs Movement," also based in California, which urged a pension for those over age 50 who were unemployed (Putnam, 1970). The passage of Social Security and the end of the Great Depression caused these age-based movements to go into eclipse. Social Security itself grew during the 1940s and 1950s, though not in response to political pressure or social upheaval.

Age-based movements again appeared in the United States in the 1960s. Today, the most prominent of these is the American Association of Retired Persons (AARP), the country's largest voluntary organization of older people (Schurenberg and Luciano, 1988). Founded in 1958 as an outgrowth of the National Retired Teachers Association, the AARP today is open to anyone over the age of 50. AARP provides a range of services and benefits to members, such as health and life insurance, prescription drugs, and travel services. Its magazine, *Modern Maturity,* is one of the most widely read periodicals in the United States. AARP is joined by other important **aging interest groups,** such as the National Council on Aging, the Gerontological Society of America, and the American Society on Aging, all prominent professional or academic societies.

A different history marked the National Council of Senior Citizens, a membership group coming out of the labor movement. Still another prominent aging interest group today is the National Committee to Preserve Social Security and Medicare, whose 5 million members helped to repeal the Medicare Catastrophic Coverage Act of 1988. This whole collection of national interest groups, along with parallel organizations at the state level, such as the "Silver-Haired Legislatures," has been called the "gray lobby" (Pratt, 1976, 1982; Hess and Kerschner, 1978). An umbrella body called the Leadership Council of Aging Organizations, based in Washington, D.C., brings together many aging interest groups. Currently, more than 1,000 aging interest groups are lobbying all levels of government (Day, 1990).

Somewhat apart from the gray lobby is the Gray Panthers, founded in 1970 by activist Maggie Kuhn with a goal of fighting ageism on an intergenerational basis (Jacobs and Hess, 1978). The Gray Panthers have occasionally criticized mainstream aging organizations as a cadre of professionals who earn their living by providing services to dependent elderly clients (Estes, 1979; Moody, 1988b). Nonetheless, the professionalized aging network remains a successful instance of "interest group liberalism" (Binstock, 1972), that is, advocacy for expanded government intervention on behalf of a group—in this case, the elderly.

The arguments raised by the Gray Panthers and other critics of the gray lobby raise a point debated today: To what extent should age-based advocacy groups press for laws or benefits to help the elderly alone as opposed to those that help people of all ages? For every person over age 65 who is disabled, a younger person with similar disabilities could benefit from home health care. When Medicare was created in 1965, many people believed it was the first step toward creating a national health insurance program

(Marmor, 1973; Feder, 1977). But more than 30 years later, we still don't have a program covering all age groups.

To understand the intensely political debates about public policies on aging, we must understand something about political attitudes in old age. It is a mistake to assume that older people are bound to be more conservative just because they are older (Cutler, 1981). A sizable body of literature in political science suggests that age in itself does not have much impact on political attitudes or behavior, and people tend to maintain their political affiliation as they age (Glenn and Hefner, 1972). Thus there seems to be little likelihood of a "generational politics" developing in which people vote according to age lines (Heclo, 1988). On the other hand, interest in politics, and certainly voting behavior, does tend to increase with age. The most active voters are in the 65- to 75-year-old age group. Remember, however, that although older Americans are likely to have a disproportionate voice in elections, they do not necessarily speak with one voice.

In addition, the sheer size and diversity of aging interest groups may weaken their ability to influence public policy. For instance, AARP is larger than any other organized interest group in the United States. With 34 million members, it has more people than Canada. But the power of AARP, which sometimes claims to speak for the elderly, is commonly overrated. Perhaps the most striking example of its limited power is the case of the Medicare Catastrophic Coverage Act of 1988. That act was intended to help older people pay high medical bills. The act was hailed at the time as the biggest expansion of Medicare in its history, and Congress expected it to be popular. But the act soon proved controversial and unpopular. More affluent elderly voters disliked the higher taxes required by the law. AARP, against the wishes of many of its own vocal members, supported the act, and the National Committee to Preserve Social Security and Medicare opposed it. In little more than a year, the Catastrophic Coverage Act was quickly repealed, not because of a powerful Washington interest group but despite it.

"Gray power" sounds impressive. Yet the skeptic might ask just how effective these interest groups are in the real world of politics. Political scientists who have studied the matter tend to argue that aging interest groups are not all that effective, except in preventing cuts in popular programs, such as Social Security (Binstock, 1972).

Trends in Public Policy and Aging

As we think about the future, it is important to keep in mind the diversity of the aging population, including dramatic differences in well-being among subgroups, and the impact of cumulative disadvantage, whereby earlier experience over the life course influences what old age will be like. Clearly, the improved economic circumstances of older people have already prompted some reassessment of aging programs. Whatever we may think about the effectiveness of political advocacy for the elderly, an increasing share of the federal government's expenditures have unquestionably been directed toward the older population. This growth in spending for older Americans has several explanations:

- Social Security and Medicare have grown rapidly because they have been available on the basis of age alone, without means testing. These programs serve all older adults without reference to need. In fact, beneficiaries of this spending are mostly the middle-class elderly, not the poor. Even the rich elderly collect Social Security, because they paid into it.

- A related point is that federal programs for the elderly continue to enjoy broad political support. Most recipients sincerely believe that they are only getting back what they are entitled to, that Social Security functions something like an annuity with every dollar contributed in the working years being returned, with interest, during retirement. This view is in fact mistaken: Social Security does not operate like a bank account. But the majority of elderly, conservative or liberal, expect their due. At the same time, many younger people are only too happy to support programs that help their parents, even if growing numbers of young adults have doubts about whether they will collect similar benefits when they retire.

- Programs for the elderly have developed incrementally for the most part, making it harder to see just how much they have grown over the years. Sometimes breakthroughs have been dramatic, as when Social Security was instituted in 1935. But equally important have been the less noticed, gradual expansions of Social Security, which have had a large cumulative impact. It is true that periods of growth have been offset by cutbacks like the Social Security amendments of 1983, when Congress agreed for the first time to tax Social Security benefits. But these technical details have not been well understood by the general public.

- The growth of benefit programs for the elderly reflects the growth in size of the aging population itself. Population aging virtually guarantees that a growing share of resources will go to older people. Age-based entitlements make such a shift natural and inevitable, not the result of special political advocacy.

The rapid growth of federal programs serving older people over the past 20 years presents a quandary. The sheer size of age-based entitlements in the budget makes planners worried. (Torres-Gil, 1992). The retirement of baby boomers, beginning around 2010, will dramatically increase the numbers of those eligible for Social Security and Medicare, while the number of working adults will be smaller. How will we find a fiscally responsible way of maintaining benefits in the face of these population pressures? One solution came in 1983, when Congress decided to raise the age of eligibility for Social Security benefits by two years early in the 21st century. But the evolution of Social Security is by no means over, as a 1997 Advisory Report on its future made clear. Among the changes being advocated are measures that would make Social Security fairer to women and that would allocate Social

Security funds to private investment, perhaps for individuals to make their own investment decisions.

Some changes seem inevitable: For instance, a bipartisan consensus has emerged to cut Medicare expenditures to safeguard the program. But the general shape of federal aging programs is unlikely to change dramatically. Many people have a strong interest in seeing these benefit programs continue, and the political pressure to maintain them will be intense. On the other hand, precisely because aging expenditures are so large and because we have other public needs, pressure to cut costs is likely to bring age-based entitlements under continuing scrutiny.

Equity. Other serious questions remain. One of them concerns equity or fairness. The most successful federal aging programs have been the ones that serve all the aged population, such as Social Security and Medicare. These programs have succeeded in improving the well-being of the average elderly person; indeed, they constitute a stunning example of how government can come to agreement and move decisively to solve a problem (Schwarz, 1983). But celebration of success should not obscure the fact that groups like older women and minorities continue to have high rates of poverty.

Furthermore, the most successful aging programs have all been based on a presumption of need or dependency. Both Social Security and Medicare arose from a "permissive consensus" that depicted the elderly as weak, needy, and dependent (Hudson, 1978). That image is what Kalish (1979) called the "failure model" of old age. To the extent that older Americans today are healthier, better educated, and more affluent, the permissive consensus is likely to be eroded (Binstock, 1985).

Related to this point is the issue of **generational equity.** The elderly already receive a substantial portion of the federal budget and will likely receive more as the retired population grows. At the same time, federal expenditures on children and families have decreased. Rates of homelessness, poverty, malnutrition, and poor health have increased among younger Americans. Is it fair or wise to continue distributing benefits on the basis of age alone, or do we need to take a more **needs-based** approach? As discussed earlier, how should universal programs, such as Social Security and the OAA, take account of differences in the financial well-being of men and women, whites and minorities? Should, for instance, women receive more in benefits because they on average have lower earnings and income in retirement?

An important lesson here is that some degree of redistribution and targeting of benefits to the most needy can be acceptable as long it remains within certain bounds. But, as the long controversy over race and affirmative action shows, once we begin targeting benefits too explicitly or giving preference to one group over another, then principles of "need" versus "universalism" do come into conflict. (See Controversy 5, "Should Age or Need Be the Basis for Entitlement?")

Productivity. In the United States, as in other advanced industrialized societies, one result of higher retirement benefits has been the movement of more older workers out of the labor force through early retirement, a move that can be attractive to workers and employers alike. Today's policies in effect push many vigorous, capable young-old out of their productive social roles. To be sure, older people often find great personal meaning in leisure, family life, and voluntary association with churches, community groups, and the like. But can our society afford to lose their contributions?

Racial and ethnic differences in aging are important when we look at the future of work and retirement. Just what does retirement mean for different subgroups within the aged population (Gibson, 1987; Zembek and Singer, 1990)? Older blacks, for instance, may respond to poor employment prospects by defining themselves as "retired." Or people who qualify for disability benefits but have no pension might withdraw from the labor force without ever being officially labeled as "retired." Finally, many minority groups exchange services among kin, but that pattern of productivity doesn't show up on official statistics about work and retirement.

Another question is how the retirement income system, both private pensions and Social Security, can take account of gains in longevity and the greater vigor and productive capability of today's older people. Age-based benefit programs such as Social Security are understood to be entitlements, just as private pensions are forms of deferred compensation. But the idea of entitlement, of benefits owed to us as a right, is different from the idea of productivity. Productivity implies that income and benefits are provided on the basis of how much a person contributes. How is it possible to maintain the integrity of retirement income while also encouraging productivity among the older population (Moody, 1990)? Questions like this will have to be more seriously explored as society considers what leisure and "productive aging" may mean in the future (Allen and Chin-Sang, 1990).

Conclusion

The overall position of older Americans has improved substantially in the past two decades. Improvements in health status have been matched by gains in pension coverage and rising home equity values. The indexing of Social Security benefits to inflation is the main reason for this improvement in income. On the other hand, income from earnings has declined as more older Americans have left the labor force for retirement.

Most older people are not affluent: 3.3 million older Americans still fall below the poverty line. There is enormous variation among subgroups of the aging and even a large group of older people who have been brought above the official poverty line but remain near-poor and vulnerable.

The new politics of aging in America has been deeply influenced by the economic condition of older people and especially by recent improvement in their average economic status. This shift in mood marks a change from the past and provokes new controversies that will command attention for years to come. As we think about the future, it is important to keep in mind the key ideas emphasized in this discussion: (a) the diversity of the aging population, including dramatic differences in well-being among subgroups; (b) the impact of cumulative disadvantage whereby earlier life course experience influences what old age will be like; and (c) the socially agreed on expectations we have about old age, including attitudes toward the meaning of retirement.

Population aging is an important and indisputable fact. But by itself, population aging does not dictate the shape of things to come, and it is certainly no cause to be gloomy about the coming of an aging society. For both individuals and society, the key point to remember is that the life one leads as a younger person will affect prospects for old age (Taeuber, 1990). The social and economic outlook for an aging society, then, is not simply something to be predicted but something to be constructed. The decisions we make today depend on thoughtful consideration of the controversies that will shape the aging society of tomorrow (Steckenrider and Parrott, 1998).

Should Age or Need Be the Basis for Entitlement?

Americans as a people have always looked to the future and expected that the next generation would do better than their parents. But in recent years, that confidence has faded in response to mounting economic problems and doubts about the future (Newman, 1993). In an era of declining expectations, questions are being raised about what the older generation is entitled to and what is fair to younger generations.

Not so long ago, the elderly as a group were thought of as uniformly poor and vulnerable. That image has changed. The condition of older Americans has improved markedly in recent decades when measured according to income, health status, and educational level. Now it is no longer surprising to see older people depicted in the media as well off or even prospering at the expense of the young, especially children (Villers Foundation, 1987). This new image leads to questions about fairness in how different generations are treated.

A Tale of Two Generations

The question of generational equity can be seen in the story of the Walton family. George and Martha Walton, members of the World War II generation, were proud of what they had accomplished: surviving the Depression and winning the war. When George got out of the army, he and Martha were able to buy a house with a VA mortgage loan. George went to college on the GI Bill, and during the 1950s and 1960s the Waltons enjoyed prosperity. When they retired, they found it possible to sell their house and use some of the capital gains, along with George's pension and Social Security benefits, to enjoy a comfortable income in retirement. The Waltons were never rich, but they are satisfied with how things turned out.

Things worked out differently for the Walton children. Carol and Robert were baby boomers born not long after World War II. They had a comfortable childhood, and when they graduated from high school they had high hopes. Both attended college and married, but they never seemed to be able to get ahead of their bills. They had trouble putting their own kids through school in the 1980s because college tuition had risen dramatically. Unfortunately, Robert lost his job because of downsizing; Carol's oldest boy finished school but couldn't find a job and ended up moving back home with Carol and her husband. Carol felt she needed to stay at work but was forced to cut back her hours when her father, George, got sick. Now she helps out her mother, Martha, a lot. Both Carol and Robert are seriously into debt and haven't managed to save much. They worry a lot about the future.

Sometimes it seems as if life hasn't been "fair" to the Walton children and grandchildren. Some things that have happened to the different Walton generations are a matter of economic circumstance, such as rising home values or losing a job. Other things are a matter of government policy—for example, the impact of the GI bill or Social Security. Whether the result is intended or not, circumstances and policies do affect different generations in different ways. How, then, can we sort out what is at stake in debates about justice between generations?

Generational Equity

In thinking about issues of equity or fairness between age groups, it is clear that two different meanings of *generation* must be kept distinct: first, a specific age group, such as "the elderly" (65+) or "children under age 18," and second, a historical cohort consisting of a group of people born in the same year or in a certain period (Ryder, 1965). **Cohort** describes those who experienced specific historical events (Mannheim, 1952), for example, the "World War II generation" or the " '60s generation."

Corresponding to these two meanings of generation are two very different concerns about the fairness of distributing benefits on the basis of age. First, are the elderly today as a group receiving too much of society's resources in comparison to children? And second, can today's workers and their successors count on economic security—for example, Social Security benefits—in the future?

Stories like the Waltons' have become familiar. When these trends were first recognized, the noted gerontologist Bernice Neugarten (1983) published a book titled *Age or Need?* that asked a provocative question: Should government benefit programs for older people be available on the basis of need rather than chronological age? Are older people today getting too much at the expense of the young?

For many years, Americans were used to thinking of older people as the "deserving poor": financially dependent for reasons beyond their control and therefore deserving of help. This assumption was the basis for many important government programs, from Social Security to the Great Society. Not all older people fit this stereotype, of course, but a picture of the old as especially needy or vulnerable did become widespread—a form of "compassionate age-ism," as some called it (Binstock, 1983). But as government programs for the elderly have become more expensive, another, less compassionate point of view was voiced. Critics began to depict the elderly as a burden on society and to worry about the negative impact of population aging now and in the future. These concerns have become part of a debate about generational equity.

The generational equity debate is basically a controversy about whether older adults are receiving an excessive share of limited government resources in comparison with other age groups. There are at least four different issues that fall under the label *generational equity* (Wisensale, 1999). First, there are questions about the allocation of resources between older adults and children: Are older people getting too much? Second, there is a concern about large government deficits, a concern recently diminished by federal budget surpluses. Third, there is the issue discussed in the first controversy in this book about rationing health care resources. And finally, there are questions about the fairness of how Social Security is financed: Is Social Security really fair to younger people?

To understand the many elements of the generational equity debate, we need to look at several trends, including the incidence of poverty among the old and the young, the relative burden of supporting a dependent aging population, and the impact of taxes and other public policies on different age groups. Finally, we will consider the question of who among the elderly are most in need of help.

Poverty Among the Old

By any measure available, there has been a dramatic reduction in the official rate of poverty among older Americans in the past three decades. Today, there are 3.3 million older people below the poverty line, but that figure represents major progress, illustrated in Exhibit 25. Note that most of the gains in income for older people took place between 1960 and 1974, long before complaints were heard that older people were getting too many benefits. For instance, in 1959 the poverty rate of older people in America was 35%, more than one out of three. According to U.S. Census figures, the poverty rate among the elderly in 1997 dropped to a historic low of 10.5%, below the poverty rate of working-age adults. The economic situation of children is quite different: 21% of children under age 18 live in poverty, twice the rate for elders. Exhibit 26 shows just how dramatically the poverty rate has dropped for older people compared with nonelderly adults.

When Medicare is taken into account, the proportion of older people who are categorized "poor" drops to only 6%. Here again we see the impact of successful entitlement programs. If we were to ignore all government cash transfer programs, such as Social Security, then 44% of Americans over age 65 would fall below the poverty line. This is another way of stating how important Social Security has been in preventing late-life poverty.

Exhibit 25. Poverty Rates of Elderly and Nonelderly Adults: 1966-1995

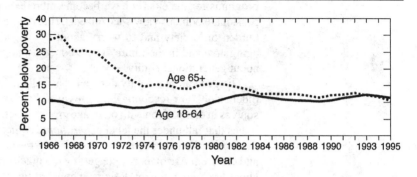

SOURCE: U.S. Bureau of the Census (1996).

Exhibit 26. Percentage of Elderly and Nonelderly Below and Near Poverty: 1995

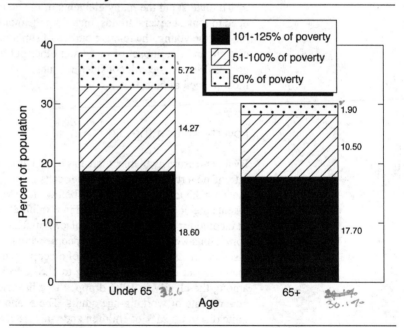

SOURCE: U.S. Bureau of the Census (1996).

The official poverty line is not the whole story (Cook and Kramek, 1986). First, consider the fact that more than 50% of older people depend on Social Security for half or more of their total income. Second, if we look at the group of elderly who could be called "near-poor"—those with an income up to one and a half times the poverty line—then more than one out of four older people are facing economic hardship. Exhibit 26 shows the proportion of people under and over age 65 who fall into this "near-poor" category.

Another group of elders has been called the " 'tweeners." They are people caught in between, the economically insecure lower-middle-class elderly. The 'tweeners are not well off economically, but they are not poor enough to be eligible for programs such as **Supplemental Security Income** (SSI)—a cash benefit program for the elderly poor, blind, and disabled that is administered by Social Security. SSI, like food stamps and welfare (AFDC), is a **means-tested** program, that is, it is available only if your income and assets fall below a designated level. But the 'tweeners do not qualify because they are slightly above the poverty level. When people in this in-between category encounter unexpected hardship, such as a rent increase, the death of a spouse, or an expensive illness requiring long-term care, they are extremely vulnerable.

The stereotype of the well-to-do elderly is, therefore, a mistaken one. Many older people have been lifted out of poverty, but they still remain precariously perched in the "near-poor" category. In fact, the near-poverty rate among older people has hardly changed since the 1970s. Furthermore, the average statistics on poverty and aging conceal some important differences among subgroups of older people. Most discussion of generational equity revolves around averages, but these can be misleading.

Poverty Among Children and Young People

The current generation of children is clearly threatened, by everything from poor prenatal care to inadequate child care and a mediocre educational system. They have been called a "generation in crisis" (Moynihan, 1986; Hamburg, 1992). International comparison shows that U.S. poverty rates among children are higher than those of every industrialized nation in the world (Smeeding, 1990). The passage of tough welfare reform legislation in 1996 suggests that more government aid for poor children is unlikely in the near future.

Poverty among young people has been going up, while poverty among the old has been declining, as Exhibit 27 clearly shows. But are government programs to help the elderly responsible for that trend? It is true that government programs to help younger poor families—such as welfare and food stamps—are unpopular and have been reduced, first during the 1980s and later by federal legislation to "end welfare as we know it" passed in 1996. Public support for children at risk has declined sharply in recent years, and means-tested programs for families have been cut. By contrast, social entitlement programs benefiting retirees, like Social Security or Medicare, have mostly withstood most attacks on them.

Nevertheless, the basic cause of rising child poverty seems to have little to do with government entitlement programs. Defenders of old-age programs point out that the high poverty rate among younger generations is caused mainly by family structure, unemployment, and declining wages. In most countries, children living in single-parent families have poverty rates more than double those in two-parent families.

Exhibit 27. Percentage of Youth and Elderly Below the Poverty Line: 1975 and 1995

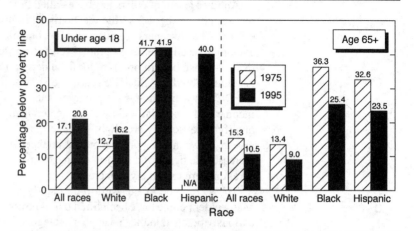

SOURCE: U.S. Bureau of the Census (1997).
NOTE: Hispanic origin may be of any race.

Some commentators have blamed the declining well-being of children on the voting power of the elderly. Demographer Samuel Preston (1984) was one of the first to worry that the political power of the elderly, along with their greater numbers, poses a threat to the well-being of American children. Many articles in the popular media have picked up this theme. But there is actually little evidence that the elderly as a group has voted to take resources from children (Rosenbaum and Button, 1989).

Still, it is a fact that families with children today form a smaller part of the electorate than in the past. The proportion of children in the population has declined with population aging, as Exhibit 28 demonstrates.

The Dependency Ratio

The changing proportion of children and elderly in the population has prompted another question: Will we as a society be able to support such a large population of older people in the future? The support ratio, or **dependency ratio,** is a numerical measure of the economic burden imposed on the working population, who must ultimately support people who are not in the labor force. If we look at elderly people alone, we can compute the elderly dependency ratio by comparing the number of people over age 65 with the number in the working-age group (18 to 64). We can compute the dependency ratio for children by comparing the number of those under age 18 with the number in the working-age group.

Exhibit 29 displays how both ratios—child dependency and elder dependency—have changed over time and are projected to change into the 21st century. Those who are fearful about the burden of an aging population

Exhibit 28. Percentage of Children and Elderly in the Population: 1900, 1980, and 2030

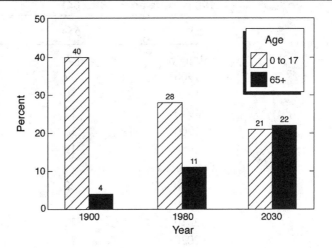

SOURCE: The 1990 figures, which exclude Alaska, Hawaii, and armed forces overseas: U.S. Bureau of the Census (1965). The 1980 and projected 2030 figures: Spencer (1989).

point out that when Social Security was created in the 1930s, there were 50 workers to support each Social Security beneficiary. They point out with alarm that today there are only 3 workers for each beneficiary. Early in this century, the proportion will go down to 2 workers for each beneficiary. Thus we will have a greater burden on a shrinking working-age population to support a larger group of elderly dependents.

To offset this scenario, it should be noted that the dependency ratio for children has declined dramatically since 1960 because of smaller family sizes. As a result, when we combine both ratios, we see an overall decline, which is projected to continue through the first decade of the 21st century until 2030 (Exhibit 28, above), when the youth and elderly dependence ratios are about equal.

The key point is that because of the declining child dependency ratio, the overall dependency ratio, including the burden of an aging population, is not excessive now and may not be into this century. Although the cost of specific programs, such as Medicare, may pose problems, we should focus on the means by which such expenditures are financed and controlled, instead of making judgments based on overall dependency ratios in the abstract.

Taxation and Generational Accounting

Discussions of generational equity usually look only at the cost of government expenditures for the elderly. But equally important is the role of the tax system with its far-reaching impact on different age groups and cohorts. Tax

Exhibit 29. Young, Elderly, and Total Support Ratios: 1900-2050 (number of people of specified age per 100 people ages 18 to 64)

Year	65+	Under 18	Total
Estimates			
1900	7	76	84
1920	8	68	76
1940	11	52	63
1960	17	65	82
1980	19	46	65
Projections			
1990	20	41	62
2000	21	39	60
2010	22	35	57
2020	29	35	64
2030	38	36	74
2040	39	35	74
2050	40	35	75

SOURCE: U.S. Bureau of the Census (1988, 1989).

expenditures are distributed much less equally than are income or benefit entitlements such as Social Security and Medicare. For example, a number of "tax breaks"—sometimes called tax expenditures—go disproportionately to older people with higher incomes. By contrast, the elderly poor (those with incomes below $5,000) get only 2% of the benefits from tax expenditures (Nelson, 1983).

A key stimulus to the generational equity debate has been a growing awareness that not all the elderly are any longer poor or needy. Taking that idea seriously might mean replacing age-based entitlement programs, such as Medicare, with those that are accessible to persons of all ages. A related question is whether benefits, such as Social Security, should be taxed at progressive rates to take into account the heterogeneity of today's older population.

An important new tool for analyzing generational equity has emerged from economics. It is a method known as **generational accounting,** as developed by economists Lawrence Kotlikoff and Alan Auerbach (Kotlikoff, 1992). The aim of this approach is to analyze how government tax and spending policies affect different cohorts. Generational accounting adds up all taxes paid to federal, state, and local governments over a lifetime and then subtracts benefits received, such as Social Security, Medicare, and schooling. For example, it turns out that baby boomers born in 1950 will pay an average lifetime tax rate about a third higher than their parents (31% as opposed to 24%). That difference means paying $200,000 more in taxes than collected in benefits over a lifetime (Nasar, 1993).

Generational accounting provides a way of thinking about the long-range impact of budget decisions made today. Many controversies about Social Security can also be analyzed in terms of generational accounting. But critics of generational accounting and the generational equity framework argue that future projections about population or the economy are filled with uncertainty. Some have warned about what they call "apocalyptic demography," namely, the belief that an increasing aging population inevitably means an increasing burden on society. This scenario is closely coupled with fear of competition between age groups (Robertson, 1997). After all, the U.S. population has already aged considerably without terrible consequences. Demography alone doesn't determine the future; economic growth and government policies are also vital in shaping the world (Friedland and Summer, 1999).

Power and Competition for Scarce Resources

Does the debate about generational equity imply that the old and young are locked in conflict? We need to distinguish between the notion of conflict between generations and competition for different public programs. Conflict and competition are not the same thing. Age conflict does occur in some societies, as when the aging patriarch of a family controls property (Foner, 1984). Similarly, it is possible to find examples of gerontocracy, or the rule of the elderly, when groups cling to positions of power as they grow older. A current instance might be Communist China with its aging party leaders. Yet even the Chinese case might better be described not so much as rule by the aged but as a case of power through incumbency and authoritarian control (Eisele, 1979).

In the United States, there is no serious evidence of conflict or polarization between age groups. On the contrary, public support for Social Security and for other benefit programs for the elderly remains high. But there can be competition over limited resources, and the political process may affect age groups differently, as when school bond issues are voted down or when Social Security benefits are taxed. But these changes in taxes and spending are not motivated by hostility among age groups, and it would be a mistake to pit age groups against one another. On the other hand, it is also a mistake to overlook the fact that competition, choice, and trade-offs are always part of political life, as periodic changes in Social Security have demonstrated (Light, 1985). The fact that changes have taken place at all is proof enough that the political power of the elderly has clear limits.

The Least Advantaged Elderly

Since the 1980s, hard questions have been asked not only about how to pay for benefits to older Americans but also who should receive them (Binstock,

1994). Are government-funded services actually helping the vulnerable elderly? How should government target its resources to those most in need? How, in fact, do we agree on who the "least advantaged" are among the elderly (Harel, Ehrlich, and Hubbard, 1990)?

Answers to this last question have included the following:

- All the elderly

- Those above a very advanced age

- Elders in minority ethnic groups

- Older women

- Rural or inner-city elderly

- The physically or mentally frail

- Older people who are vulnerable to abuse or neglect

- Seniors in poverty

The earliest answer to the question of who was least advantaged was that all elderly people should be viewed as vulnerable; in other words, age itself should be the criterion for need. This conviction originally inspired the Older Americans Act. Some said that older people, as a group, were subject to prejudice or bigotry, and their treatment could be compared with that of minority groups (Barron, 1953). Instead of racism, one could speak of age-ism, or stereotyped prejudice against older people leading to discrimination and disadvantage (Butler, 1969; Levin and Levin, 1980). But is it helpful to think about older people as a minority group? That formulation has proved controversial (Streib, 1965).

Some have therefore suggested that the age of entitlement might perhaps be raised (Torres-Gil, 1992). For example, raising the age for Medicare eligibility from 65 to 67 would over a period of years save $75 billion and prevent bankruptcy of the system, according to a Health and Human Services Department study completed in 1992. But raising the age of eligibility would have a negative impact on minority groups, whose life expectancy is, on average, lower than that of the rest of the population.

Still another answer to the question of who is least advantaged might be the aged poor (Clark, 1988; Crystal, 1986). Indeed, most of the multiple disadvantages of elderly people, regardless of gender or ethnicity, come from poverty, often a lifetime of low earning power (Nelson, 1982). Looking at disadvantage from a life course point of view underscores the importance of **socioeconomic status** (SES), a term sociologists use to describe what is often known as social class (Bendix and Lipset, 1966). Instead of simply describing older people as "rich," "poor," or "middle class," we can rank groups of people in terms of SES and then see how occupation, income, and educational background are interrelated over the course of a lifetime.

SES is one way to think about stratification, or the structured inequality in the distribution of power, prestige, or wealth among older people (Dowd,

1980; Streib, 1985). Lower SES over the life course tends to produce **cumulative disadvantage** that is perpetuated in old age. Higher SES tends to mean greater longevity and better health as well as more income (Streib, 1984). Gender and race, along with class, create interlocking hierarchies of privilege and disadvantage, making it more difficult to identify just a single characteristic that defines the "least advantaged" among the elderly.

Help for Those Most in Need

If "need" instead of age alone is to be the basis for distributing benefits or services, then how will we assess need as a practical matter? One popular method is to use a means test, that is, a measure of eligibility based on whether a person's income or assets fall below a certain amount. For example, Medicaid, SSI, and food stamps are all programs with a means test. By contrast, Medicare and Social Security are not means tested.

A common argument against means-tested programs is that they are stigmatizing; that is, people who are forced by necessity to make use of such programs feel embarrassed and degraded. Even if eligible, many older people are reluctant to apply for SSI because to them it has the image of "welfare." In the past, local governments took take care of old-age poverty through a local "poorhouse" or almshouse, a familiar institution in American life dating back to colonial times (Achenbaum, 1978). Older people who descended into poverty or who had no family to care for them could be forced into the stigma of "outdoor" relief, a predecessor of today's welfare system.

Other methods of helping the least advantaged have been less stigmatizing but have also taken account of different levels of need. The income tax system reflects a principle of progressive taxation or ability to pay: The higher your income, the higher the percentage of taxes owed. At the local level, where property taxes are important, many local governments have "circuit breaker" provisions or homestead exemptions, which offer tax reductions or exemptions for low-income older homeowners. Since 1983, half of Social Security benefits for more affluent beneficiaries have been subject to federal taxation. Both a means test and progressive taxation recognize that ability to pay for benefits differs within the older population.

Finally, **cost sharing** is an approach that combines elements of means testing and taxation. Older Americans Act programs are not permitted to charge for their services, but Congress has never appropriated enough money to reach more than a small part of those who could be served by the programs. Some program administrators believe that, to expand the services, it is reasonable to charge recipients for services based on their ability to pay. For example, elderly with incomes at least 200% above the poverty line might pay a part of the cost of a service according to a sliding scale. Opponents of cost sharing fear that it will discourage the use of services by those least able to pay and that it will also begin to erode broad public support for universal programs (Kassner, 1992).

The Targeting Debate

There are different answers to the question: Who are the least advantaged elderly? For example, the Older Americans Act explicitly directs that the aging service network target its services to "individuals with the greatest economic or social needs, with particular attention to low-income minority individuals." That legislative mandate has given rise to vigorous debate about targeting of benefits. A major legal case in the federal courts (*Meek v. Martinez*) disputed what criteria should be used for allocating resources to those "most in need."

The targeting debate has provoked strong differences of opinion about how universal programs, such as the Older Americans Act, can properly give preference to some needy groups (Jacobs, 1990). The debate has some similarity with disputes about financing and distributing the benefits of Social Security. On one side are those who believe that programs are most fair and effective when they are universal and open to all. On the other side are those who believe that the least advantaged need special consideration if they are to receive their fair share. The arguments here are reminiscent of debates about affirmative action programs. As the aging population becomes more diverse, and as long as all public expenditures remain limited, there will be controversy about age or need as a basis for entitlement.

The readings that follow present sharply different views about the fairness of social programs that help the elderly. On one side is Peter Peterson, who takes aim at the politics of aging in America. He compares population aging to a giant iceberg that threatens to sink the ship of state if we don't change course. The political power of the elderly, he believes, has caused us to spend too much on older people and not enough on children. He believes that need, not chronological age, should be the basis for how government helps people.

By contrast, Eric Kingson and his colleagues, in the reading from their book *Ties That Bind,* take a more favorable view of age-based entitlements. They argue that public benefit programs directed at the elderly actually help people of all ages, among other reasons because they relieve middle-aged children of the need to support aged parents.

Meredith Minkler believes the entire debate about generational equity is misguided. She argues that talking about "greedy geezers" is a new kind of victim blaming that distracts attention from the real issues of injustice arising from social class along with racial and gender inequalities.

Whatever we conclude about justice between generations, a practical question must be faced: How do we decide who is most in need? In her article, Louise Kamikawa argues strongly that social class by itself is not sufficient for measuring need among older people. Race and ethnicity also should be taken into account, she believes. Kamikawa identifies a variety of entitlement programs for older people, including programs for the poor, for the lower middle class, and for the upper middle class. She points out that, even in programs intended for the poor or marginal elderly, it is whites, not minorities, who tend to get most of the resources. Her argument parallels the view advanced on behalf of affirmative action programs in education and employment: Special consideration should be given to minority status to ensure that the results of participation are fair and equal.

Policymakers and service providers face hard choices about how to distribute benefits to those in greatest social or economic need. The debate about who are the least advantaged among the elderly will continue to be a challenge for the future.

READING 19

Gray Dawn
Target Benefits on the Basis of Need

Peter G. Peterson

The challenge of global aging, like a massive iceberg, looms ahead in the future of the largest and most affluent economies of the world. Visible above the waterline are the unprecedented growth in the number of elderly and the unprecedented decline in the number of youth over the next several decades. Lurking beneath the waves, and not yet widely understood, are the wrenching economic and social costs that will accompany this demographic transformation—costs that threaten to bankrupt even the greatest of powers, the United States included, unless they take action in time. Those who are most aware of the implications of this extraordinary demographic shift will best be able to prepare themselves for it, and even profit from the many opportunities it will leave it its wake.

Societies in the developed world—by which I mean primarily the countries of North America, Western Europe, Japan, and Australia—are aging for three major reasons:

Source: Gray Dawn: How the Coming Age Wave Will Transform America and the World, by Peter G. Peterson. Copyright © 1999 by Peter G. Peterson. Reprinted with the permission of Random House, Inc.

- Medical advances, along with increased affluence and improvement in public health, nutrition, and safety, are raising average life expectancy dramatically.

- A huge outsized baby boom generation in the United States and several other countries is now making its way through middle age.

- Fertility rates have fallen, and in Japan and a number of European countries are now running far beneath the "replacement rate" necessary to replace today's population. The impact of so few young people entering tomorrow's tax-paying workforce, while so many are entering benefit-receiving elderhood, is of profound consequence.

As a result, I believe that global aging will become the transcendent political and economic issue of the twenty-first century. I will argue that—like it or not, and there's every reason to believe we won't like it—renegotiating the established social contract in response to global aging will soon dominate and daunt the public policy agendas of all the developed countries.

By the 2030s, these countries will be much older than they are today. Some of them may exceed a median age of 55, twenty years older than the oldest median age (35) of *any* country on earth as recently as 1970. Over half of the adult population of today's developed countries and perhaps two-thirds of their voters will be near or beyond today's eligibility age for publicly financed retirement. So we have to ask: When that time comes, who will be doing the work, paying the taxes, saving for the future, and raising the next generation? Can even the wealthiest of nations afford to pay for such a vast number of senior citizens living a third or more of their adult lives in what are now commonly thought of as the retirement years? Or will many of those future elderly have to do without the retirement benefits they are now promised? And what happens then?

Each country's resistance is colored by its political and cultural institutions. In Europe, where the "welfare state" is more expansive, the public can hardly imagine that the promises made by previous generations of politicians can no longer be kept. They therefore support leaders, unions, and party coalitions that make generous unfunded pensions the very cornerstone of social democracy. In the United States, the problem is not so much a habit of welfare-state dependence as the peculiar American notion that every citizen has personally earned and therefore is "entitled" to whatever benefits government happens to have promised. Over the past fifty years, as this notion of "earned benefits" has expanded, America's personal savings rate has fallen from near the top to the very bottom among developed nations. From a society that once felt obliged to endow future generations, we have become a society that feels entitled to support from our children. Unless this mindset changes, Americans may one day find that all they really are "entitled to" is a piece of the national debt.

Within the next thirty years, the official projections suggest that governments in most developed countries will have to spend at least an extra 9 to 16 percent of GDP annually simply to meet their old-age benefit promises. To pay these costs through increased taxation would raise the total tax burden by an unthinkable extra 25 to 40 percent of every worker's taxable wages—in countries where total payroll tax rates often already exceed 40 percent. Or, if we resort to deficit spending, we would have to consume all the savings and more of the entire developed world.

If we don't prepare for this challenge, much of what is good about an aging society could turn sour. After all, how will young and old live happily together if they see themselves as competitors for scarce resources? And, if this comes to pass, what wisdom will the old have after all to offer the young? And who among the young will listen? I very much respect the gifts that aging individuals can give to our communities and culture: But will the aged be praised for increasing the quality of life if they are deemed responsible for bankrupting the global economy?

So how, exactly, should we arrange our affairs? It is wrong to suppose that the solution is simply a combination of across-the-board tax hikes and benefit cuts. With most younger workers already hard-pressed by taxes—and with most older workers already unprepared financially for retirement—this is not a solution at all. It is merely a restatement of the problem. Instead, we should attempt to create a new paradigm of aging, one as revolutionary as the demographic transformation we are entering. This new paradigm can best be defined by its objective: We must make aging both more secure for older generations and less burdensome for younger generations.

Today's retirement systems the world over, no matter how much they spend, redistribute little household income from rich to poor—and often offer limited benefits to large numbers of elders who are in dire need. In developing countries, the rural poor often don't qualify for benefits at all, and the rules are rigged to favor powerful urban elites. Even in the developed world, the data lend little support to the often-heard claim that universal social insurance is intrinsically progressive. In the United States, for instance, the most affluent beneficiary households receive more than twice the average government payment as do the poorest households. Some $200 billion in yearly benefits go to the most affluent quarter of all households—while one-tenth of all elders still languish below the official U.S. poverty line.

The targeting strategy would return elder entitlements to their original function—and direct more of their benefits to the poor while reducing their overall cost.

A comprehensive means test (what I call an "affluence test") is a central piece of the reform package that I have proposed for the United States. In the interest of fairness, I would impose it on *all* federal benefits no matter what the age of the recipient—including Social Security, military and civil service pensions, Medicare, housing subsidies, and unemployment compensation. Those beneath the U.S. median household income would retain full benefits. Above the median, households would lose 10 percent of their benefit for each additional $10,000 in income. The maximum reduction would be 85 percent, thus ensuring that even the most affluent would retain some minimal return on their prior personal contributions.

According to the U.S. Congressional Budget Office, affluence testing "has several pluses: straightforward interpretation, simplicity of design, apparent ease of administration, and some political appeal." The last point is worth emphasizing. Polls show that majorities of every age group—even the elderly—favor affluence testing.

When it's a question of young single mothers, everyone assumes that means-tested benefits are workable. When it's a question of elder retirees, we can no longer afford to assume otherwise. Let me put it another way: If everybody is invited onto the bandwagon (including the rich), who will be left to pull it? Targeting the needy in all phases of life can and must be a critical strategy for an aging society.

READING 20

Ties That Bind

Eric Kingson, John Cornman, and Barbara Hirschorn

Issues associated with the aging of America are best framed and analyzed if one bears in mind that

- the aging society is both a success and a challenge;

- the elderly population is greatly diversified;

- the relationship between individuals and generations is characterized essentially by interdependence and reciprocity;

- all generations have a common stake in social policies and intergenerational transfers that meet needs throughout the life course; and

- the nation's future *can* be changed and shaped by choices made today.

Source: *Ties That Bind: The Interdependence of Generations in an Aging Society* (pp. 1-14), by E. Kingson, J. Cornman, and B. Hirschorn, 1986, Arlington, VA: Seven Locks Press. Reprinted with permission.

The Trends and the Challenge

More people are living longer, largely because of better sanitation, improved public health, and the control of life-threatening diseases. In 1900 life expectancy at birth was about 47 years for men and 49 years for women. . . . In 1985 it was an estimated 71.5 years for men and 78.8 years for women. About four out of five individuals can now expect to reach age 65, at which point—all things being equal—there is a better than 50 percent chance of living past 80. Moreover, for increasing numbers of elderly people, the quality of life is vastly improved over that for previous generations.

Both the increased probability of reaching old age and the generally improving quality of life in old age can be credited to the successful advances made by past and present generations in addressing problems across the life course, notably public and private investments in research, education, public health, social policies, and economic growth. These investments were often made in policies and programs having no apparent connection with the aged as well as in those that appear to serve only the elderly. For example, although programs that have all but eliminated many life-threatening infectious diseases may have been justified previously for their benefit to children and young adults, their success also accounts for the increasing numbers who survive to old age. Similarly, although Social Security provides income directly to retirees, it also benefits younger persons in many ways.

Still, as a society we must deal with the reality that millions of older people continue to live in or near poverty and continue to be afflicted with debilitating chronic illnesses. Further, we have to recognize that the large majority of the elderly who are not poor or who are not significantly limited in their normal activities—and even many who are—wish to maintain their autonomy, to contribute as much as they can to their families and communities, even in advanced old age. Thus, we are challenged to find ways to ensure the economic well-being of the elderly; to reduce the incidence, or delay the onset, of chronic illness; to provide humane care to those who require assistance or attention on a continuing basis; and to offer opportunities for the elderly to make productive contributions to society at large.

To meet the challenge of an increasingly aging society will naturally cost increasing sums of money. Unhappily, the challenge comes at a time of painful economic uncertainty. The nation faces a seemingly intractable federal-deficit problem. Sharp budget cuts in many government programs at all levels—federal, state, and local—have particularly impaired our ability to meet the needs of poor children, and demographic changes (e.g., growth in single-parent households and increasing participation of women in the work force) are limiting the time family members can spend providing direct care to the very young or to the functionally disabled of any age. Inevitably, questions press about the quantity and quality of opportunities available to younger generations, and about the impact of the federal deficit on these opportunities.

So the challenge of an aging society extends far beyond concerns about the quality of life for the elderly. It cries for a civic commitment to improve the quality of life for *all* members of society, regardless of age. At root, the challenge is inextricably linked to the need for economic growth and for full use of the nation's productive capacity.

Diversity of the Elderly

The outstanding characteristic of the elderly, now and in the future, is their diversity. In 1984 about a fourth of elderly families reported incomes of $30,000 or more, while one-fifth reported incomes under $10,000. Among elderly individuals, about 11 percent reported incomes of $20,000 or above while 25 percent reported incomes under $5,000. At the same time, a substantial portion of the elderly occupy marginal economic status. In 1984 the incomes of 5.6 million elderly (21.2 percent) were below the near-poverty thresholds ($6,224 for a single elderly person and $7,853 for an elderly couple).

Although most noninstitutionalized elderly consider themselves to be in good or even excellent health, about one-fifth report limitations on their ability to carry on at least one major activity of daily living. Persons aged 85 and over are more than four times as likely as persons 65 to 74 to need in-home and institutional long-term care.

Understanding this diversity is critical if society is to assess accurately the various impacts of policies and proposed changes on particular groups of the elderly.

Interdependence and Reciprocity

The amount and type of resources individuals give and receive vary as they grow and age, generally in this sort of pattern: (1) in childhood individuals mainly receive resources; (2) throughout the young adult and middle years, they usually give more than they receive; and (3) in later years—particularly in advanced old age—they receive more and more resources even as they continue to give them. For any society to progress and prosper, each generation must provide assistance to, and receive assistance from, those that follow.

A comprehensive social policy, therefore, must focus not on a single moment in the life course—say, childhood or old age—but rather on the positions and needs of diverse individuals as they move through their lives. From such a perspective, the reciprocity of giving and receiving that goes on over time among individuals, and between generations, becomes a commanding principle. It is the bond of interdependence that ties society together. Prior experience thus emerges as an important determinant in the quality of life at all ages.

The Intergenerational Inequity Thesis

Regrettably, the current debate over the role of government in society has produced an approach that frames policy questions primarily in terms of competition and conflict between young and old. It is grounded not in the interdependence of gen-

erations but in an assumption of intergenerational inequity, the rationale for which goes like this:

> Due to previous circumstances of the elderly and the broad-based perceptions of the elderly as both "needy" and "worthy," there has been a flow of public resources (income, health, and social services) toward the elderly, which has successfully improved their economic status and access to health care. In fact, the elderly are (or shortly will be) financially better off than the nonaged population. In light of this improved status, of large federal deficits, of the cost to younger persons of continuing present policies, and of anticipated growth of the elderly population, the flow of resources to the elderly seems "intergenerationally inequitable" and a source of intergenerational conflict.

While seemingly neutral in approach and possessing an intuitive appeal (who can be against fairness?), the argument carries with it very pessimistic views about the implications of an aging society. It would have us believe that

- programs for the elderly are a major cause of current budget deficits and economic problems;

- the elderly receive too large a portion of public social welfare expenditures to the detriment of children and other groups;

- because of demographic trends, the future costs of programs for the elderly will place an intolerable burden on younger workers; and

- younger people will not receive fair returns for their Social Security and Medicare investments.

As articulated thus far, the "intergenerational inequity" argument frames policy questions in terms of competition for scarce resources. It assumes that it is possible to measure accurately the fairness of the flows of resources between generations; that the amount of resources available for social programs in the future will and should be comparable to or less than what is currently available; and that advances in research, education, and economic growth will not change straightline projections of the need for future health care and retirement income, nor will they change projections of our collective ability to respond. The approach evaluates costs and benefits of social policies primarily at a single point in time, measures fairness in terms of dollars rather than outcomes, and draws many of its conclusions from comparisons between broad demographic groups such as "the elderly" and "children."

Flaws and Misunderstandings

Not only are many of these assumptions based on misunderstandings, but the analytic approach itself is flawed. For example:

1. *"Intergenerational inequity" does not take into account the overall dependency ratio.* Many pessimistic arguments are based on the oft-referenced "aged dependency ratio," which measures the number of persons aged 65 and over (all of whom, for the purpose of this measure, are presumed "dependent") for every 100 persons aged 18 to 64 (all of whom are presumed to be contributing to the economy). Currently, there are 19 dependent elderly persons per every 100 persons of so-called "working ages." Using the definition above, the aged dependency ratio is projected to rise slowly to 22 persons in 2010 and then increase rather precipitously to 37 persons by 2030, leading some to conclude that the costs of programs for the elderly will be unsustainable unless drastic changes are made now.

This sounds ominous indeed, but the aged dependency ratio as described shows only part of the so-called "dependency burden." In contrast, the "overall dependency ratio," which measures the total number of persons under age 18 plus those aged 65 and over for every 100 persons aged 18 to 64, provides a very different picture. As economist Barbara Boyle Toffey points out, never at any time during the next 65 years is the overall dependency ratio projected to exceed the levels it attained in 1964. While it should be noted that the composition of governmental and private expenditures for younger and older Americans is quite different, clearly the overall dependency ratio does not paint quite so gloomy a picture about

society's ability, through public and private mechanisms, to enhance the quality of life for persons of all ages.

Further, according to Brandeis University researcher William Crown, both the aged dependency ratio and the overall dependency ratio are flawed because they fail to take into account such factors as the increasing labor force participation of women, the potential for significant portions of the elderly to work longer, or the effect of economic growth. For example, when the midrange assumptions of the Social Security Administration about the growth of the economy and the size of the future U.S. population are used, real GNP per person is projected to nearly double by 2020 and triple by 2050. Barring unforeseen disasters, the economy of the future seems likely to be able to support a mix of programs for all age groups.

2. *"Intergenerational inequity" assumes that all the elderly are well off.* Having discovered that all elderly are not poor, some journalists, academics, and policymakers have gone to the other extreme and declared that all elderly are financially comfortable, thereby justifying the position that public benefits should be reduced.

Failure to recognize the heterogeneity among the elderly—even among those aged 85 and over—leads to distortions in how social problems are defined, to misunderstandings about the implications of policy options, and ultimately to poor policy. Even so, these stereotypes persist, in part because stereotypical thinking is convenient, in part because negative attitudes about the elderly and growing old exist, and in part because, for some, stereotypes further political ends such as reducing social programs.

3. *"Intergenerational inequity" sees conflict as the rule.* Conflict between generations is the exception, not the norm. Certainly, examples of conflict can be found, such as those showing the elderly voting against a school-related tax in a particular community. Care should be taken, however, not to conclude that conflict between generations is the "rule" or that the elderly are a cohesive political group intent on forcing their will against the interests of the young (or vice

versa). Despite assertions of "senior power" by the press and by senior advocacy organizations themselves, political scientists such as Robert Binstock, Robert Hudson, and John Strate, who study the voting behavior of the elderly, generally conclude it is influenced far more by such things as lifelong party affiliation, social class, race, and political beliefs than by age. Opinion surveys show, too, that all age groups are willing to support programs for the elderly, particularly when given a choice between cutting defense spending or programs like Social Security and Medicare.

Considerable evidence also exists to show that the elderly are concerned about the needs of the young. In a 1983 poll commissioned by the American Council of Life Insurance, 88 percent of the elderly believed parents should feel a great deal or some responsibility to provide grown children with a college education, and 85 percent believed parents should feel a great deal or some responsibility to provide their grown children with a place to live if those children are unable to afford their own.

4. *"Intergenerational inequity" is based on a narrow view of fairness.* Equity between generations, while certainly desirable, is a very limited criterion on which to base the distribution of scarce resources among those with competing claims. Even if all parties could agree on what constitutes a fair distribution of resources among generations, achieving such a balance would not necessarily meet many of the nation's goals for social justice. For example, it would not guarantee (1) that poor citizens would be provided with minimally adequate resources; (2) that nonpoor citizens would be protected from the risks of drastic reduction in their standards of living due to factors beyond their control; or (3) that all citizens would be afforded equal opportunity to achieve what their potentials allow. In short, as Binstock, a professor at Case Western Reserve University, has observed, the current preoccupation with equity between generations "blinds us to inequities within age groups and throughout our society."

Similarly flawed is the notion that per capita public expenditures on children and the elderly ought to be equal. Such an equation assumes that the relative needs of children and the elderly for public expenditures are identical and that equal expenditures are the equivalent of social justice. In fact, a sense of fairness based on the concept of need may require that greater per capita expenditures be directed at children than at the elderly, or that very substantial outlays of public resources be directed at certain subgroupings of children (for example, the growing number of children living in poverty), but not at others. Further, even if the aggregate needs of each group were the same, equal per capita expenditures directed at children and the elderly in the face of substantial unmet needs are not the same as social justice, nor would they result in equal outcomes.

It is sometimes argued that Social Security is unfair because today's young, as a group, will not have as high a rate of return on their "investments" in these programs as current retirees. Still others consider it "intergenerationally inequitable" that these programs do not function like private insurance programs, in which benefits are strictly related to the amount of contributions made.

The concept of fairness incorporated in such arguments is based on a misunderstanding of the multiple purposes of Social Security and Medicare. These goals include preventing economic insecurity through the sharing of risks against which very few could protect on their own, enhancing the dignity of beneficiaries, and providing stable financing. For example, to prevent economic insecurity, Social Security must provide a floor of protection through special provisions for low-wage workers and for certain family members, thereby emphasizing social adequacy. Once this goal is accepted, it is impossible to guarantee in addition that the rate of return for all parties will be identical.

5. *"Intergenerational inequity "uses limited measures to draw broad conclusions.* Since each generation receives transfers from those that precede it and also gives transfers to those that follow, to reach accurate conclusions about equity between generations would require an examination within the context of the multiple intergenerational pub-

lic and private transfers that are occurring constantly. Further, such an examination would have to answer questions like these:

How should the economic and social investments made by previous generations be valued? What about those of current ones?

Should part of what is spent on the elderly be counted as a return on *their* investments in younger generations? Should part of what is spent on children be considered an investment in future productivity?

How should investments made in research, conservation, environmental protection, and defense be allocated among generations?

Comprehensive measurement of intergenerational transfers is virtually impossible. As an alternative, analysts sometimes measure a particular resource transfer—for example, the percent of the federal budget directed at children versus the elderly. There is nothing necessarily wrong with making such measurements. What's wrong is to use them as the basis for broad and inappropriate conclusions about equity.

6. *"Intergenerational inequity" fails to recognize the common stake in social policies.* By framing policy issues in terms of competition and conflict between generations, the intergenerational inequity perspective implies that public benefits to the elderly are a one-way flow from young to old and that there is no reciprocity between generations. This simply is not the case.

7. *"Intergenerational inequity" assumes a zero sum game.* In accepting a framework that pits young against old over the division of scarce resources, the intergenerational inequity framework assumes a "fixed pie," which apparently can only be cut from one of two places—either the elderly or the young. By doing so, the framework takes for granted, wrongly, that the federal pie cannot be increased by economic growth or more tax revenues, and/or that the slice of pie for domestic programs cannot be increased as a result of reduced defense spending.

8. *"Intergenerational inequity" distracts attention from important policy issues.* By framing issues in terms of trade-offs between young and old rather than in terms of policy goals or other trade-offs, the intergenerational inequity framework distracts attention from more useful ways of evaluating and making social policy. It also serves to deflect consideration of such important questions as (1) whether taxes should be raised; (2) whether the rapid growth and current composition of defense expenditures are in the national interest; and (3) whether new policies are needed to meet the needs of the most vulnerable citizens, regardless of age. Discussions about the unacceptably high rates of poverty among children, for instance, get obfuscated by the suggestion that declines in the elderly poverty rate are causally related to the precipitous increase in poverty among children—almost as if an increase in poverty among the elderly would somehow help children!

9. *"Intergenerational inequity" undermines the family.* Were the inequity argument to be embraced as principle and used to justify government's lack of obligation to respond to the growing pressure on families for care-giving, many families could be overwhelmed by the stresses inherent in providing care for relatives. By promoting conflict, advocacy of such a principle might even subtly weaken the bonds between generations within the family.

While those who use this approach to policymaking span the political spectrum, some proponents see it simply as a convenient rationale for an ideology that opposes all public efforts directed at meeting family and individual needs. This point of view encourages attitudes that do not fully represent either the rich mix of values in our society or the balance generally sought between private and public solutions to social problems.

In Truth, the Generations Are Interdependent

Fairer and more effective social policy, we suggest, would be based on a tacit understanding of the interdependence of generations. This approach recognizes the heterogeneity of age groups within the U.S. population, evaluates costs and benefits of social policies primarily over time rather than at just one moment in time, and stresses the importance of understanding who—indirectly as well as directly—pays for and benefits from social policies existing and proposed. Finally, the approach takes a life course perspective to help explain the seeming paradox of the autonomy and interdependence of individuals and age groups as they move through life. Consequently, it emphasizes the importance of thinking broadly about how policies directed at one age group may affect all others—at any given point in time and over time—as these groups age. And it suggests that in an interdependent and aging society, all generations have a common stake in family efforts and public policies, or intergenerational transfers, that respond to the needs of people of all ages.

The Role of Intergenerational Transfers

Intergenerational transfers are not limited to government programs and public policies that transfer income and in-kind services (e.g., Social Security, education between generations). They also include private (e.g., family care-giving, inheritances) and societal (e.g., economic growth, new technology) transfers.

To consider only transfers resulting from public policies would be to miss a major way generations assist each other. Analysis that includes the value of housework and child care along with a few other nonmoney items (e.g., imputed rent from equity in a house) as part of the contribution made by individuals in families leads University of Michigan economist James Morgan to conclude that "the family is by far the most important welfare or redistributional mechanism even in an advanced industrial country like the United States with extensive public and private income maintenance programs"; he estimates transfers within families in 1979 to be $709 billion, equivalent to 30 percent of the gross national product.

Generations also assist each other through societal intergenerational transfers. These involve, for example, the legacy (e.g., economic growth, culture, values, knowledge) older generations bequeath to younger ones as well as the improvements (e.g., economic growth, new technology) younger generations make to the benefit of older ones.

There is no guarantee that particular birth cohorts or generations (within families) will receive more than they will give through intergenerational transfers, although generally this has been the case in American society. Without intergenerational transfers, however, the very continuity and progress of society and families would cease because needs that all experience at various points in life would not be met and legacies of the past would not be transmitted.

Currently, for children, especially the very young, the family is the principal provider. This is particularly true in this country because care-giving is a special domain of the family. As a child ages, the family generally remains dominant, although formal structures (especially educational institutions) become increasingly important. Farther along the life course, society has chosen to have government play a stronger role, especially through income maintenance and health care programs. Nevertheless, the family plays a significant role in offering assistance to the elderly who are functionally disabled.

Interdependence of generations within families. Ordinary care-giving and care-receiving exchanges occur within the family every day, ranging from assisting a spouse or child with a cold to paying for a college education. These exchanges are numerous, as exemplified by findings from a Harris survey that (1) more than four-fifths of family members aged 18 to 24 run errands for parents or grandparents and help them when someone is ill; and (2) even people aged 80 and over continue to provide support to younger generations in their families, with 57 percent helping out when someone is sick and 23 percent running errands. And some of these transfers involve financial resources; Urban Institute researcher Thomas Espenshade estimates that the cost of raising a typical child in a middle-class household to age 18 is $82,400 (in 1981 dollars).

Over the course of life, many persons will also give and/or receive extraordinary care. This might happen, for example, if a child is born with Down's syndrome, if a spouse becomes a paraplegic following an automobile accident, or if an aged parent or grandparent develops a chronic and seriously debilitating heart ailment.

It is primarily the family that is asked to respond when serious support needs arise and, in most cases, to bear most of the long-term costs. About 80 percent of elderly persons requiring assistance in the normal activities of daily life live in private settings. Most of the service these persons receive comes from family members, who provide such care for a number of reasons, including a sense of reciprocity, of filial responsibility, and of duty based on assistance previously provided by the older family members.

The costs to families of providing such care are likely to increase in the future as a result of the aging of society—especially the growth of the very old population—and other demographic trends. One set of projections suggests that the elderly long-term care population will increase from 6.6 million persons today to over 9 million by the year 2000, to nearly 13 million by 2020, and to nearly 19 million by 2040. Further, other social trends are straining the family's capacity to function as a provider of care. These trends include (1) increased rates of divorce and childbirth to unmarried persons, resulting in growing numbers of single-parent households; (2) increased participation of women in the labor force; and (3) the growing preference for smaller families, resulting in fewer children to share care-giving.

The real issue facing the nation, then, is not how to ask families to give more care across the life course with the intent of reducing public expenditures. Rather, given demographic trends, the crucial question is what kinds of assistance should be offered to help the family continue in its traditional care-giving role.

Long-Term Views of Social Programs

The interdependence of generations framework primarily bases its analysis on a longitudinal approach to evaluating costs and benefits of public policies. This approach examines the flow of tax payments and benefits over time. Thus, it is quite different from the cross-sectional approach emphasized by the intergenerational inequity framework, which examines the flow of tax payments and public benefits primarily at one moment in time. And it often leads to very different conclusions about who pays for and who benefits from such policies as public education, public health, investments made in research, Social Security, and Medicare. Take public education as an example. From a cross-sectional perspective it would appear that education is primarily a transfer from working persons and other taxpayers to children and youth. From a longitudinal perspective, however, although the young clearly receive a transfer in the form of education, as they age they will also contribute to the education of those who follow as well as to economic growth and tax revenue, which will benefit the current workers as they age.

Social Security. As an outstanding example both of a program in which all generations have a common stake and of the importance of taking the long-term view of a social policy, consider Social Security. It serves these goals and values:

- the widespread preference for nonpersonal means of financial support in old age—that is, for the major responsibility for financial support of older relatives to be placed outside the family;

- the desire for a dignified and stable means of support for the elderly, the disabled, and surviving and financially dependent family members; and

- the need for a rational approach for protection against basic risks such as reduction of income due to retirement, disability, or death of a breadwinner.

The common stake in Social Security is also a result of the widespread distribution of benefits and costs among persons of all ages. To understand this common stake, it is not sufficient just to examine the direct benefits at one point in time—those that go primarily (about 85 percent), but not exclusively, to retired workers and their spouses and to widows and widowers aged 60 and over. When time is "frozen" in this fashion, it may appear as if the distribution of burdens and benefits is unfair—with the young mostly paying and the elderly mostly taking. But identifying the direct and indirect benefits and the costs of Social Security over time presents a far different picture. The long-term perspective of Social Security shows that

- retirement benefits for today's younger workers will, on average, have greater purchasing power than those of today's retirees;

- Social Security introduces a critical element of stability into the retirement plans of young and middle-aged workers because even before benefits are first received, their value is kept up-to-date with rising wages and increases in the standard of living;

- disability and survivors protection alike have tangible worth to covered workers and their families;

- by providing cash benefits to older family members, Social Security frees up younger and middle-aged family members to concentrate more financial resources on their children; and

- by enabling family members and individuals to protect themselves against some major financial risks, Social Security stabilizes family life and the society.

Summary and Recommendation

These observations do not lead to the conclusion that such transfers are flawless and should never be changed. On the contrary, because of the basic functions they serve and because demographic and economic change is an ongoing process, policies should be reviewed carefully and options vigorously debated. Of critical importance now, however, is that those who are considering changes understand both who benefits from these policies and the common stake that prevails in these intergenerational transfers.

At best, the framing of issues in terms of competition and conflict between generations is based on a misunderstanding of relations between generations and distracts attention from more useful ways of examining social problems. At worst, it is a cynical and purposely divisive strategy put forth to justify and build political support for attacks on policies and reductions in programs that benefit all age groups. In contrast, we advocate an approach that assumes the interdependence of generations and emphasizes the importance of thinking broadly about how policies directed at one age group affect all others, at any given point in time and over time, as these groups age. Among our more important conclusions are these:

1. It is erroneous to think of Social Security as a one-way flow of resources from young to old, or of education as a one-way flow from adults to children.

2. The elderly, now and in the future, have at least two important stakes in programs that respond to the needs of children, young adults, and the middle aged. First, they benefit directly and indirectly from education, training, and health programs that help increase the productivity of the workforce. Second, it is in their political interest to pursue strategies that do not pit generations against each other.

3. Younger generations have two important stakes in programs that assist the elderly to maintain a decent quality of life. First, they will be served by those programs when they become old. Second, such programs relieve young and middle-aged family members of financial burdens and intrafamily stresses.

4. For both humanitarian and practical reasons, advocates for the elderly and others concerned with preparing for the retirement of the baby boomers have a special responsibility to support policies that respond to the needs and aspirations of the many poor and near-poor children in America. Failure to provide adequate educational, health, and employment opportunities to these children could undermine their future pro-

ductivity and reduce the quality of life for the baby boomers during their retirement years.

Granted our preference for the interdependence framework, this report deals with a more basic issue—the importance of framing properly the policy debate necessary to meet the challenge of an aging society. Our single recommendation is that all those concerned understand the power of various frameworks to define the terms of this debate, and that they give careful consideration to the implications of each approach.

"Generational Equity" and the New Victim Blaming

Meredith Minkler

This policy and reverence of age makes the world bitter to the best of our times;
keeps our fortunes from us till our oldness cannot relish them.
I begin to find an idle and fond bondage in the oppression of aged tyranny,
who sways, not as it hath power, but as it is suffer'd.
—*King Lear, 1, ii, 47*

Stereotypic views of the elderly in the United States as a wealthy and powerful voting block have replaced earlier stereotypes of this age group as a poor, impotent, and deserving minority (1). Capitalizing on and contributing to these changing perceptions, the mass media and a new national organization, Americans for Generational Equity (AGE), prophesize a coming "age war" in the United States, with Social Security and Medicare as the battleground (2). Like Gloucester's young son in *King Lear,* they argue that entitlement programs for today's affluent elderly "mortgage our children's future" and contribute to high poverty rates among the nation's youth.

The framing of complex public policy issues in terms of conflict between generations, however, tends to obscure other, far more potent bases of inequities in our society. Indeed, in Binstock's words (1, pp. 437-438):

> To describe the axis upon which equity is to be judged is to circumscribe the major options available in rendering justice. The contemporary preoccupation with . . . intergenerational equity blinds us to inequities within age groups and throughout society.

This [essay] will examine the assumptions underlying the concept of generational equity, with particular attention to notions of fairness and differential stake in the common good. Tendencies by policy makers, scholars, and the mass media to statistically homogenize the elderly and to utilize inadequate and flawed measures of poverty further will be examined and seen to contribute to

---

Source: " 'Generational Equity' and the New Victim Blaming," by Meredith Minkler, in *Critical Perspectives on Aging* (pp. 67-79), edited by Meredith Minkler and Carroll Estes. Amityville, NY: Baywood, 1991. Reprinted by permission of the author.

the myth of a monolithic and financially secure elderly population. Finally, the false dichotomy created between the interests of young and old will be found to illustrate a new form of victim blaming, whose employment is inimical not only to the elderly but to the whole of society.

The Making of a Social Problem

In his trenchant look at the cyclical nature of social problems, O'Conner noted that when the economy is perceived in terms of scarcity, social problems are redefined in ways that permit contracted, less costly approaches to their solution (3). Thus, while the economic prosperity of the 1960s permitted us to discover and even declare war on poverty, the recession of 1973 and its aftermath resulted in a redefinition of poverty and the subsequent generation of less costly "solutions."

The discovery of high rates of poverty and poor access to medical care among America's elderly in the economically robust 1960s and early 70s helped generate a plethora of ameliorative programs and policies including Medicare and Social Security cost of living increases (COLAs). By the mid-1970s however, amid high inflation and unemployment, Social Security and Medicare were themselves being defined as part of the problem. By implication, the elderly beneficiaries of these programs frequently were characterized by the mass media as targets of special resentment. The "compassionate ageism" which had enabled the stereotyping of the elderly as weak, poor and dependent, from the 1930s through the early 1970s, (1) gave way to new images of costly and wealthy populations whose favored programs were "busting the federal budget."

In the mid-1980s, a new dimension was added to this socially constructed problem when the rapidly increasing size of the elderly population and the costliness of programs like Social Security and Medicare were directly linked to the financial hardships suffered by younger cohorts in general and the nation's children in particular. Indeed, in a widely publicized article in *Scientific*

American, Samuel Preston, then President of the Population Association of America, argued that the elderly now fare far better than children in our society (4): In the twelve years from 1970 to 1983, he pointed out, the proportion of children and elders living in poverty was reversed, with the proportion of children under fourteen living in poverty growing from 16 percent to 23 percent and the percent of elderly poor dropping from 24 percent to only 15 percent, while public outlays for the two groups had remained relatively constant through 1979. Moreover, many public programs for children were cut back in the 1980s, at the same time that programs for the politically powerful elderly were expanded. Preston's widely quoted paper went on to compare the elderly and children on a variety of parameters including suicide rates and concluded with a plea for redressing the balance of our attentions and resource allocations in favor of youth.

Following closely on the heels of Preston's analysis, the President's Council of Economic Advisors reported in February of 1985 that the elderly were "no longer a disadvantaged group," and indeed were better off financially than the population as a whole (5).

These two publications helped generate a new wave of media attention to the "costly and wealthy elderly." They further provided much of the impetus for a new, would-be national organization devoted to promoting the interests of younger and future generations in the national political process. With the backing of two prominent congressmen and an impressive array of corporate sponsors, Americans for Generational Equity (AGE) attacked head on government policies which, under pressure from a powerful gray lobby, were seen as creating a situation in which "today's affluent seniors are unfairly competing for the resources of the future elderly" (6).

The mass media, AGE, and other proponents of an intergenerational conflict framework for examining current U.S. economic problems have successfully capitalized on growing societal concern over certain facts of life which have coincided with the graying of America. These include:

- a massive federal deficit;

- alarming increases in poverty rates among children, with one in five American children now living in poverty (7); and

- a 76 million strong "baby boom" generation whose real incomes have declined 19 percent over the last fifteen years.

These statistics have been coupled with another set of facts and figures used to suggest that the growing elderly population is itself part of the problem:

- The elderly, while representing only 12 percent of the population, consume 29 percent of the national budget and fully 51 percent of all government expenditures for social services (8);

- Since 1970, Social Security benefits have increased 46 percent in real terms, while inflation-adjusted wages for the rest of the population have declined by 7 percent (9).

The picture presented is one of a host of societal economic difficulties "caused," in part, by a system of rewards that disproportionately benefits the elderly regardless of their financial status.

The logic behind the concept of generational equity is flawed on several counts, each of which will be discussed separately. In addition to these specific inaccuracies, however, a broader problem will be seen to lie in an approach to policy which lays out the issues in terms of competition among generations for scarce resources. Each of these problems will now be discussed.

The Myth of the Homogeneous Elderly

Basic to the concept of generational equity is the notion that elderly Americans are, as a group, financially secure. Borrowing statistics from the President's Council of Economic [Advisors], proponents of this viewpoint argue that the 1984 poverty rate for elderly Americans was only 12.4 percent (compared to 14.4 percent for younger Americans), and dropped to just 4 percent if the

value of Medicare and other in-kind benefits was taken into account (5).

While the economic condition of the elderly as a whole has improved significantly in recent years, these optimistic figures obscure several important realities. First, there is tremendous income variation within the elderly cohort, and deep pockets of poverty continue to exist. Close to a third of black elders are poor, for example (32%), as are 24 percent of older Hispanics and 20 percent of all women aged eighty-five and above (10).

Minority elders and the "oldest old," aged eighty-five and above, not only have extremely high rates of poverty but also comprise the fastest growing segments of the elderly population. Thus, while only about 8 percent of blacks are aged sixty-five and over, compared to over 13 percent of whites, the black elderly population has been growing at a rate double that of the white aged group. The number of black elders further is increasing at twice the rate of the younger black population (11). In a similar fashion, the "oldest old" in America—those aged eighty-five and above—are expected to double in number by the turn of the century, from 2.5 million in 1985 to some 5 million by the year 2000 (12). The very high rates of poverty in the current generation of "old old" may reflect in part a Depression-era cohort effect. At the same time, however, the heavy concentration of women in the eighty-five and over age group, coupled with continued high divorce rates and pay and pension inequities, suggest a significant continuing poverty pocket as the population continues to age (13).

The myth of a homogenized and financially secure elderly population, in short, breaks down when the figures are disaggregated and the diversity of the elderly is taken into account.

Problems in the Measurement of Poverty

Analyses which stress the low poverty rates of the aged also are misleading on several counts. First, as Pollack has noted, comparisons which stress the favorable economic status of the aged vis-à-vis younger cohorts fail to acknowledge the use of two separate poverty lines in the United States—one for those sixty-five and above and the other for all other age groups (14). The 1987 poverty line for single persons under sixty-five thus was $5,905—fully 8 percent higher than the $5,447 poverty line used for elderly persons living alone (15). If the same poverty cutoff had been used for both groups, 15.4 percent of the elderly would have fallen below the line, giving the aged a higher poverty rate than any other age group except children.

The inadequacy of even the higher poverty index also merits attention. It is telling, for example, that Molly Orfshanksy, the original developer of the poverty index, dismissed it some years ago as failing to accurately account for inflation. By her revised estimates, the number of elderly persons living in or near poverty almost doubles (16).

Discussions of the role of Social Security and other in-kind transfers in lifting the elderly out of poverty also are problematic. Blaustein thus has argued that while Social Security and other governmental transfers helped lift millions of elders out of poverty, they for the most part succeeded in "lifting" them from a few hundred dollars below the poverty line to a few hundred dollars above it (17). Indeed, some 11.3 million elders, or 42.6 percent of the elderly, live below 200 percent of the poverty line, which for a person living alone is about $10,000 per year (15).

Recent governmental attempts to reduce poverty by redefining it also bear careful scrutiny in an effort to uncover the true financial status of the elderly and other groups. The argument that poverty in the aged drops to 4 percent where Medicaid and other in-kind transfers are taken into account thus is extremely misleading. By such logic, an elderly woman earning less than $5,000 per year may be counted as being above the poverty line if she is hit by a truck and has $3,000 in hospitalization costs paid for by Medicaid. The fact that she sees none of this $3,000 and probably incurs additional out-of-pocket health care costs in the form of prescription drugs and other deductibles is ignored in such spurious calculations (14).

The continuing high health care costs of the elderly are themselves cause for concern in any attempt to accurately assess the income adequacy of the elderly. The elderly's out-of-pocket health care costs today are about $2,400 per year—three and one-half times higher than that of other age groups, and higher proportionately than the amount they spent prior to the enactment of Medicare and Medicaid more than two decades ago (18). Contrary to popular myth, Medicare pays only about 45 percent of the elderly's medical care bills, and recipients have experienced huge increases in cost sharing (e.g., a 141 percent increase in the Part A deductible) under the Reagan administration (14). Inflation in health care at a rate roughly double that of the consumer price index further suggests that the de facto income adequacy for many elderly may be significantly less than the crude figures imply.

Moral Economy and the Cross-Generational Stake in Elderly Entitlements

Another criticism of the logic behind intergenerational equity lies in its assumption that the elderly alone have a stake in Social Security, Medicare, and other governmental programs which are framed as serving only the aged. Arguing that the nation's future "has been sold to the highest bidder among pressure groups and special interests" (6), Americans for Generational Equity and the mass media thus cast Social Security and other income transfers to the aged in a narrow and simplistic light. For even if one disregards the direct benefits of Social Security to nonelderly segments of the society (e.g., through survivors benefits to millions of persons under age sixty-five), the indirect cross-generational benefits of the program are significant. By providing for the financial needs of the elderly, Social Security thus frees adult children from the need to provide such support directly. As such, according to Kingson et al., it may reduce interfamilial tensions while increasing the dignity of elderly family members who receive benefits (19). Research by Bengtson et al. has suggested that the family is not perceived by any of the major ethnic groups in America as having major responsibility for meeting the basic material needs of the elderly (20). Rather, families are able to provide the support they do in part because of the availability of government programs like Social Security. When these programs are cut back, the family's ability to respond may be overtaxed, to the detriment of young and old alike (21).

Programs like Social Security are not without serious flaws. . . . Yet despite these problems, and contrary to recent media claims, there has been little outcry from younger taxpayers to date about the high costs of Social Security and Medicare. Indeed, in an analysis of some twenty national surveys conducted by Louis Harris and Associates over a recent two-year period, Taylor found no support for the intergenerational conflict hypothesis (22). While the elderly appeared somewhat more supportive of programs targeted at them than did younger age groups, and vice versa, the balance of attitudes in all generations was solidly on the same side. The majority of both elderly people, and young people under thirty, thus opposed increasing monthly premiums for Medicare coverage, opposed increasing the deductible for Medicare coverage of doctors' bills, and opposed freezing Social Security cost of living increases. Similarly, both young and old Americans opposed cutting federal spending on education and student loans, and overwhelmingly opposed cutting federal health programs for women and children (22). In short, while young and old differ significantly on questions relating to values and lifestyle, issues of government spending and legislation affecting persons at different stages of the life course appeared to evoke intergenerational *consensus* rather than *conflict.*

The strong support of younger Americans for Social Security and Medicare is particularly enlightening in the wake of recent and widely publicized charges that these programs may be bankrupt before the current generation of young people can reap their benefits. Such charges, while poorly substantiated, have made an impact: poll data suggest that today's younger workers are pessimistic about the chances of Social Security and Medicare being there for them when they retire. In light of this pessimism, how might their continued high level of support for elderly entitlements be explained?

As noted earlier this phenomenon reflects in part the fact that younger people in the workforce prefer to have their parents indirectly supported than to shoulder this burden themselves in a more direct way.

Yet on a more fundamental level, the continued support of younger generations for old-age entitlements they believe will go bankrupt before their time reflects what Hendricks and Leedham describe . . . as a moral economy grounded in use value—one whose central goal is "to structure a society so as to maximize possibilities of a decent life for all." As these analysts go on to note, moral economies grounded in use value envision the public interest as "a negotiated rule structure, to which people adhere *even though it may run counter to their own immediately desired satisfactions* since it improves overall opportunities of obtaining satisfaction" (emphasis added). Further, a moral economy based on use value or individual and social utility views citizens "not as passive recipients or consumers of public policy, but as active moral agents." Within such a vision of moral economy, resource allocation would be viewed not in terms of competition between generations, but in Rawls' sense, as allocations appropriate to ourselves at various points over the life course (23). . . .

Generational equity proponent Daniel Callahan has argued that such life course perspectives are flawed in their failure to adequately address the fact that the huge demands made by unprecedented numbers of elders in recent years "threaten to unbalance any smooth flow of an equitable share of resources from one generation to the next" (24, p. 207). Yet he and other proponents of generational equity similarly evoke a notion of moral economy in support of their arguments that the purpose of old age in society should be reformulated as involving primarily service to the young and to the future—in part through an acceptance of the need for "setting limits" on government support for lifesaving medical treatment for those over a given age.

Callahan indeed proposes a shifting of the existing moral economy and a questioning of some of its basic assumptions. In particular, a fundamental tenet of the existing moral economy—that health care not be rationed on the basis of age—should, he argues, be reconsidered in light of current and growing inequities in the distribution of scarce public resources for health care between young and old (24).

The strong public outcry against age-based rationing, coupled with the considerable evidence of the continued popularity of Social Security and Medicare among young and old alike, suggests, however, that the older moral economy notions of what is just and "due" the old have continued to hold sway. For both young and old, it appears, elderly entitlement programs like Social Security are not simply the way things are, but the way they should be. The reality, in short, stands in sharp contrast to the rhetoric which claims that Social Security is "nothing less than a massive transfer of wealth from the young, many of them struggling, to the elderly, many living comfortably" (25). Instead, the program, firmly grounded in American moral economy, is one which all generations appear to support, and from which all see themselves as receiving some direct or indirect benefit.

Age/Race Stratification and Inter-ethnic Equity

Arguments that young and old alike have a stake in programs like Social Security and Medicare may break down, according to some analysts, when the element of ethnicity is introduced.

Indeed, Hayes-Bautista et al. suggest that there may be strong resentment of entitlement programs for the elderly thirty to fifty years from now in age/race stratified states like California (26). Within such states, the burden of support for the large, predominantly white elderly population is expected to fall heavily on the shoulders of a young workforce composed primarily of Latinos and other minorities.

Utilizing California demographic projections as a case in point, Hayes-Bautista et al. note that unless major shifts take place in fertility and immigration patterns, and/or in educational and job policy achievements, the working-age population of the future will not only be heavily minority but also comprised of individuals whose lower total wage base will require that larger proportions of their income go simply to maintaining current Social Security benefit levels for the white elderly baby boom generation. Under such conditions, they argue, the nation may be ripe for an "age-race collision."

While these investigators go on to suggest policy measures that might avert such a catastrophe, the "worst case scenarios" which they and other analysts (27, 28) describe have unfortunately received far more media attention than their recommended policy solutions. It is precisely because of the popularity of these "age wars" predictions, moreover, that a deeper look at the current reality is in order.

While it is of course impossible to project attitudinal shifts in the population in the way that demographic changes can be forecasted, current national opinion poll data on the attitudes of Latinos and other minorities toward entitlement programs for the elderly are instructive.

If the hypothesis is correct that there may be substantial resentment of Social Security and Medicare in the future on the part of a large minority working-class population left to shoulder this burden, one might expect hints of such resentment now. Contrary to expectation, however, opinion poll data show Hispanics, blacks, and other minorities to be strongly supportive of Social Security and Medicare and indeed often more opposed than whites to proposed budget cuts in these programs (22).

The hypothesis of growing minority resentment of elderly entitlement programs also may be questioned on demographic grounds. Thus, while minorities make up only about 10 percent of the aged population today, that figure is expected to increase by 75 percent by the year 2025. [The (c)omparable increase among white elders will be only about 62 percent (29).] Elderly Hispanics, already the fastest growing subgroup within the older population, will see their numbers grow even more rapidly, quadrupling by the year 2020 (30). From 2025 to 2050, the period corresponding to the graying of the huge baby boom generation, the proportion of elderly within the non-white population is projected to increase another 29 percent, compared to only 10 percent for the white population (29). While the minority aged population will remain small numerically compared to the elderly cohort, the fact that greater proportions of working-aged Latinos, blacks, and other minorities will have parents and grandparents reaching old age suggests again an important phenomenon which may work against the reification of an age/race wars scenario.

A final factor which may mitigate against the likelihood of increasing minority resentment of elderly entitlement programs concerns the differential importance of programs like Social Security to the economic well-being of whites, blacks, and Hispanics. The disadvantaged economic position of elderly blacks and Hispanics relative to whites, for example, means that higher proportions rely on Social Security as their only source of income, and that far fewer have private insurance and other nongovernment resources to cover the costs of medical care. Under such conditions, more rather than less support for elderly entitlement programs might be expected among these economically disadvantaged minority groups, and that is indeed what the survey data appear to suggest.

Guns Versus Canes?

A common theme throughout the intergenerational equity movement is that the elderly are not only numerous but also expensive: The high cost of Social Security, amounting to about 20 percent of the federal budget, is juxtaposed against a $2 trillion national debt and a massive federal deficit, with the implicit and often explicit message that the costly elderly are a central part of our economic crisis.

As Pollack has noted, however, such equations are misleading at best (14). Social Security, for example, is not a contributor to the deficit and in fact brings in considerably more money than it pays out. Indeed, throughout the 1990s, when the small Depression-era cohort is elderly, the system will bring in literally hundreds of billions more than it will spend (14).

Ironically, the nation's military budget, while a major contributor to the deficit is virtually excluded from discussions by many analysts of the areas necessary for scrutiny if we are to achieve a balanced budget. AGE President Paul Hewitt indeed has spoken out against a congress which, under pressure from aging interest groups, will "weaken our national defense before it will cut cost of living allowances (COLAs) for well to do senior citizens" (6).

Tendencies by the mass media and others to overlook defense spending in discussions of the costliness of programs for the elderly continue . . . a tradition described earlier by Binstock when he noted that we are taught to think in terms of how many workers it takes to support a dependent old person, but not how many it takes to support an aircraft carrier (16). Citing an OMB fiscal analyst, Binstock further pointed out that classic political economic trade-off, "guns vs. butter," has been reframed "guns vs. canes," in reference to the perceived costliness of the aged population.

In the relatively few years since Binstock's initial analysis, a further reframing has occurred with "canes vs. kids" constituting the new political economic trade-off.

As Kingson et al. (19) have noted, such an analysis assumes a zero sum game in which other possible options (e.g., increased taxes or decreased military spending) are implicitly assumed to be unacceptable (19). It is worthy of note that such traditionally conservative analysts as Meyer and Ein Lewin of the American Enterprise Institute (31) have begun arguing in favor of cutbacks in defense spending as a means of balancing the federal budget without in the process decimating needed social programs. While favoring increased taxation of Social Security and some initial taxing of Medicare benefits, the AEI analysts appear to have come down hardest on the need for massive reductions in military spending if the United States is to cease "protecting sacred cows and slaughtering weak lambs" (31, p. 1).

Still other analysts have urged the closing of tax loopholes for corporations and the rich as a means of redressing huge national deficits. Noting that corporate taxes dropped from 4.2 percent of the GNP in 1960 to 1.6 percent in the 1980s, and that money lost to the treasury through tax loopholes grew from $40 billion to $120 billion over the period 1980-86 alone, Pollack thus has argued that tax breaks for the rich, rather than Social Security COLAs for the elderly, should be viewed as the real culprits in the current economic crisis (14).

Finally, national opinion poll data show overwhelming public support for cutting military spending and closing tax loopholes, rather than cutting programs for the elderly and other population groups as a means of addressing America's economic difficulties (32).

The "canes vs. kids" analytical framework, in short, does not appear to have wide credence in the larger society, and where a hypothetical "guns vs. canes" trade-off is proposed, the American public overwhelmingly supports the latter.

Victim Blaming Revisited

. . . The new victim blaming is particularly well illustrated in the application of a market theory perspective to determinations of appropriate resource allocations for the different age groups. Demographer Samuel Preston thus has argued that, "Whereas expenditure on the elderly can be thought of *mainly as consumption,* expenditure on the young is a combination of consumption and investment" (4, p. 49; emphasis added). Leaving aside the inaccuracies of such statements from a narrow, worker productivity perspective (since many of the elderly continue to be employed full- or part-time), the moral and ethical questions raised by such an approach are signifi-

cant. While it is true that the elderly "consume" about a third of all health care in the United States, for example, such figures become dangerous when used to support claims of the differential "costs" of older generations, and the need for the rationing of goods and services on the basis of age (1).

The scapegoating of Social Security and Medicare as primary causes of the fiscal crisis has served to deflect attention from the more compelling and deep-seated roots of the current economic crisis. At the same time, and wittingly or unwittingly fueled by recent mass media and groups like AGE, it has been used as a political tool to stoke resentment of the elderly and to create perceptions of a forced competition of the aged and younger members of society for limited resources. As Kingson et al. have noted, (19, p. 4):

> . . . while the concept of intergenerational equity is seemingly neutral and possesses an intuitive appeal (who can be against fairness?), its application, whether by design or inadvertence, carries with it a very pessimistic view about the implications of an aging society, which leads to particular policy goals and prescriptions.

These "policy goals and prescriptions" as we have seen, reflect a "new victim blaming" mentality in their suggestion that we must cut public resources to the elderly in order to help youth and to avert conflict between generations.

For as noted elsewhere, to trade the victim blaming approaches of the 1980s for those of the 1960s and 70s is not a solution to problems which ultimately are grounded in the skewed distribution of economic and political power within the society (33). Ultimately, as Pollack has argued, the central issue is not one of intergenerational equity but of income equity (14). Cast in this light, inadequate AFDC payments and threatened cuts in Social Security COLAs which would plunge millions of elderly persons into poverty are part of the same problem. Programs and policies "for the elderly" like education and health and social services "for youth" must be redefined as being in fact not "for" these particular subgroups at all, but for society as a whole. Conversely, threatened cutbacks in programs for the elderly, under the guise of promoting intergenerational equity, must be seen as instead promoting a simplistic, spurious and victim blaming "solution" to problems whose causes are far more fundamental and rooted in the very structure of our society.

Conclusion

In the short time since its inception, the concept of generational equity has become a popular framework for analysis of contemporary economic problems and their proposed solutions. Yet the concept is based on misleading calculations of the relative financial well-being of the elderly vis-à-vis other groups and on questionable assumptions concerning such notions as fairness and differential stake in the common good. Predictions that young people, and particularly minority youth, may be increasingly resentful of elderly entitlement programs are unsubstantiated by current national survey data which show strong continued support for these programs across generational and ethnic lines. The reframing of political economic trade-offs in terms of "canes vs. kids" indeed appears to have little credence with the public at large, despite its popularity in the mass media, and with a growing number of scholars, policy makers and new, self-described youth advocates.

Proponents of an intergenerational equity approach to policy have performed an important service in calling attention to high rates of poverty in America's children, and to the need for substantially greater societal investment in youth and in generations as yet unborn. At the same time, however, their tendency to blame the costliness of America's aged for economic hardships experienced by her youth is both misguided and dangerous. The call for intergenerational equity represents a convenient smokescreen for more fundamental sources of inequity in American society. By deflecting attention from these more basic issues, and by creating a false dichotomy between the interests of young and old, the ad-

vocates of a generational equity framework for policy analysis do a serious disservice.

References

1. Binstock, R. H. The oldest old: A fresh perspective or compassionate ageism revisited? *Milbank Mem. Fund Q.* 63:420-541, 1983.
2. Longman, P. Age wars: The coming battle between young and old. *The Futurist* 20:8-11, 1986.
3. O'Connor, J. *The Fiscal Crisis of the State.* St. Martin's, New York, 1973.
4. Preston, S. Children and the elderly in the U.S. *Scient. Am.* 251:44-49, 1984.
5. *Annual Report of the President's Council of Economic Advisors.* U.S. Government Printing Office, Washington, D.C., 1985.
6. Hewitt, P. A Broken Promise. Brochure of Americans for Generational Equity. AGE, Washington, D.C., 1986.
7. Edelman, M. W. Meeting the needs of families and children: Structural changes that require new social arrangements. (Statement before the Consumer Federation of America.) Children's Defense Fund, New York, March 15, 1990.
8. Longman, P. Justice between generations. *Atlantic Monthly,* pp. 73-81, June 1985.
9. Taylor, P. The coming conflict as we soak the young to enrich the rich.
10. Villers Foundation, *On the Other Side of Easy Street: Myths and Facts about the Economics of Old Age.* The Villers Foundation, Washington, D.C., 1987.
11. U.S. Bureau of the Census. Current reports: Poverty in the U.S. Series P 60, No. 163. U.S. Government Printing Office, Washington, D.C., 1989.
12. Bould, S., Sanborn, B., and Reif, L. *Eighty Five Plus: The Oldest Old.* Wadsworth Publishing Company, Belmont, California, 1989.
13. Minkler, M., and Stone, R. The feminization of poverty and older women. *Gerontologist* 25:351-357, 1985.
14. Pollack, R. F. Generational equity: The current debate. Presentation before the 32nd

Annual Meeting of the American Society on Aging, San Francisco, March 24, 1986.

15. U.S. Bureau of the Census, *Statistical Abstract of the U.S.* (109th edition). U.S. Government Printing Office, Washington, D.C., 1989.

16. Binstock, R. The aged as scapegoat. *Gerontologist* 23:136-143, 1983.

17. Blaustein, A. I. (ed.). *The American Promise: Equal Justice and Economic Opportunity.* Transaction Books, New Brunswick, New Jersey, 1982.

18. Margolis, R. J. *Risking Old Age in America.* Westview Press, Boulder, Colorado, 1990.

19. Kingson, E., Cornman, J., and Hirschorn, B. *Ties That Bind: The Interdependence of Generations in an Aging Society.* Seven Locks Press, Cabin John, Maryland, 1986.

20. Bengtson, V., Burton, L., and Mangen, D. Family support systems and attributions of responsibility: Contrasts among elderly blacks, Mexican-Americans, and whites. Paper presented at the Annual Meeting of the Gerontological Society of America, Toronto, Canada, November 1981.

21. Pilisuk, M., and Minkler, M. Social support: Economic and political considerations. *Social Policy* 15:6-11, 1985.

22. Taylor, H. Testimony before the House Committee on Aging, Washington, D.C., April 8, 1986.

23. Rawls, J. *A Theory of Justice.* Belknap Press, Cambridge, Massachusetts, 1971.

24. Callahan, D. *Setting Limits: Medical Goals in an Aging Society.* Simon and Schuster, New York, 1987.

25. Schiffres, M. The Editor's Page, "Next: Young vs. old?" *U.S. News and World Report,* p. 94, November 5, 1984.

26. Hayes-Bautista, D., Schinck, W. O., and Chapa, J. *The Burden of Support: The Young Latino Population in an Aging Society.* Stanford University Press, Palo Alto, California, 1988.

27. Longman, P. The youth machine vs. the baby boomers: A scenario. *The Futurist* 20:9, 1986.

28. Lamm, R. D. *Mega-Traumas, America at the Year 2000.* Houghton Mifflin Company, Boston, Massachusetts, 1985.

29. U.S. Senate Special Commission on Aging. *Aging America: Trends and Projections, 1985-86.* U.S. Department of Health and Human Services, Washington, D.C., 1986.

30. Andrews, J. Poverty and poor health among elderly Hispanic Americans. Commonwealth Fund Commission on Elderly People Living Alone, Washington, D.C., 1989.

31. Meyer, J. A., and Levin, M. E. Poverty and social welfare: Some new approaches. Report prepared for the Joint Economic Committee. American Enterprise Institute, Washington, D.C., 1986.

32. Ryan, W. *Blaming the Victim* (1st edition). Random House, New York, 1972.

33. Minkler, M. Blaming the aged victim: The politics of retrenchment in times of fiscal conservatism. In *Readings in the Political Economy of Aging,* edited by M. Minkler and C. L. Estes, pp. 254-269. Baywood Publishing, Amityville, New York, 1984.

Public Entitlements
Exclusionary Beneficence

Louise Kamikawa

In the land of "our" forefathers the notion of class has traditionally been and continues to be an overriding consideration in public policy formation. With its roots in the Northeast, this orientation—and the underlying belief system about how peoples coexist—is woven into the fabric of our social contract; class is implicitly assumed to be the major factor affecting all public and private spheres of living.

While more than a grain of truth exists in this hypothesis—and it certainly did apply in eighteenth-century New England—it is anachronistic to continue to allow the subtle application of "classism" to permeate public policy in the United States of today. The focus on class—traditionally and certainly in the latter part of this century—has obviated the necessity to consider color as an essential variable in the formulation of public policy. Class and color often function in tandem with each other, but the idea that they are the same is an illusion.

In the last four decades, the elderly population has grown exponentially, outpacing any other segment of our society. This has placed greater demands on government, requiring that policy makers reevaluate the needs of this particular population. The risks and vulnerabilities incurred with old age have generated greater demands for public service/welfare measures. Government

Source: "Public Entitlements: Exclusionary Beneficence," by Louise Kamikawa, *Generations* (Fall/Winter 1991), pp. 21-24. Copyright ©1991 by the American Society on Aging. Reprinted with permission from *Generations*, 833 Market St., Suite 512, San Francisco, CA 94103.

has had to assume an increased protective role. Correspondingly, the expenditures for the elderly have resulted in the "graying of the federal budget" (Hudson, 1978; Califano, 1978; Samuelson, 1987). With the expenditures to the elderly representing a major component of all social welfare expenditures (McMillan and Bixby, 1980), public resistance and criticism have been mounting.

The combination of class-rooted public policy orientation and the recent developments regarding the elderly raises some important issues, particularly as they relate to older minorities:

1. How are beneficiaries of government intervention defined?

2. Are benefits based on need?

3. What is the impact of needs- and nonneeds-based benefits on older minorities?

This article theorizes that public policy currently targets benefits for the elderly by class and serves as "an intervening variable to ensure status maintenance in old age" (Nelson, [1980]). Moreover, using class as a public policy mechanism serves to exclude consideration of minority populations.

Social Class, Race, and Aging

There is a pervading belief that all the variables of old age are experienced fairly uniformly and that seniority is the demarcation line beyond which all class and status attainment variables become moot. Class variables such as family origin, education, occupational attainment, and income are all examined (Sewell and Hauser, 1975) to define an individual's status, but only to the point of his or her seniority. More alarming is that the status attainment literature on people of color is sparse and obscure and often treated as undifferentiated information, relegating its use to a limited audience. The outcome of the lack of attention to social status and stratification of the elderly is to objectify them as a social class unto themselves, thus obscuring social and economic inequalities and further exacerbating the relative negative status of people of color. Henretta and Campbell (1976) examined income variation among the elderly, finding that the factors that determine income differences are the same before and after retirement. The effects of attainment variables on income are not reduced in old age, negating the posture that all persons experience the impact of aging evenly. Studies conducted by various minority organizations (Pacific/Asian Elderly Research Project, 1977; Lacayo, 1980, for the Asociación Nacional Pro Personas Mayores; National Indian Council on Aging, 1980) not only document the disparate impact of attainment variables on older minorities but suggest that these variables have a worsening effect on that segment of the elderly population. Such variables as assets accumulation, tax policies, health insurance measures, pension policies, and other governmental interventions have served to ensure the persistence of social class differences into old age (Henretta and Campbell, 1976).

Social welfare measures for the elderly parallel those welfare measures for nonelderly, attributing approved and disapproved classes of public dependency (Titmuss, 1965). "Approved" classes receive entitlements as a right resulting from preretirement occupational status, i.e., health insurance, private pensions, Social Security, income transfers such as tax protected retirement savings, property tax relief, and tax exemptions. "Disapproved" classes receive benefits as a measurement of "paternalism" (Friedman, 1962), not right. Such programs generally are means-tested and provide a "minimal level of care and sustenance" (Nelson, 1980).

Entitlements: Class Versus Race

Although the needs of various segments of the elderly population are quite different and access to resources to meet the needs uneven, very little is done to discriminate need within the population. Since social provisions are determined by socioeconomic status, the inequalities experienced in preretirement years are sustained.

Entitlement benefits/programs, composed primarily of income maintenance interventions, are the mainstay of public efforts to support the elderly. Nelson (1980), in his analysis of benefits to the elderly, conceptualizes a three-tiered network of benefits for this population. He also identifies three separate and distinct groups of elderly recipients of these benefits/programs.

Poor elders' benefits. The first tier is composed of means-tested welfare programs, which are directed to the poorest or "marginal elderly" class (Nelson, 1980). These programs are the most invasive in establishing participation eligibility, punitive in their treatment of participants, and complex in their requirements. The continuum of benefits/programs includes Supplemental Security Income (SSI), Medicaid, Title XX, and food stamps.

The needs of the "marginal" elderly are absolute; many remain poor even after receiving public income transfers. The data show that minorities, women, single persons, and "old" old are disproportionately represented in this group (Tissue, 1977). Even after the passage of SSI, those older persons living at or above the poverty line had increased only 6 percent between 1973 and 1984.

The health care program for the poor is Medicaid, also means-tested. Thirty percent of Medicaid expenditures are directed to the poor elderly, primarily for institutional care (Nelson, 1980). The provision of service is uneven and limited. Medicaid falls under state jurisdiction, with some states like Arizona opting to formulate their own health program. Expenditures vary by states, as do the regulations, creating unevenness in the service system. The bias toward institutional care limits outlays for other medical interventions; in 1978, 1 percent of all Medicaid expenditures went to home health services (General Accounting Office, 1991). The elderly poor paid more in out-of-pocket costs for health care than did nonelderly poor (Feder and Holahan, 1979).

Title XX of the Social Security Administration (SSA) provides the mainstay of social services to the poor, "marginal" elderly. Their participation in the Older Americans Act (OAA) programs has been minimal; the primary beneficiaries of OAA programs have been nonpoor, white, lower-middle/middle-class elderly (Estes and Newcomer, 1978). Further, when the programming has been targeted to the poor, the participation rate of minorities has been minimal and far below levels necessary to address the needs of the particular group.

Lower-middle- and middle-class elders' benefits. This second tier includes both lower-middle class and middle class; there is a perceived need based on relative deprivation as opposed to the objective need experienced by the poor elderly (Townsend, 1973). With the onset of old age and retirement, they attempt to maintain their preretirement middle class lifestyle and do so through public support. This group relies primarily on earnings-related Social Security benefits, Medicare, and the OAA program. Other private resources are minimal, generally limited to savings. Without Social Security, approximately 60 percent would fall below the poverty threshold (Ball, 1978).

All programs targeted for this class are assumed to be integrative, either improving or maintaining the standard of living and status that recipients had during their working years. Service interventions seek either to reintegrate the individual or compensate him or her for losses in linkages to the community and resources. Individual beneficiaries perceive services as a right, and the system responds to that perception.

Social Security and Medicare require no arduous or extensive eligibility process and no income or assets tests are applied. This group is not perceived to be a welfare class with the ascribed stigmas. It is apparent in their utilization patterns of Medicare; in 1970 the National Opinion Research Center reported that per capita Medicare expenditures were approximately 70 percent higher for elderly with incomes above $11,000 than for those with incomes below $6,000. The per capita outlays for hospital costs are twice as high for high-income groups than low-income groups (Davis and Schoen, 1977). Physician visits commensurately increase with income. This parallels service utilization patterns of those individuals prior to their retirement.

Middle- and upper-middle-class elders' benefits. Nelson (1980) refers to this tier as the integrated class. This group not only receives government-supported pensions, they also have private pensions, assets, and income and benefits from favorable tax policies. They are able to maintain the socioeconomic status they had during their preretirement years. With such status, they retain the roles and community relationships necessary for social integration.

Health care coverage is comprehensive for this class and ensures optimum availability and access to necessary services. This is provided at the cost of Medicare and Medicaid patients, as physicians and hospitals will limit Medicaid/Medicare patients to serve higher-paying, private insurance patients. It must also be noted that private insurance subscribers are provided tax subsidies that undergird their ability to pay higher costs, serving to raise health care costs generally. . . .

Benefits: Class Versus Race

The application of class as a measure of analyzing public policy is a necessary, but not a sufficient, criterion for ensuring appropriateness and adequacy of intervention mechanisms for all elderly. It assumes homogeneity of experience, perception, and participation in, and benefit from, the full spectrum and hierarchy of institutions and resources. Clearly, for people of color, who are disproportionately represented among the poor and disenfranchised, the use of class as a sole criterion serves to deny access to goods and services as it assumes a similarity of color and class. Minority status implicitly places groups outside the structure as separate entities. They are treated differentially and [gain] access to class status on a fragmented basis, as reflected in our national educational crisis and our employment practices in the social order.

Public policy measures directed at the elderly clearly demonstrate this phenomenon; even in programs for the poor/marginal class, the representation of minorities is far less than their reported objective needs would indicate. Census figures show that in 1989 over 30 percent of all blacks over 65, 20 percent of Hispanics, and 14.5 percent of Pacific/Asians were poor, yet they represent less than 3 percent of all poverty programs for the elderly. Ten percent of older whites were poor in 1989, yet they consume 97 percent of those benefits outlays for the poor. For non-means-tested programs such as those of the OAA, the picture has been more severe. Programs with no income or asset tests have most consistently served all classes of white populations. Class allows the illusion that everyone is being served because the poor are included in the system. But the resources are provided from a white perspective incorporating majority values and behavior relegating the minority population to [a] position of nonalignment and nonmembership. Moreover, service providers, predominantly white, are unable to adapt or to reconcile differences brought about by minority participation and therefore create exclusionary programs, ones allowing the status quo. As a result, minorities have been consistently underserved in the OAA programs. It has taken legislative mandates and litigation to rectify the low participation rate of minorities. Policy makers and service providers have not provided leadership in their efforts. It has taken efforts within minority groups to have an impact on the system and bring about change. But reliance on such efforts is both shortsighted and self-defeating vis-à-vis the public policy infrastructure.

Public Benefits Integration

A benefit structure based on political and subjective entitlement standards like class is not effective for all older persons. Such a structure has a serious negative impact on people of color, irrespective of their "class" standing. We can no longer abide by the hypothesis that class participation cross-cuts races. We do not have a monolithic universe of older persons. Therefore, a structure that identifies minority status as a measure for determining public policy interventions must be instituted. The objective need of all minority groups must be delineated and appropriate service measures created, and these measures must be monitored and evaluated. With the perceived limitation of resources, it will be necessary to address the needs of the most needy if we are to ensure quality maintenance for all. The high degree of deterioration of certain populations in this country is too closely paralleling what is seen in underdeveloped countries.

It may be necessary to consider a guaranteed annual income, a national health care program, and a reconsideration of tax policies that now favor high-income beneficiaries. We cannot continue a policy of "benign neglect"; it is becoming an observable and metastasizing cancer.

References

Ball, R., 1978. *Social Security Today and Tomorrow*. New York: Columbia University Press.

Califano, J., 1978. "U.S. Policy for the Aging—A Commitment to Ourselves." *National Journal* 10:1575-81.

Davis, K. and Schoen, C., 1978. *Health and the War on Poverty*. Washington, D.C.: Brookings Institution.

Estes, C. and Newcomer, R., 1978. *State Units on Aging Discretionary Policy and Action in Eight States*. San Francisco: Administration on Aging Report.

Feder, J. and Holahan, J., 1979. *Financing Health Care for the Elderly*. Washington, D.C.: Urban Institute.

Friedman, M., 1962. *Capitalism and Freedom.* Chicago: University of Chicago Press.

General Accounting Office, 1991. "Minority Participation in AoA Programs." Washington, D.C.: Subcommittee on Aging. Senate Testimony.

Henretta, J. and Campbell, R., 1976. "States Attainment and States Maintenance: A Study of Stratification in Old Age." *American Sociological Review* 41:981-92.

Hudson, R., 1978. "The Graying of the Federal Budget and Its Consequences for Old Age Policy." *Gerontologist* 18:428-40.

Lacayo, C. G., 1980. *A National Study to Assess the Service Needs of the Hispanic Elderly.* Los Angeles, Calif.: Asociación Nacional Pro Personas Mayores.

McMillan, A. and Bixby, A., 1980. "Social Welfare Expenditures, Fiscal 1978." *Social Security Bulletin* 35:746-57.

National Indian Council on Aging, 1980. *Needs Assessment in Older American Indians.* Albuquerque, N.M.

Nelson, G., 1980. "Contrasting Service to the Aged." *Social Service Review* 54:376-89.

Pacific/Asian Elderly Research Project, 1977. *Critical Factors in Service Delivery: Preliminary Findings.* Los Angeles, Calif.

Samuelson, R., 1987. "The Elderly: Who Will Support Them?" *National Journal* 10:1712-17.

Sewell, W. H. and Hauser, R. M., 1975. *Education, Occupation and Earnings: Achievement in the Early Career.* New York: Academic Press.

Tissue, T., 1977. "The Effect of SSI on the Life Situation of the Aged." San Francisco: National Gerontological Society. Paper.

Titmuss, R., 1965. "The Role of Redistribution in Social Policy." *Social Security Bulletin* 28:14-20.

Townsend, P, 1973. *The Social Minorities.* London: Allen Lane.

FOCUS ON PRACTICE   INTERGENERATIONAL PROGRAMS

Interest in intergenerational programs today is a response to changes in relationships among age groups in modern society. In the past, the family or the local community typically provided informal opportunities for contact across age groups, especially between the very old and the very young. But one of the consequences of modernization has been the rise of age grading and grouping. For example, the educational system introduces bureaucratic categorization and separation of children by age (Eisenstadt, 1956). Moreover, a youth culture and popular media, combined with the rapid pace of technological change, all tend to accentuate cultural separation between young and old.

Another important tendency has been **age segregation,** or the residential separation of people of different ages. Age segregation has been promoted by trends such as migration, urbanization, and income transfer programs like Social Security, which enable aged parents to live apart from their children. Age segregation may, however, pose problems in a society where young and old are both competing for limited public resources.

The challenge of the generational equity debate has been one factor stimulating programs to bring together young and old (Wilson, 1992). Such deliberate programs seem more necessary because children today often lack the opportunity for close and frequent contact with grandparents. Intergenerational programs can meet a vital need for age integration (Haber and Short-DeGraff, 1990).

One example of a successful intergenerational program is the Foster Grandparents Program, a federally funded effort that recruits older volunteers to work in such settings as schools, day care centers, hospitals, and homes for the handicapped. Foster grandparents provide one-on-one nurturing for children who need affection and personal attention. Foster grandparents are trained for and supervised in their tasks. They are drawn from the low-income elderly and therefore receive a modest but significant cash stipend as well as a transportation allowance and a hot meal. Evaluation studies have shown that the Foster Grandparents Program can help reintegrate older people into society and give them meaningful and appreciated roles in helping younger generations (Ziegler and King, 1982).

Intergenerational programs have been successfully demonstrated in a wide variety of settings, including nursing homes (Newman, Lyons, and Onawola, 1984; Melvin and Ryder, 1989). In some instances, nursing homes have also served as sites for child care programs (Sommers, 1985), sparking the idea of intergenerational day care (Kopac, 1987). Some prominent corporations, such as the Stride Rite Company, have sponsored on-site intergenerational day care (Leibold, 1989). The National Council on Aging has sponsored an initiative known as "Family Friends," a nationwide outreach program to enlist seniors to visit homeless shelters (Davis, 1992). Schools have proved to be a particularly attractive site for intergenerational programs (Aday, Rice, and Evans, 1991). The National School Volunteers Program has recruited thousands of older people to tutor children in classrooms (Tierce and Seelback, 1987).

The real benefits of intergenerational programs seem to be of two kinds: direct service, allowing young and old to serve as resources for vulnerable members of other generations, and attitude change, overcoming some of the feelings of cultural distance between old and young. On the direct service side, elderly people with time available during the day have been a source of social contact for latchkey children (Anderson, 1989) and at-risk youth (Ventura-Merkel and Friedman, 1988). But the young, too, have shown themselves to be a valuable source of volunteers for aging network service organizations (Firman, Gelfand, and Ventura, 1983).

With respect to attitude change, there is evidence that positive opportunities for contact between old and young can help reduce ageism and prejudice on the part of the young (Peacock and Talley, 1984; Dellman-Jenkins, 1986; Dobrosky and Bishop, 1986). For instance, in oral history programs, older people can become vital resources for improving the education and cultural knowledge of young people. Among the most successful efforts at intergenerational communication are the Full Circle Theater Company in Pittsburgh and the Roots and Branches Theatre in New York, which enlist old and young actors in portraying intergenerational issues, relationships, and attitudes.

Apart from services and attitude changes, intergenerational programs also help renew the bond between generations. That bond is needed for support for important public policies, such as Social Security and public education.

Significantly, the American Association of Retired Persons (AARP) and other senior advocacy groups have come to the forefront in vigorously supporting more government spending for children's programs. In addition, AARP and the National Council on the Aging have been active in coalition with the Children's Defense League on behalf of Generations United, a national coordinating body for intergenerational programs (Thursz, Liederman, and Schorr, 1989). This interest in intergenerational programs is part of an ongoing dialogue between young and old, including the debate around generational equity. By overcoming stereotypes and misunderstanding, it is possible to strengthen the bonds between age groups in decades to come, leading to more enlightened policies for taking care of both young and old.

FOCUS ON THE FUTURE   WALLED RETIREMENT VILLAGES?

Separate living arrangements for the elderly have long been a feature of nuclear families in Western societies (Laslett, 1972). But intentionally segregated housing is a more recent pattern. National surveys of retirement destinations frequently cite places like Sun City, Arizona and Leisure World, California as among the most attractive places for retirees to live. Such communities offer an age-segregated, recreation-oriented lifestyle that some older people find attractive.

Consider Leisure World in Laguna Hills, California, a private retirement community of 21,000 residents. Residents are largely conservative, middle-class, white retirees above age 75, with women outnumbering men. Security at Leisure World is tightly controlled, and the grounds and recreational facilities are attractively maintained. There are nearly 200 social or philanthropic organizations, and the local community college offers courses to Leisure World residents.

Leisure Village, in Ocean County, New Jersey, is a similar community. It has nearly tripled the local county population. Changes have been made in new retirement subdivisions to keep up with housing preferences and to appeal to younger, more active retirees. Century Village, in Florida, has also grown despite some conflicts with neighboring towns, and it is second in size only to Sun City, Arizona.

Since opening in 1960, the original Sun City has grown continuously. Successive stages of development have kept up with demands from increasingly affluent retirees. Sun City provides a comfortable home for thousands of affluent, active, and healthy residents, along with those who are ill or no longer affluent. Sun City also embraces a vast volunteer network, which enhances services provided by the government and formal organizations. Recreation centers and golf courses are always crowded. But beneath the recreation-oriented lifestyle, unanswered questions face all age-segregated communities.

One question is how a retirement village can maintain its active lifestyle. Not surprisingly, new residents tend to be among the young old (ages 65-74). Over time, however, the population of retirement communities is "aging in," and that raises questions about long-term care and other supportive services. Retirement community residents are less likely than peers to have children, and when they do, their adult children tend to live at too great a distance to help with chores or to assist in the event of an illness. Limited short-term assistance comes from friends and neighbors (Sullivan, 1986), but long-term illnesses present a problem. Some retirement complexes have become full-scale life care communities with levels of care ranging from housing amenities for independent elders to nursing home support for those requiring constant care and supervision.

Social critic Lewis Mumford was one of many who argued early against the whole idea of age segregation. Yet people in deliberately age-segregated communities voluntarily choose to live there. Why do they make that choice? People often hear about a retirement community through relatives, but in selecting a place to live, only a small proportion cite proximity to friends and relatives as a reason. Climate, recreation facilities, health, cleanliness, and age segregation are commonly cited as reasons for migrating to Sun City (Gober and Zonn, 1983). Still, more than 90% of people who reach retirement age do not choose to move away but continue to stay right where they have lived all their lives. For the most part, older people remain integrated in communities consisting of people of all ages. But some older people end up in age-segregated communities anyway. For instance, many housing developments evolve into **naturally occurring retirement communities** (NORCs), defined as housing that was not originally planned for older residents but that evolved in that direction over time. Location, especially proximity to shopping and family or friends, is a major attraction of NORCs. In rural areas, NORCs appeal to some residents because of amenities and a natural environment remote from the big city, while others are attracted by convenience or proximity to relatives (Hunt, Merrill, and Gilker, 1994).

There has long been debate about the virtues of age-integrated versus age-segregated approaches to serving the elderly. Arguments in favor of age-integrated services are that age integration reduces ageism and improves efficiency of service delivery. But some evidence suggests that elderly people prefer and benefit more from being with their peers. In age-integrated groups, the needs of the elderly may too easily be neglected (Lowy, 1987). Some studies have suggested that age segregation in itself can actually be a positive factor promoting social integration and a sense of community (Osgood, 1982).

Informal relationships play a big part in most age-segregated communities, whether planned commercial ventures like Sun City or NORCs, like apartment buildings that have "aged in" over time. Age-segregated patterns of association do bring many benefits: a chance for self-expression, a sense of security, and a peer network that can help people cope with problems of aging (Jerrome, 1992).

Hidden Costs of Age Segregation

Another issue is the question of the effect that high-density retirement villages have on communities around them. One study did find that apartment buildings occupied mostly by people over age 60 tended to exclude or impose restrictions on families with children. Elderly respondents sharing older city housing with families with young children and teenagers expressed concern for their own well-being. As a result, families with children sometimes confront a serious problem of housing availability (Margulis and Benson, 1982).

One ominous sign of intergenerational tension was the "adults only movement" that arose in Arizona. For some older people, the appeal of age-segregated communities is that there are no schools or recreation facilities crowded with teenagers playing loud radios. But what happens when families with youngsters want to move in? In Arizona in 1973, a court case was brought by a group of neighbors against a family with a minor who had bought land in a mobile home subdivision in the town of Apache Wells, despite a restrictive covenant intended to keep out anyone under age 21. The "politics of age exclusion" caused age groups to be in opposition to one another in disturbing ways (Anderson and Anderson, 1978).

When people are forced to make hard choices, there is a danger of generational confrontation. For instance, one study found that Florida retirees tend to vote against bond issues for public schools much more often than younger voters. But different studies in other geographic areas found no such correlation. One explanation for the difference may be that Florida has many recent migrants, whereas long-term residents in other areas are more sympathetic to schools than new residents without children. That hypothesis is supported by studies of elderly voting patterns (Button, 1992). Another Florida study found differences between older and younger residents around topics such as community development, zoning regulations to ban nursing homes, and lifestyle issues, such as elderly drivers. However, negative images of the elderly were rarely shared across age groups; in fact, different age groups often saw the elderly as a positive economic influence (Rosenbaum and Button, 1992).

There are significant generational differences around the economic impact of population aging at the local level. Immediate windfalls from attracting higher-income elders who demand few services may give way later to higher expenditures for an older population needing public services, especially health and long-term care. But targeting service programs to segregated groups of elderly people can present problems. In that case, polls show that younger respondents are more likely to agree that older adults in their county or city are a divisive influence or a selfish voting bloc (Rosenbaum, 1993). Tensions between young and old are magnified at the local level by competition for shrinking public budgets. Conversely, improved intergenerational communication could overcome some of these problems.

Another glimpse of the future may be visible in the nation's most populous state, California. The elderly in California are overwhelmingly (three-quarters) Anglo, but among children under age 17, Anglos number less than half the population. In the future, interethnic and intergenerational conflict could emerge if a well-educated, elderly Anglo population has to be supported in retirement by contributions from a poorer, younger Latino population. The well-being of the elderly population will be linked to the financial success or failure of the minority population (Hayes-Bautista, 1991), a link that suggests a need for intergenerational coalition building.

Part of the answer may be to avoid walled retirement villages and instead favor residential patterns to connect generations. One attractive option along these lines is **cohousing,** or planned communities that offer self-sufficient housing units tied to shared common spaces. Cohousing is already popular in Scandinavia and can be attractive to elders who want to live independently. In this multigenerational environment, older people can serve as mentors, friends, or surrogate grandparents to younger people. A retirement housing complex linked to a college or university could offer similar advantages. This approach is found in mixed-use retirement communities, where services are shared and supported by the broader public, and the elderly do not live in isolation or at a distance from the larger community.

QUESTIONS FOR WRITING, REFLECTION, AND DEBATE

1   Some have criticized Peter Peterson and others who are worried about generational equity for being too gloomy and pessimistic about the future of American society. Is this a valid criticism? How might Peterson reply to such a charge of "pessimism"?

2   If a political conservative were to agree with Peterson's picture, what would a likely conservative response to the problem be? If a political liberal were to agree with Peterson's picture, what would a likely liberal response to the problem be?

3   Eric Kingson and his colleagues believe that both young and old have a "common stake" that should overcome generational differences. Prepare a short article for a local community newspaper in which you outline ideas and examples that support this "common stake" point of view.

4   Public opinion suggests that Meredith Minkler may be right when she says the public at large does not much agree with the idea of generational equity. What does this fact suggest about public opinion or the programs government officials should implement for children and the

elderly? As an exercise, try writing opinion poll questions about generational equity and rephrase the same idea in two different ways. Then test the two different ways of framing the issue by asking the questions of people not enrolled in a gerontology class.

5   Consider the following difficult task. Imagine that you are in charge of a meals-on-wheels program providing home-delivered meals to the elderly in your community. Your agency has just received a 50% budget cut for next year, and now you must recommend which of the current meal recipients should continue to receive food. Write a detailed memorandum explaining how you would decide who are the least advantaged elderly deserving of continued service.

6   Is there a way of targeting benefits to those in greatest social and economic need that doesn't make use of factors like race, which tends to be divisive, or income, which tends to be stigmatizing? What factors might work in such an approach to targeting?

7   Assume that you are the new superintendent of a school district with a larger proportion of senior citizens among the voters, who are about to be asked to approve a new school bond issue that will raise taxes. Prepare a letter to be distributed to senior citizens in the community in which you set forth reasons why they should vote in favor of the school bond issue.

8   What might be the consequences of adopting what Peter Peterson calls an "affluence test" instead of a "means test"? Based on what you know about financial aid in higher education, how would you estimate the possible consequences of either an affluence test or a means test instead of an age-based entitlement? Give arguments in favor of, or against, introducing either of these tests.

9   Visit a Web site devoted to cross-cultural and global perspectives on aging at http://www.stpt.usf.edu/~jsokolov/. Drawing on material available on this Web site, what cultural factors can you identify that help explain how different societies mobilize resources to help people based on age?

SUGGESTED READINGS

Bengston, Vern, and Harootyan, Robert, *Intergenerational Linkages: Hidden Connections in American Society,* New York: Springer, 1994.

Johnson, P., Conrad, C., and Thomson, D. (eds.), *Workers Versus Pensioners: Intergenerational Justice in an Ageing World,* New York: St. Martin's, 1989.

Penny, Timothy, and Schier, Steven, *Payment Due: A Nation in Debt, a Generation in Trouble,* Boulder, CO: Westview, 1996.

Thau, Richard D., and Heflin, Jay S., *Generations Apart: Xers vs. Boomers vs. the Elderly,* New York: Prometheus, 1999.

Williamson, John, and Kingson, Eric (eds.), *The Generational Equity Debate,* New York: Columbia University Press, 1999.

What Is the Future for Social Security?

Social Security is the public retirement pension system administered by the federal government, the largest domestic program it operates. Social Security covers almost all U.S. workers except for some state and local government employees. To be eligible for benefits, an older person must be age 65 (62 for early retirement) and have worked for a total of 10 years in a job where Social Security taxes were deducted. The age of eligibility will rise slightly over the next two decades.

Today, annual Social Security retirement benefits average over $8,000 for an individual and over $14,000 for a couple. It was never intended that Social Security would be the sole income source for people in retirement, and the large majority of beneficiaries have other income from a pension, savings, or continued part-time employment. For most retired people, the retirement annuity part of Social Security is the most important because it provides a foundation for retirement income. The broad outlines of the Social Security system are familiar to most Americans, and it remains enormously popular, widely supported by Americans of all ages.

But many people wonder: Will Social Security be there later in the 21st century? A 1997 *Newsweek* survey showed that 61% of adult Americans are "not confident" that Social Security will be there for them. Another widely reported poll showed that, among younger people, more are inclined to believe in the existence of UFOs than in the likelihood of receiving Social Security at retirement age.

Opinion polls aside, the federal government will be facing difficult choices as the baby boom generation moves into retirement. The number of beneficiaries will rise, but the proportion of contributors to Social Security will decline. Benefits of future Social Security beneficiaries might be lowered; alternatively, the age of eligibility for full retirement benefits could be raised; or again, future annual cost-of-living adjustments might be diminished. Currently, the federal budget shows a surplus because of Social Security taxes. But after the year 2008, deficits are likely to emerge and grow larger (U.S. Congressional Budget Office, 1998).

The 1983 Social Security reforms responded to earlier anxiety and succeeded in putting the program on a more secure footing (Light, 1985). But the public rhetoric of "crisis" has continued, and public confidence has eroded. Part of the problem is that Social Security was created more than 60 years ago under different historical conditions. The Social Security Act of 1935 was a centerpiece of the New Deal, a response to the Great Depression at a time when only 5% of the U.S. population was over age 65. This legislation was notable because it acknowledged government's role in providing income support to individuals outside the labor market. Social Security from the outset was conceived as a form of social insurance. Social Security not only helped replace income lost and thereby provided a cushion or an incentive to leave the labor force (Ball, 1978; Myers, 1985). It also legitimized age 65 as a date when it was customary and predictable to leave the labor force (Stewart, 1982).

Main Features of Social Security

Social Security is actually more than just a retirement income program. It includes other features important to younger age groups. For example, Social Security wage earners are covered by a disability insurance policy worth the equivalent of $203,000 on the private market. For an average wage earner with two children, Social Security also provides the equivalent of nearly $300,000 in life insurance. However, what most people think of when they hear the term *Social Security* is the retirement annuity part of the program, which is what is under consideration here.

The money to fund Social Security comes from its own separate payroll tax, which is compulsory for almost everyone who receives wages or salary, including those who are self-employed. Other kinds of earnings—such as interest and dividends, partnership income, and so on—are excluded from the tax. The payroll tax is divided equally between employer and employee. From 1937 until 1950 the combined payroll tax rate was 2%, but today it has risen to 12.4%, with another tax for Medicare hospital insurance. Payroll taxes are paid by 132 million workers, whose wages are taxed up to the first $68,000 received.

Critics have often pointed out that the Social Security payroll tax is a **regressive tax.** That is, a person earning $20,000 a year and someone earning $50,000 a year both pay at the same 6.2% rate. By contrast, in a more progressive tax system—such as the federal income tax—the percentage rises as income goes up, so that wealthier people, at least in principle, pay a greater percentage as well as a greater absolute amount of money in taxes. But Social Security, as a flat percentage, becomes a heavier burden for poorer people than for those earning more money.

On the other hand, Social Security is modestly progressive in its distribution of benefits because of the **replacement rate,** or the proportion of wages replaced by Social Security at the point of retirement. For instance, a worker earning an average wage could expect to receive Social Security payments of about 43% of salary before retirement. Someone earning only half the average would have a replacement rate of 56%; a high wage earner would receive only 28%. Although the percentage replacement rate for higher wage workers is lower, they do receive more back in absolute dollars.

Today, annual Social Security retirement benefits average around $8,000 for an individual and $14,000 for a couple. Since 1975, Social Security benefits have been indexed to the consumer price index, so benefits automatically increase with inflation. A package of the current Social Security and Medicare benefits would cost half a million dollars to buy on the private marketplace, and some features—including inflation protection—would be difficult or impossible to buy at all.

But these benefits come at a price. In 1960, less than 15% of the federal budget was spent on the aging; by the 1990s, the proportion had risen to more than 30%. Social Security payroll taxes now bring in about $400 billion each year, an amount larger than the entire military budget.

The large reduction in the poverty rate among older Americans that has taken place since the 1960s is partly due to the increase in social insurance benefits like Social Security. For example, in a recent year, 8 of every 10 older families would have fallen below the poverty line without these benefits (U.S. Bureau of the Census, 1990).

The relative income of over-65 households has improved faster than for younger people, and government policies have begun to shift in response. Social Security was revised in 1993 to tax up to 85% of Social Security benefits for individuals with incomes above $25,000 or couples above $32,000. But at present, Social Security benefits are subject to taxation for only about a quarter of older people, an indication that the other three-quarters of older Americans in fact have quite modest incomes. The elderly as a group are hardly uniformly affluent.

Success—and Doubts

More than a half century after its founding, Social Security remains America's most successful and perhaps its most popular domestic government program (Barrett and Cook, 1988). One book on Social Security characterized it as "the system that works," and most Americans would agree with that positive judgment.

Despite its success and popularity, Social Security remains the subject of debate (Achenbaum, 1986; Boskin, 1986; Berkowitz, 1987). One fundamental question concerns the purpose of Social Security: Is it a welfare program designed to prevent impoverishment in old age? Or is it an annuity program that entitles everyone who pays into it to receive proportional benefits? Social Security as it actually exists has come to embody both purposes. On the one hand, Social Security provides a floor, or minimum income, for almost all older Americans. In this way, it mildly redistributes income

(Choi, 1991). Social Security helps those who are at risk of total disability and helps families with only one wage earner. On the other hand, Social Security is a universal program that benefits both poor and affluent older people. As a result, nearly everyone has a stake in the system.

Any program that tries to accomplish such fundamentally different goals is bound to have its critics. Thus some people question the basic fairness and integrity of the Social Security system. For example, proponents of the generational equity idea have argued that Social Security is unfair to future generations. They argue that these future cohorts will get back less than current beneficiaries of the system. According to their view, it might be better for people to have a private pension system instead of a compulsory one like Social Security.

Under one plan (Ferrara, 1985), people could drop out of Social Security and sign up for a so-called Super IRA, hoping to collect a better return than Social Security offers. But defenders of Social Security point out that better returns are not at all guaranteed by the private marketplace.

A related criticism is the idea that Social Security is not stable and may not be there for future recipients because the costs will go out of control (R. Campbell, 1977; C. Campbell, 1984; Aaron, Bosworth, and Burtless, 1989). There has been much discussion about the **dependency ratio,** or proportion of younger workers to retirees (Crown, 1985; U.S. General Accounting Office, 1986). Beginning in the mid-1980s, public opinion polls have repeatedly suggested that the public, particularly younger people, are worried about the future of the system, whether rightly or wrongly (Yankelovich, Skelly, & White, 1985).

Social Security is funded by payroll taxes that go into a large account called the Social Security Trust Fund (actually several such funds). Despite the name, the Trust Fund is not actually a big bank account where money is saved for the future. In fact, Social Security was originally designed to operate on a modified pay-as-you-go approach; that is, the money collected each year mostly pays for people who receive benefits in that same year. Younger workers don't actually "save up" for their own Social Security benefits; instead, they pay for current beneficiaries. If more money is collected from payroll taxes than is paid out that year, then the Trust Fund runs a surplus.

The 1983 Social Security amendments put in place payroll tax rates that would create a $5.5 trillion reserve fund by the year 2025; in other words, the payroll tax rate is now higher than needed to pay current benefits. For example, in 1997 the Social Security System brought in $458 billion and paid out $362 billion in benefits. Almost all of the difference went to increase the level of the Trust Fund. By law, that surplus money in the Trust Fund must go to buy U.S. Treasury notes. In effect, the federal government is borrowing the money and promising to pay it back at a certain time, with interest (Stein, 1991).

To understand what this means, imagine that a family is setting aside money to pay for the children's college education. As college savings accumulate, we can compare the savings with the family's debts for car payments, credit cards, and so on. We might say that the college savings fund reduces the family's outstanding debt. But putting the matter that way would be misleading, since the savings fund will be rapidly depleted at some time in the not-too-distant future.

The Social Security Trust Fund works the same way. Depending on accounting assumptions, Social Security can be viewed as reducing or paying for part of the current federal budget deficit, just like a family could "borrow" from its college fund to pay off current debts. In this way, the surplus Trust Fund money reduces the need for the government to borrow the money from somewhere else. But the "real" deficit is not reduced at all.

There has been considerable debate about just how the Social Security Trust Fund should be viewed: whether as part of the budget, thus reducing the combined federal deficit, or as something completely separate. Defenders of Social Security point out that the program does not increase the federal budget deficit. On the contrary, Social Security collections actually reduce the federal budget deficit, because the amount of money collected in payroll taxes each year exceeds what Social Security pays out. In 1993, that **Social Security surplus** was more than $50 billion.

Not everyone is happy with the fact that Social Security is generating a surplus. In 1990, U.S. Senator Daniel P. Moynihan proposed to cut the Social Security payroll tax and convert the system more completely to pay-as-you-go financing—in other words, take in just enough money from taxes to cover current obligations. His proposal generated some support; after all, it was a proposed tax cut. But it also aroused opposition, first because it would reduce government revenues (thereby driving up the federal deficit), and second, because it would abandon the goal of partly "saving up" for retirement later in the 21st century.

If the payroll tax is a burden, then we might ask why we need a surplus anyway. One answer can be found in the Bible's story of Joseph, in which the ancient Egyptians saved up grain during seven fat years to prepare for seven lean years. So, too, today's Social Security surplus is really a collection of "IOUs" that will be needed when the baby boom generation starts to retire in large numbers. It is estimated that the cost of benefits will exceed income after the year 2013. By the year 2034, the system will run out of reserves and taxes will cover only three-quarters of benefits to be paid, unless changes are made.

Members of the baby boom cohort will probably pay higher taxes on their benefits or else receive somewhat lower benefits for two reasons that have nothing to do with the Trust Fund surplus. In the first place, the $25,000 income threshold for taxing Social Security is not indexed for inflation, so in the future a much larger proportion of Social Security recipients are likely to have benefits taxed. In the second place, Congress in 1983 decided that the age of eligibility for full Social Security benefits will rise from the present 65 first to 66 and then to 67 in the years after the year 2000. A couple retiring today can recover the money they contributed to Social Security taxes in only four and a half years. But for those retiring after 2010, it will take seven and a half years—in short, not as good a rate of return.

Whether this difference in benefits from one generation to the next is seriously inequitable is another question. Increased life expectancies and levels of wealth between historical cohorts make comparisons difficult.

None of these arguments about fairness has affected the basic popularity of Social Security with the American public, however, as demonstrated not only by polls but by the votes of Congress in more than half a century since Social Security came into existence (Day, 1990). Despite broad support, however, in recent years there have been serious questions raised about some aspects of Social Security, and these controversies are at the center of the discussion about its future (Olsen and Baylyff, 1998):

- Should eligibility for Social Security be restricted to people who are most in need?

- Should Social Security be changed, at least in part, into a privatized system of retirement to ensure its integrity in the future?

- Should Social Security be changed to make it more fair in its treatment of women compared to men?

Eligibility

One way to reduce the cost of Social Security and improve its financing would be to raise the age for those eligible to receive benefits. To some extent, that shift has already begun and will go into effect in this century. But some are asking whether the age of eligibility should be raised even higher, to 69 or 70.

Some of those arguing for an increased age of eligibility cite rising life expectancy. In 1940, a 21-year-old man had a 54% chance of living long enough to collect Social Security. But a 21-year-old male in the 1990s has a 72% chance of living to age 65, and a 21-year-old woman has an 83% chance.

What about longevity after the point of retirement? In 1940, the life expectancy for people surviving to 65 was 12.7 years for men and 14.7 years for women. Today, however, men at 65 can expect to live 15.3 years and women 19.6 years. Raising the age of eligibility by two or three years would bring the program back to the years of coverage anticipated at the time it was created. On the other hand, raising the age of eligibility could create special hardship for minority groups, whose life expectancy is lower than whites. Lower-income people might have to work longer than before at difficult jobs but still be more likely to die earlier than other Americans, and in effect their benefits would be cut.

Still another approach under consideration would be to reduce Social Security benefits to make them reflect the actual rate of inflation. In 1996, an official government commission examining inflation found that the consumer price index has for years been overstating the rise in the cost of living by 1.1%. The commission estimated that by reducing the consumer price index to a level equal to actual inflation, the federal government would save $1 trillion in Social Security benefits (which are linked to the consumer price index) over a 12-year period. As a result, Social Security would be solid until the middle of the 21st century. However, an across-the-board reduction in benefits would create the greatest hardship for the poorest beneficiaries.

Another possible solution is to make eligibility for Social Security means tested, that is, available only to people whose income falls below some threshold, such as the Supplemental Security Income (SSI) program. However, we should note that the flat SSI benefit paid in 1998 was only $494 per month for an individual, which is a very low amount to live on. Another variation of this approach is the proposal that Social Security benefits might be eliminated for people above some threshold: a so-called **affluence test.** This approach is in some ways an extension of the present policy of taxing benefits for higher-income beneficiaries.

Any of these approaches would either reduce expenses or increase revenues. The result might be to place Social Security on a sounder footing. All three approaches would keep Social Security a publicly financed, age-based entitlement program. But they would shift eligibility in ways that might put the least advantaged at risk in unpredictable ways.

Still another eligibility factor for Social Security is its so-called retirement test or **earnings test** (Rejda, 1990). Social Security law discourages people in their 60s from collecting benefits while they are still working. The limits were recently liberalized, but those ages 65 to 69 still lose $1 for each $3 earned above $12,500. Beneficiaries over age 70 face no reduction in benefits. By the year 2002, this earning limitation level will rise to $30,000. The effect of this liberalization, supported by both Democrats and Republicans, is to make Social Security more of an age-based entitlement unrelated to need and also to give stronger incentives for work and productivity.

Privatization

In 1994, a 13-member Advisory Council was appointed to look into the future of Social Security and recommend ways of ensuring its integrity. In 1997, the Advisory Council issued a report offering three different proposals for overhauling Social Security. All three plans involved some degree of privatization—that is, putting Social Security taxes into private investment in the stock market. Since 1926, stocks have earned an average of 7.5% after inflation. This is a level that is much more than the rate of 2% to 3% earned by Social Security funds currently invested in Treasury bonds. The potential for greater gain from private investment is what makes privatization attractive to many people.

One plan proposed would keep the traditional system intact but would permit the Social Security Trust Fund to be invested partly in a broad index of the stock market. The two other proposals would let people invest some of their own Social Security contributions, an idea favored by 71% of Americans (1997 *Newsweek* poll). One would institute a new 1.6% tax on wages now covered by Social Security and have people invest it in a small number of government-approved mutual funds. The other plan, a big departure from traditional Social Security financing, would require that wage earners save 5% of their income in some type of stocks.

To finance the transition from today's Social Security toward this mostly privatized system, the federal government would have to borrow money to make up for retirement benefits already promised. Those "transition costs" would mean higher payroll taxes on top of those currently paid for Social Security. Under the boldest privatization plan, the transition costs would require higher taxes equal to $6.5 trillion over a 70-year period.

Nearly half the members of the Social Security Advisory Council supported a proposal to put up to 40% of the Trust Fund into an index of the stock market. The result might be to boost public confidence in the future of Social Security. But other changes would come as well. By the year 2015 the federal Social Security Fund would own $800 billion in shares, or 10% of the entire stock market, which would be a dramatic shift toward national influence over the capital markets. Critics of the plan note that, although investing in a broad stock index should provide some diversification and safety, putting Social Security funds at risk in the stock market is not necessarily prudent. True, stocks have risen at an average annual rate of 10% since 1926. But in the short term there can be severe drops. For example, the Japanese stock market has plummeted 50% from the high reached in 1988.

Conservative critics of Social Security, such as economist Martin Feldstein, have long argued that a public pension program weakens private savings and capital formation. They often point to Chile as an example of successful transition to a privatized system. The United Kingdom, like Finland, has already shifted large portions of its retirement financing to the private sector. Similar experiments are under way in Chile, Brazil, and Australia. But questions have been raised about investing Social Security funds in the stock market. What impact would forced savings plans really have on other voluntary savings and capital formation? Could federal government ownership of stocks lead to other intervention in the markets—for example, forbidding Social Security from buying tobacco stocks? What happens in a crash or prolonged market downturn, such as we experienced after 1929 or in 1973-1974?

The Advisory Council's proposals amount to making Social Security a **funded system** instead of a modified **pay-as-you-go system.** These plans all end up with tax increases, whether direct or indirect. The plans for outright privatization through individual investment accounts would require additional new taxes to cover transition costs. Even the proposal to invest Trust Fund monies in the stock market would not be cost free, because the federal government would have to borrow directly from the public, thus raising taxes indirectly.

What about allowing workers to invest part of their Social Security taxes in private retirement accounts? On the positive side, this plan would give individuals the freedom to make their own decisions about investing for retirement, as they do with 401(k) plans now. But a study by the Employee

Benefit Retirement Institute suggests that lower-income workers tend to be much too cautious in their investments, and as a result their savings do not grow as much over time. On the other hand, if people do make more risky investments, they are vulnerable to losing their retirement savings. Still another problem is how to help investors ride out the stock market's periodic ups and downs over time. What would holders of individual accounts do if the market took a long downturn?

The effect of changing Social Security into private retirement accounts would be to emphasize equity over adequacy in the operation of the system as a whole. Social Security has always embodied two different, sometimes contradictory, principles: **equity,** which means a fair return to beneficiaries depending on how much they contribute to the system, and **adequacy,** which means maintaining a decent minimum of income for everyone. Some degree of privatization might make Americans more confident in Social Security. But by favoring equity over adequacy, privatization could be the first step toward dismantling a system that has been popular and successful for over 60 years.

Women and Social Security

Not all concerns about Social Security revolve around expectations for the future. Some issues have come to the forefront now because of changing social conditions, such as the role of women (MacDonald, 1998). A major issue arises from the fact that the traditional family assumed by Social Security at its inception in the 1930s has now changed. The Social Security program was originally planned for the one-earner family, but today more than 70% of women between the ages of 20 and 44 are in the labor force. Social Security seeks to treat both men and women fairly, but there are troublesome equity problems related to caregiving, divorce, and two-earner couples (B. Johnson, 1987).

The rate of poverty and near poverty among older women is shockingly high. Women constitute almost three-fourths of older people who live in poverty. Widowhood is a distinct threat to well-being: Almost four times more widows live in poverty than do married women of comparable age (Older Women's League, 1998).

Women's wages remain about three-quarters of men's, and that gap widens in retirement. Taking time out to raise families or to care for older relatives reduces the primary insurance amount credited under Social Security (Kingson and O'Grady, 1993). Leaving the workforce to care for others, whether early or late in a career, is more costly for women with low and moderate earnings. As a result, women may fail to earn enough during their working lives to be able to save on their own for retirement. A basic problem is that the Social Security system recognizes only paid work for determining benefits. The nonmonetized work done by women in caring for family members receives no acknowledgment. These facts lead some observers to recommend earnings sharing for Social Security or even credit for years of lost wages due to caregiving.

Another equity issue arises from the higher divorce rate today. Under Social Security, women who have been married fewer than 10 years and who were out of the labor force during those years receive no credits toward Social Security, meaning lower benefits at retirement. As a result of past reforms, women who are divorced are eligible for a spousal benefit if they were married at least 10 years. Nevertheless, those who are divorced receive only a third of what the couple would have received had they stayed together.

Still another issue arises from the way that Social Security treats married couples. When she retires, a woman automatically receives a spousal benefit equivalent to half of what her husband is entitled to. Unless married women have earned a great deal, their spousal benefits are higher than the level they would get from their own work history. Social Security will give benefits to a woman for work outside the home only when her accumulated benefits are greater than her husband's. Typically, then, older women's lifetime economic contribution to Social Security is totally disregarded and two-earner couples may receive proportionately lower retirement benefits than one-earner couples under the present system, and some critics find that inequitable (U.S. Congress, 1983).

This issue here is related to the question of fairness in Social Security, namely, equity versus adequacy. Women who are eligible for Social Security receive a benefit based on their own earnings record. But if they have been married, they are also entitled to a benefit based on the earnings record of their spouse. In other words, a married woman (or widowed or divorced), can be *dually entitled* to Social Security benefits. In 1960, only 5% of women beneficiaries were in this category, but by 1995 one-quarter were dually entitled to benefits. As a result, dropping out of the labor force to care for children or other dependents may be offset by a share of the spouse's earnings record.

Some suggestions have been made to reform the Social Security system to take into account a woman's life cycle (Wolff, 1988). Some critics have urged that Social Security give credit for time taken out for caregiving (Buckley, 1990). For example, a *child care dropout option* has been proposed, whereby years spent at home caring for children are not counted in determining an average benefit level. A related proposal is for Social Security caregivers to simply eliminate up to five years of low earnings if those years were devoted to caregiving responsibilities.

One problem is that a child care dropout credit might favor economically advantaged women, who can afford to take time off for childrearing, more than those who are disadvantaged. But many European countries have a similar system of implicitly subsidizing child care through children's allowances. Another suggestion to help women would be the so-called *double-decker system,* under which a retiree would receive a minimum fixed amount of money along with a benefit related to work history and prior contributions (Kahne, 1981).

Finally, some women's advocates have urged an *earnings sharing plan,* which would divide the total earnings of the married couple between the Social Security accounts of both spouses (U.S. Congress, 1984). Earnings sharing is attractive because it treats marriage as a partnership of equals, and it also helps improve the retirement income of women who may be impoverished by divorce or widowhood. But the idea of earnings sharing brings us back to a fundamental question concerning the rationale for Social Security: Is the program to be viewed as a means for replacement of earnings or as an investment judged by equity and rate of return? Would complete privatization of Social Security be good for women (Williamson, 1997)? This is the same question that arises regarding the earnings test for Social Security benefits. People have different ways of thinking about fairness and adequacy, and basic social values are at stake. However these debates are resolved, Social Security will remain a key issue for women.

Debate Over Social Security

In the readings that follow, we encounter some very different views about the future of the Social Security system. One view favors actual privatization of Social Security, that is, introducing a new system of personal accounts owned by workers and invested according to their wishes. Carolyn Weaver argues that privatization does have its risks, but she is unhappy about the idea of letting the Social Security Trust Fund earn the low yields it has in the past. Whatever risks private investors bear should be compared with the real risks of leaving Social Security in the hands of Congress, who could reduce benefits in the future. Gary Burtless takes a different view. He believes that the best way to minimize risk is a collective system like Social Security where risks are spread across different generations.

If we do not privatize Social Security, there remains the looming problem of how a public system will be able to support the retiring baby boom generation. One answer, proposed by Henry Aaron, is to invest a portion of the Social Security Trust Fund monies in the stock market. This plan would produce higher returns than investing in Treasury bonds. But again, not all are persuaded by this approach. Robert Myers worries that government investment of Social Security may eventually lead to federal interference, as happened with public pension plans controlled by state governments.

The impact of Social Security on women is another topic addressed in the readings that follow. Economist Barbara Bergmann argues that feminist thinking should be a basis for changing the Social Security system to reflect new realities of gender instead of the family structure taken for granted when Social Security was initiated in 1935. Such changes would provide greater equity for women, she believes. By contrast, Robert Myers believes that Social Security should not be expanded to take into account all equity claims. He believes that the present system is satisfactory and represents the best approach to reconciling the competing values of equity and adequacy.

Private Accounts
Political Vs. Market Risk

Carolyn L. Weaver

Similar to 401(k) plans in the private sector, personal accounts would be owned by workers and invested in by private financial institutions. Workers would make regular contributions to these accounts (with a portion of their payroll taxes) and would accumulate financial wealth on which they could draw in retirement.

Low-Yield System

The idea behind personal accounts is to move away from our current low-yield system of income transfers—which shifts the cost of retirement income for elders to workers and future generations—toward a system based squarely on saving and capital investment. The goal is to generate a stronger national economy and larger and more secure retirement incomes for younger workers.

There is widespread agreement that substantial economic benefits would flow from accumulating real assets against Social Security's accruing liabilities. Increased saving and capital investment would increase labor productivity and the wages of American workers and lead to higher future living standards. Further, investing in private capital would generate substantially higher returns than investing in Social Security. Over the long term, mixed portfolios of stocks and bonds have yielded an average return of 5%–

Source: "Private Accounts: Political Vs. Market Risk," by Carolyn L. Weaver, in *Aging Today* (January-February 1999). Reprinted with the permission of the author and publisher.

6% annually (after adjusting for inflation), which is substantially higher than the 1%–2% younger workers are projected to earn under Social Security. (The real pretax return to private capital, which is the return to society as a whole, is closer to 8%–9%.)

Personal accounts would have other benefits as well. Giving workers at all income levels the opportunity to invest and to become shareholders—and thus stakeholders—in the U.S. economy would enhance opportunities for risk diversification among lower-income Americans and would reduce their dependence on wages and government transfers.

Furthermore, since workers would have a legal claim to their contributions and investment earnings, they would have the peace of mind of knowing that the money they put away for retirement was theirs, period, shielded from political manipulation. This would improve public confidence in the system and promote informed retirement-income planning. For at least this portion of Social Security, periodic financing crises would be a thing of the past. Personal accounts would be fully funded at all times.

Personal accounts would not get us around the problem of having to close long-range deficits or dig out from under the debt created by the current system. Social Security has extended trillions of dollars of unfunded benefit promises to workers and retirees. Personal accounts would, however, create a light at the end of the tunnel—a beacon of hope that Social Security can be of significant value in the future as it has been in the past.

Social Security's Risks

Critics complain that a system of personal accounts would be risky, whereas Social Security is safe. But this line of reasoning is disingenuous at best. Both kinds of systems involve risks. Personal accounts involve financial risks, risks that can be controlled by holding broadly diversified portfolios and by investing for the long term. With these risks comes the opportunity to accumulate wealth—not just government benefit promises to be made good by future workers—and the potential to generate larger retirement incomes.

Social Security, though, entails political risks, risks that Congress will reduce benefits or raise taxes—and there is no way for individuals to control these risks. Political risks can be very large. The benefit reductions imposed in 1977, for example, resulted in reductions in lifetime benefits for younger workers that swamp anything sustained by investors as a result of periodic stock market "corrections." The same can be said about the benefit reductions that would be required to shore up the system today on a sustained, long-term basis.

In thinking about the riskiness of reforms involving personal accounts, it is important to keep in mind that workers would not be required to invest entirely or even heavily in stocks. Those concerned with security, such as people nearing retirement who are more sensitive to short-term fluctuations in asset values, would be free to invest more heavily in fixed-income instruments. Furthermore, low-income workers would not be left to fend for themselves. Under all proposals being discussed, a safety net would be retained that would boost retirement incomes for low-income workers or those who accumulated low account balances. Proposals for small personal accounts retain much more generous safety nets, which, of course, come at a higher cost to workers. Finally, older workers and retirees would not be required to participate in personal accounts. Benefits for these people would be continued with little modification.

It is ironic that many of those who argue most forcefully that workers should be denied personal accounts because of the riskiness of the stock market are peddling the idea that the government should invest in the stock market—to the tune of $1 trillion or more under one leading proposal. But stock market risks are stock market risks. Centralizing them, sharing them, spreading them, or in other ways socializing them does not make them go away.

Who Bears These Risks?

The great unanswered question is who bears these risks if not Social Security taxpayers and retirees. If the stock market experienced a sharp or prolonged drop, resulting in substantially less investment earnings than anticipated, would taxes be increased or benefits reduced? If the stock market performed better than expected, would benefits be increased or taxes reduced? Persistent underfunding or overfunding would necessitate changes in taxes or benefits, changes that imply additional risks for workers and retirees. Just what these changes would be is anyone's guess, because proponents of centralized investment have not been forthright about the ongoing risks. With some of the finest mutual funds in the world at their disposal, workers have an efficient and low-cost means of investing in broadly diversified portfolios. They can, if they wish, invest in precisely the same broad-based equity (or fixed-income security) funds the government can. This means they can manage their assets so as to bear precisely the same risks. The government can reduce an individual's risk only by shifting it to somebody else, and who that somebody is goes unstated.

The government also can create serious new risks with centralized investment—the risk of politicizing investment decisions and matters of corporate governance and the risk of distorting the allocation of capital in the economy. The resulting cost would be borne by everyone. Moving toward a system of private accounts that are fully funded with a share of workers' taxes and managed by private financial institutions is not the only way to reform Social Security for the 21st century, but it's the best way.

Conventional reforms involving tax increases or benefit reductions will not ensure solvency (any more than they did in 1977 and 1983); they will not enhance the value of Social Security for younger workers; and they will not boost the confidence of workers in the long-term viability of the program—nor will conventional reforms coupled with the nonconventional idea of allowing the government to invest directly in the stock market.

American workers should be given the opportunity to draw on modern financial markets—and on the wide array of investment products that make investing cheaper, easier and safer—to enhance their retirement income security.

READING 24

Private Accounts
Putting Retirement at Risk

Gary Burtless

The public is uneasy about the future of Social Security. Young workers fear that the present system is not sustainable. Their fear is exaggerated but not completely unfounded. To pay promised Social Security benefits, the contribution rate must eventually be increased. Future voters might resist paying higher taxes, and benefits would then have to be cut or the budget deficit would soar.

The expected revenues of Social Security will fall short of anticipated benefit payouts by about 15% over the next 75 years, a shortfall that is equivalent to 2.2% of taxable wages during this period. Shortly after 2030, benefit payments would need to be cut by nearly one-quarter to keep the program solvent with the current payroll tax rate. This does not mean Social Security pensions will have to be eliminated, as some young workers fear. It does mean, however, that their taxes will have to be increased or their benefits trimmed if the system is to be preserved.

Source: "Private Accounts: Putting Retirement at Risk," by Gary Burtless, in *Aging Today* (January-February 1999). Reprinted with the permission of the author and publisher.

Political Risks Overstated

Future tax rates and benefit payments will be determined by legislators who have not yet been elected (and in some cases have not even been born). This fact introduces substantial political uncertainty around future benefit levels and tax burdens. Future voters and elected officials may reject the structure of Social Security that has prevailed from the 1930s to the present. They may wish to scale back the system's promises, including those to people who are already retired or are on the threshold of retirement.

These political risks are easy to overstate, however. Elected officials are keenly aware of public opinion. Social Security has long been one of the most popular programs run by the federal government. Its popularity is deep and extends across the age spectrum. The program enjoys nearly as much support among people under age 35 as it does among elders. Large majorities of people in all age groups express satisfaction with paying Social Security payroll taxes. This is probably because most voters recognize that disabled and elderly Americans rely on the program for a significant portion of their income: 44 million people collect Social Security every month, and a large percentage of them vote in every election. Most of the 140 million contributors to Social Security have friends or relatives who collect benefits, so even among contributors there would be wide resistance to major benefit cuts.

If Social Security enjoys broad political support today, when comparatively few voters draw benefits, it is hard to believe the popularity of the program will disappear when a sharply higher percentage of voters reaches retirement age, beginning around 2010.

Private alternatives to Social Security, such as individual retirement accounts, also face sizable political risks. Since 1980 Congress has twice made major changes in the eligibility requirements for tax-favored contributions into existing IRAs. It has altered the conditions under which workers can make penalty-free withdrawals from such accounts. Congress is free in the future to make additional changes in the taxation of IRA contributions or withdrawals.

Of course, Congress also is free to change the entire basis of the federal tax system. For example, were it to abolish the income tax system and replaced it with a comprehensive consumption tax, as many conservatives urge, the tax burdens on older Americans would almost certainly rise, thus reducing their net incomes. Americans' retirement incomes are therefore subject to significant political risk regardless of whether Social Security is maintained as a single public system or is replaced by a system of private individual accounts.

The Public Advantage

The notable advantage of a single public system is that political pressures tend to keep benefits relatively stable—though not completely constant—over time. Benefits have been trimmed and contributions increased in line with the changing demographic and economic realities facing the retirement system, but the changes have rarely been sudden and have always been phased in gradually. The economic and demographic risks are shared between active workers and retired beneficiaries and are distributed broadly among members of several generations rather than concentrated on only one.

In contrast, a system of individual, defined-contribution accounts distributes the risk of adverse financial outcomes much more haphazardly and unequally. Pension replacement rates of male workers would have varied over the 20th century if their pensions had been derived from individual retirement accounts invested solely in U.S. stocks. The chart [shown here demonstrates] what would have happened to the pension return of a typical man who entered the labor force on his 22nd birthday and worked for 40 years until he turned 62. (The entrance of a large proportion of women into the workforce is a relatively recent development, hence this focus on male employment through most of this century.) This calculation is based on the lifetime earnings profile of the male workforce in 1996.

Year worker reaches 62	Income replaced (%)	Year worker reaches 62	Income replaced (%)
1912	50	1960	79
1915	34	1965	89
1920	29	**1969**	**104**
1925	33	1970	90
1930	69	1975	39
1935	25	1980	47
1940	30	1985	42
1942	**19**	1990	57
1945	25	1995	51
1950	27	1997	72
1955	53		

For each year in the chart, the typical male worker saves 6% of his earnings and invests those savings exclusively in common stocks. All stock dividends are reinvested and are free of individual income taxes when received. On his 62nd birthday the worker converts his accumulation into a single-life annuity. The insurance company selling the annuity bases its charge on the expected mortality experience of American males reaching age 65 in 1995, using mortality projections of the Social Security actuary.

The chart shows the percentage of income that the earnings on a personal account would have replaced for workers in retirement from 1912 to 1997. The replacement rate is the real value of the annuity divided by the worker's real average earnings when he was between age 54 and 58 (that is, when he was earning his peak lifetime wage). For example, the figure shows a replacement rate of 50% in 1912. This reflects the real value of the 1912 annuity available to a worker who began to work in January 1872, worked and saved for 40 years and retired in January 1912.

As the figures demonstrate, hypothetical replacement rates have varied enormously over relatively short periods of time. The replacement rate was slightly over 100% for workers retiring in 1969, but only 39% for workers retiring in 1975. Pensions from individual accounts depend crucially on when workers buy stocks and when they convert their nest eggs into annuities. In an individual-account system, virtually all of this risk is borne by individual workers.

In a collective retirement system, such as Social Security, these risks are shared among the members of several generations. The Social Security replacement rate for full-career workers earning average wages has fluctuated in a much narrower range than the one shown in the table. (The replacement rate of average-wage workers is currently about 42% for people who retire at age 65.) While future Social Security benefits are subject to unknown political risks, these risks seem comparatively small in a mature democracy like the United States. Similar political risks would surround any privately managed, publicly regulated system of individual accounts. A key advantage of a single collective retirement system is that it spreads the financial and demographic risks facing a retirement system much more broadly across workers and retirees and among members of successive generations.

READING 25

Should a Portion of Social Security Funds Be Invested in the Stock Market?
Yes: It Means Higher Future Benefits

Henry Aaron

[The] proposal to invest a small portion of Social Security reserves in common stocks deserves the

Source: "Should a Portion of Social Security Funds Be Invested in the Stock Market? Yes: It Means Higher Future Benefits," by Henry Aaron. In *AARP Bulletin* (March 1999). Reprinted with permission of the publisher. Henry Aaron is senior fellow in the Economic Studies Department of the Brookings Institution in Washington.

support of all Americans. Building a reserve and investing part of that reserve in stocks will result in higher pensions for each dollar of workers' payroll taxes than would be possible without reserves or if reserves continue to be invested only in government bonds.

The reason is simple. On the average, stocks have yielded much more than government bonds for decades. Even large drops in asset values would not threaten the payments of benefits, because benefits are tied to earnings and because Social Security would continue to hold reserves in government bonds sufficient to ride out any market decline. In short, a policy of building reserves and investing them in a prudently diversified portfolio of government bonds and stocks means larger pensions for workers tomorrow at no risk to current pensioners.

Nonetheless, some people have expressed two fears about such a policy. The first is that such stock market investments might lead to federal interference in private business. This fear is misplaced.

- The investments would not be managed by the government, but by professional funds managers.

- These managers would be hired not by federal bureaucrats, but by a new independent board, modeled on the Federal Reserve Board, which would be financially independent of Congress. Like Federal Reserve governors, its members could be removed only for malfeasance, not for political reasons.

- The private managers would merge funds managed for Social Security with funds they managed for private clients and would be legally required to distribute investments equally among all traded stocks—no picking favorites.

- Stocks purchased for Social Security would be accumulated gradually over 15 years under the president's plan and would never exceed 4 per-

cent of traded securities. This is a smaller share of stocks than the portion now owned by the Fidelity family of funds alone. These safeguards would eliminate any realistic chance of political interference in private business decisions.

The second fear is that growing reserves would lead Congress to enact imprudent benefit increases or tax cuts. To reduce the chances of such behavior, the independent investment board should be charged to report to the American public on how every proposed legislative change in Social Security benefits would affect the solvency of the system in the short, medium, and long runs.

Any bill that reduces the system's financial balance over any of these periods would require a super-majority to pass the Senate. Simply reporting that a proposal would threaten solvency would reduce chances of enactment. The special voting requirements would lower chances still further.

Congress has managed Social Security with great prudence for more than six decades. It can do so in the future at the same time that American workers enjoy the returns of a diversified investment portfolio.

American workers deserve to have their Social Security assets invested to generate returns as high as every prudent private pension manager is expected to deliver. [A] plan to invest a small portion of Social Security reserves in common stocks is a significant step toward this goal.

Should a Portion of Social Security Funds Be Invested in the Stock Market?
No: Possible Advantages Not Worth the Risk

Robert J. Myers

In recent years, some influential persons have advocated investing a portion of the assets of the Social Security trust funds in the stock market.

The sole reason for such action is to strengthen the financing of the Social Security program, as a preferable alternative to increasing its dedicated taxes or decreasing benefit costs (or both). This is, of course, very appealing at first glance and is "justified" as a proper course of action because such procedure is followed in other pension plans, including those for state and local government employees, as well as in the Thrift Savings Plan for federal workers. Admittedly, it is very likely that investing in the market would produce higher returns for the Social Security trust funds. However, serious potential dangers are present that, in my view, do not make the possible gains worth the risks involved. It should be realized that the potential increased financing so arising is only a small portion of that necessary to restore the program to long-range actuarial balance. Such an estimate indicates that the trust funds will, under present law, become exhausted in 2032; the proposed investment procedure, if successful, would extend this date by only about 10 years.

Under present law, the assets of the trust funds are invested entirely in special-issue obligations of the federal government. These are part of the recognized national debt and, although not marketable, are redeemable on demand, along with accrued interest. Such special issues bear an equitable, reasonable interest rate related to the average long-term interest rate on all government bonds, determined at the time of issue by a formula in the law.

Under the proposal, a portion of the assets of the trust funds would be invested in the stock market under a mechanism intended to ensure that the investments are made independent (and with minimal administrative cost). The hope is to avoid such things as government interference in the management of companies, the purchase of the stock of companies solely because they are doing "desirable social" things (or vice versa), and seeking "proper" geographical distribution of companies (so as to keep all members of Congress satisfied). It is very likely that, over the long run, governmental interference would occur. This has already taken place in California and Texas pension plans for state government employees. Once "the camel's nose gets into the tent," there would be no stopping its expansion. Still another problem arises in connection with federal debt financing—who will purchase the government obligations that the trust funds would otherwise have bought, and what effects will this have? Also, investment-timing problems would likely occur because, in times of economic recessions when payroll taxes fall off, sale of the stock investments would involve large capital losses.

Source: "Should a Portion of Social Security Funds Be Invested in the Stock Market? No: Possible Advantages Not Worth the Risk," by Robert J. Myers. From *AARP Bulletin* (March 1999). Reprinted with permission of the publisher. Robert J. Myers was chief actuary at the Social Security Administration from 1947 to 1970.

In summary, I do not believe that the relatively small possible advantages of investing some of the assets of the Social Security trust funds in the stock market are worth the risks inherent in the federal government in essence owning or having control of a significant portion of private industry.

Certainly, other ways involving relatively small and painless changes can be found to solve the likely long-range financing problems of the program without the possible risk of, at the extreme, having "socialism by the backdoor method."

The Housewife and Social Security Reform
A Feminist Perspective

Barbara R. Bergmann

If we were to ponder the list of major complaints which are currently being voiced concerning the present set-up of the social security system—the "inequity" in benefits between one- and two-earner couples, the treatment of the divorced spouse, the "wasted" social security taxes of the working wife—we would find that virtually all of them, in one way or another, involve the housewife. It is the system's method of provision for the housewife—in some instances its lack of provision—that is at the heart of almost all of the complaints.

Paradoxically, it is the *decreasing* number of full-time housewives that has pushed the problem of their treatment under social security onto center stage. As long as most adult men were husbands and most adult women were housewives, the system's provision for a wife through a benefit which was supplementary to her husband's benefit seemed straightforward to most people. The spouse benefit, which gave a married male retiree 50% more than an unmarried male retiree with the same earnings record, was advantageous to the vast majority of men and the vast majority of women. True, the system's treatment of the working wife was no less anomalous and the system's treatment of the divorced wife was only slightly more shabby than it is today. But working wives and divorced wives were less numerous, and there was little public concern about their problems.

Along with the rise in the labor force participation of married women, the fall in the marriage rate, and the increase in the divorce rate has come a trend of feminist thinking concerned with the economic, social, and psychological relations between men and women and with the institutions through which those relations are policed and expressed. Feminists now seek redress for what they

Source: "The Housewife and Social Security Reform: A Feminist Perspective," by Barbara R. Bergmann, in *A Challenge to Social Security: The Changing Roles of Women and Men in American Society* (pp. 229-233), edited by R. V. Burkhauser and K. C. Holden. New York: Academic Press, 1982. Reprinted by permission of the Institute for Research on Poverty, University of Wisconsin–Madison.

perceive as previous neglect of women's satisfaction and well-being. They ask that women's interests be more faithfully represented in discussions of issues and that institutional structures be revamped to serve those interests. Whether this wave of feminist thought has been an important part of the cause of these social trends or is in reality more of an effect is something we need not debate here. What needs to be understood, however, is that feminist ideas have a considerable contribution to make to the discussion of issues like social security reform, and in fact are indispensable to a cogent discussion of any set of issues in which gender roles figure prominently. Of course, feminist thought has done more than provide an intellectual framework for the discussion of reform. It has been a source of political action to get the issue of reform onto the national agenda and will be needed to mobilize enough political power to enact reforms.

The role of and treatment of the housewife, which is really the major bone of contention in social security reform, has, of course, a major place in feminist thought. Betty Friedan's book, *The Feminine Mystique* (1963), which was influential in initiating the current wave of feminism in the United States, centered on the disadvantages to women of assuming the housewife's role. All feminists believe that women should not be forced into assuming it, and that alternative choices should be available. Many feminists, such as the present writer, go further and believe that the disadvantages of the role of housewife are so great that it would be better if younger women were to avoid entering the role even temporarily and if the "option" to assume the role were to disappear.

There is a second strand of feminist thought concerning housewives, which derives from the solidarity which feminists feel with all women, housewives included. . . . This solidarity expresses itself in a concern to alleviate injuries (physical and psychological as well as financial) inflicted on housewives by their husbands and by the institutions of society. This second strand is not logically contradictory to the first; it is possible to love the sinner (the housewife herself) while hating the sin (playing the role). Nevertheless, the two strands do tend to cut different ways in terms of policy. Moreover, individual feminist thinkers differ in the emphasis they place on each.

These two strands of feminist thought inspire two kinds of complaints against the social security system—that some housewives are treated too well and that some housewives are treated not well enough. The housewives who are treated too well are those married to retired men, who are enabled by the system to live at a higher standard than retired working wives whose family had comparable total covered earnings. The housewives who are treated not well enough are those whose dignity is scanted by treatment as a dependent, or those whose marriages end, and whose husbands retain all rights to social security (and private pensions) earned during the marriage.

The solidarity-with-housewives strand of feminist thought results in attitudes which emphasize the housewife's productiveness and give dignity to the position of housewife. It results in policy suggestions which would have the effect of making the woman who becomes and remains a housewife safer, more comfortable, less subject to financial shipwreck, more able to hold up her head as a productive member of society. The most characteristic product of this line of thought is the suggestion that housewives be awarded social security credits for the homemaking work they do. Some credit schemes would require the household to pay taxes in return for the credit; others would not. One merit of homemaker credits in the eyes of the solidarity-with-housewives advocates is that it makes housework and "paid work" more alike, thereby raising the status of housework psychologically and financially. A second merit, of course, is that in the case of divorce the homemaker would keep her credits, and thus would be more financially independent than is the case now.

Earnings sharing, whereby social security credits for paid work are shared between spouses, would also give housewives earnings credits under their own names. In the event of divorce there would be no cases in which the housewife would lose all social security protection, as can happen under present arrangements. While earnings sharing is probably much easier to implement than homemaker credits, it does not go as far in protecting and dignifying housewives. Most earnings-sharing schemes call for sharing 100% of the earnings credit, and no more. For one-earner couples who retire still married, sharing 100% rather than 150% of earnings credit would result in lower pensions than the present spouse benefit or the proposed homemaker credit would provide.

One may also view the two-tiered system (or the double-decker system), in which entitlement is given to all persons of a certain age, regardless of work history, as a protective measure for the housewife and as a potential substitute for the 50% spouse benefit. Homemaker credits are based on the idea that housework should be counted as paid work in figuring pensions. Earnings sharing is based on the idea that housework earns one the right to share the pension entitlement due to the paid work of one's spouse. On the other hand, the two-tiered and double-decker schemes are based on the idea that a pension should be given to all people who reach a certain age, regardless of work history. These two schemes are not based on a concept of the value of housework; rather they are based on the assumption that work history should be less important in determining a person's pension than it now is. This attitude increases the housewife's dignity as a person, if not as a worker. The two-tiered system can also be thought of as bringing the position of the husband closer to the present position of the housewife, instead of moving the position of the housewife towards that of the husband by giving her work a market value, which is the case with homemaker credits.

The role-avoidance strand of feminist thought on the housewife suggests that the concerns of the working wife should get priority over those of the housewife because the wife with a job outside the home works harder than the housewife. The housewife and her family should not get higher benefits than two-earner families who have contributed the same amount to the social security system. This line of thought leads to an advocacy of the abandonment of the 50% spouse benefit.

The role-avoidance theme is probably inconsistent with the proposal for untaxed homemaker credits, but not necessarily with any of the other forms of reform that have been mentioned. The role-avoidance strand of thought suggests that it may be detrimental to the long-run interests of women to make the housewife's position a great deal safer and more comfortable [than] it is now. However, none of the proposals for earnings sharing or a two-tier system would accomplish this in any significant degree and thus do not provoke feminist opposition.

Most informed feminists would probably choose one or another of these two programs of social security reform:

1. The sharing between spouses of earnings credits plus the elimination of the 50% spouse benefit

2. The same as 1 plus the provision of a substantial tier or deck of benefits unrelated to work history, with concomitant scaling back of benefit dollars awarded per dollar of earnings credit

The first program is more "antihousewife" than the second. While it would insure that housewives get a share of benefits earned by their spouses, it would mean that there would be less to share. The second plan makes the pension less dependent on work history, and so favors those with little or no work history—the housewife, par excellence.

Feminist thought on the housewife is not only a useful guide in organizing our thoughts about social security reform, it is indispensable if certain mistakes are to be avoided. The history of thought on social policy demonstrates that women and their concerns have tended to slip out of sight, even in cases where gender roles are central to the policy being debated. Where the women involved are housewives, the tendency to ignore them is apparently almost irresistible. An egregious example occurred in the debate on welfare reform. When social scientists approached this issue, they apparently forgot that most of the adult clients of the present system are women who stay home with their children—housewives or housewives manqué. This forgetfulness resulted in the concentration of research and thought on the issue of work incentives, with little attention to child-care issues. It also resulted in proposals to expand the number of clients to include anyone of low income, with little attention paid to ways of getting adequate resources to the existing clients of the program. Some of the leading thinkers on welfare reform have recently become interested in social security reform, and once again the problematic issues connected with the housewife are being ignored. . . .

Instead of keeping up with feminist thought, social scientists have been busy learning the anti-feminist "new home economics," which is for the most part a fatally oversimplified theory of the traditional form of family life. It is the passing away of this traditional form which is occasioning the need for the very reforms we are studying. A familiarity with feminist thought and attitudes is necessary at a minimum as a corrective to ingrained and unexamined sexist attitudes concerning issues which have gender roles at their core, as social security reform does. This does not mean that only women or only feminists are fit to deal with these issues. It does mean, however, that social scientists of both genders and all persuasions need to understand what the feminists are saying.

READING 28

Incremental Change in Social Security Needed to Result in Equal and Fair Treatment of Men and Women

Robert J. Myers

In continuing contemporary discussion of the treatment of men and women in various aspects of our social and economic life, one of the major topics is social security. This [essay] will examine that subject in depth: its basic nature, past developments, and various proposals.

Source: "Incremental Change in Social Security Needed to Result in Equal and Fair Treatment of Men and Women," by Robert J. Myers, in *A Challenge to Social Security: The Changing Roles of Women and Men in American Society* (pp. 235-245), edited by R. V. Burkhauser and K. C. Holden. New York: Academic Press, 1982. Reprinted by permission of the Institute for Research on Poverty, University of Wisconsin–Madison.

Nature of OASDI and Medicare

To judge whether or not the social security program provides equal treatment by sex, one must first understand the basic nature of the current program: Old-Age, Survivors, and Disability Insurance and *Medicare*. OASDI and the hospital-insurance portion of Medicare (HI) are social insurance programs, whereas the supplementary medical insurance portion of Medicare is subsidized voluntary insurance (and as such will not be considered further in this [essay]).

A social insurance program generally is a mix of individual equity and social adequacy, with more emphasis on the latter. Specifically, "individual equity" means that each participant receives protection actuarially equivalent to the contributions or premiums paid on his or her behalf. This does not necessarily involve, in all cases, an exact return of contributions, plus interest. On the other hand, "social adequacy" means that benefits are paid to meet presumptive needs, regardless of length and amount of contribution payments.

Frequently, individuals say that OASDI and HI are improperly structured, because they contain a mix of what they refer to as "insurance" and "welfare." By these phrases, they mean individual equity and social adequacy, although frequently they misuse "insurance" to mean a money-back plan. (Perhaps this view is prevalent among those in the academic community because of their familiarity with TIAA-CREF, which is a defined-contribution plan, a form not widely used throughout the private pension field.) They advocate splitting out the individual-equity and social-adequacy aspects, apparently for purposes of neatness, consistency, and public understanding. Yet most long-time students of social insurance believe that the best results can come from the skillful blending of these two elements into one system.

From the start of social security in 1935, different views have been expressed publicly on how to balance individual equity against social adequacy. Over the years, a gradual trend has occurred toward greater social adequacy and less individual equity. At times, however, this trend has been reversed, such as by the introduction of the delayed-retirement credit in 1972. Nonetheless, there are often general public pressures for instilling more individual equity, such as proposals to eliminate the retirement test and to eliminate the spouse benefit.

I believe that social security has the major role of providing a broad system of social benefits protecting against the long-term risks associated with old-age retirement, disability, and death of insured workers. Such benefits should provide a floor of economic security, with considerable emphasis on social adequacy. As such, the program will effect significant income redistribution (as does any insurance system, to a greater or lesser extent), but it should not be considered that this is its primary purpose—as some assert.

Accordingly, I believe that too much emphasis should not be laid on individual-equity considerations—i.e., on whether people exactly get "their money's worth." I am satisfied that there must be some consideration of individual equity. I believe that, as long as there is not too great a discrepancy between the amount an employee participant pays and the value of the protection furnished, the program is properly balanced.

History of Equal Treatment of Men and Women Under Social Security

There have, in the past, been a number of instances where different (unequal) treatment by sex was introduced by OASDI. Interestingly, the original 1935 act had completely equal treatment by sex, essentially because benefits were provided only for retired workers.

Beginning with the 1939 act, which introduced auxiliary and survivor benefits, the sexes were treated differently. Husbands and widowers were protected on the basis of the wife's earnings record *only* if dependency could be proved. Also, benefits to children were payable on behalf of women workers under much more restrictive conditions than were applied to male workers. Further, for a time, women had a lower minimum retirement age for reduced benefits and, for a much longer period, had more favorable conditions as to insured status and computation of retirement benefit amounts (because these were calculated for a shorter period of time—namely, the number of years after 1950, or age 21 if later, and up to age 62 rather than 65 as for men, although for both sexes earnings credits after age 61 could be utilized).

Over the years, owing to both legislative changes and court decisions, virtual equality of treatment of the sexes has now been achieved. The only exceptions are for relatively minor matters—such as that widows can waive payment of federal benefits based on military service before

1957 (so as to count such service under OASDI), but widowers cannot do so. Incidentally, the House version of the 1977 act provided complete equality of the sexes in all respects. However, this provision was dropped in conference, and instead a study by the Department of Health, Education, and Welfare was requested, which resulted in the report *Social Security and the Changing Roles of Men and Women*. . . .

Criticism of Present Treatment of Men and Women

A number of critics assert that the social security system unfairly discriminates against women. The very foundation for their belief is that the program was constructed almost half a century ago, at a time when the roles of men and women in our society were completely different from those that obtain at present. They seem to assume that no married women worked in the paid labor market in the mid-1930s whereas now (or certainly in the near future) the reverse is the case. This is not true, of course, although admittedly there has been a rapidly growing trend of employment of married women and of women reentering the paid labor force after their children have grown up or after widowhood. But this trend was anticipated by the original planners of the social security system, and the benefit structure was developed taking it into account.

Some people assert that, even though the benefit provisions might apply equally in all respects between men and women, equal treatment is still not present because women have both lower wages and more breaks in service, as a result of unfair discrimination in the marketplace. The solution to this problem should not be sought from OASDI. Rather, the remedies should come through altering the underlying causes. (Moreover, this argument has no validity when HI is considered, because all insured persons receive exactly the same benefit protection.)

Other people are concerned about what they believe to be the unfair treatment of two-worker families compared to one-worker families under OASDI. Any such unfairness is equally present when the one-worker family consists of a male worker and spouse or when it consists of a female worker and spouse, so there is no question of unequal treatment by sex. In this discussion, "worker" is used to refer only to workers in paid employment in the labor market outside the home.

As to relative treatment of one-worker and two-worker families, consider what the problem is stated to be by those who believe there is one. Usually, very simplistic assumptions are made, such as that the husband and wife are the same age and both retire at age 65 and that the one-worker family and the two-worker family have the same total combined earnings, but in the two-earner family the earnings are split equally. The total of the two primary benefits for the latter family is generally smaller than the primary benefit plus the spouse benefit for the former family. For example, for the cohort of persons attaining age 62 or becoming disabled or dying before age 62 in 1980, Average Indexed Monthly Earnings (AIME) of $1,000 produce a primary benefit of $432.60 in the early part of 1980, so that the combined primary and spouse benefit for both, retiring at age 65, is $648.90. In contrast, an AIME of $500 produces a primary benefit of $272.60, so that the total benefit for the two workers in a two-worker family is $545.20, or 16% less than the benefits for the one-worker family. Because both families paid the same amount of social security taxes, it is then argued that the two-worker family is treated unfairly.

The weaknesses of the argument are that it is based solely on the individual-equity principle and that the advantages accruing to the two-worker family are not considered. The argument for individual equity is faulty because in many other instances it can be shown that one person is not receiving as good an "actuarial" deal from OASDI as another. This is inevitable in a system that, desirably, is founded primarily on social-adequacy principles. If individual equity were the overriding aim of social security, there would be no need for a governmental program, because the private sector could just as readily handle it. Therefore, just because complete individual equity is not present in a particular situation is no reason why an injustice is present and why a change should be made. Moreover, I would argue that, although the one-worker family and two-worker family have the same total income, from an economic standpoint they are not really in equivalent positions. The one-worker family actually has a higher real income, because of the greater time at home of the "nonworker" spouse and the resulting increased productivity for home-consumption items (and thus the lessened need for expenditures). As a result, in keeping with the principle that benefits should be somewhat greater as earned income increases, there is no reason to be disturbed about the one-worker family versus the two-worker family.

Still further, it could be argued that the two-worker family with each having equal earnings is unduly advantaged as compared with a one-person, one-worker family with the same total earnings. Although both families contribute the same, the total benefits for the former are $545.20, or 26% more than the benefit of $432.60 for the latter. Once again, this absence of individual equity is nothing to be disturbed about!

But is the two-worker family in any sense receiving less than its fair share? The two-worker family in fact receives more insurance protection for its "investment" than does the one-worker two-person family with an equal income. If one worker in such a family retires before the other, then benefits will be paid to that worker. On the other hand, in the one-worker family, no benefits are payable to the nonworker unless the worker retires. Also, child survivor benefits are payable in the event of the death of *either* spouse in a two-worker family, but only on the death of one spouse (the worker) in the one-worker family. Further, prior to retirement, both spouses in the two-worker family have disability insurance, whereas in the one-worker family only the working spouse does.

Finally, I think that an important social principle requires that a nonworking spouse who is taking care of the home and raising the children have an OASDI benefit. Then, if such a spouse also has a benefit based on earnings outside the home, it is only fair that the larger of the two available bene-

fits should be paid—without consideration of the taxes that were or were not paid.

Proposed Solutions and Their Weaknesses

Several proposals have been made . . . to remedy what are believed to be either the unequal or inequitable treatment of women under OASDI. Little discussion has been given to the similar situation under HI, but this too should be considered.

Those who believe that gross inequities are involved recommend what might be called sweeping structural changes. There are three general types of such proposals—earnings-sharing credits, wage credits for homemakers, and the "double-decker" approach. All of these proposals would, to one extent or another, provide social-benefit protection for the "nonworking" wife (or full-time homemaker), but so too does the present spouse benefit. Which approach is best depends upon many factors, some objective and some subjective. Among these factors are cost, administrative feasibility, public understanding, and (very important) the problems involved in any transition required from the existing provisions.

Before discussing each of these proposals in turn, I want to clear up one matter. It is frequently argued that it is degrading for persons who have made a life career as a homemaker to receive OASDI and HI benefits on the basis of dependency. As I see it, a straw-person has been set up by terming these auxiliary benefits as "dependent benefits." The law does not contain (and never has contained) the designation of these auxiliary benefits as "dependent benefits." Nor, for that matter, has there ever been any dependency requirement for wives and widows. The various types of spouse benefits are now payable as a right on the basis of legal status (although 10 years of marriage is required for divorced spouses); they are not based on proof of dependency.

Now consider the proposals which have been made to solve what is said to be the inequitable treatment of two-worker families compared to one-worker families. These proposals have usually been quite simplistic. They have not considered all the complex situations that can arise, including not only those mentioned previously but also termination of the marriage through divorce or death. Separation, too, can cause serious problems under these proposals.

Usually involved are either equally splitting the combined earnings records of the couple (earnings sharing) or providing wage credits for homemakers. The earnings-sharing approach, even though superficially attractive, would create other anomalies and inequities. If all benefit rights, both accrued and expected, were preserved for present participants, the costs involved would be very high. If such rights are not preserved, there would be grave, divisive political and social problems. Furthermore, regardless of how an earnings-sharing plan was instituted and phased in, there would be tremendous administrative problems and difficulties in explaining the program to the public (in a system which is already having troubles with public relations).

The earnings-sharing proposals would result in giving higher benefits to two-worker families by *reducing* the benefits for one-worker families. In some ways, this could be viewed as taking benefits away from men to give them to women. However, in actuality, what is involved is taking benefits away from certain women (traditional homemakers) and giving them to other women (married women working in the paid labor market).

Some might say that such a result would be good, while others would say that this would be bad. In my opinion, if one group is to be favored over another (but not to an unfairly great extent), it should be the traditional homemaker, because otherwise we *may* be endangering the familial structure of the nation and its future development. And, once again, I question whether we should care so much about apparent individual equity in a social-insurance program that we create divisive situations of benefit losses. I strongly believe that any resulting gain in individual equity is not worth the loss, especially a loss bound to shake the public's confidence in the viability and integrity of the system. If the OASDI system had just now been initiated, it might have been possible to develop a satisfactory earnings-sharing~ plan. However, with OASDI having been in operation for over 40 years, it just is "not possible to get from here to there!"

Some have said that earnings sharing would eliminate the alleged demeaning nature of the present program. I fail to see any difference in this respect between getting *earnings credits* from a spouse's earnings record and getting *benefit rights* from a spouse's earnings record. Some might point out that, in the case of divorces, the earnings credits would always be available under earnings sharing, but that benefit rights would not be if the marriages lasted less than 10 years. The answer to this, essentially, is that such a requirement should be reduced to 5 years (the House version of the 1977 amendments). The absence of deferred-benefit rights for very short marriages broken by divorce does not seem vital, because the individuals involved will almost certainly obtain OASDI benefit rights in other ways.

Concern has also been expressed over the unfair treatment of homemakers under OASDI. It has been argued that homemakers should receive earnings credits for their home work which reflects the value of the services they render, because the present basis of OASDI benefits as "dependents" is degrading. Although this proposal has considerable appeal, it involves insurmountable problems of administration and/or costs. If it is offered on a voluntary basis, few will elect it—and those who do so will be the high-cost cases (i.e., women who are near retirement age or who have eligible children and are in very poor health). If it is on a compulsory contributory basis, great difficulties will arise in devising an equitable method of determining the earnings to be attributed—and then also in collecting the applicable taxes, which could be heavy financial burdens for many families. If a homemaker-credit plan is on a compulsory noncontributory basis, with the credits financed from the general treasury, a large cost is involved.

Another proposal intended to solve the alleged discrimination of OASDI against women is the so-called double-decker approach. This is by no means new, having been discussed first some 40 years ago. A flat benefit would be paid to all persons who are eligible by reason of age or other demographic condition, to be financed from general revenues. The second deck would provide wage-related benefits, financed by payroll taxes.

Although there is a certain appeal to this approach, I do not favor it. Under some circumstances, the benefit level of the first deck could become too high, and thus too costly, because of the absence of fiscal constraints (such as are inherent in earmarked, highly visible payroll-tax financing). Under other circumstances, there might be pressures to make the first deck subject to a needs test, which would be undesirable because it would discourage private savings and private pension plans.

Solutions Through Incremental Change

Despite the foregoing discussion, I believe that certain changes should be made to alleviate the problems of homemakers under OASDI. These involve such matters as the distribution of OASDI benefits between spouses, more consistent and equitable treatment with regard to termination of benefits because of marriage or remarriage, and computing average earnings by taking into account child-care years.

At present, a retired worker and a spouse who has not worked in the paid labor market can receive, at their choice, either a combined benefit check or two separate ones. In the latter case, the amounts of the checks will not be equal, being larger for the retired worker than for the spouse. I propose that, when spouses are living together, the total family benefit amount should be divided equally between them. This would apply in all cases of retirement benefits when an auxiliary spouse benefit is payable, including those cases in which both spouses are eligible for benefits on their own earnings and those in which children's benefits are payable. There would, of course, be no cost effect on OASDI.

At present the marriage (or remarriage) of a beneficiary can in some instances terminate benefits. Marriage after age 60 is not a terminating event, and neither is marriage between two survivor beneficiaries. However, when a survivor beneficiary under age 60 marries a retired worker, the survivor benefit terminates, and any subsequent benefit eligibility is based on the benefit of the new spouse as long as that spouse is living. Also, when a young survivor beneficiary (with eligible child or children) marries any person (other than certain categories of beneficiaries), her or his benefit rights end. Considering that, currently, there are widely different ethical and moral views about living together without benefit of marriage; it is unfair to penalize those who hold to tradition. Accordingly, both marriage and remarriage should be eliminated as causes of termination of benefit rights. Such a change would have a favorable effect for others beside homemakers (e.g., child student beneficiaries). There would be the continuing cost control for OASDI in that individuals can, in essence, draw only the largest of any benefits to which they are entitled, so that overlapping of benefits will not occur.

Also, as mentioned previously, the duration-of-marriage requirement for a divorced spouse to be eligible for benefits on the earnings record of the insured worker should be reduced from 10 years to 5 years.

Persons who do not engage in paid gainful work while caring for their young children can be at a disadvantage under the present benefit-computation~ methods. This is so because the average earnings used in the calculations are determined over a long period. This period should be shortened somewhat by allowing "child-care drop-out years"—years to be skipped in making the calculation—for periods during which the individual takes full care of a preschool child at home or a child under age 16 in school. The number of child-care drop-out years should be limited to, say, 20 years. Thus, over the long run, the average earnings for retirement cases would be computed over not less than 15 years (and not more than 35 years, as at present).

A problem in connection with child-care drop-out years is how to define such years so that the provision can be properly administered and well understood by the public. It may perhaps be the case that, although the principle is good, it is not operable. In lieu thereof—but only partially solving the problem—the period for computing the AIME could be shortened somewhat (say, for retirement benefits, from 35 years ultimately to 25 or 30 years).

Provisions for child-care drop-out years are contained, to a limited extent, in P.L. 96-265, enacted on June 9, 1980 (which deals with changes in the DI program). This law *reduces* the normal drop-out years for computing the Primary Insurance Amount for disabled-worker cases from the previous uniform 5 years to less than this for persons disabled in the year in which age 46 is attained or in an earlier year (e.g., 4 years for ages 42-46, 3 years for ages 37-41, 2 years for ages 32-36, 1 year for ages 27-31, and none for ages 26 and under). Child-care years with respect to children under age 3 can be used to "build up" the drop-out years to a maximum of 3 years (i.e., this is applicable only to those disabled at ages 36 and under). A child-care year is defined as one in which a child under age 3 was living in the same household as the individual substantially throughout the entire year, during which time the individual did not engage in *any* outside employment.

Persons who are widowed before age 60 will probably be at a disadvantage, because the indexing of the deceased spouse's pension in the deferred period (from age at widowhood to age 60) is now by prices, rather than by wages. This could be remedied by indexing the deceased worker's earnings record by wages up to the earlier of (a) when the worker would have attained age 60; or (b) when the survivor beneficiary attains age 58. This will produce a larger widow's or widower's benefit and is quite logical. (Under the present unusual economic conditions, a larger benefit would not result—but it is to be hoped that such conditions will not prevail over the long run.)

If it is felt imperative to solve the putative "equity" problem between one-worker and two-worker families, the best approach is to provide an *additional* "working-spouse" benefit for the spouse who has the smaller primary benefit. This benefit would be 25% of the smaller of (a) the spouse's own primary benefit, or (b) the benefit coming from the other spouse's earnings record. This provision was contained in the Republican alternative bill put forth when the House of Representatives was considering the 1977 amendments. The principal drawback is that it involves substantial additional cost—an estimated long-range cost of approximately 0.8% of taxable payroll.

Conclusion

I have a moderate philosophy of social security. I hold that the existing program—and especially its scope and level of benefits—is more or less proper and adequate. In contrast, holders of an expansionist philosophy feel that the benefit level particularly should be increased significantly, so as to provide for the full economic needs of covered workers. The other extreme, the contractionist or laissez-faire proponents, oppose governmental social insurance and support only a limited public assistance program. They feel that individuals should provide for their own economic security through the private sector (or at least have the opportunity of opting out of social security and using this alternative).

I believe that a moderate social security program is not just desirable, it is essential. Such a program must meet presumed social needs and therefore must be primarily based on principles of social adequacy rather than individual equity. This is the kind of social security program we now have.

There is no need for radical changes in the structure of the program to solve existing problems. In fact, many things which are seen as problems by some individuals are not really problems at all.

I realize that, in intellectual circles, the defense of the status quo is often assailed on the grounds that change is always desirable and that criticism is always constructive. However, change is not always necessarily beneficial, and even when it may be beneficial in some ways, the net effect produced may be harmful. Further, although those advocating radical change in the structure of social security may see the system's problems as serious, I believe the "solutions" examined [by some] would, on balance, be damaging to our whole social security system. Who can say that the repudiation of the Ten Commandments, which have borne the test of time, would be desirable for the sake of change?

FOCUS ON PRACTICE   INVESTMENT DECISIONS FOR
RETIREMENT INCOME

"Investing for retirement? Oh that's so far off! I've got more important things to worry about right now." Does that statement sound familiar? If you're young, it may sum up your sentiments about investing for retirement. If you're a bit older, you might have different thoughts that are no more realistic: "Investing for retirement? Oh, I'm already in a pension plan, and besides I'm covered by Social Security."

Ignoring the problem of retirement income because it's far off or assuming it's already "taken care of" are both unwise. For one thing, the proportion of American workers covered by employer-paid pension plans has not been growing in recent years. As more and more employees who have pensions are under defined-contribution plans, retirement income becomes less predictable and individuals need to plan more carefully.

In short, when it comes to pension coverage, more and more workers are on their own. In the early years of the 21st century, the shift is away from "someone else" taking care of retirement planning toward individuals making more investment decisions on their own.

As for Social Security, we know that a large proportion of younger Americans lack confidence in its future. Even if their pessimism is mistaken, Social Security was never intended to cover more than a portion of retirement income. Social Security benefits and private pensions, taken together, constitute an important part of the assets of older people. For three-quarters of men in their 60s, retirement income wealth represented by Social Security and pensions was greater than all other wealth, including even home equity (Quinn, 1985). Decisions about retirement—such as assigning pension survivor rights and choosing whether to accept an early retirement offer—are some of the most important financial decisions a person will make over the course of life.

If we take account of all these factors, the conclusion is conveyed by the title of a book by Robert Butler and Kenzo Kiikuni: *Who Is Responsible for My Old Age?* (1992). The answer is "I am responsible," and retirement in the future will require more careful financial planning than in the past.

A key idea for investment planning is to invest with a life course perspective in mind, that is, to think about age and tolerance for risk. Psychological studies tell us that people tend to become more risk averse as they grow older. Some risk aversiveness is quite rational. With advancing age, the bad consequences for risky behavior become more severe. If you have a skiing accident, it takes longer for bones to heal; if you're widowed or divorced, the odds on remarriage become worse; and if you make a bad investment, it's more difficult to recover.

What does risk aversiveness suggest about investing for retirement? One response might be to shift savings away from more volatile and risky assets—such as the stock market—in favor of safe, fixed-income investments, such as savings accounts, certificates of deposit, or U.S. Treasury bills.

But is that advice practical? Someone retiring at 60 years of age may have a life expectancy of 20 or 25 more years. Would a nest egg of $600,000 at age 62 be enough to last 20 or 25 years? Suppose you put the nest egg in "safe" investments (Treasury bills or corporate bonds), paying a historical yield of 5.5%—or $33,000 a year. If you decide you need a total family income of $50,000, why not just take the interest and withdraw an additional $17,000 a year from savings? Taking $17,000 over 25 years would still leave a big cushion of $175,000 in principal, wouldn't it? And you would have the advantage of safety for the principal.

Actually, this example shows the difficulty of retirement planning. To begin with, each time you withdrew money from the principal, there would be less money left to generate interest. The $33,000 yield would get smaller each year as the principal shrank. Second, the original calculation failed to take account of inflation. At a 3.14% inflation rate, the historical average for inflation, the original $600,000, would, in real dollars, be completely gone in only 14 years if you took out the $17,000 supplement each year. In other words, if you retired at age 62, you'd be completely broke by age 76.

Another problem is the rate of return on this "safe" investment. One mistake people make nearing retirement is to put too much into safe investments, neglecting the likelihood that they will live 20 or 25 years. A better strategy is to invest for both current income and capital gains. Fixed-income investments are part of a strategy, but they should not dominate the portfolio. Let's look at the $600,000 nest egg again, this time assuming that it is invested in a mixed stock and bond portfolio generating a pretax yield of 7.5%. Here's how much you could withdraw from the portfolio each year (again, assuming a 3.14% annual inflation rate):

If you withdraw	Your money will last
$30,000	40+ years
$40,000	23.7 years
$50,000	16.7 years
$60,000	12.9 years

But doesn't investing in the stock market involve too much risk for someone who is nearing retirement? In any given year, there may be more risk. But over a period of decades, risk goes down because volatility—the ups and downs of the stock market—tends to be absorbed by overall average gains. Historically, stocks have returned gains of around 10% since the year 1920. Of course, that historical average must take account of huge drops, like the market downturn after 1929 or the 1973-1974 slump. But all things considered, it might make more sense to accept a higher degree of short-term risk to gain more inflation protection over the long run.

The point of this exercise is to underscore a simple point. There are several different kinds of risk: risk of losing principal, risk of inflation, risk of not being able to convert an asset into cash when needed. There is no way to avoid all types of risk in investing. The only question is how much risk a person is willing to take for some investment objective. To make reasonable investment decisions about risk, you need to consider many factors, and age is certainly one of them.

In addition to overestimating how much money they will receive from a pension and Social Security, most people underestimate retirement expenses. Because people are living longer, they may end up spending as many years in retirement as they did working. Because many people are having children later in life, they may be putting their children through college while simultaneously caring for their aging parents. The amount of money needed for retirement must take into consideration current expenses, future living expenses, life expectancy, taxes, and inflation.

Financial advisers generally recommend that people of all ages should make stocks some part of an investment program. They also recommend diversifying an investment portfolio and investing on a regular basis to soften the impact of market price swings. One favored approach is dollar cost averaging, where the same dollar amount is invested each month, regardless of whether stock prices are high or low. Another way to reduce risk is asset allocation, which splits investments among stocks, bonds, and fixed rate investments, taking account of age and other factors.

Students of financial gerontology remind us that decisions about saving for retirement are influenced by a variety of factors. Some economists have favored a **life cycle model of savings,** which predicts that people in their 40s will begin to put more money into savings as retirement looms on the horizon. But savings and investment also depend on cohort characteristics and the historical period or economic environment, not to mention individual variations in attitudes toward planning for the future. As people take on more responsibility for their own retirement investment decisions, the practical need for better planning will become greater in years to come.

FOCUS ON THE FUTURE   TWO SCENARIOS FOR THE
FUTURE OF SOCIAL SECURITY

Scenario 1: Trouble ahead. The year now is 2021 and the oldest of the baby boomers are now in their mid-70s. But the world isn't at all what most of them expected to find in old age.

Looking back, it's easy to see signs of today's problems. First came the Medicare shortfall in 2004, then Medicare was merged with Medicaid three years later. Today, health care costs consume 20% of the gross national product, but still there are millions with Alzheimer's disease or kept alive in a persistent vegetative state. Of course, the worst shock was the stock market collapse in 2012 brought on when baby boomers started cashing in their mutual funds. The Dow Jones Industrial Average went from a high of 30,000 down to 9,000, where it's been ever since. Most people lost their Social Security savings in the stock market crash.

After the great Baby Boomers Social Security March on Washington, Vice President Chelsea Clinton was appointed to head a special commission to restore solvency to the system. Drastic cuts were enacted, but no one's very happy with the result. Most everyone nowadays stays in the labor force until age 70 in order to receive full benefits, but lots of people in their mid-70s are also desperately trying to work again, part-time, because cost-of-living increases have been frozen for the next five years. Middle-aged adults have mixed feelings about the Social Security crisis. They never expected to collect benefits in the first place, but their taxes are too high, and now they're in no position to support their elderly parents as new laws require them to do.

The economy has been in a shambles since the Great Flooding began. For the past two decades, ocean levels have been steadily rising as a result of global warming. More recently, the collapse of the Ross Ice Shelf in Antarctica led to abandonment of the World Trade Center in Manhattan and to the resettling of the population in what used to be the Netherlands. These events have plunged industrialized countries into the worst depression in the 21st century, so people have other things to worry about besides Social Security. Older people will just have to look out for themselves.

Scenario 2: The best is yet to be. It's funny to look back now, in the year 2021, on all those gloomy predictions that were so common just after the turn of the century. People at that time were actually afraid of the coming of an aging society.

It's true, we had some close calls, but everyone learned as a result. After near collapse in 2004, Medicare was finally put on a sound footing. Through a combination of outcomes research and health promotion under managed care, costs to the system were cut and larger numbers were served. By the year 2010, Social Security was again bringing in surpluses because of the booming stock market and investment of part of the Trust Fund in index funds. The Dow is now at 30,000 and still climbing.

Another big factor was the swelling number of job holders, including hard-working immigrants from Asia and Latin America and growing numbers of black college graduates. People today also routinely work past 70, usually at new jobs for which they've been retrained, some of them working from home over the Internet. Almost as many people in their 50s and 60s are in college today as young people, so lots of people are having second or third careers.

Looking back at the gloom after the turn of the century, you can't help but be reminded of similar fears during the late 1970s about running out of oil and natural resources. Sometimes the things we fear the most don't turn out that way at all.

QUESTIONS FOR WRITING, REFLECTION, AND DEBATE

1 What are the key differences between the American population now and the U.S. population in 1935, when Social Security was first introduced? Should these differences prompt changes in the Social Security system for the future?

2 Define at least three different interpretations that can be given to what it might mean to "privatize" Social Security. Give a reason for and a reason against each of these three different ideas of privatizing.

3 If a substantial part of the Social Security Trust Fund were invested in the stock market, what are some reasons why this plan might make people more confident in the future of Social Security? What are some reasons why this plan might make people less confident in the future?

4 Critics of Social Security argue that the program does not adequately help the least advantaged elderly. Some have urged a means test to be sure that Social Security goes to those who are poorest. Imagine that you are a staff assistant to the U.S. Commissioner on Social Security and have been asked to prepare a memorandum on this issue. Examine the evidence for, or against, this proposal for means testing.

5 Those who believe that it is wrong to have a large surplus in the Social Security Trust Fund say they are unhappy with the fact that money in the trust fund is invested in Treasury certificates. In that respect, they say, the surplus simply funds the federal budget deficit. Is this claim correct? If the funds were invested in the stock market, what might be the positive, and the negative, results of that move?

6 Imagine that you are chair of the United Taxpayers Association of America and that your organization is about to take a position in favor of changing the payroll tax rate for Social Security. Prepare a draft version of the position paper you will urge to your membership to adopt. Outline in detail the reasons why you think it is in the interest of taxpayers to change the payroll tax.

7 One proposal to make Social Security more fair to women is to give credit for the work mothers and housewives do at home. Is this proposal fair to women who work outside the home?

8 Imagine that you are president of the local chapter of the National Association of Women. Prepare a detailed statement as the basis for a public petition campaign aiming to make Social Security more fair to women. Highlight the key arguments to be used to convince the public to sign the petition.

SUGGESTED READINGS

Achenbaum, W. Andrew, *Social Security: Visions and Revisions,* Cambridge, UK: Cambridge University Press, 1986.

Kingson, Eric, and Schulz, James (eds.), *Social Security in the 21st Century,* New York: Oxford University Press, 1997.

Kohler, Peter A., et al. (eds.), *The Evolution of Social Insurance,* New York: Cambridge University Press, 1986.

Myers, Robert J., *Social Security* (3rd ed.), Homewood, IL: Richard D. Irwin, 1985.

U.S. Department of Health and Social Services, *Social Security Handbook,* Washington, DC: Author, 1988.

Is Retirement Obsolete?

The 20th century could well be called the age of retirement. Never before in history has retirement in old age become such a widespread, almost universal pattern of behavior. As recently as 1950, the average retirement age was 67, by 1980 it had gone down to 63, and by the 1990s it declined further to around 60. In all industrialized countries since World War II, there has been a consistent decline in labor force participation with advancing age. But does this trend toward retirement represent progress or is it a sign of problems to come (Schnore, 1985)? Will the 21st century continue the prevailing pattern or has retirement become obsolete?

For society, the steady decline in labor force participation represents a loss of productivity by older people—who, on average, are now living longer, are better educated, and are in better health than ever before. Individuals who withdraw from the workforce often face many years without any clearly defined purpose in society (Sheppard, 1990). As the cost of Social Security and private pensions continues to rise, it is understandable that people are asking whether retirement makes sense.

But if we ask, "Is retirement obsolete?" we are actually asking two different questions. First is the question of whether retirement is a wise choice for a specific individual—for example, a person who is considering taking early retirement, which is an option to retire before some conventional age for retirement. Second is the question of whether the systematic practice of retirement in our society is good policy; that is, does it make sense for the economy or the good of society as a whole (Blau, 1985)?

Retirement, as Rosow (1967) observed, means entering a "roleless role." It signifies the withdrawal of individuals from work during the later period of life. Whether a person reduces his or her workload gradually or stops working abruptly, retirement often leads to new options in later life: leisure pursuits, voluntary action, part-time employment, a second career. Typically, retirement is accompanied by reliance on pension income instead of salary as the primary means of support. In the previous discussion of investment and preretirement planning, we stressed the importance of individual decision making.

But emphasis on individual planning fails to take into account an important point: People have a personal choice about retiring only if they can count on enough income to support themselves without working. Someone who wins the lottery might have that choice at a younger age, but for most people retirement is not an option until much later in life. Middle-aged or older workers can choose to retire only if there is a social or institutional policy supporting the choice by paying them to no longer be in the workforce. In that respect, retirement remains very much an issue for public policy debate (Munnell, 1991).

As we saw in debates about the future of Social Security, critics have raised questions about whether, in the 21st century, we as a society can or ought to maintain retirement as it has been known in the past (Clark, 1988). That questioning has already resulted in some important changes. For example, in 1986 the common practice of mandatory retirement was abolished by law.

Today, people tend to take retirement for granted and assume it is a natural and appropriate pattern for later life. But in fact retirement as a social practice or institution is historically quite recent. We need to understand the origins of retirement as an institution and to better appreciate how work and retirement are now being transformed by changes in the U.S. economy. Instead of taking for granted retirement as a natural phase of life, we need to consider current trends that will determine what work and retirement mean in the 21st century.

History of Retirement

Widespread retirement by workers became possible only after the industrial revolution of the 19th century. It was Prussian Chancellor Otto von Bismarck who first introduced age 65 as the basis for a pension. By the early 20th century, many European countries began to institutionalize retirement through government pension systems. The United States followed with Social Security in 1935, a development that made leaving the labor force much more attractive to people. In 1890, 68% of men over age 65 were in the labor force. But that number dropped to 54% in 1930. In 1950, after improvements in Social Security, the number of men in the labor force dropped further to 46% and has continued to decline to under 17% in 1989. Exhibit 30 shows the major trends over the past 45 years.

Several points are clear from the data. First, beyond age 65, the overwhelming majority of both men and women are retired from work, although a small minority continues in the labor force. Second, among older men, the trend has clearly been away from work and toward retirement, and the decline in labor force participation applies equally to men in their 50s. Early retirement has become a major phenomenon in its own right (Dworaczek and Wong, 1989). Third, for women over age 65, labor force participation has not changed much in recent years. In fact, women in the 55-64 age

Exhibit 30. Labor Force Participation Rates for Older Men and Women, by Age: 1950-1995 (annual averages)

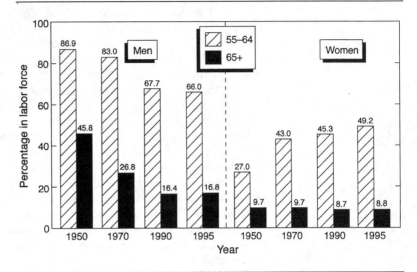

SOURCE: 1950 and 1970 data: U.S. Department of Labor (1985); 1990 and 1995 data: U.S. Department of Labor (1996).

bracket have counteracted the male trend in that they have joined the work force in larger numbers. The earlier discussion of gender and aging illuminates some reasons for these contrasting trends. Older men tend to have earned higher pension and Social Security benefits, but older women must face a longer life span with lower average income expectations.

Some insight into these trends comes from one of the first major longitudinal studies of work and retirement, the Cornell Study of Occupational Retirement, which was carried out between 1952 and 1962 (Streib and Schneider, 1971). That study helped challenge previously accepted but mistaken beliefs, such as the idea that retirement has a negative effect on people's health or that it causes feelings of worthlessness. The Cornell study found no evidence for the idea that retirement causes ill health, yet that idea continues to persist (Ekerdt, 1987). The study did document a drop in income upon retirement, but a large majority of retirees still reported that their income was sufficient, and a quarter even felt their standard of living was better than earlier. Overall, the Cornell study showed that retirement is not a negative event for most people, and subsequent studies have confirmed its main findings (Palmore et al., 1985; Parnes et al., 1985). These results help explain the trend toward earlier retirement. Older people retire for many different reasons, but we should not overlook the growing appeal of leisure as a desirable option.

Origins of Late-Life Leisure

Retirement has come to mean an expansion of leisure time, most of it during the retirement years. Futurist Graham Molitor, of Public Policy Forecasting, estimates that by 2030 more than half of an American's waking hours over a lifetime will be spent in leisure, in contrast to 41% today. But leisure can be defined in different ways. Leisure can be viewed not merely in a negative sense as time away from work but as free time perceived in a positive sense and containing opportunities for recreation, relaxation, personal development, and service to others (Kaplan, 1979).

Retirement as a time of leisure is only feasible with a certain degree of wealth. From a historical standpoint, widespread retirement first became possible when the industrial economy was productive enough to support sizable numbers of nonworking adults. At the same time, the economy no longer needed so many workers in the labor force and companies believed that older workers were not as quick or as productive as the young. Governments, corporations, labor unions, and older workers themselves found retirement to be a desirable policy, and it soon became the normal practice (Graebner, 1980).

Since 1900, the average life expectancy for Americans has risen from around 47 years to 76 years. With longer lives, people have spent increased time in education, work, and retirement. But when we look at the different uses of time over the life course during the 20th century, the most significant trend has been the growth in the amount of leisure time. Exhibit 31 shows how time use has changed in the 20th century.

The figures in Exhibit 31 show that, although life expectancy has increased by over 50% since 1900, the period spent in retirement has increased even more dramatically. Work now accounts for a smaller percentage of a man's life than it did in the year 1900. By contrast, for women, the big change has been a substantial increase in the number of years spent in the paid workforce. But for both men and women, years in retirement constitute a larger and growing portion of life.

How did this pattern come to be? Free time, along with higher wages, was always a potential by-product of industrialization and economic progress. Trade-offs always exist: free time versus higher wages. From 1900 until the 1930s, the workweek and the workday gradually became shorter across the industrialized world. Subsequently, free time has also increased, but not through a reduction of the workweek. Instead, free time has taken different forms over the life cycle: increased vacation time, later entry into the workforce for the young, and earlier retirement for the old (Hunnicutt, 1982).

In the 1920s, there was a "shorter hours movement," which remains an unexplored chapter in liberal reform movements of this century. It was followed by a "share-the-work" plan during the Depression. Reformers favored shorter working hours and more leisure as a vehicle for self-development. This goal of self-development had much in common with ideas that would later be advocated by writers such as Fred Best, Willard Wirtz, Gosta Rehn,

Exhibit 31. Life Cycle Distribution of Education, Labor Force Participation, Retirement, and Work in the Home: 1900-1980

	Year					
Subject	*1900*	*1940*	*1950*	*1960*	*1970*	*1980*
Number of years spent in activity						
Men						
Average life expectancy	46.3	60.8	65.6	66.6	67.1	70.0
Retirement/work at home	1.2	9.1	10.1	10.2	12.1	13.6
Labor force participation	32.1	38.1	41.5	41.1	37.8	38.8
Education	8.0	8.6	9.0	10.3	12.2	12.6
Preschool	5.0	5.0	5.0	5.0	5.0	5.0
Women						
Average life expectancy	48.3	65.2	71.1	73.1	74.7	77.4
Retirement/work at home	29.0	39.4	41.4	37.1	35.3	30.6
Labor force participation	6.3	12.1	15.1	20.1	22.3	29.4
Education	8.0	8.7	9.6	10.9	12.1	12.4
Preschool	5.0	5.0	5.0	5.0	5.0	5.0
Percentage distribution by activity type						
Men						
Average life expectancy	100%	100	100	100	100	100% of life
Retirement/work at home	3	15	15	15	18	19
Labor force participation	69	63	63	62	56	55
Education	17	14	14	15	18	18
Preschool	11	8	8	8	7	8
Women						
Average life expectancy	100%	100	100	100	100	100% of life
Retirement/work at home	60	60	58	51	47	40
Labor force participation	13	19	21	27	30	38
Education	17	13	14	15	16	16
Preschool	10	8	7	7	7	6

SOURCE: U.S. Bureau of the Census (1984; median years of school for persons 25 years or older, 1940-1980); Best (1981, p. 8; 1900 estimates of median years of school for persons 25 years or older); National Center for Health Statistics (1990; life expectancy data); U.S. Department of Labor (1986).

NOTE: Data may not add to 100% due to rounding.

and Max Kaplan, who have advocated more flexible boundaries between work and leisure. When we ask, "Does retirement, as it currently exists, make sense?" we are asking whether a flexible and humanistic goal of self-development is still a possibility.

In the past, economic forces quickly foreclosed any debate on that question. U.S. business leaders during the 1920s saw a combined threat to economic prosperity from overproduction and expanding leisure time. They feared that consumer markets were becoming oversaturated and that workers would demand more free time rather than continuing to work. Declining working hours along with declining production spelled lower profits and slower economic growth. Against this view were the "optimists," who argued that consumption demand could be driven higher, primarily through advertising and marketing techniques to stimulate new purchasing power.

In fact, it was the consumer view that triumphed, as the emergence of the affluent society after World War II came to testify. But the consumer society of rising demand and stable working hours was also supported by actions of the government. The stimulus for government action was, of course, the Great Depression. With the New Deal and World War II, the U.S. government took on new responsibility for managing the economy to moderate the business cycle and ensure aggregate consumer demand.

The passage of the Social Security Act, and later the spread of private pensions, ratified the practice of a fixed retirement age, typically age 65. Public policy promoted the idea of displacing leisure into later life and enlarging the period of education in early life, presumably as preparation for work. Purchasing power for goods and services would be maintained during retirement by transfer payments—Social Security—disbursed in such a fashion as to keep older people out of the labor market. Work would increasingly be compressed into the middle period of life.

With the establishment of a standard 40-hour week by 1945, the movement toward a shorter workweek lost popularity. Productivity gains were channeled into higher wages and fringe benefits; gains in free time became converted into longer vacations and, above all, earlier retirement. The amount of free time available in old age increased by about five years during the 20th century, chiefly from gains in life expectancy but also from earlier retirement.

The spread of leisure in retirement is related to a debate about Social Security, namely, the earnings test for people collecting benefits. Social Security's function was always in part to remove older workers from the labor market, and the earnings limitation has indeed had this effect (Honig and Reimers, 1989). Because Social Security has always intended to remove people from the labor force, some suggest that retirement is forced on people and therefore not really leisure (Hunnicutt, 1982). This view reflects a debatable assumption that work is desirable and meaningful for the majority of people. But in fact just the opposite seems true (Terkel, 1985). Most people are eager to leave their jobs and, contrary to popular stereotype, retirement is not dangerous to one's health. Except for displaced workers or elite groups who leave their jobs reluctantly, people generally prefer to retire rather than continue working at jobs that are unsatisfying (Boaz, 1987). What is problematic about retirement is not that work is always better but that the abundance of free time in late life is not adequately structured for any larger social purpose or meaning.

Overall, most people applaud the fact that the amount of time devoted to leisure has increased in this century through reductions in the workweek, longer vacations, and early retirement. But a few dark clouds lurk on this pleasant horizon.

First is a phenomenon sometimes described as "the overworked American." More and more married women have entered the labor force, and more workers are taking on second jobs to maintain their standard of living (Schor, 1991). One result is that people have less time for volunteer activities or adequate leisure during their middle years.

Second, since the late 1980s the proportion of workers covered by pension plans has stalled at about half the workforce. If half of all workers lack pension coverage, future cohorts of older Americans may not be able to enjoy early retirement at levels comparable to those today (McGoldrick and Copper, 1989).

Third, there are concerns about the base of economic productivity that supports a sizable old-age population devoted to leisure pursuits (Kleiler, 1978). These concerns range from future financing for Social Security to international economic competitiveness and the quality of the present and future workforce.

Changes in the American Economy

The U.S. economy is in the midst of far-reaching changes that will affect retirement in the future. A new postindustrial economy shaped by information technology and global competition has reshaped American society. Large corporations routinely engage in downsizing, that is, letting go of employees through layoffs and early retirement incentive programs. Employers have encouraged early retirement as a way of restructuring the labor forces in favor of younger, less costly, and technologically more sophisticated workers. By the year 2000, blue chip corporations such as IBM, General Motors, and Sears had drastically cut their workforces.

Increasingly, large companies can no longer guarantee employment or a predictable work life based on the patterns of the past. Smaller companies are even less secure employers because of the new competitive environment. This loss of security and predictability in the labor market has severe consequences for older workers. In the first place, older workers face a leveling off earlier in their careers as they compete for a diminishing number of good jobs (Morgan, 1981). When companies downsize and eliminate middle-management positions, older workers easily find themselves pushed aside. Many opt for early retirement rather than face unemployment.

For the organization, corporate downsizing often means a loss of older employees' experience and skills. Ironically, companies that try to decrease operating costs by pressuring older workers to retire have already begun finding themselves with unexpected skill gaps. The U.S. Conference Board, a major industry organization, reported that few companies have age-conscious downsizing policies. On the other hand, some enlightened companies, such as Travelers Insurance Company of Hartford, Connecticut, have developed ways of using older workers by arrangements such as consulting, job sharing, flex time, and temporary work (Estabrook, 1993).

For individuals, early retirement is not necessarily good or bad. A "push-and-pull" factor usually prompts the decision (Williamson, Rinehart, and Blank, 1992). The trend toward early retirement continues for many reasons. Health status, perceived retirement income, financial plans of one's spouse, peer-group pressure to retire, the psychological attractiveness of the workplace, and strength of family ties are among the most important factors that influence the decision to retire (LaRock, 1993). Early retirement incentive packages can also be influential.

The volatility of the labor market today is harder for older workers to cope with than it is for younger workers. Statistically, older workers actually have lower unemployment rates than younger workers, but when older workers are displaced, it takes them much longer to find new jobs. Furthermore, statistics measuring unemployment rates may be deceptive. Many older people give up trying to find a job and become "discouraged workers"; that is, they are not even counted as part of the official unemployment rate. Still others declare themselves "retired," so that retirement itself becomes a disguised form of unemployment. Indeed, one of the prime reasons for adopting the Social Security system in the United States during the Depression was to reduce the level of official unemployment by drawing older people out of the labor market and thus opening up jobs for young people.

Looking at the labor force as a whole, long-range changes are clearly visible. In 1979, total manufacturing jobs constituted 23% of the labor force, but by 1992 the proportion had shrunk to 17%. Meanwhile, jobs in the service sector rose from 19% to 27% (U.S. Department of Labor, 1993, reported in Uchitelle, 1993). But the service sector jobs on average paid less and offered fewer benefits than older jobs in manufacturing. In addition, job growth is increasingly found not in big corporations but in small companies that can move quickly and flexibly. Typically, the new jobs are much less likely to offer full fringe benefits or pension coverage.

In recent years, the pattern of pension income has been changing. During the 1950s and 1960s, the most common type of retirement programs were defined-benefit programs that guaranteed to pay a specified level of income in retirement. In the 1990s, this guaranteed approach to retirement income had changed in two ways. First, fewer employers offered pensions as part of a fringe benefit package. Second, there is a trend toward defined-contribution plans in all major industrial sectors and for all firms with pension plans. This trend may reduce the effects of an aging workforce by reducing barriers to job mobility for older workers. Displaced workers or others who wanted to move to new jobs would then not lose pension coverage as a result of moving.

Some pension changes are dramatic. For instance, personal plans, such as **401(k) pension plans,** have spread rapidly. Around half of all American workers are eligible for a 401(k) or some other form of defined-contribution plan, and 86% of eligible workers are actually participating in a plan—an astonishingly high proportion. In 1984, the total amount of 401(k) plan assets was $92 billion. By 1998, this amount had increased by more than 15 times to one and a half trillion, and the average 401(k) plan balance reached nearly $100,000. In 1998, there were nearly six times as many 401(k) plans as a decade before.

When we look at government, we see incentives for moving older employees out of the labor force (Quinn, 1990). But there is a serious question about whether such practices are financially sustainable in the future. A striking example is military personnel, who can retire after 20 years of service and receive half their salary for the remainder of their lives. These military commitments amount to nearly half of the federal government's pension debts, and the Pentagon expects to spend an increasing amount to fund these pensions. Estimates are that the cost will grow from just over $11 billion in 1992 to $296 billion by 2041.

Similar patterns of early retirement are common in state and local government jobs, especially for police and firefighters. Faced with budget problems, state and local governments have begun using early retirement as a staff reduction technique. Early retirement yields short-term savings but may turn out to be a very expensive proposition in the long run. There are now large costs extending into the future for inadequately funded pension plans of state and municipal governments. Federal civil service pension plans aside from the military are underfunded by more than $1 trillion. The Pension Benefit Guaranty Corporation now insures the private pensions of 40 million American workers (Schieber and Shoven, 1997).

A New View of Retirement

The American economy, whether in government or private industry, has found retirement a convenient tool for managing the labor force (Schulz, 1995). On the positive side, the availability of retirement has meant expanded leisure and opportunities for self-fulfillment in later life. On the negative side, the practice of retirement entails large hidden costs, both in funding required for pension systems and in the loss of the accumulated skills and talents of older people.

Critics of retirement as it exists today have pointed to the rigidity of retirement practices. Retirement is typically an all-or-nothing proposition. Would it not be better to have some form of flexible, **phased retirement,** in which employees gradually reduce their work hours or take longer vacations? Such an approach might enable older workers to adjust better to retirement and permit employers to make gradual changes instead of coping with the abrupt departure of a well-integrated employee. Retirement could be radically redefined in the future if phased retirement were to take hold (Schmahl, 1989).

Earlier criticism of **mandatory retirement** at a fixed age led to legal abolition of the practice in 1986. Mandatory retirement is still permitted for high-level policy-making employees in private industry and for jobs where age is a bona fide occupational qualification. But critics still point to pervasive age discrimination in employment (Levine, 1989). The Age Discrimination in Employment Act forbids older workers from being limited or treated in any way that would harm their employment possibilities. Nonetheless, most observers recognize that age discrimination in the workplace remains widespread (Montgomery, 1991). Negative stereotypes of older workers have made employers reluctant to hire or train older people, who are often believed to be less productive (Yankelovich, Skelly, & White, 1985). In fact, empirical studies have not shown older workers to be less effective in their job performance (Stagner, 1985).

The average age of retirement fell throughout the 20th century, and the trend holds not just in America but internationally. Between 1965 and 1995, the average age of retirement among both men and women went down in most advanced industrialized countries (Gendell, 1998). As a result, people have been spending more and more of the years of their lives in retirement.

But that trend may not continue in the future. With the graying of the baby boomers, there is evidence that the long post-World War II trend of earlier retirement may be coming to an end. For instance, labor force participation rates in later life have held steady since the mid-1980s and even increased a bit in recent years. More older people are working than earlier trends would have predicted. Some surveys suggest that new attitudes may be developing about work late in life. An AARP-Roper survey in 1997 revealed that up to 80% of aging baby boomers expect to work at least part-time after what used to be normal retirement age.

Changes in the relative attractiveness of work and retirement may encourage continued employment into later life. One problem in the past has been that policies have encouraged a trend toward earlier retirement and have discouraged older workers from continuing to work. However, there have been some positive changes in recent years. Mandatory retirement has been eliminated, and Social Security benefits have become more age neutral; that is, Social Security no longer penalizes those who keep working or delay benefits until after age 65. Moreover, the spread of defined-benefit plans means fewer work disincentives than the typical defined-benefit plan (Quinn, 1999).

These trends offer promise for the future. If employers are willing to revise compensation and job structures to meet the needs of potential older workers, then they can draw on a growing pool of experienced and willing workers for years to come. Too often, companies respond to new challenges of technology or of the marketplace by favoring younger employees. As a result, whether older workers stay in place or retire early, companies lose the rich life experience embodied in proven, valued workers (Buonocore, 1992).

Managing an older workforce will clearly be a challenge for the future (Dennis, 1988). As labor shortages arise from declining numbers of young people in the workforce, that fact could stimulate a need for older workers and reverse the trend toward early retirement (Clark and Barker, 1981). There is growing support for the idea of *work-life extension,* that is, adaptations of retirement rules or employment practices to enable older people to become more productive (Doering, Rhodes, and Schuster, 1983). In favor of this idea is the fact the labor force is growing older: The median age will rise from 35 in 1980 to over 40 by 2005.

We have also seen the movement from an industrial to a postindustrial economy. For example, three-quarters of employees over age 65 are in white-collar occupations in service industries, which are less physically demanding than agriculture or manufacturing jobs. As a result, older people can remain in productive jobs longer than in the past. On the other hand, changes brought by information systems and telecommunication technology continue to bring rapid shifts in methods of production. Older workers who are decades away from school are likely to become victims of skills obsolescence. Without retraining, older workers may not be in a position to take up jobs that might open up in the future.

There is an even more fundamental question about whether work life extension is a valid goal in the first place. After all, why shouldn't the economic surplus from improved productivity be taken in the form of leisure time, either earlier in the course of life or in retirement years? The assumption that old age is unsatisfactory unless people continue to work seems an uncritical extension of the work ethic that originated in capitalist ideology, as sociologist Max Weber argued. Although those older people who love their work may find the work ethic compelling, declining labor force participation for most older people suggests that the attraction is not universal. A substantial body of literature in gerontology suggests that late-life leisure has important meaning and deserves attention as an activity in its own right (Kleemeier, 1961; Teague and MacNeil, 1992).

Productive Aging

As we have seen, the question, "Does retirement make sense?" is complicated. For both individuals and society, the alternative of work versus retirement is in many ways a false choice. The real question may be how to enable older people to lead lives of greater productivity, whether in employment or in retirement. Interest in this question about productive aging has grown in recent years (Butler and Gleason, 1985; Bass and Caro, 1993).

First of all, we should recognize that people over age 65 are already productive in many different ways. When we include unpaid work, such as housework or volunteer roles, three-quarters of older people are actually engaged in productive activity. In 1991, Louis Harris and Associates, with support from the Commonwealth Fund, carried out a national survey of 3,000 adults over age 55 to explore involvement in productive activities such as work, volunteer roles, and caregiving for a sick or disabled spouse, relative, neighbor, or friend. The survey showed that among people over 55, 27% were working, 26% were volunteering, 42% were helping children or grandchildren, and 29% were assisting the sick and disabled. Such findings are in stark contradiction to myths that depict older Americans as dependent, depressed, and isolated.

The Commonwealth study also found that Americans over age 55 represent an overlooked national resource. The total value of their contribution to society is equal to nearly 12 million full-time workers, and in caregiving activities alone, the equivalent of over 7 million full-time workers. The Commonwealth study discovered that men play a bigger role as volunteers and caregivers than they are usually credited with, including helping sick or disabled relatives as well as helping children or grandchildren. Informal caregiving may be viewed as a barrier to other productive activities (O'Reilly and Caro, 1994), but it can also be considered as an important form of productivity. Some critics have charged that the ideal of productive aging may devalue the contributions of women outside the paid workforce in maintaining relationships and providing care to others, activities that enrich all of society (Holstein, 1992).

Another important recent finding of the Commonwealth study is the remarkable vitality of many people over age 75. Health problems do increase in this group and limit some activities (Herzog et al., 1989). But even among the old-old, over half reported being in "excellent or good health," and nearly a quarter were still volunteering through organizations, or involved in caregiving for family or neighbors.

Finally, the Commonwealth study confirmed that, along with current productive roles, older people are eager to be even more actively involved: 31% were not yet employed but wanted to be. A similar picture has emerged for volunteers, reaffirming the importance of the older volunteer activities documented in earlier studies (Chambre, 1987). This rise in the number of able elders has optimistic implications that deserve consideration (Hudson, 1987).

One organized vehicle for productive aging already exists in public service employment programs sponsored by government. Two of the largest programs are the Senior Community Service Employment Program (SCSEP), created under Title V of the Older Americans Act, and the Job Training Partnership Act (JTPA). SCSEP supports part-time, government-subsidized jobs for low-income people over age 55, who are placed in local community service agencies. SCSEP provides only minimal training for those eligible, but the JTPA program has a 3% set-aside reserved exclusively for older workers. JTPA has worked closely with private industry councils representing employers, and the program includes job search and placement help. The latter service can be especially helpful for older workers trying to get back into the workforce, as shown by the successful experience of Project ABLE in Chicago, a model employment agency specializing in older workers.

Organized efforts can also enhance productive roles for older people in volunteer activities. The Office of Older American Volunteer Programs is the largest of the operating units within ACTION, the federal agency that coordinates volunteer activities. One of the older volunteer programs run by ACTION is the Senior Companions Program, similar to Foster Grandparents but directed toward impaired adults needing help to continue living in their own homes. The largest ACTION-sponsored initiative is the Retired Senior Volunteer Program (RSVP), offering community volunteer service opportunities in day care centers, nursing homes, libraries, and adult education programs.

A larger proportion of older people are volunteering today than was true a generation ago, and that trend seems likely to continue in the future (Chambre, 1993). Most of those who do volunteer are middle-class people who are continuing a lifetime pattern (Cnaan and Cwikel, 1992). A major national study recently found that personal ideals, such as altruism and the wish to be useful to others, is a key to volunteerism (Okun, 1994). Several studies reveal a strong correlation between volunteerism and higher life satisfaction, but the higher health and economic status of those who volunteer may confound any conclusion about causal connections (Fengler, 1984).

Another challenge for productive aging lies in the workplace. Most older workers perform as well as younger workers—welcome news since one-third of the U.S. workforce now consists of workers over the age of 40. This graying of working America poses a challenge for the economy. In the past, companies have relied on younger workers to bring in the new skills and knowledge that are key to raising productivity. If the U.S. economy is to prosper in the future, managers will have to pay more attention to making use of older workers, who will constitute an increasing proportion of the workforce during a period when technological change will be accelerating (Kieffer, 1983).

Experience in industry over many years has demonstrated that middle-aged and older workers can be trained or retrained to acquire new skills as previous skills or knowledge become obsolete (Davies and Sparrow, 1985). This potential for retraining is called **plasticity.** The positive experience in older-worker retraining serves to contradict a common prejudice that "you can't teach an old dog new tricks." Laboratory tests do show a decline in test performance, but in the real world, any decline in speed or accuracy tends to be compensated for. In addition, older workers have other positive attributes such as less absenteeism, lower job turnover, and a lower accident rate. Older people typically demonstrate some declines in motor performance and speed of comprehension as new information is acquired. Such effects sometimes discourage older workers, who may themselves come to believe the stereotype. But modest changes in teaching techniques can serve to offset most of these problems.

For example, the *discovery method of training* has proven successful with older workers (Belbin and Belbin, 1972). In this method, trainees discover for themselves how to carry out a task to be learned. They make decisions actively and then receive immediate corrective feedback. This method has been used successfully in operations such as post office mail sorting, stone masonry, and machine work. It has also been used in fields such as data processing and interpretation of engineering designs (Belbin, 1969). Examples such as these are encouraging because of the projected dramatic growth of jobs in the information sector of the postindustrial economy.

Debate Over Retirement Policy

The volatility of the U.S. economy and the aging of the workforce make predictions difficult. But the vitality of the aging population today already constitutes a positive sign for the future, which can be optimized if there is greater attention to the potential of productive aging. Community service employment, second careers, volunteer opportunities, and retraining of older workers may all be part of the picture in years to come.

In the readings that follow, we hear different voices in the debate over retirement policy. Caro, Bass, and Chen argue that under today's new conditions, we need to think again about the meaning of retirement and, in particular, to design social institutions that can open up new possibilities for productive aging. Making better use of the talents of older people would represent a new social policy goal for American society.

Rhonda Montgomery and her colleagues remind us that all social policies depend on shared assumptions and values. What are these assumptions and values? On the positive side, older workers may be considered entitled to a justified reward in the form of retirement leisure. On the negative side, older workers may be considered less valuable than younger workers. It is interesting that both the positive and the negative assumptions would probably lead us to encourage early retirement. But both assumptions can be called into question. As we think about alternative social policies, we need to ask especially about the relevance of chronological age. For instance, a 30-year-old who decides not to work might be judged "lazy." But a 70-year-old with the same preference might be judged "retired."

Age is not the only factor involved in the value judgments we make. A key assumption in debates around work and retirement is the idea that people are somehow ethically better if they continue to be active and productive. In fact, this moral valuation of work and productivity has deep roots in American culture in the Puritan ethic: the idea that hard work is a virtue in itself. David Ekerdt highlights what he calls the "busy ethic" and shows that for many Americans both work and retirement are characterized by the same style of activity and productive engagement, whether in a paid job or not.

But the busy ethic is not the only image of human fulfillment. Nancy Osgood provides us with a historical view of how the concept of leisure has changed over the centuries. Just as paid work is not the only form of productivity, so recreation and relaxation are not the only forms that leisure might take. Through the ages, philosophers and social thinkers have dreamed about what a society might look like if the burden of work were lifted from humankind. Today, that dream has come to pass. In the 20th century, with mass retirement as a normal social institution, we witnessed what happens when vast numbers of people are given leisure in their later years. The experiment goes on, and the results are debatable. In fact, controversies about work and leisure demonstrate that we have not yet agreed on the key social values at stake when we ask, "Is retirement obsolete?"

READING 29

Achieving a Productive Aging Society

Francis G. Caro, Scott A. Bass, and Yung-Ping Chen

Older people face a prolonged period in life in which they are relatively healthy and vigorous but lack a recognized role in the economic and social life of the society. Although elders, especially older women, are encouraged to provide support to their extended families, they too frequently are left without a significant role in late adulthood. This ambiguous status of retirement and explicit devaluation may last for a period as long as twenty or thirty years, which in some cases may be as long as a working career. . . .

A so-called productive aging perspective views older people as a major and valuable resource. In the United States and certain other nations, within this large and diverse group of older individuals, many are becoming increasingly dissatisfied with a life primarily structured around leisure. But even these people too frequently experience serious barriers as they seek significant societal roles.

Most older people are relatively healthy and robust well into their sixties and seventies, and in some cases beyond. Although, as a group, they tend to experience chronic ailments, they are capable of sustaining most of the intellectual and many of the physical activities in which they participated during their fifties. . . .

Source: "Introduction: Achieving a Productive Aging Society," by Francis G. Caro, Scott A. Bass, and Yung-Ping Chen, in *Achieving a Productive Aging Society*, edited by Scott A. Bass, Francis G. Caro, and Yung-Ping Chen. Copyright © 1993 by Auburn House. Reproduced with permission of Greenwood Publishing Group, Inc., Westport, CT.

Defining Productive Aging

The term *productive aging* has emerged over the past decade as a rallying cry for elder advocates, policymakers, and academicians dissatisfied with the stereotype of older people as dependent and frail. . . .

This more positive approach to the examination of aging seeks to identify the changes associated with aging and to maximize the human potential throughout the life course. At the center of the discussion is the fact that, in many activities, chronological age, up and into the advanced ages, is not necessarily a strong predictor of performance. Compelling evidence indicates that the aging process is highly individualistic, with enormous differences in the way various individuals age and in their subsequent performance in physical and mental activities. Some individuals in their seventies and eighties may be very active and produce their most significant contributions, while others in their fifties and sixties may be unable to function fully in society or may choose to withdraw from productive activity. Age as a sole predictor of performance is simply too crude a tool to reflect the actual capability of older people.

Productive aging, not unlike other terms such as *successful aging* or *normative aging,* has reflected an intellectual direction or theme that has attempted to attract individuals from many different perspectives. . . .

More recently, A. Regula Herzog (1989) has defined productive aging as "any activity that produces goods or services, whether paid or not, including activities such as housework, child care, volunteer work, and help to family and friends."

The major difference among the definitions is the range of activities they include. The broadest includes nearly all activities of older people. The most restrictive includes only paid employment and formal volunteer work.

A definition we prefer is the following: Productive aging is any activity by an older individual that produces goods or services, or develops the capacity to produce them, whether they are to be paid for or not. This definition builds on Herzog's by including only voluntary or paid service or goods produced but excluding activities of a personal enrichment nature. Our definition expands upon Herzog's to encompass activities that provide training or skills to enhance one's capacity to perform paid or volunteer work; it does not include education for personal growth as that would not directly contribute to enhanced skills for paid or volunteer labor.

While we acknowledge the many facets of productive aging, we particularly emphasize paid employment and volunteering because they are sectors in which older people experience significant barriers. In other sectors, productive involvement of older people is usually expected. The role of older people in providing long-term care to disabled spouses is a good example. . . . [H]ealthy spouses of the disabled are *expected* to provide care to their partners. In fact, the public policy issue concerns how public intervention should complement that responsibility. In the case of employment, however, the issue is how to reverse skepticism about the capabilities of older people and even the loss of confidence of older people in their ability to be effective in the world of work. In the employment sector, the issue is also how to address a whole set of institutional forces that encourage early departure from the workforce. In the case of volunteering, the question is how volunteer roles can be made significantly more attractive so that volunteering among older people will expand.

The definition we have selected sufficiently excludes many important and constructive activities undertaken by the elderly, such as worship-ing, meditation, reflection, reminiscing, reading for pleasure, carrying on correspondence, visiting with family and friends, traveling, and so forth. It is not to say that these are not valuable activities and part of healthy and fulfilling aging experience . . . ; they simply are outside the bounds of productive aging as we define it. Activities undertaken in our definition can be counted, aggregated, and assigned some economic value. Productive aging, therefore, is not for all older people, only for those who are interested, and that interest may vary at different times, ages, or even seasons. In our search for words that embody all that gives aging meaning, *productive aging* may be only one of several components. . . .

Historical Origins

Nonproductive aging, as evidenced by retirement and an absence of a role in late life, is a relatively recent phenomenon in America. In other developed nations, it is a concept that dates back no earlier than the late nineteenth century. Prior to these times and dating back to antiquity, older people were engaged in some form of work until they were unable to continue with it. Throughout the centuries, the old were expected to work or to beg until they were simply too ill or enfeebled, leaving their care to the family, neighboring community, poorhouses, or no one (Axinn & Stern, 1988). . . .

The first reported social security system came into being in the 1890s in Bismarck's Germany. By 1913, Australia, Belgium, Great Britain, Denmark, France, New Zealand, and Sweden also had public pension systems for the elderly. The United States was among the last of the industrial nations to institutionalize a national pension program to provide economic security to the elderly. . . . But prior to the establishment of Social Security in 1935, older people, for the most part, were expected to work or to seek shelter and care from almshouses, or they were cared for by their families. . . .

In the late nineteenth and early twentieth centuries in the United States, the nonworking elderly were not usually accorded favorable consideration. In fact, David Hackett Fisher (1977) notes that expressions of hostility toward the poor, nonworking elderly continued to grow during the nineteenth century. The opinion at the time was that there was enough work for all who could work. Those who could not placed a burden on the family and society. Little was available other than personal family charity for those who could not work, including the frail aged.

Within the first fifty years of Social Security, a relatively short time in history, all had changed. From a situation where the elderly had no option but to continue to work or be dependent on others, we arrived at a place where retirement had become an institution rather than a luxury (U.S. Senate, [1990]).

Near-universal work for the aged has been replaced by near-universal retirement. The contrast and extremes remain stark. The contemporary pattern of nonparticipation of the elderly in the work force is particularly remarkable in light of the growth of the elderly population and the number of years older people now typically live in retirement. The fact that many elderly are able to live comfortably on the basis of pensions and savings is a reflection of the strength of the economy (Schulz, Borowski, & Crown, 1991). The ability of the U.S. economy to function adequately without the presence of most older people in the work force also is consistent with the assumptions that Patten advanced nearly 100 years ago. But will these assumptions hold true as we look to the economic future of America?

Appropriateness of the Past in Today's Policy

To what extent is there a labor-supply abundance? Since the late 1960s the economy has absorbed large numbers of new women workers, and new supplies of labor for economic growth are limited as a result of the low birthrate of the 1970s and 1980s and recent restrictions on immigration (Schulz, Borowski, & Crown, 1991). If the nation faces modest economic growth, from where will labor support come? Older people are one nontraditional population to consider (McNaught, Barth,

& Henderson, 1989). For the most part, they have good work habits and extensive on-the-job experience. With the older population increasingly in better health, could it not be an important economic resource to the nation (Bass & Barth, 1992)? Further, in light of the vast array of social needs and the declining public willingness to provide tax support for human service programs, could not interested older people be trained to fill certain important, but currently unmet, social needs, and if so, to what extent? We are not advocating that older volunteers replace paid workers, but we do believe that there are societal functions that may be performed by trained older volunteers or stipend workers.

Such a scenario for older people is not without its problems. There are family and societal expectations of the aged. And no equivalent of career counseling is available for those who leave their primary employment at age sixty or sixty-five and seek an alternative. Retirement is thought of as the terminal work experience; in fact, it may be a transitional one. Career planning for paid or volunteer roles after retirement is not yet common. Part-time or flexible work hours which many older workers want remain elusive and are considered unconventional. Training programs and higher educational opportunities are designed for younger people, with little thought to the needs of older workers seeking work past retirement. . . .

Obstacles to Productive Aging

How is the limited participation of older people in paid work and volunteering to be explained? To what extent do older people prefer not to work and not to volunteer? To what extent are important opportunities for employment and volunteer work denied elders? Are elders tracked out of mainstream roles in subtle and discriminatory ways?

One hypothesis is that the limited participation of older people in paid work and volunteering is the result of "institutional ageism"—that societal institutions have structures, rewards, and sanctions that value certain cultural norms. These idealized and otherwise unspoken values and cultural traditions are inclusive of certain behaviors and groups and exclusive of others. Indeed, some individuals may overcome these barriers, but they are the exceptions rather than the rule.

The forces that exclude older people on bases other than merit are widespread. Some have been documented, such as age discrimination in employment. However, institutional ageism may be such a pervasive aspect of all major institutions in our society that we often do not recognize it. In fact, many older people themselves have internalized ageism. Too often they underestimate their own capabilities and accept the notion that older adults should leave productive roles at certain prescribed ages.

The major force at the root of institutional ageism may be the conflicting interests of the elderly and the nonelderly. Embedded in existing institutional arrangements may be management's desire to remove the elderly from attractive jobs and other positions of power and influence to facilitate greater access for younger people. Conflict theory suggests that such removal can be explained in part by economic competition between the nonelderly and elderly. It hypothesizes that pressure to exclude the elderly is affected by labor market conditions. During recessions, when jobs are scarce, pressure to remove the elderly is expected to increase. In periods of economic boom, when workers are in short supply, conflict theory predicts that older workers will be seen in a much more favorable light and the employment of older people is more likely to be actively encouraged.

Cultural lag is a second potential explanation for the limited participation of older people in attractive paid-work roles. The cultural-lag hypothesis differs from the conflict hypothesis on the basis of its assumptions about the underpinnings of institutional patterns. The cultural-lag hypothesis suggests that, as a society, we are slow to adjust our institutions in response to changing conditions. We may be slow, for example, in modifying our retirement policies moving from an era of labor oversupply to one of labor shortages. We may be slow in reorganizing our educational institutions to provide the lifelong training for work necessary in an economy characterized by sharper competition and rapid technological advances. Further, our society may take too long to recognize that people now have the potential for remaining productive later in life than in the past as a result of their improved health and of reduced physical demands in the workplace.

A third explanation, which might be called the defective-institutions hypothesis, is that employment and volunteer options are so badly flawed that people who can choose to depart from jobs as early as they can and generally avoid extensive volunteer commitments. A factor here is the quality of the work environment itself. In many fields, working people of all ages in this country complain about their work environments and compensation. Further, many of the volunteer assignments are unattractive, having unappealing tasks, insufficient challenges, or heavy demands, and training and support are inadequate.

A fourth explanation, which we will call the alternate-preferences hypothesis, is that many older people organize their lives around alternatives to the work ethic. According to this hypothesis, many older people subscribe to values other than those that lead to employment and community service. They find personal expressive activities highly attractive and, when given a choice, are not interested in paid employment or volunteering options. According to this hypothesis, some advocates for productive aging may be overestimating the number of older people currently interested in access to work and volunteer roles. . . .

Both the conflict and cultural-lag theories can provide explanations of the alternate-preferences hypothesis. Both of these theories would argue that alternate preferences are learned either through the popular culture or through direct experience with the negative aspects of work environments and volunteer opportunities. Both theories predict that older people would regard paid employment more favorably if work environments were made more attractive. Further, as a change strategy, the infusion into the society of more positive views about employment of older people might trigger increased public support for the employment of older people.

Because we suspect that both conflict theory and cultural-lag theory help explain current arrangements that discourage participation of older people in paid employment and meaningful volunteer work, we believe that both confrontation and public education are useful strategies for directed change. Political action may help break down discriminatory policies and practices and create improved employment options for the elderly. Public education also may be effective in encouraging older people to seek to remain active in both paid employment and volunteering, it may stimulate employers and voluntary organizations to be more creative in recognizing older people as resources, and it may lead educational institutions to develop attractive retraining programs.

Preferences among the elderly that cause them to focus their interests and activities on sectors other than paid employment and volunteering must be recognized. Our hypothesis is that, if work and volunteering are made more attractive as later-life options, many more older people would pursue them. How many more people actually would work or volunteer would then depend both on the attractiveness of work and volunteer options and the pull of competing alternatives.

Like any other reform movement, productive aging can have perverse effects on its intended beneficiaries. Our emphasis is on expanded opportunities for the elderly for paid employment and volunteering. . . . At this point, we would not endorse blanket proposals to expand either work obligations or reduced pensions for the elderly premised on an extended work life. A great deal has to be accomplished in extending work opportunities before there is a sound basis for debating whether work obligations should be increased.

Similarly, we advocate improved volunteer opportunities for older people to address serious human needs that currently are not being met. But we do not regard elderly volunteers as substitutes for paid workers. If efforts to recruit and retain older volunteers were spectacularly successful in some sectors, some might conclude that fewer paid workers are needed in those fields. We prefer to wait until large, effective cadres of older volunteers actually threaten to displace paid workers and debate the specific issues on their merits.

References

Axinn, J., & Stern, M. J. (1988). *Dependency and poverty: Old problems in a new world.* Lexington, MA: Lexington Books.

Bass, S. A., & Barth, M. (1992). *The next educational opportunity: Career training for older adults.* Draft for the Commonwealth Fund. New York: The Commonwealth Fund.

Fisher, D. H. (1977). *Growing old in America.* New York: Oxford University Press.

Herzog, A. R. (1989). Age differences in productive activity. *Journal of Gerontology: Social Sciences, 44,* S129-S138.

McNaught, W., Barth, M., & Henderson, P. (1989, Winter). The human resource potential of Americans over 50. *Human Resources Management, 28*(4), 455-473.

Schulz, J., Borowski, A., and Crown, W. H. (1991). *Economics of population aging.* New York: Auburn House.

U.S. Senate, Special Committee on Aging. (1990). *Aging America.* Washington, DC: U.S. Government Printing Office.

Social Policy Toward the Older Worker
Assumptions, Values, and Implications

Rhonda J. V. Montgomery, Edgar F. Borgatta, and Karl D. Kosloski

The role of the older worker is coming under increasing scrutiny by employers, unions, policymakers, and researchers. Among the developments which have stimulated this interest are a changing demographic makeup of the work force, due to shifts in birth rates and increased length of life for most persons; medical advances, with accompanying increases in medical costs, primarily associated with older persons; compression in the upper ages among workers in some industries; and the trend toward earlier retirement among certain groups of workers.

Some observers see an increase in the proportion of older workers as cause for alarm, others as a burgeoning resource. Before it is possible to make a pronouncement on whether there is a coming "crisis" in the workplace or whether dramatic shifts in policy are necessary, it is useful to consider not only where we are as a society with respect to a defined role for the older worker but also how we got there. We will look at examples that illustrate the implicit value system that appears to underlie present social policy with respect to older workers. We will then suggest possible policy initiatives that are consistent with

both the new demographics and attitudinal changes toward the older worker.

The Present Role of the Older Worker

An Aging Society

The American population is changing demographically, with persons generally surviving longer. At the turn of the century, less than one in every ten Americans was 55 years old or older. Presently, the figure is one in five. By the beginning of the next century, the size of this segment of the population will increase yet another 20 percent, from 47 million to roughly 55 million, and by the year 2010, according to the Census Bureau (1983), fully 25 percent of the population will be 55 years old or over.

The aging of the population roughly parallels the aging of the baby boomers, that cohort born from the mid-1940s to the early 1960s. Almost one-third of the current U.S. population (nearly 75 million) was born during this period. Due to their large numbers and increasing life expectancy, the baby boomers are expected to be the dominant age cohort well into the next century.

The effect of the population bulge caused by this cohort is heightened by a smaller than expected succeeding cohort, often referred to as the "baby bust" generation. While the fertility rate soared during the two decades from 1945 to 1964, reaching a high of 3.7 in 1957, it dropped to a low of 1.7, substantially below the replacement rate, in 1976 (U.S. Bureau of the Census, 1982). Partly as the result of these demographic shifts, the aver-

Source: Reprinted from "Social Policy Toward the Older Worker: Assumptions, Values, and Implications," by Rhonda J. V. Montgomery, Edgar F. Borgatta, and Karl D. Kosloski, in *The Aging of the American Workforce*, edited by Irving Bluestone, Rhonda J. V. Montgomery, and John Owen. Copyright © 1990 by Wayne State University Press, Detroit, MI 48202. Reprinted by permission of the Wayne State University Press.

age age of the population has been steadily increasing.

The major concern here is the change produced in the dependency ratio (the number of dependents in society supported by each working member). There are various ways of computing this ratio (see, e.g., Adamchak and Friedmann 1983), but no matter how it is conceptualized, two considerations should not be overlooked. First, as the proportion of older adults increases, there is a corresponding reduction in the number of dependent young, which tends to offset, at least in part, the impact of the older group. The exact trade-off in costs at the individual and societal levels is, as yet, unknown. Second, there are conditions other than changing fertility rates that affect the dependency ratio. These include perturbations in the economy, legislation affecting Social Security and Medicare, and restrictive public and private policies that reduce the ability of older workers to adapt to changing conditions.

In short, demographic shifts in the population structure produce a population with a higher proportion of older persons. Though the implications of this shift for good or ill are not yet apparent, there has been much debate of the merits of alternative solutions to the "problems" created by an aging society.

An Aging Work Force

Since the composition of the work force is determined, in part, by the composition of the larger population from which it is drawn, the median age of the labor force is slowly increasing. It is important to bear in mind that much of the increase is because the baby boomers are aging, not because older workers are staying in the work force longer. At the beginning of this century, more than two-thirds of American men aged 65 and over were employed. In 1960, the proportion had dropped to roughly one-third (Back 1969); by 1979 the proportion was 19 percent and dropping (Smedley 1979); the figure is expected to fall below 10 percent by the year 2000 (Fullerton 1987).

American workers are opting for retirement at an earlier age. In 1966, 38 percent of workers retired before age 65 under Social Security; by 1976 the number had increased to 66 percent (*U.S. News & World Report* 1978). And even though recent amendments to the Age Discrimination in Employment Act of 1986 remove the age-70 cap in the law and prohibit mandatory retirement based on age for most workers, the trend toward earlier retirement continues. . . .

Currently, labor force participation begins to decline as early as age 45 for both men and women, as health problems and early retirement options begin to thin the ranks of the employed (Sandell 1987). However, the trend toward earlier retirement is particularly pronounced for males. The parallel for women is not direct, since the labor force participation of women has been changing. Work rates for women below the age of 55 continue to rise, and the work rates of older women remain relatively unchanged (Clark 1988).

As Kutscher and Fullerton point out in their [chapter in the book from which this reading is drawn], the median age of the post-World War II labor force reached its apex in 1962, at 40.6 years. With the entry of the baby boom generation, the median age dropped dramatically. Since then, it has been increasing steadily. In spite of this increase, however, voluntary decisions by older workers to leave the work force are more than offsetting the effect of the aging of the baby boomers, and the median age of 1962 is unlikely to be matched in the foreseeable future.

Planners wonder whether society will have the ability to finance such a retirement level without a negative impact on the economy and the standard of living. The most frequently invoked scenario, related to the dependency ratio, is that as the average age of workers increases and older workers depart prematurely, fewer workers will be left to support an increasing proportion of retirees. As a result, workers will eventually be unable to afford to retire, and the work force will be inundated with older workers.

Objective data do not support this view. The greatest disparity in the dependency ratio occurred in the early 1960s, when there were over 150 nonworkers for every 100 workers. Since then the ratio has steadily declined, in large part because of increasing labor force participation by women. This trend is expected to continue for the next twenty years before slowly reversing itself. Even when it does, however, the ratio of non-workers to workers is not expected to exceed 115 nonworkers for every 100 workers. So even when the baby boomers reach retirement age, the dependency ratio is expected to be much more favorable than in the 1960s and 1970s (Sandell 1987). This relatively optimistic view of the future must be tempered somewhat by the expectation that older dependents will be more expensive than younger dependents. High-tech medical advances that increase the length of the dependency period will contribute substantially to health care costs for this group.

Thus the notion of an aging work force is somewhat of a misnomer at present. Although certain sectors have older than average work forces (e.g., the auto industry), this phenomenon largely is caused by union-negotiated work and seniority rules, rather than demographic change. Age compression in industry should not be confused with demographic shifts in the population. Since they have different causes, they are likely to have different solutions. For the most part, aging trends within the general population are being offset by trends toward earlier retirement. The result has been a less rapid aging of the work force. In a similar fashion, increased participation by females in the labor force appears to have forestalled an economically debilitating dependency ratio. Indeed, Adamchak and Friedmann, in their analyses of differing conceptions of the dependency ratio, conclude: "Whatever the reasons for the revolt against the alleged increases in 'dependency' loads resulting from population aging and the institutionalization of retirement, *the argument cannot be justified on the basis of a demonstrable increase in dependency load employing any appropriate measure*" (p. 336).

Intergenerational Tension

A number of analysts have raised the specter of intergenerational conflict as a logical conse-quence of the present support for older Americans. Groups such as Americans for Generational Equity (AGE), with the ostensible purpose of protecting the economic rights of younger hAmericans, have been cited as evidence that battle lines are being drawn. Impetus for such movements is fueled by such inflammatory statements as this: "The baby boomers are paying an unprecedented proportion of their incomes to support the current older generation in retirement, and they will expect today's children to support them in turn. The likely result, unless many fundamental trends are soon reversed, will be a war between young and old" (Longman 1987, p. 2).

In reality, the prospect of such intergenerational conflict seems remote. For example, the tradition of intrafamilial responsibility for informal caregiving appears as strong as ever (Brody 1985; Shanas 1979). In addition, private transfers of money are more likely to proceed from old to young than vice versa (Gibbs 1988). In fact, it has been contended that the whole "intergenerational inequity" argument is based on a series of false assumptions such as the belief that all the elderly are well-off, that allocation of federal monies is a zero-sum game, that conflict is the rule rather than the exception, and that there is no common stake between generations (Kingson et al. 1986).

Other factors that have nothing to do with economic support also promote negative attitudes toward the old by the young. For example, there are prevailing myths that older workers "wear out"; that their knowledge becomes superannuated or even obsolete; that they are accident-prone, forgetful, and so on. One of the achievements of modern social gerontology has been the successful challenging of such myths. Indeed, it might be argued that the heightened awareness of gerontological issues has created a renewed sense of egalitarianism and an advocacy by some policymakers of the view that older workers must be given an opportunity to remain in the workplace. Given their retirement patterns, however, older workers show little sign of wanting or needing such an opportunity.

Implicit Values in Contemporary Social Policy

Some Historical Notes on Retirement

On the face of it, then, there would seem to be no compelling need for a radical revision of the role of the older worker based solely on demographic trends. This is consistent with Graebner's (1980) observation that the aging of the general population occurs too slowly to account for such historical movements in any more than a general way.

According to Graebner, formal occupational retirement emerged in the American workplace for three main reasons. First, retirement was an assault on the system of permanence that employees attempted to build into their positions, as exemplified by tenure in teaching, seniority on the railroad, and the spoils system in civil service. Retirement served to lessen the "right" of individuals to such occupational permanence.

Second, retirement weakened the effort of "personal influence" and personal relationships in institutions. In other words, a worker's ability came to be more important than his or her family and social connections. Prior to the institutionalization of retirement, public and private corporations were assumed to be providing for the welfare of their older workers; that is, income, status, and activity were to be dispensed to older workers as part of the job. Unfortunately, provision of these gratifications was never uniform. With retirement, these functions were transferred to senior citizens' groups, nursing homes, and retirement communities.

Third, says Graebner, "retirement has historically been sanctioned as a form of unemployment relief; older workers have been retired to create places for younger ones" (p. 266), a policy most blatant in the railroad industry, but applied to other occupations experiencing technological unemployment. To note this function of retirement is not to minimize the discrimination inherent in the process; however, the process is, in large part, implicitly accepted among all age groups.

From Graebner's perspective, certain social and economic values were instrumental in the eventual institutionalization of a retirement role; and, extending this line of reasoning, shifting values will most likely be responsible for any changes in the perceptions or operationalization of this role. In order to explain the renewed interest in the older worker in America, Graebner again points to the economy: "Mandatory retirement was established over the course of the last century because it served real and perceived needs; it is now being dismantled because it is increasingly seen as economically counterproductive for the firm and the nation; because the proposed alternatives seem to offer substantial benefits; and because it is generally accepted that mandatory retirement can be eliminated without significant social dislocation" (p. 250).

From this perspective, the role of the older worker can be seen as being influenced by social values that are based, at least in part, on economic considerations. According to Graebner, it would be a distinct mistake to interpret recent legislation removing mandatory retirement ages as a belated victory for older workers who want to continue working but have been barred by arbitrary age discrimination. Rather, such a change in policy became possible only when those in positions of power in corporate America decided that current retirement policies were too expensive and inefficient in their utilization of the labor supply. In short, in order to understand the role of the older worker, it is important to identify which values are presently being represented and whose values they are.

Conventional Policy Development and Implicit Values

To illustrate where we are, as a society, with respect to a defined role for the older worker, it may be useful to examine certain contemporary policies and practices in the workplace, raise questions about the values reflected, and ask whether or not these are the values that should be implemented. The purpose of this exercise is not to engage in a systematic analysis of current policy, but to begin such an endeavor by focusing on several current practices and the implications of these practices. Then it may be possible to begin a dialogue about which values we as a society would like to support and the policies and practices that could be implemented to achieve these goals.

For the past few decades, there has been a movement in labor and industry toward the practice referred to as "30-and-out." Implementation of this policy was a victory for the worker who had spent long years at physically exhausting labor and was given an opportunity to retire before literally working himself to death. The "30-and-out" policy has been most conspicuous in the older manufacturing industries, where modernization has led to a decrease in the labor force and where there are few new opportunities for younger workers.

The benefits of the "30-and-out" policy are numerous and clearly transcend the original goal of assuring at least some time for retirement for laborers. For example, "30-and-out" tends to make room for younger workers and for promotion of those in the middle years. It has the potential to create an orderly influx of new members into the labor organizations and assure the continued need and support for such organizations. The practice also reinforces the societal belief that retirement is an earned right which workers may exercise even before reaching the age qualifying them for Social Security. For its part, industry has benefited to the extent that those in the system for a shorter time command lower salaries and fewer benefits.

On the surface, then, "30-and-out" would appear to be a practice that is desirable. However, careful scrutiny raises questions about the long-term costs of such a practice and the values that are being reinforced. For example, if an individual is capable of continued work and is not prepared for a reduction in income, this practice may be limiting his or her opportunities. Such a person is not only restricted from working but is less well able to prevent economic dependency in the future. In principle, "30-and-out" may appear to be a humane provision; in practice, it threatens the older person's access to continued employment. If there are not enough jobs to go around, the no-

tion of full employment can be maintained if some groups are defined as outside the work force. Those groups could be the young, women, or minorities. And at various times in various ways, many groups have been prohibited access to employment. It may be convenient to treat the group of old people in this way.

It may be argued that legislation was passed in 1986 to prevent forced retirement in most employment settings. However, the law does not prevent enticements to retire such as bonuses and what are often referred to as "golden parachute" packages. Furthermore, the statistics reported above show that the average retirement age has been and continues to be below that required for Social Security eligibility. In reality, then, while there may be virtues associated with retirement, "30-and-out" and related policies may create expectations within society about who should retire and when, thereby placing a limitation on all future income for these persons.

It is the latter aspect of retirement (i.e., a limitation on future income) that may be problematic for individuals and society. As long as individuals live only a few years beyond retirement, initially adequate pensions will probably remain adequate as time passes. However, as larger numbers of persons live longer and the retirement period is extended, it becomes questionable whether existing pension programs will be able to meet the needs of individuals over their retirement life, particularly if inflationary pressure is substantial and there is no provision for cost of living allowances. When people outlive pension resources, government or other resources will be called upon to meet unmet needs, including substantial health care costs. In either case, the public purse will be drawn upon to pay for perhaps unanticipated consequences of early retirement, since these individuals will not be in a position to contribute to their own care.

In addition to the practice of "30-and-out," there are other private and public policies that encourage elders to leave the work force to make room for others. For example, persons who work part-time are limited in how much they can earn before their Social Security benefits are reduced for the period in which they are most likely to continue working, i.e., the years right after formal retirement. Further, recent changes in the tax law require recipients of Social Security to pay taxes on their benefit payments if they secure employment that raises their income over a designated maximum. The stated purpose of this practice is to ensure that elders with sufficiently high incomes are not equal beneficiaries of a tax transfer system. Another consequence of this law is that older workers are "penalized" for going into the work force. This set of circumstances is also mirrored by recent changes in federal employees' benefit packages. Essentially, a federal employee who elects to earn and then draw Social Security benefits after leaving government service is penalized for such an action. The message given by current practices is clear, whether intended or not: older persons should leave the work force.

Is this the message that we want current policy to send? Once this initial question is asked, a series of other questions emerges, all of which deserve serious consideration if we are to create policies concerned with older workers in a proactive way. Do we want workers to leave the work force at ever earlier ages? Are older persons the most appropriate group economically to force out of the work force? Do we need to force a selected subgroup out of the labor force? If not, will we need to do so in the future? Are there alternative ways of achieving full employment?

A second employment practice that is intricately tied to retirement and older worker policies is the pervasive and growing tendency to hire part-time employees. The benefits of this practice to employers are clear. They gain scheduling flexibility and major savings because part-time employees are frequently paid low hourly wages and usually are not provided key benefits. From the perspective of older workers, such jobs can be viewed favorably because they allow retired persons to supplement their retirement income on a flexible schedule. One might be tempted to assert that this practice reflects an increasing value placed on older persons. However, in reality, it reflects underlying values similar to those described earlier. Specifically, older persons are employed as marginal participants in the labor market, and often the jobs are available only because other persons are unable or unwilling to take them.

Apart from the question of whether this is the value we want to foster, there are questions related to the long-term consequences of these practices for retirement policy. Older persons are not the only group employed as part-time help without benefits. Women, youths, minorities, and those with lower levels of education are also employed in such a manner. When these persons progress through their work lives to retirement age, they arrive there with no planned retirement benefits except for minimal Social Security coverage—and even that assurance continues to be questioned. Hence the savings incurred by these service industries are likely to be at a substantial cost to the public purse. If large numbers of these marginal workers live extended lives, it is likely that minimal Social Security benefits will need to be supplemented by government programs.

The Future Role of the Older Worker

Value-Driven Policy Development

All too often, when policy analysts and policymakers address difficult issues, they approach their task as one of fine tuning rather than one of asking more basic and difficult questions about which values are being supported by a policy and whether or not they should be supported. This reluctance to raise questions about values stems directly from the fact that many social issues are complex, involve a diverse set of values, and may be conflicting. The employment and retirement of older workers is one such issue. Debate concerning the rights and privileges of older persons as workers and retired citizens will not only reflect differences in values among different interest groups but will also reveal conflicting values among individuals.

In a brief presentation it is not possible to develop new directions for policy with regard to the older worker. However, we will suggest a few ways in which values can be stated in a forthright and direct way.

First, let us emphasize the simple notion that older persons are people like everyone else, and should not be treated any differently merely on the basis of age—that is to say, there should be no discrimination. Such a statement is more easily accepted as a generality than in application. It implies that older persons who wish to work should be judged on the basis of their qualifications, and the process of determining qualifications may create some costs. This value is now reasonably well incorporated in our federal legal system, and is reflected at other levels of government as well.

However, the other side of the coin is that older persons also should not be treated preferentially. For some, this is a position that is harder to accept. To hire without prejudice, it may be necessary to test persons' ability to do tasks. This adds administrative costs, but is fairer than making the prejudicial assumption that older persons will learn more slowly, perform more slowly, and lack the energy and alertness of young people. On the other hand, in many cases there are rewards for seniority that are routinized and may be applied without having any bearing on the efficiency of a given individual. If rewards were to be distributed on the basis of merit rather than seniority, assessment procedures would be necessary, and such procedures would add cost. It is a two-way street, and both practices, although less arbitrary and prejudicial, would add to operating costs.

In the area of retirement policies, one of the major politically sensitive issues is whether Social Security should be treated as a universal benefit or as a form of insurance. Presumably, the latter view was a prominent notion at the initiation of the program, and is evident in its title, Old Age and Survivors Insurance (now called Retirement Survivors Disability Health Insurance, or RSDHI). Many changes have occurred in the program over the years, including coverage by SSI for those not eligible by earnings, which bring the program closer to a notion of a universal entitlement. Consideration will need to be given to the question of whether the system should be moved fully to a universal entitlement. If this conclusion is reached, then attention will need to be given to how to make it work. If it is designed to provide baseline support only, then the assumption that people should get benefits on the basis of payments into the system would need to be negated. Similarly, the fiction that the payments are not a tax would need to be dispelled. Consequences of moving in such a direction would lead to other questions of consistency. For example, with the RSDHI program there are two parallel tax collection systems, and they could be combined. Presumably, the less regressive tax system would be the one to survive.

If clarification of the Social Security system were to occur, it could well have consequences for savings for retirement. On this score, again, policy has not been generated by broad reflection and planning, but has arisen out of historical circumstances. There is no reason why a parallel retirement savings plan as a form of insurance cannot exist, run either by the government or by the private sector. The principle has been established with individual retirement accounts (IRAs), and could be generalized further by being made a required benefit of employment.

What is unique about the IRAs is that they constitute a notion equivalent to immediate vesting. One of the great problems that has been created for older workers is that retirement benefits have not been treated as other forms of compensation, i.e., as belonging to the worker just as wages do. Pension benefits have often been associated with funds controlled by industry or unions, and thus have been subject to many forms of abuse, ranging from actual criminal exploitation of the funds to control of workers by control of access to benefits. If pension benefits are truly a part of wages, the worker should have access to them in the form of immediate vesting and transportability.

The previous sentence may be a strong statement, but it is one that should be considered. The point is that policy development rarely, if ever, begins with such a direct statement. Most often a problem becomes apparent, and then solutions are considered within the context of the political and power structures that exist. This does not necessarily lead to good policy reflecting thoughtful consideration of values.

In sum, changes may well be on the horizon with regard to the role of older workers in America. However, it would be a mistake to view these changes as the inevitable result of demographic and economic forces in the marketplace. Such a model is not only overly simplistic and short-sighted: It has a more insidious effect. It suggests that society in general, and policymakers in particular, are somehow not responsible for the present role of the older worker in the workplace. The view presented here suggests otherwise: that social policy directly shapes roles and expectations. Unfortunately, the values shaping policy are often implicit and ill-considered. Thus the challenge confronting us is not how to respond to forces largely beyond our control. Rather, the challenge is how to develop policy on the basis of explicit statements about how we, as a society, intend to meet the economic and social challenges awaiting us now and in the years to come.

References

Adamchak, D., and E. Friedmann. 1983. "Societal Aging and Generational Dependency Relationships: Problems of Measurement and Conceptualization," *Research on Aging* 5: 319-38.

Back, K. 1969. "The Ambiguity of Retirement." In *Behavior and Adaptation in Late Life,* edited by E. W. Busse and E. P. Pfeiffer, pp. 93-114. Boston: Little, Brown.

Brody, E. 1985. "Parent Care as a Normative Family Stress," *The Gerontologist* 25: 19-29.

Clark, R. 1988. "The Future of Work and Retirement," *Research on Aging* 10: 169-93.

Fullerton, H. 1987. "Labor Force Projections: 1986-2000," *Monthly Labor Review,* September, pp. 19-29.

Gibbs, N. 1988. "Grays on the Go," *Time,* February 22, pp. 66-75.

Graebner, W. 1980. *A History of Retirement.* New Haven, CT: Yale University Press.

Kingson, E., B. Hirschorn, and J. Cornman. 1986. *Ties That Bind: The Interdependence of Generations.* Washington, D.C.: Seven Locks Press.

Longman, P. 1987. *Born to Pay: The New Politics of Aging in America.* Boston: Houghton Mifflin.

Sandell, S. 1987. "Prospects for Older Workers: The Demographic and Economic Context." In *The Problem Isn't Age,* edited by S. Sandell, pp. 3-14. New York: Praeger.

Shanas, E. 1979. "Social Myth as Hypothesis: The Case of the Family Relations of Old People," *The Gerontologist* 19: 3-9.

Smedley, L. 1979. "The Patterns of Retirement," *AFL-CIO American Federationist* 86: 22-25.

U.S. Bureau of the Census. 1982. *Population Profile of the United States: 1981.* Current Population Reports, Series P-20, No. 374. Washington, D.C.: U.S. Government Printing Office.

———. 1983. *America in Transition: An Aging Society.* Current Population Reports, Series P-23, No. 128. Washington, D.C.: U.S. Government Printing Office.

U.S. News & World Report. 1978. "Work Beyond Age 65? Most Would Rather Not." April 3, pp. 50-55.

The Busy Ethic
Moral Continuity Between Work and Retirement

David J. Ekerdt

There is a way that people talk about retirement that emphasizes the importance of being busy. Just as there is a work ethic that holds industriousness and self-reliance as virtues so, too, there is a "busy ethic" for retirement that honors an active life. It represents people's attempts to justify retirement in terms of their long-standing beliefs and values.

The modern institution of retirement has required that our society make many provisions for it. Foremost among these are the economic arrangements and mechanisms that support Social Security, private pensions, and other devices for retirement financing. Political understandings have also been reached about the claim of younger workers on employment and the claim of older people on a measure of income security. At the same time, our cultural map of the life course has now been altered to include a separate stage of life called retirement, much as the life course once came to include the new stage of "adolescence" (Keniston, 1974).

Among other provisions, we should also expect that some moral arrangements may have emerged to validate and defend the lifestyle of re-

tirement. After all, a society that traditionally identifies work and productivity as a wellspring of virtue would seem to need some justification for a life of pensioned leisure. How do retirees and observers alike come to feel comfortable with a "retired" life? In this [essay] I will suggest that retirement is morally managed and legitimated on a day-to-day basis in part by an ethic that esteems leisure that is earnest, occupied, and filled with activity—a "busy ethic." The ideas in this [essay] developed out of research on the retirement process at the Normative Aging Study, a prospective study of aging in community-dwelling men (Bosse et al., 1984).

The Work Ethic in Use

Before discussing how the busy ethic functions, it is important to note a few aspects about its parent work ethic. The work ethic, like any ethic, is a set of beliefs and values that identifies what is good and affirms ideals of conduct. It provides criteria for the evaluation of behavior and action. The work ethic historically has identified work with virtue and has held up for esteem a conflation of such traits and habits as diligence, initiative, temperance, industriousness, competitiveness, self-reliance, and the capacity for deferred gratification. The work ethic, however, has never had a single consistent expression nor has it enjoyed universal assent within Western cultures.

Another important point is that the work ethic historically has torn away from its context, become more abstract and therefore more widely useful (Rodgers, 1978). When the work ethic was

Source: "The Busy Ethic: Moral Continuity Between Work and Retirement," by David J. Ekerdt, *The Gerontologist,* vol. 26, no. 3, pp. 239-244, 1986. Copyright © The Gerontological Society of America. Reprinted by permission. This research was supported in part by the Medical Research Service of the Veterans Administration and by grants from the Administration on Aging (90-A-1194) and the National Institute on Aging (AG02287). The author thanks Raymond Bosse, Thomas Cole, and Linda Evans for helpful comments.

Calvinist and held out hope of heavenly rewards, believers toiled for the glory of God. When 19th century moralists shifted the promise toward earthly rewards, the work ethic motivated the middle class to toil because it was useful to oneself and the common weal. The coming of the modern factory system, however, with its painful labor conditions and de-emphasis on the self-sufficient worker, created a moral uncertainty about the essential nobility and instrumentality of work that made individuals want to take refuge in the old phrases and homilies all the more. As work ideals became increasingly abstract, they grew more available. Rodgers (1978) pointed out that workingmen now could invoke the work ethic as a weapon in the battle for status and self-respect, and so defend the dignity of labor and wrap themselves in a rhetoric of pride. Politicians of all persuasions could appeal to the work ethic and cast policy issues as morality plays about industry and laziness. Thus, despite the failed spiritual and instrumental validity of the work ethic, it persisted in powerful abstraction. And it is an abstract work ethic that persists today lacking, as do many other of our moral precepts, those contexts from which their original significance derived (MacIntyre, 1981). While there is constant concern about the health of the work ethic (Lewis, 1982; Yankelovich & Immerwhar, 1984), belief in the goodness of work continues as a piece of civic rhetoric that is important out of all proportion to its behavioral manifestations or utilitarian rewards.

Among persons approaching retirement, surveys show no fall-off in work commitment and subscription to values about work (Hanlon, 1983). Thus, assuming that a positive value orientation toward work is carried up to the threshold of retirement, the question becomes: What do people do with a work ethic when they no longer work?

Continuity of Beliefs and Values

The emergence of a busy ethic is no coincidence. It is, rather, a logical part of people's attempts to manage a smooth transition from work to retirement. Theorists of the life course have identified several conditions that ease an individual's tran-

sitions from one status to another. For example, transitions are easier to the extent that the new position has a well-defined role, or provides opportunities for attaining valued social goals, or when it entails a formal program of socialization (Burr, 1973; Rosow, 1974). Transitions are also easier when beliefs are continuous between two positions, that is, when action in the new position is built upon or integrated with the existing values of the person. Moral continuity is a benefit for the individual who is in transition, and for the wider social community as well.

In the abstract, retirement ought to entail the unlearning of values and attitudes—in particular, the work ethic—so that these should be no obstacle to adaptation. Upon withdrawal from work, emotional investment in, and commitment to, the work ethic should by rights be extinguished in favor of accepting leisure as a morally desirable lifestyle. Along these lines, there is a common recommendation that older workers, beginning in their 50s, should be "educated for leisure" in preparation for retirement. For example, the 1971 White House Conference on Aging recommended that "Society should adopt a policy of preparation for retirement, leisure, and education for life off the job . . . to prepare persons to understand and benefit from the changes produced by retirement" (p. 53).

But the work ethic is not unlearned in some resocialization process. Rather, it is transformed. There are two devices of this transformation that allow a moral continuity between work and retired life. One—the busy ethic—defends the daily conduct of retired life. The other—an ideology of pensions—legitimates retirees' claim to income without the obligation to work. As to the latter, a special restitutive rhetoric has evolved that characterizes pensions as entitlements for former productivity. Unlike others, such as welfare recipients, who stand outside the productive process, whose idleness incurs moral censure, and who are very grudgingly tendered financial support (Beck, 1967), the inoccupation of retirees is considered to have been *earned* by virtue of having *formerly* been productive. This veteranship status (Nelson, 1982) justifies the receipt of income without work, preserves the self-respect of retirees, and keeps retirement consistent with the dominant societal prestige system, which rewards members primarily to the extent that they are economically productive.

The Busy Ethic: Functions and Participants

Along with an ideology that defends the receipt of income without the obligation to work, there is an ethic that defends life without work. This "busy ethic" is at once a statement of value as well as an expectation of retired people—shared by retirees and nonretirees alike—that their lives should be active and earnest. (Retirees' actual levels of activity are, as shall be explained, another matter altogether; the emphasis here is on shared values about the conduct of life.) The busy ethic is named after the common question put to people of retireable age, "What will you do (or are you doing) to keep yourself busy?" and their equally common reports that "I have a lot to keep me busy" and "I'm as busy as ever." Expressions of the busy ethic also have their pejorative opposites, for example, "I'd rot if I just sat around." In naming the busy ethic, the connotation of busyness is more one of involvement and engagement than of mere bustle and hubbub.

The busy ethic serves several purposes: It legitimates the leisure of retirement, it defends retired people against judgments of obsolescence, it gives definition to [the] retirement role, and it "domesticates" retirement by adapting retired life to prevailing societal norms. Before discussing these functions of the busy ethic, it is important to emphasize that any normative feature of social life entails endorsement and management by multiple parties. There are three parties to the busy ethic.

First, of course, are the subjects of the busy ethic—older workers and retirees—who are parties to it by virtue of their status. They participate in the busy ethic to the degree that they subscribe to the desirability of an active, engaged lifestyle. When called upon to account for their lives as retirees, subjects of the busy ethic should profess to be "doing things" in retirement or, if still working, be planning to "do things." Retirees can testify to their level of involvement in blanket terms, asserting: I've got plenty to do, I'm busier than when I was working. Or they can maintain in reserve a descriptive, mental list of activities (perhaps exaggerated or even fictitious) that can be offered to illustrate a sufficient level of engagement. These engagements run heavily to maintenance activities (e.g., tasks around the house, shopping) and involvement with children and grandchildren. Obviously, part-time jobs, volunteering, or major life projects ("I've always wanted to learn how to play the piano") can be offered as evidence of an active lifestyle. Less serious leisure pursuits (hobbies, pastimes, socializing) can also contribute to a picture of the busy life as long as such pursuits are characterized as involving and time consuming. In honoring the busy ethic, exactly what one does to keep busy is secondary to the fact that one purportedly *is* busy.

A second group of parties to the busy ethic comprises the other participants—friends, relatives, coworkers—who talk to older workers and retirees about the conduct of retired life. Their role is primarily one of keeping conversation about retirement continually focused on the topic of activity, without necessarily upholding ideals of busyness. Conversation with retirees also serves to assure these others that there is life after work. Indeed, apart from money matters, conversation about retired life per se is chiefly conversation about what one does with it, how time is filled. Inquiries about the retiree's lifestyle ("So what are you doing with yourself?") may come from sincere interest or may only be polite conversation. Inquiries, too, can be mean-spirited, condescending, or envious. Whatever the source or course of discussion, it nonetheless frequently comes to assurances that, yes, it is good to keep busy.

The third group can be called institutional conservators of the busy ethic, and their role is more clearly normative. These parties hold up implicit and explicit models of what retired life should be like, models that evince an importance placed on being active and engaged. Prominent institutional conservators of the busy ethic are the marketers of products and services to seniors, the gerontology profession, and the popular media. More shall be said about these later.

Returning to the purposes that the busy ethic serves, its primary function is to legitimate the leisure of retirement. Leisure without the eventual obligation of working is an anomalous feature of adulthood. Excepting the idle rich and those incapable of holding a job, few adults escape the obligation to work. Retirement and pension policies, however, are devised to exclude older adults from the labor force. In addition, age bias operates to foreclose opportunities for their further employment. How can our value system defend this situation—retirement—when it is elsewhere engaged in conferring honor on people who work and work hard? The answer lies in an ethic that endorses leisure that is analogous to work. As noted above, leisure pursuits can range from the serious to the self-indulgent. What legitimates these as an authentic adult lifestyle is their correspondence with the *form* of working life, which is to be occupied by activities that are regarded as serious and engaging. The busy ethic rescues retirement from the stigma of retreat and aimlessness and defines it as a succession to new or renewed foci of engagement. It reconciles for retirees and their social others the adult obligation to work with a life of leisure. This is the nature of continuity in self-respect between the job and retirement (Atchley, 1971).

In an essay that anticipates some of the present argument, Miller (1965) took a stricter view about what justifies retirement leisure. Mere activity is not meaningful enough; it must have the added rationale of being infused with aspects of work that are culturally esteemed. Activity legitimates retirement if it is, for example, economically instrumental (profitable hobbies), or contributes to the general good (community service), or is potentially productive (education or skill development). Whether people in fact recognize a hierarchy of desirable, work-correlative activities at which retirees can be busy remains to be determined. What Miller's essay and the present argument have in common, nonetheless, is the view

that what validates retirement, in part, is activity that is analogous to work.

The busy ethic serves a second purpose for its subjects, which is to symbolically defend retirees against aging. Based on the belief that vigor preserves well-being, subscription to the norm of busyness can recast retirement as "middle-age like." Adherence to the busy ethic can be a defense—even to oneself—against possible judgments of obsolescence or senescence. To accentuate the contrast between the vital and senescent elder, there is an entire vocabulary of pejorative references to rocking chairs and sitting and idleness. As an illustration, a recent piece in my local newspaper about a job placement service for seniors quoted one of the program's participants, who said: "I am not working for income. I am working for therapy, to keep busy. There is nothing that will hurt an elderly person as much as just sitting alone all day long, doing nothing, thinking about nothing." It is appropriate to note here that, in scope, the busy ethic does not apply to all retirees. The busy life is more likely to be an expectation on the conduct of the "young-old" retiree, or at least the retiree who has not been made frail by chronic illness.

A third purpose of the busy ethic is that it places a boundary on the retirement role and thus permits some true leisure. Just as working adults cycle between time at work and time off, retirees too can have "time off." Because the busy ethic justifies some of one's time, the balance of one's time needs no justification. For example, if the morning was spent running errands or caring for grandchildren, one can feel comfortable with napping or a stretch of TV viewing in the afternoon. The existence of fulfillable expectations allows one to balance being active with taking it easy—one can slip out of the retirement role, one is allowed time offstage. Being busy, like working, "pays" for one's rest and relaxation.

The busy ethic serves a fourth function, and this for the wider society by "domesticating" retirement to mainstream societal values. It could be otherwise. Why not an ethic of hedonism, nonconformity, and carefree self-indulgence as a logical response to societal policies that define older workers as obsolescent and expendable? Free of adult workaday constraints, retirees could become true dropouts thumbing their noses at convention. Or why not an ethic of repose, with retirees resolutely unembarrassed about slowing down to enjoy leisure in very individual ways? Retirees do often describe retirement as a time for sheer gratification. In response to open-ended questions on Normative Aging Study surveys about the primary advantages of retirement, men overwhelmingly emphasize: freedom to do as I wish, no more schedules, now I can do what I want, just relax, enjoy life. Such sentiments, however, do not tend to serve drop-out or contemplative models of retired life because retirees will go on to indicate that their leisure is nonetheless responsibly busy. The busy ethic tames the potentially unfettered pleasures of retirement to prevailing values about engagement that apply to adulthood. For nonretirees, this renders retirement as something intelligible and consistent with other stages of life. Additionally, the busy ethic, in holding that retirees can and should be participating in the world, probably salves some concern about their having been unfairly put on the shelf.

The active domestication of retirement is the province of the institutional conservators of the busy ethic. The popular media are strenuous conservators. An article in my local newspaper last year bore the headline, "They've retired but still keep busy," which was reprised only a few months later in another headline, "He keeps busy in his retirement." Both articles assured the reader that these seniors were happily compensating for their withdrawal from work. It is common for "senior set" features to depict older people in an upbeat fashion, though in all fairness the genre of newspapers' lifestyle sections generally portrays everybody as occupied by varied and wonderful activities regardless of age. The popular media are also staunch promoters of aged exemplars of activity and achievement—Grandma Moses, Pablo Casals, George Burns, and so on through such lists (Wallechinsky et al., 1977). A current National Public Radio series on aging and creativity bears the perceptive title: "I'm Too Busy to Talk Now: Conversations with American Artists over Seventy."

Marketers, with the golf club as their chief prop, have been instrumental in fostering the busy image. A recent analysis of advertising in magazines designed specifically for older people found that the highest percentage of ads in these magazines concerned travel and more often than not portrayed older people in an active setting such as golfing, bicycling, or swimming (Kvasnicka et al., 1982). Calhoun (1978) credited the ads and brochures of the retirement home industry, in particular, with promoting an energetic image of older Americans. This industry built houses and, more importantly, built a market for those houses, which consisted of the dynamic retiree. While few retirees ever live in retirement communities, the model of such communities has been most influential in the creation of an active, if shallowly commercial, image of the elderly. One writer (Fitzgerald, 1983), visiting Sun City Center in Florida ("The town too busy to retire"), reflected:

> Possibly some people still imagine retirement communities as boarding houses with rocking chairs, but, thanks to Del Webb and a few other pioneer developers, the notion of "active" retirement has become entirely familiar; indeed, since the sixties it has been the guiding principle of retirement-home builders across the country. Almost all developers now advertise recreational facilities and print glossy brochures with photos of gray-haired people playing golf, tennis, and shuffleboard. (p. 74)

The visitor noted that residents talked a great deal about their schedules and activities. The visitor also noted how their emphasis on activities was an attempt to legitimate retirement and knit it to long-standing beliefs and values:

> Sun Citians' insistence on busyness—and the slightly defensive tone of their town boosterism—came, I began to imagine, from the fact that their philosophies, and, presumably, the [conservative, work ethic] beliefs they had grown up with, did not really support them in this enterprise of retirement. (p. 91)

The gerontological community has been an important conservator of aspects of the busy ethic. Cumming and Henry (1961) early on pointed out the nonscientific presuppositions of mainstream gerontology's "implicit theory" of aging, which include the projection of middle-aged standards of instrumentality, activity, and usefulness into later life. This implicit, so-called "activity theory" of aging entailed the unabashed value judgment that "the older person who ages optimally is the person who stays active and manages to resist the shrinkage of his social world" (Havighurst et al., 1968, p. 161). Gubrium (1973) has noted the Calvinistic aura of this perspective: "Successful aging, as the activity theorists portray it, is a life style that is visibly 'busy' " (p. 7). Continuing this orientation over the last decade, gerontology's campaign against ageism has, according to Cole (1983), promoted an alternative image of older people as healthy, sexually active, engaged, productive, and self-reliant.

Institutional conservators of the busy ethic are by no means monolithic in their efforts to uphold ideals of busyness. Rather, in pursuing their diverse objectives they find it useful to highlight particular images of retirement and later life that coalesce around the desirability of engagement.

Sources of Authority

The busy ethic is useful, therefore, because it legitimates leisure, it wards off disturbing thoughts about aging, it permits retirees some rest and relaxation, and it adapts retirement to prevailing societal norms. These benefits to the participants of the busy ethic are functional only in an analytic sense. No one in daily life approves of busy retirements because such approval is "functional." It is useful at this point to ask why people ultimately assent to the notion that it is good to be busy.

The busy ethic has moral force because it participates in two great strong value complexes—ethics themselves—that axiomatize it. One, of course, is the work ethic, which holds that it is ennobling to be exerting oneself in the world. The other basis for the busy ethic's authority is the profound importance placed on good health and the stimulating, wholesome manner of living that is believed to ensure its maintenance. The maintenance of health is an ideal with a deep tradition that has long carried moral as well as medical significance. Haley (1978), for example, has pointed out how Victorian thinkers promoted the tonic qualities of a robust and energetic lifestyle. The preservation of health was seen to be a duty because the well-knit body reflected a well-formed mind, and the harmony of mind and body signified spiritual health and the reach for higher human excellence. Ill, unkempt, and indolent conditions, by contrast, indicated probable moral failure. Times change, but current fashions in health maintenance still imply that a fit and strenuous life will have medical benefits and testify as well to the quality of one's will and character. Thus, admonitions to older people that they "keep busy" and "keep going" are authoritative because they advocate an accepted therapy for body and soul.

Correspondence With Behavior

One crucial issue is the correspondence between the busy ethic and actual behavior. It is important to mention that not all self-reports about busy retirements are conscious presentations of conformity to a busy ethic. There are retirees who by any reckoning are very active. But in the more general case, if people believe it is important to keep busy, should they not therefore *be* busy by some standard or another?

This [essay's] argument in favor of the busy ethic has implied that belief is not necessarily behavior. On one hand, the busy ethic may—as any ethic should—motivate retirees to use their time in constructive or involving pursuits. It may get them out of the unhealthful rocking chair or away from the can-of-beer-in-front-of-the-TV. On the other hand, the busy ethic can motivate people to *interpret* their style of life as conforming to ideals about activity. An individual can take a disparate, even limited, set of activities and spin them together into a representation of a very busy life. It would be difficult to contradict such a manner of thinking on empirical grounds; "engagement" is a subjective quality of time use that simple counts of activities or classifications of their relative seriousness or instrumentality are not likely to measure. Indeed, gerontologists should be wary about the extent to which the busy ethic may shape people's responses on surveys about their leisure, frequency of activities, and experience in retirement.

In posing the question, "How busy do retirees have to be under such a set of values?" the answer is they don't objectively have to be very busy at all. Just as with the work ethic, which has been an abstract set of ideals for some time (Rodgers, 1978), it is not the actual pace of activity but the preoccupation with activity and the affirmation of its desirability that matters. After all, all of us are not always honest, but we would all agree that honesty is the best policy. The busy ethic, like the work ethic and other commonplace values, should be evaluated less for its implied link with actual behavior than for its ability to badger or comfort the conscience. The busy ethic, at bottom, is self-validating: Because it is important to be busy, people will say they are busy.

Conclusion

The busy ethic is an idea that people have about the appropriate quality of a retired lifestyle. It solves the problem of moral continuity: how to integrate existing beliefs and values about work into a new status that constitutes a withdrawal from work. The postulation of a busy ethic is an attempt to examine sociologically people's judgments of value and obligation regarding the conduct of daily life—their expectations of each other and of themselves.

To be sure, there are other superseding expectations on the conduct of retirees. Writing about the duties of a possible retirement role, Atchley (1976) has noted that a stability of behavior is expected, as well as self-reliance and independence in managing one's affairs. Such normative preferences are fairly vague and open-ended. Rosow (1974) surveyed the prospects for socialization to later life, in which the retirement role is nested,

and found that behavioral prescriptions for older people are open and flexible, and norms are limited, weak, and ambiguous. Even admonitions to be active carry virtually no guidance about the preferred content of such activity. Perhaps this is just as well. Streib and Schneider (1971), summarizing findings from the Cornell Study of Occupational Retirement, pointed out that the vagueness of retirees' role expectations may protect retirees from demands that they might be disinclined to fulfill or from standards that diminished health and financial resources might not allow them to meet.

The busy ethic, too, comprises vague expectations on behavior. It is a modest sort of prescription—less a spur to conformity and more a way to comfortably knit a new circumstance to long-held values. Social disapproval is its only sanction. Not all retirees assent to this image of retirement, nor do they need to. Judging by the ubiquity of the idea, however, subscribers to the busy ethic are probably in the majority; one cannot talk to retirees for very long without hearing the rhetoric of busyness. The busy ethic also legitimates the daily conduct of retired life in a lower key than has been claimed by some gerontologists, who propose that work substitutes and instrumental activity are essential to indemnify retirement. While some retirees do need to work at retirement to psychologically recoup the social utility that working supplied (Hooker & Ventis, 1984), for most it is enough to participate in a rather abstract esteem for an active lifestyle and to represent their own retirement as busy in some way.

To conclude, the busy ethic, as an idealization and expectation of retired life, illustrates how retirement is socially managed, not just politically and economically but also morally—by means of everyday talk and conversation as well as by more formal institutions. Drawing its authority from the work ethic and from a traditional faith in the therapeutic value of activity, the busy ethic counsels a habit of engagement that is continuous with general cultural prescriptions for adulthood. It legitimates the leisure of retirement, it defends retired people against judgments of senescence, and it gives definition to the retirement role. In all, the busy ethic helps individuals adapt to retirement, and it in turn adapts retirement to prevailing societal norms.

References

Atchley, R. C. (1971). Retirement and leisure participation: Continuity or crisis? *The Gerontologist, 11,* 13-17.

Atchley, R. C. (1976). *The sociology of retirement.* New York: Halsted.

Beck, B. (1967). Welfare as a moral category. *Social Problems, 14,* 258-277.

Bosse, R., Ekerdt, D. J., & Silbert, J. E. (1984). The Veterans Administration Normative Aging Study. In S. A. Mednick, M. Harway, & K. M. Finello (Eds.), *Handbook of longitudinal research. Vol. 2, Teenage and adult cohorts.* New York: Praeger.

Burr, W. R. (1973). *Theory construction and the sociology of the family.* New York: John Wiley.

Calhoun, R. B. (1978). *In search of the new old: Redefining old age in America, 1945-1970.* New York: Elsevier.

Cole, T. R. (1983). The "enlightened" view of aging: Victorian morality in a new key. *Hastings Center Report, 13,* 34-40.

Cumming, E., & Henry, W. H. (1961). *Growing old: The process of disengagement.* New York: Basic Books.

Fitzgerald, F. (1983, April 25). Interlude (Sun City Center). *New Yorker,* pp. 54-109.

Gubrium, J. F. (1973). *The myth of the golden years: A socioenvironmental theory of aging.* Springfield, IL: Charles C Thomas.

Haley, B. (1978). *The healthy body and Victorian culture.* Cambridge, MA: Harvard University Press.

Hanlon, M. D. (1983). Age and the commitment to work. Flushing, NY: Queens College, City University of New York, Department of Urban Studies (ERIC Document Reproduction Service No. ED 243 003).

Havighurst, R. J., Neugarten, B. L., & Tobin, S. S. (1968). Disengagement and patterns of aging. In B. L. Neugarten (Ed.), *Middle age and aging: A reader in social psychology.* Chicago: University of Chicago Press.

Hooker, K., & Ventis, D. G. (1984). Work ethic, daily activities, and retirement satisfaction. *Journal of Gerontology, 39,* 478-484.

Keniston, K. (1974). Youth and its ideology. In S. Arieti (Ed.), *American handbook of psychiatry. Vol. 1, The foundations of psychiatry.* 2nd ed. New York: Basic Books.

Kvasnicka, B., Beymer, B., & Perloff, R. M. (1982). Portrayals of the elderly in magazine advertisements. *Journalism Quarterly, 59,* 656-658.

Lewis, L. S. (1982). Working at leisure. *Society, 19* (July/August), 27-32.

MacIntyre, A. (1981). *After virtue: A study in moral theory.* Notre Dame, IN: University of Notre Dame Press.

Miller, S. J. (1965). The social dilemma of the aging leisure participant. In A. M. Rose & W. Peterson (Eds.), *Older people and their social worlds.* Philadelphia: F. A. Davis.

Nelson, D. W. (1982). Alternate images of old age as the bases for policy. In B. L. Neugarten (Ed.), *Age or need? Public policies for older people.* Beverly Hills, CA: Sage.

Rodgers, D. T. (1978). *The work ethic in industrial America: 1850-1920.* Chicago: University of Chicago Press.

Rosow, I. (1974). *Socialization to old age.* Berkeley: University of California Press.

Streib, G. F., & Schneider, C. J. (1971). *Retirement in American society: Impact and process.* Ithaca, NY: Cornell University Press.

Wallechinsky, D., Wallace, I., & Wallace, A. (1977). *The People's Almanac presents the book of lists.* New York: William Morrow.

White House Conference on Aging. (1971). *Toward a national policy on aging: Proceedings of the 1971 White House Conference on Aging, Vol. II.* Washington, DC: U.S. Government Printing Office.

Yankelovich, D., & Immerwahr, J. (1984). Putting the work ethic to work. *Society, 21* (January/February), 58-76.

Life After Work
Retirement, Leisure, Recreation, and the Elderly

Nancy J. Osgood

Work: Past, Present, and Future

Work in Classical and Preindustrial Society

Work has not always been exalted as the noblest of institutions. To the ancient Greeks, who forced slaves to do their work for them, work was nothing more than a curse (Tilgher, 1930). Leisure was the highest aim in life. As Aristotle noted: "We should not be able only to work well but to use leisure well; for as I repeat once more, the first principle of all action is leisure. Both are required, but leisure is better than work and its end" (DeGrazia, 1962, p. 15). The Greeks classified work and other obligations as nonleisure, unlike many today who classify leisure as nonwork. To the Greeks, leisure was the noblest activity, and music, the arts, and contemplation were the highest of all activities, exemplifying the human aspect that was most godlike and that most distinguished humans from other animals (DeGrazia, 1962). Work, on the other hand, was seen as brutalizing the mind, rendering one unfit to consider truth or practice virtues (DeGrazia, 1962, p. 115).

Like the ancient Greeks, the Hebrews viewed work as a trial and tribulation, Adam's punishment for the fall. They placed no intrinsic value or meaning on work. It was merely necessary toil that had to be endured as punishment.

How has the nature and meaning of work changed since early days? What place will work

hold in our lives as we enter what Daniel Bell (1973) has called the postindustrial society? . . .

In *The Coming of Post-Industrial Society,* Bell presents a detailed analysis of the distinguishing features of postindustrialism. Postindustrial society is, above all, a knowledge-based, service-oriented society whose major hallmarks are the increasing bureaucratization of science and specialization of intellectual work.

The supremacy of mind over body is one of the cornerstones of Bell's postindustrial society. As the acquisition and utilization of knowledge and information achieves a larger place in our society, new modes of life that depend on cognitive and theoretical knowledge inevitably result in individual self-enhancement and self-expression.

Writers describing modern day America have suggested that we are in the midst of a value revolution in which the Protestant work ethic, appropriate in earlier days of industrialization but sorely outdated today, is being replaced by a new system of hedonistic values that emphasize fun, consumption, play, and instant pleasure as ends in themselves. Yankelovich (1974) suggests that today success is defined differently than it was 50 years ago. As he points out, from World War I until recently, most Americans defined achievement in terms of material things. Mizruchi's study of success values conducted 20 years ago (1964) also confirmed that materialism was a dominant measure of success in former times. Today, Yankelovich suggests, self-fulfillment and quality of life are more important than higher earnings. If the motif of the past was "keeping up [with] the Joneses," today it is "I have my own life to live."

Let Jones shift for himself" (1974, p. 81). Self-actualization has become a major value in today's society as more and more individuals resist the standardization, regimentation, and specialization characteristic of work in industrial society. Today many are choosing to work part time (roughly 45 percent of all Americans according to Eli Ginzberg) or to find jobs in which they can "do their own thing," be more creative, and "express themselves," even if it means a cut in pay. Fifty million Americans now participate in some form of amateur art activity, a further testimony to the move toward "doing your own thing." . . .

Since 1900, the percentage of a man's life spent in work activities has declined from 66.6 percent to 58.4 percent, the bulk of the reduction due to the institutionalization of retirement. The percentage of a man's total life spent in retirement has increased nearly 150 percent since 1900, from 6.5 percent to 16.8 percent (McConnell, 1980, p. 69). Best [1978] presents an interesting analysis of dramatic changes in the proportion of life spent in work through the centuries in a recent article in *The Futurist*. He states that work absorbed about 33 percent of the average person's life span in primitive times (before 4000 B.C.), 29 percent during the agriculture era (4000 B.C.–1900 A.D.), and about 14 percent during the agricultural era (past 1900 A.D.). In the twentieth century, work time for U.S. males as a proportion of their overall working and sleeping lifetime was cut almost in half between 1900 and 1970, from 23.7 to 13.4 percent (1978, p. 5).

The drastic reductions of work life for U.S. males is a result of several factors besides the institutionalization of retirement. Drastically reduced workweeks coupled with longer vacations and more holidays are a factor. As Best (1979) points out, the average workweek has declined over the last century from about 60 hours in 1870 to 39 hours today. . . .

Wilensky (1961), in his oft quoted article, "The Uneven Distribution of Leisure: The Impact of Economic Growth on 'Free Time,'" presents an interesting historical analysis of changes in the amount of time spent in work, comparing the present century not only to the 1900s but also to earlier centuries. Figures presented by Wilensky convincingly indicate that we are only barely beginning to achieve the amount of leisure time enjoyed by the Romans and by primitive agriculturists. In the old Roman calendar, nearly 109 of the 355 days, or one-third, were designated as nonwork days (p. 109). It is only when we compare work time today with hours spent in work during the late 1800s and early 1900s, when industrialization was at its peak, that we can correctly conclude that the amount of time spent working has been significantly reduced. It is probable, however, that during the next century we may more nearly approximate the work-leisure distribution enjoyed by our ancestors in earlier centuries.

Other significant changes in the organization and structure of work have also been occurring since 1900. Due to the increased length of time spent in education preparing for the jobs characteristic of our new knowledge-based scientific society and to trends toward earlier retirement, workers enter the labor force later and exit earlier now than they did in 1900. The effect is a compression of work into the middle years of life. . . .

Another change is the adoption of the four-day week. Between 1973 and 1977, according to the Bureau of Labor Statistics, the number of U.S. workers on a four-day workweek increased by more than 50 percent, although such workers still represent only 1.4 percent of the U.S. labor force. Another change is the increase in part-time work. Almost nonexistent at the turn of the century, part-time work includes 17 million persons, mostly women. Both of these changes allow more leisure for the American worker and more flexible integration of work and play. . . .

The New Leisure Society

These changes in the organization and structure of work and leisure reflect the larger values of the society and impact on other social institutions, particularly on the family, education, and economic institutions. Roberts (1970), Bacon (1975), Dumazedier (1967), Parker (1976), and others have recently suggested that we are entering a new leisure age, characterized by a new leisure ethic or fun morality. The conceptualization of our society as a new leisure society implies more than simply an increase in the amount of time for leisure. These writers are referring to a major value change, a shift in the way we view work and leisure in our lives. Signs of change can be seen in increased worker dissatisfaction with jobs, absenteeism, part-time work, and midcareer job changing. The new leisure ethic emphasizes leisure as the central life interest, replacing the former centrality of work. Leisure is the most important social institution through which we achieve identity and self-expression, not through work. Finally, leisure has the most important effect on how we structure the other domains of our life (family and work, for example). Leisure is viewed as an end in itself rather than as subordinate to work.

Dumazedier, probably the best known exponent of this argument, suggests that the growth of leisure has nurtured

> a new social need for the individual to be his own master and please himself.... What used to be considered idleness when confronted with the requirements of the firm is now defined as dignity, what used to be called selfishness when confronted with the requirements of the family is now perceived as respect for the personality of one of its members. Part of what used to be considered sinful by religious institutions is now recognized as the art of living. (1974, p. 42)

The development of the new leisure ethic has been made possible primarily by improved technology, which has resulted in shorter workweeks, retirement, pension plans, and relative affluence for large numbers. Two other conditions necessary to the development of such an ethic, according to Dumazedier (1967), are the disappearance of rituals governing social activities and a clear line of demarcation between labor and other activities.

Many writers (Kaplan, 1960; Wilensky, 1964) suggest that modern society is moving in the direction of a fusion of labor and leisure in which work is becoming more like play and play more like work. With this idea in mind, Gregory Stone (1972) has asserted "more and more we play at our work and work at our play." Riesman explains this fusion in terms of the changing U.S. character from inner-directedness to other-directedness. He writes: "The other-directed person has no clear core of self to escape from; no clear line between production and consumption; between adjusting to the group and serving private interests; between work and play" (1953, p. 185). . . .

The historical relationship of work and leisure can be diagrammed as a circular one. In the beginning, there was fusion and integration. Work and leisure were part of the whole and not distinct, observable units of behavior. The Greeks identified leisure as a behavior distinct from and superior to work. The shift was from the fusion of work and leisure to leisure as a priority. With the Industrial Revolution, the gradual change from leisure as a priority to work as the ultimate goal was complete. However, change was inevitable, and gradually work was demoted as leisure achieved prominence. This change reached its peak during the late 1960s and 1970s, when leisure and "doing your own thing" were exalted. . . .

Fourastié writes that "to choose one's leisure will be to choose one's life" (quoted in Dumazedier, 1974, p. 148). If Fourastié is correct, we are currently embarking upon a happier era in the history of civilization. But not all students of leisure agree that the increased amount of leisure time is a positive phenomenon. Another Frenchman, Tocqueville, writing at an earlier time, expressed his fears about the tyrannizing effect of mass affluence resulting from industrialization:

> I seek to trace the novel features under which despotism may appear in the world. The first thing that strikes the observation is an innumerable multitude of men, all equal and alike, incessantly endeavoring to procure the petty and paltry pleasures with which they glut their lives. Each of them, living apart, is as a stranger to the fate of all the rest; his children and his private friends constitute to him the whole of mankind. (1945, p. 10)

Since Tocqueville made his classic statement, numerous others have expressed similar concern over the negative effects of leisure in our mass society. Hedonism, says Daniel Bell (1973), is one of the cultural contradictions of capitalism. Capitalism fosters hedonism through its emphasis on consumption, but the hedonistic individual becomes a less dedicated worker and family worker, thereby jeopardizing future ability to produce and consume. Others have criticized our mass culture for providing spurious gratification, reducing the level of cultural quality and civilization and encouraging totalitarianism and dehumanization by creating a passive public responsive to mass persuasion. . . .

As we approach a new era of labor-leisure relationships, one more closely approximating the situation of ancient Greek and Roman civilizations in which work and leisure were merged and in which leisure enjoyed an exalted status, certain questions are suggested.

Will leisure be a liberating or an alienating social institution?

What new norms will develop to structure labor-leisure relations?

How will new values regarding work and leisure affect other major social institutions, particularly the family, educational, and economic institutions?

What new patterns of social organization and social structures will characterize the new leisure society?

What new cultural values and individual lifestyles will result from these fundamental changes in the structure and organization of work and leisure?

In what ways will patterns of production and consumption be altered in this new society and with what effects?

In the new society, what social institution, if any, will restore the authority of a common code of ethics and social discipline formerly provided by the family, then by work?

How will the new leisure ethic affect our conceptions of aging and retirement in the future? . . .

Retirement makes available a range of options in all life sectors; work role is not necessarily the only one. Continuity theory postulates the inevitability of retirement as a normal noncrisis con-

comitant of our industrial society and emphasizes the necessity to adapt successfully to that condition, involving as it does a change in roles. Those who view retirement as one of the most disturbing crises of their lives, it is claimed, probably had difficulty adapting to other role changes. Adaptive flexibility and a sense of well-being in the middle years of life predict the probable display of these same characteristics in later years. In fact, the entire life cycle may be conceptualized as a process in which success predicts success. Proponents of the continuity theory maintain that for retirees there is a range of options. If life has meaning only when one contributes to it, such a contribution need not be measured in economic or occupational terms. Most retirees, in fact, adapt successfully (Bultena and Wood, 1969; Streib and Schneider, 1971).

Most recent research has indicated that for most people retirement has become a normal, expected part of the occupational cycle. Retirement is not necessarily a traumatizing crisis. If the financial disadvantages of retirement could be eliminated and inflation controlled, people would look forward to retirement in an even more positive sense. The decision to retire is a function of the individual's income, health, family status, and prospects for life after retirement—in other words, what the individual is retiring to as well as from is also important. Hard, dirty, or hazardous work is a factor affecting early retirement, as are increased private and public pension programs and increased social security benefits. . . .

Many researchers whose findings lend support to the continuity theory have found that work is no longer a central life interest for men in U.S. society. Rather, work represents only a means of earning the money necessary to pursue leisure or family activities. For many blue-collar and white-collar workers, as well as professionals, work has become an alienating and dissatisfying experience. In their study of the meaning of work to individuals, Friedman and Orbach conclude that "work does not seem to take precedence over other life areas for most workers" (1974, p. 613). Blauner's review of attitudes of U.S. workers (1964) revealed that many are alienated from their work and see no purpose in it. Similarly Williams and Wirths (1965) found that the world of work was the central element in lifestyle for only 15 percent of their subjects, echoing much earlier findings by Dubin (1956), who found that for three out of four industrial workers, work was not a central life interest. . . .

The studies reviewed here discount the belief that work is currently the most important social institution in our society and that loss of the work role results in a severe crisis of identity for the individual. What these and other recent studies reveal is the changing nature and meaning of work, leisure, and retirement in U.S. society. As retirement becomes a more widespread phenomenon in our society, norms develop around the role of retiree, and more role models are available, thus facilitating socialization and smooth transition into the role. As we enter the new leisure age, which Kaplan (1975) and others describe, and as leisure assumes greater importance and credibility as a legitimate source of personal identity, one suspects that attitudes toward and effects of retirement upon individuals will undergo profound change.

References

Bacon, W. 1975. "Social Caretaking and Leisure Provision." In *Sport and Leisure in Contemporary Society*, edited by S. Parker, mimeograph. London: Polytechnic of Central London.

Bell, Daniel. 1973. *The Coming of Post-Industrial Society.* New York: Basic Books.

Best, F. 1978. "Recycling People: Work Sharing Through Flexible Life Scheduling." *The Futurist* 12 (February):5-16.

————. 1979. "The Future of Retirement and Life Time Distribution of Work." *Aging and Work* 2 (Summer):172-81.

Blauner, Robert. 1964. *Alienation and Freedom.* Chicago: University of Chicago Press.

Bultena, Gordon, and Vivian Wood. 1969. "The American Retirement Community: Bane or Blessing?" *Journal of Gerontology* 24 (January):209-18.

DeGrazia, S. 1962. *Of Time, Work, and Leisure.* New York: Twentieth Century Fund.

Dubin, R. 1956. "Industrial Worker Worlds: A Study of Central Life Interests of Industrial Workers." *Social Problems* 3 (January):131-42.

Dumazedier, J. 1967. *Toward a Society of Leisure.* Amsterdam: Elsevier.

————. 1974. *Sociology of Leisure.* New York: Collier-Macmillan.

Friedman, Eugene, and Harold Orbach. 1974. "Adjustment to Retirement." In *American Handbook of Psychiatry,* edited by Silvano Arieti, pp. 609-45. New York: Basic Books.

Kaplan, Max. 1960. *Leisure in America.* New York: John Wiley.

————. 1975. *Leisure: Theory and Policy.* New York: John Wiley.

McConnell, S. R. 1980. "Alternative Work Patterns for an Aging Work Force." In *Work and Retirement: Policy Issues,* edited by P. Ragan, pp. 69-86. Los Angeles: University of Southern California, Ethel Percy Andrus Gerontology Center.

Mizruchi, Ephraim H. 1964. *Success and Opportunity.* Glencoe, Illinois: Free Press.

Parker, Stanley. 1976. *The Sociology of Leisure.* New York: International Publishers Service (G. Allen).

Riesman, David. 1953. *The Lonely Crowd.* New York: Doubleday.

Roberts, K. 1970. *Leisure.* London: Longman.

Stone, Gregory R. 1972. "American Sports: Play and Display." In *Sport: Readings From a Sociological Perspective,* edited by E. Dunning, pp. 47-65. Toronto: University of Toronto Press.

Streib, Gordon, and Clement J. Schneider. 1971. *Retirement in American Society: Impact and Process.* Ithaca, N.Y.: Cornell University Press.

Tilgher, Adriano. 1930. *Work: What It Has Meant to Men Through the Ages.* Translated by D. Fischer. New York: Harcourt, Brace.

Tocqueville, Alexis de. 1945. *Democracy in America.* New York: Vintage Books.

Wilensky, Harold L. 1961. "The Uneven Distribution of Leisure: The Impact of Economic

Growth on 'Free Time.'" *Social Problems* 9 (Summer):32-55.

———. 1964. "Mass Society and Mass Culture: Interdependence or Independence." *American Sociological Review* 29 (April):173-97.

Williams, Richard H., and Claudine Wirths. 1965. *Lives Through the Years.* New York: Atherton Press.

Yankelovich, D. 1974. *The New Morality: A Profile of American Youth in the 70's.* New York: McGraw-Hill.

———. 1979. "The Future of Retirement and Lifetime Distribution of Work." *Aging and Work* 2 (Summer):31-45.

FOCUS ON PRACTICE   PRERETIREMENT PLANNING

Retirement itself has become a longer and more important part of the life course. In 1900, around 3% of an average man's lifetime was spent in the retirement years, but by 1980 that proportion had increased to 20%, or between 10 and 30 years. For those who retire early, the number of years in retirement can even approach the number of years in the workforce. Yet although we prepare for the world of work through schooling, few people give comparable attention to planning or preparing for retirement.

Taking advantage of opportunities and achieving secure retirement income demand a degree of planning and preparation. Here lies the rationale for preretirement planning as an educational practice with benefits for both workers and employers.

Preretirement planning is becoming more and more common today. The National Council on Aging, the American Association of Retired Persons (AARP), and Retirement Advisors, Inc., are a few of the groups that market their own retirement planning packages. Brokerage firms, outplacement consultants, and other financial groups are increasingly entering the field as well. One professional body, the International Association of Preretirement Planners, seeks to promote improved retirement education. The growth of interest in the field is illustrated by the increase in membership of that group from 150 in 1983 to more than 750 by the end of the decade.

Approximately one-third of business corporations offer some kind of formal program to their workers for preretirement planning (Morrison and Jedriewski, 1988), but the proportion is probably higher among Fortune 500 companies. Current preretirement planning programs typically cover issues such as financial planning, housing options, use of leisure time, and adjustment to the retirement role. Participants may engage in clarification of their own values and also receive factual knowledge during a class that meets 12 to 16 hours over a period of weeks (Giordano and Giordano, 1983).

Some recent trends in preretirement planning include the following (Dennis, 1989):

- Individualized instruction and counseling

- Use of educational technology, such as computer software, to model financial decisions

- Attention to special needs of women in retirement

- Recognition of options for positive growth and productive aging, such as second careers and volunteerism

But after three decades of experience with preretirement planning programs, it is now clear that there are major problems with preretirement planning as it currently exists. Some of these problems include the following:

- *Low participation rate.* A study by AARP revealed that less than a quarter of workers over age 40 reported that their employers were offering any kind of preretirement planning program (American Association of Retired Persons, 1986). Most retirement planning programs are offered by large corporations, so those who are self-employed or work for small businesses are much less likely to participate. What is more, one study found that only 10% of those with access to preretirement planning actually participated in a program (Campione, 1988).

- *Need for earlier planning.* Employers fail to offer, and employees fail to acquire, preretirement planning information early enough in workers' careers. It is harder to start accumulating retirement savings if you begin at 60 than at 35.

- *Ability to reach the least advantaged.* Programs typically reach only the more educated and well-off older people, for whom financial planning makes obvious sense. But poor people also need education about the benefits and entitlements for which they may be eligible, particularly if they are forced to retire early because of ill health. Minority group members report that preretirement planning is not relevant to their needs and concerns (Torres-Gil, 1984). Early retirement among minorities, instead of being a sign of wealth, is often a sign of disability (Stanford, Happersett, and Morton, 1991).

- *Vulnerability of older workers.* Early retirement incentive plans are increasingly being used as a tool for staff reduction and downsizing by major corporations. It is not unusual for older workers to be forced to make irrevocable choices under a tight deadline and with minimum information or help in planning. In these circumstances, educating and protecting the rights of older workers are of paramount concern. Choices about work and retirement reflect the cumulative advantage or disadvantage experienced by workers of different social classes over the course of a lifetime (Crystal, Shea, and Krishnaswami, 1992).

In summary, preretirement planning has established itself as a valuable educational strategy for helping older people achieve greater security in and control over their lives. But preretirement planning and consumer education continue to be limited to the more advantaged older workers. In addition, preretirement planning by itself cannot change the distribution of power or wealth, nor can it create new opportunities for the last stage of life. Thinking about these questions demands a more far-reaching assessment of the role of work and retirement in later life.

FOCUS ON THE FUTURE   THE U.S. WISDOM CORPS?

Dateline: 2021. Washington, DC. United Press International.

Reporters gathered today on the White House lawn for a ceremony to hear the president proclaim the 10th anniversary of the U.S. Wisdom Corps. Former President Bill Clinton, now age 75, was on hand to receive an award for his part in establishing the U.S. Wisdom Corps, a group designed to enlist the talents of retired people for guiding the country during the 21st century.

In his remarks, former President Clinton noted that exactly 60 years ago President John Kennedy established the U.S. Peace Corps, which attracted idealistic young people. Clinton's own efforts to create the Wisdom Corps, he said, were inspired by the idea of doing something like what Kennedy had done, this time for seniors.

The audience was moved by Clinton's reminiscence about his own odyssey since leaving the White House:

"I was only 54 when my term as President was finished, and I have to admit that when I left the White House, it wasn't quite what I expected. I kept busy but I was still trying to find a role for myself. I couldn't just limit myself to the golf course, like some former presidents had done. So I began to look for an organized way to make use of the talents of all former chief executives. That's when we started lobbying Congress to create the U.S. Wisdom Corps.

"At first we ran into a lot of criticism—you know, this was just an elephant's graveyard, a boondoggle for bored CEOs—that kind of thing. But eventually people started listening, especially when large numbers of us baby boomers began to retire. Gradually, we expanded the idea to include retired judges, ministers, all kinds of leaders. There's enormous talent out there, but we weren't attracting that talent through conventional volunteer roles. We needed to come up with roles to make use of the wisdom of a lifetime.

"The U.S. Constitution does not provide a role for former presidents. But in our history, we've seen some very interesting examples. One of my favorites is John Quincy Adams, who went on to become a congressman after leaving the presidency. I didn't feel that option would work for me, and I couldn't exactly run for my local school board—although at times I considered it! As it's turned out, the Wisdom Corps has been the most exciting thing I've done since leaving the White House."

In his speech Clinton detailed examples of how the Wisdom Corps has used the accumulated life experience of retired leaders:

- *Conflict mediation.* By the early years of the 21st century, Americans were getting fed up with lawsuits and the breakdown of the legal system. They found an alternative approach for conflict resolution in a program originating in Boulder, Colorado, where senior citizens were being trained to serve as mediators in tenant-landlord disputes, business conflicts, and other areas where good judgment can overcome antagonism.

- *Proxy decision making.* More and more people are surviving into old age without anyone to make health care decisions on their behalf if they lose mental capacity. A program that began in New Mexico trains retired social workers and teachers to become surrogate decision makers for those with diminished mental capacity who have no family members to speak for them. Difficult end-of-life decisions require all the wisdom available.

- *Oral history.* Only a handful of people in their 90s have firsthand memories of World War II. The Wisdom Corps, in its "Alternatives to War," has been making efforts to ensure that their oral history testimonies are preserved on videotape for future generations, as an inspiration to help us find alternatives to violence in human affairs.

- *Community leadership roles.* The Wisdom Corps has a roster that furnishes board members for libraries, schools, social service agencies, and nonprofit groups of all kinds. In a particularly successful part of its program, the Wisdom Corps sends long-experienced nonprofit executives to agencies needing a temporary CEO while an executive search is going on. These agencies are looking for a strong person who has no interest in permanent power. Retired leaders have proved to be just what was needed.

Is the U.S. Wisdom Corps just a fantasy? Not necessarily. A forerunner already exists. The Service Corp of Retired Executives (SCORE), a program by the U.S. Small Business Administration, enlists retired business executives for volunteer roles as counselors and advisers helping small business owners. SCORE now comprises 13,000 older volunteers in 750 offices around the country. SCORE volunteers rely on life experience to give advice on all aspects of business: writing a business plan, devising a marketing strategy, avoiding pitfalls in expansion, and so on. Through free counseling sessions and low-cost workshops, SCORE volunteers are now serving as mentors to more than a quarter of a million entrepreneurs each year. Building on this pattern of success, SCORE volunteers have expanded to serve new community needs: developing rural communities, assisting businesses filing papers for Chapter 13 bankruptcy, and counseling business owners in the aftermath of natural disasters.

QUESTIONS FOR WRITING, REFLECTION, AND DEBATE

1 The French poet Baudelaire once said, "Work is less boring than pleasure." Was Baudelaire right? Write a short discussion of Baudelaire's statement as you think it applies to the question of work versus leisure among older people. If possible, give examples of people you've known during their retirement years.

2 Imagine you've become the marketing director for a new $100 million residential complex called Retirement City, USA, located in Florida. Your job is to produce a brochure describing the benefits of retirement in this unique residential environment. The idea is to attract a new group of retirees who are looking for a distinctive lifestyle. Prepare a draft of the brochure highlighting the points that would be most attractive to potential residents of Retirement City, USA.

3 The words we use to describe the same action can make a big difference in how we see it. For instance, what is the real difference between *leisure, free time,* and *recreation*? Are the distinctions just a matter of semantics?

4 Imagine a single middle-aged individual who stays at home all day long. What is the difference between describing that person as "on a sabbatical," "on vacation," "unemployed," or "taking early retirement"? Does the individual's age make a difference in what term might be most appropriate?

5 Assume that you've just read a long editorial in a local newspaper that calls on senior citizens to avoid the "rocking chair" approach to retirement living. You find the editorial profoundly disturbing. Write a long letter to the editor of the paper identifying the reasons why you think retirement makes sense today and in the future.

6 Based on your observation of family members or people you've seen in the workplace, what are the biggest problems middle-aged or older workers would face if they were forced to change jobs and go into a completely new field? What steps could be taken to make such changes easier for people?

7 Some people believe that, if there are not enough jobs to go around for everyone, it makes sense to encourage older people to retire and "get out of the way" to make room for the young. What are the arguments for and against this approach to older people in the labor force? What are the costs and benefits of encouraging or discouraging early retirement?

SUGGESTED READINGS

Atchley, Robert C., *The Sociology of Retirement,* New York: Schenkman, 1976.

Bass, Scott, and Caro, Francis J. (eds.), *Toward a Productive Aging Society,* Westport, CT: Auburn House, 1993.

Bluestone, Irving, Montgomery, Rhonda, and Owen, John (eds.), *The Aging of the American Work Force,* Detroit, MI: Wayne State University Press, 1990.

De Grazia, Sebastian, *Of Time, Work and Leisure,* New York: Doubleday, 1964.

Graebner, William, *A History of Retirement: The Meaning and Function of an American Institution,* New Haven, CT: Yale University Press, 1980.

Sandell, Steven H. (ed.), *The Problem Isn't Age: Work and Older Americans,* New York: Praeger, 1987.

A Life Course Perspective on Aging

T ry to conjure a mental image of a college student. Now imagine a recent retiree, a grandmother, a first-time father. Hold those images in mind, and then consider the following facts:

- Each year, half a million people over age 60 are studying on college campuses.

- Retirees from the military are typically in their 40s or 50s.

- In some inner-city neighborhoods, it is not at all unusual to meet a 35-year-old grandmother whose own daughter is a pregnant teenager.

- It is no longer surprising for men in second marriages to become a father for the first time over age 40 or 50.

Did some of those facts contradict the images you conjured, particularly your images about how old people are when they fill certain roles? What this exercise tells us is that roles such as "student," "retiree," "grandmother," or "first-time father" are no longer necessarily linked to chronological age. Today, what we are learning about aging is forcing us to reexamine traditional ideas about what it means to grow old. Both biomedical science and social behavior among older adults departs from stereotyped images of what is "right" or "appropriate" for old age.

Although we tend to think of old age as a stage at the end of life, we recognize that it is shaped by a lifetime of experience. Such conditions of living as social class, formal education, and occupational experience are determinants of the individual's experience in old age. In other words, the last stage of life is the result of all the stages that came before. The implication is that we no longer accept the quality of life in old age, or even the meaning of old age, as a matter of destiny. Rather, we view it as a matter of individual choice and social policy. Whether older people feel satisfaction and meaning in their last years may therefore depend on what they do and what social institutions do to give them new purpose after retirement.

Recent biological research demonstrates that indeed people do not suddenly become old at the time we have defined as "old age." Aging is a gradual process, and many human capabilities survive long past the time when Americans are considered of an age to retire. We are learning more everyday about how and why people grow old, with the hope that we can make the last stage of life just as meaningful in its own way as earlier stages have been.

Age Identification

A central concept in any discussion of aging is age itself. Age identification is partly an acknowledgment of chronological age, or years since birth, but it is also a powerful social and psychological dimension of our lives.

From early childhood, we are socialized to think about what it means to "act your age," a process described as **age differentiation.** We learn that different roles or behaviors are considered appropriate depending on whether we are a toddler, a teenager, an adult, or an elderly person. **Age grading** refers to the way that people are assigned different roles in society depending on their age (Streib and Bourg, 1984). Theorists of *age stratification* emphasize that a person's position in the age structure affects behavior or attitudes (Riley and Foner, 1972).

People also come to define themselves, at least in part, in terms of their age. Consider when you started thinking of yourself as an adult instead of a kid. Did you suddenly lose interest in some of the things that had once fascinated you, because you considered them "childish" interests? Do you anticipate that when you become "middle aged" or "old" you will no longer be quite the same person you are now?

People within a culture have widely shared expectations about the "right time" for an event to happen. In Western society, for example, marriage at age 13 or retirement at age 30 would be considered "off time," but graduation from college at 22 or retirement at age 65 would be "on time." In other words, we have a shared **social clock** concerning the appropriate age for life events (Helson, Mitchell, and Moane, 1984). However, the timetable for life events varies somewhat with social class and occupation; the career timetable of a medical student, for instance, is quite different from that of a migrant farm worker (Bortner, 1979). In addition, age norms change over time (Breytspraak, 1984). For example, Americans today tend to first marry in their mid- to late 20s, but a century ago, people that age (particularly women) would have been considered rather old for first marriage.

Cultural understandings about what is "age appropriate" is part of a tradition going back to antiquity (Falkner and de Luce, 1992). In the comedy of ancient Rome, for example, the elderly are often ridiculed for unseemly behavior, and hostility is expressed toward old men who take young lovers, a theme often repeated in medieval literature (Bertman, 1976).

What do we think is appropriate for "older people" in our culture today? For one answer, we can look to the images in our symbols, rituals, and myths. Storytellers and minstrels have expressed traditional societies' concepts of age, but today in advanced industrial societies those concepts are frequently transmitted and reinforced by television and other mass media. As a rule, people on TV are young and good-looking; older people are not visible on television in anything like their proportion in the actual population (Davis and Davis, 1985). When they are depicted, they tend to be one step removed from the action. Even when TV advertisers try to appeal to the "gray market" of older consumers, they present idealized images of good health and vigorous activity. It seems sometimes that we are trying to ignore the inevitability of old age. On the other hand, some analysts find that older people themselves use TV in ways that connect public concerns with their everyday lives (Riggs, 1998).

Beyond stereotypes, electronic media have a latent effect both more subtle and more pervasive. Television occupies a perpetual present dominated by novelty and momentary images (Meyrowitz, 1985). The effect is to weaken any sense of continuity over the life course and to undercut any authority or meaning for old age (Moody, 1988a). Traditional cultures tend to prize their older members as links in a historical chain reaching back to the ancestors. But the contemporary culture of television, like the Internet, tends to put all age groups on an equal footing. The result is the "disappearance of childhood" and perhaps of old age too (Postman, 1982).

Mythic images of aging are, of course, oversimplified and based on fantasy. But sometimes they examine the deeper meaning of the last stage of life. The Western view of old age tends to be ambivalent. In Ancient Hebrew religious literature, for instance, old age is venerated as a reward for righteous living: the Fifth Commandment to honor one's parents contains a promise of long life. On the other hand, there is a realistic dread of frailty and a fear that children may reject aged parents (Isenberg, 1992). The Book of Job even questions the assumption that old age brings wisdom and recognizes that the wicked can live just as long as the righteous.

The Greek and Roman views of late life also reflect profound ambivalence. In the first great work of Western literature, Homer's *Iliad,* we find worship of youth in the figure of the young, strong warrior Achilles, but the aged Nestor is revered for his wisdom. In the philosophical tradition, Plato and Aristotle took opposing views on aging. For Plato, later life offered a possibility of rising above the body to attain insight into the eternal nature of reality. On the other hand, Aristotle saw middle age as the summit of life, a time when creative intellectual powers were at their peak, but later life as a time of decline.

In our culture today, we explore similar issues, especially in feature-length films. The myths of aging range from the quest for rejuvenation through the fountain of youth (*Cocoon*) to the psychological self-fulfillment of the aged hero returning home (*Wild Strawberries* or *The Trip to Bounti-*

ful). At its best, film can present images of the older person as a genuine hero triumphing over circumstance (*Driving Miss Daisy*). The images of old age purveyed by mass media have a profound effect on attitudes toward aging in all industrialized societies (Featherstone and Wernick, 1995). (See Controversy 10, "Does Old Age Have Meaning?")

The Stages of Life

Since the dawn of civilization, human beings have recognized a progression to the life course, from infancy through old age. The overall progression appears universal, yet the time between birth and death has been organized in distinctive ways by different societies (Boyle and Morriss, 1987). The simplest concept of the life course has been a division into two stages: childhood and adulthood. But as societies become more complex, they tend to develop a greater number of life stages.

Greek and Roman ideas were influential in shaping how we think today about aging and the life course. One of the greatest Greek tragedies is the three-part Oedipus cycle, the last play written when its author, Sophocles, was 90 years old himself. In this story, Oedipus became king because he solved the famous riddle of the Sphinx: "What creature walks on four legs in the morning, two legs at noon, and three legs in the afternoon?" The answer is the human being at successive life stages: infancy (crawling on all fours), adulthood (walking on two), and old age (using a cane, a third leg, to support the other two). The Greek medical writer Hippocrates described four stages of life, or "ages," corresponding to the four seasons of the year. Similar ideas were put forward by the Roman physician Galen and by the astronomer Ptolemy. Ptolemy developed an idea of seven stages of life, which had great influence during the Middle Ages.

During the Middle Ages, Christian civilization balanced the image of multiple stages with the metaphor of life as a journey or a spiritual pilgrimage. From that standpoint, no single stage of life could be viewed as superior to another. Just as the natural life cycle was oriented by the recurrent cycle of the seasons, so the individual soul would be oriented toward the hope of an afterlife (Burrows, 1986). The human life course as both cycle and journey was thereby endowed with transcendent meaning and wholeness (Cole, 1992).

With the coming of the Reformation and the Renaissance, ideas about the life course changed into forms we recognize as modern. Writing in this epoch, Shakespeare expressed the traditional idea of the "Seven Ages of Man":

> All the world's a stage
> And all the men and women merely players,
> They have their exits and entrances;
> And one man in his time plays many parts,
> His acts being seven ages.
>
> (*As You Like It*, Act 2, scene 7)

To Shakespeare, the periods of life were merely "roles" acted out on the stage of society, and the role losses of old age appeared as the final act of the play. Thus a theatrical metaphor replaced the ideal of a cosmic cycle or a spiritual journey.

At the dawn of modern times, a generation after Shakespeare, drawings and engravings began to depict the stages of life in a new way. The traditional image of a completed circle became an image of a rising and falling staircase, where midlife occupied the peak of power. That image promoted the idea of life as a "career," in which individuals could exercise control over later life through, for example, extended education, good health care, and capital accumulated through savings during earlier stages.

During the 16th and 17th centuries, the stages of life began to be demarcated in ways we recognize today. Childhood became a period of life in its own right, separate from adulthood and old age (Aries, 1962). By the 20th century, as the practice of retirement became well established, old age became a distinct phase as well. Some sociologists argue that such stages reflect patterns of socialization tied to dominant institutions such as the school or workplace (Dannefer, 1984); in other words, retirement exists as a separate phase of life partly because society needs to make way in the workplace for younger workers.

Today, a person will spend, on average, at least one-fourth or even one-third of adulthood in retirement (Kohli, 1987). Partly as a consequence, new distinctions are made between the young-old, the old-old, and now the oldest-old. Demarcating a stage of life following the working years is more important to us than ever, yet we have simultaneously become less certain about what it means to grow older or to "act your age" at any point in life.

The Life Course and Aging

The study of aging as a historical phenomenon reveals a variety of views about the stages of life, about when old age begins, and about what it involves (Minois, 1989). When we read about aging in the Bible or in works by such writers as Shakespeare or Cicero, we might imagine that "old age" is a fixed stage of life, always part of the natural pattern of things, like birth or death. But now at the beginning of the 21st century, it has become clear that human aging is far more ambiguous than might have been imagined in earlier epochs. We can most fruitfully understand old age not as a separate period of life but as part of the total human life course from birth to death.

Increasingly, aging is seen from this **life course perspective.** In other words, we look at old age as one phase of the entire course of life and the result of influences that came earlier than old age. We distinguish here between the span of a lifetime, the total number of years we live, and the course of life, which refers to the meaningful pattern seen in the passing of time. Gerontology is enriched and broadened by the life course perspective.

Instead of merely describing the limited characteristics of old age, we shift the framework to include all phases of life, from childhood, adolescence, and adulthood right up through the last period of old age. We also view the complex interaction of age, social status, cohort effects, and history (Riley and Riley, 1994). Longitudinal research, which follows individuals over long periods of time, is one manifestation of the life course perspective.

The life course perspective insists that to make sense of later life we need to understand the entire life history. As people move through the life course, they are socialized to act in ways appropriate to successive social roles: student, parent, worker, retiree, and so on. But these structural factors only set boundaries; the meaning and experience of aging varies significantly by culture and is influenced by powerful factors such as gender, socioeconomic status, and ethnicity. There is also room for individual variety and freedom of choice as human beings interpret age-related roles in distinctive ways.

Life Transitions

A life course perspective will recognize markers of the passage through life: important life events or transition points, such as graduation from school, first job, marriage, and retirement. In some respects, life transitions have become more predictable than was true earlier in history. For example, today people commonly die in old age, whereas in an earlier era, death was not unusual at any time of life. Thus an event such as the death of a spouse or of a parent is now a more predictable marker of later adulthood than it once was.

At the same time, however, certain transitions are less often tied to a particular age or stage of life than they might have been in earlier times. For example, during the 1950s and 1960s, college students were expected to graduate at the age of about 21. But today's college students graduate at any age from the early 20s to the 30s and beyond, and news photos of gray-haired grandparents wearing a cap and gown are no longer uncommon. Graduation may occur either before marriage, sometime during child rearing, or well after. Whatever the age or circumstance of the graduate, however, the transition still marks a major role change.

Special events that mark the transition from one role to another—such as a bar mitzvah, confirmation, graduation ceremony, or wedding—are known as **rites of passage** (Van Gennep, 1960). These rituals reinforce shared norms about the meaning of major life events. Some traditional rites of passage, such as the sequestration of adolescents prior to induction into adult society, are no longer commonly observed in our society. However, we continue to observe a great many, including such markers of old-age transitions as retirement parties, 50th wedding anniversaries, and funerals.

How are we to understand the significance of life transitions? As the human life course became an object for scientific study, the stages of life were no longer seen as part of a cosmic order of meaning (Cole and Gadow, 1986). Instead, life span developmental psychology attempts to explain psychological change over the course of life as a natural process unfolding through time. Erik Erikson (1963), an influential developmental psychologist, depicted the life course as a series of psychological tasks, each requiring the person to resolve conflicting tendencies. For middle age, Erikson posited a conflict between stagnation and generativity—roughly, being trapped by old habits versus going beyond self-absorption to nurture the next generation (Kotre, 1984). For old age, Erikson saw a conflict between ego integrity and despair—that is, accepting one's life versus feeling hopeless and depressed about the limited time remaining.

Related to Erikson's basic ideas has been the attention on psychological changes during midlife transition, a time when people in middle age confront facts about mortality and the limits of youthful dreams (Jacques, 1965). Psychologist Daniel Levinson (1978) has described life transitions characteristically associated with ages such as 30, 40, and 50. These are times when people at midlife reassess themselves and ask, "Where have I come from and where am I going?" Many of these psychological "passages" or changes of adult life have been popularized by journalists. However, doubts have been raised about just how universal such passages and age-related transitions actually are (Braun and Sweet, 1984). Even Erikson's theory has never been fully demonstrated by empirical study.

In contrast, many theorists today see personality in terms of continuity or flexible adaptation over the life course. These theories are more optimistic than those that see old age as a time of loss resulting in either passive adjustment or dependency and depression. Today, most gerontologists believe that people bring positive resources to aging, including a personal sense of meaning. Empirical studies show that people generally cope well with such life transitions as retirement, widowhood, and the health problems of later life. When problems come, styles of coping tend to remain intact, and people adapt. Because of this capacity for adaptation, old age is not usually an unhappy time.

Nevertheless, those behavioral or psychological problems that do arise come about because of the difficulties of preparing for life transitions without the help of widely observed rites of passage or institutional structures. For example, the transition from adolescence to adulthood is typically marked by events such as marriage, parenthood, and employment (Hogan and Astone, 1986). While schools, job orientation, or marriage counseling help people make transitions to adulthood, few social institutions exist to help people with the transitions of the second half of life.

In addition, we now have no consensus about how people are supposed to act when in late life they confront events that have traditionally been linked to younger ages (Chudakoff, 1989). How are older widows supposed to go about dating? How much help should elderly parents expect from their children who are themselves at the point of retirement? When confronted with a 70-year-old newlywed or a 60-year-old "child," we realize how unsettled are the norms relating to many of the transitions in later adulthood (Featherstone and Hepworth, 1993).

Theories of Aging

Modernization Theory

How do we make sense of the contradictory images of aging found in modern culture? One influential account of aging that tries to do so is **modernization theory** (Cockerham, 1997). According to this theory, the status of the elderly declines as societies become more modern. The status of old age was low in hunting and gathering societies, but it rose dramatically in stable agricultural societies, where older people controlled the land. With the coming of industrialization, it is said, modern societies have tended to devalue older people. Modernization theory of aging suggests that the role and status of the elderly are inversely related to technological progress. Factors such as urbanization and social mobility tend to disperse families, while technological change tends to devalue the wisdom or life experience of elders, leading to a loss of status and power (Cowgill and Holmes, 1972). Some investigators have found that key elements of modernization were in fact broadly related to the declining status of older people in different societies (Palmore and Manton, 1974).

This account strikes a responsive chord because it echoes the "golden age" picture, which depicts the old as honored in preindustrial societies (Stearns, 1982), a version of the "world-we-have-lost" syndrome (Laslett, 1965/1971). But the truth is more complex than modernization theory might suggest, and in fact the theory has been widely criticized (Haber, 1983; Quadagno, 1982). As we have seen already, in primitive, ancient, and medieval societies, the elderly were depicted and treated in contradictory ways: sometimes abandoned, sometimes granted power. The history of old age includes variations according to race, gender, social class, and culture. Modernization has clearly reshaped the meaning of old age, yet image and reality have never entirely coincided, as the cross-cultural study of aging confirms (Holmes and Holmes, 1995).

At the core of the history of old age, there has always been ambivalence: resentment and guilt, honor and oppression. The psychological basis for ambivalence is understandable. Why shouldn't adults feel guilt and dread at the sight of vulnerable old age stretching before them? And why shouldn't they harbor ambivalent feelings toward those who accumulate power and wealth over a long lifetime? We see the same ambivalence today. Older people as a group receive widely popular benefits from the welfare state, yet they are sometimes depicted, perhaps unfairly, as selfish or unconcerned with other generations. The truth is different from what popular images convey.

A decisive change with industrialization has been a growing rationalization and bureaucratization of the life course itself—a greater rigidity among the "three boxes of life" of childhood, adulthood, and old age (Bolles, 1981). At the same time, as we have seen, mass media and rapid flux in cultural values have begun to erode any special qualities linked to distinctive life stages. With rising longevity, more people are living to old age, and the elderly as a group are becoming a larger proportion of the total population. The power of older people has grown by sheer numbers. Meanwhile, the achievement of old age has been devalued simply by becoming more familiar. Perhaps most important, old age itself has been stripped of any clear or agreed-on meaning because the entire life course itself has changed in ways that will have unpredictable effects on what aging may be in the 21st century.

The problem of constructing an overall theory of aging for social gerontology can be compared with a parallel problem in the biology of aging. The difficulty for evolutionary biology begins with a paradox: Why does aging appear at all? From the standpoint of survival of the fittest, there seems to be no reason for organisms to live much past the age of reproduction. Old age, in short, should not exist. Yet human beings do live long past the period of fertility; indeed, human beings are among the longest-living mammals on earth.

Thus the meaning of old age is a problem even for biology, and biologists have put forward a whole variety of theories to explain it: somatic mutation theory, error catastrophe theory, autoimmune theory, and so on. No single theory has proved decisive, but all have stimulated research enabling us to better understand the biology of aging. Similarly, the changing condition and meaning of old age has provoked a variety of theories in social gerontology. Just as with the biology of aging, there is no clear agreement that a single theory is best. But two early theories of aging are still worth closer examination because they demonstrate just how deeply held values affect all theories of aging and how these theories are related to enduring questions about the meaning of old age.

Disengagement Theory

One of the earliest comprehensive attempts to explain the position of old age in modern society was **disengagement theory** (Cumming and Henry, 1961). Disengagement theory looks at old age as a time when both the older person and society engage in mutual separation, as in the case of retirement from work. This process of disengagement is understood to be a natural and normal tendency reflecting a basic biological rhythm of life. In other words, the process of disengagement is assumed to be "functional," serving both society and the individual. Disengagement theory is in fact related to modernization theory: Because the status of the elderly declines when society becomes more modern and efficient, it is natural for the elderly to disengage.

Disengagement theory grew out of an extensive body of research known as the Kansas City Studies of Adult Life, a 10-year longitudinal study of the transition from middle age to old age (Williams and Wirths, 1965). The idea of disengagement presented itself not only as an empirical account based on those findings but also as a theory to explain why the facts turned out the way they have. But the theory of disengagement has been criticized by gerontologists (Hochschild, 1975), including those who point out that the theory evolved during the 1950s and reflected social conditions quite different from those today.

Even though the original theory is no longer widely accepted, the pattern of disengagement does describe some behavior of older people—for example, the popularity of early retirement. But there are growing numbers of older people whose behavior cannot be well described as withdrawal or disengagement from society. Disengagement as a global pattern of behavior can hardly be called natural or inevitable.

Another problem arises when we describe disengagement as "functional," which is a synonym for useful. The same process that might be functional or useful for an organization—for instance, compulsory retirement at a predictable age—may not be at all useful for individuals, who might prefer flexible retirement. In fact, it was widespread resentment at being forced to retire at a fixed age that led Congress to end mandatory retirement in 1986.

There is also a difficulty about what behavior is actually being described by the concept of disengagement. For example, individuals might partially withdraw from one set of activities, such as the workplace, to spend more time on other activities, such as family and leisure pursuits. Later life today, at least for those who remain healthy, is often filled with a rich range of activities. Total withdrawal is quite uncommon. Advancing age at some point is usually accompanied by losses in health, physical ability, and social networks. Those who age most successfully adjust to and compensate for these losses by putting the changes of later life into a wider perspective: an attitude sometimes described as "wisdom."

The Kansas City Study investigators found that, with advancing age, there is in fact a trend toward greater *interiority,* meaning increased attention to the inner psychological world (Neugarten et al., 1964). Individuals appear to reach a peak of interest in activity and achievement in their middle years. As they anticipate later life, they may become more detached, more inclined to "ego transcendence," as if in anticipation of predictable role losses in later life (Peck, 1968).

Understood in this way, "disengagement" need not necessarily describe the outward behavior of individuals but may refer to an inner attitude toward life. Furthermore, there is no reason to assume that all older people are inclined toward even a psychological stance of disengagement; some may have ambivalence about their own activities and attachments. Perhaps the greatest example in literature of that ambivalence is the tragic fate of Shakespeare's King Lear, who tried to give up his role as king but was not quite able to withdraw from power and prestige. As a result, he brought disaster on his family. King Lear's example suggests that disengagement depends on having some sense of personal meaning that is distinct from the office one holds. The ability to achieve some degree of detachment, at any age, is a matter of wide individual difference. In later life, disengagement is the preferred style for some, while continued activity remains attractive for others.

Activity Theory

At the opposite pole from disengagement theory is the **activity theory** of aging, which argues that the more active people are, the more likely they are to be satisfied with life. Activity theory assumes that how we think of ourselves is based on the roles or activities in which we engage: We are what we do, it might be said. Activity theory recognizes that most people in old age continue with the roles and life activities established earlier because they continue to have the same needs and values.

A similar point is made by the **continuity theory** of aging, which notes that people who grow older are inclined to maintain as much as they can the same habits, personality, and style of life they developed in earlier years (Costa and McCrae, 1980). According to both activity theory and continuity theory, any decreases in social interaction are explained better by poor health or disability than by some functional need of society to "disengage" older people from their previous roles (Havighurst, Neugarten, and Tobin, 1968).

A large body of research seems to support some aspects of activity theory. Continued exercise, social engagement, and productive roles all seem to contribute to mental health and life satisfaction. But other studies indicate that informal activity or even merely perceived social integration may be more important in promoting subjective well-being. In other words, our attitude and expectations about activity or detachment may be more important than our formal participation patterns (Longino and Kart, 1982). In fact, what counts as "activity" depends partly on how we look at things, not on external behavior alone. This point is emphasized by those who adopt a phenomenological standpoint underlying the interpretation theory of aging.

If retirement or age limitations make actual participation impossible, activity theory suggests that people will find substitutes for earlier roles or activities that had to be given up (Atchley, 1985). A great many social activities encouraged by senior centers or long-term care facilities are inspired by an assumption that, if older people are active and involved, then all will be well. This "busy ethic" and its hostility to retirement is expressed in similar terms and the sentiment seems widely shared. For instance, former *Cosmopolitan* magazine editor Helen Gurley Brown, in a self-help book for older women titled *The Late Show* (1993), writes that work is "our chloroform . . . our life . . . our freedom from pain . . . supplier of esteem." Along the same lines, essayist Malcolm Cowley in his book *The View From 80* (1980) also expressed the ideal of the activity theory of aging when he wrote: "Perhaps in the future our active lives may be lengthened almost to the end of our days on earth; that is the most we can hope for."

But such active involvement may be more feasible for the young-old than for the old-old. Biological limitations cannot be altogether overcome by voluntary effort: for example, no amount of health promotion is likely to prevent Alzheimer's disease. Similarly, the ideal of active aging seems in many respects a prolongation of middle age rather than something special or distinctive about the last stage of life. Finally, despite some progress in recent years, society still places obstacles to social engagement in old age. For example, remarriage is statistically more difficult for older women than for older men, and in the labor market age discrimination is a very real barrier preventing middle-aged and older people (anyone over 40 is officially an "older worker") from taking up second careers. More realistic recognition of these facts might allow the elderly to live out their years with greater dignity.

Influences on the Life Course

There are obvious limitations to theories of aging: None of them fully explains the variety of old age, and many theories seem to reflect social values in uncritical ways—for example, by holding up activity or disengagement as ideal end points of later life. The advantage of thinking in terms of age transitions is that we can see adult development as more open ended than people have tended to see it in the past. As a result, the meaning of old age is less fixed, and the choices are more varied. We can contrast this wider social freedom with stereotypes that still persist about human development in the second half of life.

The most pervasive and popular view of adulthood is not based on positive development at all but assumes continuous deterioration and decline: After youth, it's all downhill. This pessimistic, age-as-decline model gives priority to biological factors and is the basis for the widely shared prejudice called "ageism." We are better off appreciating how social class, life history, and social institutions and policies create variation in the experience of aging. Although aging is negative for some people, for others it opens the door to meaningful new roles and activities.

Social Class and Life History

The pathway through life depends very much on social class, which is strongly related in turn to the number of years spent in the educational system. Socioeconomic position predicts not only how long people remain in school but also, for instance, whether they will be "late" parents—that is, with a first child born after age 30.

Earlier life events have long-lasting effects. The basic rule of accumulated advantage or disadvantage is that "the rich get richer and the poor get poorer." For example, early completion of college and entry into a favorable occupation is converted during middle age into increased wealth in the form of home ownership and pension vesting (Henretta and Campbell, 1976). Women who enter the labor force at the beginning of childbearing usually have to accept career interruptions and tend to have diminished income later in life; thus gender differences in old-age poverty are explainable partly as the result of life course choices made decades earlier.

History also plays a profound role in shaping lives. For example, a large historical event like the Great Depression caused a dramatic and unexpected drop in income and status for many people (Elder, 1974). Members of the cohort who were in their prime working years at the time were typically worse off financially in old age than their children, the current generation of retirees. This recognition of the influence of historical events has stimulated new interest among sociologists in using interviews and oral history to understand how social forces affect people's lives (Bertaux, 1981).

Unpredictable or nonnormative life events, such as getting divorced or losing a job, also have a significant effect on the life course. A longitudinal study during the 1970s showed that around one-third of people experienced an unexpected but very significant drop in income due to such nonnormative life events (Duncan, 1988). Research has also shown that negative life events like widowhood or job loss can cause a dramatic downturn in personal health and can profoundly affect an individual's financial status during retirement. Such events induce a psychosomatic response to stress, and negative life events therefore become risk factors that predict the onset of illness (Holmes and Rahe, 1967). Yet the impact of life events is not a simple process. The same stressful life event—for example, bereavement—may have different effects on different people (George, 1980). The impact depends on whether the event was expected or anticipated and also on what kind of personal or family resources are available. Support from family and friends can help older people cope with stress and maintain self-esteem.

Social Institutions and Policies

The structure of the life course in modern times has been shaped by the power of the educational system and the workplace. In the 19th century, the rise of public schools began to lengthen the period of formal education and introduce credential requirements for most types of work. The United States, a self-consciously "modern" nation, took a lead in these progressive developments (Fischer, 1977; Achenbaum, 1978). Early in the 20th century, adolescence was recognized as a distinct phase of life and became more prolonged, while middle age became an important period of the life course (Neugarten, 1968).

The industrial revolution brought far-reaching demographic and economic changes, as well as new cultural ideas about age-appropriate behavior (Hareven and Adams, 1982). Bureaucratic institutions, from local school systems to the Social Security Administration, always favor rule-governed, predictable procedures, so it is not surprising that with the rise of bureaucracy came an emphasis on defining life stages by chronological age.

Today, social policies and institutions still define transitions throughout life. The educational system defines the transition from youth to adulthood, just as retirement defines the transition from middle age to old age. Like progression through the school system, the movement into retirement seems more orderly than midlife transitions because retirement is closely regulated by employment policies and pension coverage. But the timing of retirement today is becoming less predictable than in the past because of turbulence in the U.S. labor market as well as the disappearance of mandatory retirement. Economic pressures force some to retire early, while others are encouraged to go back to school or take on part-time employment. The result is that clear roles—"student," "retiree," and so on—are becoming blurred.

If the life course is shaped by societal forces, then it is reasonable to think that some of the negative features of old age may be due, at least in part, to institutional patterns that could be changed. A good example is the pattern known as **learned helplessness,** or dependency and depression reinforced by the external environment (Seligman, 1975). It has been suggested that some of the disengagement often seen in old age is not inevitable but comes from social policies and from practices in institutions that care for the dependent elderly (Baltes and Baltes, 1986). For instance, nursing home residents often suffer a diminished **locus of control,** where they lose the ability to control such basic matters as bedtime and meal choices. When residents feel manipulated by forces beyond their personal control, they may become more withdrawn, fail to comply with medical treatment, and become fatalistic and depressed.

Without interventions to reduce dependency, elderly people in ill health all too commonly lose hope and self-esteem as they experience declining control (Rodin, Timko, and Harris, 1985). But this downward spiral is not inevitable. The institutional structures responsible for such dependency can be changed. In an experiment with nursing home residents, psychologists offered small opportunities to increase locus of control—for example, allowing elderly residents to choose activities or giving them responsibility for taking care of plants. The result was a dramatic improvement in morale and a decline in mortality rates (Rodin and Langer, 1980).

Aging in Postindustrial Society

Today, at the beginning of the 21st century, we no longer have a shared timetable for the course of life. The timing of major life events has become less and less predictable at all levels of society. In upper socioeconomic groups, for example, a woman with a graduate degree and career responsibilities may delay having a first child until age 35 or later; in other parts of society, where teenage pregnancy rates have soared, a 35-year-old woman may well be a grandmother. We are no longer so surprised when a 60-year-old retires from one career and takes up a new one, perhaps in consulting if the retiree has been an executive or professional or in small electronics repair if the retiree has been a technician. In many other ways as well, the life course is becoming more "deinstitutionalized," more fragmented, disorderly, and unpredictable (Held, 1986). Major events of life are no longer parts of a predictable or natural pattern.

Although the rigidity of the linear life plan has failed to keep up with new demographic realities, it did offer a degree of security. In the new, "postindustrial" life course, we are increasingly each on our own. Familiar social institutions like marriage and employment can no longer be counted on for security throughout adulthood, and therefore the last stage of life also becomes less predictable.

Society has not yet come to terms with the meaning of "aging" in such unpredictable times. Optimists believe that medical science will soon permit us to delay aging-related decline until later and later in life. Yet economic forces seem to move in the opposite direction. In science and engineering, knowledge becomes obsolete within 5 or 10 years, so life experience counts for less than exposure to the latest technical advances. On the one hand, biology promises to postpone aging, but on the other hand, social forces, like age discrimination, make the impact of aging on individuals more important than ever.

Time and the Life Course

Note that expectations about time remain a major element in how we think about aging and the life course today (Hendricks and Peters, 1986). Just as industrialization imposed time schedules on workers to improve efficiency in the workplace, so the life course became "scheduled" by differentiated life stages. The factory and the assembly line had their parallel in the linear life plan. But that mode of organization has itself become outdated. In a postindustrial "information economy," the pace of life is speeding up, and flexible modes of production require a more flexible life course. The volatile economy demands multiple job changes and thereby makes every career unpredictable. Individuals at any age may be called on again and again to rewrite their biographies, although reinventing oneself gets more difficult as the résumé gets longer.

Another example of our contemporary time orientation is the prolonged period of life devoted to education. The knowledge explosion and pressure for specialization put a premium on added years of schooling, and the job market has fewer places for those without advanced skills. Our post-industrial economy is increasingly based on "knowledge industries," where emerging fields, such as computer software and biotechnology, favor cognitive flexibility.

The trend toward cognitive flexibility also poses a distinct challenge for an aging society. Middle-aged and older workers, who are perceived to be less creative than younger workers, may be at a disadvantage in the fast-moving labor market. For instance, in some branches of media or advertising, an employee is viewed as "old" over the age of 40. But if retirement, the defining institutional feature of old age, is to remain economically feasible, then we will have to develop ways to keep people working as long as they remain productive. Retraining for displaced workers and displaced homemakers, of whatever age, will become imperative in the future. These trends underscore the importance of adaptability and lifelong learning.

Parenthood offers still another example of our changing time orientation. In the 1830s, demographers estimate, 90% of a woman's years after marriage were spent raising dependent children (Gee, 1987). But by the 1950s, that proportion had dropped to 40%, giving rise to what some observers dubbed the "empty nest" syndrome: an extended postparental period of life that occurs after children have grown up and left home (Lowenthal and Chiriboga, 1972). Because of women's roles and responsibilities in the family, their later lives typically have greater variability than men's (Rindfuss, Swicegood, and Rosenfeld, 1987). This makes the impact of gender on the life course a complex subject (Rossi, 1985).

Another change has been the postponement of child rearing. People often spend more of their lives in their roles as adult children of aging parents than as parents themselves (Brubaker, 1985). But what does it mean, in psychological and social terms, when a "child" is 50 or 60 years old or even older? Even to ask these questions shows that the human life course has changed in ways that are still not fully recognized.

The Moral Economy of the Life Course

The changing structure of the life course has profound implications for obligations and expectations across generations. Martin Kohli (1986, 1987), for example, has analyzed the evolution of retirement in terms of what he calls the "moral economy" of the life cycle. The moral economy embodies expectations of what is fair or right: Stay in school and you'll get a good job, become a senior citizen and you'll have a right to retirement income, and so on. But the old "moral economy," with its characteristic distribution of work and leisure according to chronological age, is losing its power, and we do not have anything as well defined to replace it.

We need to develop bolder ideas about the positive social contributions that can be made by the old; we also need to think more deeply about the meaning of life's final stage. Cicero (106-43 B.C.), author of the classic essay "On Old Age," offered a realistic account of both the gains and losses of aging. Cicero was inspired by the hope that the mind can prevail over the body. Thus he viewed old age not exclusively as a time of decline or loss but also as an opportunity for cultivating compensatory wisdom. Cicero, in fact, was one of the first and most eloquent proponents of the ideal of "successful aging" (Baltes and Baltes, 1990).

We should not sentimentalize the status of old age in the past. But at least in the past, those who had lived a full life span could take for granted shared values and shared experience across the generations, simply because the pace of change was slower. With the rapid social changes of postindustrial society, we can too easily stereotype those who are older as people who are "behind the times" or lacking in creativity and wisdom. The challenge of an aging society in the 21st century is to nurture the special strengths of age in an environment that prizes change, novelty, and flexibility.

One role well suited to older people in such an environment might be mentoring, or guiding the next generation in the capacity of teacher, coach, or counselor. This idea is attractive for several reasons: It encourages intergenerational relationships, and it takes advantage of generativity and wisdom, the virtues to be cultivated in the second half of life, according to Erikson. Mentors, however, still have to develop up-to-date skills and attitudes if their advice is to be respected by younger workers.

The point is that the mismatch between the flexibility of the individual aging experience and the rigidity of outdated social structures, such as retirement practices, does not need to limit opportunities in later life (Riley and Riley, 1994). Instead of treating the life course as fixed, we are coming to see aging as susceptible to intervention and improvement. Instead of viewing age as decline, it is possible to provide incentives that modify the lifestyles and behaviors of older people. The goal will be to move from an age-differentiated society to an age-integrated society, where opportunities in education, work, and leisure are open to people of every age. (See Controversy 7, "Is Retirement Obsolete?")

The Biology of Aging

The life course perspective on aging offers an optimistic view of possibilities open to older people in our society. That view is sensible, given the prolongation of vigor among older people in our times. But it also feeds into a popular myth that denies aging itself. For instance, the film *Cocoon* tells the story of elderly people who gain access to a drug that can reverse the process of aging and make them young again. In the movie, the audience has the experience of seeing famous elderly actors Don Ameche and Hume Cronyn grow young before their eyes. The film, of course, is science fiction. It's only the latest version of a recurrent hope as old as humanity: the search for the fountain of youth. Sometimes the dream takes the shape of the "hyperborean theme": a conviction that people in a remote part of the earth—for example, the Asian Caucasus or the mountains of Peru—live extremely long lives. James Hilton's novel *Lost Horizon* (1933) popularized the idea of a place called Shangri-La that harbored the secret of longevity, and a movie based on the book had wide appeal.

But researchers have never found groups of people who live beyond the normal life span. Scientists who have diligently examined the facts have failed to find any place on earth where people live beyond the maximum human life span of around 120 years. Death certainly remains a biological inevitability, and so far we have not even figured out how to forestall until the very end the physiological decline that we know as aging.

The biology of aging remains one of the great unsolved mysteries of science. Scientists ask how the same process that leads to decline and death can be intrinsic to life itself. From an evolutionary point of view, aging poses a puzzle: How can a process detrimental to the survival of organisms be preserved by natural selection? Biologists who study how aging takes place have accumulated a large body of knowledge, and experiments with lower organisms have proved that genetic and environmental manipulations can change life expectancy and maximum life span. Thus scientists are now beginning to confront the question of whether it is possible to postpone, or even reverse, the process of biological aging.

Aging and Longevity

Normal aging is a process of progressive changes that usually, but not inevitably, increase the risk of mortality. For example, hair typically turns gray with advancing age, but this change does not diminish survival prospects. By contrast, other progressive changes lead to losses in functional capacity, or the ability of biological structures to perform their proper jobs. For example, as blood vessels age, they gradually lose their elasticity, a tendency known as arteriosclerosis or hardening of the arteries. Over time, arteriosclerosis can increase the likelihood of blockage and therefore the risk of damage we describe as a stroke or heart attack.

At the biological level, aging seems to result from changes in molecular, cellular, tissue, and whole organism function. The simplest way to study the effects of aging at these levels is to compare younger and older organisms and note the differences. Such studies employ a **cross-sectional methodology**; that is, they look at physical function of people at different chronological ages but at a single point in time. The general conclusion from such studies of human beings suggests that most physiological functions decline after age 30, with some individual variations.

A purely cross-sectional design is not necessarily the best way, however, to measure the changes presumably brought about by aging. For one thing, it is hard to be sure we have taken into account changes in all the possible variables that might affect the organism. Thus a contrasting methodological approach, a longitudinal design, is sometimes used. The same individuals are followed over a long period to measure changes in physical function at different ages. This approach also has problems; for instance, with human beings, we need to consider the influences of a changing external environment. Furthermore, carrying out longitudinal studies is expensive and not easy when the subject is a long-lived organism like a human being. But the results can be of great importance.

The Baltimore Longitudinal Study of Aging, sponsored by the National Institute on Aging and now directed by Dr. James Fozard (Shock et al., 1984), has been one of the most important studies to date. Its scientists have been looking at 24 distinct physiological functions (Sprott and Roth, 1992). One important focus of the Baltimore Study has been **biomarkers,** biological indicators that can identify features of the process of aging. More formally, biomarkers can be defined as specific physiological or functional processes that may remain stable but often decline with chronological age (Shock, 1962). Some of the most commonly measured biomarkers are vital capacity, grip strength, diastolic and systolic blood pressure, and auditory or visual acuity. Others include the ability of the kidney to excrete urine and the behavior of the immune system.

Many age-related changes in physical function have already been documented, some of them familiar. For instance, with increased age, height tends to diminish while weight increases; hair becomes thinner, and skin tends to wrinkle. Another change is the loss in vital capacity, or the maximum breathing capacity of the lungs. With aging, both respiratory and kidney function decrease. But this decline chiefly results in a loss of **reserve capacity,** or the ability of the body to recover from assaults and withstand peak-load demands, as during physical exertion. It is important to note, however, that diminished reserve capacity may not have any discernible impact on the normal activities of daily living (Masoro, 1981). For instance, not having reserves to run a marathon race is probably irrelevant to most activities of daily life.

A key finding from studies of biological aging is that chronological age itself is not a good predictor of functional capacity. In other words, people of the same chronological age may differ dramatically in their **functional age,** which can be measured by biomarkers (Anstey, Lord, and Smith, 1996).

Scientists have not yet identified a single overall mechanism that gradually reduces functional capacity. Increasingly, however, they have come to believe that the process of aging is controlled at the most basic level of organic life. The key to reversing the process of aging may lie in the strands of the molecule called DNA, the basis for heredity in living cells.

Interestingly, however, what happens as we age may not be linked to how long we live. That is, the maximum human life span, or longevity, may be determined by biological processes separate and distinct from those that bring about the time-related declines we see as aging. In fact, it might turn out that maximum life span is determined by factors much simpler than whatever degrades functional capacity. At this point, it seems likely that longevity is genetically determined. Some scientists have argued that natural selection may have promoted longevity-assurance genes (Sacher, 1978). In other words, evolution may have arranged for us to live as long as we do but not necessarily for us to have the signs and symptoms of aging that we do.

Medawar (1952) was one of the first to advance the idea that a species might carry harmful genes whose time of onset was delayed until after the period of reproduction. If those same genes had the positive virtue of promoting reproduction, then such genes would be transmitted to future generations. This idea of a trait beneficial in early life but harmful in later life is known as **antagonistic pleiotropy.** The idea helps explain how senescence could be the product of natural selection through evolution (Williams, 1957).

Much remains to be discovered about genetic links between evolution and longevity. Genes with a favorable influence early in life, perhaps by maintaining reproductive capacity for a longer time, could have a harmful influence later on by allowing individuals to pass on linked genes with a negative impact, such as a shorter life span. On the other hand, the genes that determine maximum life span could turn out to be linked to genetic factors that forestall the degenerative diseases of late life. Thus, under the most favorable scenario, if we were to discover and intervene in the genetic causes of longevity, we might also find the key to reducing the disabilities and dysfunctions of old age.

Scientists studying genetic influences on aging and longevity have moved in a number of suggestive research directions. From an evolutionary point of view, for example, there seems to be no obvious reason that human beings should live beyond 30 or 40 years, which gives them enough time to reproduce. From the standpoint of species survival, it is hard to see what biological advantage any species would gain from having aged organisms around. In fact, we see from population studies of animals in the wild that aging rarely exists. On the other hand, there seems to be no fundamental genetic program ensuring death at a relatively young age for the good of the species. Animals in the wild exhibit survival curves very similar to those of human populations—that is, most individuals die during a certain age range, but others die when very young and when very old. What follows from this evolutionary argument is that there is no intrinsic biological necessity for aging and thus no reason that the extension of maximum life span would be impossible.

According to one optimistic view, most of the decremental changes associated with aging—including potentially preventable diseases, such as Alzheimer's—are not the result of any preprogrammed, built-in requirement for decline but are the result of environmental causes (Cutler, 1983). However, maximum life span seems to be largely shaped by specific genetic endowment rather than environmental factors. Perhaps, then, aging is merely a passive or indirect result of biological processes, whereas maximum life span is a positive or direct result of evolution. From this perspective, it follows that both the rate of aging and the maximum life span of a species could change, and change relatively quickly.

A couple of questions follow: Would it be possible by direct intervention to alter the genetic code and thus delay the onset of age-dependent illnesses and perhaps to retard the rate of aging itself? With deeper biological knowledge, could maximum life span be extended to 150 or 200 years or beyond? Even to ask these questions shows just how far we have come from a traditional view of the human life course, in which birth, aging, and death were simply taken for granted as part of the unalterable nature of things. (See Controversy 8, "Why Do We Grow Old?")

Mechanisms of Physical Aging

We sometimes think of aging as a process applying uniformly to the whole organism. Yet physiological studies show that different parts of the body age at different rates. For example, white blood cells die and are replaced within 10 days, but red blood cells last 120 days. The stem cells that produce all blood cells reveal no signs of aging at all. Cells in the brain have been thought to last as long as the body lives, with limited capacity for regeneration. But apart from long-living stem cells and brain cells, most parts of the body are constantly subjected to damage and repair. The mechanisms that contribute to this process of aging include wear and tear, the effects of free radicals, and the decline of the immune system.

Wear and Tear

The organic process of life is a delicate balance between forces that wear down structures—forces that lead to cell death, for instance—and those that repair damage at the molecular and cellular levels. This balance is maintained by the structure and metabolism of each living thing over time. But over time the balance begins to shift: Damage occurs faster than it can be repaired. Moreover, repair capacity is not unlimited; mechanisms for maintenance and repair can be maintained only at a certain cost. In other words, there are trade-offs involved in longevity. As a result, damage tends to accumulate with age, and the body gradually loses its capacity to repair that damage.

Like other components of the body, DNA in the nucleus of cells is always being damaged and repaired, although not always perfectly. Among mammals, the longer-lived species are the ones that have greater capacity to repair damaged DNA. But as DNA replicates over and over, those small errors, or mutations, progressively alter the organism's genetic code.

Can we conclude that aging could possibly be controlled by reprogramming our genes? Perhaps, but manipulating genes to retard aging might not increase the human life span. Imagine that an older person starts to exhibit signs of arteriosclerosis, and so we "fix" the individual's DNA. We might prolong one person's life, but we haven't really done anything to prolong the lives of that person's children or successor generations. They will also need DNA fixes when they become older. The problem is that a harmful mutation expressed at an advanced age, only after reproduction, will not be removed from the gene pool. In fact, we may want to leave a mutation that contributes to aging in place for the next generation, because the mutated gene could have positive effects at an earlier age. In other words, the same biological processes promoting health and vigor among young organisms can have a negative impact in later life.

Free Radicals

Like the effects of wear and tear, the action of free radicals contributes to physical aging. As they engage in metabolism, all cells produce waste products. Among those waste products are free radicals, or molecules of ionized oxygen, which have an extra electron. Those ionized oxygen molecules cause damage because they more readily bond with proteins and other physiological structures. Sometimes the proteins become inactive and unable to carry out their functions. Even oxygen, the essential element required for energy transformation in living organisms, can become a destructive force.

Certain physiological processes can fight the effects of free radicals, but over time, the reduction of functional capacity damages the organism. Free radicals have been implicated in many processes of physical aging (Armstrong et al., 1984).

A similar mechanism of physical aging is **glycosylation.** Among the most universal of all chemical changes in living things are those involving sugar (glucose). Along with oxygen, glucose is the basis for metabolism in all organisms. When foods like meat or bread are heated, the proteins combine with sugar and turn brown, in a process known as caramelization. In our bodies, the sticky by-products of this chemical reaction can literally gum up our cells. Glycosylation is behind much of the damage created in adult-onset diabetes, as well as stiffened joints and blocked arteries.

Is it possible to reverse the symptoms of aging caused by free radicals or glycosylation? Perhaps so, but that intervention is not likely to be simple—at least not as simple, for instance, as taking an "antiaging pill."

Immune System

The decline of the immune system is another important mechanism of physical aging. The immune system's job is to defend the body from invaders like viruses, bacteria, and parasites. To perform this job, it sends a variety of cells, which are categorized as T cells, B cells, and accessory cells, coursing through the body. These cells interact in complex ways to destroy or neutralize antigens, the foreign organisms that trigger an immune response. The cells of the immune system also remove damaged and mutant cells produced within the body, which may become cancers.

With normal aging, the immune system's ability to fight off invaders and mutants gradually declines; it may even begin mistakenly attacking healthy cells. The process begins at puberty, when the levels of a certain hormone begin to decrease. The components of the immune system, particularly the T cells, gradually lose their efficiency. In general, the immune system declines because its cells and their proportions change, not because their total numbers decrease (Crew, 1995).

The aging immune system leaves the body increasingly vulnerable. No longer does it mount the maximum response to very small doses of antigen; below a certain dose, it may no longer even recognize some antigens. It seems to develop an especially sluggish response to some tumor cells. Thus infection and age-related cancers, such as prostate and colon cancer, become more likely. In addition, the immune system becomes more likely to attack healthy cells, which may lead to an increase in rheumatoid arthritis and other autoimmune diseases. However, most autoimmune diseases do not seem to be a function purely of age, and so it is thought that genetic predispositions also play a role (Heidrick, 1995). In any case, the gradual decline of the immune system leaves the body more and more susceptible to a wide variety of diseases, each of which takes its toll on the functioning and vigor of the organism as a whole.

Aging and Psychological Functioning

Research continues into ways to forestall physical aging, in the hopes that someday we will discover a way to stay young as long as we live. The crusade against decrepitude and death is particularly appealing to Americans, who idealize success. The sentiment that "you're only as old as you think you are!" expresses an optimistic outlook that fits well with our "can-do" attitude toward life. According to this optimistic picture of later life, both physical and psychological decline can be offset by vigorous exercise and engagement with the world. "Use it or lose it!" seems to be the motto here, a philosophy that has been applied to everything from "sex after 60" to life-long learning.

No wonder that the strategy called "successful aging" has become the goal of many gerontologists. Partly they wish to reject age-based stereotypes, and partly they wish to counter the assumption that aging means a rapid decline into frailty and senility (Rowe and Kahn, 1997). They are certainly right to reject such stereotypes. But the idea of successful aging should never be based on denial of real losses in functioning in the last stage of life. The importance of the idea of successful aging is that it encourages older people to optimize the capacities that remain while compensating for inevitable losses (Baltes and Baltes, 1990). The measure of successful aging is life satisfaction and a sense of well-being in the face of decline. Successful aging therefore involves the psychological side of aging, including self-concept, social relationships, and cognitive processes.

Some aspects of self-concept change with age, as do social relationships because of transitions due to retirement and widowhood. But the most dramatic age-related changes occur in cognitive functioning.

Self-Concept and Social Relationships

The way people see themselves has several facets, including personality, self-esteem, body image, and social roles. The aspect of self-concept that changes least with age seems to be personality. For instance, an extroverted person, one who enjoys interacting with other people, is likely to remain extroverted from childhood into the final stage of life. An older person who is skeptical or gullible is likely to have been that way all along.

However, other aspects of self-concept do tend to change. The aging mind is not so much the impetus for change as is the progression of circumstances in which people find themselves. Take body image, for example. Naturally, the image of one's body changes as it becomes grayer, lumpier, and more wrinkled. Self-esteem varies throughout life with one's successes, whether they are interpersonal, occupational, intellectual, or otherwise.

Social relationships in old age tend to exhibit the most predictable types of change. For one thing, people's social networks become smaller as time goes on. With retirement, work relationships disappear. An elderly person may have survived a great many friends and family members. In addition, it is hard to add new members to the network when one is no longer engaged in work or community life.

Another aspect of self-concept that changes rather predictably with age is the roles one fills. Growing up and growing older, we leave behind earlier roles, such as child, student, employee, parent, and eventually, perhaps, spouse and friend. In the process, whether as an adolescent or a recent retiree, it's natural enough to ask: Who am I? Psychologist Carl Jung described the psychological task of the second half of life as *individuation*—that is, becoming more and more our genuine individual self as opposed to carrying out the social roles required of people in middle life (Chinen, 1989).

Gerontologists have spoken about this late life transition as a matter of role loss or role discontinuity. In earlier life transitions, role losses are typically accompanied by new roles that take their place: Ceasing to be a child in one's family of birth, one grows up and takes on the role of parent oneself. But in old age some roles, such as those ended by widowhood or retirement, may never be replaced.

From one sociological standpoint, then, old age can be described as a "roleless role" (Burgess, 1960; Blau, 1981). Once defined in this way, it is a natural step to see aging as a "social problem." But a different perspective is possible. Other sociologists look on old age as a period when individuals maintain informal roles that are individually negotiated and perhaps continually redefined and constructed (George, 1980). In other words, the meaning of age, subjectively experienced, would not be decisively determined by the external roles, such as spouse, employee, or parent, that typically shape behavior earlier in the life course. On the contrary, once freed from conventional roles, the development of the self in later life may become a highly individual matter (Breytspraak, 1984). From a philosophical point of view, old age can actually appear as an unexpected form of "late freedom" (Rosenmayr, 1984).

The importance of the meaning we bring to situations encountered in life has been underscored by several theories of aging. For example, Hans Thomae has developed his **cognitive theory** of aging based on empirical results of the Bonn Longitudinal Study of Aging (Ruddinger and Thomae, 1990). The cognitive theory of aging argues that it is perception of change, rather than actual objective change itself, that has the most impact on behavior. The very same life event—such as retirement—might be perceived by one person as loss but another could perceive it as freedom from an oppressive work situation. Cognitive, emotional, and motivational factors shape the way we perceive any event, and adjustment depends on a balance that changes over the course of life. Studies of stress and coping in old age reveal individual differences in mastery depending on perception and adaptation.

The subjective experience of meaning is closely related to individual well-being, as Carol Ryff (1989) has argued. She defines multiple psychological dimensions including self-acceptance, which may come from reviewing one's life; positive relations with other people; autonomy and self-determination; mastery of the surrounding environment; beliefs that give purpose to life; and a sense of personal growth and development over the life course. Ryff's conceptualization gives a new approach to the definition of *activity* by shifting our attention to the inner dimension of relationship between ourselves and the world. But the old theory of disengagement has received some support as well: for example, through Tornstam's idea of "gero-transcendence." Tornstam (1992) suggests that people find the deepest meaning in the last stage of life by overcoming self-centeredness and fear of death in favor of a spiritual focus in life.

Cognitive Functioning

The search for interpretive meaning in later life underscores the importance of cognitive functioning in old age. Contrary to popular stereotype, we don't "lose a million neurons every day" as we grow older. Most people over age 65 do not suffer from memory defects or dementia. Among all those over 65 there are a significant number—perhaps one in five—who have mild or moderate mental impairment. That means the overwhelming majority of older people have no mental impairment. Memory defects are actually quite limited among the large majority of normal older people. Nevertheless, some thinking processes do decline with age. Cognitive skills like remembering, solving complex problems, paying attention, and processing language are affected by age- and disease-related changes in the brain.

Cognitive functioning is a critical issue because it is the aspect of psychological functioning most affected by aging. In addition, cognition has a greater effect than the other types of psychological functioning on the ability to perform the activities of daily living. Those whose memories fail may not be able to keep up with needed medications or remember to turn off the stove when they've finished cooking. People who lose their judgment or become more impulsive may make extremely foolish decisions about how to spend their money or whom to trust. What's worse, they may lose the ability to recognize their own mental shortcomings.

The picture for most older people, however, is considerably more positive. Although memory, reaction time, and basic information-processing and problem-solving ability appear to decline with normal aging, other cognitive functions seem to remain stable or even improve. Wisdom and knowledge about the ways of the world, for example, are typical strengths of older people. In addition, training and practice in problem-solving skills, memory techniques, and other cognitive strategies can noticeably improve the abilities of older people. (See Controversy 9, "Does Creativity Decline With Age?")

It is important to remember the influence of life history and context as well. Older people who never learned a foreign language, for example, might have a harder time doing so in retirement than would an older person who had been bilingual from childhood. A person who worked as a carpenter in middle age might later be able to solve simple geometry problems faster than someone who had worked as a nurse, simply because the retired carpenter had been called on to solve geometry problems all his life.

Older people also remain adaptive and learn ways to cope with losses in cognitive functioning. For example, other people may help them compensate for cognitive losses through a social process dubbed "interactive minds" or "collaborative cognition." Imagine that two old sisters have been asked by a young relative about their parents. One may start out with the story of how their parents met but be stymied by the issue of who introduced them. The other sister may say, "Remember, it was their friend from the old neighborhood. What was his name? He always used to bring us butterscotch candies." "Oh, I know who you mean," says the first sister. "The man who played the accordion." The other sister then remembers his name: "Yes, Mr. Catano. His family lived next door to Mother's family, and he was in the band that Dad played in." Similar teamwork helps older people function cognitively much better than they might on their own. That is one of the reasons why losing a spouse, another relative, a close friend, or some other central member of one's social network can be such a problem for the elderly.

Another form of cognitive adaptation is "selective optimization with compensation" (Baltes and Baltes, 1990). The idea of selective optimization is that older people gradually narrow the scope of the capabilities they seek to maintain to those that are most useful, just as we all do throughout life. For instance, a freshman college student may begin studying engineering. But by the time she begins to pursue a career, she may decide to specialize in the microchips that make appliances work and forget about becoming knowledgeable about hydraulics or engines or other aspects of engineering.

The idea of compensation is that people seek new ways of accomplishing things that become difficult or impossible because of losses in functional capacity. An example of selective optimization with compensation is the case of pianist Arthur Rubinstein. As Rubinstein grew older, he reduced the music he played to those piano pieces he knew best and then practiced just those pieces more often (selective optimization). When it came time to play the faster passages, he would slow down his playing speed just beforehand to maintain the apparent difference between the slower and faster passages (compensation).

Although much research remains to be done on cognitive capacity in old age, particularly among the oldest-old, it is safe to say that the old stereotypes of feebleminded seniors is not only counterproductive but inadequate as description of cognitive functioning in later life. Older people do lose some thinking abilities, but the losses through normal aging are gradual and for the most part can be accommodated until very late in life. What is more, older people often have other cognitive gains to offer. Their experience of living gives them an understanding of the world and an ability to apply its lessons that younger people typically have not had time to develop.

Conclusion

As long as there have been old people, there has been ambivalence about old age. Why shouldn't people dread the prospect of becoming vulnerable? On the other hand, why shouldn't they look forward to a time when it seems possible to finally drop the burdens of coping with the complications of life? We see the same ambivalence today, but the truth is different from what popular images often convey. Old age in our day cannot easily be characterized. Especially in early old age, just past retirement, most people remain active and capable despite their removal from productive roles. Inevitably, people do decline and die, but normally even in middle and late old age they retain more capabilities than they are often given credit for.

Industrialization brought growing rationalization and bureaucratization of the life course, a greater rigidity that took the shape of stronger demarcations between youth and adulthood and adulthood and old age. At the same time, rapid developments in medical science and in cultural values have begun to erode the concept of distinctive life stages. With rising longevity, more people are living to old age, and the elderly as a group are becoming a larger, more influential proportion of the total population. Today, because the entire life course is changing, the meaning of old age is ambiguous.

Along with the problem of understanding what it means to be old in postindustrial society is the problem of understanding why physical aging occurs: There seems to be no reason for organisms to live much past the age of reproduction, yet humans do. But the challenge is not just to discover why we live so long—or even how to allow people to live longer. It is to understand how we can make the final phase of the life course more satisfying—for our elders and, eventually, for our future selves.

Toward a New Map of Life

We can think of the stages of life as a kind of "map" of unknown territory through which we must move. Until recently, some regions of that territory, such as midlife transition, were completely "unmapped" and unacknowledged. Other regions, such as adolescence, have been delineated or cultivated only in the past century, though now they seem familiar and predictable. The symbolism of life stages was once easily understood in societies where a map could be understood to depict a common social "space" that was stable and enduring, the same for each generation. This familiar ideal of life stages reappears in popular forms of life span development psychology, such as the theories of Erikson and Levinson. The ideal seems to correspond to a fundamental and universal fact about human psychology: the need to define the predictability of life (Marris, 1975). Now, however, some are questioning this whole approach to the life course. Perhaps the metaphor of a "map" is mistaken.

Timing of major life events has become less and less predictable. As a result, we may need a new "map of life" corresponding to the changed conditions of demographic circumstances, economics, and culture in a postindustrial society (Laslett, 1991).

The meaning of "aging" has changed in contradictory ways. Optimists believe that medicine will soon permit us to displace aging-related disease and declines until later and later in life: a pattern known as **compression of morbidity.** Yet economic forces seem to move in the opposite direction from biology. Changes in the job market or technology can make previous skills irrelevant. Biology promises to postpone aging, but social forces, like age discrimination, make the impact of aging more important than ever.

To overcome limitations of the old map of life, we need to develop bolder ideas about the contributions of older people to society. We also need to think more deeply about the meaning of life's final stage. Without such new understanding, there is a risk that older people may be dismissed as "uncreative" or that people will lose any shared sense of the positive meaning from survival into old age. Successful aging in the future will involve new ways of tapping the creative potential of later life (Adams-Price, 1998).

Creativity and wisdom depend on cognitive development over the life course. Whether our society cultivates such qualities among older people will depend, in the end, on more imaginative policies and institutions. The challenge of an aging society in the 21st century is to nurture the special strengths of age in an environment that prizes change, novelty, and flexibility. That challenge is what is ultimately at stake in debates about the meaning of the last stage of life (Roszak, 1998).

Why Do We Grow Old?

Oliver Wendell Holmes, in his poem "The Deacon's Masterpiece; or, the Wonderful 'One-Hoss Shay,' " invokes a memorable image of longevity and mortality, the example of a wooden horse cart, or shay, that was designed to be long-lasting:

> Have you heard of the wonderful one-hoss shay,
> That was built in such a logical way,
> It ran a hundred years to a day?

This wonderful "one-hoss shay," we learn, was carefully built so that every part of it aged at the same rate and didn't wear out until the whole thing fell apart all at once. Exactly a century after the carriage was produced, the village parson was driving this marvelous machine down the street, when

> What do you think the parson found,
> When he got up and stared around?
> The poor old chaise in a heap or mound,
> As if it had been to the mill and ground!
> You see, of course, if you're not a dunce,
> How it went to pieces all at once,
> All at once, and nothing first,
> Just as bubbles do when they burst.

The wonderful one-horse shay is the perfect image of an optimistic hope about aging: a long, healthy existence followed by abrupt cessation. But where does this limit on longevity come from? Is it possible to extend life beyond what we know? The living organism with the longest individual life span is the bristlecone pine tree found in California, more than 4,500 years old, with no end in sight.

The maximum human life span appears to be around 120 years. In fact, we have no valid records of anyone living much beyond that length. There have been claims of people living into advanced age of 150 or even more. Some claims have persuaded the *National Enquirer,* while others convinced investigators at Harvard Medical School. But whatever the *Enquirer* or

Harvard wanted to believe, there has never been proof of such longevity. Quite the contrary: Despite the fact that we have millions upon millions of verified birth records in the 20th century, until recently there were no proven cases at all of any human being living above age 120. But in 1995, a French-woman named Jeanne Louise Calment reached the proven age of 120. Madame Calment actually remembered seeing Van Gogh as a child!

Some scientists argue that even the idea of maximum life span is based only empirical observation. With biological breakthroughs in the future, might we someday surpass that limit? Indeed, optimists ask, why settle for the one-horse shay?

On the face of it, prolonging the human life span sounds good. But is it feasible? Will it make our lives better? One cartoon in the *New Yorker* shows a middle-aged man at a bar complaining to his companion: "The problem with doing things to prolong your life is that all the extra years come at the end, when you're old." Another cartoon depicts two nursing home residents in wheelchairs confiding to each other: "Just think. If we hadn't given up smoking we'd have missed all this."

These cartoons point to the fact that often the symptoms of aging appear well before reaching maximum life span. Some believe that the proper aim of medicine should therefore be to intervene, perhaps even to slow down the rate of aging, so that more and more of us can remain healthy up to the very end of life. At that point, the body would simply "fall apart" all at once, like the wonderful one-horse shay (Avorn, 1986). This view is known as the compression of morbidity idea.

The compression of morbidity hypothesis looks forward to greater numbers of people who postpone the age of onset of chronic infirmity (Brooks, 1996). In other words, we would aim for a healthy old age followed by rapid decline and death. Sickness or morbidity would be compressed into the last few years or months of life. But things don't always work out that way. We may succeed in postponing deaths from heart disease, cancer, or stroke. But what happens if we live long enough to get other diseases? The same preventive measures can have, as an unintended result, increased rates for chronic conditions such as dementia, diabetes, complications from hip fracture, and arthritis (Roush, 1996). Many observers worry that as increasing numbers of people live to advanced ages, the challenge of compressing morbidity will become more and more difficult. One study of mortality in the Netherlands did find some evidence that over a period from 1950 to 1992 survival curves became more rectangular; that is, deaths became concentrated around a point later in life (Nusselder and Mackenbach, 1996). However, a study of mortality data in Alameda County, California found a pattern of increased survival accompanied by increased morbidity and disability (Kaplan, 1991).

Compression of morbidity is attractive because delaying dysfunction would enhance the quality of life, extend life expectancy, and reduce health costs (Butler, 1995). A compression of morbidity strategy would move life expectancy closer to the hypothetical upper bound of maximum life span. Instead of expecting to live only to 85, people who reached 65 could expect to become centenarians, yet in good health nearly to the end of life. Such a

Exhibit 32. Some Organisms' Maximum Life Spans

Organism	Maximum Life Span (in years)
Tortoise	150
Human being	110
African elephant	78
Golden eagle	50
Chimpanzee	48
Horse	40
Domestic cat	30
American buffalo	26
Dog	20
Kangaroo	16
Domestic rabbit	12
House mouse	3.5
Fruit fly	25 days

SOURCE: Data from Walford (1983).

gain in active life expectancy would have dramatic consequences for our society (Seltzer, 1995).

To judge whether or not this strategy for compression of morbidity is actually feasible, we need to examine in more detail what is involved in normal aging. We need to understand what is known about the biology of aging and may be discovered in the future.

The Process of Biological Aging

Normal aging can be defined as an underlying time-dependent biological process that, though not itself a disease, involves functional loss and susceptibility to disease and death. One way to measure susceptibility to death is to look at death rates, which in humans today double every eight years. This pattern is known as **Gompertz law.** In other words, a 38-year-old is about twice as likely to die as a 30-year-old, a 46-year-old is four times more likely as a 30-year-old, and so on. At any given age, there is an important gender difference: Men are around twice as likely to die as women. Although men and women age at the same *rate,* women at every age are less biologically fragile than men—just the contrary to what our cultural stereotypes might suggest.

Studies of different species of organisms show that aging is almost universal, but the causes of aging are complex. For instance, among animals whose body mass and metabolism are comparable, the rate of aging varies greatly. Consider the differences in maximum life span among some familiar animal species, as shown in Exhibit 32.

The rate of aging can be correlated, in a general way, with the amount of time it takes for the mortality rate of a species to double. The doubling time is around eight years for humans today but only 10 days for a fruit fly and three months for a mouse. In rough terms, we can say that a mouse ages at around 25 times the rate of the human being.

What accounts for these clear differences in aging and life span across species? Comparative anatomy—the study of the structure of different species—generates some insights into this question. For example, among mammals and other vertebrates, an increase in relative brain size is positively related to an increased life span. Other factors correlated with life span are lifetime metabolic activity, body size, body temperature, and the rate of energy use. For example, a tiny hummingbird has a rapid heartbeat and high rate of energy metabolism; it also lives a comparatively short time, as if it were using up more quickly its total lifetime energy or action potential (Sacher, 1978).

Biologists have discovered intriguing relationships among life span, body size, relative brain size, and metabolic intensity. For example, a chipmunk has a maximum life span of 8 years, but an elephant can achieve 78 years. These facts suggest a more general idea known as the **rate of living** concept: roughly, the concept that metabolism and life expectancy are closely correlated. Smaller organisms, which tend to have a more rapid metabolism for each unit of body mass, also tend to have shorter life spans. A short-lived mouse and a long-lived elephant both have approximately the same temperature, but the mouse produces more heat per unit of mass. At the other extreme, slow-moving turtles are likely to have life spans longer than the more active mammals. Another fascinating fact is that no matter what their total body mass, mammals have approximately the same number of heartbeats in a lifetime. Still, despite these tantalizing correlations the rate-of-living theory has largely been rejected by biologists, along with the notion that biological aging is somehow necessary for the good of the species (Austad, 1997).

In comparison to other species of mammals, the human being has the longest life span and also expends more energy per body weight over the total life span than any other mammal. Energy metabolism per body weight across the life span in humans is about four times greater than for most other species of mammals. Human beings have an average life expectancy and a maximum life span about twice as great as those of any other primate.

Compare the chimpanzee and the human being. The maximum human life span appears to be around 110 to 120 years; the chimpanzee's is close to 50 years. But when we look at DNA from both species, we find that their DNA is more than 99% identical. These figures suggest that the rate of aging may be determined by a relatively limited part of the genetic mechanism. Calculations suggest that, if a cell is determined by around 100,000 genes, then perhaps no more than a few hundred alterations in the genetic code are needed to change the rate of aging.

Scientists have judged that a large increase in maximum human life span occurred fairly recently—probably within the past 100,000 years. The speed of this development suggests that only a tiny portion of the human genome, representing less than 1% of the genetic code, was likely to be involved. If so few genetic mechanisms determine aging, then we can perhaps hope to intervene to delay the process of aging (Finch, 1990).

Biological Theories of Aging

The facts about aging and maximum life span have led many biologists to believe that aging or senescence may have a single fundamental cause. In their efforts to find such a single primary process to explain those time-dependent changes we recognize as biological aging, they have developed many different ideas. Biologist Zhores Medvedev enumerated over 300 biological theories of aging. At present, no single theory of aging explains all the complex processes that occur in cells and body systems, but ongoing research is under way that is leading to new insights into why we grow old.

Broadly speaking, we can distinguish between two kinds of theories of aging:

- *Chance:* Some theories see aging as the result of external events, such as accumulated random negative factors that damage cells or body systems over time. For example, these factors might be mutation or damage to the organism from wear and tear.

- *Fate:* Some theories see aging as the result of an internal necessity, such as a built-in genetic program that proceeds inevitably to senescence and death.

In either case, the question remains open: Is it possible to intervene to correct damage to the aging body or modify the genetic program? The most likely interventions are those that would make sense depending on which theory best explains the facts about aging (Ludwig, 1991).

Wear-and-Tear Theory

The **wear-and-tear theory** sees aging as the result of chance. The human body, like all multicellular organisms, is constantly wearing out and being repaired. Each day, thousands of cells die and are replaced, and damaged cell parts are repaired. Like components of an aging car, parts of the body wear out from repeated use, so the wear-and-tear theory seems plausible.

The wear-and-tear theory is a good explanation for some aspects of aging—for example, the fact that joints in our hips, fingers, and knees tend to become damaged over the course of time. A case in point is the disease of osteoarthritis, in which cartilage in joints disintegrates. Another is cataracts, in which degeneration causes vision loss. Our hearts beat several billion times over a lifetime, so with advancing age the elasticity of blood vessels gradually weakens, causing normal blood pressure to rise and athletic performance to decline.

The wear-and-tear theory of aging goes back to Aristotle, but in its current form was expounded by one of the founding fathers of modern biogerontology, August Weismann (1834-1914). He distinguished between the two types of cells in the body: germ plasm cells, such as the sperm and egg, which are capable of reproducing and are in some sense "immortal," and somatic cells comprising the rest of the body, which die. Weismann, in his treatise *On the Duration of Life* (1882), argued that aging takes place because somatic cells cannot renew themselves, and so living things succumb to the wear and tear of existence.

What we see as aging, then, is the cumulative statistical result of wear and tear. Consider the case of glassware in a restaurant, which follows a curve similar to that for human populations. Over time, fewer and fewer glasses are left unbroken, until finally all are gone. The "life expectancy" or survival curve of the glassware follows a linear path over time. But the result for each individual glass comes about because of chance. Nothing decrees in advance that a specific glass will break at a fixed time. Glasses are just inherently breakable, so normal wear and tear in a restaurant will have its inevitable result. Just like everyone born in a certain year, for example, 1880, the glasses disappear one by one until none are left.

Some modern biological theories of aging are updated versions of this original wear-and-tear theory. For example, **somatic mutation theory** notes that cells can be damaged by radiation and as a result mutate or experience genetic changes (Szilard, 1959). The somatic mutation hypothesis would seem to predict higher cancer rates with age. Yet survivors of the atomic bomb at Hiroshima showed higher rates of cancer but no acceleration of the aging process.

Even without actual mutation, over time, cells might lose their ability to function as a consequence of dynamic changes in DNA. According to the so-called **error accumulation theory,** or error catastrophe theory, decremental changes of senescence are essentially the result of chance or random changes that degrade the genetic code (Medvedev, 1972). The process is similar to what would happen if we were to use a photocopy to make another copy. Over time, small errors accumulate. The errors eventually make the copies unreadable. Similarly, the error catastrophe theory suggests that damaged proteins eventually bring on what we know as aging through dysfunction in enzyme production.

Accumulative waste theory points to the buildup in the cells of waste products and other harmful substances. The accumulation of waste products eventually interferes with cell metabolism and leads to death. Although waste products do accumulate, there is little evidence of harm to the organism. The key to longevity may be the extent that cells retain the capacity to repair damage done to DNA. In fact, DNA repair capacity is correlated with the metabolic rate and life span of different species. Some studies suggest that DNA damage in excess of repair capacity may be linked to age-related diseases such as cancer.

Autoimmune Theory

The immune system is the body's defense against foreign invaders such as bacteria. The immune system protects and preserves the body's integrity, and it does this by developing antibodies to attack hostile invaders. We know that the immune system begins to decline after adolescence, and the weakening of immune function is linked to age-related vulnerability. According to the **autoimmune theory,** the system may eventually become defective and no longer distinguish the body's own tissues from foreign tissues. The body may then begin to attack itself, as suggested by the rising incidence of autoimmune diseases, such as rheumatoid arthritis, with advancing age (Kay and Makinodan, 1981),

Aging Clock Theory

According to the **aging clock theory,** aging is programmed into our bodies, like a clock ticking away from the moment of conception. One of the best examples of an aging clock in humans is the menstrual cycle, which begins in adolescence and ends with menopause. The aging clock theory is part of programmed aging, in which aging is seen as a normal part of a sequence leading from conception through development to senescence and finally to death.

One version of the aging clock theory emphasizes the role of the nervous system and the endocrine system. This version postulates that aging is timed by a gland, perhaps the hypothalamus, the thymus, or the pituitary gland. Such a gland acts like an orchestra conductor or a pacemaker to regulate the sequence of physiological changes that occur over time. Some support for this idea comes from observations that the hormone dehydroepiandrosterone (DHEA) is found in higher levels among younger people. Experimenters have also discovered that DHEA supplements help laboratory rats live longer.

The aging clock theory has encouraged research on the role of hormones secreted by the thyroid, pituitary, and thymus glands (Lamberts, van den Beld, and van der Lely, 1997). These include human growth hormone, which can now be manufactured in quantity through genetic engineering. In experiments, volunteers injected with growth hormone lost flabby tissue and grew back muscle, essentially reversing some manifestations of the aging process for a time. Other investigators are interested in hormones produced by the pineal gland, which may help regulate the "biological clock" that keeps time for the body.

Hormones and the endocrine system clearly play a major role in the process of aging. Growth, development, and reproduction in plants and animals are controlled by hormones. Biologists recognize a phenomenon here called *semelparity*. The best example is the Pacific salmon, which swims upstream to lay its eggs and then dies. So-called annual plants also exhibit semel-parity: The tomato plant flourishes, produces fruit, then dies away as the autumn leaves begin to fall.

But we find no comparable biological process in humans. We do recognize the profound age-related hormonal change of menopause, which comes with the loss of cells in the ovary that produce estrogen. Female mammals are born with a finite number of egg cells, so menopause is an example of a "preprogrammed" life event linked to age. Menopause is tied to health problems of aging because the loss of estrogen often weakens bone-mineral metabolism, resulting in thinner bone structure—a condition known as osteoporosis. When thin bones lead to fractures, an elderly person may end up in a nursing home.

Cross-Linkage Theory

Connective tissue in the body, such as the skin or the lens of the eye, loses elasticity with advancing age. We recognize the result as wrinkling of skin and cataracts. The explanation for this change lies in a substance known as **collagen,** a natural protein found in skin, bones, and tendons. According to the **cross-linkage theory** of aging, the changes we see result from the accumulation of cross-linking compounds in the collagen, which gradually become stiff. As in the waste accumulation theory, the piling up of harmful molecules is thought to eventually impair cell function. Some of this cross-linking may be caused by free radicals, which are cited in several different theories of aging.

Free Radical Theory

Free radicals are unstable organic molecules that appear as a by-product of oxygen metabolism in cells (Armstrong et al., 1984). Free radicals are highly reactive and toxic when they come in contact with other cell structures, thus generating biologically abnormal molecules. The result may be mutations, damage to cell membranes, or damage by cross-linkage in collagen.

Free radical damage has been related to many syndromes linked with aging, such as Alzheimer's disease, Parkinson's disease, cancer, stroke, heart disease, and arthritis. According to the **free radical theory** of aging, damage created by free radicals eventually gives rise to the symptoms we recognize as aging.

An important point about this theory is the fact that the body itself produces so-called **antioxidant** substances as a protection against free radicals. These antioxidants "scavenge" or destroy free radicals and thus prevent some of the damage to cell structures. The production of antioxidants is in fact correlated with the life span of many mammals.

Free radical theory has prompted some to believe that consuming antioxidant substances, such as Vitamin E, might retard the process of aging.

Genetic engineering techniques can now be used to produce antioxidants in vast quantities, but ordinary nutrients also supply them in our diet. Vitamins A, C, and E as well as less familiar enzymes play a role as antioxidants. Animal studies to date, however, show that consumption of antioxidants produces only minimal effect on aging.

Cellular Theory

A major finding from cell biology is that normal body cells have a finite potential to replicate and maintain their functional capacity. This potential appears to be intrinsic and preprogrammed, part of the genetic code. The **cellular theory** of aging argues that aging ultimately results from this progressive weakening of capacity for cell division, perhaps through exhaustion of the genetic material. That cellular limit, in turn, may be related to the maximum life span of species (Stanley, Pye, and MacGregor, 1975).

One of the major milestones in the contemporary biology of aging was the discovery that cells in laboratory culture have a fixed life span. In 1961, Leonard Hayflick and associates found that normal human cells in tissue culture go through a finite number of cell divisions and then stop (Hayflick, 1965). This maximum number of divisions is known as the **Hayflick limit.** Hayflick found that cells replicate themselves around 100 times if they are taken from fetal tissue. But if taken from a 70-year-old, they reach their limit of "aging" after 20 or 30 divisions.

Cells taken from older organisms divide proportionately fewer times than those taken from younger ones. Normal human cells that are frozen at a specific point in their process of replication and later thawed seem to "remember" the level of replication at which they were frozen. Furthermore, normal cells from a donor animal that are transplanted will not survive indefinitely in the new host.

Cell division in the laboratory sheds light on an interesting question: Can human bodies become immortal? The answer is yes, but there's a catch. We have to get cancer in order to do it. The classic instance is the case of so-called "HeLa" cells—an immortal remnant of a terminally ill young woman named Henrietta Lacks (HeLa), who died in Baltimore in 1951. Before she died, a few cancerous cells were removed from her body and put into tissue culture: essentially, put down on a glass lab dish and supplied with cell nutrients. Scientists were surprised to find that these HeLa cells just kept dividing and growing. In the years since, the cells haven't stopped growing. So we might say that a little piece of Henrietta Lacks has achieved immortality in a laboratory dish.

By contrast, in normal cell differentiation, cells divide and become more specialized, and their ability to live indefinitely simultaneously declines. The Hayflick limit may not so much be an intrinsic limit on living cells as a limit when cells begin to differentiate, as in development of the embryo. When cells approach a limiting point, a genetic program normally shuts down the capacity for further division. If the genetic program doesn't work, the result is uncontrolled multiplication, or cancer. The Hayflick limit does not keep all cells from dividing—after all, germ cells such as eggs and sperm continue to divide—but it may give a clue about why aging brings an increase in cancer and a weakening of the immune system.

Studying aging by examining cells in a test tube raises some questions. For instance, the nutrient medium in a cell culture does not contain all the nutrients and hormones that a cell would normally receive. In addition, cells in the body become differentiated tissues and organs and remain in equilibrium in ways quite different from the way cells replicate in a test tube.

Fundamentally, the cellular theory of aging sees aging as somehow "programmed" directly into the organism at the genetic level. In this view, it is just as "natural" for the body to grow old as it is for the embryo or the young organism to develop to maturity, as we see in annual plants or the Pacific salmon. Does the program theory of aging therefore apply to higher organisms such as mammals and specifically human beings? Perhaps, but it does not apply as obviously as it does in organisms where rapid aging is tied to reproduction.

Recently, one of the most intriguing points in favor of the cellular approach to aging is the discovery that tiny tips at the ends of chromosomes—structures known as *telomeres*—become shorter each time a cell divides. Telomeres, it seems, comprise a biological clock marking the unique age of a cell as it divides. Studies are under way to explore the link between aging at the cellular level and what we recognize as aging in complete organisms (Bodnar et al., 1998).

The Inevitability of Aging

The aging process may not be the result of a rigid genetic program; it may simply be the complex and indirect result of multiple traits in the organism tied to normal development. In other words, the body may not be preprogrammed to acquire gray hair, wrinkles, or diminished metabolic functions. Rather, these signs of aging may simply be telltale side effects of activities of the organism.

Consider the analogy of an aging car. Suppose a distinctive "species" of automobile were designed to burn fuel at a fixed temperature with an efficient rate of combustion. That specific rate of combustion is required for appropriate acceleration, cruising speed, fuel mileage, and so on. But, alas, when the car performs this way, it also inevitably produces certain emission by-products. Over time, these by-products clog the cylinders, reduce efficiency, and lead to the breakdown and final collapse of the machine.

In the case of the human "car," burning oxygen in normal metabolism generates harmful by-products—namely, free radicals that prove toxic to the organism. The trade-off is that oxygen is both essential for life yet harmful to our long-term well-being. Although the human car is not intentionally designed to accumulate toxic emissions in order to collapse, the car cannot function at optimum levels without creating destructive by-products.

Now suppose we could find some special fuel additive that eliminates toxic emissions. Would we then have an "immortal" car? Probably not. Changing the fuel in your car won't prevent accidents, nor will any fuel additive prevent rusting or the wearing down of springs and shock absorbers.

The "human car" analogy has its limits because an organism, unlike a manufactured object, has a capacity for repair and self-regeneration, at least up to a certain point. Nevertheless, to find out how we might modify or retard biological aging we must find out why capacity for self-repair seems unable to keep up with the damage rate—in short, why aging and death appear to be universal.

Ways to Prolong the Life Span

Most theories of aging depict biological aging as an inevitable process, like a disease to which we must all eventually fall victim. Some theories look on the organism as succumbing to chance events; others see it as driven by a built-in biological clock. Yet whether aging is thought to occur by chance or by fate, most theories seem to reach a pessimistic conclusion about the inevitability of aging.

But aging is not a disease; it is, rather, a process of change, part of which may make us vulnerable to disease. Instead of being driven by a single primary process timed through a single biological clock, aging is driven by many different clocks, each on a different schedule and unfolding in parallel developmental patterns.

Biological theories of aging could have enormous importance for an aging society. For example, the compression of morbidity idea assumes that there is a finite human life span, roughly 85 years with a broad range of from 70 to 100 years. But today, basic research in the biology of aging is challenging assumptions about a fixed maximum life span and the inevitability of aging as a biological process. Two approaches have been found that could extend the maximum life span for a species: one based on environmental intervention through diet, the other on a genetic approach.

Environmental Approach

For more than 60 years, scientists have known of only one environmental intervention, restricting food intake, to extend life span in mammals. Dietary restriction produces gains in longevity in laboratory animals, even doubling normal life span. The existence of one such intervention disproves the idea that the maximum life span for a species is unalterable (Weindruch and Walford, 1988).

As long ago as the 1930s, scientists discovered that the life span of rats can be extended by restricting food intake after weaning. Caloric restriction in mice has similar effects even when it is begun in midlife (Walford, 1983). Rodents live longer if they eat a diet with 40% fewer calories than normal, as long as their diet remains otherwise nutritionally sound. When caloric intake is restricted, age-related deterioration slows down and age-related diseases, such as kidney problems and autoimmune syndromes, are diminished (Bronson and Lipman, 1991). The rats' condition does not deteriorate until very late in a long life. Under such a diet, both average life expectancy and maximum life span increase by 30%. Apparently, the rate of acceleration of aging has been reduced.

What accounts for this dramatic, well-established impact of dietary restriction in enhancing longevity? The longevity gain is achieved not through reduction in any specific component of the diet but simply because of fewer total calories consumed. One possible explanation is that caloric reduction slows metabolism, or the rate at which food is transformed into energy. With caloric reduction, the basic biological clock slows down. But we cannot be sure of the explanation because caloric restriction is consistent with many different mechanisms of biological aging, including DNA, free radicals, and a stronger immune system. The results are clear enough for rodents and experiments with primates are under way to confirm whether caloric restriction is effective there as well (Couzin, 1998).

In human terms, caloric reduction would mean surviving on a diet of 1,400 calories a day but in return gaining 30 extra years of life. To achieve this goal, Roy Walford, one of the premier investigators of the biology of aging, has proposed a so-called high-low diet that incorporates high nutritional value with low calories (Walford, 1986).

A similar approach is suggested by cryobiology, or the study of organisms at low temperatures. Lowering internal body temperature can increase life span in fruit flies as well as vertebrates, such as the fence lizard, an animal that lives twice as long in New England as its cousins do in sunny Florida. Experiments with fish demonstrate that, with lower temperature, life span is prolonged in the second half of life. Lower temperature can significantly reduce DNA damage. We don't yet know if cryobiological processes apply to warm-blooded animals like humans. However, calorie restriction also seems to lower body temperature a small amount. Calorie-restricted mice have a lower average body temperature, and the temperature itself changes according to biorhythm.

Caloric restriction somehow protects genes from damage by the environment and perhaps serves to strengthen the immune system. Caloric restriction also reduces the incidence of cancer. The experimental findings on caloric reduction converge with what is known about indirect regulation of genetic expression that controls the aging process.

Do the findings on dietary restriction and longevity have importance for humans? Very likely, but immediate practical implications are not yet clear. The National Institute on Aging has allocated $30 million for biomarker studies in the next few years to see if this approach works in primates and later perhaps in humans (Ingram et al., 1990). In the meantime, dietary change remains an attractive option for those concerned with increasing longevity.

Genetic Approach

Many lines of evidence point toward the central role of genetics in fixing the longevity for each species, though for any individual, length of life will be the result of both genetic and environmental factors. We often think of genetic inheritance as the element that is fixed and unalterable. But some genetic studies have shown a dramatic ability to improve maximum life span over generations.

For example, studies have been conducted on bread mold, fruit flies, mice, and nematode worms. In all these different species, genetic manipulation has been shown to modify maximum life span. For example, some mutated forms of nematode worms have exhibited substantial increases. Among mice, large differences in average life expectancy and maximum life span exist among different strains because of hereditary differences. In the fruit fly, scientists have achieved an increase in average as well as maximum life span by using artificial selection as a breeding technique.

Some recent genetic experiments have produced astonishing gains in longevity. For example, Michael Rose, a population geneticist, used artificial selection to produce fruit flies whose life span of 50 days is double the normal average of 25 days—the equivalent would be a human being living to 240 years of age. Rose, in effect, has in the laboratory mimicked an increase in the evolutionary rate of change. As a result, successive generations of fruit flies passed along genes favoring prolonged youth and longevity.

Thomas Johnson, a behavioral geneticist, went further and altered a single gene (known as Clock-1) out of the roundworm's 10,000 genes. He also achieved a doubling of the worm's three-week life span (Johnson, 1990). Still other recent studies suggest that, in some fruit fly populations, the risk of mortality may actually decrease with advancing age, a finding that challenges previous assumptions about maximum life span (Barinaga, 1992). These dramatic successes, through breeding or direct genetic manipulation, point to the way that genetic change may have come about rapidly through natural selection.

Whether any of these findings can be applied to humans is, again, unknown. But we can draw some conclusions about the genetics of aging. For instance, in at least several of the animal studies cited here, the genes involved governed antioxidant enzymes and mechanisms for repair of damage to DNA, which have been at the center of several theories about the biology of aging. Second, in the species benefiting from genetic change, a small number of genes has been involved in determining longevity. Thus these results could possibly be applied to higher animal species.

New horizons for genetic application are already visible. Scientists have found a way to double the life of skin cells by switching off the gene that regulates production of a specific protein responsible for manifestations of aging. A similar method of genetic engineering has been used with tomatoes, permitting them to be stored and shipped without decay. The key here is the so-called mortality genes, which determine the number of times cells divide. Thus this intervention addresses the Hayflick limit, which remains central to aging at the cellular level. Even without affecting maximum life span, this sort of gene therapy could have major applications in the future, perhaps leading to a cure for age-related diseases such as Parkinson's, Alzheimer's, and cancer (Anderson, 1992; Freeman, Whartenby, and Abraham, 1992).

The current Human Genome Project, supported by the U.S. government and one of the most ambitious scientific projects ever undertaken, is intended to yield a comprehensive "map" of the entire sequence of genes on the human chromosome. Genetic engineering could draw on that knowledge in ways that might dramatically change what we have thought of as the process of aging and even our assumptions about the maximum human life span (Watson, 1992). Such speculations, however, belong to the future.

Compression or Prolongation of Morbidity?

Biology has not yet succeeded in unraveling the mystery of aging, so it is not surprising that medical science has produced no technology or method for raising the maximum life span of human beings. Caloric reduction and genetic methods have worked with lower organisms, but they have no proven impact for human beings. To extend life expectancy and promote healthy aging we may need to identify genes responsible for harmful mutations, whether expressed early or late in life. A parallel approach would be to identify those environmental agents, such as diet, sunshine, and smoking, that have a cumulative impact on sickness and survival. Health promotion might then succeed in postponing chronic illness, thereby making more possible the idea of the one-horse shay.

Progress in these directions depends on answering the question of why we age. In the reading "Why We Age," Steven Austad highlights some basic facts about the biology of aging that are relevant to our hopes for compressing morbidity or extending our longevity.

In the readings that follow, we hear different voices in the compression of morbidity debate. On one side, James Fries and Lawrence Crapo take the optimistic position that improving life expectancy will also lead to compressed morbidity: People will live longer and not be sick until the very end of their natural life span. Fries (1988) believes that successful aging involves optimizing life expectancy while reducing physical, psychological, and social morbidity. Fries's "sunny" view of aging is paradoxical, in a way, because it presumes that the maximum life span remains fixed, a limitation other biologists might reject. In support of Fries's view, we can note that some postponement of morbidity has already occurred: Declining death rates from heart disease and stroke reflect improvements in health due to lifestyle, diet, hypertension detection, and so on.

But not everyone is persuaded by Fries's interpretation of the evidence on morbidity and death rates. Researchers and demographers disagree about whether compression of morbidity is actually occurring and whether maximum human life span is really finite, as Fries believes. Edward Schneider and Jacob Brody point to other diseases, such as degenerative bone and joint disease, Parkinson's, and Alzheimer's, that cannot easily be prevented or postponed by any obvious interventions. Still other conditions, such as depression or sensory losses, are not linked to causes of improved life expectancy at all, so we remain haunted by the fear that longer life might mean only prolongation of morbidity (Verbrugge, Lepkowski, and Imanaka, 1989; Olshansky, Carnes, and Cassel, 1990).

The debate over compression of morbidity shows us that scientific facts are rarely as simple as we imagine. The meaning of the facts depends on our theories and interpretations and is therefore subject to debate and construction in different ways. As Kenneth Manton reminds us, different views of the facts about illness and survival in old age today are leading us to new ways of thinking about mortality and morbidity among the elderly. Indeed, the debate about compression of morbidity is rooted in biology, but it has implications for health care economics in an aging society. What can we expect in the future if medical technology succeeds in prolonging life still more? How much emphasis should we give to health promotion as opposed to curing diseases in old age? Whatever our view, the compression of morbidity theory stands out as an important reminder of how critical biological research will be for the future of an aging society.

READING 33

Why We Age

Steven N. Austad

Aging represents a biological paradox that few people appreciate, and for such a nearly universal process, it is nearly limitless in its variety. A mayfly lives a day, a fly a week, a dog a decade, a human a century, a tree a millennium or two. Salmon live a few years, then spawn and die within a few days. For turtles, to get older may be

Source: Excerpted from *Why We Age: What Science Is Discovering About the Body's Journey Through Life,* by Steven N. Austad. Copyright © 1997 by Steven N. Austad. Reprinted with the permission of John Wiley & Sons, Inc.

to get better. Is there a pattern here? What is it and why? Is the pattern fixed or can we alter it?

Nothing would alter human life more dramatically (whether for better or worse isn't exactly clear to me) than our learning to delay aging—if we had an active working life of a century, if athletes remained in their prime for 50 years, if we could live with six or eight generations of our family, if we might live to suffer the long-term consequences of short-sighted political foolishness.

Remember, aging is not just developing diseases, it is generalized deterioration. Postmenopausal hormone therapy and certain diets (low fat, lots of fruits and vegetables) are known to reduce your chances of developing specific diseases, such as heart disease and cancer. A large group of people taking hormones or eating such diets would on average live a bit longer than they would if they were not watching their diet, because so many of us die of heart disease and cancer. But we couldn't really say that these treatments had retarded aging per se, unless they also slowed the rate at which their practitioners lost their hearing and sprint speed and knack for picking up new languages. Also, treatments that truly retarded aging would not only increase average longevity, they would also increase maximum longevity—that is, how old their longest-lived practitioners lived to be. Nothing to date has been demonstrated to live up to this expectation.

Let me emphasize one thing clearly at the outset so that whatever I may say later will not be misunderstood. *There are currently no diets, no vitamin or mineral or hormone supplements, no attitudes, and no behaviors or lifestyle choices that have been demonstrated to slow aging in humans!* Some currently advertised antiaging treatments and behaviors consist of sound health tips, even though they may have nothing at all to do with slowing aging. Others are unproven even with respect to health, and still others can be dangerous. But given what we know about life's damaging processes, there are some likely candidates for real antiaging treatments for humans in the not-too-distant future.

It's not just a guess that within a few years the entire human genome will be mapped and sequenced. Currently projected to be completed early in the next century, the Human Genome Project has consistently progressed more rapidly than projections. Using these maps and sequences, gene therapy, in which defective genes are destroyed or replaced with normal genes, will become commonplace. We are already routinely transplanting human genes into bacteria, pigs, and mice and fiddling with regulating the action of individual genes in fruit flies.

It is in our increasing control over our genes and the deciphering of what certain gene products do that holds the best hope for retarding aging in the near future. Few of us think that controlling one or a few human genes will stop aging, but a measurable slowing seems within the realm of possibility.

Fruit flies genetically engineered to produce additional amounts of two different antioxidants within their cells have already been shown to outlive nonengineered flies by about 25 percent. It's a long step from fruit flies to humans, but who knows how general such phenomena might be? Studies are already under way to determine whether similarly engineered mice will be similarly long-lived.

Vitality and Aging
Implications of the Rectangular Curve

James F. Fries and Lawrence Crapo

Why do we age? Why do we die? How can we live longer? How can we preserve our youth? Questions about life, aging, and death are fundamental to human thought, and human beings have speculated about the answers to these questions for centuries. Our own age values the methods of science—the methods of gathering evidence, of observation, of experiment—above the musings of philosophy. Yet, philosophical speculation and scientific theory may interact and enhance each other. The scientific theories of Copernicus and the conception of a sun-centered solar system, of Newton and an orderly universe, of Einstein and the relationship between matter, energy, and spacetime, of Darwin and the evolution of species have influenced our notions of who we are, where we are, how we came to be here, and the meaning of life itself. Similarly, the study of health and aging may contribute a new philosophical perspective to these age-old questions about life and death.

The implications of new scientific discoveries are often not widely appreciated for many years. Scientific knowledge develops by small increments within a relatively cloistered scientific community, whose members are sometimes more interested in the basic ideas than in their social implications. . . .

So it is with the study of human aging. The ancient philosophical questions have largely fallen to those who search for the biological mechanisms that affect our vitality and that cause our death. The study of aging as a separate scientific discipline is relatively new and is not yet the province of any single science. Independent observations have been made in medicine, in psychology, in molecular biology, in sociology, in anthropology, in actuarial science, and in other fields. There are remarkable parallels in the ideas that have emerged from these independent fields of research. It is our intention to review these parallel developments and to present a synthesis of scientific ideas about human aging that will offer insights into the fundamental questions about the nature and meaning of the life process, aging, and death.

The Incomplete Paradigm

The growth of scientific knowledge historically has been impeded by thought systems (paradigms) that worked well for a time but that increasingly failed to explain new observations. For the study of aging, the contemporary paradigm is often called the *medical model*. The medical model defines health as the absence of disease and seeks to improve health by understanding and eradicating disease. This model of life and health, while useful, has obscured a larger perspective. There are four prevalent beliefs in the medical model that have proved to be limiting (see box [p. 354]). Certainly, few present scholars hold these beliefs literally, but these ideas nonetheless have largely defined contemporary opinion about the aging process.

Source: Excerpted from *Vitality and Aging: Implications of the Rectangular Curve,* by James F. Fries and Lawrence Crapo. New York: W. H. Freeman, 1981. Reprinted by permission of the authors.

These four premises seem to imply the following conclusions. If the human life span is increasing, then our scientific goal can be the achievement of immortality. If death results from disease, our objective must be the elimination of disease. If disease is best treated with medication, our strategy is to seek the perfect drug or surgical procedure. With regard to aging, the medical model suggests that we should perform basic research to understand the genetic, neurologic, or hormonal mechanisms that control the process, and then learn to modify them.

Historically, these premises, objectives, and strategies have been useful. They are still worthy and deserving of study and hope. But they are certainly incomplete, and, taken literally, they are misleading. The human life span is not increasing; it has been fixed for a period of at least 100,000 years. The popular misconception of an increasing life span has arisen because the average *life expectancy* has increased; the *life span* appears to be a fixed biological constant. Three terms must be understood. The maximum life potential (MLP) is the age at death of the longest-lived member of the species—for human beings, 115 years. The life span is the age at which the average individual would die if there were no disease or accidents for human beings, about 85 years and constant for centuries. The life expectancy is the expected age at death of the average individual, granting current mortality rates from disease and accident. In the United States, this age is 73 years and rising.

Death does not require disease or accident. If all disease and all trauma were eliminated, death would still occur, at an average age not much older than at present. If premature death were eliminated, and it may be in large part, we would still face the prospect of a natural death.

Medical treatment is not the best way to approach current national health problems. The major chronic diseases (atherosclerosis, cancer, emphysema, diabetes, osteoarthritis, and cirrhosis) represent the major present health threats. They are deserving of continued medical research, and further advances are to be expected. But abundant evidence points to personal health habits as the major risk factors for these diseases. Preventive approaches now hold far more promise than do therapeutic approaches for improving human health.

Aging does not appear to be under direct control of the central nervous system or the genes. Rather, the aging process occurs in cells and in organs. The aging process is most likely an essential characteristic of biological mechanisms. The process of aging, or *senescence,* is an accumulation in cells and organs of deteriorating functions that begins early in adult life. Aging may result from error-prone biological processes similar to those that have led to the evolution of species.

So the prevailing ideas about aging are incomplete. An increasing body of new scientific information requires revision and extension of these ideas. The time for a new synthesis has arrived, heralded by a number of new discoveries that do not fit well into the old paradigm but that as yet lack a coherent paradigm of their own.

Competing Themes

Changes in our ideas about health and aging are now being reflected in our social institutions and lifestyles. Change in a prevalent system of thought is often turbulent, and such turbulence is now manifest in health by a set of new movements. Within the medical community, there has been increasing recognition of the importance of preventive medical approaches. Such technical strategies as mass screening have been promoted. New departments of preventive medicine have been developed within medical schools; previously, such efforts were largely carried out within schools of public health. These developments are not entirely successful (screening efforts have proved disappointing, and some departments of preventive medicine have not thrived), but their very creation acknowledges the ferment of new approaches to health care.

The public has asked for more active involvement in consumer choices and for more accurate information on which to base such choices. In response, a self-care movement in health has developed, which now represents a considerable social force. At its best, this movement encourages critical consumption of medical services and increased autonomy from professional dominance. At its worst, the self-care movement takes an adversary stance and would replace professional medical treatment with idiosyncratic folk remedies. Still, the growth of these movements indicates discontent with the prevailing medical orthodoxy.

Recent changes in personal lifestyles have been even more significant. Joggers organize footraces in which tens of thousands compete, and cocktail party conversations concern the number of miles run per week. The number of militant antismokers has grown, and the nonbelievers are being packed into smaller and smaller spaces in the back of the airplane. Such spontaneous social changes are very likely to have constructive effects on health, and we applaud them, but the point is that the phenomenon itself represents a profound changing of the public consciousness.

Within professional medicine, new themes are evident. There is an increased interest in long-term patient outcome as a goal and less interest in correcting the trivial laboratory abnormality that does not materially affect the patient. Benefit-cost studies are sometimes advocated as a solution to the astronomical increases in the cost of medical care. Many observers have pointed out that orthodox medical approaches have reached the area of diminishing returns. The quality of life, rather than its duration, has received increasing emphasis.

Both psychologists and physicians have recently described strong relationships between psychological factors and health, and theories explaining such relationships have been developed that emphasize life crises, helplessness, loss of personal autonomy, depression, and other psychological factors. Correction of some psychological problems, it is implied, will improve health, and indeed the circumstantial evidence that this may be true is quite convincing. Again these approaches are outside the orthodoxy of the medical model.

Two new research areas have recently been emphasized—chronic disease and human aging. Increasingly, researchers recognize the central roles that aging and chronic disease play in our current health problems. The study of aging and chronic disease is oriented toward long-term outcomes, is interdisciplinary, requires preventive strategies, seeks to demonstrate the relevance of psychological factors, and uses lifestyle modification as a major tactic. The student of aging and the student of the diseases of the aged now have a unique opportunity to harmonize the incomplete old orthodoxy and the emerging new themes.

A New Syllogism

Using new knowledge of human aging and of chronic disease, we attempt here to provide a model that harmonizes these competing and chaotic themes, one that points toward new strategies of research and of health attainment. Our theoretical structure allows predictions to be made, and the predictions are strikingly different from those traditionally expected.

Figure 1 shows the actual data. Quite . . . startling conclusions follow from these data. The number of extremely old persons will not increase. The percentage of a typical life spent in dependency will decrease. The period of adult vigor will be prolonged. The need for intensive medical care will decrease. The cost of medical care will decrease, and the quality of life, in a near disease-free society, will be much improved.

Adult life may be conveniently divided into two periods, although the dividing line is indistinct. First, there is a period of independence and vigor. Second, for those not dying suddenly or

Figure 1. Human Survival Curves for 1900, 1920, 1940, 1960, and 1980

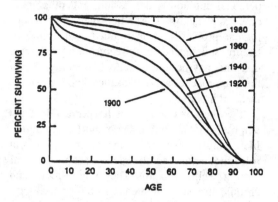

SOURCE: U.S. Bureau of Health Statistics.

NOTE: These curves are correct. They converge at the same maximum age, thereby demonstrating that the maximum age of survival has been fixed over this period of observation.

prematurely, there is a period of dependence, diminished capacity, and often lingering disease. This period of infirmity is the problem; it is feared, by many, more than death itself. The new syllogism does not offer hope for the indefinite prolongation of life expectancy, but it does point to a prolongation of vitality and a decrease in the period of diminished capacity.

There are two premises to the syllogism; if they are accepted, then it follows that there will be a reversal of the present trend toward increasing infirmity of our population and increased costs of support of dependency. . . . The first premise is almost certain; the second is very probable. If, after careful evaluation of the supporting data, one accepts the premises of this syllogism, then one must accept the conclusion and the implications of the conclusion.

Some Questions of Semantics

Nuances of meaning may mask the substance of a subject, and slight changes in emphasis may allow a new perspective to be better appreciated. There are problems with several of the terms

often used to describe health, medical care, and aging. Among these are *cure, prevention, chronic, premature death,* and *natural death.* We will use these terms in slightly different senses than is usual.

Cure is a term with application to few disease processes other than infections. The major diseases of our time are not likely to be cured, and we have tried to avoid this term. *Prevention* is better but is unfortunately vague; this term, as we shall see, is sometimes misleading. We prefer the term *postponement* with regard to the chronic diseases of human aging, since prevention in the literal sense is difficult or impossible. *Chronic* is a term usually used to denote illnesses that last for a long period of time. It serves as a general but imprecise way of distinguishing the diseases that may be susceptible to cure (such as smallpox) from those better approached by postponement (as with emphysema). Regrettably, this important distinction cannot be based solely on the duration of the illness, since some diseases that last a long time both are not chronic conditions and might eventually be treatable for cure (such as rheumatoid arthritis and ulcerative colitis). We limit our use of the term *chronic* to those conditions that are nearly universal processes, that begin early in adult life, that represent insidious loss of organ function, and that are irreversible. Such diseases (atherosclerosis, emphysema, cancer, diabetes, osteoarthritis, cirrhosis) now dominate human illness in developed countries. We have defined *premature death* simply as death that occurs before it must, and we have used *natural death* to describe those deaths that occur at the end of the natural life span of the individual. . . .

A New Syllogism

1. The human life span is fixed.
2. The age at first infirmity will increase.
3. Therefore the duration of infirmity will decrease.

The Rectangular Curve

Survival curves for animals show a similar pattern of *rectangularization* with domestication or

Figure 2. Theoretical Survival Curves for an Animal Become Progressively More Rectangular as the Environment Progresses From Wild to Domestic

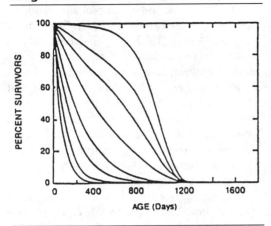

SOURCE: Redrawn from G. A. Sacher, "Life Table Modification and Life Prolongation," in L. Hayflick and C. E. Finch, eds., *Handbook of the Biology of Aging,* Van Nostrand Reinhold, 1977. Redrawn with permission.

Figure 3. The Linear Decline of Organ Function With Increasing Age

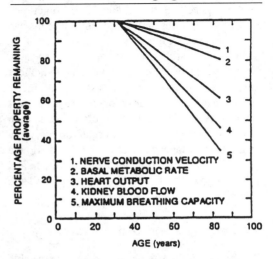

SOURCE: Redrawn from N. Shock, "Discussion on Mortality and Measurement of Aging," in B. L. Strehler, S. D. Ebert, H. B. Glass, and N. W. Shock, eds., *The Biology of Aging: A Symposium.* Copyright © 1960, American Institute of Biological Sciences. Redrawn with permission.

better care. Old age in wild animals is very rare, as it probably was for prehistoric man living in a dangerous environment. In uncivilized environments, accidental deaths and violent deaths account for a greater proportion of deaths than the biologically determined life-span limit. For the great majority of wild animal species, there is a very high neonatal mortality, followed by an adult mortality rate that is almost as high and is nearly independent of age. In such environments, death occurs mostly as a result of accidents and attacks by predators. One day is about as dangerous as the next.

By contrast, animals in captivity begin to show survival curves much more rectangular in shape. Such animals are removed from most threats by accident or predator, and for them the second term of the equation, that of the species' life span, begins to dominate. Figure 2 shows theoretical calculations of this phenomenon after Sacher (1977). Such rectangularization has been documented for many animals, including dogs, horses, birds, voles, rats, and flies. . . .

Figure 3 is drawn from the data Shock developed in 1960, and it is modified only slightly from what has been called "the most frequently shown data in the field of gerontology." The data show that many important physiological functions decline with age, and the decline is quite close to being a straight line. It is important to emphasize that these data were obtained from healthy human subjects in whom no disease could be identified that was related to the function being measured. Thus, the observed decline does not depend on disease.

Figure 3 is a major oversimplification of complex data. . . . The lines are not actually as straight as portrayed, and some of the data have been contested. The point is that a considerable body of research supports a gradual, nearly linear decrease in organ function with age.

Normal, healthy organisms maintain an excess organ reserve beyond immediate functional needs. We have four to ten times as much reserve function as we need in the resting state. The heart during exercise can increase its output sixfold or more. The kidneys can still excrete waste products adequately if five-sixths of the functional units, the nephrons, are destroyed. Surgeons can remove one entire lung, and sometimes part of the second, and still have an operative success. Three-fourths of the liver can be removed, under some circumstances, and life is still maintained.

However, the mean level of reserve in many of our organs declines as we grow older. We seldom notice this gradual loss of our organ reserve. Only in the circumstances of exceptional stress do we need all that excess function anyway. Shock and others suggest that the decline may be plotted as a straight line.

Homeostasis and Organ Reserve

The human body may be viewed as a remarkable assembly of components functioning at various levels of organization. Systems of molecules, cells, and organs are all marvelously integrated to preserve life. The eminent nineteenth-century physiologist Claude Bernard emphasized that these integrated components act to maintain a constant internal environment despite variable external conditions. Bernard saw life as a conflict between external threats and the ability of the organism to maintain the internal milieu.

These fundamental observations have stood well the test of time. Indeed, the human organism cannot survive if the body temperature is more than a few degrees from normal, if acid-base balance is disturbed by a single pH unit, or if more than 20% of the body water is lost. Body chemicals are regulated closely, often to within 2% or 3% of an average value. A change in one direction in body constituent is often followed by a complicated set of responses that act to restore equilibrium.

Bernard also noted that living beings change from a period of development to a period of senescence or decline. He stated that "this characteristic of a determined development, of a beginning and an end, of continuous progress in one direction within a fixed term, belongs inherently to living beings."

The regulation of bodily functions within precise limits was termed *homeostasis* by Cannon (1932). Living organisms under threat from an extraordinary array of destructive sources maintain their internal milieu despite the perturbations, using what Cannon called the "wisdom of the body." Dubos (1965) has pointed out that this "wisdom" is not infallible. Homeostasis is only an ideal concept; regulatory mechanisms do not always return bodily functions to their original state, and they can sometimes be misdirected. Dubos sees disease as a "manifestation of such inadequate responses." Health corresponds to the situation in which the organism responds adaptively and restores its original integrity.

The ability of the body to maintain homeostasis declines inevitably with decreasing organ reserve. Figure 3 shows the decline for lungs, kidneys, heart, and nerves. The decline is not the same for all individuals, nor is the decline the same for all organs. For example, nerve conduction declines more slowly than does maximal breathing capacity. And some organs, such as the liver, intestinal lining cells, and bone marrow red cells, seem to show even less decline with age.

The important point, however, is that with age there is a decline in the ability to respond to perturbations. With the decline in organ reserve, the protective envelope within which a disturbance may be restored becomes smaller. A young person might survive a major injury or a bacterial pneumonia; an older person may succumb to a fractured hip or to influenza. If homeostasis cannot be maintained, life is over. The declining straight lines of Figure 3 clearly mandate a finite life span; death must inevitably result when organ function declines below the level necessary to sustain life. . . .

Implications of the Rectangular Curve

The rectangular curve is a critical concept, and its implications affect each of our lives. The rectangular curve is not a rectangle in the absolute sense, nor will it ever be. The changing shape of the curve results from both biological and envi-

Figure 4. Sequential Survival Curves in the United States

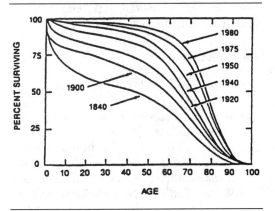

SOURCE: U.S. Bureau of Health Statistics.

NOTE: The progressive elimination of premature death allows these curves to begin to approximate the curve that would be found in the absence of any premature death.

Figure 5. Ideal Mortality Curve in the Absence of Premature Death

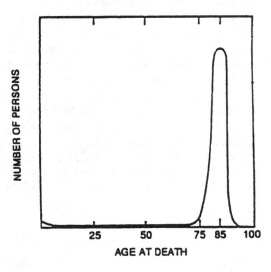

SOURCE: U.S. Bureau of Health Statistics.

NOTE: The average death occurs at age 85, with a standard deviation of about 4 years. Ninety-five percent of all deaths occur between the ages of 77 and 93.

ronmental factors. Many biological phenomena describe what is often called a normal distribution. This is the familiar bell-shaped or Gaussian curve. If one studies the ages at death in a well-cared-for and relatively disease-free animal population, one finds that their ages at death are distributed on both sides of the average age of death, with the number of individuals becoming less frequent in both directions as one moves farther from the average age at death. A theoretical distribution of ages at death taking the shape of such a curve in humans is shown in Figure 5. This simple bell-shaped curve, with a mean of 85 years and a standard deviation of 4 years, might exemplify the age at death of an ideal disease-free, violence-free human society. The sharp downslope of the bell-shaped survival curve is analogous to the sharp downslope of the rectangular curve.

In Figure 4, the first part of the curve becomes ever flatter, reflecting lower rates of infant mortality. Several factors prevent the total elimination of infant mortality and thus prevent the curve from becoming perfectly horizontal. These premature deaths are the result of birth of defective babies, premature disease, and violent death. Improvements in medicine can lower but never elim-

inate the birth of defective babies and premature disease. It seems likely that the ever dominant proportion of violent deaths during early life will prove recalcitrant to change and will form an ever larger fraction of total premature deaths.

So, the rectangular curve has an initial brief, steep downturn because of deaths shortly after birth, a very slow rate of decline through the middle years, a relatively abrupt turn to a very steep downslope as one nears the age of death of the ideal Gaussian curve, and a final flattening of the curve as the normal biological distribution of deaths results in a tail after the age of 90. . . .

Thus, two profound characteristics of the mortality of man, the elimination of premature disease and the development of the sharp downslope representing natural death, have remained far from the public consciousness. These data have been available for many years. The first solid comments about rectangularization of the human survival curve can be found in prophetic statements in the 1920s. Many statisticians and actuaries working with national health data since that time have noted the increasingly rectangular shape of the curve, and many have speculated that it represents a natural species life limit. Entire theories of the aging process . . . have been built around the observed fact of a natural life span in man and animals. Yet, the public has remained largely ignorant of these developments.

A society in which life expectancy is believed to increase at every age and in which one becomes increasingly feeble as one grows older is a society heading for trouble. A society moving according to the curves of Figure 4, as our society is, is a society moving toward a world in which there is little or no disease, and individuals live out their natural life span fully and vigorously, with a brief terminal period of infirmity. . . . Dramatic changes in mortality patterns result in equally dramatic social changes.

References

Cannon, W. B. *The Wisdom of the Body.* New York: Norton, 1932.

Dubos, R. *Man Adapting.* New Haven: Yale University Press, 1965.

Sacher, G. A. Life Table Modification and Life Prolongation. In Birren, J., and Finch C., eds. *Handbook of the Biology of Aging,* pp. 582-638. New York: Van Nostrand Reinhold, 1977.

READING 35

Aging, Natural Death, and the Compression of Morbidity
Another View

Edward L. Schneider and Jacob Brody

In a compelling and articulate Special Article published in the [*New England Journal of Medicine*] over three years ago, Fries[1] outlined a set of predictions indicating that the number of very old people would not increase, that the average period of diminished vigor would decrease, that chronic diseases would occupy a smaller proportion of the life span, and that the needs for medical care in later life would decrease. Such predic-

tions have important implications for planning the future allocation of health resources. The evidence that we will review supports quite different conclusions: that the number of very old people is increasing rapidly, that the average period of diminished vigor will probably increase, that chronic diseases will probably occupy a larger proportion of our life span, and that the needs for medical care in later life are likely to increase substantially.

Life Span and Life Expectancy

It is important to define the terms "life span" and "life expectancy" before proceeding with discus-

Source: "Aging, Natural Death, and the Compression of Morbidity: Another View," by Edward L. Schneider and Jacob Brody, *New England Journal of Medicine,* 1983, 309(14): 854-856. Copyright © 1983 by the Massachusetts Medical Society. All rights reserved. Reprinted by permission.

sions of these concepts. Life span is best defined as the maximum survival potential of a particular species.[2] For human beings, there is documented survival of between 110 and 115 years.[3] Claims for enclaves with longevity past these ages have been demonstrated to be inaccurate.[4] Life expectancy is the average observed years of life from birth or any stated age. At present, life expectancy at birth in the United States is approximately 70.7 years in males and 78.3 years in females.[3]

Are There Biologic Limits to Life Span?

One important cornerstone to Fries' predictions[1] is that there is a genetically defined human life span that we are rapidly approaching. Hayflick and Moorhead demonstrated in an elegant series of experiments that human fetal lung fibroblasts, when placed in tissue culture, underwent a predictable and finite number of cell-population doublings and then ceased replication.[5,6] Fries[1] offers this limited in vitro replicative ability of cultured human cells as evidence for an internal cellular limit on the human life span. However, examination of several aging cell populations in vivo reveals that there is no evidence that aging of any organ or group of cells is caused by a limited number of replications. In fact, it has been amply demonstrated that some replicating cell populations have life spans that far exceed the replicative life span of the parent organism, often by several fold.[7,8]

A Natural Death?

Fries[1] suggests that the decline in function that occurs in most organs with aging can lead to "natural death" without disease. Although this fulfills Oliver Wendell Holmes' "one hoss shay" metaphor,[9] there is no documentation of its occurrence in human beings. A recent article suggested that in 30 percent of autopsies of patients over the age of 85, no acceptable cause of death was ascertained.[10] However, at autopsy, these patients had bronchopneumonia, pulmonary edema, pulmo-

nary infarctions, and aspirations.[10] Their deaths were attributed to aging because no lesions were found of the magnitude "that would cause death in middle-aged persons." [10] Although most organs undergo functional declines with aging,[11] none is compromised sufficiently, even at extreme ages, for death to result in the absence of disease. Therefore, the compromised physiology of the elderly still requires a specific pathologic insult, such as pulmonary edema or pulmonary infarction, for death to occur.

Is the Population Rapidly Approaching a Maximum Life Expectancy?

The basis for Fries' predictions is his premise that the human survival curve will continue to "rectangularize." [1] This includes two assumptions: that death rates will remain low until a certain age (the horizontal component of the rectangle), and that the majority of deaths will occur over a short span of years (the vertical component of the rectangle). Fries predicts that this rectangularization will result in an average life expectancy of approximately 85 years in the first part of the next century.[1] We agree with Fries that chronic disease has replaced acute disease.[1] Improvements in general living conditions, diet, sanitation, and other public-health measures, as well as in the control of infectious diseases and in the reduction of infant mortality, have resulted in a gradual rectangularization of the survival curve, particularly for white women in the 20th century. However, the evidence that we will present indicates that life expectancy is increasing and will continue beyond the ninth decade if present trends persist. Fries' assertions were based on actuarial predictions that mortality rates were reaching a plateau. However, mortality rates resumed their decline in the 1970s after the plateau observed in the early 1960s.[12,13] According to recent actuarial data from the Social Security Administration,[14] life expectancy at birth may be longer than 90 years for white females by the year 2080. This is probably an underestimate, since the calculation did not take into account the rapid decline in mortality rates for the elderly that has occurred in the past 10 years.[13,15]

Of particular importance, the mortality rate of persons over age 85 is decreasing faster than that of any other older age group (i.e., 55 to 65, 65 to 75, or 75 to 85).[13] In addition, the absolute numbers of persons in this age group and the percentage of the population in this age group are increasing.[15] For the survival curve to continue to rectangularize toward a maximum life expectancy of 85 years, there must be very high, stable mortality rates in the age groups immediately below and above 85, to produce the vertical drop at the end of the survival curve. However, the observed much more rapid decrease in mortality at 85 and above, when compared with 75 to 84, indicates that there is a horizontal trend at age 85 and above, causing a "derectangularization" of the survival curve. Manton's examination of survival curves from 1940 to 1978 clearly demonstrates this trend away from increased rectangularization at 50 and older.[16] . . .

Will There Be a Compression of Morbidity?

Fries' prediction of a compression of morbidity is based on two assumptions: that rectangularization of the survival curve will continue and will result in a compression of mortality (which is opposed by the evidence presented above), and that there will be a postponement of the onset of chronic diseases. Fries suggests that this can be achieved by preventive approaches such as stopping smoking and undergoing treatment for hypertension. We strongly support preventive approaches with the goal of postponing the onset of chronic diseases, and we assume that this is occurring to a limited extent. However, this optimistic view must be tempered by two realities: the absence of evidence of declining morbidity and disability in any age group, particularly those aged 45 to 64 years,[17] and the increasing numbers of people who are reaching advanced age. If current trends continue, the fastest growing segment of the population will be those most vulnerable to chronic diseases, the group over age 85. This

group has the greatest need for health care; although it represents only 0.8 percent of the overall population, 21.6 percent of this group are currently residing in nursing homes.[18] Recent evidence indicates that the incidence of one of the major chronic diseases of aging, Alzheimer's disease, may be as high as 3 percent per year for persons in the ninth decade of life and that the prevalence of the disease in persons over 80 is above 15 percent.[19]

Obviously, any compression of morbidity would have to result from a postponement of chronic diseases or a reduction of the disabilities that they produce. Interviews with members of older populations during the past decade have revealed no substantial change in the percentage reporting poor health[20] and no decline in morbidity or disability.[17] If the percentage of the elderly who are in poor health at specific ages (e.g., 60, 65, and 70) remains the same or increases and the numbers of individuals at advanced ages continue to increase, more people will spend longer proportions of their lives afflicted with chronic diseases. Unless preventive measures are extraordinarily fruitful or successful methods of treating or minimizing the impact of the chronic diseases of aging are developed, we will be faced with a burgeoning number of patients in need of long-term care.

Implications for Health Policy

If current demographic trends continue we will clearly be faced with increased numbers of people at advanced ages. The unknown variable will be the health of this group. If the health of this group in the future is not considerably different from the health of the present cohort, a huge proportion of the population will be suffering from chronic diseases. Today, health-care resources are stretched to the point at which federal entitlement programs for the health care of the elderly have become a major political issue. Increased pressures on the limited resources of our society will require difficult decisions in terms of the quantity and quality of health care for older Americans. The only approach that can forestall these consequences of increased life expectancy is for substantial inroads to be made in the prevention, treatment, or management of the common chronic diseases of aging. We write this article in the hope that Fries' seductive predictions will not be used for health-care planning and policy decisions and that valuable resources will not be diverted from programs directed at the prevention and treatment of chronic diseases.

Notes

[Only the notes that are included in the excerpted material appear here.]

1. Fries JF. Aging, natural death, and the compression of morbidity. N Engl Jour Med 1980; 303: 130-135.

2. "Life span." *Encyclopedia Britannica* Vol. 13. Chicago: William Benton, 1969:1098.

3. Population characteristics of the United States. Age, sex, race and Spanish origin of the population by regions, divisions, and states. Supplementary reports. 1980 census of population. Bureau of the Census, 1981.

4. Leaf A. Long-lived populations: Extreme old age. Jour Am Geriatr Soc 1982, 30:485-487.

5. Hayflick L., Moorhead PS. The serial cultivation of human diploid cell strains. Exp Cell Res 1961; 25:585-621.

6. Hayflick L. The limited *in vitro* lifetime of human diploid cell strains. Exp Cell Res 1965; 37:614-36.

7. Harrison DE. Normal production of erythrocytes by mouse marrow continuous for 73 months. Proc Natl Acad Sci USA 1973; 70:3184-8.

8. Daniel CW, Young Lit. Influence of cell division on an aging process: Life span of mouse mammary epithelium during serial propagation in vivo. Exp Cell Res 1971: 65:27-32.

9. Holmes OW. The deacon's masterpiece; or the wonderful "one-hoss shay." Cambridge, Mass.: Houghton Mifflin, 1881.

10. Kohn RR. Causes of death in very old people. JAMA 1982; 247:2793-7.

11. Shock NW. Systems integration. In: Finch CE, Hayflick L, eds. Handbook of the biology of aging. New York: Van Nostrand Reinhold, 1977:639-65.

12. United States National Center for Health Statistics. The change in mortality trend in the United States. Hyattsville, Md.: National Center for Health Statistics, 1964. (Vital and Health Statistics. Series 3, No. 1). (DHHS publication no (PHS)1000).

13. United States National Center for Health Statistics. Changes in mortality among the elderly: United States, 1940-1978. Hyattsville, Md.: National Center for Health Statistics, 1982. (Vital and Health Statistics. Analytical Studies. Series 3, No. 22). (DHHS publication no. (PHS)82-146).

14. Faber JF, Wilkin JC. Social Security area population projections 1981. Washington, D.C.: Social Security Administration, 1981:42, Actuarial study no. 85.

15. Rosenwaike I, Yaffe N, Sagi PC. The recent decline in mortality of the extreme aged: An analysis of statistical data. Am J Public Health 1980; 70:1074-80.

16. Manton KG. Changing concepts of morbidity and mortality in the elderly population. Milbank Mem Fund Q 1982; 60:183-244.

17. Colvez, A, Blanchet M. Disability trends in the United States population 1966-76: Analysis of reported causes. Am J Public Health 198 1; 71:464-71.

18. United States National Center for Health Statistics. The national nursing home survey: 1977 summary for the United States. Hyattsville, Md.: National Center for Health Statistics, 1979. (Vital and Health Statistics. Series 13, No. 43). (DHEW publication no. (PHS)79-1794).

19. Hagnell O, Lanke J, Rorsman B, Ojesjo L. Does the incidence of age psychosis decrease: A prospective longitudinal study of a complete population investigated during the 25-year period 1947-1972; the Lundby study. Neuropsychobiology 1981; 7:201-11.

20. Health: United States, 1979. Hyattsville, Md.: Public Health Service, 1979. (DHEW publication no. (PHS)801232).

The Sunny Side of Aging

James F. Fries

When confronting the health and medical care costs of the aging of America, there are optimists and there are pessimists. In a most curious way the "optimists" have become those who believe that life is limited and that the average life expectancy of seniors is unlikely to grow rapidly in the future. "Pessimists" are those who believe that life expectancy increases will continue, and perhaps will even increase in the future. In a thoughtful article in this issue of *JAMA,* Schneider and Guralnik[1] beat the pessimistic drum loudly and clearly. Medicare costs may rise sixfold by the year 2040 in constant 1987 dollars. Dementia might ultimately afflict 28% or more of the senior population. We might expect 800,000 hip fractures annually by the year 2040. Research funding for the conditions that will pose the largest health care problems in the next century, including osteoarthritis, osteoporosis, and Alzheimer's disease, is woefully inadequate. Schneider and Guralnik emphasize the mental senescence of Alzheimer's disease; I would add an equal concern for the problems of osteoarthritis and musculoskeletal disability.

Are they right? In large part they are. There is no avoiding the fact that the national health burden is shifting toward problems of the elderly, or that these problems will increasingly dominate the health burdens of the next century. The overwhelming majority of health difficulties will become the physical (osteoarthritis and musculoskeletal disability) and mental (Alzheimer's disease) conditions associated with senescence. More of everything will be needed to deal with emerging problems in this area. More research, more prevention, more care, more facilities, and more money. It is already past time to admit the magnitude of the problem, as well as the inappropriateness and inadequacy of present facilities and training, and to declare war on infirmity. There can be no disagreement about this.

I, however, am an optimist. Granting that we make the necessary investments, the pessimistic future may be ameliorated by two "optimistic" trends. First, increases in longevity may slow, and, second, disability, on average, may occur later in life. There is already strong evidence that gains in life expectancy are slowing in females.[2-4] There are increasing data on the ability to move infirmity farther into the life span, shortening its overall duration. A theoretical framework for intervention into these serious problems, the compression of morbidity, is emerging.[2,5,6] Many gerontologists, including Schneider, are involved in programs with names like "Successful Aging," implying a prevalent belief that the problems are indeed accessible and that solutions are possible. The history of the next 50 years is not yet written. There are options for research and for the implementation of new interventions based on behavioral principles, on social adaptation, and on the new biomedical information and techniques that will become available over this period.[2,6]

Source: "The Sunny Side of Aging," by James F. Fries, 1990, *Journal of the American Medical Association,* 263:17, pp. 2354-2355. Copyright © 1990 American Medical Association. Reprinted by permission. This article was supported by Grant AM21393 to the Arthritis, Rheumatism, and Aging Medical Information System (ARAMIS), Stanford, Calif., and the National Institutes of Health.

The Number of Elderly

There are two numbers that, when multiplied together, yield the health or illness burden of the future. The first is the absolute number of elderly. The second is the average health of the elderly individual. The firmest estimates are for the absolute number of individuals aged 65 and older that we may expect. Here there is little room for major disagreement. The number of future elderly is driven by the number of individuals who pass 65 years of age each year. These individuals, through the next 65 years, are already born and, barring catastrophe, nearly all will reach 65 years of age. The proportion of a birth cohort that reaches 65 years of age has steadily risen. Birth cohorts in the United States increased steadily and even dramatically through 1963. These increases will be passed forward into the senior population, and it is this factor that drives the estimates for the aging of America. To be sure, there are differences in estimates of future life expectancy from 65 years of age, and the Social Security Administration's Office of the Actuary provides a range of alternative projections to encompass this uncertainty. But whether life expectancy for those aged 65 years increases to about 20 years, as we expect, or 25 years, as Schneider and Guralnik predict, this 25% difference in estimates does not account for more than a small fraction of the 600% increase in costs that Schneider and Guralnik foresee. The main issue is that there are going to be many more seniors. Even the most fervent optimist cannot but fully agree with the call for action.

The Health of the Elderly

It is not only how long seniors live that determines the overall health burden, however; it is additionally how well they live. At what average age does first physical infirmity occur? At what age is first mental impairment, on average, noted? At what average age does dependence on others become a problem? The health burden of the elderly is made up of age-dependent, fatal chronic diseases that include heart disease, cancer, and stroke, and also of a variety of nonfatal, age-dependent conditions, led by osteoarthritis, Alzheimer's disease, falls, incontinence, and others. There are well-known risk factors for the prevalent fatal diseases, and there is general agreement that, in part, because of changes in health behaviors of the public, there has been a marked decrease (now about 40% in cardiovascular disease) in age-specific risk of some major problems such as heart attack, stroke, and lung cancer in men and that these conditions have been pushed later into life.[2,7,8]

The nonfatal diseases present a new frontier, and one that now appears approachable. Our group has been carefully investigating risk factors for musculoskeletal infirmity in four large senior populations that involve thousands of subjects.[9,10] Risk factors for future infirmity include the preventable problems of lack of exercise, obesity, and the presence of chronic comorbid conditions that have risk factors themselves. Fractures, as discussed by Schneider and Guralnik, have many well-defined risk factors. Osteoporosis is amenable to prevention with exercise, estrogens, avoidance of corticosteroids, maintenance of adequate dietary calcium, and other measures.[3,10] The fall that results in the fracture is related to risk factors of bone density, muscular strength, presence of handrails, absence of household clutter, and restraint in medication use, among others. If we can put helmets on motorcyclists, we ought to be able to find some effective ways to reduce the incidence of osteoporotic fractures by prevention.

Alzheimer's disease represents a substantial exception to an optimistic view. It does not have recognized risk factors. Its prevalence increases as the number of seniors increases and as the senior population increases its average age, even though its incidence may not change. Alzheimer's disease may prove amenable to biomedical solutions, although this observer does not anticipate much success in attempting to revitalize atrophic brains and suspects that any effective biomedical interventions will have to be employed in preclinical stages of illness. Is it possible to be optimistic, even a little bit, about Alzheimer's? Perhaps. There may be some hope that nonspecific factors that influence health also influence the incidence of Alzheimer's disease, and that as these change there might be an increase in the average age of onset. Conjecture, but optimistic conjecture. We desperately need data on trends in incidence of chronic disease. Perhaps more importantly, life expectancy from 65 years of age in females has plateaued over the past decade. Despite decreasing mortality rates from specific chronic diseases, life expectancy has not improved significantly. This provides an important perspective for the individual patient. If life expectancy for females (who make up the great majority of patients with Alzheimer's disease) remains essentially constant and the age-specific incidence of Alzheimer's disease also remains constant, then the chance of Alzheimer's disease developing in a given individual does not increase. The national health burden of Alzheimer's disease increases because of the larger number of individuals at risk and the slowly increasing average age of these individuals, but the risk for the individual remains constant.

The research agenda must contain three major components. First, there must be data that support an epidemiology of morbidity. We must know what is happening to incidence rates of disability, disease, and dementia, and we need to know what is happening to mortality rates. Second, we need, as Schneider and Guralnik urge, an increased effort to understand the fundamental basis of age-associated conditions and of nonfatal chronic diseases, with the hope of discovery of biomedical solutions. Finally, we need research into prevention of chronic infirmity, research into delaying the onset of morbidity, and research into using interventions that already exist. The obvious interventions include exercise, diet, self-efficacy, and other life-style risk modification. It is neglect of this research arena, perhaps even more than neglect of a biomedical research agenda for age-associated disease, that limits our ability to foresee and control our future health.

Half Empty or Half Full?

Ninety-nine percent of individuals below the age of 75 years are not in nursing homes. Pretty healthy bunch. Eighty percent of those over age 85 years, with an average age of nearly 90 years, are *not* in nursing homes.[1] Half of all individuals in nursing homes are there because of chronic conditions and do not necessarily have to be there; their conditions have definable and modifiable antecedent risk factors.

It will help if we have better scientific knowledge to confront the coming problems. It will help if we have good data on the prevalence and incidence of specific types of morbidity, and good data on changes in these incidence rates over time. But managing old age better is not an issue best handled by waiting for the cure. It requires healthy life-styles to prevent morbid disease; healthy life-styles to preserve fitness, vigor, and independence; environmental improvements to render the surroundings less hazardous; and living wills and durable powers of attorney for health care to limit inappropriate and inhumane terminal care. I hope that Dr. Schneider receives funding and that he and his colleagues find a cure for Alzheimer's disease. But aging well, with vigor and vitality toward the end of life, is already a reasonable prospect. Many seniors do it now, and more can.

Notes

1. Schneider EL, Guralnik J. The aging of America: Impact on health care costs. *JAMA.* 1990; 263:2335-2340.

2. Fries JF. The compression of morbidity: Near or far? *Milbank Q.* 1990; 67:208-232.

3. *Monthly Vital Statistics Report.* Hyattsville, Md: National Center for Health Statistics; 1989; 37:1-15.

4. Metropolitan Life. Changes in life expectancy. *Statistical Bull.* 1987; 68:10-17.

5. Fries JF. Aging, natural death, and the compression of morbidity. *N Engl J Med.* 1980; 303: 130-136.

6. Fries JF. Aging, illness, and health policy: Implications of the compression of morbidity. *Perspect Biol Med.* 1988; 31:407-423.

7. Pell S, Fayerweather WE. Trends in the incidence of myocardial infarction and in associated mortality and morbidity in a large employed population, 1957-1983. *N Engl J Med.* 1985; 312:1005-1011.

8. Horm JW, Kessler LG. Falling rates of lung cancer in men in the United States. *Lancet.* 1986; 2:425-426.

9. Lane NE, Bloch DA, Wood PD, et al. Aging, long-distance running, and the development of musculoskeletal disability: A controlled study. *Am J Med.* 1987; 82:772-780.

10. Lane NE, Bloch DA, Jones HH, et al. Long-distance running, bone density, and osteoarthritis. *JAMA.* 1986; 225:1147-1151.

READING 37

Changing Concepts of Morbidity and Mortality in the Elderly Population

Kenneth G. Manton

There is little doubt that the aging of the population of the United States is a demographic phenomenon that holds profound implications for both private and public American institutions. In order to best adapt those institutions to serve the aging of the population, it is necessary to understand the dynamics that underlie this phenomenon. One component of those population dynamics, mortality, is of particular importance since it has implications for both individual and institutional planning. At the individual level mortality determines the number of years of life a person can expect to live past a given age—an important factor in planning career, retirement, and investment goals. At the institutional level, mortality is important since it is the prime dynamic factor de-

Source: "Changing Concepts of Morbidity and Mortality in the Elderly Population," by Kenneth G. Manton, 1982, *Milbank Memorial Fund Quarterly*, 60:2, pp. 183-191. Copyright © Milbank Memorial Fund. Reprinted by permission.

termining short-run changes in the size and age structure of the elderly population. Since health and social service requirements for individuals change dramatically and rapidly after the age of 65, accurate predictions of the changes [in] age distribution at advanced ages are especially important to social policy. . . .

Current Theories of Human Mortality and Longevity

A primary goal of a model of human mortality is to anticipate changes in mortality rates and human life expectancy. Many current models of human mortality predict that life expectancy in the U.S., with the present organization of medical science, is unlikely to increase much beyond present levels—a view that has strongly influenced forecasts of the rate of population aging and federal planning. Two mechanisms are proposed to explain this "ceiling" on life expectancy, one involving limitations on life span due to cellular processes of senescence and one involving an increased societal risk from chronic degenerative diseases. In the following we discuss basic principles of each type of model.

Biological Constraints on Human Mortality Changes

A number of theorists (Fries, 1980; Keyfitz, 1978; Hayflick, 1975) argue that mortality reductions and life expectancy increases in the U.S. population will cease in the near future because of biological constraints on the length of the human life span that are due to species specific processes of senescence. A prime implication of this perspective is that current efforts to increase life expectancy through disease control serve mainly to "rectangularize" the survival curve (Comfort, 1964). Thus, the curve describing the proportion of a cohort surviving to any given age will become nearly square with the surviving proportion remaining near 1.0 until the age range where mortality due to biological senescence occurs. Then the curve will drop rapidly to 0.0. Thus, life expectancy is increased by eliminating "premature death" due to specific diseases, so that large proportions of a cohort survive to their biologically determined life span to die a "natural death." As Fries (1980:133) concludes, "The surprising fact is that we are already approaching the limits."

The argument that senescence will soon limit life expectancy change is based upon four types of evidence. First, historically, the maximum human life span has not been observed to change except in populations where age documentation is poor and the literacy rate is low (Fries, 1980; Hayflick, 1975). Second, the risk of death seems to increase as an exponential function of age with a doubling time of about eight years, so that the likelihood of observing persons at extreme ages is small (Fries, 1980; Sacher, 1977). Third, standard actuarial computations indicate that the elimination of cancer and heart disease would increase the average life expectancy, at most, by 20 years (Hayflick, 1975). Finally, there is experimental evidence to suggest that at least certain types of human cells are internally programmed

for only a limited number of reproductions (Hayflick, 1965, 1975, 1977). The weight of this evidence leads to an important conclusion—that mortality is not necessarily linked to disease processes, or, in Fries's (1980:130) words:

> The bioscientific, medical model of diseases, our prevalent model, assumes that death is always the result of a disease process; if there were no disease, there would be no death. This view is hard to defend.

Therefore, once we are close to the elimination of disease-related, premature death, then the average life expectancy in the population is unlikely to change significantly unless we discover the key to altering the basic biological aging rate of human organisms—an accomplishment viewed as unlikely at least in the near future (Fries, 1980; Hayflick, 1975).

An important corollary to the model of biological constraints on population life expectancy is the implication it holds for the age distribution of chronic disease morbidity. Two basic principles of this model (i.e., that mortality and morbidity are not necessarily linked and that changing disease risks do not alter the underlying aging rate of the organism) give rise to distinct and contradictory views on future changes of chronic disease morbidity. It is useful to present and contrast these views.

A distinctly pessimistic perspective is presented by Kramer (1980) and Gruenberg (1977; 1980:1304-1305), who suggest that chronic disease prevalence and disability will increase as life expectancy is increased. This conclusion is reached because increases in life expectancy are viewed as not being accomplished either by reducing the incidence or by retarding the rate of progression of chronic degenerative disease, but by controlling the lethal sequelae of those diseases (i.e., primarily early terminal infections such as pneumonia). Therefore, Gruenberg (1977:3) concludes that "the net effect of successful technical innovations used in disease control has been to raise the prevalence of certain diseases and disabilities by prolonging their average duration." This will lead to what Kramer (1980) has labeled as a "pandemic of mental disorders and chronic disease."

A more optimistic appraisal is offered by Fries (1980). He argues that, in analogy to the rectangularization of the survival curve, there can be a rectangularization of the age at onset of chronic degenerative diseases. Thus, although medical science is viewed as not being effective in increasing the human life span, hope is offered that personal participation in health maintenance can help "postpone chronic illness, to maintain vigor, and to slow social and psychological involution" (Fries, 1980:134). Consequently, while the growth of the elderly population will be limited by biological constraints on the human life span, the requirements for health and social services for the elderly can be reduced by eliminating or postponing chronic disease, so that smaller portions of the life span will be affected (Fries, 1980:130). Unfortunately, the optimism with which Fries's arguments have been accepted needs to be tempered due to a critical omission in Fries's arguments. Specifically, he does not indicate how society is to deal with the increased social and health service demands currently manifest, and emerging, between the present time and the time of occurrence of his "utopian" stage where chronic disease onset can be delayed till age 85 and beyond.

Despite the differences in the degree of optimism with which Gruenberg and Fries view the future, there are several important commonalities in their perspectives. Most important is their view that chronic illness and not mortality should be the prime focus of public health efforts. Each, however, has a somewhat different perspective on how we should proceed in this effort and the difficulty in achieving significant progress. Gruenberg views chronic diseases as distinct pathological states, and emphasizes the search in epidemiological studies for preventable causes of chronic illness. Fries (1980:133) views chronic illness as a physiological process accelerating loss of organ reserve for which "postponement," rather than "cure," is likely to be effective. That is, for Fries a "cure" is achieved by delaying the age at which a disease reaches the symptomatic threshold beyond the age programmed for "natu-

ral death." Both Fries and Gruenberg suggest that alternatives to clinical treatment of chronic diseases need to be developed in the effort to control illness and disability; Gruenberg emphasizes the importance of epidemiology and prevention, while Fries emphasizes the role of geriatric medicine and personal responsibility for self care.

In part, the differences in optimism seem to be a function of what Fries and Gruenberg perceive to be our present state of knowledge concerning mechanisms for slowing chronic disease progression. For example, though one might agree that "personal autonomy" could be the "probable final common pathway to improved health" (Fries, 1980:134)—say, by better nutrition, exercise, and reduced smoking—it is not clear from Fries's exposition how such personal responsibility is to be engendered in the population. For example, we know that in certain population groups such as the Mormons mortality rates are 30 percent below the nation as a whole—largely as a consequence of a religious and social ethic that emphasizes personal responsibility for health (Lew, 1980). Though the success of such groups in improving health is well known, fostering such a health ethic nationally is a difficult task. Fries gives few directions on how such goals are to be accomplished programmatically. Indeed, though Fries argues that we are near the elimination of premature death, he acknowledges that currently 80 percent of mortality, and a higher proportion of disability, are due to chronic illness. Thus, though he suggests that "present approaches to social intervention, promotion of health and personal autonomy" (Fries, 1980:135) may serve to compress morbidity and senescence, and points to recent declines in circulatory disease mortality as possible signs of such improvement, it must be recognized that current social conditions have led to the majority of our health problems being due to what Fries views as "preventable" causes. Given the difficulties in achieving reductions in such an apparent health hazard as smoking we would be inclined to agree with Gruenberg's and Kramer's more pessimistic outlook. Furthermore, Gruenberg points out that certain chronic conditions (e.g., Down's syndrome) are genetically programmed. Consequently, there may be significant chronic morbidity that cannot be altered by personal choice. Such arguments reach a logical extreme in the thesis of P. R. J. Burch (1976), who argues that a major component of all chronic disease risks is genetically determined through individual variation in the immune system.

Fries and Gruenberg also seem to differ in their belief about future increases in life expectancy. Fries sees these as constrained by the biological processes of senescence. Gruenberg suggests an imbalance between lifesaving technology and health-preserving technology so that continuing life expectancy changes presently serve to greatly increase the demand for health service. Thus, Gruenberg seems to argue for further life expectancy changes. However, it seems reasonable to assume that future improvements in life expectancy will be limited since the progression of chronic diseases is unaltered. Both views posit that chronic disease morbidity and at least certain components of mortality have no necessary connection.

Societal Constraints on Human Mortality Changes

A second theoretical position is that, historically, major declines in mortality have resulted from reductions in infectious disease risk due to improvements in lifestyle, hygiene, nutrition, and other public health factors—and not due to innovations in medical technology (Omran, 1971; McKeown, 1976; McKinlay and McKinlay, 1977). Omran proposed a model of epidemiological transition in which the correlation between the economic, demographic, and public health changes of a society were described as a series of stages, with the U.S. and other developed nations having reached an "end" stage, the "Age of Degenerative and Manmade Diseases." In this end stage, mortality slowly declines (to rates below 20/1000) and eventually approaches stability at relatively low levels, while life expectancy at birth increases slowly until it exceeds 50 years

(Omran, 1971:517). At this stage, fertility "becomes the crucial factor in population growth" and heart disease, cancer, and other chronic diseases become the prominent public health hazards—with little said about the prospects for reducing chronic disease risks. Indeed, the nature of developed industrial societies is viewed by certain authors as having positive health risks for chronic diseases due both to societal, public health factors—such as environmental deterioration or occupational stress—and to factors involving choice at the individual level, such as smoking (Dubos, 1965).

Models of societal determinants of mortality also have implications for aging changes in U.S. society because they imply that a societal health state has been reached in which major improvements in life expectancy in the near future are unlikely. In contrast to the view that life expectancy is biologically bounded, however, the potential for reductions in infectious disease and maternal mortality due to improvements in hygiene, nutrition, and sanitation is viewed as having been largely fulfilled, while societal factors relevant to chronic disease risks have recently shown either marginal improvements (e.g., smoking rates) or actual deterioration (e.g., environmental toxicological hazards). Thus, while there is nothing in the societal model to preclude the existence of a biologically determined limit, societal constraints on life expectancy are viewed as becoming operational before biological constraints. As in the biological model, medical science is argued to have little potential for increasing life expectancy through the treatment of chronic degenerative diseases. Consequently, it cannot serve to compensate for possible increases in societal risks. Often both perspectives are combined to suggest an even more limited potential for life expectancy change than could be projected under a pure biological model. Fries's optimism seems to result from his belief that societal constraints on both life expectancy increases and health improvement can be overcome.

References

Burch, P. R. J. 1976. *The Biology of Cancer: A New Approach.* Baltimore: University Park Press.

Comfort, A. 1964. *Ageing.* New York: Holt, Rinehart and Winston.

Dubos, R. 1965. *Man Adapting.* New Haven: Yale University Press.

Fries, J. F. 1980. Aging, Natural Death, and the Compression of Morbidity. *New England Journal of Medicine* 303:130-135.

Gruenberg, E. M. 1977. The Failures of Success. *Milbank Memorial Fund Quarterly/Health and Society* 55:3-24.

————. 1980. Mental Disorders. In Last, J., ed., *Public Health and Preventive Medicine.* New York: Appleton-Century-Crofts.

Hayflick, L. 1965. The Limited *In Vitro* Lifetime of Human Diploid Cell Strains. *Experimental Cell Research* 37:614-636.

————. 1975. Current Theories of Biological Aging. *Federation Proceedings of American Societies for Experimental Biology* 34:9-13.

————. 1977. Perspectives on Human Longevity. In Neugarten, B., and Havighurst, R., eds. *Extending the Human Life Span: Social Policy and Social Ethics,* pp. 1-12. Chicago: Committee on Human Development, University of Chicago.

Keyfitz, N. 1978. Improving Life Expectancy: An Uphill Road Ahead. *American Journal of Public Health* 68:954-956.

Kramer, M. 1980. The Rising Pandemic of Mental Disorders and Associated Chronic Diseases and Disabilities. In Epidemiologic Research as Basis for the Organization of Extramural Psychiatry. *Acta Psychiatrica Scandinavica,* Suppl. 285, Vol. 62.

Lew, E. 1980. Discussion Comment in Implications of Future Mortality Trends: Follow-Up to Ideas Presented at the Chicago Mortality Symposium. *Record* of the Society of Actuaries, Montreal meeting, October 20-22, 1980, pp. 1365-1366.

McKeown, T. 1976. *The Role of Modern Medicine: Dream, Mirage or Nemesis?* London: Nuffield Provincial Hospitals Trust.

McKinlay, J. B., and McKinlay, S. M. 1977. Questionable Contribution of Medical Measures to the Decline of Mortality in the United States in the Twentieth Century. *Milbank Memorial Fund Quarterly/Health and Society* 55:405-428.

Omran, A. R. 1971. The Epidemiological Transition: A Theory of the Epidemiology of Population Change. *Milbank Memorial Fund Quarterly* 49:509-538.

Sacher, G. A. 1977. Life Table Modification and Life Prolongation. In Birren, J., and Finch, C., eds. *Handbook of the Biology of Aging,* pp. 582-638. New York: Van Nostrand Reinhold.

FOCUS ON PRACTICE   HEALTH PROMOTION

Can we take steps now to control our own longevity? The consumer market for life-extension products is growing, and magazines on the subject can be found on newsstands. But claims for life-extending products exceed what science has proved. Melatonin, antioxidants, human growth hormone, and DHEA have all been hailed as antiaging breakthroughs, but proof has rarely lived up to the promise. There are no diets, hormone injections, or vitamin or mineral supplements that have so far been proven to slow down the process of aging. However, it is possible that a breakthrough in our knowledge of the biology of aging could give us ways to slow down aging in the 21st century.

When we think about the prospect of slowing the process of aging or dramatically extending maximum life span, many questions present themselves. Would people really want to triple their life spans? Would they want to hold the same job or be married to the same person for 150 years? What would society be like if people lived for centuries instead of decades (Fossel, 1996)?

If altering process of aging is possible, what are the implications for practice? Some interventions have already been shown to promote health and longevity (Haber, 1999). For example, the death rate from cardiovascular disease has been cut in half in the past two decades, chiefly because of a reduction in such high-risk behaviors as smoking. Changes in diet or exercise patterns could provide further gains in adult life expectancy. The key point is that most of the causes of lost years of life today are not only environmental; they are related to lifestyle choices: alcohol, tobacco, and exercise (Arking, 1991).

One promising approach is dietary. Millions of Americans have already started eating a low-fat, high-fiber diet, just as they have given up smoking. Others go further and seek to minimize free radical damage to cells by including more antioxidant carotenes in their diets. Dr. Roy Walford (1986), well known for his immunological theory of aging, has for years been eating according to a calorie-restricted diet based on findings from studies of laboratory animals. Walford's diet is a low-fat, high-fiber one, used in combination with regular exercise and vitamin and mineral supplements. The diet permits no smoking and little drinking. Walford hopes to live beyond the century mark. But even if he doesn't, he is likely to be healthier in old age.

The topic of health promotion and aging engenders a familiar argument between "optimists" and "pessimists." On the one hand, Hayflick argues that calorie-restricted, long-living mice are merely living out their fixed natural life span. In the end, our genetic program prevails and environmental interventions, like diet, can accomplish only a limited amount. If Hayflick is right, then Walford, like Ponce de León, has embarked on a vain search for the fountain of youth.

But the optimists hold a different view. According to one scenario for the future, as a result of prudent nutrition and more exercise, after the year 2000, the average life span could rise from 75 up to 80 years. Then, early in this century, through hormone replacement and genetic engineering, the maximum life span could push well beyond the current limit of 110 or 120 years. Optimists believe that lifestyle enhancement and new technologies could combine to delay or even reverse aging, thus extending youthfulness and pushing the limits of the life span itself.

Steps to improve longevity are already becoming part of the popular culture (Brody, 1984). Changes in diet and exercise, reductions in smoking, and health promotion activities of many kinds are now far more common than two decades ago. As baby boomers experience middle age, these activities are likely to spread and have an impact on longevity.

In thinking about these scenarios for the future, we should retain a measure of skepticism. We should also focus on practical steps that are proven and feasible right now. Health promotion has to be based on science, not on conjecture or hopes for the future.

Health promotion seems clearly to be a desirable trend, but it also raises some difficult questions about personal and social responsibility (Walker, 1994). What should we do about groups in our society who cannot or will not change their unhealthy behaviors? Are harmful behaviors ultimately a matter of free choice, or do environmental and social factors also shape behavior? The cost of Medicare depends a great deal on the cost of chronic illnesses. If we embrace an ethic of personal responsibility for health care, might we be less willing to support public funding for medical care? Should health promotion take account of inequality in income, education, and access to health care? And how do we motivate people in favor of health promotion when the results of "bad choices"—such as smoking, poor diet, lack of exercise, or use of alcohol—don't show up until decades later? These questions will remain both personal and societal issues for years to come.

FOCUS ON THE FUTURE   "I DATED A CYBORG!"

Dateline: 2020. As Tony walked back to the college dormitory, his feelings were confused. He needed to talk to his roommate.

"You know, I really like her," Tony began. "I mean I really fell for her. And now . . . I just don't know. . . ." Tony's voice trailed off.

"What's the problem?" Tony's roommate asked.

"Well, you know that girl I've been dating—Cynthia? It turns out she's a lot older than I thought she was."

"So. How much older?" asked his roommate.

"Hey, she remembers the assassination of President Kennedy, which happened when she was 10. That makes Cynthia 67 years old. She's 45 years older than me! Can you believe that?"

Tony's roommate was aghast. He'd seen Cynthia. He figured she was around 30, not much more. Tony was pleased about going out with an "older" woman. But neither Tony nor his roommate had guessed just how much older she really was.

"I don't believe it! I mean, how could she be so old?" stammered Tony's roommate.

"Well, I found out she's had skin grafts and plastic surgery on her face; that's why there are no wrinkles. And of course her hair is dyed so there's no gray at all. But it's the rest of her that's . . . I don't how to say it . . . that's all been replaced. It's weird. It's like Cynthia's body is artificial, the way it is with a cyborg.

"To begin with, she's got silicone breast implants. OK, not so unusual. But inside she's artificial, too: all plastic valves in her heart, a liver transplant, hip replacements, and a lot of artificial bones. She's been on estrogen replacement for years and on other antiaging hormones, too. That's why she looks so young.

"Cynthia never talked much about things that happened before the turn of the century, and now I see why. I never suspected that she was born in the early 1950s. She admitted it to me last night. I came home and suddenly realized I've been dating a cyborg!"

* * *

Many science fiction stories have had titles like "I Married a Martian," and the film *Star Trek: First Contact,* featured a female Borg (a cyborg species) as a leading character. *Star Trek* fans remember that the alien species known as the Borg are creatures who are part human and part machine. Like Tony, in *First Contact* Captain Picard found himself in a relationship with a Borg and faced perplexing questions. Are the experiences of Tony and Captain Picard a glimpse of things to come?

Cyborgs are not outside the realm of possibility (Gray, 1995). In fact, the era of modern bioethics may be said to have started in 1967, when Louis Washkansky received a heart transplant from Dr. Christiaan Barnard. Tissue transplants have long become a standard part of modern medicine. Some tissues—such as cartilage and the cornea of an eye—are transplanted easily. With proper safeguards, blood can be safely transfused. Modern medicine has also shown success in transplanting skin, bone, kidneys, and more recently, lungs, livers, and hearts. The development of monoclonal antibodies, which help suppress rejection of transplanted tissues, has opened up a vast field of surgery to replace organs diseased or worn out with age.

At the same time, biomedical scientists are developing artificial tissues and organs, some of which have been successfully inserted into the human body. Bioengineering has already made possible a variety of "replacement parts":

- *Skin.* Skin tissue has been successfully grown in the laboratory, and biotechnology companies are now producing it in quantity for use with burn victims.

- *Cartilage.* One of the most common effects of aging is the wear and tear on cartilage. Surgeons can now use cartilage grown in the lab to treat joint injuries.

- *Bone.* Hip replacements have long been a staple of geriatric medicine; even Elizabeth Taylor has one. Today, biotechnology companies are selling bone substitutes manufactured from artificial substances. Companies are working on grafts that would enable the body to replace living tissue with artificial bone.

More exciting innovations are on the horizon:

- *Breasts.* Breast implants made of silicone have long been in use, but the results have been controversial. Tissue engineers are working on new techniques to stimulate women's bodies to grow new breast tissue. Already, plastic surgery has become enormously popular. Tissue engineering and "body sculpting" is likely to become even more important in years to come.

- *Artificial vision.* In the TV series *Star Trek: The Next Generation,* the character Geordi (played by LeVar Burton), who is blind, is able to see by wearing a device called a VISOR (Visual Instrument and Sensory Organ Replacement) over his eyes. Today, the elderly are the age group most likely to have impaired vision or total blindness. But in the future, electronic devices may replace lost visual capacity.

- *Heart valves.* Cardiovascular disease is the biggest cause of death among older Americans. Researchers have long been at work on a totally implantable artificial heart. Today, heart valves from pigs have been transplanted into humans. Researchers have discovered how to grow valves from blood vessel cells in the laboratory, and these lab-grown valves work well in lambs. In the future, thousands of people could benefit from artificially grown heart valves.

- *Bladder.* Urinary incontinence is one of the most troubling afflictions for the elderly, and it is a factor in nursing home placement. But scientists are working on producing molded lab-grown cartilage that could function as a valve to keep urine flowing in the proper direction.

- *Pancreas.* Late-life diabetes is one of the most serious diseases of old age, entailing complications such as blindness, amputation, and heart failure. Diabetes results from basic organ failure. The pancreas doesn't produce enough insulin to metabolize sugar properly. Bioengineers are now working on implants made of pig islet cells, which could produce insulin without injections for people who develop diabetes.

- *Brain.* No one expects medical science to produce anything like "Donovan's brain," a tissue-culture brain that was the centerpiece of a 1950s science fiction movie. But drugs to stimulate nerve growth are under investigation today, and techniques may soon be available to implant cells or introduce growth factors that would reverse damage to the central nervous system.

So far, cyborgs, like *Star Trek,* are just science fiction. But bioengineering work on transplants and artificial organs is not fictional. Moreover, other scenarios are possible. For instance, Bruce Sterling's novel *Holy Fire* (1997) has as its heroine a wealthy 94-year-old woman who gets total cellular rejuvenation based on new genetic material added to chromosomes in her body. The result is an organism constructed from "designer genes," which is very different from Cynthia and her replacement parts. Stay tuned in the 21st century as biomedical technology reshapes our vision of what human aging is all about.

QUESTIONS FOR WRITING, REFLECTION, AND DEBATE

1   What are the arguments for and against the view that aging itself is a disease? Pick one side of this issue and then try listing the points that can rebut the opposing point of view.

2   What do James Fries and Lawrence Crapo mean by *natural death*? What is the relationship between *natural death* and the *natural life span*? Should we consider the natural life span to be identical to the maximum life span?

3   In criticizing Fries and Crapo's predictions, Edward Schneider and Jacob Brody still seem to support Fries's point that preventing or postponing the chronic diseases of old age would be desirable. If they all agree that health promotion is a good idea, what is the real basis of debate between the two sets of authors? Does their disagreement matter in any practical way? Write your own summary of the opposing views and then explain what the implications might be for such practical matters as medicine, health care policy, and personal decisions about diet.

4   Kenneth Manton points to the importance of "societal constraints" on raising life expectancy. What are some examples of such constraints, and how do societal factors relate to personal responsibility factors? What can we learn from the AIDS epidemic about future steps to raise life expectancy?

5   Swedish data have turned up the surprising fact that death rates for the oldest-old (85+) have actually been going down. Some scientific studies suggest an ever-increasing life expectancy is quite possible (Kolata, 1992). These findings sound like good news. Do we have any reasons to believe that these findings are not good news? What would Fries's response be to these claims?

6   The Human Genome Project will soon produce a complete map of all human chromosomes. Considering the different theories of aging, what are some of the ways in which new genetic knowledge might change how we think about the causes of biological aging? What are the social and ethical implications of that knowledge?

7   Write a science fiction scenario or imaginary picture of how the United States might look in the year 2030 if dramatic breakthroughs in the genetics of aging occur. In developing this picture, be sure to state the year you expect the key discoveries or inventions to occur and describe the likely social consequences of those discoveries or inventions.

8   What is the best scientific evidence in favor of, or against, the compression of morbidity thesis? Visit the Web site on this subject at aspe.os.dhhs.gov/daltcp/reports/trends/htm where you can read a report by Timothy Waidmann and Kenneth Manton examining international evidence on disability trends among the elderly. What questions are left open by this Web site's report—for example, what exactly is "disability" as measured across different societies?

9   The National Institute on Aging has a booklet titled "In Search of the Secrets of Aging," which you can get directly from their Web site at http://www.nih.gov/health/chip/nia/aging. Based on what you see there, what advice would you give to your grandmother about how she can remain healthy in old age? What *different* advice would you give to your own young children?

SUGGESTED READINGS

Austad, Steven N., *Why We Age: What Science Is Discovering About the Body's Journey Through Life,* New York: Wiley, 1997.

Hayflick, Leonard, *How and Why We Age,* New York: Ballantine, 1994.

Masoror, Edward J., *Challenges of Biological Aging,* New York: Springer, 1999.

Ricklefs, Robert E., and Finch, Caleb E., *Aging: A Natural History,* New York: Scientific American Library, 1995.

Sprott, R. L., Warner, H. R., and Williams, T. F. (eds.), "The Biology of Aging" [special issue], *Generations* (1992), 16:4.

Does Creativity Decline With Age?

We shall not cease exploring
And the end of all our exploring
Will be to arrive where we started
And know the place for the first time.

—*T. S. Eliot*, The Four Quartets

The view that people become less creative as they grow older is widely shared. Albert Einstein won a Nobel prize for his contribution to quantum theory, a creative breakthrough that appeared in published form when he was only 26 years old. He later remarked that "a person who has not made his great contribution to science before the age of thirty will never do so." Was Einstein right?

The question of age and creativity is an important one for individuals who worry about becoming irrelevant in a fast-paced world. The question is also important for society. The French demographer Alfred Sauvy (1976) feared that an aging society would result in a "population of old people ruminating over old ideas in old houses." In coming decades, the U.S. population will become older. The workforce will be aging in a period when companies are being pushed to adopt new methods to improve competitive performance. Can we expect middle-aged and older workers to exercise creativity and initiative, or can we expect them to resist new ideas? What will happen to American inventiveness and scientific creativity as the average age of scientists goes up (Stephan and Levin, 1992)? These questions are disturbing for those who see in an aging America the "specter of decline" (Pifer and Bronte, 1986; Moody, 1988a).

Some of these fears have a foundation in fact. For instance, there is a common stereotype that older people take longer to learn new things, and this is a stereotype that turns out to be true. Compared with younger people, older people *do* tend to proceed more slowly in new learning situations. But slower speed is partly explained by lack of practice, differences in learning style, or motivation. In addition, reaction time itself tends to slow down with age, probably the result of "hardware" limits in the nervous system. By itself, chronological age doesn't explain much about learning ability. In any case, slower speed or reaction time usually isn't a factor in everyday performance.

Along with the stereotype of low creativity, there is a common assumption that older people overall are just plain bored. Yet the Duke Longitudinal Study of Aging found that nearly 9 out of 10 respondents said they had never been bored at all in the previous week (Palmore, 1981). Another stereotype suggests that the elderly cannot adapt to change. Yet a little reflection shows this stereotype to be wrong: Consider only the enormous changes that most people are likely to face in their later years, changes such as retirement, widowhood, adapting to chronic illnesses, and so on.

The debate about age, intelligence, and creativity is important for America's future. A number of gerontologists, perhaps with one eye on their own advancing years and the other on a changing society, have tried to determine whether creativity declines with age. They have faced a number of practical obstacles in their research, the most basic being an acceptable definition of creativity. Other types of cognitive function, notably intelligence, have proved easier to pinpoint, though not without debate.

Elements of Cognitive Function

Creativity has been related to intelligence, specifically, **fluid intelligence,** which is intelligence applied to new tasks or the ability to come up with novel or creative solutions to unforeseen problems (Horn, 1982). Some believe the key to fluid intelligence is divergent thinking, which is the ability to come up with lots of different ideas in response to a problem-solving challenge.

The other side of the coin is **crystallized intelligence,** which reflects accumulated past experience and socialization (Horn, 1982). Whereas fluid intelligence denotes a capacity for abstract creativity, crystallized intelligence may signify the acquisition of practical expertise in everyday life—in short, wisdom. Some components of wisdom have long been familiar. Philosophers going back to Socrates have argued that wisdom lies in a balanced attitude toward what we think we know: knowing what one does not know, but at the same time, refusing to be paralyzed by doubt (Meacham, 1990). Another key feature of wisdom would seem to be the ability to transcend bias or personal needs that may distort one's perception of a given situation (Orwoll and Perlmutter, 1990). Wisdom, then, involves more than cognitive development alone; it requires a degree of detachment and freedom from self-centeredness that has been described as "ego transcendence" (Peck, 1968).

Older people, if they develop a degree of detachment, might be in a position to achieve such wisdom. But, of course, no one has suggested that wisdom is a universal or inevitable result of chronological age alone. Something more is required than merely living a certain number of years, but psychologists do not agree about what that "something more" might be.

Some psychologists have wondered if there is a trade-off between creativity and wisdom, with one declining while the other increases with advancing age. In this view, wisdom and creativity are seen in opposition to one another. Other psychologists argue that the cognitive processes involved in wisdom, intelligence, and creativity are all basically the same but are put to different uses by different kinds of people. Wise people, we might say, have a high tolerance for ambiguity because they appreciate how difficult it is to make reliable judgments. They see the world "in depth." By contrast, the creative person seeks to go beyond whatever is given in the immediate environment to create something new.

Yet genuine creativity need not be identified with novelty for its own sake, as contemporary Western societies often do. In some societies of the East—for example, India, China, and Japan—old age is viewed as an appropriate time for spiritual exploration and artistic development. Late-life disengagement is balanced by opportunities for personal growth and creativity. "A Confucian in office, a Taoist in retirement," goes the Chinese proverb, so retirement roles might include meditation or traditional landscape painting. In the Hindu doctrine of life stages as well, later life is a period culminating in spiritual insight and wisdom.

What happens when a creative artist grows older and also develops a measure of wisdom applied to the creative process itself? Part of the answer may be found by looking at those creative artists who continued to be productive in old age. One of the greatest examples was the Dutch painter Rembrandt, whose style changed and deepened as he grew older. The aged Rembrandt practiced looser brush work and became more preoccupied with the inner world of the people he painted. Another example is the impressionist Monet, who continued to paint his famous water lilies even after he was confined to his home in his 70s. Frail health also plagued the aging Matisse, who was forced to give up painting in favor of creating colored cardboard "cutouts" that distilled a lifetime of artistic experience into simple, powerful designs. It is as if the older artist is able to discard mere technical achievement in favor of some essential and elemental quality of art. We see a similar development of "late style" among poets like Goethe and W. B. Yeats. All these examples suggest that in the last stage of life many of the greatest creative minds experience a change or a deepening of their creative style that could be attributed to an accumulation of wisdom.

The sources of creativity and productivity in later life are complex and result from many different factors. For example, most productive individuals produce both successes and failures; they have more successes than less productive individuals partly because they have more failures as well. There is no law of fate that decrees that creativity must decline with age. Late-life creativity is unquestionably real, but it is far from universal and it takes unpredictable forms. For example, it is well known that so-called late bloomers—such as the painter Grandma Moses—may attain the peak of their career much later in life than others. What is known about creativity in later life suggests that individual differences in creative potential are so substantial that they largely go beyond the effect of aging itself (Simonton, 1998).

The Classic Aging Pattern

Creativity in itself is difficult to define or measure. But psychologists have had long experience in measuring human intelligence or cognitive function. The **Wechsler Adult Intelligence Scale** (WAIS) is the most influential measure of global or general intelligence in use today. The WAIS includes a verbal scale and a performance scale, which are combined to assess IQ. The verbal part focuses on learned knowledge including comprehension, arithmetic, and vocabulary; the performance part measures ability to solve puzzles involving blocks or pictures. As people grow older, their verbal scores on the WAIS tend to remain stable but their performance scores tend to decline (Sattler, 1982). This persistent difference between the two components has been found so often that it is called the **classic aging pattern.**

Some leading researchers have cautioned against taking the classic aging pattern too seriously. They question what is actually being measured by IQ tests. In other words, they challenge the very validity of IQ tests as a measure of the "real" intelligence of older adults. Perhaps test performance should not be equated with real differences in intelligence at all, they say. This controversy has a familiar ring. It is the same kind of challenge that has been heard about the use of IQ tests and SAT tests when those tests show poorer scores for some minority groups. Critics argue that "intelligence" is a more complex, multidimensional capacity than the tests measure (Gardner, 1985).

The evidence certainly indicates that age and intelligence have a complex relationship. In a test of basic memory skills of young and older adults, the average 70-year-old will take three or four times longer than a 20-year-old to identify a mental picture linking a word and a location and will tend to make more mistakes. But things are completely different when we test people for knowledge transmitted across generations through culture. Older people do well on language skills as well as knowledge about how to handle life's ups and downs. For example, when presented with a difficult hypothetical dilemma, older adults score much better than do younger adults. How, then, do we develop a valid measure of late-life intellectual ability?

Measures of Late-Life Intelligence

Interest in the validity problem, or the problem of measuring "real" intelligence, has helped stimulate psychologists to ask whether any positive cognitive developments come with age. The long debate has at least confirmed that conventional methods of measuring intellectual abilities have not always acknowledged the skills used by adults in coping with the demands of everyday life. As a result, some psychologists have become interested in devising new approaches and methods, such as an age-relevant intelligence test.

Tests to measure the relation of wisdom or creativity to age are seeking to capture something very elusive. Everyday intelligence is a multidimensional capacity involving more than logic or information processing alone. Everyday intelligence—what we sometimes call common sense—involves pragmatic or social judgment, which is more than abstract reasoning (Cornelius, 1990). What is involved is something akin to "everyday problem solving" (Cornelius and Caspi, 1987) or "expertise in life planning." Some of these same cognitive capacities are evident in what we call wisdom. The wisdom of later life probably includes several distinct attributes—reflective judgment in the face of uncertainty, "problem finding" (as opposed to solving an already given problem), integrated thought about one's life, and intuition, or the empathic ability to understand a concrete situation. These qualities are obviously difficult to measure on a test.

Paul Baltes, perhaps the leading psychologist investigating wisdom today, has tried to develop a psychological test to measure wisdom. Baltes and his associates presented adult test subjects with questions like this one: "A fourteen-year-old girl is pregnant. What should she, what should one, consider and do?" In scoring the test, Baltes was not looking for any specific answer but instead was trying to measure how wise people go about dealing with difficult questions. Not all older people are wise, but over half of the top responses on Baltes's "wisdom test" came from people beyond 60 years of age (Baltes, 1992).

Baltes went on to define wisdom as an expert knowledge system derived from experience and capable of dealing with pragmatic problems. That definition is similar to the commonsense understanding of wisdom as consisting of good judgment in response to uncertain problems of living. If we follow this approach, we can understand why wisdom, potentially at least, might increase with age. The reason goes back to the distinction between fluid intelligence, which operates by the mechanics of information processing, and the content-rich, pragmatic knowledge of crystallized intelligence.

Steps toward defining or measuring wisdom are still in the early stages, but the effort holds promise. Research on the aging mind has moved from a simple view of growth versus decline to a more complex assessment of potential and limits. The cognitive mechanics of the computer—information processing—can be compared to fluid intelligence, which is biology based and tends to decline with age. On the other hand, cognitive pragmatics—factual knowledge and problem solving—can grow with age and can compensate for losses in processing power. We could say that with advancing age hardware declines while software becomes enriched (Baltes, 1993).

Studies of Age and Cognitive Function

Different methodologies have been used to measure changes associated with aging. Cross-sectional studies look at groups of young and old people at a single point in time, and longitudinal studies follow subjects over many years. Optimists on the subject of creativity and age point out that cross-sectional studies of intelligence may be revealing differences that do not come from age itself but from characteristics of different cohorts.

For instance, young people taking IQ tests tend to be quite familiar with test taking from recent experience in school. As a group, they show far less "test anxiety" than do older people (Whitbourne, 1976). Furthermore, many older people accept the prejudices of ageism and believe that, with advancing age, intelligence inevitably declines. Older people also tend to be more cautious than younger people, and thus they may be more reluctant to guess at the right answers on an IQ test (Birkhill and Schaie, 1975). Finally, the current cohort of older people, on average, lacks the formal schooling enjoyed by younger age groups (Granick and Friedman, 1973).

Given the tendency of cross-sectional studies to overestimate the impact of chronological age, longitudinal studies make sense. One of the most extensive sources of knowledge about intelligence and aging comes from the Seattle Longitudinal Study, which followed individuals ranging from age 25 to age 81 over two decades (Schaie, 1996). That investigation and others have found that the steepest average intellectual declines come after age 60. Averages conceal large differences among individuals, but even on longitudinal studies the classic aging pattern emerges. Still, research findings do challenge the idea of inevitable, global intellectual decline for all individuals. Even more important, intellectual decline in older people may be halted or reversed by specific interventions, such as training and education. These findings suggest that intellectual decline in later life is by no means irreversible or inevitable.

Indeed, longitudinal studies show that successive cohorts of older people are in fact improving their performance on intelligence tests, perhaps reflecting higher educational attainment. In addition, anywhere from 60% to 85% of those tested maintain their scores over time or even improve specific abilities. Among those over age 80, only between 30% and 40% of participants in the Seattle study had declining scores.

These studies indicate that very few people show any global decline in intelligence as they age, suggesting that people can optimize their cognitive functioning by drawing on their strengths or compensating for losses. Perhaps most important, even in their 80s and 90s, people tend to remain quite competent in familiar, everyday situations. Both cross-sectional and longitudinal studies, however, do show the classic aging pattern, with uniform decline among subjects beyond their 70s.

Studies of creativity, as opposed to cognitive function in general, have been harder to conduct. Again, the problem is defining *creativity*. Both cross-sectional and longitudinal studies, using many different kinds of tests, have shown that divergent thinking does decline with advancing age, and the decline is not attributable simply to reductions in speed of response (McCrae, Arenberg, and Costa, 1987). These tests are not a completely satisfactory measure of creativity, however. Harvey Lehman (1953), in his classic study of creativity and aging, used a public consensus approach instead.

First, he recognized public consensus about products that clearly demonstrate superior creativity—for example, Mozart's symphonies, Newton's theory of gravity, Thomas Edison's invention of new electrical devices. Lehman found that the curves of publicly acknowledged creativity followed exactly the curves of fluid intelligence: They both peaked after age 30 and declined with each subsequent decade (Lehman, 1962).

Wayne Dennis (1966), a critic of Lehman's work, looked at different data and found that for most people the decades of the 40s and 50s were the most productive period. Dennis's conclusions were based on quantitative measures of productivity (for example, how many publications), not on qualitative measures (how important the contribution was). Therefore, Dennis's results do not actually refute Lehman's findings.

Still other investigators, measuring scientific creativity, found that productivity among scientists peaked in the early 40s—later than Lehman said—and then declined slowly after age 50 (Cole, 1979; Diamond, 1986). A longitudinal study of creativity among mathematicians found that those who published a great deal when young did continue to publish as they became older, at least through middle age.

The evidence thus shows that age does not necessarily mean loss of cognitive function. Nevertheless, performance on intelligence tests does decline. Psychologists speculating about the reasons cite strong evidence that declining speed with advancing age does have a negative effect on performance on intelligence tests, but the precise reasons remain unclear (Salthouse, 1985a). Aging is, in fact, accompanied by a clear loss in **cognitive reserve capacity**—that is, the degree of unused potential for learning that exists at any given time. Studies of reaction time in training also show that the speed of information processing definitely declines with age. Older adults, for instance, do not reach the same peak of performance in reaction time as do younger adults (Salthouse, 1985b). Nor do older people achieve comparable performance when trained in memory skills (Baltes and Baltes, 1990).

Optimists counter that, although fluid intelligence abilities decline with age, crystallized abilities tend to increase. In addition, declines in cognitive ability among older people can often be compensated for by the expertise acquired with aging: a phenomenon that has been called *decrement with compensation.* In other words, wisdom and pragmatic knowledge compensate for declines in speed or fluid intelligence. For instance, despite declines in typing speed, some older typists demonstrate superior typing productivity. They apparently compensate for loss of speed by reading farther ahead in the manuscript they are typing, which is a pragmatic response demonstrating knowledge of how to type more effectively (Salthouse, 1984).

Correlates of Cognitive Stability

The debate about the causes and meaning of the measurable decline in IQ scores with age comes down to a difference between those who think of themselves as "realists" and those who take a more optimistic view. On the optimistic side, some psychologists speak of the "myth of the twilight years." They suggest that intelligence actually need not decline in later life at all (Baltes and Schaie, 1974). But other, equally expert psychologists bitterly reject this conclusion (Horn and Donaldson, 1977). These "realists" contend that declines in fluid intelligence in the classic aging pattern are empirical facts to be accepted, no matter how unpleasant. Although we might find individuals who do not exhibit the pattern, the "realists" insist, such cases do not refute an overall decline in average performance.

Taking another tack, the optimists have explanations other than chronological age for the classic aging pattern. One possible factor could be ill health, which does become more frequent with aging, though not universally so. A major study revealed consistent differences in IQ test performance depending on even modest declines in health status (Botwinick, 1973). Poor health and disability also tend to cause retirement and therefore probably weaken learning opportunities. Note then that both biological changes, such as health status, and social changes, such as retirement, may be responsible for changing cognitive abilities. It may be possible to change these biosocial factors to such a degree that the classic aging pattern no longer holds true.

The ability to adapt or compensate for decrements in cognitive function is probably related to cognitive style or personality. Basic personality dispositions include traits such as being neurotic, extroverted, open to experience, and conscientious. These dispositions predict how people adapt to changing life circumstances. Surprisingly, basic personality changes very little after the age of 30 (Costa and McCrae, 1980; McCrae and Costa, 1990). Longitudinal studies show that personality is stable throughout adulthood, even in response to health problems, economic setbacks, and bereavement (Costa, Metter, and McCrae, 1994).

However, psychological characteristics over the life span do not emerge entirely from the isolated individual. Behavior often reflects social conditions and socially structured transitions in the life course (Schooler and Schaie, 1987). For example, retirement may boost the cognitive performance of people who retire from very routine or boring jobs, but accelerate cognitive decline for those who have held complex jobs. In addition, some psychological traits can be intensified by life course transitions. For instance, middle-aged people with flexible attitudes are less likely to experience a decline in psychological competence as they grow older than those who could be described as cognitively rigid (Schaie, 1984).

We should thus be skeptical of any broad generalizations or unqualified claims about either the decline or the stability of intelligence with aging. Experiments in training have shown that declines in intellectual functioning among older people can be reversed. In the Seattle Longitudinal Study, investigators found that 40% of participants who showed a decline in mental abilities benefited from training; following training, they achieved intelligence scores at least as high as those measured at the beginning of the 14-year study (Cunningham and Torner, 1990). Critics question, however, whether the reversal reflects practice or a genuine reversal of changes induced by aging.

Despite the criticism, psychological studies with older people have demonstrated that intelligence, defined as the ability to think and learn new things, has a great measure of plasticity, or potential for growth, even at advanced ages. Data from groups of healthy people between ages 60 and 80 show that they benefit from practice and show performance gains just as younger people do. One series of studies showed that elderly people could even be trained to become memory experts (Baltes and Baltes, 1990). When older people are stimulated and intellectually challenged, this capacity for learning is impressive.

Creativity in an Aging Population

These experiments suggest that the debate about the effect of aging on creativity and intelligence is by no means settled. The readings that follow represent the classic positions in this debate. The selection by Harvey Lehman gives some of the data from his public consensus studies and provides Lehman's major conclusions. Wayne Dennis, one of Lehman's strongest critics, attacks the claim that creativity must decline with age. Dean Simonton's article provides an up-to-date summary of scientific studies of age and creativity in the four decades since Lehman published *Age and Achievement.* As Simonton shows, some of Lehman's factual points have been supported over the years, but the issue turns out to be more complicated than might have been imagined at the time of the early debate on this subject.

Finally, the piece by Douglas Powell looks at the question of whether aging brings wisdom. Powell gives an ambivalent answer to this question: "It all depends," he seems to tell us. Powell draws our attention to a paradox about wisdom that goes back to the life of the Greek philosopher Socrates. People told Socrates that he had been called "the wisest man alive," but Socrates replied that he felt he knew nothing for sure. The point is that those who are wisest are also the most modest because they truly understand how little they know.

This answer to the question about wisdom and aging should remind us of how little we too know about what is possible in old age. It was during the 20th century that we first saw gains in longevity on a massive scale. Only in recent decades have substantial numbers of people experienced old age in relatively good health and with high levels of education. Therefore, studies of older people in previous decades may not be a good basis for judging what older people are capable of today or in the future.

We are left to take hope from examples of individual achievement in the past. A number of creative artists made outstanding contributions in their old age. At age 71, Michelangelo was named chief architect of St. Peter's in Rome. Titian painted some of his greatest works in his 80s, and Picasso produced drawings and paintings into his 90s. Martha Graham continued her choreography into her 80s, and Jessica Tandy won an Oscar at age 80.

With improving opportunities to practice the arts and to pursue lifelong learning, tomorrow's elders could take up the challenge of creativity in the later years in ways unimagined today. The creative old age once reserved for an elite could become an opportunity for all. As art critic Ananda Coomaraswamy put it, it is not that the artist is a special kind of person, it is that each person is a special kind of artist. Viewed in those terms, the real debate about age and creativity has barely begun.

READING 38

Age and Achievement

Harvey Lehman

What are man's most creative years? At what ages are men likely to do their most outstanding work? In 1921, Professor Robert S. Woodworth, of Columbia University, published this statement in his book, *Psychology: A Study of Mental Life*: "Seldom does a very old person get outside the limits of his previous habits. Few great inventions, artistic or practical, have emanated from really old persons, and comparatively few even from the middle-aged. . . . The period from twenty years up to forty seems to be the most favorable for inventiveness" (p. 519). . . .

Assuming that the method by which one arrives at a conclusion is no less important than is the conclusion itself, let us see what is found when the inductive method is employed in the study of man's most creative years. Let us first examine the field of creative chemistry and attempt to answer the question whether chemists display more creative thinking at some chronological age levels than at others.

In his book, *A Concise History of Chemistry* . . . , Professor T. P. Hilditch, of the University of Liverpool, presents the names of several hundred noted chemists and the dates on which these chemists made their outstanding contributions to the science of chemistry. . . .

When the birth dates of the chemists listed by Hilditch were ascertained, insofar as data were available, it was possible to determine the ages at which the world's most renowned chemists made their most significant contributions, both theoretical and experimental, to the science of chemistry. A sample of the findings is set forth graphically in Figure 1.

Figure 1. Average Number of Contributions by Chemists During Each Five-Year Interval of Their Lives

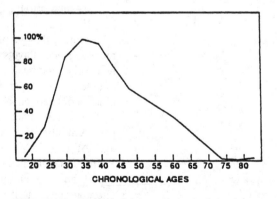

NOTE: Based on 993 significant contributions by 244 chemists now deceased.

Source: Excerpted from *Age and Achievement,* by Harvey Lehman. Princeton, NJ: Princeton University Press, 1953. Reprinted by permission of the American Philosophical Society.

Figure 2. Average Number of Practical Inventions During Each Five-Year Interval of the Inventors' Lives

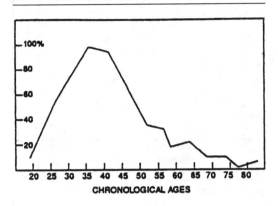

CHRONOLOGICAL AGES

NOTE: Based on 554 inventions by 402 inventors now deceased.

Figure 3. Age Versus Inventions Patented in the U.S.A.

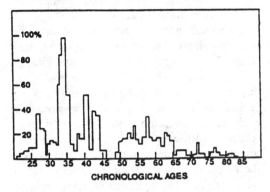

CHRONOLOGICAL AGES

NOTE: Based on a total of 1,086 patents.

Figure 1 presents, by five-year intervals, the chronological ages at which 244 chemists (now deceased) made 993 significant contributions to the science of chemistry. In studying Figure 1 it should be borne in mind that it sets forth the average number of chemical contributions per five-year intervals. Full and adequate allowance is thus made for the larger number of youthful workers. . . .

Figure 2 presents the ages at which 554 notable inventions were made by 402 well-known inventors. . . . When Figure 2 was displayed to interested friends and colleagues, several persons immediately said, "What about Edison?" It is, of course, well-known that Thomas A. Edison was very active as an inventor throughout his entire life. Figure 3 reveals, however, that 35 was Mr. Edison's most productive age. Moreover, during the four-year interval from 33 to 36, Edison took out a total of 312 United States patents. This was more than a fourth (28 per cent) of all the United States patents taken out by him during an inventive career that lasted for more than 60 years. . . .

The shape of a performance age-curve varies with a number of things: (1) the type of performance, (2) the excellence of the performance, and (3) the kind of measurement employed. This last fact can perhaps best be illustrated by use of an analogy. Thus, one might construct an age-curve setting forth the average ability of individuals within each of the several age-groups to do the ordinary high jump. At almost every age level some persons would be found who are more or less able to perform this feat. One might, therefore, test out large numbers at each age level and with the resultant data it would be quite possible to construct age-curves disclosing the *average* height that could be attained by the members of each age group.

But there are several other possible procedures which might be employed for comparing the several age groups. Thus, within each of the age groups, one might ascertain the per cent of individuals able to high-jump six feet, the per cent able to high-jump five feet, etc. With the obtained data it would then be possible to construct one curve that would show for each age group the per cent of individuals able to do six feet, another curve showing the per cent able to do five feet, and so on. If a number of these curves were to be constructed, it seems obvious that that curve which set forth age differences in the ability to do six feet would start its rise later and would fall off both earlier and much more rapidly than would another curve showing age differences in the ability to do, say, two feet. It is evident that very superior high jumping is likely to occur during a narrower age-range than would be found for a much lower degree of ability.

If we think in terms of actual performance, the foregoing situation seems to exist in such diverse fields of endeavor as athletics, mathematics, invention, science, chess, the composition of enduring music, and the writing of great books. For each of these types of behavior, very superior achievement seems most likely to occur during a relatively narrow age-range, and the more noteworthy the performance, the more rapidly does the resultant age-curve descend after it has attained its peak. The findings with . . . reference to sculptured works, oil paintings, and etchings suggest similarly that there is an optimal chronological age level for superlatively great success within these particular fields also. . . .

The work of the genius in his old age may still be far superior to the best work that the average man is able to do in his prime. Therefore, for the study of age differences in creativity, it is not valid merely to compare the achievements of the aged genius with the more youthful accomplishments of the average person. If one wishes to ascertain when men of genius have done their very best work, it is necessary to compare the earlier works of men of genius with their own later works. . . .

Sculpture. Effort was made to ascertain the ages at which the most noted sculptors of early Greece executed their most famous works, but this information could not be obtained. Data for Figure 4 were found in Lorado Taft's *The History of American Sculpture* . . . , which attempts to list the best works of the most famous American sculptors. It seems safe to assume that Taft's list contains no age bias. From his book the dates of execution were found for 262 sculptured works by 63 sculptors now deceased. For these 262 works Figure 4 sets forth the average number executed during each five-year interval of the artists' lives. . . .

By means of statistical distributions and graphs [we] show the ages (1) at which outstand-

Figure 4. Age Versus Famous Sculpture

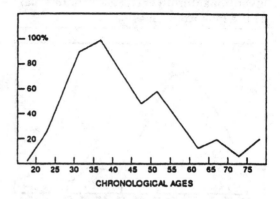

CHRONOLOGICAL AGES

NOTE: Based on 262 works by 63 sculptors.

ing thinkers have most frequently made (or first published) their momentous creative contributions, [and] (2) at which leaders have most often attained important positions of leadership. . . .

The most notable creative works of scientists and mathematicians were identified by experts in the various specialized fields of endeavor. For such fields as oil painting, education, philosophy, and literature, a consensus of the experts was obtained by a study of their published writings. In each field listed below the maximum average rate of highly superior production was found to occur not later than during the specified range of ages. For example, item 1 of this list, chemistry, 26-30, is to be interpreted as follows: in proportion to the number of chemists that were alive at each successive age level, very superior contributions to the field of chemistry were made at the greatest average rate when the chemists were not more than 26-30. The remaining items here and those in the tabular lists that follow are to be interpreted in similar manner.

Physical Sciences, Mathematics, and Inventions:

1. Chemistry, 26-30

2. Mathematics, 30-34

3. Physics, 30-34

4. Electronics, 30-34

5. Practical Inventions, 30-34

6. Surgical Techniques, 30-39

7. Geology, 35-39

8. Astronomy, 35-39

Biological Sciences:

9. Botany, 30-34

10. Classical Descriptions of Disease, 30-34

11. Genetics, 30-39

12. Entomology, 30-39

13. Psychology, 30-39

14. Bacteriology, 35-39

15. Physiology, 35-39

16. Pathology, 35-39

17. Medical Discoveries, 35-39 . . .

For most types of superior music, the maximum average rate of good production is likely to occur in the thirties. Here are the maxima.

18. Instrumental Selections, 25-29

19. Vocal Solos, 30-34

20. Symphonies, 30-34

21. Chamber Music, 35-39

22. Orchestral Music, 35-39

23. Grand Opera, 35-39

24. Cantatas, 40-44

25. Light Opera and Musical Comedy, 40-44

For the study of literary creativity, fifty well-known histories of English literature were canvassed. The works most often cited by the fifty literary historians were assumed to be superior to those cited infrequently. Best-liked short stories were identified similarly by use of 102 source books, and "best books" were ascertained by study of a collation of fifty "best book" lists. As is revealed by the following tabulation, literary works that are good and permanently great are produced at the highest average rate by persons who are not over 45 years old. It is clear also that most types of poetry show maxima 10 to 15 years earlier than most prose writings other than short stories.

26. German Composers of Noteworthy Lyrics and Ballads, 22-26

27. Odes, 24-28

28. Elegies, 25-29

29. Pastoral Poetry, 25-29

30. Narrative Poetry, 25-29

31. Sonnets, 26-31

32. Lyric Poetry, 26-31

33. Satiric Poetry, 30-34

34. Short Stories, 30-34

35. Religious Poetry (Hymns), 32-36

36. Comedies, 32-36

37. Tragedies, 34-38

38. "Most Influential Books," 35-39

39. Hymns by Women, 36-38

40. Novels, 40-44

41. "Best Books," 40-44

42. Best Sellers, 40-44

43. Miscellaneous Prose Writings, 41-45 . . .

Although the maximum average rate of output of the most important philosophical books occurred at 35-39, the total range for best production extended from 22 [to] 80, and for mere quantity of output—good, bad, and indifferent—the production rate was almost constant from 30 [to] 70. . . .

A very large proportion of the most renowned men of science and the humanities did their first important work before 25, and . . . in general the earlier starters contributed better work and were more prolific than were the slow starters. . . .

For most types of creative work the following generalizations have been derived. Within any given field of creative endeavor: (1) the maximum production rate for output of highest quality usually occurs at an earlier age than the maximum rate for less distinguished works by the same individuals; (2) the rate of good production usually does not change much in the middle years and the decline, when it comes, is gradual at all the older ages—much more gradual than its onset in the late teens or early twenties; (3) production of highest quality tends to fall off not only at an earlier age but also at a more rapid rate than does output of lesser merit. . . .

Item 62 in the following tabulation shows that, in proportion to the number of men who were still alive at each successive age level, presidents of American colleges and universities have served most often at 50-54. The other items in this tabulation are to be interpreted similarly.

62. Presidents of American Colleges and Universities, 50-54

63. Presidents of the U.S. Prior to Truman, 55-59

64. U.S. Ambassadors to Foreign Countries From 1875 to 1900, 60-64

65. U.S. Senators in 1925, 60-64

66. Men in Charge of the U.S. Army From 1925 to 1945, 60-64

67. Justices of the U.S. Supreme Court From 1900 to 1925, 70-74

68. Speakers of the U.S. House of Representatives From 1900 to 1940, 70-74

69. Popes, 82-92

An analysis of age data for the most highly successful athletes reveals that their modal ages differ less from the norms for intellectual proficiency than is commonly supposed. The following comparisons are illustrative.

70. Professional Football Players, 22-26

71. Professional Prizefighters, 25-26

72. Professional Ice Hockey Players, 26

73. Professional Baseball Players, 27-28

74. Professional Tennis Players, 25-29

75. Automobile Racers, 26-30

76. Leading Contestants at Chess, 29-33

77. Professional Golfers, 31-36

78. Breakers of World Billiards Records, 31-36

79. Winners at Rifle and Pistol Shooting, 31-36

80. Winners of Important Bowling Championships, 31-36 . . .

When seven groups of earlier-born athletic champions were compared with seven groups of those more recently born, the field of sport being kept constant in each comparison, the later-born were found to be older than the earlier-born. The changes that have taken place in the modal ages of creative thinkers, leaders, and athletes all evidence the fact that these modal ages are not due solely to genetic factors. Whether the modal ages will continue to change and whether they can be subjected to some kind of human control are quite different questions.

A mere increase in man's longevity should not change greatly the modal ages at which man exhibits his greatest creative proficiency since, both for long-lived and for short-lived groups, the modal age occurs in the thirties. . . .

Possible Causes for the Early Maxima in Creativity

At present we are in no position to explain these curves of creativity that rise rapidly in early maturity and then decline slowly after attaining an earlier maximum. Undoubtedly multiple causation operates in these complex behaviors and no discovered contributing condition is likely to be of itself a sufficient or necessary cause. Nevertheless, it is profitable here to list sixteen of the factors which have been suggested as contributing to these representative functions with their early maxima, for such factors indicate possible lines for further research. Here is the list.

(1) A decline occurs prior to 40 in physical vigor, energy, and resistance to fatigue. This decline is probably far more important than such normal age changes as may occur in adult intelligence prior to outright senility.

(2) A diminution in sensory capacity and motor precision also takes place with advance in age. For example, impaired vision and hearing handicap the older individual in many cumulative ways, and writing by hand also becomes more difficult with advance in age.

(3) Serious illness, poor health, and various bodily infirmities more often influence adversely the production rates of older than of younger age groups.

(4) Glandular changes continue throughout life. It is conceivable that hormone research may some day reveal a partial explanation for the changes and especially for the early maxima.

(5) In some instances unhappy marriages and maladjustment in the sex life, growing worse with advance in age, may have interfered with creative work.

(6) The older age groups, more often than the younger, may have become indifferent toward creativity because of the death of a child, a mate, or some other dear one.

(7) As compared with younger persons, older ones are apt to be more preoccupied with the practical concerns of life, with earning a living, and with getting ahead.

(8) Less favorable conditions for concentrated work sometimes come with success, promotion, enhanced prestige, and responsibility.

(9) In some cases the youthful worker's primary ambition may not have been to discover the unknown or to create something new but to get renown. Having acquired prestige and recognition, such workers may try less hard for achievement.

(10) Too easy, too great, or too early fame may conceivably breed complacency and induce one to rest on his previously won laurels before he has done his best possible creative work.

(11) Some older persons may have become apathetic because they have experienced more often the deadening effect of non-recognition and of destructive criticism.

(12) As a result of negative transfer, the old generally are more inflexible than the young. This inflexibility may be a handicap to creative thinking, even though it is dependent on erudition.

(13) Perhaps in part because of the foregoing factors, some older persons experience a decrease in motivation which leads to a weaker intellectual interest and curiosity.

(14) Younger persons tend to have had a better formal education than their elders, they have grown to maturity in a more stimulating social and cultural milieu, and they have had less time to forget what they have learned.

(15) In some few cases outright psychosis has clouded what was previously a brilliant mind. Psychoses occur more often in the latter half of the normal life span.

(16) In other extreme cases, the individual's normal productive powers may have been sapped by alcohol, narcotics, and other kinds of dissipation. Here, as elsewhere, it is difficult to separate cause from effect. . . .

Upon the basis of all these statistics what is one to conclude? Whatever the causes of growth and decline, it remains clear that the genius does not function equally well throughout the years of adulthood. Superior creativity rises relatively rapidly to a maximum which occurs usually in the thirties and then falls off slowly. Almost as soon as he becomes fully mature, man is confronted with a gerontic paradox that may be expressed in terms of positive and negative transfer. Old people probably have more transfer, both positive and negative, than do young ones. As a result of positive transfer the old usually possess greater wisdom and erudition. These are invaluable assets. But when a situation requires a new way of looking at things, the acquisition of new techniques or even new vocabularies, the old seem stereotyped and rigid. To learn the new they often have to unlearn the old and that is twice as hard as learning without unlearning. But when a situation requires a store of past knowledge then the old find their advantage over the young.

Possibly every human behavior has its period of prime. No behavior can develop before the groundwork for it has been prepared, but in general it appears that the conditions essential for creativity and originality, which can be displayed in private achievement, come earlier than those social skills which contribute to leadership and eminence and which inevitably must wait, not upon the insight of the leader himself, but upon the insight of society about him.

Age and Achievement
A Critique

Wayne Dennis

The recent book by Lehman (1), *Age and Achievement,* seems to indicate that in many fields relatively little creative work of importance is done by persons past 45 or 50 years of age. This generalization does not hold in all fields of creativity, but the preceding sentence expresses Lehman's most striking finding.

That the production of first-rate work in poetry, art, science, and other creative areas decreases markedly with age is a matter of prime importance. If correct, it suggests that the creative worker in many fields should plan for early superannuation. If the conclusion drawn by Lehman is erroneous, the impression which it has created should be corrected with dispatch, for a conviction that early deterioration is inevitable may itself have deleterious consequences. Clearly the relationship of age to achievement is a topic in regard to which conclusions should be drawn with extreme care.

It is the thesis of this [essay] that much of the apparent decline in creative achievement revealed by Lehman's tables and graphs is due to factors other than age. We believe Lehman's data give a spurious appearance of age decrement in creativity.

Let us note first that the studies presented by Lehman are so numerous and so varied that it is difficult to do justice to them in a brief recapitula-

Source: "Age and Achievement: A Critique," by Wayne Dennis, *Journal of Gerontology,* 2(3): 331-333, 1956. Copyright © The Gerontological Society of America. Reprinted by permission. Publication of this article was supported by a grant from the Forest Park Foundation to the *Journal of Gerontology.*

tion. However, it is not incorrect to say that Lehman has been interested primarily in determining the 5 or 10 year age-period in which important creative works have most often been produced. The first step in his procedure, typically, consists in identifying important works in some field. To avoid introducing a bias of his own, he always uses a list of works drawn up by some other person. Lehman then determines the age at which each item was produced. He has done this for many creative fields, including mathematical discoveries, contributions to chemistry, lyric poems, and operas, to mention only a few. The first six chapters of his book are devoted to presenting the results of these analyses.

The graphs in these chapters almost all indicate that the production of outstanding works rises to a peak relatively early in the adult years and then declines. The age at which the peak of productivity is reached varies from field to field. It is as early as ages 22-26 for lyrics, ballads, and odes, and as late as 40-45 for novels, metaphysics, and miscellaneous prose writings. However, for a considerable number of fields the top rates for the production of outstanding works occur between ages 30 and 39.

Many aspects of these curves are worthy of attention, but we are concerned chiefly with the decrements which follow the peaks. In most instances, as presented by Lehman, the decrements are very striking. For example, . . . at ages 40-45 chemists produce, per man [*sic*], only one half as many significant contributions as they produce between ages 30-35. By ages 60-65 their rate of production is only 20 per cent of their peak rate.

Other graphs give very similar data for other sciences. The fine arts also show a severe decrement. For example, . . . by ages 45-50 the production of orchestral music judged to be of highest merit is only about 10 per cent as great as it was 10 years earlier. By ages 55-60 the composition of orchestral music of high quality decreases to 20 per cent of the maximum rate.

Examination of such findings, page after page, creates an impression of inevitable decline. If these charts are taken at their face value, we must conclude that in most kinds of creative work the output of work of first-rate quality is greatly reduced after the thirties.

But should these charts be taken at their face value? Let us consider this question.

A major methodologic weakness in Lehman's treatment of data lies in the fact that in most instances a table or graph combines information pertaining to men of different degrees of longevity. Thus a table usually presents data for men nearly all of whom reached age 30, but only part of whom attained age 40, and still fewer of whom completed half a century of life. To equate for differences in numbers of subjects at different ages, Lehman found the mean number of important contributions per person for persons surviving each decade. We shall attempt to show that this method of treating data acts in part to produce the productivity differentials which Lehman discovers.

Let it be noted that each man whose record is used by Lehman is required to produce only one important work in order to qualify for inclusion. In most lists of outstanding works used by Lehman, each individual contributes one, or only a few items. In his collections of data, the mean number of contributions per man is often only two or three. Furthermore, the mean number of "significant" contributions per man is only slightly greater for the men who lived to age 70 than it is for the men who died relatively early.

In order to be included the short-lived man must have produced a significant work at an early age. To qualify for inclusion, a long-lived man was required to produce one significant work but this could have been done either early or late. In other words, in order to achieve a certain degree of eminence, the short-lived man must have fulfilled in a few years what the longer-lived achieved in a more leisurely fashion. We shall show that the consequence of combining data for men of different longevities is a higher average productivity in the early decades.

In this connection Lehman says . . . , "Adequate allowance for the unequal numbers of individuals alive at successive age levels was made. . . ." It seems to us that no adequate allowance can be made for the fact that all of the significant contributions of short-lived people occur in the early decades, whereas the long-lived can contribute both early and late. In tabulating entries for different decades, the twenties or thirties receive a score for each short-lived person. On the other hand, the later decades, such as the sixties, contain no entries for short-lived persons and only part of the entries for the septuagenarians. When data from men of different degrees of longevity are included in the same table, the early decades have an inevitable loading which is not shared by the later decades. To give the later decades a similar loading, it would be necessary to adopt the rule of including a long-lived person only if he made a significant contribution in his later years, because, conversely, the short-lived person is included only if he made a significant contribution in the early decades of life. This is a somewhat subtle point, but one which is essential to the correct evaluation of Lehman's data.

From the point of view of the consideration presented above, a very interesting table is presented by Lehman in his penultimate chapter. . . . This table represents 1,540 notable contributions to various sciences. In this case, the data for persons of different longevity are treated separately. For this reason, the criticism presented above does not apply.

The table shows that for each group the decade . . . of the thirties is most productive but the differences between the thirties and the forties are not large. The largest difference between the thirties and forties occurs among those dying in the forties. In this group ill-health may have contributed to the decrement. For longer-lived groups, even the decrements in the fifties, compared to the thirties, are not dramatic. No group in the fifties drops to the extent which is found when persons are not segregated according to longevity. In other words, this table shows that the combining of data for men of unequal longevity in other tables seems to have exaggerated the apparent age decrement. Nevertheless, even when data refer to men of equal life-spans some age decrement is still found.

This table is so significant in regard to age decrement that it is surprising that Lehman makes no reference to it when discussing the striking decrements reported in his earlier chapters. Nor are its findings adequately reflected in the summary chapter of his book. For these reasons it seems necessary here to emphasize the importance of the data which it contains.

We believe that much of this residual decrement is the product of other deficiencies in methodology. For one thing, it seems likely that the very high peaks of productivity which Lehman reports in his early chapters may be due to errors in sampling and to choosing age-intervals in such a way as to maximize the effects of sampling errors.

Many, but not all, of the curves presented by Lehman are based upon a relatively small number of entries. Thus figure 14 is the result of only 52 entries, figure 16, 30, figure 51, 53, figure 53, 67, and figure 56, 40. These entries are divided among age-intervals, usually 5-year periods, extending from age 20 to age 70 and beyond. With small numbers of entries divided among 10 or more age intervals, one would expect that, even though no true age differences are present, high values in some age-intervals would frequently be obtained through the operation of sampling errors. This fact is important because the highest age score in any body of data is taken as the peak from which decrement is measured. Therefore any exaggeration of the peak naturally results in finding exaggerated decrements.

This factor is further aggravated by the fact that Lehman did not limit himself to a fixed set of age-intervals, but apparently altered them in order to determine the particular "peak years" which seem to characterize a particular set of data. Thus, as the final chapter indicates, the step-intervals for peak years for different activities are variously reported as 22-26, 24-28, 25-29, 26-31, 30-34, 32-36, etc. The modification of age-intervals in order to find "ages of maximum productivity" would be legitimate if the findings were cross-validated against new data, but this was seldom done. Hence the extent to which "peak years" are affected by random errors of sampling is unknown.

There can be little doubt that some part of the decrements reported by Lehman are to be explained by the considerations just presented. The reader of Lehman's book will note that decrements are less precipitous in the graphs which are based upon numerous data and in the construction of which the step intervals follow the decimal system instead of being varied to maximize the peaks.

The preceding arguments have been of a mathematical or statistical sort. Those which follow are of a different kind, but, we think, no less cogent.

Lehman used as a criterion for inclusion of a work as a "significant contribution" the appearance of the work in histories of the appropriate area, or its appearance in lists of "best" books, "best" operas, etc. Perhaps, no better indices of importance are available, but it should be pointed out that these criteria may have certain weaknesses from the point of view of the study of age differences. It is possible that biographies, histories, and lists of best works contain systematic errors somewhat favoring a man's early work at the expense of his later products, and Lehman's findings may reflect these biases. For example, the art historian may be more likely to mention a painter's first significant contribution than he is to mention his last important piece of work. Likewise, an historian of science may be more likely to mention a young man's pioneering research which opened a new vista than he is to describe the subsequent painstaking investigations which were necessary to develop and validate the promise of the pioneering study. It is difficult to know to what extent an apparent age decrement may be due to the proclivities of anthologists and historians rather than to age itself.

In this connection, the possibility of a bias against the evaluation of recent contributions should be considered. It is our impression that critics and historians tend to consider the evaluation of recent contributions to be more difficult than the evaluation of more remote works. They may, therefore, suspend judgment in connection with recent contributions. Now a considerable number of Lehman's subjects were born after 1800. . . . Their later works were recent works at the time of the preparation of the source books from which Lehman obtained his data. Unwillingness, on the part of historians and editors, to evaluate recent works would therefore lessen the number of significant works recorded for the later years of some of Lehman's subjects. Consonant with this interpretation is Lehman's report that in former centuries the decrement with age in several fields seems not to have been as great as in recent times. . . . A century or more ago the apparent decline of creativity with age was slight.

Let us note, too, that the assessment of the relative excellence of work done early and late in a man's career is made exceedingly difficult, if indeed not impossible, by the changes in standards which occur during a man's lifetime. For example, the situation in biology in 1880, when Darwin was 71, was extremely different from what it was when "The Origin of the Species" appeared in 1859 when Darwin was 50. In fact, the difference was due in large part to Darwin's own work. It seems relatively meaningless to compare biologic contributions made before and after the publication of the theory of evolution. This argument, of course, is not limited to biology. Changing standards characterize all fields, whereas judgments of quality in regard to works separated by several decades seem to imply absolute standards.

Standards for the judgment of quality are further complicated by the great increase in the number of creative workers in most fields which has taken place in recent times. Thus the best psychologist in America in 1900 was the best in a group of approximately 100. The best psychologist today, if he were ascertained, would have to be judged the best among 13,000. A psychologist living in 1900 and still living today, had 99 competitors for distinction in his youth and has 12,999 rivals (or thereabouts) in his later years. Similar, if perhaps less striking, increases in personnel have taken place in other fields. Curves for age changes in number of significant contributions do not, and probably cannot, correct for changes in standards of evaluation which occur during a lifetime.

In summary, we have presented several reasons for skepticism in regard to accepting the view that there is a decrement with age in the production of creative works of high level. We have not attempted to be exhaustive in this treatment. We submit, however, that there is a reasonable doubt that the curves presented by Lehman depict an age decline. Quality of creative work *may* decrease with age, but data presently available do not offer satisfactory evidence.

We would like to be able to suggest a method by which valid conclusions concerning changes in the quality of creative contributions with age could be reached, but we are unable to do so. All sources of data, and all methods of evaluation which we have considered seem to suffer from one or more of the difficulties discussed above. Nevertheless, it has been noted that as the methodologic difficulties in Lehman's work are reduced, the apparent decline with age becomes smaller. Whether ideal data would show no decline prior to extreme old age it is at present impossible to say, but this possibility should not be ignored.

Reference

1. Lehman, H. C.: *Age and Achievement,* Princeton University Press, 1953.

Creative Productivity Through the Adult Years

Dean Keith Simonton

All too often the years in the latter part of life are seen as a phase of decline in creative powers. Supposedly once an individual enters his or her 40th year, society cannot and should not expect much, for the best years have been left behind. This notion is expressed cruelly in Shakespeare's words, "When the age is in, the wit is out." No wonder that many otherwise productive individuals sense a "midlife crisis" coming on as they pass into the putative region of decline and deterioration. Indeed, some commentators have aggravated matters by claiming that the downhill slide normally begins in the 30s rather than the 40s, as is evident in a little poem written by Paul Dirac, who received the Nobel Prize for Physics when only 31 years old for work he had completed when just 25:

> Age is, of course, a fever chill that every physicist must fear. He's better dead than living still when once he's past his thirtieth year. (quoted in Jungk, 1958, p. 27)

Presumably these conceptions of the superiority of youth to maturity are based on straightforward empirical observations—solid facts rather than prejudicial stereotypes. But is that necessarily so? One can always offer anecdotes, about the exceptional accomplishments of youth, such as Newton's *annus mirabilis* that reportedly occurred before his 24th year, but such instances

can always be balanced by stories of phenomena] achievements by personalities in advanced age; for example, Copernicus saw his treatise on the heliocentric system published as he lay on his deathbed in his 70th year. So what is required is not the compilation of anecdote and counteranecdote, but rather the systematic investigation of how creative productivity changes over the life span.

Interestingly enough, scientific inquiries on this very question have been going on for over a hundred years (e.g., Beard, 1874; Quetelet, 1835/ 1968). The classic study in this area is Harvey C. Lehman's (1953) well-known *Age and Achievement,* in which the connection between creative productivity and chronological age is examined for virtually every endeavor under the sun. Although Lehman's work suffered from a number of methodological problems—not surprising for such a pioneer effort—recent years have seen a resurgence of investigations that exploit more sophisticated techniques. Indeed, the fact that so many children of the baby boom generation are now entering the latter half of life may have made this a hot issue in life-span developmental psychology. Accordingly, despite the existence of several published reviews of the most current literature in the past few years (see, especially, Simonton, 1988, 1990a, 1990b), the burst of activity has already rendered these surveys somewhat obsolete! An updated summary of key findings is thus in order.

Let us begin with one solid empirical generalization that was first promulgated in 1835 and that remains robust today. If one plots the number of creative products, such as articles, paintings, or plays, as a function of a creator's chronological age, the output rate first increases rather quickly, attaining a peak in the late 30s or early 40s of life; thereafter, productivity gradually declines. It is the latter portion of the age curve, naturally enough, that seems to shatter the hopes of those wanting to continue creativity in the final half of life. Indeed, ever since Beard (1874), this downward tendency has led to pessimistic expectations about the utility of advanced maturity. Nevertheless, while the observed age curve has been replicated hundreds of times, more detailed theoretical and empirical analyses reveal that the picture is not as bad as first meets the eye. Six considerations, discussed below, are paramount.

Exceptions Expected

It cannot be stressed too much that the typical age curve is merely a statistical average of hundreds of separate age curves for individual creators. Like any statistical summation, the result is far from deterministic; no creative person is forced to have his or her career trajectory follow the exact same course. Rather, these averaged age curves can be taken to represent merely the probability of creative output at particular stages in a human life. Because we are dealing solely in probabilities, "exceptions to the rule" must be necessarily expected, not categorically denied. This point takes on special force when we introduce a central finding of the recent empirical literature: The generalized age curve is not a function of chronological age but rather it is determined by *career age* (e.g., Simonton, 1991, in press). People differ tremendously on when they manage to launch themselves in their creative activities. Whereas those who get off to an exceptionally early start may—if circumstances to be discussed later are held constant—find themselves peaking out early in life, others who qualify as veritable "late bloomers" will not get into full stride until they attain ages at which others are leaving the race. It is for this reason that some creative personalities have failed to reach the acme of their achievements until near the close of their lives.

Magnitude of Decline

But to make matters simpler, let us now suppose that we are confining our analysis to individuals who all initiated their creative activities at the same chronological age, such as the mid-20s, thus taking the respective career ages of these individuals as identical—what then? Notwithstanding the general occurrence of an age decrement in productivity in the final decades of life, the magnitude of this decline is seldom so substantial that an individual must become devoid of creativity at life's close. On the contrary, the average rate of output in the seventh decade of life falls to around half the rate seen at the career optimum in the 30s and 40s (Simonton, 1988). Consequently, even an octogenarian can expect to produce many notable contributions to a chosen creative endeavor. Indeed, even though a 50% decrement may look depressing, the drop by no means necessitates the last decade of a typical career to suffer in comparison to the first decade of that same career. Quite the contrary: Creators in their 60s and 70s will most often be generating new ideas at a rate exceeding that of the very same creators in their 20s (e.g., Dennis, 1966). In fact, toward the end of life the postoptimum decrease in output decelerates, so that rather than a plummeting we witness a leisurely asymptotic approach to the zero productivity level (Simonton, 1984). Of course, those persons who experience severe disabilities may exhibit a "terminal drop," but such an unfortunate happenstance is far from normal so long as a creator's health holds out. As a consequence, it is easy to list impressive accomplishments by people who were well along in years, yet not necessarily late bloomers (Lehman, 1953, chap. 14).

Variation Across Disciplines

The overall age curve described earlier is not only the statistical average of hundreds of separate career trajectories that can depart from the norm in manifold ways, but in addition the generalized trend represents a kind of rough summary of age curves that vary substantially across disciplines (Simonton, 1988). Especially noteworthy is the realization that the expected age decrement in creativity in some disciplines is so minuscule that we can hardly talk of a decline at all. Although in certain creative activities, such as pure mathematics and lyric poetry, the peak may appear relatively early in life, sometimes even in the late 20s and early 30s, with a rapid drop afterwards, in other activities, such as geology and scholarship, the age optimum may occur appreciably later, in the 50s even, with a gentle, even undetectable decrease in productivity thereafter (e.g., Dennis, 1966). Expressed in precise terms, whereas in some endeavors the last decade of life may see output rates only 10 percent as high as witnessed at the career maxima, in other endeavors the productivity seen in the closing years may remain quite near the magnitude of output reached in the supposed productive prime.

The occurrence of such interdisciplinary contrasts endorses the conjecture that the career course is decided more by the intrinsic needs of the creative process than by generic extrinsic forces, whether physical illness, family commitments, or administrative responsibilities. This conclusion is bolstered further by the fact that the distinctive age curves for various disciplines tend to replicate across different nationalities and historical periods (Lehman, 1962; Simonton, 1975). Now clearly, if creativity in some domains can persist until the final days, it becomes obvious that we cannot speak of broad decrements in psychological functioning required for creative output (Simonton, 1988). Significantly, a theoretical model that quite accurately predicts such interdisciplinary differences in the career trajectories does so solely by taking into consideration the information-processing requirements of distinct fields (Simonton, 1989a).

Admittedly, for creators whose aspirations fall into fields that feature early career optima, these empirical findings may still look discouraging. A lyric poet, after all, will yet be "over the hill" at a relatively youthful age. Even so, nothing prevents a person from switching fields in order to preserve creative vitality. By carefully designed mid-career changes, individuals may resuscitate their creative potential (cf. Root-Bernstein, 1989).

Quantity or Quality

One critical question lies lurking in the preceding discussion, namely, whether we are speaking of quantity or quality when publicizing the age trends. Lehman's (1953) classic summary of his extensive empirical findings has often been attacked for excessive reliance on tabulations of only those creations recognized as notable or influential, ignoring the much larger body of potential contributions that underlie the few works that are thus singled out (Simonton, 1988). Dennis (1966), in particular, argued that, whereas tabulations of famous contributions may exhibit sharp declines in the later years, truly exhaustive tallies display far more gradual decreases. Therefore, if we choose to reject the judgments of posterity and focus on strictly behavioral measures, the age decrement in creativity is much less substantial.

This criticism has two deficiencies, however. First, if the term "creative" is to have any genuine meaning, it must ultimately be tied to real social value, and thus mere behavioral productivity is largely irrelevant. Second, and more profound, empirical studies actually demonstrate that quality of output across the life span is strongly associated with quantity of output (e.g., Over, 1989; Simonton, 1977, 1985). In other words, those periods in a creative career in which an individual is generating the most total works tend to be, on the average, the same periods in which the most successful pieces emerge. In fact, if one calculates the ratio of creative products to the total number of offerings at each age interval, one finds that this "quality ratio" exhibits no systematic change with age. As a consequence, the success rate is the same for the senior colleague as it is for the young whippersnapper. Older creators may indeed be producing fewer hits, but they are equally producing fewer misses as well. Hence, on a contribution-for-contribution basis—that is, by determining the probability that a particular product will prove influential in a given domain of cultural endeavor—we cannot speak of an age decrement at all! This probabilistic connection between quantity and quality, which has been styled the "constant probability of success" principle

(Simonton, 1988), strongly implies that an individual's creative powers remain intact throughout the life span.

Individual Variation

Individuals vary immensely in what may be termed *creative potential,* which may be roughly defined here as the maximum number of attempted contributions an individual is capable of making given an unlimited life span (Simonton, 1988). The primary behavioral manifestation of this variable is the sheer rate at which ideas are generated throughout the career: The higher the creative potential, the faster the output per annum. Now because this individual difference variable is independent of the age of career onset (Simonton, in press), it provides yet another factor that can enhance the creativity of the later years. In particular, given a set of persons having all launched their careers at the same chronological age, that subset of individuals who score high on this attribute will tend to generate possible contributions at a more prolific rate in the closing years and thus, according to the constant-probability-of-success principle, manage to produce more truly notable works as well. The age curves do not really differ for those highest in creative potential, but rather the curves function at a larger scale; thus a person with exceptional potential will be producing at rates in the final years that can surpass the productivity of an individual with lower potential who is operating at his or her career peak. Consequently, predictions about the expected creativity in the last decade cannot be made without reference to substantial cross-sectional variation in both the age at which the career commences and the individual's total creative capacity (see, e.g., Over, 1982a, 1982b).

A Secondary Peak

In all of the preceding points we continued to speak of an age decrement in the last years of life, the main thrust of the arguments being that certain factors can intervene to impede the seemingly inevitable decline. Yet empirical research actually suggests that creative productivity can undergo a substantial renaissance in the final years, especially toward life's close. For example, some time after the late 60s a resurgence in output often appears (Simonton, 1988). This secondary peak, to be sure, is not nearly so pronounced as that appearing in the so-called prime of life. Even so, its very existence contradicts the supposed inevitability of the downhill slide.

This contradiction gains even greater force when we consider the recent demonstration of the swan-song phenomenon, or "last works" effects (Simonton, 1989b). After subjecting 1,919 works by 172 classical composers to detailed quantitative scrutiny, one striking pattern emerged: As the composers neared their final years, when death was becoming more than an abstract contingency, they began to create compositions that were more concise, with simpler and more restrained melodic lines; yet these compositions scored extremely well in esthetic significance, as judged by musicologists, and eventually joined the popular mainstays of the classical repertoire. It is as if each composer, when seeing the end approaching fast on life's horizon, put the utmost into everything undertaken, with the knowledge that among the current works-in-progress dwelt a last artistic testament. Whatever the motivation, the mere fact that dying creators can pull off such feats provides another argument on behalf of the theory that the general decline in output need not be synonymous with a deterioration in creative powers.

The foregoing six points by no means exhaust all that might be said on this critical life-span developmental issue (cf. Simonton, 1988, 1990b). But these empirical findings should enable us to appreciate that the final phase of life can be, and often is, a period of phenomenal creativity. At the very least we should understand how it can come to pass that certain creators manage to leave posterity with monumental creations that would have been sorely missed had their late-life endeavors been summarily dismissed. Thus in the arts, Cervantes could complete Part II of *Don Quixote* at age 68, Verdi compose *Falstaff* in his 80th year, and Titian paint *Christ Crowned With Thorns* when approaching 90 years of age. And turning to science, Laplace finished his *Celestial Mechanics* at age 79, Humboldt put out the last volume of his *Cosmos* when 89, and, most remarkably, the chemist Chevreul took up the study of gerontology in his 90s and published his last scientific paper when 102! Nor are such examples restricted to a bygone era, as the recent example of Elizabeth Layton well exemplifies: At the age of 68, she combated thoughts of suicide by taking up artistic expression, propelling herself on an enterprise of distinctive creativity at an age when most would be contemplating retirement.

The important implication of these examples is that the career trajectory reflects not the inexorable progression of an aging process tied extrinsically to chronological age, but rather entails the intrinsic working out of a person's creative potential by successive acts of self-actualization.

References

Beard, G. M., 1874. *Legal Responsibility in Old Age.* New York: Russell.

Dennis, W., 1966. "Creative Productivity Between the Ages of 20 and 80 Years." *Journal of Gerontology* 21: 1-8.

Jungk, R., 1958. *Brighter Than a Thousand Suns* (trans. J. Cleugh). New York: Harcourt Brace.

Lehman, H. C., 1953. *Age and Achievement.* Princeton, N.J.: Princeton University Press.

Lehman, H. C., 1962. "More About Age and Achievement." *Gerontologist* 2(3): 141-48.

Over, R., 1982a. "Does Research Productivity Decline With Age?" *Higher Education* 11: 511-20.

Over, R., 1982b. "Is Age a Good Predictor of Research Productivity?" *Australian Psychologist* 17: 129-39.

Quetelet, A., 1835/1968. *A Treatise on Man.* New York: Franklin. (Reprint of 1842 Edinburgh translation of original 1835 publication.)

Root-Bernstein, R. S., 1989. *Discovering.* Cambridge, Mass.: Harvard University Press.

Shakespeare, W. "Much Ado About Nothing." In R. M. Hutchins, ed., *Great Books of the Western World.* Chicago: Encyclopedia Britannica, 1952, p. 520.

Simonton, D. K., 1975. "Age and Literary Creativity: A Cross-Cultural and Transhistorical Survey." *Journal of Cross-Cultural Psychology* 6(3): 259-77.

Simonton, D. K., 1977. "Creative Productivity, Age, and Stress: A Biographical Time-Series Analysis of 10 Classical Composers." *Journal of Personality and Social Psychology* 35(3): 791-804.

Simonton, D. K., 1984. "Creative Productivity and Age: A Mathematical Model Based on a Two-Step Cognitive Process." *Developmental Review* 4: 77-111.

Simonton, D. K., 1985. "Quality, Quantity, and Age: The Careers of 10 Distinguished Psychologists." *International Journal of Aging and Human Development* 21(4): 241-54.

Simonton, D. K., 1988. "Age and Outstanding Achievement: What Do We Know After a Century of Research?" *Psychological Bulletin* 104(2): 251-67.

Simonton, D. K., 1989a. "Age and Creative Productivity: Nonlinear Estimation of an Information-Processing Model." *International Journal of Aging and Human Development* 29: 23-37.

Simonton, D. K., 1989b. "The Swan-Song Phenomenon: Last-Works Effects for 172 Classical Composers." *Psychology and Aging* 4: 42-47.

Simonton, D. K., 1990a. "Creativity and Wisdom in Aging." In J. E. Birren and K. W. Schaie, eds., *Handbook of the Psychology of Aging,* 3d ed. New York: Academic Press.

Simonton, D. K., 1990b. "Creativity in the Later Years: Optimistic Prospects for Achievement." *Gerontologist* 30(5): 626-31.

Simonton, D. K., 1991. "Career Landmarks in Science: Individual Differences and Interdisciplinary Contrasts." *Developmental Psychology* 27(1): 119-27.

Simonton, D. K., in press. "The Emergence and Realization of Genius: The Lives and Works of 120 Classical Composers." *Journal of Personality and Social Psychology.*

Does Aging Bring Wisdom?

Douglas H. Powell

Some of today's most influential thinkers about the life cycle believe that wisdom accumulates with age. Erik Erikson, the first American psychologist to extend developmental theory into older age, believed that wisdom is unique among the generally declining curves of our physical and intellectual capabilities as a power that actually can increase with age.

During the past decade, Paul Baltes and his colleagues at the Max Planck Institute for Human Development and Education in Berlin have been studying wisdom. They focused their efforts on distinguishing between wisdom based on knowledge only and that rooted in "excellent judgment and advice about important and uncertain matters of life." They believed that the highest wisdom-related skills, which they have called cognitive pragmatics, may well be associated with the last season of life.

Most wise individuals don't think of themselves as possessing any special powers of wisdom. They are modest. And they will tell you that their modesty about their powers to understand the complex and uncertain matters of human experience is well deserved. The more they learn, the less they know for certain.

Lessons from my own experience confirm these sentiments. A quarter-century of counseling young people has taught me that there are many individuals that will be impervious to my best efforts to help them. A month after writing a paper setting down the precise steps for treating

Source: "Does Aging Bring Wisdom?" in *The Nine Myths of Aging: Maximizing the Quality of Later Life* by Douglas H. Powell. 1998. New York: Freeman. Reprinted with the permission of W. H. Freeman and Company.

students with performance anxiety, the method failed with the next two undergraduates I saw. The same scenarios have played out in other parts of my life. From these experiences, I have discovered just how fragile my self-confidence is, how quickly it can dissolve into uncertainty, panic, and despair. I can't honestly say that I have enjoyed the pain associated with the deflation of my young adult arrogance, by the failure of some of my best notions, by the recognition that others close to me have had ideas better than mine, or from the feedback that what I was doing was not working. Neither have I liked confronting the fact that I sometimes fail at just those things that I think I am best at. But, as the years have passed, humility has gradually filled the void left by my eroding certainty. Maybe that humility is where we all begin to find wisdom. Humility, perplexity, and modesty are not weaknesses. Considerable strength lies in being uncertain about the nature of truth.

A contemporary example of the strength of humility can be found at every AA meeting. The first step to sobriety for alcoholics is to admit their powerlessness over their urge to drink.

For the last three decades, social scientists have been searching for a more precise definition of wisdom. For the most part, their approach has consisted of asking people what traits they thought wise people might possess. Many of the words used to describe wise people are traits of kindness. Subjects in a study at Yale described wisdom as having attributes of "concern for others." Research in California found that words used to describe wise individuals were often not intellectual: "gentle," "compassionate," "empathic," "nonjudgmental," and "having a sense of humor." These characteristics have more in common with qualities of the heart than of the head.

For example there was John, the young professor who taught me freshman English. When I began his class in September, I stuttered badly. Years of working on this problem had met with no success. The class required us to read the Greats and discuss their ideas. Every day was terrifying for me because I had trouble articulating what I wanted to say. The professor never entered into my struggles with stuttering. Instead, John stood apart, quietly encouraging me to share my thoughts with others in the class, however halting and inept the words must have seemed. He usually found something in what I said that he could agree with. By the end of the term, my stuttering problem of more than a decade was hardly noticeable.

Suffering forces us to find ways to cope with adversity; it is a source of resilience. These reactions to the hard times in our lives become the cornerstones of our character. And suffering leads to experience from which we learn important things about ourselves and the world around us.

If suffering is one source of wisdom, and suffering is an ordinary human experience, are there other ordinary events all of us ordinary people confront in our lives that are wellsprings of wisdom? Again, both ancient and modern thinkers have identified a list that can be condensed into those additional ordinary experiences that lie on the pathway toward wisdom: a life fully lived, self-knowledge, and learning from growing older.

A Life Fully Lived

Wisdom grows out of a life rich in experience and passion, as well as in suffering. I know that now, in my young-old years, I can comfortably lose a tennis match, play second fiddle on a committee, or brake at a yellow light rather than scream through the intersection as I would have done twenty years ago. It is not that winning or controlling these parts of my life aren't fun anymore, but I can savor the playing now, not just the winning.

Coming to Know Yourself

Opinion is almost unanimous that self-knowledge is an essential source of wisdom. A psychological thinker who has described this life-long journey to self-knowledge is Erik Erikson. He coined the term *identity crisis.* He was also interested in wisdom. He saw it as a unique adaptive strength of older age. He made the critical point that the emergence of wisdom as a late-blooming power depends on adequate psychological adjustment in the earlier portions of our lives. He asserted the formation of wisdom follows from successfully confronting particular developmental challenges associated with earlier age and moving on.

Successful transition through earlier periods of the life cycle prepares the individual for the final phase, where wisdom is the principal virtue to be developed. Erikson said that at every new stage of the life cycle we again confront and resolve those problems left over from earlier periods of our life. If in our youth we never really developed a sense of identity, this problem will resurface at this final phase of our lives. We may again face this problem, perhaps finally forming an idea of who we are and what our purpose has been in this life. Or we may have to live with the sense of not knowing.

Nearly a half-century ago, the American writer Langston Hughes said, "Age has nothing to do with wisdom," a sentiment expressed by the great German writer Goethe two hundred years earlier.

More birthdays do not guarantee greater wisdom. It emanates from continuing to be open to experience, to learn from it, and to change in small ways as a result. Wisdom evolves from a life fully lived, enabling us to understand the passions of others, and from our own suffering, which provides a basis for judgment and intuition. Wisdom emerges from the self-knowledge that grows out of living with ourselves through the epochs of our life span.

Wisdom accumulates as long as we can continue to learn while aging—about ourselves and about others, about the world around us.

Increasingly, education is not limited to the first stage of life but is instead extended over the life course. One obstacle to late-life education, however, is a stereotype that the elderly are too old to learn. Sometimes older people themselves accept the stereotype. But we have seen that continued involvement in learning helps to maintain the ability to learn.

Today's opportunities for late-life learning are more plentiful than ever before. Along with organized educational programs, many informal opportunities for older people also abound. One example of a successful program is Elderhostel, founded in 1975 as a summer residential college program for people over age 55. It offers noncredit courses in the liberal arts and now attracts a quarter million participants each year at 1,000 campuses around the United States and in 70 countries overseas. Elderhostel involves no homework, papers, or grades. But it does offer an opportunity for low-cost travel and an intellectual challenge for those interested in learning.

For those who do not want to travel to another community, tuition-free, space-available courses are offered at most public universities. In addition, a national survey of community colleges showed that up to a quarter of two-year institutions provide some offerings for older adults, mostly in the areas of personal financial planning; health and life enrichment (e.g., arts and humanities, exercise, and nutrition); and contemporary civic or political issues (Ventura-Merkel and Doucette, 1993).

Still another approach is the local "learning in retirement" institute, where retired people with special skills or knowledge teach courses to one another. This mutual-aid model has been replicated in 280 communities around the United States and is now sponsored by Elderhostel. In the Scandinavian countries, France, Spain, and other countries, older people have created similar "Universities of the Third Age" affiliated with institutions of higher education.

In the future, we can expect that older-adult education will increase substantially. One reason is the rising level of prior education among successive cohorts of older people. Previous education is the best predictor of interest in lifelong learning. The median level of education for people over 65 in the year 1900 was only 8 years, while by the 1980s it had risen to 12 years (U.S. Senate, 1991). Between 1970 and 1994, the proportion completing high school rose from 28% to 62%. Today, younger people have comparatively higher levels of education, but after the year 2000, Americans over 65 will have nearly as many years of schooling as the general adult population (U.S. Bureau of the Census, 1984).

An explosion in lifelong learning among mature adults is already taking place. In 1984, there were 2.7 million people age 55 and over who had taken adult education courses, and nearly a million of these were persons 65 and over. The number of older people participating in adult education courses is growing rapidly. The expanding population of educated adults should make lifelong learning even more appealing over the entire life course.

Dateline: May 1, 2005, Washington, DC. Associated Press.

Today, President Martha Jefferson welcomed 30,000 delegates to the
White House Conference on Aging. At the same time on a specially dedicated Web site she announced the beginning of Older Americans Month.

President Jefferson noted that this White House Conference on Aging,
the first in the 21st century, was held exactly one decade after the last conference. The big difference, she noted, is that this time there were 10 times
as many official delegates—far more than any hotel in Washington could
accommodate.

In fact, conference "delegates" didn't meet face to face at all but "con-
vened" in cyberspace. They used high-speed fiber-optic connections made
possible by Internet III CyberSystem.

President Jefferson also took special note of the more than 1,000 older
people at the conference who had earned an advanced degree through distance learning under Internet III or its predecessors. She noted that students
over the age of 55 are now the fastest-growing segments in U.S. higher
education.

* * *

The likelihood of this scenario all depends on how quickly new computer
and telecommunications technologies achieve acceptance and widespread
use among the aging population. The technology is advancing rapidly, and
signs of late-life learning in an information society were already evident at
the close of the 20th century. Today, many older people still have anxiety
about using a computer. But technophobia is a stereotype, and their anxiety
can be overcome.

Studies have shown that computer communication can be an aid to independence for older adults. For instance, one study looked at a sample of
women ages 55 to 95 in a Florida community, a group with no prior experience with computers. Participants in the study were given at first a simplified electronic mail and text editor system, and their software was later
upgraded to offer news, weather, movie reviews, health information, and
entertainment news. A follow-up survey showed that participants easily
learned to use the system and came to value it as a means of social interaction (Czaja et al., 1993).

Another study looked at older adults' ability to learn a specific computer
skill: using the Lotus 1-2-3 spreadsheet program (Garfein, Schaie, and Willis, 1988). Participants, whose average age was 58, were tested on measures
of fluid and crystallized intelligence and given training on computer tasks.
More than half of the participants performed well on criterion tasks, suggesting that older individuals can benefit from formal educational experiences as
well as trial-and-error learning. As might be expected, fluid intelligence
scores were the key predictor of success.

A survey in 1995 of computer users subscribing to *Modern Maturity* found that three-quarters of respondents used their computer daily, and a majority reported that computer literacy had definitely enhanced their lives (Cole, 1996). Of these older users, nearly two-thirds used an online service daily to download information, engage in discussion groups, or communicate by e-mail. Interestingly, even many of these intensive users had to overcome an initial fear of new technology, but the computers helped them overcome physical and other limitations.

One of the leaders in the "seniors in cyberspace" movement is SeniorNet, a nonprofit organization founded in San Francisco in 1986 to teach computer skills to older persons (Furlong and Lipson, 1996). SeniorNet has grown rapidly as a membership organization with over 70 learning centers around the country supporting more than 15,000 individual members. SeniorNet publishes its own educational materials, holds annual conferences, and operates its own online network. SeniorNet Learning Centers, run by senior volunteers, are found in community centers, in senior centers, at schools and on college campuses, in libraries, and at health care facilities. Through America Online, SeniorNet also offers classes and discussion forums, live chats, and file downloading.

SeniorNet is not the only service for elders in cyberspace. CompuServe offers its own "Retirement Living Forum" with online discussions about Social Security and health, and Prodigy has a "Seniors Bulletin Board" listing topics on retirement and travel. The Cleveland Free Net has become a nationally recognized example of how an entire city can be "wired" to promote maximum access by all groups, with prominent participation from the elderly and disabled. For example, the local Cleveland Alzheimer's support groups are plugged in to the Free Net, providing a combination of "high tech" and "high touch." In this way, the "virtual community" of cyberspace becomes a means of reinforcing and extending face-to-face mutual support networks.

In growing numbers, older people are using computers to entertain themselves, improve their productivity, and enhance quality of life (Lawhon, Ennis, and Lawhon, 1996). People age 55 and older are using the Internet and World Wide Web in a variety of creative projects, including writing for fun and profit, preparing family histories, communicating with distant family members, and maintaining community involvement through bulletin boards. Typical computer projects may involve recipe files, personalized children's books, bridge tallies, computer portraits, genealogies, family newsletters, and computer-related poems.

The spread of computer use among elders isn't confined to the United States. A recent European study confirmed that computer literacy is helping to reduce social isolation and is providing access to services such as "teleshopping," home entertainment, and home banking in Europe. Computer use is also a source of intellectual exercise and helps promote self-esteem and communication across generations (James et al., 1995).

For older people to realize the benefits of new computer and telecommunications technologies those technologies must be made widely available, easy to use, accessible to people with disabilities, reasonably priced, and capable of supporting a wide variety of applications. Among the new technologies that might benefit older adults are self-paced distance learning with feedback via modems, computerized technologies to allow older workers to work at home, online networks organized by support groups for specific diseases or impairments, and monitoring services and automated check-ins that help the frail elderly maintain their independence (Koch, 1992).

The key to lifelong learning in an information society will be to perceive older adults as active users of new technologies rather than as passive recipients (Czaja and Barr, 1989). Two-way interactive TV can address loneliness and isolation among the elderly. For instance, a two-way television system in Reading, Pennsylvania has been programmed, operated, and financed by senior citizens. The Leisure World retirement community in California has long operated its own cable TV station and generated local programming. Interactive and self-directed activities using new technologies can enhance knowledge, skills, and adaptability—a "high tech/high touch" world with great promise for older people in years to come.

QUESTIONS FOR WRITING, REFLECTION, AND DEBATE

1   Harvey Lehman's data about the peak years of creativity for different fields are derived from creative people who lived in the past. Would it be reasonable to argue that his conclusions don't apply to older people today because health and life expectancy in recent decades have increased rapidly? Does Wayne Dennis succeed in refuting Lehman's argument that age generally means declining creative power? What are Dennis's strongest points in his criticism of Lehman?

2   Dean Simonton, like Lehman, assumes that in judging late-life creativity we should measure how many "masterpieces" or "breakthroughs" are produced by older people. Do you think this standard is the right one for judging late-life creativity? Would other standards or definitions of creativity be more appropriate?

3   What are the most important points in which Simonton's article supports or modifies Lehman's conclusions about age and achievement? Assume that you are Harvey Lehman looking today at the question of late-life creativity. Write a statement describing how your views have been changed or been maintained by the aging of America in recent years.

4   Imagine that you are writing a long obituary for "Louise Bachelard" (an imaginary name), who died recently at age 78. "Bachelard" was a famous painter whose style changed dramatically in her later years. In

the obituary, describe the ways in which the painter's creativity changed as she grew older and connect this with what you have learned about the psychology of aging.

5 Paul Baltes and his colleagues define wisdom as accumulated expertise. But this definition makes no reference to character or the ethical behavior exhibited by a wise person. Could a bank robber, like Willie Sutton, be judged to have "wisdom" if he showed skillful judgment in crime based on long experience? In developing your answer, draw on what Douglas Powell says about the relationship between wisdom and humility.

6 Pick an example of an older person who seems to you to have developed some of the traits of wisdom, whether in general or in some specific field of activity. Write to a stranger explaining why this wise older person is someone whose advice should be taken seriously.

7 If we were designing classes or educational programs for older adults based on the conclusions of Simonton and Powell, how would we organize the learning activities? How would such an older adult educational program differ from what is offered in schools and colleges today?

8 Visit three Web sites: www.elderhostel.org, www.thirdage.com, and SeniorNet's Web site at www.seniornet.org. What similarities do you see in these three sites concerning age-appropriate behavior for older adults? What issues do you see not reflected in these three sites that seem important for successful living in later life?

SUGGESTED READINGS

Arieti, Sylvano, *Creativity: The Magic Synthesis,* New York: Basic Books, 1976.

Greenbery, Reva M., *Education for Older Adult Learning: A Selected Annotated Bibliography,* Westport, CT: Greenwood, 1993.

Manheimer, Ronald, Snodgrass, Denise, and Moskow-McKenzie, Diane, *Older Adult Education: A Guide to Research, Programs and Policies,* Westport, CT: Greenwood, 1995.

Simonton, Dean K., *Genius, Creativity, and Leadership: Historiometric Inquiries,* Cambridge, MA: Harvard University Press, 1984.

Sternberg, Robert (ed.), *The Nature of Creativity: Contemporary Psychological Perspectives,* New York: Cambridge University Press, 1988.

Does Old Age Have Meaning?

*A human being would certainly not grow to be seventy or eighty
years old if this longevity had no meaning for the species. The
afternoon of human life must also have a significance of its own
and cannot be merely a pitiful appendage to life's morning.*

—*Carl Jung,* The Structure and Dynamics of the Psyche

The Meaning of Age

Most of the characteristic qualities of old age are uniquely human. For
instance, among animal species in the wild, we never see offspring take care
of the aging parents who gave birth to them. On the contrary, young animals
typically abandon their parents when they themselves reach maturity, like
baby birds who leave the nest to fly on their own. It is only the human being
who cares for and honors the oldest members of the species, just as only
human beings care for and remember their dead. In both cases we might ask,
Why?

The answer is that human beings live in a symbolic world of shared meaning, and the power of meaning can be a matter of life and death. For example,
acts of bravery in crisis or wartime prove that people are willing to sacrifice
their lives for what outlives the individual self, whether they act on behalf of
family, religion, patriotism, or something else. Outliving the self—what Erik
Erikson called *generativity*—is not limited to acts of sacrifice (Kotre, 1984).
Awareness of a meaning that transcends individual life is a universal human
quality. Transcendence and the search for meaning are what make us human.

Human beings contemplate aging and death, and they reach backward
and forward in time to pose questions about the meaning of existence. In
remembering the dead and in caring for the elderly, we express our deepest
convictions about the meaning of life. Old age is a time when we are likely to
come face-to-face with questions about ultimate meaning. In fact, it is only
since the 20th century that a sizable proportion of the population has survived to experience old age, and it is therefore natural that in our time the
meaning of old age has become an issue.

The question about whether old age itself has meaning is both a personal
question and a challenge for social gerontology. The personal question is
ultimately a matter of values: What is it that makes my life worth living into

the last stage? Put in this way, it may seem like an abstract or philosophical question. But as we saw in the earlier discussion about end-of-life decisions, this question becomes very practical for families and health professionals.

Whether old age itself has meaning is central to what we understand to be life satisfaction or morale in old age (Kaufman, 1986). If aging threatens deeply held values—such as the desire to be independent, to have control, or to be socially esteemed—then both society and individuals will seek to avoid age or deny it as much as possible. The denial of aging and the denial of death are central problems for our society (Becker, 1973).

Thus there are two questions we need to examine: "Does old age have a meaning for society?" and "How do individuals actually experience their lives as meaningful in the last stage of life?" Both questions are related, and both pose a challenge to social gerontology. A key issue is whether we have a theory of aging that can explain the facts about old age, including the different meanings old age takes on over the course of life and through history. To focus on these questions about meaning and aging, we can begin with two domains, leisure and religion, that express contrasting values of activity and disengagement and thereby offer alternative perspectives on how people find meaning in later life.

Leisure Activities in Later Life

Old age is characteristically a time when the work role becomes less constricting. Leisure may take its place as a way of finding meaning in life. We might think of leisure simply as "discretionary time," which becomes more available during the retirement years. But more deeply, leisure can be defined as activity engaged in for its own sake, as an end in itself. Leisure is not simply "leftover time" but a multidimensional quality of life different from paid employment, household maintenance, or other instrumental activities. Aristotle described leisure as a realm where human beings gain freedom for self-development when the necessities of life have been taken care of.

Does leisure in retirement actually replace the work role in later life? Does it become a powerful source of meaning in its own right? The answer to these questions depends on the quality of subjective experience during leisure. Leisure may be an end in itself, but moments of leisure also have a developmental structure—they are not complete in themselves. For example, if we play sports or perform music or read a book, each moment leads to the next in some purposeful developmental pattern. By contrast, other common leisure activities, like television viewing, take up a lot of time for elderly people but tend to be passive or less demanding. If leisure activity is to be a path to deeper meaning, then it must have some dimension of growth or personal development.

As people get older, they usually engage in the same activities as earlier in life, but with advancing age, there tends to be an overall decline in participation rate. It is a mistake to think in stereotypes about "old people's" activities, like shuffleboard, bingo, or singing old-time songs. That stereotype is wrong because age alone does not serve as a good predictor of what people do with their leisure in later life. Old people are not all alike. Variations and individual differences, along with the influence of gender and socioeconomic status, play a big part.

Changing Leisure Participation Patterns

How do patterns of leisure activity change over the life course? Broadly speaking, people over age 65 continue to engage in the same activities with the same people as they did in middle age. Although there is some selective age-related withdrawal, active engagement remains a key to life satisfaction and positive meaning in later life. But subgroups among the elderly display markedly different patterns. For instance, the young-old (ages 65-74) can generally be categorized as the "active old," an age group of increasing interest to advertisers and marketers.

Social structures, not age itself, determine the uses of time in later life. According to surveys of time use, as people age they spend varying proportions of time in paid work, family care, personal care, and free time. Most of the variation comes from a decrease in time spent working, not from any demonstrable effects of aging. People who are still in the labor force above age 65 have time use patterns similar to those of younger people. But retirement frees up time: on average, up to 25 hours a week for men and 18 hours a week for women. After taking account of household labor, most of this gain in time is taken up by media use (TV, radio, and newspapers) (Robinson, 1991).

Some leisure activities decline with age, but others remain the same. A Canadian study of leisure found that the number of people starting new activities does diminish as we get older (Iso, Jackson, and Dunn, 1994). In addition, certain activities show a marked decline in participation rates; for example, participation in going to movies drops from 38% in midlife to 17% after age 65. Involvement in indoor fitness shows a decline, and travel diminishes significantly among people over age 75. Other activities, such as outdoor gardening, show only modest declines, and still others, such as TV viewing, watching sports, and engaging in informal discussion, show no age-related decline at all. Church participation and community activities tend to be maintained. Age-related declines appear to come partly from barriers to physical exertion or access. Activities based in the home, such as reading or socializing with familiar people, remain strong until well into advanced old age.

Patterns of late-life leisure have important implications for the economy in an aging society. Americans over the age of 50 offer a huge market for business: They command more than half of all discretionary income and account for 40% of consumer demand (Doka, 1992). Older consumers are highly heterogeneous, varying by family status, ethnicity, education, geography, and social class. However, the "gray market" is itself stratified by age. The young-old are much more likely to be interested in travel than are the **old-old** (ages 75-84). Old-age leisure is often advertised as a consumption good or a status symbol. But leisure is also a means of affirming one's identity, a vital dimension of our phenomenological "life world," at a time when other roles may be lost (Hendricks and Cutler, 1990). Leisure time activities, then, are an important part of our personal world of meaning, and also part of a shared horizon of social and economic transactions that shape the meaning of leisure over the entire life course.

Explaining Patterns of Leisure

A study of activity patterns in old age sheds interesting light on different theories of aging, such as activity theory, disengagement theory, and continuity theory. The Ontario Longitudinal Study of Aging found that most people engage in activities that are familiar and that they maintain stable activity patterns, as continuity theory would predict (Singleton, Forbes, and Agwani, 1993). But the Ontario study also found that education and income are big factors. Retired people who have more choice are likely to change their activity patterns more often.

We also find some support for the idea of disengagement from the world as people age, but not as a global generalization or stereotype. Disengagement, in other words, is not a universal pattern but highly selective: an example of selective optimization with compensation (Baltes and Baltes, 1990). As long as leisure activities remain accessible, people will go on doing what they find worthwhile and meaningful as long as they can. When physical impairments impose obstacles, most people adapt to optimize whatever is still possible. Most people don't simply disengage altogether from meaningful activities.

Other explanations for the decline in leisure participation can also be found. For an important segment of the older population with limited income, travel or cultural activities may be economically out of reach. Another cause for constricted activity is declining health, which limits participation in sports and curtails driving at night. Even among those who remain healthy, loss of companions for leisure activities can be a limiting factor. As a result, decline in leisure, as we might expect, is most severe among the oldest-old (age 85+).

Religion and Spirituality

Public opinion surveys tell us that more than three-quarters of people over age 65 say religion is "a very important part of their lives." But to understand the role of religion, different aspects of "religion" must be recognized. In particular, we need to distinguish formal religious behavior from an inner attitude of spirituality. Across these distinct dimensions religion plays a vital role in the lives of older Americans and helps people find meaning in later life (Levin, 1997).

Religion Over the Life Course

Religious involvement in old age displays a pattern some investigators have called "multidimensional disengagement." What this phrase means is that as people grow older, they may withdraw from some activities—such as attending church—but at the same time show an increase in personal religious practice, such as Bible study or listening to religious TV and radio. The number who report praying "once a day" or "several times a day" increases steadily from age 55 to the highest levels among those over 75. By contrast, other empirical studies show declining frequency of church attendance after age 75, perhaps reflecting frailty and physical limitations among the old-old. Older people seem to disengage from some organized religious roles but make up for this loss by intensifying their nonorganizational religious involvement—for example, personal prayer, meditation, and other forms of spirituality.

As they grow older, Americans continue to display patterns of religious identification similar to those among younger age groups: 65% identify themselves as Protestant, 25% as Catholic, and 3% as Jewish. But older women tend to have higher levels of religious participation and belief than do men. Overall, 50% of all elderly attend religious services at least once a week, and attendance tends to be positively related to measures of personal adjustment. When we look at church attendance from a life course perspective, we see the influence of family structure. Parents with young children often get involved in church activities, but after middle age attendance falls off.

Despite these variations, older people are still more likely to be involved with church or synagogue than with other kinds of community organizations. Among mainstream Protestant and Catholic churches as well as Jewish synagogues, a large proportion of the congregation is over age 50. Adults over age 65 are twice as likely to attend church regularly as those under 30. But it is a mistake to assume that people simply become more religious as they get older. Today's older generation appears to be more religious, but that effect may be due more to cohort or generational effects than to age. Today's older generation, for instance, may have gone to Sunday school or been involved in religion throughout life. Such lifelong religious identification explains higher religiosity in old age.

Churches and religious organizations play many different roles in the lives of older people: in formal religious programs, through pastoral care programs, and as sponsors or providers of social services. Elders find fulfillment in a variety of church-sponsored volunteer activities, even though organized religion has often emphasized services and activities for youth. Innovative programs—like Bible classes geared to older people, intergenerational programs, and new volunteer roles—could change that picture in the future. Some successful national initiatives, such as the Faith in Action Program and the Federation of Volunteer Interfaith Caregivers, remind us that religious organizations represent a great, partly untapped resource for older people to find deeper meaning in life.

Religion and Well-Being

Researchers have been interested in the benefits that religion can have for older people. Cross-sectional studies have found a positive correlation between measures of well-being and religious beliefs among the old. Those with high levels of religious commitment also have higher levels of life satisfaction than those with no such sense of meaning. This relationship holds true even controlling for age, marital status, education, and perceived health status.

But the significance of these correlations may be less than meets the eye. How do we define or measure what "religiousness" actually means in people's lives? Another difficulty is the partial confounding of religious involvement with measures of functional health status. Does religious engagement actually promote physical health? The answers to these questions are elusive.

Empirical studies have shown that religion can serve as a means of helping older people cope with stress. For example, the Duke Longitudinal Study found that older persons who used religion as a coping mechanism were more likely to exhibit higher levels of adjustment than others, even during intense life stress, such as bereavement and chronic illness. Nearly half of the respondents in the Duke study reported that religious attitudes or behavior helped them cope with stressful life events. Among those who relied on religion, coping strategies reflect different patterns of disengagement or activity. Private religious behaviors, such as trust, faith in God, or prayer, were cited as coping strategies more frequently than church-related or religious social activities.

Investigators theorize that religion helps older adults cope in a variety of ways (Ellison, 1994):

- By reducing the impact of stress in late-life illness

- By providing a sense of order and meaning in life

- By offering social networks tied to religious groups

- By strengthening inner psychological resources, such as self-esteem

Spirituality and the Search for Meaning

Habits of religiosity, like other behavior, tend to remain stable as people move into later life, but faith itself can take on new meanings with age. One research team found that among those who had undergone some distinct change in religious faith, 40% reported experiencing such a change after the age of 50. The researchers concluded that changes in religious faith are not limited to youth but can occur at any time in the life course (Koenig, 1994).

Often the personal search for meaning leads to deeper understanding of religious faith. James Fowler (1981) developed a framework of "faith stages" describing how people move from simpler, more literalist ideas of religion to levels where they see themselves and their lives in more universal terms, as the greatest saints and mystics have preached. For examples of those who have reached the highest stage of faith, Fowler cites such personalities as Dag Hammarskjöld, Abraham Heschel, Thomas Merton, and Mahatma Gandhi.

Theologians who have reflected on the life course tend to view aging not as a problem that calls for a solution but as an existential condition to be accepted for personal growth, or what some have called a "spiritual journey" (Bianchi, 1982) that can lead to a contemplative dimension for aging (Tornstam, 1997). In terms of Erik Erikson's developmental theory, older adults struggle with a psychological conflict of ego integrity versus despair. Faith can be a way of enhancing ego integrity—an attitude of acceptance toward life and the world that is part of positive mental health. Stressing the importance of religion for mental health, Blazer (1991) has identified six dimensions of **spiritual well-being:** self-determined wisdom, self-transcendence, the discovery of meaning in aging, acceptance of the totality of life, revival of spirituality, and preparation for death. None of these tasks is easy, but the fact that some older people undertake this spiritual journey makes us believe that the effort can yield a profound sense of meaning for the later years.

Social Gerontology and the Meaning of Age

As a branch of the social sciences, gerontology tries to depict the facts about old age as a way of understanding the meaning of aging. A good place to begin is to ask, What do older people themselves say about what gives meaning to their lives? When a sample of participants at a senior center was asked that question, nearly 90% of respondents described their lives as meaningful (Burbank, 1992). For most of them (57%), the meaning came from human relationships followed by service to others (12%), religion, and leisure activities. Another study revealed that the most damaging threat to well-being in later life is loss of life purpose and boredom, not fear of absolute destitution or poor health. Responses show that people find purpose or meaning in a variety of ways: work, leisure, grandparenting, and intimate adult relationships. Respondents reported that unless they were sick or depressed, they "didn't feel old" (Thompson, 1993), which suggests what has been called "the ageless self" (Kaufman, 1986).

Looking at verbal responses or patterns of behavior is suggestive but may not get us any closer to understanding meaning in the last stage of life. Questionnaires about life satisfaction tell us only a limited amount about these deeper issues (Gubrium and Lynott, 1983). Inevitably, values and philosophical assumptions reveal themselves in our discourse.

According to one widely shared view, the agenda for social gerontology should be to promote better social integration of the aged (Rosow, 1967) by means of group activities, social involvement, and participatory roles of all kinds. We see that view in the popularity of "productive aging," intergenerational programs, and other strategies. The ideal of an "age-integrated society" is a comprehensive enunciation of the same goal (Riley and Riley, 1994). Whether through work, leisure, or attendance at religious services, the aim of social integration is for people to stay engaged throughout life. Workers in senior centers and nursing homes often share this outlook. But if we view the role losses of old age as an opportunity for self-development that goes beyond conventional roles, then integration in group activities may no longer seem so compelling. Other values might assume greater importance.

We might still encourage older people to maintain social connections or affiliate with groups, but the form of that engagement would be based on a strategy for individual development, not conformity to social norms or activities. An example of such individual development might be a creative arts program designed to encourage self-expression; another might be a religious retreat designed to permit individual prayer and meditation. These last kinds of pursuits seem in keeping with the potential for interiority and individuation in later life. Whether individual contemplation or social activity is the more desirable approach still remains debatable, of course. But that is precisely what is at issue in the controversy about whether old age has meaning or offers some special opportunity not readily available at other stages of life. The question is what makes it appropriate for gerontology to look more deeply at what inspires a shared sense of meaning in life's last stage (Cole and Gadow, 1986).

The Meaning of Aging in the 21st Century

The life course perspective tends to view "stages of life" as social constructions reflecting broader structural conditions of society. As conditions change, so will our view of how people find meaning at different stages of life. Consider the weakening of age norms and beliefs about what is "appropriate" for different stages of life. In a world where retired people can go back to college and women can have a first child at age 40, it makes less sense to link education or work with strict chronological ages. Indeed, one attractive strategy for an aging society might well be to introduce more flexibility for people of all ages to pursue education, work, and leisure over the entire course of life rather than link these activities stereotypically to periods of youth, middle life, and old age, as modern societies have done in the past.

It is not clear how the meaning of old age will change in contemporary postindustrial societies. On the one hand, older Americans have achieved gains in income levels, health, and political power. On the other hand, as the stages of life have evolved and become blurred, the entire image of "old age" is giving way to more of an "age-irrelevant" image of the life course (Neugarten, 1983). As an empirical matter, chronological age, by itself, loses predictive value and importance for many purposes.

Does this trend mean that old age, as a distinct stage of life, no longer has any special meaning or significance? Here we again must distinguish between a meaning that society ascribes to old age as opposed to what individuals find meaningful in their own lives. In "postmodern" culture, it is increasingly hard to ascribe anything special to the last stage of life. But if nothing special is to be found in later life, we wonder, does it follow that personal meaning in old age must simply be "more of the same"—that is, continuing whatever values gave meaning earlier in life (Moody, 1997)? Or does lifelong growth imply a constant effort to overcome old habits and change our view of what offers meaning in life? These questions have no easy answers.

Activity or Reflection?

The previous discussion initially looked at two classical theories of aging—disengagement and activity. We saw how both theories implicitly appeal to deeply held values but point in opposite directions. When we think about the question of whether old age has meaning, we come back, over and over again, to two fundamental alternatives: on the one hand, continuation of midlife values into old age, and on the other hand, discovering some new or special challenge that belongs to the last stage of life.

In the readings that follow, Simone de Beauvoir represents the view of those who insist on continuity with midlife activity, and Carl Jung represents the view of those who insist that detachment from midlife roles is the path to deeper meaning. Erik Erikson, with his concept of "vital involvement," occupies a position somewhere between these two opposing ideas. Finally, there is the testimony of Florida Scott-Maxwell, whose journal was written while she was in a nursing home. Her work reveals the importance of the personal construction of meaning in old age (Berman, 1986), even under adverse conditions of frailty and loss. Her contribution underscores the validity of understanding the meaning of aging through a subjective or phenomenological viewpoint (Gubrium and Buckholdt, 1977).

The selection by Simone de Beauvoir offers the view of a philosopher who rejects traditional ideals of old age as a time of tranquility or detachment. On the contrary, she believes that only continued activity on behalf of new goals gives life meaning, in old age or at any other time of life. Erik Erikson, one of our most distinguished psychologists, takes a different approach. Erikson and his colleagues see each stage of life as a period with its own special purpose or psychological task to be achieved. Old age is different from other stages because it offers a kind of culmination to life as a whole. Erikson et al. believe that through concern for the welfare of future generations older people find a sense of meaning in later life.

Carl Jung offers the perspective of a psychologist fascinated by the unconscious as revealed in dreams, myths, and human personality over the life span. Jung argues that the second half of life must have its own distinctive psychological challenge. Maturity, in his view, is a time for detachment and reflection as we turn inward. In the selection from Florida Scott-Maxwell's personal journal, we see a record of that inward journey during advanced age. Her rich description and reflections prove that, even when outer activity is cut off, it is possible to find deep meaning in the last stage of life.

It seems ironic that modernization has made it possible for people to live a greater portion of their lives in old age than ever before in history. At the same time, the distinctive stance of postmodern culture tends to preclude finding any special meaning or purpose for the last stage of life. Whether modernization has reduced the power of the old seems debatable. Public spending for old-age benefits suggests that just the opposite may be true. But there is no doubt that modernization has helped to erode traditional ideas about fixed "stages of life" once based on shared meaning (Gruman, 1978). The result is a sense of openness or uncertainty about the meaning of old age. Such openness to new ideas and to contradictory answers is disconcerting to some, exhilarating to others. However, the future of an aging society will be shaped by all of us because in the end the old are simply "our future selves."

READING 42

The Coming of Age

Simone de Beauvoir

Die early or grow old: there is no other alternative. And yet, as Goethe said, 'Age takes hold of us by surprise.' For himself each man is the sole, unique subject, and we are often astonished when the common fate becomes our own—when we are struck by sickness, a shattered relationship, or bereavement. I remember my own stupefaction when I was seriously ill for the first time in my life and I said to myself, 'This woman they are carrying on a stretcher is me.' Nevertheless, we accept fortuitous accidents readily enough, making them part of our history, because they affect us as unique beings: but old age is the general fate, and when it seizes upon our own personal life we are dumbfounded. 'Why, what has happened?' writes Aragon. 'It is life that has hap-

pened, and I am old.' . . . When we are grown up we hardly think about our age any more: we feel that the notion does not apply to us; for it is one which assumes that we look back towards the past and draw a line under the total, whereas in fact we are reaching out towards the future, gliding on imperceptibly from day to day, from year to year. Old age is particularly difficult to assume because we have always regarded it as something alien, a foreign species: 'Can I have become a different being while I still remain myself?' . . .

Thus the very quality of the future changes between middle age and the end of one's life. At sixty-five one is not merely twenty years older than one was at forty-five. One has exchanged an indefinite future—and one had a tendency to look upon it as infinite—for a finite future. In earlier days we could see no boundary-mark upon the horizon: now we do see one. 'When I used to dream in former times,' says Chateaubriand, harking back to his remote past, 'my youth lay before me; I could advance towards the unknown that I was looking for. Now I can no longer take a single step without coming up against the boundary-stone.' . . .

A limited future and a frozen past: such is the situation that the elderly have to face up to. In many instances it paralyses them. All their plans have either been carried out or abandoned, and their life has closed in about itself; nothing requires their presence; they no longer have anything whatsoever to do. . . .

Clearly, there is one preconceived notion that must be totally set aside—the idea that old age brings serenity. From classical times the adult world has done its best to see mankind's condition in a hopeful light; it has attributed to ages that are not its own, virtues that they do not possess: innocence to childhood, serenity to old age. It has deliberately chosen to look upon the end of life as a time when all the conflicts that tear it apart are resolved. What is more, this is a convenient illusion: it allows one to suppose, in spite of all the ills and misfortunes that are known to overwhelm them, that the old are happy and that they can be left to their fate. . . .

Why should an old person be better than the adult or child he was? It is quite hard enough to remain a human being when everything, health, memory, possessions, standing and authority has been taken from you. The old person's struggle to do so has pitiable or ludicrous sides to it, and his fads, his meanness, and his deceitful ways may irritate one or make one smile; but in reality it is a very moving struggle. It is the refusal to sink below the human level, a refusal to become the insect, the inert object to which the adult world wishes to reduce the aged. There is something heroic in desiring to preserve a minimum of dignity in the midst of such total deprivation. . . .

On the intellectual plane, old age may also bring liberation: it sets one free from false notions. The clarity of mind that comes with it is accompanied by an often bitter disillusionment. In childhood and youth, life is experienced as a continual rise; and in favourable cases—either because of professional advancement or because bringing up one's children is a source of happiness, or because one's standard of living rises, or because of a greater wealth of knowledge—the notion of upward progress may persist in middle age. Then all at once a man discovers that he is no longer going anywhere, that his path leads him only to the grave. He has climbed to a peak; and from a peak there can be a fall. 'Life is a long preparation for something that never happens,' said Yeats. There comes a moment when one knows that one is no longer getting ready for anything and one understands that the idea of advancing towards a goal was a delusion. Our personal history had assumed that it possessed an end, and now it finds, beyond any sort of doubt, that this finality has been taken from it. At the same time its character of a 'useless passion' becomes evident. A discovery of this kind, says Schopenhauer, strips us of our will to live. 'Nothing left of those illusions that gave life its charm and that spurred on our activity. It is only at the age of sixty that one thoroughly understands the first verse of Ecclesiastes.' . . .

If *all* were vanity or deceit there would indeed be nothing left but to wait for death. But admitting that life does not contain its own end does not mean that it is incapable of devoting itself to ends of some kind. There are pursuits that are useful to mankind, and between men there are relationships in which they reach one another in full truthfulness. Once illusions have been swept away, these relationships, in which neither alienation nor myth form any part, and these pursuits remain. We may go on hoping to communicate with others by writing even when childish images of fame have vanished. By a curious paradox it is often at the very moment that the aged man, having become old, has doubts about the value of his entire work that he carries it to its highest point of perfection. This was so with Rembrandt, Michelangelo, Verdi and Monet. It may be that these doubts themselves help to enrich it. And then again it is often a question of coincidence: Age brings technical mastery and freedom while at the same time it also brings a questioning, challenging state of mind. . . .

Freedom and clarity of mind are not of much use if no goal beckons us any more: but they are of great value if one is still full of projects. The greatest good fortune, even greater than health, for the old person is to have his world still inhabited by projects: then, busy and useful, he escapes both from boredom and from decay. The times in which he lives remain his own, and he is not compelled to adopt the defensive or aggressive forms of behaviour that are so often characteristic of the final years. . . .

There is only one solution if old age is not to be an absurd parody of our former life, and that is to go on pursuing ends that give our existence a meaning—devotion to individuals, to groups or to causes, social, political, intellectual or creative work. In spite of the moralists' opinion to the con-

trary, in old age we should wish still to have passions strong enough to prevent us turning in upon ourselves. One's life has value so long as one attributes value to the life of others, by means of love, friendship, indignation, compassion. When this is so, then there are still valid reasons for activity or speech. People are often advised to 'prepare' for old age. But if this merely applies to setting aside money, choosing the place for retirement and laying on hobbies, we shall not be much the better for it when the day comes. It is far better not to think about it too much, but to live a fairly committed, fairly justified life so that one may go on in the same path even when all illusions have vanished and one's zeal for life has died away.

Vital Involvement in Old Age

Erik H. Erikson, Joan M. Erikson, and Helen Q. Kivnick

Elders have both less and more. Unlike the infant, the elder has a reservoir of strength in the wellsprings of history and storytelling. As collectors of time and preservers of memory, those healthy elders who have survived into a reasonably fit old age have time on their side—time that is to be dispensed wisely and creatively, usually in the form of stories, to those younger ones who will one day follow in their footsteps. Telling these stories, and telling them well, marks a certain capacity for one generation to entrust itself to the next, by passing

on a certain shared and collective identity to the survivors of the next generation: the future. Trust, as we have stated earlier, is one of the constant human values or virtues, universally acknowledged as basic for all relationships. Hope is yet another basic foundation for all community living and for survival itself, from infancy to old age. The question of old age, and perhaps of life, is how—with the trust and competency accumulated in old age—one adapts to and makes peace with the inevitable physical disintegration of aging.

After years of collaboration, elders should be able to know and trust, and know when to mistrust, not only their own senses and physical capacities but also their accumulated knowledge of the world around them. It is important to listen to the authoritative and objective voices of professionals with an open mind, but one's own judgment, after all those years of intimate relations with the body and with others, is decisive. The ultimate capacities of the aging person are not yet determined. The future may well bring surprises.

Elders, of course, know well their own strengths. They should keep all of these strengths in use and involved in whatever their environment offers or makes possible. And they should not underestimate the possibility of developing strengths that are still dormant. Taking part in needed and useful work is appropriate both for elders and for their relationship to the community.

With aging, there are inevitably constant losses—losses of those very close, and friends near and far. Those who have been rich in intimacy also have the most to lose. Recollection is one form of adaptation, but the effort skillfully to form new relationships is adaptive and more rewarding. Old age is necessarily a time of relinquishing—of giving up old friends, old roles, earlier work that was once meaningful, and even possessions that belong to a previous stage of life and are now an impediment to the resiliency and freedom that seem to be requisite for adapting to the unknown challenges that determine the final stage of life.

Trust in interdependence. Give and accept help when it is needed. Old Oedipus well knew that the aged sometimes need three legs; pride can be an asset but not a cane.

When frailty takes over, dependence is appropriate, and one has no choice but to trust in the compassion of others and be consistently surprised at how faithful some caretakers can be.

Much living, however, can teach us only how little is known. Accept that essential "not-knowingness" of childhood and with it also that playful curiosity. Growing old can be an interesting adventure and is certainly full of surprises.

One is reminded here of the image Hindu philosophy uses to describe the final letting go—that of merely being. The mother cat picks up in her mouth the kitten, which completely collapses every tension and hangs limp and infinitely trusting in the maternal benevolence. The kitten responds

instinctively. We human beings require at least a whole lifetime of practice to do this. The religious traditions of the world reflect these concerns and provide them with substance and form.

The Potential Role of Elders in Our Society

Our society confronts the challenge of drawing a large population of healthy elders into the social order in a way that productively uses their capacities. Our task will be to envision what influences such a large contingent of elders will have on our society as healthy old people seek and even demand more vital involvement. Some attributes of the accrued wisdom of old age are fairly generally acknowledged and respected. If recognized and given scope for expression, they could have an important impact on our social order. We suggest the following possibilities.

Older people are, by nature, conservationists. Long memories and wider perspectives lend urgency to the maintenance of our natural world. Old people, quite understandably, seem to feel more keenly the obstruction of open waterfronts, the cutting of age-old stands of trees, the paving of vast stretches of fertile countryside, and the pollution of once clear streams and lakes. Their longer memories recall the beauty of their surroundings in earlier years. We need those memories and those voices.

With aging, men and women in many ways become less differentiated in their masculine and feminine predilections. This in no way suggests a loss of sexual drive and interest between the sexes. Men, it seems, become more capable of accepting the interdependence that women have more easily practiced. Many elder women today, in their turn, become more vigorously active and involved in those affairs that have been the dominant province of men. Some women come to these new roles by virtue of their propensity to outlive the men who have been their partners. Many younger women have made a similar transition by becoming professional members of the work force. These women seem capable of managing parenting and householding along with their jobs, particularly if they have partners who learn cooperation in these matters as an essential component of the marriage contract.

Our subjects demonstrate a tolerance and capacity for weighing more than one side of a question that is an attribute of the possible wisdom of aging. They should be well suited to serve as arbiters in a great variety of disputes. Much experience should be a precursor of long-range vision and clear judgement.

The aged have had a good deal of experience as societal witnesses to the effects of devastation and aggression. They have lived through wars and seen the disintegration of peace settlements. They know that violence breeds hatred and destroys the interconnectedness of life here on our earth and that now our capacity for destruction is such that violence is no longer a viable solution for human conflict.

Ideally, elders in any given modern society should be those who, having developed a marked degree of tolerance and appreciation for otherness, which includes "foreigners" and "foreign ways," might become advocates of a new international understanding that no longer tolerates the vicious name-calling, depreciation, and distrustfulness typical of international relations.

It is also possible to imagine a large, mature segment of the aging population, freed from the tension of keeping pace with competitors in the workplace, able to pursue vigorously art activities of all varieties. This would bring an extraordinary liveliness and artfulness to ordinary life. Only a limited portion of our adult population now has either the time or the money to be involved in activities of art expression or as appreciative supporters of the performing arts. Widespread participation in the arts is possible only if children are encouraged to develop those roots of imaginative play that arise from stimulating sensory experience. Elders learn this as they undertake to open these new doors of experience and could promote the inclusion of the arts in the educational system. The arts offer a common language, and the learning of that language in childhood could contribute to an interconnection among the world's societies.

The development of a new class of elders requires a continued upgrading of all facilities for the health care and education of people at all stages of life, from infancy to old age. Organisms that are to function for a hundred years need careful early nurturing and training. Education must prepare the individual not only for the tasks of early and middle age but for those of old age as well. Training is mandatory both for productive work and for the understanding and care of the senses and the body as a whole. Participation in activities that can enrich an entire lifetime must be promoted and made readily available. In fact, a more general acceptance of the developmental principle of the life cycle could alert people to plan their entire lives more realistically, especially to provide for the long years of aging.

Having started our "joint reflections" with some investigation of the traditional themes of "age" and "stages," a closing word should deal with the modern changes in our conception of the length and the role of old age in the total life experience. As we have described, modern statistics predict for our time and the immediate future a much longer life expectancy for the majority of old individuals rather than for a select few. This amounts to such a radical change in our concept of the human life cycle that we question whether we should not review all the earlier stages in the light of this development. Actually, we have already faced the question of whether a universal old age of significantly greater duration suggests the addition to our cycle of a ninth stage of development with its own quality of experience, including, perhaps, some sense or premonition of immortality. A decisive fact, however, has remained unchanged for all the earlier stages, namely, that they are all significantly evoked by biological and evolutionary development necessary for any organism and its psychosocial matrix. This also means that each stage, in turn, must surrender its dominance to the next stage, when its time has come. Thus, the developmental ages for the pre-adult life stages decisively remain the same, although the interrelation of all the stages depends somewhat on the emerging personality and the psychosocial identity of each individual in a given historical setting and time perspective.

Similarly, it must be emphasized that each stage, once given, is woven into the fates of all. Generativity, for example, dramatically precedes the last stage, that of old age, establishing the contrast between the dominant images of generativity and of death: one cares for what one has generated in this existence while simultaneously preexperiencing the end of it all in death.

It is essential to establish in the experience of the stages a psychosocial identity, but no matter how long one's life expectancy is, one must face oneself as one who shares an all-human existential identity, as creatively given form in the world religions. This final "arrangement" must convince us that we are meant as "grandparents," to share the responsibility of the generations for each other. When we finally retire from familial and generational involvement, we must, where and when possible, bond with other old-age groups in different parts of the world, learning to talk and to listen with a growing sense of all-human mutuality.

READING 44

The Stages of Life

Carl Jung

The nearer we approach to the middle of life, and the better we have succeeded in entrenching ourselves in our personal attitudes and social positions, the more it appears as if we had discovered the right course and the right ideals and principles of behaviour. For this reason we suppose them to be eternally valid, and make a virtue of unchangeably clinging to them. We overlook the essential fact that the social goal is attained only at the cost of a diminution of personality. Many—far too many—aspects of life which should also have been experienced lie in the lumber-room among dusty memories; but sometimes, too, they are glowing coals under grey ashes.

Statistics show a rise in the frequency of mental depressions in men about forty. In women the neurotic difficulties generally begin somewhat earlier. We see that in this phase of life—between thirty-five and forty—an important change in the human psyche is in preparation. At first it is not a conscious and striking change; it is rather a matter of indirect signs of a change which seems to take its rise in the unconscious. Often it is something like a slow change in a person's character; in another case certain traits may come to light which had disappeared since childhood; or again, one's previous inclinations and interests begin to weaken and others take their place. Conversely—and this happens very frequently—one's cherished convictions and principles, especially the moral ones, begin to harden and to grow increasingly rigid until, somewhere around the age of fifty, a period of intolerance and fanaticism is reached. It is as if the existence of these principles were endangered and it were therefore necessary to emphasize them all the more.

The wine of youth does not always clear with advancing years; sometimes it grows turbid. All

Source: "The Stages of Life," in *The Structure and Dynamics of the Psyche* (pp. 12-21), by Carl Jung. Copyright © 1960 by Bollingen. Copyright © 1969 by Princeton University Press. Reprinted by permission of Princeton University Press.

the phenomena mentioned above can best be seen in rather one-sided people, turning up sometimes sooner and sometimes later. Their appearance, it seems to me, is often delayed by the fact that the parents of the person in question are still alive. It is then as if the period of youth were being unduly drawn out. I have seen this especially in the case of men whose fathers were long-lived. The death of the father then has the effect of a precipitate and almost catastrophic ripening. . . .

The very frequent neurotic disturbances of adult years all have one thing in common: they want to carry the psychology of the youthful phase over the threshold of the so-called years of discretion. Who does not know those touching old gentlemen who must always warm up the dish of their student days, who can fan the flame of life only by reminiscences of their heroic youth, but who, for the rest, are stuck in a hopelessly wooden Philistinism? As a rule, to be sure, they have this one merit which it would be wrong to undervalue: they are not neurotic, but only boring and stereotyped. The neurotic is rather a person who can never have things as he would like them in the present, and who can therefore never enjoy the past either.

As formerly the neurotic could not escape from childhood, so now he cannot part with his youth. He shrinks from the grey thoughts of approaching age, and, feeling the prospect before him unbearable, is always straining to look behind him. Just as the childish person shrinks back from the unknown in the world and in human existence, so the grown man shrinks back from the second half of life. It is as if unknown and dangerous tasks awaited him, or as if he were threatened with sacrifices and losses which he does not wish to accept, or as if his life up to now seemed to him so fair and precious that he could not relinquish it.

Is it perhaps at bottom the fear of death? That does not seem to me very probable, because as a rule death is still far in the distance and therefore somewhat abstract. Experience shows us, rather, that the basic cause of all the difficulties of this transition is to be found in a deep-seated and peculiar change within the psyche. In order to char-

acterize it I must take for comparison the daily course of the sun—but a sun that is endowed with human feeling and man's limited consciousness. In the morning it rises from the nocturnal sea of unconsciousness and looks upon the wide, bright world which lies before it in an expanse that steadily widens the higher it climbs in the firmament. In this extension of its field of action caused by its own rising, the sun will discover its significance; it will see the attainment of the greatest possible height, and the widest possible dissemination of its blessings, as its goal. In this conviction the sun pursues its course to the unforeseen zenith—unforeseen, because its career is unique and individual, and the culminating point could not be calculated in advance. At the stroke of noon the descent begins. And the descent means the reversal of all the ideals and values that were cherished in the morning. The sun falls into contradiction with itself. It is as though it should draw in its rays instead of emitting them. Light and warmth decline and are at last extinguished.

All comparisons are lame, but this simile is at least not lamer than others. A French aphorism sums it up with cynical resignation: *Si jeunesse savait, si vieillesse pouvait.*

Fortunately we are not rising and setting suns, for then it would fare badly with our cultural values. But there is something sunlike within us, and to speak of the morning and spring, of the evening and autumn of life is not mere sentimental jargon. We thus give expression to psychological truths and, even more, to physiological facts, for the reversal of the sun at noon changes even bodily characteristics. Especially among southern races one can observe that older women develop deep, rough voices, incipient moustaches, rather hard features and other masculine traits. On the other hand the masculine physique is toned down by feminine features, such as adiposity and softer facial expressions.

There is an interesting report in the ethnological literature about an Indian warrior chief to whom in middle life the Great Spirit appeared in a dream. The spirit announced to him that from then on he must sit among the women and children, wear women's clothes, and eat the food of women. He obeyed the dream without suffering a loss of prestige. This vision is a true expression of the psychic revolution of life's noon, of the beginning of life's decline. Man's values, and even his body, do tend to change into their opposites.

We might compare masculinity and femininity and their psychic components to a definite store of substances of which, in the first half of life, unequal use is made. A man consumes his large supply of masculine substance and has left over only the smaller amount of feminine substance, which must now be put to use. Conversely, the woman allows her hitherto unused supply of masculinity to become active. . . .

The worst of it all is that intelligent and cultivated people live their lives without even knowing of the possibility of such transformations. Wholly unprepared, they embark upon the second half of life. Or are there perhaps colleges for forty-year-olds which prepare them for their coming life and its demands as the ordinary colleges introduce our young people to a knowledge of the world? No, thoroughly unprepared we take the step into the afternoon of life; worse still, we take this step with the false assumption that our truths and ideals will serve us as hitherto. But we cannot live the afternoon of life according to the programme of life's morning; for what was great in the morning will be little at evening, and what in the morning was true will at evening have become a lie. I have given psychological treatment to too many people of advancing years, and have looked too often into the secret chambers of their souls, not to be moved by this fundamental truth.

Aging people should know that their lives are not mounting and expanding, but that an inexorable inner process enforces the contraction of life. For a young person it is almost a sin, or at least a danger, to be too preoccupied with himself; but for the aging person it is a duty and a necessity to devote serious attention to himself. After having lavished its light upon the world, the sun withdraws its rays in order to illuminate itself. Instead of doing likewise, many old people prefer to be hypochondriacs, niggards, pedants, applauders of the past or else eternal adolescents—all lamentable substitutes for the illumination of the self, but inevitable consequences of the delusion that the second half of life must be governed by the principles of the first.

I said just now that we have no schools for forty-year-olds. That is not quite true. Our religions were always such schools in the past, but how many people regard them as such today? How many of us older ones have been brought up in such a school and really prepared for the second half of life, for old age, death and eternity?

A human being would certainly not grow to be seventy or eighty years old if this longevity had no meaning for the species. The afternoon of human life must also have a significance of its own and cannot be merely a pitiful appendage to life's morning. The significance of the morning undoubtedly lies in the development of the individual, our entrenchment in the outer world, the propagation of our kind, and the care of our children. This is the obvious purpose of nature. But when this purpose has been attained—and more than attained—shall the earning of money, the extension of conquests, and the expansion of life go steadily on beyond the bounds of all reason and sense? Whoever carries over into the afternoon the law of the morning, or the natural aim, must pay for it with damage to his soul, just as surely as a growing youth who tries to carry over his childish egoism into adult life must pay for this mistake with social failure. Money-making, social achievement, family and posterity are nothing but plain nature, not culture. Culture lies outside the purpose of nature. Could by any chance culture be the meaning and purpose of the second half of life?

In primitive tribes we observe that the old people are almost always the guardians of the mysteries and the laws, and it is in these that the cultural heritage of the tribe is expressed. How does the matter stand with us? Where is the wisdom of our old people, where are their precious secrets and their visions? For the most part our old people try to compete with the young. In the United States it is almost an ideal for a father to be the brother of his sons, and for the mother to be if possible the younger sister of her daughter.

I do not know how much of this confusion is a reaction against an earlier exaggeration of the dignity of age, and how much is to be charged to false ideals. These undoubtedly exist, and the goal of those who hold them lies behind, and not ahead. Therefore they are always striving to turn back. We have to grant these people that it is hard to see what other goal the second half of life can offer than the well-known aims of the first. Expansion of life, usefulness, efficiency, the cutting of a figure in society, the shrewd steering of offspring into suitable marriages and good positions—are not these purposes enough? Unfortunately not enough meaning and purpose for those who see in the approach of old age a mere diminution of life and can feel their earlier ideals only as something faded and worn out. Of course, if these persons had filled up the beaker of life earlier and emptied it to the lees, they would feel quite differently about everything now; they would have kept nothing back, everything that wanted to catch fire would have been consumed, and the quiet of old age would be very welcome to them. But we must not forget that only a very few people are artists in life; that the art of life is the most distinguished and rarest of all the arts. Who ever succeeded in draining the whole cup with grace? So for many people all too much unlived life remains over—sometimes potentialities which they could never have lived with the best of wills, so that they approach the threshold of old age with unsatisfied demands which inevitably turn their glances backwards. . . .

I have observed that a life directed to an aim is in general better, richer, and healthier than an aimless one, and that it is better to go forwards with the stream of time than backwards against it. To the psychotherapist an old man who cannot bid farewell to life appears as feeble and sickly as a young man who is unable to embrace it. And as a matter of fact, it is in many cases a question of the selfsame childish greediness, the same fear, the same defiance and willfulness, in the one as in the other. As a doctor I am convinced that it is hygienic—if I may use the word—to discover in death a goal towards which one can strive, and that shrinking away from it is something unhealthy and abnormal which robs the second half of life of its purpose. I therefore consider that all religions with a supra-mundane goal are eminently reasonable from the point of view of psychic hygiene. When I live in a house which I know will fall about my head within the next two weeks, all my vital functions will be impaired by this thought; but if on the contrary I feel myself to be safe, I can dwell there in a normal and comfortable way. From the standpoint of psychotherapy it would therefore be desirable to think of death as only a transition, as part of a life process whose extent and duration are beyond our knowledge.

The Measure of My Days

Florida Scott-Maxwell

Age puzzles me. I thought it was a quiet time. My seventies were interesting, and fairly serene, but my eighties are passionate. I grow more intense as I age. To my own surprise I burst out with hot conviction. Only a few years ago I enjoyed my tranquillity; now I am so disturbed by the outer world and by human quality in general that I want to put things right, as though I still owed a debt to life. I must calm down. I am far too frail to indulge in moral fervour.

Old people are not protected from life by engagements, or pleasures, or duties; we are open to our own sentience; we cannot get away from it, and it is too much. We should ward off the problematic, and above all the insoluble. These are far, far too much, but it is just these that attract us. Our one safety is to draw in, and enjoy the simple and immediate. We should rest within our own confines. It may be dull, restricted, but it can be satisfying within our own walls. I feel most real when alone, even most alive when alone. . . .

Age is truly a time of heroic helplessness. One is confronted by one's own incorrigibility. I am always saying to myself, "Look at you, and after a lifetime of trying." I still have the vices that I have known and struggled with—well it seems like since birth. Many of them are modified, but not much. I can neither order nor command the hubbub of my mind. Or is it my nervous sensibility? This is not the effect of age; age only defines one's boundaries. Life has changed me greatly, it has improved me greatly, but it has also left me practically the same. I cannot spell, I am over critical, egocentric and vulnerable. I cannot be simple. In my effort to be clear I become complicated. I know my faults so well that I pay them small heed. They are stronger than I am. They are me. . . .

Another day to be filled, to be lived silently, watching the sky and the lights on the wall. No one will come probably. I have no duties except to myself. That is not true. I have a duty to all who care for me—not to be a problem, not to be a burden. I must carry my age lightly for all our sakes, and thank God I still can. Oh that I may to the end. Each day then, must be filled with my first duty, I must be "all right." But is this assurance not the gift we all give to each other daily, hourly? . . .

Another secret we carry is that though drab outside—wreckage to the eye, mirrors a mortification—inside we flame with a wild life that is almost incommunicable. In silent, hot rebellion we cry silently—"I have lived my life haven't I? What more is expected of me?" Have we got to pretend out of noblesse oblige that age is nothing, in order to encourage the others? This we do with a certain haughtiness, realising now that we have reached the place beyond resignation, a place I had no idea existed until I had arrived here.

It is a place of fierce energy. Perhaps passion would be a better word than energy, for the sad fact is this vivid life cannot be used. If I try to transpose it into action I am soon spent. It has to be accepted as passionate life, perhaps the life I never lived, never guessed I had it in me to live. It feels other and more than that. It feels like the far side of precept and aim. It is just life, the natural intensity of life, and when old we have it for our reward and undoing. It can—at moments—feel as though we had it for our glory. Some of it must go beyond good and bad, for at times—though this comes rarely, unexpectedly—it is a swelling clarity as though all was resolved. It has no content, it seems to expand us, it does not derive from the body, and then it is gone. It may be a degree of consciousness which lies outside activity, and which when young we are too busy to experience. . . .

It has taken me all the time I've had to become myself, yet now that I am old there are times when I feel I am barely here, no room for me at all. I remember that in the last months of my pregnancies the child seemed to claim almost all my body, my strength, my breath, and I held on wondering if my burden was my enemy, uncertain as to whether my life was at all mine. Is life a pregnancy? That would make death a birth.

Easter Day. I am in that rare frame of mind when everything seems simple. When I have no doubt that the aim and solution of life is the acceptance of God. It is impossible and imperative, and clear. To open to such unimaginable greatness affrights my smallness. I do not know what I seek, cannot know, but I am where the mystery is the certainty.

My long life has hardly given me time—I cannot say to understand—but to be able to imagine that God speaks to me, says simply—"I keep calling to you, and you do not come," and I answer quite naturally—"I couldn't, until I knew there was nowhere else to go." . . .

I am uncertain whether it is a sad thing or a solace to be past change. One can improve one's character to the very end, and no one is too young in these days to put the old right. The late clarities will be put down to our credit I feel sure.

It was something other than this that had caught my attention. In fact it was the exact opposite. It was the comfortable number of things about which we need no longer bother. I know I am thinking two ways at once, justified and possible in a note book. Goals and efforts of a lifetime can at last be abandoned. What a comfort. One's conscience? Toss the fussy thing aside. Rest, rest. So much over, so much hopeless, some delight remaining.

One's appearance, a lifetime of effort put into improving that, most of it ill judged. Only neatness is vital now, and one can finally live like a humble but watchful ghost. You need not plan holidays because you can't take them. You are past all action, all decision. In very truth the old are almost free, and if it is another way of saying that our lives are empty, well—there are days when emptiness is spacious, and non-existence elevating. When old, one has only one's soul as company. There are times when you can feel it crying, you do not ask why. Your eyes are dry, but heavy, hot tears drop on your heart. There is nothing to do but wait, and listen to the emptiness which is sometimes gentle. You and the day are quiet, and you have no comment to make. . . .

I don't like to write this down, yet it is much in the minds of the old. We wonder how much older we have to become, and what degree of decay we may have to endure. We keep whispering to ourselves, "Is this age yet? How far must I go?" For age can be dreaded more than death. "How many years of vacuity? To what degree of deterioration must I advance?" Some want death now, as release from old age, some say they will accept death willingly, but in a few years. I feel the solemnity of death, and the possibility of some form of continuity. Death feels a friend because it will release us from the deterioration of which we cannot see the end. It is waiting for death that wears us down, and the distaste for what we may become.

These thoughts are with us always, and in our hearts we know ignominy as well as dignity. We are people to whom something important is about to happen. But before then, these endless years before the end, can we summon enough merit to warrant a place for ourselves? We go into the future not knowing the answer to our question.

But we also find that as we age we are more alive than seems likely, convenient, or even bearable. Too often our problem is the fervour of life within us. My dear fellow octogenarians, how are we to carry so much life, and what are we to do with it?

Let no one say it is "unlived life" with any of the simpler psychological certitudes. No one lives all the life of which he was capable. The unlived life in each of us must be the future of humanity. When truly old, too frail to use the vigour that pulses in us, and weary, sometimes even scornful of what can seem the pointless activity of mankind, we may sink down to some deeper level and find a new supply of life that amazes us.

All is uncharted and uncertain, we seem to lead the way into the unknown. It can feel as though all our lives we have been caught in absurdly small personalities and circumstances and beliefs. Our accustomed shell cracks here, cracks there, and that tiresomely rigid person we supposed to be ourselves stretches, expands, and with all inhibitions gone we realize that age is not failure, nor disgrace; though mortifying we did not invent it. Age forces us to deal with idleness, emptiness, not being needed, not able to do, helplessness just ahead perhaps. All this is true, but one has had one's life, one could be full to the brim. Yet it is the end of our procession through time, and our steps are uncertain.

Here we come to a new place of which I knew nothing. We come to where age is boring, one's interest in it by-passed; further on, go further on, one finds that one has arrived at a larger place still, the place of release. There one says, "Age can seem a debacle, a rout of all one most needs, but that is not the whole truth. What of the part of us, the nameless, boundless part who experienced the rout, the witness who saw so much go, who remains undaunted and knows with clear conviction that there is more to us than age? Part of that which is outside age has been created by age, so there is gain as well as loss. If we have suffered defeat we are somewhere, somehow beyond the battle." . . .

A long life makes me feel nearer truth, yet it won't go into words, so how can I convey it? I can't, and I want to. I want to tell people approaching and perhaps fearing age that it is a time of discovery. If they say—"Of what?" I can only answer, "We must each find out for ourselves, otherwise it won't be discovery." I want to say— "If at the end of your life you have only yourself, it is much. Look, you will find."

FOCUS ON PRACTICE   REMINISCENCE AND LIFE REVIEW

As people grow older, it is not unusual for them to reminisce about the "good old days." Feelings of both nostalgia and regret are commonly part of this attitude toward the past. A stereotypical response to reminiscence is to assume that older people are only interested in the past or, still worse, to see those who dwell on past memories as showing signs of escapism or even mental impairment. But late-life reminiscence may be a normal form of **life review,** which Robert Butler (1963) defines as a natural, even universal process stimulated by awareness of approaching death:

> The life review is characterized by a progressive return to consciousness of past experience, in particular the resurgence of unresolved conflicts which can now be surveyed and integrated. . . . If unresolved conflicts and fears are successfully reintegrated they can give new significance and meaning to an individual's life. (Butler, 1974, p. 534)

Butler's view is similar to that of Erik Erikson, who sees the psychological task of late life as achieving ego integrity, a reintegration of all aspects of the individual's life. Both Erikson and Butler based their psychological theories on the importance of finding meaning in the last stage of life. But do the facts support their theories? Just how important is reminiscence in old age?

Some studies have shown that elderly people actually do not spend much more time daydreaming about the past than do people of other ages (Gambria, 1977). So it may be a mistake to see life review as a universal process. On the other hand, regardless of frequency, reminiscence may have adaptive value; that is, it may promote better mental health in old age. One early study of reminiscence found that people who spend time thinking about the past are less likely to suffer depression (McMahon and Rhudick, 1967). Some psychologists who have studied life review feel it may be a psychological defense mechanism that helps some people adjust to memories of an unhappy past. In that sense, reminiscence could be described as an adaptive feature of old age (Coleman, 1974), something to be encouraged (Brennan and Steinberg, 1983-1984).

Finally, reminiscence and life review appear to help some older people bolster their self-image (Lewis, 1971). By recalling the past, older adults can improve self-esteem and establish solidarity with others of their own generation. We might interpret older people's interaction with the young as a way to help the old maximize perceived power or status, just as the **exchange theory** of aging predicts. When activity is the preferred style, then older people are likely to downplay reminiscence in favor of talking about present or future events. But when disengagement is the preferred style, older people may emphasize past accomplishments.

Some gerontologists recommend that reminiscence and life review can have great value for older people who can no longer remain active (Haight, 1991). For that reason, reminiscence groups have been encouraged as a form of therapy among some nursing home residents and senior center participants. Guided autobiography is a method used as a basis for education in the later years (Birren and Deutschman, 1991). Spiritual autobiography groups have played a similar role in religious congregations.

All these methods can be useful for practitioners who work with older people. But techniques to encourage reminiscence as a form of practice must not divert us from a basic question: Is reminiscence or life review the best way of achieving a sense of meaning in old age? The response to that question cannot be a scientific answer but depends on basic values and philosophy of life. For example, if we follow Simone de Beauvoir's view, then activity and future orientation are the best approach to finding meaning in old age. She would therefore discourage people from spending time reminiscing about the past, unless past memories can somehow contribute to improving the world. Jung, on the other hand, would see great value in inwardness or interiority in old age. The purpose or meaning of old age, in his view, is not necessarily to be active but to know ourselves better and to accept ourselves as individuals. If life review can promote that goal, then Jung would encourage it.

Do the reminiscence and life review by older people have meaning for people of other ages? Clearly, there is something special about old age precisely because it is the final stage of life. The last stage includes an awareness of finitude and a shortened time perspective (Kastenbaum, 1983). Furthermore, as the pace of social change increases, older people can no longer take for granted that their values will be shared by other cohorts; the " '60s generation" and the "World War II generation" may be quite different, not only from one another but from "Generation X," born during the baby bust after the mid-1960s. The old may be perceived by others, or perceive themselves, as belonging to "the past," regardless of their own subjective time orientation. Young people may assume that reminiscence is something appropriate only for the old.

In fact, the process of life review or autobiographical consciousness is not limited to old age but occurs at transitions across the adult life course—for instance, in self-assessment after a job loss or bereavement. The life course perspective helps us appreciate links between subjective and objective time orientations and to see life review in broader terms. The search for meaning in life occurs not only at the end of life but every time human beings become aware of their limited time on earth. It is perhaps for that reason that in the Bible the Psalms include a prayer for God to help us all to "number our days" and thus to cherish each passing moment whatever our age may be.

FOCUS ON THE FUTURE   CONSCIOUS AGING

As we approached the millennial year 2000, there was a surge of public interest in spiritual topics, as shown by the popularity of best-sellers such as *The Road Less Traveled* (Peck, 1980/1993) and *The Care of the Soul* (Moore, 1992). This interest in things spiritual takes different forms, ranging from an interest in exotic New Age phenomena to a revival of traditional mystical teachings from Judaism and Christianity.

Some recent research suggests that mystical experience is becoming more common, with broad implications for an aging society. For example, Jeffrey Levin (1993) looked at age differences in reports of extrasensory perception, spiritualism, and numinous experience, which he defined as being "close to a powerful, spiritual force that seemed to lift you out of yourself." Using data from a representative cross-sectional population survey, Levin found that between 1973 and 1988 composite mysticism scores have been increasing with successive age cohorts. Private and subjective religiosity is positively related to overall mystical experience, but organizational religiosity is inversely related—suggesting that those pursuing spiritual growth may find it in places other than church on Sunday.

Compared with European societies, the United States has historically been more religiously oriented. But spiritual revival today goes beyond mainstream religion. *Individual growth* is the new watchword. In keeping with that trend, one of the most fascinating developments today is the rise of "conscious aging," an idea based on an assumption that late life can be a period for positive spiritual growth. Zalman Schachter-Shalomi, a pioneer of the Jewish Renewal Movement, and Ram Dass, once a Harvard psychology professor and later a spiritual teacher, emerged as national leaders of the conscious aging movement. Holistic health care, life review, and mystical religion are all important elements in conscious aging (see, e.g., Schachter-Shalomi and Miller, 1995).

One of the earliest initiatives on behalf of conscious aging was a self-help project known as Senior Actualization and Growth Explorations (SAGE), developed in California in 1974 to promote holistic health activities among the elderly. In that project, weekly group activities drew on methods of humanistic and transpersonal psychology, such as meditation, guided discussions, yoga, massage, dream analysis, and exercises built around nutrition and holistic health care. SAGE was founded by Gay Luce, who was inspired to share her enthusiasm for meditation and biofeedback techniques with her 71-year-old mother (Luce, 1979). Exercises in visualization, meditation, and relaxation helped participants move toward self-discovery while confronting fears of dying.

A central practice of conscious aging is personal meditation (Goleman, 1988), whether it takes the form of yoga, Zen or other Eastern disciplines, or the form of contemplative prayer, which has a long history in the Christian church. Meditation as a spiritual discipline is a way of looking at ourselves as beings with depths beyond the conscious mind or ego. The same outlook permeates the work of Jungian psychiatrist Allan Chinen (1989), who has opened up new vistas for the interpretation of fairy tales about the second half of life. Conscious aging represents a coming together of religion and psychology so that each can enrich the other.

Conscious aging goes beyond conventional assumptions about adaptation or personality development over the life course. An early proponent of this view was Abraham Maslow, founder of humanistic psychology. Maslow believed that most people use only a small part of human potential, a potential demonstrated in what Maslow called "peak experiences." At these high points in our life, we have a chance to move toward self-actualization—that is, to become more fulfilled as a human being. Maslow himself believed that most people who are self-actualized are to be found among those who are mature in years—middle-aged or elderly.

Mainstream psychology has for the most part not looked closely at the higher reaches of human potential, whether in young people or old. One result of that limitation may be the "decline-and-fall" view of aging criticized by researchers who have looked at the emergence of wisdom in later life (Baltes, 1993). But some life span developmental psychologists go further. They argue that mature thought in adulthood entails a dimension of "transcendence" (Miller and Cook-Greuter, 1994), the province of *transpersonal psychology* (Walsh and Vaughan, 1993). Transpersonal psychology includes such elements as attention training, emotional transformation, refining awareness, and the achievement of wisdom through detachment and integration.

The conscious aging perspective may have something to contribute to gerontology on matters such as health care, intergenerational relations, and adult education. For example, research over the past two decades has documented the tangible benefits of meditation for physical and mental health. What happens in meditation has long been familiar to medical and psychological researchers under the name of *autogenic training,* or self-induced modification of lower brain centers. More than two decades ago, Dr. Herbert Benson of Harvard Medical School published his groundbreaking article on "the relaxation response" that explained altered states of consciousness in yoga and Zen in terms of the central nervous system. Since then, extensive research on biofeedback and alpha waves in the brain has confirmed the feasibility of studying consciousness.

There has also been some interesting experimental confirmation of strategies of conscious aging as a means of overcoming what psychologist Robert Kastenbaum (1984) calls **habituation.** In Kastenbaum's view, the essence of aging is a process of becoming gradually deadened or more mechanical in our response to life because of the power of habits. By contrast, meditation can be viewed as a progressive growth in powers of attention to overcome habituation in old stimulus-response patterns.

Conscious aging is a struggle to establish new cognitive structures, new ways of looking at the world. Researcher Arthur Deikman (1966/1990) has described how the process of deautomization can come from practicing meditative disciplines like yoga or Zen. Deikman, for instance, conducted a procedure of "experimental meditation" after which subjects reported sensory experience that was more vivid and luminous. Deikman's work and other experiments like it suggest that deliberate concentration and meditation can modify the selectivity of sensory input to the brain.

These findings could have implications for an aging society. In a geriatric population, one controlled study found that meditation-relaxation techniques can have a major impact in reducing anxiety and depression, an impact superior to conventional cognitive/behavioral techniques (DeBerry, Davis, and Reinhard, 1989). Another study, funded by the National Institute of Mental Health, looked at the impact of transcendental meditation to see if it can have benefits beyond simple relaxation. That study confirmed the point that cultivation of "mindfulness," a state of consciousness free of content but alert, does have measurable consequences for learning, cognitive flexibility, and for overall mental health. These results remained with the individuals years later (Alexander et al., 1989).

Proponents of conscious aging are trying to apply these lessons from research and practice to a growing elderly population. Interest in health promotion, productive aging, and lifelong learning is likely to make conscious aging a subject of continuing importance as America becomes an aging society in the 21st century. It may prove an intriguing glimpse of things to come.

QUESTIONS FOR WRITING, REFLECTION, AND DEBATE

1 Some critics have argued that disengagement may have described some behavior in the elderly population in the 1950s, but that it was a mistake to infer that the pattern was universal. According to this view, activity theory or continuity theory might well be a better description of how older people actually live today. If this view is correct, does it mean that any "theory of aging" simply expresses the way aging appears at a certain time in history? If so, how would it be possible to develop an account that is more general and not limited to a certain time and place?

2 Most observers agree that America as a society places a high value on success and achievement. Does that fact suggest that the goal of "successful aging" is an appropriate approach to thinking about growing old in America? Are there aspects of growing older that the idea of successful aging may not adequately deal with?

3 Jung believed that the psychological goal of later life is to become more and more oneself as an individual. What does this goal mean in practice? What drawbacks to this idea can you think of? If we adopt Jung's approach, how would we evaluate older people who remain very much as they have always been in contrast to others who dramatically change their lives, say, after retirement or widowhood?

4 Imagine that you are now 80 years old and have discovered that you may not have long to live. Your grandchildren have asked you to write a statement about what you've learned about the meaning of life, especially in the past few years. In your statement, contrast what you believe now (as a future 80-year-old) with what you believed in the past (at what is your present age).

5 Assume that you are the activities director of a church-affiliated nursing home that prides itself on promoting the quality of life of residents. Write a memorandum for the nursing home director outlining a range of activities that would help enhance the residents' sense of the meaning of life in the long-term facility.

6 Is the idea of "meaning" in life something purely personal and private, or does it have some wider social importance? Does discussing the question of meaning give us an understanding of older people's behavior, or is it simply confusing? In addressing this question, consider other issues discussed in this book, such as assisted suicide, work and leisure, and the allocation of health care resources for life prolongation. How would the idea of a "meaning" for old age affect one's view of these questions?

7 Visit the Web site devoted to an overview of old age and religion at www.trinity.edu/mkearl/geron.html. Based on what you see at this site, what recommendations would you make to a reporter whose editor has given an assignment to write a general article titled "Religion and Old Age"?

8 Consider carefully Lars Tornstam's concept of "gerotranscendence" as this idea is expressed and developed on his Web site, http://www.soc.uu.se/research/gerontology/gerotrans.html. Now do the following exercise. Using only the simplest and most everyday language, give an explanation of gero-transcendence to a friend or relative who knows nothing about gerontology and is not particularly sympathetic to religion.

SUGGESTED READINGS

Frankl, Victor, *Man's Search for Meaning: An Introduction to Logotherapy* (trans. Ilse Lasch), New York: Pocket Books, 1973.

Haight, B. K., and Webster, J. D., *The Art and Science of Reminiscing: Theory, Research, Methods, and Applications,* Washington, DC: Taylor & Francis, 1995.

Kelly, J. R. (ed.), *Activity and Aging: Staying Involved in Later Life,* Newbury Park, CA: Sage, 1993.

Kimble, M. A., McFadden, S. H., Ellor, J. W., and Seeber, J. J. (eds.), *Aging, Spirituality and Religion: A Handbook,* Minneapolis, MN: Fortress, 1995.

Koenig, Harold G., *Research on Religion and Aging: An Annotated Bibliography,* Westport, CT: Greenwood, 1995.

How to Research a Term Paper in Gerontology

Research and writing can be intimidating to many students, especially in a field such as gerontology, which is a new subject to most. But research and writing needn't be frightening. Skillful research is the key to good writing, and careful thinking is the foundation for both.

Doing the background research for a term paper in gerontology is more than half the task of actually writing the paper itself. If you are successful in the research, you end up having other people do your work for you! Of course, that does not mean plagiarism or simply copying what other people have written without giving proper credit. But the trick in writing is to save yourself the trouble of reinventing the wheel. You want to avoid floundering around trying to rediscover a fact or idea that someone else has already worked out before you. Wasting time that way is not necessary at all. In fact, it detracts from the real job of research and writing—namely, thinking about what others have written and deciding what to take and put into your own work.

The key is not to work harder but to work smarter. By building on other people's work, and giving credit to them where credit is due, you save yourself time and devote your best efforts to expressing what you really have to say. The process is the same as the one that takes place in science. All science and all scholarship stand on the work of others. This point holds true for the beginning student no less than for great thinkers. Indeed, the great physicist Isaac Newton himself once said, "If I have seen further than others, it is because I have stood on the shoulders of giants."

How does this approach apply to your writing a term paper? Conducting library research for a term paper is a bit like looking for buried treasure. If you don't know *exactly* where the treasure is buried, you end up spending a lot of time digging in places where you imagine the treasure *might* be. You rely on guesswork instead of careful thought. Once you have a hunch about where the treasure lies, then the actual digging takes practically no time at all. It is just the same with library research. Once you have developed your search strategy—your map for where treasure might be found—then the information sources at your fingertips will guide you quickly to where the treasure lies. The rest of the work—including writing up your findings—will actually take very little time, because you can build on the work of others.

Defining Your Topic

At every stage in the research process, you need to ask yourself, What is the question I am asking? (What information am I trying to find?) You don't ask this question only once. For example, suppose you are trying to find out what percentage of people are retired at ages 60 and 70. At first, the question may seem simple. But as you dig deeper, you find that there may be uncertainty about how to count people as "retired" instead of "unemployed" or "disabled." As you look into the statistics, you discover that, behind the solid numbers, differing assumptions are involved. In effect, you ask your basic question over and over again as you look through bibliographic sources.

When you are planning your topic, you might find it helpful first to free-associate, or let your mind wander. You need to think about points related to your topic, but also about other subject terms and ideas related to your topic. This process of cross-referencing is at the heart of research and creative thinking. For example, suppose you're interested in writing a paper on retirement. Retirement is a big subject, maybe too big for one paper. Social scientists have written whole books on the subject; some have devoted their entire careers to it. But stay with the big subject for a while. Then, think about all the other subjects—the "key words"—that are related to retirement: *work, pensions, Social Security,* and so on. Each of these could also be a term paper or indeed a whole book.

As you look over all your key words, look for connections that interest you; for instance, maybe you see a connection between *pensions* and *retirement.* You might begin to put together a hypothesis or a theme; for example, What is the relationship between pensions and retirement behavior?

When you ask yourself research questions, it is helpful if you write down some tentative answers. That's the first step toward making an outline, or a plan, for your work. Carrying out research is a bit like building a house. In constructing the house, it pays to put time into planning and thinking. You don't wait to draw up blueprints until you are halfway finished constructing the house. To write a term paper, you also need a plan. Write down your ideas first without worrying too much about whether your plan is adequate or complete; you're likely to change it later anyway. Then start consulting other sources.

Starting Your Search

In constructing a fruitful search strategy, you face a catch-22. You can't really narrow your research question until you know the subject matter better. But you can't define the subject matter without carving it down to size with the right research question. Imagine how discouraging your task would be if you didn't realize that pension levels and retirement behavior might be related. In gerontology, as in all fields, the amount of knowledge is simply too vast for you to master all of it. To make matters worse, gerontology is a multidisciplinary field, involving specialized subjects such as economics, biology, and psychology. Without a clear plan for research, you can simply get lost.

The secret of research is to keep widening your search process while also narrowing it at the same time. For example, the topic you've picked has two key ideas: "pensions" and "retirement." Some of the references you find may lead you in directions that don't interest you—for instance, "pension fund investments" or "mandatory retirement." But other references will be right on target and will lead you to refine your topic even further. There lies the real process of thinking: testing your ideas against a "map" of knowledge that sums up facts about the world. The mistake that people often make is to construct, at the beginning, a search that is either too narrow or too broad.

So, what to do? By all means, carve your topic down to size. But then, as you're searching for information on your refined topic, also be willing to follow the concept to related topics. In looking at "pension income," you might find references to Social Security, IRAs, and so on. Perhaps you'll come upon a term that isn't very familiar, like *Keogh plan.*

As you review what you find, you'll begin to see connections among concepts. But the connected concepts may or may not be exactly the ones listed in computer printouts or abstract summaries. You have to develop a "sixth sense," constantly looking for clues. The result of this process is a more complete cross-referencing of your subject matter; in effect, you're creating a dense network of concepts that fully captures your topic and prepares you to write your paper.

A number of resources are available to help you build your network of concepts. One is the library's own classification system; another is the librarians themselves. The Library of Congress subject headings present a uniform method of classifying documents, and that can be a useful place to begin. But the real clues will come as you examine the books and journals themselves. *Don't* simply go to the library card catalog or start browsing through the latest issue of a periodical related to your subject. Doing that will just waste your time, unless you have done some preliminary planning. By all means, enlist librarians to help you, but don't rely exclusively on librarians. They can't be specialists in all subject matters, and they can help you the most if you've already done some thinking about the question you want to pursue. If you've thought about your question, then a librarian can help guide you to the information sources you need.

Another kind of resource that might be helpful is the computerized online database. But because searching and researching are not mechanical processes, a computer search won't solve all your problems, and it may even give the illusion of completeness. Computer searches also present the student with certain dangers. There are two general kinds of dangers in online searching. The first is summarized in a slogan familiar to computer special-ists: Garbage in, garbage out. That is, you can only get an answer to the ques-tion you ask; if your question or hypothesis is badly framed—for example, if it's too vague—then you won't get useful information. The second danger is that you may get too much information, including lots of references that are irrelevant or useless. For both dangers, the cure is the same: good strategies for searching and for eliminating what is extraneous to your search. The main message here is that you can't do bibliographic research just by look-ing for simple terminology, by looking up words in an index, card catalog, or database. One reason is that there are so many related but distinct terms in gerontology: *aged, older persons, elderly, senior citizens,* and so on. But if you can formulate a research question and remain alert to the meanings of the terms you encounter, you can find the sources that will help you answer your question. Once you find the spot you've been looking for, the buried treasure will be lying at your feet.

Eight Steps for Carrying Out Library Research

Step 1. Consult *The Encyclopedia of Aging* for the lead article on your sub-ject. Be sure to make note of the relevant bibliography citations.

Step 2. Consult one of the handbooks on aging (from biology, the social sci-ences, the humanities, etc.) or a current textbook to see if there is a chapter or a section of a chapter devoted to your subject. The handbook's index can be useful here. (Be sure also to check the more detailed resource list provided at the end of Appendix A.)

Step 3. Review the bibliography references you have found and organize them by date, starting with the most recent. Look for titles that focus directly on your topic but approach the subject in a broad way. A literature review article is often an excellent way to get started. Many published articles begin with a literature review or "state-of-the-art" summary of what is known about a topic.

Step 4. Consult some recent issues of one of the abstract volumes listed in the resource list below, such as *Abstracts in Social Gerontology,* to find the most up-to-date literature on your subject. Looking at abstracts is a quick and handy way to see a summary of what's in a possible reference without wast-ing time reading the entire article. You get more than just a title, and you can find out quickly if the publication could have value for you.

Step 5 (optional). To be truly comprehensive and up-to-date, ask a friendly librarian to conduct a computerized search on your subject through AgeLine or a similar online database. From your previous bibliographic work, you should have a good collection of key words or authors to help the librarian focus on your topic as precisely as possible.

Step 6. By now, you are ready to go to your college library to find the most up-to-date, relevant books and articles on your tentative topic. But note: Do not judge a book by its cover or a reference by its title. Remember to browse through any book you find, looking at the table of contents, the index, the introduction, a summary chapter, and so on, maybe even sampling a few chapters in between. Don't make the mistake of reading straight through the entire text of what looks like the "perfect" book or article on your subject. Instead, zero in on the essential information and let the rest go. You can always come back later if you need to. It's good to get other points of view on your topic.

Step 7. When you are browsing through books or articles, be sure to check their bibliographies or reference lists for interesting titles. Using ideas from these books or articles, you will then be able to "fine-tune" your topic while taking notes and picking up additional ideas that you can incorporate into your paper.

Step 8. In most cases, you will find the references you need in your local college library. But if you cannot find them, don't hesitate to request books or articles on interlibrary loan, for example, from a wider university system or from other libraries. But don't fall into the trap of the perpetual scholar, who keeps searching forever and never quite finds the "perfect" reference source. In most cases, you will find what you need close to home. When writing a term paper, you have a deadline to meet.

Ending the Search

At some point in this process, you are likely to find yourself coming up again and again with the same books, articles, and author names as you look through new information sources. Don't be discouraged by this. It isn't a sign of failure or that you are "going around in circles." On the contrary, it may be a sign of success. If you have gone far enough in your search, it may mean that you've struck pay dirt. When you have gone really deeply into any subject area, you are bound to start seeing the same authors' names coming up again and again.

At that point, it is time to look through the references on hand and decide which ones are high quality and which ones are relevant for your now refined topic area. Decide which ones are really the most useful to you and gather the key ideas, always giving credit but putting the ideas into your own words. When you have found the treasure you are looking for, go home and start writing.

Resources for Papers in Gerontology

Encyclopedias and Handbooks

The best one-volume reference source for gerontology is *The Encyclopedia of Aging,* edited by George L. Maddox (New York: Springer, 1995). It contains more than 500 entries written by leading authorities in each field. This volume is accessible to students as well as more advanced scholars, and its vast list of references makes it extremely useful. Also worthwhile is the *Dictionary of Gerontology,* by Diana K. Harris (Westport, CT: Greenwood, 1988), a short volume that even beginning students will find easily understandable.

Among the most useful single-volume reference works are the many handbooks that focus on aging and the biological sciences, social sciences, psychology, and human services. These include the following:

Robert H. Binstock and Linda K. George (eds.), *Handbook of Aging and the Social Sciences* (4th ed.), San Diego, CA: Academic Press, 1996. Contains updated versions of articles that appeared in earlier editions as well as material in new areas. Covers the life course and social context, stratification and generational relations, work and economy, politics and policy analysis, as well as applied topics of aging and social intervention.

James E. Birren and K. Warner Schaie (eds.), *Handbook of the Psychology of Aging* (3rd ed.), New York: Academic Press, 1990. Covers theory and measurement, influences of behavior and aging, perceptual and cognitive processes, and applications to the individual and society.

Laura L. Carstensen, Barry A. Edelstein, and Laurie Dornbrand, *The Practical Handbook of Clinical Gerontology,* Thousand Oaks, CA: Sage, 1996. Covers a wide range of clinical issues for those working with older people. Chapters address normal aging, psychiatric disorders, common medical problems, behavior problems, and social issues.

Thomas R. Cole, David D. Van Tassel, and Robert Kastenbaum (eds.), *Handbook of the Humanities and Aging,* New York: Springer, 1992. Covers aging through history, comparative religion, arts and literature, and contemporary topics in humanistic gerontology.

Abraham Monk (ed.), *Handbook of Gerontological Services,* New York: Columbia University Press, 1990. Primarily relevant for those interested in social work and human services. Contains chapters by specialists on home- and community-based services, long-term care, and social work intervention forms.

Edward L. Schneider and John W. Rowe (eds.), *Handbook of the Biology of Aging* (3rd ed.), San Diego, CA: Academic Press, 1990. Covers all aspects of biogerontology from molecular biology, cell biology, and genetics through the physiology of major organic systems of the human body.

Abstracts and Databases

Each issue of *Abstracts in Social Gerontology: Current Literature on Aging* contains 250 abstracts, or short summaries, of the most important recent literature, cross-indexed and organized by topics, along with 250 other (non-annotated) bibliographic citations. *Abstracts in Social Gerontology* is issued four times each year by Sage Publications in cooperation with the National Council on Aging. Another important resource is *Gerontological Abstracts,* which covers chiefly biology and health sciences.

AgeLine is a computerized online database, accessible by telephone line and modem anywhere in the world. References in AgeLine cover all aspects of the social sciences, health care, and human services. The database includes books, articles, government documents, and dissertations as well as reports on government-sponsored research in gerontology.

For references to biomedical subjects and other health-related topics, another good source is MedLine, produced by the National Library of Medicine. A college library or other research-oriented library will be able to provide computer search services. A librarian can access both AgeLine and MedLine through DIALOG, an online information company that provides many different databases. For more direct information, contact DIALOG Information Services, Inc., 3460 Hillview Avenue, Palo Alto, CA 94304.

A useful companion volume is the *Thesaurus of Aging Terminology: AgeLine Database on Middle Age and Aging* (3rd ed.) (Washington, DC: American Association of Retired Persons, 1986). See also *Age Words: A Glossary on Health and Aging,* published by the National Institutes of Health, Washington, D.C.

Statistics

The conventional sources for U.S. statistics are the publications of the U.S. Census Bureau, for example, *Current Population Reports,* which updates information from the 1990 census. Census documents are available in most college libraries. The Health Care Financing Administration and the special committees of the U.S. Senate and House Committees on Aging also publish periodic reports, which can often be obtained by writing to these agencies or by visiting a large library. Documents from specialized sources may be difficult to obtain in local libraries, and they are not always easy to understand.

For the student, the best single source is probably the simple and comprehensive work published by the U.S. Administration on Aging, *Aging America: Trends and Projections* (Washington, DC: U.S. Senate, Office of Management and Policy, 1991). This book is a compilation of the most recent data covering population trends, economic status, work and retirement, as well as data on health and illness, federal expenditures, and international comparisons. It is clear, easy to understand, and extremely useful for the research purposes of beginners.

For statistics and interesting facts, see also Elizabeth Vierck, *Fact Book on Aging* (Santa Barbara, CA: ABC-CLIO, 1990). Useful but now somewhat outdated are the following: Frank L. Schick (ed.), *Statistical Handbook on Aging Americans* (Phoenix, AZ: Oryx, 1986). This handbook provides statistical data on the United States for a variety of variables, but it needs to be updated for the 1990 census figures. Also see Paul E. Zopf, Jr., *America's Older Population* (Houston, TX: Cap & Gown, 1986).

Guides to Research and Information

One volume that is valuable, easy to follow, and reasonably up-to-date is Dorothea R. Zito and George V. Zito, *A Guide to Research in Gerontology: Strategies and Resources* (Westport, CT: Greenwood, 1988). See also Joan Nordquist, *The Elderly in America: A Bibliography* (Contemporary Social Issues: A Bibliographic Series, no. 23) (Santa Cruz, CA: Reference & Research Services, 1991).

Among older works are John B. Balkema (ed.), *Aging: A Guide to Resources* (Syracuse, NY: Gaylord, 1983); and Linna Funk Place, Linda Parker, and Forrest Berghorn, *Aging and the Aged: An Annotated Bibliography and Library Research Guide* (Boulder, CO: Westview, 1980), the latter written as a research and study tool for undergraduates. Both volumes are out-of-date, but they are still valuable for learning about the field of aging to approach term paper topics.

Other Valuable Reference Works

J. Chrichton, *The Age Care Source Book: A Resource Guide for the Aging and Their Families,* New York: Simon & Schuster, 1987.

Edward Duensing (ed.), *America's Elderly: A Sourcebook,* New Brunswick, NJ: Center for Urban Policy Research, 1988.

Ronald Manheimer (ed.), *Aging Almanac,* Detroit, MI: Gale Research, 1993. An up-to-date overview of different special subject areas in the field of aging. Written for a popular audience but based on solid academic sources.

Marilyn D. Petersen and Diana L. White (eds.), *Health Care of the Elderly: An Information Sourcebook,* Newbury Park, CA: Sage, 1989.

R. Wasserman, P. B. Koehler, and Y. Lev (eds.), *Encyclopedia of Senior Citizens Information Sources,* Detroit, MI: Gale Research, 1987.

The 1968 volume by Matilda White Riley and Anne Foner, *Aging and Society: An Inventory of Research Findings* (New York: Basic Books), gives a comprehensive summary of knowledge through the late 1960s—out-of-date now, but an important accomplishment nonetheless. See also Matilda White Riley, Beth B. Hess, and K. Bond (eds.), *Aging in Society: Selected Review of Recent Research* (Hillsdale, NJ: Lawrence Erlbaum, 1983); and Sarah Beguns et al., *An Annotated Bibliography of Recent Research on the Elderly* (Monticello, IL: Vance Bibliographies, 1982).

See also Diana K. Harris, *The Sociology of Aging: An Annotated Bibliography and Sourcebook* (Reading, MA: Addison-Wesley, 1990). This volume covers culture and society, social inequality, social institutions, and environment and aging. Special chapters cover demography, death and dying, crime and deviance, racial and ethnic groups, and many other topics. The book also covers periodicals and source materials on aging.

Finally, the federal government is an important source of information. See, for example, the U.S. Senate Special Committee on Aging, *Publications List* (Washington, DC: Government Printing Office).

Textbooks

Current textbooks on aging and gerontology are valuable sources of information and further reference for students. The following is a partial list of textbooks that may prove useful:

Robert C. Atchley, *Social Forces and Aging: An Introduction to Social Gerontology* (6th ed.), Belmont, CA: Wadsworth, 1991.

Georgia Barrow, *Aging, the Individual and Society,* St. Paul, MN: West, 1989.

Arnold Brown, *The Social Processes of Aging and Old Age,* Englewood Cliffs, NJ: Prentice Hall, 1990.

Diana K. Harris, *The Sociology of Aging: An Annotated Bibliography and Sourcebook,* Reading, MA: Addison-Wesley, 1990.

Jon Hendricks and C. Davis Hendricks, *Aging in Mass Society: Myths and Realities,* Boston: Little, Brown, 1986.

Nancy Hooyman and H. Asuman Kiyak, *Social Gerontology: A Multidisciplinary Perspective,* Boston: Allyn & Bacon, 1991.

Cary S. Kart, *The Realities of Aging: An Introduction to Gerontology* (4th ed.), Boston: Allyn & Bacon, 1993.

Judah Matras, *Dependency, Developments and Entitlements: A New Sociology of Aging, the Life Course and the Elderly,* Englewood Cliffs, NJ: Prentice Hall, 1990.

Important Journals and Other Periodicals

For an overview of important periodicals in the field of gerontology, see Shirley B. Hesslein, *Serials on Aging: An Analytical Guide* (Westport, CT: Greenwood, 1986). This book covers general periodicals as well as periodicals specializing in social gerontology, health and biomedicine, retirement and pensions, and statistics and reference tools. It includes a geographic index and a list of publishers.

Among the many notable periodicals available, the following can be recommended:

Ageing and Society. New York: Cambridge University Press, quarterly. Edited in Great Britain with an international and interdisciplinary perspective; strong on humanities and social science.

Contemporary Long-Term Care. Nashville, TN: Advantage, monthly. Covers all aspects of long-term care, with an emphasis on applied and practical problems.

Educational Gerontology. Washington, DC: Hemisphere, quarterly. Covers both gerontology instruction and education for older adults.

The Gerontologist. Washington, DC: Gerontological Society of America, bimonthly. Interdisciplinary and focused on social gerontology.

Gerontology and Geriatrics Education. Useful for educational issues, including training for the different professional fields involved in aging.

International Journal of Aging and Human Development. Farmingdale, NY: Baywood, eight times annually. Interdisciplinary in the social sciences, but articles with clinical and practical application as well.

Journal of the American Geriatrics Society. A technical medical journal for geriatricians. Many articles are above the level of the beginning student, but some are accessible.

Journal of Gerontological Nursing. Leading periodical that covers clinical health care issues of interest to many health care providers.

Journal of Gerontological Social Work. New York: Haworth, quarterly. The leading periodical covering all aspects of social welfare policy and clinical practice in the field of aging.

Journal of Women and Aging. New York: Haworth, quarterly. The only periodical covering all aspects of gender and aging.

Journals of Gerontology. Gerontological Society of America, bimonthly. Actually four separate journals that cover the biological sciences, medical sciences, psychological sciences, and social sciences. Very technical and specialized; only for very advanced inquiry.

Psychology and Aging. Washington, DC: American Psychological Association, quarterly. Covers all aspects of adult life span development and aging, including behavioral, clinical, and experimental psychology.

Research on Aging. Thousand Oaks, CA: Sage, quarterly. Covers a broad range of inquiry for gerontology in the social sciences. Accessible for the educated reader but contains mainly specialized articles.

Internet Resources
on the Aging

The Concepts and Controversies examined in this book are in a constant state of change as a result of new information and new events coming to the fore. As a result and to keep pace with this change, we have prepared an exhaustive annotated list of online resources in aging, available through the publisher's Web site at www.pineforge.com.

Simply click to that Web site and look for the Online Appendix On Aging associated with *Aging: Concepts and Controversies, Third Edition.*

References

Aaron, Henry J., Bosworth, B., and Burtless, Gary, *Can America Afford to Grow Old? Paying for Social Security,* Washington, DC: Brookings Institution, 1989.

Aaron, Henry J., and Schwartz, W. B., *The Painful Prescription: Rationing Hospital Care,* Washington, DC: Brookings Institution, 1984.

AARP and National Alliance for Caregiving, *Family Caregiving in the U.S.: Findings From a National Survey,* Washington, DC: American Association of Retired Persons, 1997.

Achenbaum, W. Andrew, *Old Age in the New Land: The American Experience Since 1790,* Baltimore: Johns Hopkins University Press, 1978.

Achenbaum, W. Andrew, *Social Security: Visions and Revisions,* Cambridge, UK: Cambridge University Press, 1986.

Adams, Rebecca, and Blieszner, Rosemary, "Aging Well With Friends and Family," *American Behavioral Scientist* (1995), 39(2): 209-224.

Adams-Price, Carolyn, *Creativity and Successful Aging: Theoretical and Empirical Approaches,* New York: Springer, 1998.

Aday, R., Rice, C., and Evans, E., "Intergenerational Partners Project: A Model Linking Elementary Students With Senior Center Volunteers," *The Gerontologist* (1991), 31(2): 263-266.

Aleman, Sara, *Hispanic Elders and Human Services,* New York: Garland, 1997.

Alexander, C. N., Chandler, H. M., Langer, E. J., Newman, R. I., and Davies, J. L., "Transcendental Meditation, Mindfulness, and Longevity: An Experimental Study With the Elderly," *Journal of Personality and Social Psychology* (December 1989) 57(6): 950-964.

Allen, Katherine R., and Chin-Sang, Victoria, "A Lifetime of Work: The Context and Meaning of Leisure for Aging Black Women," *The Gerontologist* (1990), 30: 734-740.

Alliance for Aging Research, *Seven Deadly Myths: Uncovering the Facts About the High Cost of the Last Year of Life,* Washington, DC, 1997.

Altman, Stuart, Reinhardt, Uwe, and Shactman, David (eds.), *Regulating Managed Care: Theory, Practice and Future Options,* San Francisco: Jossey-Bass, 1999.

American Association of Retired Persons, *Work and Retirement: Employees Over 40 and Their Views,* Washington, DC: Author, 1986.

Anderson, L., "Brighter Afternoons for Latchkey Children," *Aging* (1989), 359: 20-21.

Anderson, W. French, "Human Gene Therapy," *Science* (1992), 256: 808-813.

Anderson, William A., and Anderson, Norma D., "The Politics of Age Exclusion: The Adults Only Movement in Arizona," *The Gerontologist* (1978), 18: 6-12.

Anetzberger, G. J., *The Etiology of Elder Abuse by Adult Offspring,* Springfield, IL: Charles C Thomas, 1987.

Anstey, Kaarin J., Lord, Stephen R., and Smith, Glen A., "Measuring Human Functional Age: A Review of Empirical Findings," *Experimental Aging Research* (September 1996), 22(3): 245-266.

Applewhite, S. R. (ed.), *Hispanic Elderly in Transition: Theory, Research, Policy and Practice,* New York: Greenwood, 1988.

Aries, Philippe, *Centuries of Childhood,* New York: Random House, 1962.

Arking, Robert, "Modifying the Aging Process," in Rosalie Young and Elizabeth Olson (eds.), *Health, Illness and Disability in Later Life: Practice Issues and Interventions,* Newbury Park, CA: Sage, 1991.

Arking, Robert, *Biology of Aging: Observations and Principles* (2nd ed.), Sunderland, MA: Sinauer Associates, 1998.

Arling, Greg, et al., "Medicaid Spenddown in Nursing Home Residents in Wisconsin," *The Gerontologist* (1991), 31(2): 174-182.

Arling, Greg, and McAuley, William J., "The Feasibility of Public Payments for Family Care-Giving," *The Gerontologist* (1983), 23: 300-306.

Armstrong, D., Sohal, R. S., Cutler, R. G., and Slater, T. F. (eds.), *Free Radicals in Molecular Biology, Aging, and Disease,* New York: Raven, 1984.

Atchley, Robert, *Social Forces and Aging: An Introduction to Social Gerontology* (4th ed.), Belmont, CA: Wadsworth, 1985.

Austad, Steven N., *Why We Age: What Science Is Discovering About the Body's Journey Through Life,* New York: John Wiley, 1997.

Avorn, Jerome, "The Life and Death of Oliver Shay," in Alan Pifer and Lydia Bronte (eds.), *Our Aging Society,* New York: Norton, 1986.

Avorn, Jerry, "Benefit and Cost Analysis in Geriatric Care: Turning Age Discrimination Into Health Policy," *New England Journal of Medicine* (1984), 310: 1294-1301.

Baker, F. M., "Suicide Among Ethnic Minority Elderly: A Statistical and Psychosocial Perspective," *Journal of Geriatric Psychiatry* (1994), 27(2): 241-264.

Ball, Robert, *Social Security Today and Tomorrow,* New York: Columbia University Press, 1978.

Baltes, Margaret M., and Baltes, Paul B. (eds.), *The Psychology of Control and Aging,* Hillsdale, NJ: Lawrence Erlbaum, 1986.

Baltes, Paul B., "Wise, and Otherwise," *Natural History* (February 1992).

Baltes, Paul B., "Aging Mind: Potential and Limits," *The Gerontologist* (October 1993), 33(5): 580-594.

Baltes, Paul B., and Baltes, Margaret M., "Psychological Perspectives on Successful Aging: The Model of Selective Optimization and Compensation," in Paul B. Baltes and Margaret M. Baltes (eds.), *Successful Aging: Perspectives From the Behavioral Sciences,* New York: Cambridge University Press, 1990, pp. 1-34.

Baltes, Paul B., and Schaie, K. Warner, "The Myth of the Twilight Years," *Psychology Today* (March 1974): 35-40.

Bandon, Alexandra, "Longer, Healthier, Better," *New York Times Magazine* (March 9, 1997): 44.

Banner, Lois W., *In Full Flower: Aging Women, Power, and Sexuality: A History,* New York: Vintage Books, 1993.

Barinaga, Marcia, "Mortality: Overturning Received Wisdom," *Science* (October 16, 1992), 258: 398-399.

Barrett, Edith J., and Cook, Fay Lomax, "Public Support for Social Security," *Journal of Aging Studies* (1988), 2(4): 339-356.

Barron, Milton L., "Minority Group Characteristics of the Aged in American Society," *Journal of Gerontology* (1953), 8: 477-482.

Bass, Scott, and Caro, Francis J. (eds.), *Toward a Productive Aging Society,* Westport, CT: Auburn House, 1993.

Battin, Margaret P., "Choosing the Time to Die: The Ethics and Economics of Suicide in Old Age," in Stuart F. Spicker and Stanley Ingman (eds.), *Ethical Dimensions of Geriatric Care,* Dordrecht: Reidel, 1987.

Becker, Ernest, *The Denial of Death,* New York: Free Press, 1973.

Belbin, E., and Belbin, R. M., *Problems in Adult Retraining,* London: Heinemann, 1972.

Belbin, R. M., *The Discovery Method: An International Experiment in Retraining,* Paris: OECD, 1969.

Bell, I. P., "The Double Standard: Age," in J. Freeman (ed.), *Women: A Feminist Perspective* (4th ed.), 1989, pp. 236-244.

Bell, W. G., Schmidt, W., and Miller, K., "Public Guardianship and the Elderly: Findings From a National Study," *The Gerontologist* (1981), 21(2): 194-202.

Bendix, Reinhard, and Lipset, Seymour Martin (eds.), *Class, Status and Power,* New York: Free Press, 1966.

Berkowitz, Edward D. (ed.), *Social Security After Fifty: Success and Failures,* New York: Greenwood, 1987.

Berman, Harry J., "To Flame With Wild Life: Florida Scott-Maxwell's Experience of Old Age," *The Gerontologist* (1986), 26: 321-324.

Bertaux, D. (ed.), *Biography and Society: The Life History Approach in the Social Sciences,* Beverly Hills, CA: Sage, 1981.

Bertman, Stephen (ed.), *The Conflict of Generations in Ancient Greece,* Atlantic Highlands, NJ: Humanities Press, 1976.

Best, Fred, "Work Sharing: Issues, Policy Options, and Prospects," Kalamazoo, MI: Upjohn Institute for Employment Research, 1981.

Bianchi, Eugene C., *Aging as a Spiritual Journey,* New York: Crossroads, 1982.

Binstock, Robert H., "Interest-Group Liberalism and the Politics of Aging," *The Gerontologist* (1972), 12: 265-280.

Binstock, Robert H., "The Aged as Scapegoat," *The Gerontologist* (1983), 23: 136-243.

Binstock, Robert H., "The Oldest-Old: A Fresh Perspective on Compassionate Ageism Revisited?" *Milbank Memorial Fund Quarterly* (1985), 63: 420-451.

Binstock, Robert H., "Old-Age-Based Rationing: From Rhetoric to Risk?" *Generations* (Winter 1994), 18(4): 37-41.

Birkhill, W. R., and Schaie, K. W., "The Effect of Differential Reinforcement of Cautiousness in Intellectual Performance Among the Elderly," *Journal of Gerontology* (1975), 30: 578-583.

Birren, James E., and Deutschman, Donna E., *Guiding Autobiography Groups for Older Adults: Exploring the Fabric of Life,* Baltimore: Johns Hopkins University Press, 1991.

Blau, Zena S., *Aging in a Changing Society,* New York: Franklin Watts, 1981.

Blau, Zena S. (ed.), *Work, Retirement and Social Policy,* Greenwich, CT: JAI, 1985.

Blazer, Dan G., "Spirituality and Aging Well," *Generations* (Winter 1991), 15(1): 61-65.

Blazer, Dan G., *Depression in Late Life* (2nd ed.), St. Louis, MO: C. V. Mosby, 1993.

Bloom, J., Ansell, P. and Bloom, M., "Detecting Elder Abuse: A Guide for Physicians," *Geriatrics* (1989), 44(6): 40-44.

Blumenthal, H. T. (ed.), *Handbook of Diseases of Aging,* New York: Van Nostrand, 1983.

Boaz, Rachel F., "Early Withdrawal From the Labor Force: A Response Only to Pension Pull or Also to Labor Market Push?" *Research on Aging* (1987), 9(4): 530-547.

Bodnar, A. G., Ouellete, M., Frolkis, M., et al., "Extension of Life-Span by Introduction of Telomerase Into Normal Human Cells," *Science* (1998), 279: 349-352.

Bolles, Richard N., *The Three Boxes of Life and How to Get Out of Them,* Berkeley, CA: Ten Speed, 1981.

Bonifazi, Wendy, "Who Pays for Long Term Care?" *Contemporary Long Term Care* (October 1998), 21(10): 76-78.

Bortner, R., "Notes on Expected Life-History," *International Journal of Aging and Human Development* (1979), 9: 291-294.

Boskin, Michael J., *Too Many Promises: The Uncertain Future of Social Security,* Homewood, IL: Dow Jones-Irwin, 1986.

Bosworth, Barry, and Burtless, Gary (eds.), *Aging Societies: The Global Dimension,* Washington, DC: Brookings Institution, 1998.

Botwinick, J., *Aging and Behavior,* New York: Springer, 1973.

Boyle, Joan, and Morriss, James, *The Mirror of Time: Images of Aging and Dying,* Westport, CT: Greenwood, 1987.

Braun, P., and Sweet, M., "Passages: Fact or Fiction?" *International Journal of Aging and Human Development* (1984), 18: 161-176.

Brennan, Penny L., and Steinberg, L. D., "Is Reminiscence Adaptive? Relations Among Social Activity Level, Reminiscence, and Morale," *International Journal of Aging and Human Development* (1983-1984), 18: 99-110.

Breytspraak, Linda M., *The Development of Self in Later Life,* Boston: Little, Brown, 1984.

Brickner, Philip W., et al., *Long-Term Health Care: Providing a Spectrum of Services to the Aged,* New York: Basic Books, 1987.

Brody, Elaine, "Parent Care as a Normative Family Stress," *The Gerontologist* (1985), 25: 19-29.

Brody, Elaine, *Women in the Middle: Their Parent-Care Years,* New York: Springer, 1990.

Brody, Jane E., "Hope Grows for Vigorous Old Age," *New York Times* (October 2, 1984).

Bronson, R. T., and Lipman, R. D., "Reduction in Rate of Occurrence of Age-Related Lesions in Dietary Restricted Laboratory Mice," *Growth, Development and Aging* (1991), 55: 169-184.

Brookings/ICF, "Long-Term Care Financing Model" (unpublished data). Washington, DC: Author, 1990.

Brooks, Jeffrey D., "Living Longer and Improving Health: An Obtainable Goal in Promoting Aging Well?" *American Behavioral Scientist* (January 1996), 39(3): 272-287.

Brown, Helen Gurley, *The Late Show,* New York: William Morrow, 1993.

Brown, L. D., "The National Politics of Oregon's Rationing Plan," *Health Affairs* (Summer 1991), 10: 28-51.

Brown, Randall S., et al., *The Medicare Risk Program for HMOs,* Princeton, NJ: Mathematica, 1993.

Brubaker, Timothy H., *Later Life Families,* Beverly Hills, CA: Sage, 1985.

Brubaker, Timothy H., *Aging, Health and Family: Long-Term Care,* Newbury Park, CA: Sage, 1987.

Buchanan, R. J., "Medicaid: Family Responsibility and Long Term Care," *Journal of Long Term Care Administration* (1984), 12(3): 19-25.

Buckley, William F., "Oversight Time," *National Review* (June 11, 1990).

Budish, Armond D., *Avoiding the Medicaid Trap: How to Beat the Catastrophic Cost of Nursing Home Care,* New York: Henry Holt, 1989.

Buonocore, A. J., "Older and Wiser: Mature Employees and Career Guidance," *Management Review* (September 1992), 81(9): 54-57.

Burbank, P. M., "Exploratory Study: Assessing the Meaning in Life Among Older Adult Clients," *Journal of Gerontological Nursing* (September 1992), 18(9): 19-28.

Burgess, E. W., *Aging in Western Societies,* Chicago: University of Chicago Press, 1960.

Burke, Gerald, "Changing Health Needs of the Elderly Demand New Policies," *Journal of American Health Policy* (1993), 3(5): 22-26.

Burrows, James, *The Ages of Man,* New York: Oxford University Press, 1986.

Burton, Linda (ed.), *Families and Aging,* Amityville, NY: Baywood, 1993.

Busse, Ewald W., and Blazer, Dan G. (eds.), *Handbook of Geriatric Psychiatry,* New York: Van Nostrand Reinhold, 1980.

Butler, Robert N., "The Life Review: An Interpretation of Reminiscence in the Aged," *Psychiatry* (1963), 26: 65-76.

Butler, Robert N., "Age-ism: Another Form of Bigotry," *The Gerontologist* (1969), 9: 243-246.

Butler, Robert N., "Successful Aging and the Role of the Life Review," *Journal of the American Geriatrics Society* (1974), 22: 529-535.

Butler, Robert N., "Strategies to Delay Dysfunction in Later Life," in J. L. C. Dall et al. (eds.), *Adaptations in Aging,* San Diego, CA: Academic Press, 1995, pp. 289-297.

Butler, Robert N., "Dangers of Physician-Assisted Suicide," *Geriatrics* (July 1996) 51(7): 14-15.

Butler, Robert N., and Gleason, Herbert P. (eds.), *Productive Aging: Enhancing Vitality in Later Life,* New York: Springer, 1985.

Butler, Robert N., and Kenzo, Kiikuni, *Who Is Responsible for My Old Age?* New York: Springer, 1992.

Butler, Robert N., and Lewis, Myrna I., *Aging and Mental Health* (3rd ed.), St. Louis, MO: C. V. Mosby, 1982.

Butler, Robert N., and Lewis, Myrna I., *Love and Sex After 60* (rev. ed.), New York: Ballantine, 1993.

Button, James W., "Sign of Generational Conflict: The Impact of Florida's Aging Voters on Local School and Tax Referenda," *Social Science Quarterly* (December 1992), 73(4): 786-797.

Byers, Bryan, and Hendricks, James, *Adult Protective Services: Research and Practice,* Springfield, IL: Charles C Thomas, 1993.

Callahan, Daniel, "What Do Children Owe Elderly Parents?" Hastings Center Report (April 1985), 15(2): 32-33.

Callahan, Daniel, *Setting Limits: Medical Goals in an Aging Society,* New York: Simon & Schuster, 1987.

Callahan, Daniel, "Setting Limits: A Response," *The Gerontologist* (June 1994), 34(3): 393-398.

Campbell, Colin D., *Controlling the Costs of Social Security,* Lexington, MA: Lexington, 1984.

Campbell, Rita R., *Social Security: Promise and Reality,* Stanford, CA: Hoover Institute, 1977.

Campione, Wendy A., "Predicting Participation in Retirement Preparation Programs," *Journal of Gerontology: Social Sciences* (1988), 43(3): 91-95.

Cantor, Marjorie H., "The Informal Support System: Its Relevance in the Lives of the Elderly," in Edgar F. Borgatta and Neil McCluskey (eds.), *Aging and Society: Current Research,* Beverly Hills, CA: Sage, 1980, pp. 131-144.

Cantor, Marjorie H., "Families and Caregiving in an Aging Society," *Generations* (Summer 1992), 67-70.

Capitman, J., "Case Management in Long-Term and Acute Medical Care," *Health Care Financing Review* (1988), Annual Supplement, 75-81.

Cassel, Christine, Rudberg, M., and Olshansky, J., "The Price of Success: Health Care in an Aging Society," *Health Affairs* (1992), 11(2): 87-99.

Chambre, Susan M., *Good Deeds in Old Age: Volunteering by the New Leisure Class,* New York: Free Press, 1987.

Chambre, Susan M., "Volunteerism by Elders: Past Trends and Future Prospects," *The Gerontologist* (April 1993), 33(2): 221-228.

Chellis, Robert D., Seagle, James F., and Seagle, Barbara M. (eds.), *Congregate Housing for Older People,* Lexington, MA: Lexington, 1982.

Cheung, M., "Elderly Chinese Living in the United States: Assimilation or Adjustment?" *Social Work* (1989), 14: 457-461.

Chinen, Allan B., *In the Ever After: Fairy Tales and the Second Half of Life,* Wilmette, IL: Chiron, 1989.

Choi, N. G., "Does Social Security Redistribute Income? A Tax-Transfer Analysis," *Journal of Sociology and Social Welfare* (1991), 18(3): 21-38.

Chu, Cyrus, "Age-Distribution Dynamics and Aging Indexes," *Demography* (November 1997), 34(4): 551-563.

Chudakoff, Howard P., *How Old Are You? Age Consciousness in American Culture,* Princeton, NJ: Princeton University Press, 1989.

Clark, Brian, *Whose Life Is It Anyway? A Play,* London: Samuel French, 1978.

Clark, Robert L., "The Future of Work and Retirement," *Research on Aging* (1988), 10(2): 169-193.

Clark, Robert L., and Barker, David T., *Reversing the Trend Toward Early Retirement,* Washington, DC: American Enterprise Institute, 1981.

Clark, Robert L., Maddox, G., Schrimper, R., and Sumner, D., *Inflation and the Economic Well-Being of the Elderly,* Baltimore: Johns Hopkins University Press, 1984.

Clark, William F., et al., *Old and Poor: A Critical Assessment of the Low Income Elderly,* Lexington, MA: Lexington, 1988.

Cnaan, R., and Cwikel, J. G., "Elderly Volunteers: Assessing Their Potential as an Untapped Resource," *Journal of Aging and Social Policy* (1992), 4: 125-147.

Cockerham, William C., *This Aging Society* (2nd ed.), Upper Saddle River, NJ: Prentice Hall, 1997.

Cohen, Marc A., Tell, Eileen, Greenberg, Jan N., and Wallack, Stanley S., "The Financial Capacity of the Elderly to Insure for Long-Term Care," *The Gerontologist* (1987), 27(5): 494-502.

Cole, Al, "High-Tech Anxiety," *Modern Maturity* (March-April 1996), 39(2): 14-16.

Cole, S., "Age and Scientific Performance," *American Journal of Sociology* (1979), 84: 958-977.

Cole, Thomas, *The Journey of Life: A Cultural History of Aging in America,* Cambridge, UK: Cambridge University Press, 1992.

Cole, Thomas, and Gadow, Sally (eds.), *What Does It Mean to Grow Old? Views From the Humanities,* Durham, NC: Duke University Press, 1986.

Coleman, P. G., "Measuring Reminiscence Characteristics From Conversation as Adaptive Features of Old Age," *International Journal of Aging and Human Development* (1974), 5: 281-294.

Coles, Robert, *The Old Ones of New Mexico,* Albuquerque: University of New Mexico Press, 1974.

Consumer Reports, "How Will You Pay for Your Old Age?" (October 1997), 62(10): 35-50.

Cook, Fay L., and Kramek, Lorraine M., "Measuring Economic Hardship Among Older Americans," *The Gerontologist* (1986), 26: 38-47.

Corbin, J. M., and Strauss, A., *Unending Care and Work: Managing Chronic Illness at Home,* San Francisco: Jossey-Bass, 1988.

Cornelius, S. W., and Caspi, A., "Everyday Problem Solving in Adulthood and Old Age," *Psychology and Aging* (1987), 2: 14-153.

Cornelius, Steven W., "Aging and Everyday Cognitive Abilities," in Thomas Hess (ed.), *Aging and Cognition: Knowledge Organization and Utilization (Advances in Psychology,* No. 71), Amsterdam: North Holland, 1990, pp. 411-459.

Costa, Paul T., Jr., and McCrae, Robert R., "Still Stable After All These Years: Personality as a Year to Some Issues in Aging," in Paul B. Baltes and O. G. Brim (eds.), *Life-Span Development and Behavior* (Vol. 3), New York: Academic Press, 1980, pp. 65-102.

Costa, Paul T., Jr., Metter, M., and McCrae, Robert R., "Personality Stability and its Contribution to Successful Aging," *Journal of Geriatric Psychiatry* (1994), 27(1): 41-59.

Couzin, J., "Low-Calorie Diets May Slow Monkey's Aging," *Science* (1998), 282: 1018.

Covey, H. C., "Perceptions and Attitudes Toward Sexuality of the Elderly During the Middle Ages," *The Gerontologist* (February 1989), 29(1): 93-100.

Cowgill, Donald O., *Aging Around the World,* Belmont, CA: Wadsworth, 1986.

Cowgill, Donald O., and Holmes, Lowell, *Aging and Modernization,* New York: Appleton-Century-Crofts, 1972.

Cowley, Malcolm, *The View From 80,* New York: Viking, 1980.

Coyle, Jean M. (ed.), *Handbook on Women and Aging,* Westport, CT: Greenwood, 1997.

Crew, Mark D., "Immune Cells," in George L. Maddox (ed.), *The Encyclopedia of Aging,* New York: Springer, 1995, pp. 494-496.

Crimmins, Eileen M., and Ingegneri, Dominique G., "Trends in Health Among the American Population," in Anna M. Rappaport and Sylvester J. Schieber (eds.), *Demography and Retirement: The Twenty-First Century,* Westport, CT: Praeger, 1993, pp. 225-253.

Crown, William H., "Some Thoughts on Reformulating the Dependency Ratio," *The Gerontologist* (1985), 25: 166-171.

Cruzan v. Director of Missouri Department of Health, 497 U.S. 261, 110 S. Ct. 2841 (1990).

Crystal, Stephen, *America's Old Age Crisis: Public Policy and the Two Worlds of Aging,* New York: Basic Books, 1982.

Crystal, Stephen, "Measuring Income and Inequality Among the Elderly," *The Gerontologist* (1986), 26: 56-59.

Crystal, Stephen, "Elder Abuse: The Latest Crisis," *The Public Interest* (1987), 88: 56-66.

Crystal, Stephen, and Shea, Dennis, "Cumulative Advantage, Cumulative Disadvantage, and Inequality Among Elderly People," *The Gerontologist* (1990), 30: 437-443.

Crystal, Stephen, Shea, Dennis, and Krishnaswami, Shreeram, "Educational Attainment, Occupational History, and Stratification: Determinants of Later-Life Economic Outcomes," *Journal of Gerontology* (September 1992), 47: S213-S221.

Cumming, Elaine, and Henry, William E., *Growing Old: The Process of Disengagement,* New York: Basic Books, 1961.

Cunningham, Walter R., and Torner, Adrian, "Intellectual Abilities and Age: Concepts, Theories and Analyses," in Eugene A. Lovelace (ed.), *Aging and Cognition: Mental Processes, Self-Awareness, and Interventions* (Advances in Psychology, No. 72), Amsterdam: North-Holland, 1990, pp. 379-406.

Cutler, Neal, "Political Characteristics of Elderly Cohorts in the Twenty First Century," in S. B. Kiesler (ed.), *Aging and Social Change,* New York: Academic Press, 1981.

Cutler, Neal, Gregg, Davis W., and Lawton, M. Powell, *Aging, Money, and Life Satisfaction: Aspects of Financial Gerontology,* New York: Springer, 1992.

Cutler, Richard, "Species Probes, Longevity and Aging," in *Intervention in the Aging Process* (Part B), New York: Alan Liss, 1983.

Czaja, Sara J., and Barr, Robin, "Technology and the Everyday Life of Older Adults," *Annals of the American Academy of Political and Social Science* (May 1989), 503: 127-137.

Czaja, Sara J., Guerrier, J. H., Nair, S. N., Landauer, T. K., "Computer Communication as an Aid to Independence for Older Adults," *Behaviour and Information Technology* (July-August 1993), 12(4): 197-207.

Daniels, Norman, *Am I My Parents' Keeper? An Essay on Justice Between the Young and the Old,* New York: Oxford University Press, 1988.

Dannefer, Dale, "Adult Development and Social Theory: A Paradigmatic Reappraisal," *American Sociological Review* (1984), 49: 100-116.

Davies, D. R., and Sparrow, P. R., "Age and Work Behaviour," in N. Charness (ed.), *Aging and Human Performance,* Chichester, UK: Wiley, 1985.

Davis, Richard, and Davis, Jim, *TV's Image of the Elderly,* Lexington, MA: Lexington, 1985.

Davis, T. J., "Seniors Reach Out to Troubled Youth," *Secure Retirement* (November-December 1992), 1(5): 30-31.

Davis, T. J., "Investment Scam Line," *Secure Retirement* (September 1993), 2(6): 34-36.

Day, Christine, *What Older Americans Think: Interest Groups and Aging Policy,* Princeton, NJ: Princeton University Press, 1990.

DeBerry, S., Davis, S., and Reinhard, K. E., "Comparison of Meditation- Relaxation and Cognitive/Behavioral Techniques for Reducing Anxiety and Depression in a Geriatric Population," *Journal of Geriatric Psychiatry* (1989), 22(2): 231-247.

Deikman, Arthur J., "De-automization and the Mystic Experience," *Psychiatry* (1966), 29: 324-338. Reprinted in Charles Tart (ed.) *Altered States of Consciousness* (3rd ed.), San Francisco: Harper, 1990.

Dellman-Jenkins, M., "Old and Young Together: Effect of Educational Programs on Preschoolers," *Childhood Education* (1986), 62: 206-208.

Dennis, Helen, *Fourteen Steps in Managing an Aging Work Force,* Lexington, MA: Lexington, 1988.

Dennis, Helen, "The Current State of Preretirement Planning," *Generations* (1989), 13(2): 38-41.

Dennis, W., "Creative Productivity Between the Ages of 20 and 80 Years," *Journal of Gerontology* (1966), 21: 1-8.

Diamond, Arthur M., Jr., "The Life-Cycle Research Productivity of Mathematicians and Scientists," *Journal of Gerontology* (1986), 41: 520-525.

Dill, Ann E. P., et al., "Coercive Placement of Elders: Protection or Choices," *Generations* (1987), 11(4): 48-66.

Dilworth-Anderson, Peggye, "Extended Kin Networks in Black Families," *Generations* (Summer 1992), 16: 29-32.

Dobris, Joel C., "Medicaid Asset Planning by the Elderly: A Policy View of Expectations, Entitlements, and Inheritance," *Real Property, Probate and Trust Journal* (Spring 1989), 24(1): 1-32.

Dobrosky, B., and Bishop, J., "Children's Perceptions of Old People," *Educational Gerontology* (1986), 12: 429-439.

Doering, Mildred, Rhodes, Susan R., and Schuster, Michael, *The Aging Worker: Research and Recommendations,* Beverly Hills, CA: Sage, 1983.

Doka, Kenneth J., "When Gray Is Golden: Business in an Aging America," *Futurist* (July-August 1992), 26(4): 16-20.

Dowd, James J., "Aging as Exchange: A Preface to Theory," *Journal of Gerontology* (1975), 30: 584-594.

Dowd, James J., *Stratification Among the Aged,* Monterey, CA: Brooks/Cole, 1980.

Dowd, James J., "Beneficence and the Aged," *Journal of Gerontology* (1984), 39(1): 102-108.

Dowd, James J., and Bengtson, Vern L., "Aging in a Minority Population: An Examination of the Double Jeopardy Hypothesis," *Journal of Gerontology* (1978), 33: 427-436.

Dressel, Paula L., "Gender, Race, and Class: Beyond the Feminization of Poverty in Later Life," *The Gerontologist* (1988), 28(2): 177-180.

Duke University, Center for the Study of Aging and Human Development, *Multidimensional Functional Assessment: The OARS Methodology* (2nd ed.), Durham, NC: Author, 1978.

Duncan, G., "The Volatility of Family Income Over the Life Course," in Paul B. Baltes, David L. Featherman, and Richard M. Lerner (eds.), *Life-Span Development and Behavior* (Vol. 9), Hillsdale, NJ: Lawrence Erlbaum, 1988, pp. 337-358.

Durkheim, Émile, *Suicide* (trans. J. A. Spaulding and G. Simpson), Glencoe, IL: Free Press, [1897] 1951.

Dworaczek, Marian, and Wong, Helen, *Early Retirement: A Bibliography,* Monticello, IL: Vance Bibliographies, 1989.

Eisele, F. R., "Origins of Gerontocracy," *The Gerontologist* (1979), 19: 4.

Eisenstadt, S. N., *From Generation to Generation: Age Groups and Social Structure,* New York: Free Press, 1956.

Ekerdt, David J., "Why the Notion Persists That Retirement Harms Health," *The Gerontologist* (1987), 27(4): 454-457.

Elder, Glen H., *Children of the Great Depression,* Chicago: University of Chicago Press, 1974.

Ellis, R. Darin, et al., "Gero-informatics and the Internet: Locating Gerontology Information on the World Wide Web (WWW)," *The Gerontologist* (1996), 36(1): 100-105.

Ellison, C. G., "Religion, the Life Stress Paradigm, and the Study of Depression," in J. S. Levin (ed.), *Religion in Aging and Health: Theoretical Foundations and Methodological Frontiers,* Thousand Oaks, CA: Sage, 1994, pp. 78-121.

Erikson, Erik, *Childhood and Society,* New York: Macmillan, 1963.

Estabrook, Madeleine A., "False Economies: Downsizing as Cure Costs Valuable Older Workers," *Pension World* (May 1993), 29(5): 10-12.

Estes, Carroll, *The Aging Enterprise,* San Francisco: Jossey-Bass, 1979.

Estes, Carroll, "Aging, Health, and Social Policy: Crisis and Crossroads," *Journal of Aging and Social Policy* (1989), 1(1-2): 17-32.

Eustis, N., Grenberg, J., and Patten, S., *Long-Term Care for Older Persons: A Policy Perspective,* Monterey, CA: Brooks/Cole, 1984.

Evans, John Grimley, "Health Care Rationing and Elderly People," in Michael Tunbridge (ed.), *Rationing of Health Care in Medicine,* London: Royal College of Physicians, 1993, pp. 43-53.

Falkner, Thomas, and de Luce, Judith, "A View From Antiquity," in Thomas Cole, David Van Tassel, and Robert Kastenbaum (eds.), *Handbook of the Humanities and Aging,* New York: Springer, 1992.

Fama, T., and Kennell, D. L., "Should We Worry About Induced Demand for Long-Term Care Services?" *Generations* (Spring 1990): 37-41.

Family Caregiver Alliance, *Caregiver Resource Center System Annual Report, Fiscal Year 1997-98.* San Francisco: Author, 1999.

Featherstone, Mike, and Hepworth, Mike, "Images of Ageing," in Bond, John, Coleman, Peter, and Peace, Sheila (eds.), *Ageing in Society: An Introduction to Social Gerontology,* Newbury Park, CA: Sage, 1993, pp. 304-332.

Featherstone, Mike, and Wernick, Andrew (eds.), *Images of Aging: Cultural Representations of Later Life,* New York: Routledge, 1995.

Feder, Judith, *Medicare: The Politics of Federal Hospital Insurance,* Lexington, MA: D. C. Heath, 1977.

Fengler, A. P., "Life Satisfaction of Sub-populations of Elderly: The Comparative Effects of Volunteerism, Employment, and Meal Site Preparation," *Research on Aging* (1984), 6: 208.

Ferrara, Peter J. (ed.), *Social Security: Prospects for Real Reform,* Washington, DC: Cato Institute, 1985.

Ferraro, K. F., and LaGrange, R. L., "Are Older People Most Afraid of Crime? Reconsidering Age Differences in Fear of Victimization," *Journals of Gerontology* (1992), 47(5): S233-S244.

Filene, Peter G., *In the Arms of Others: A Cultural History of the Right-to-Die in America,* Chicago: Ivan R. Dee, 1998.

Finch, C. E., *Longevity, Senescence and the Genome,* University of Chicago Press, 1990.

Firman, J., Gelfand, D., and Ventura, C., "Students as Resources to the Aging Network," *The Gerontologist* (1983), 23(2): 185-191.

Fischer, David Hackett, *Growing Old in America,* New York: Oxford University Press, 1977.

Fisher, Christy, "Coming Home to Assisted Living: Desire for Homelike Care Drives Growth," *Provider* (October 1995), 21(1): 57-60.

Fix, Janet L., "Wealth in New Hands," *Foundation News* (January-February 1994), 35(1): 18-23.

Folstein, M. F., Folstein, S. E., and McHugh, P. R., " 'Mini-Mental State': A Practical Method for Grading the Cognitive State of Patients for the Clinician," *Journal of Psychiatric Research* (1975), 12: 189-198.

Folts, W. Edward, and Streib, Gordon F., "Leisure-Oriented Retirement Communities," in W. Edward Folts and Dale E. Yeatts (eds.), *Housing and the Aging Population: Options for the New Century,* New York: Garland, 1994, pp. 121-144.

Foner, Nancy, *Ages in Conflict: A Cross-Cultural Perspective on Inequality Between Old and Young,* New York: Columbia University Press, 1984.

Fossel, Michael, *Reversing Human Aging,* New York: William Morrow, 1996.

Fowler, James W., *Stages of Faith: The Psychology of Human Development and the Quest for Meaning,* New York: Harper & Row, 1981.

Freedman, Robert M., et al., "Why Won't Medicaid Let Me Keep My Nest Egg?" (case study), *Hastings Center Report* (April 1983), 13(2): 23-25.

Freeman, Scott M., Whartenby, Katharine, and Abraham, George N., "Gene Therapy: Applications to Diseases Associated With Aging," *Generations* (1992), 16: 45-48.

Friedland, Robert, and Summer, Laura, *Demography Is Not Destiny,* Washington, DC: National Academy on an Aging Society, 1999.

Fries, James F., "Aging, Illness, and Health Policy: Implications of the Compression of Morbidity," *Perspectives in Biology and Medicine* (Spring 1988), 31:3.

Fuchs, Victor R., "Health Care for the Elderly: How Much? Who Will Pay for It?" *Health Affairs* (January-February 1999), 18(1): 11-21.

Fujii, Sharon, "Older Asian Americans: Victims of Multiple Jeopardy," *Civil Rights Digest* (1976), 9: 22-29.

Furlong, Mary S., and Lipson, Stefan B., *Young@heart: Computing for Seniors,* Berkeley, CA: Osborne McGraw-Hill, 1996.

Gale, W. G., and Scholz, J. K., "Intergenerational Transfers and the Accumulation of Wealth," *Journal of Economic Perspectives* (Fall 1994), 8(4): 145-160.

Gambria, L. M., "Daydreaming About the Past: The Time Setting of Spontaneous Thought Intrusions," *The Gerontologist* (1977), 17: 35-38.

Gamzon, Mel, "Senior Housing Comes of Age," *Contemporary Long Term Care* (June 1995), 18(6): 46-51.

Garber, Alan M., MaCurdy, Thomas, and McClellan, Mark, "Diagnosis and Medicare Expenditures at the End of Life," in David A. Wise (ed)., *Frontiers in the Economics of Aging,* Chicago: University of Chicago Press, 1998, pp. 247-274.

Gardner, Howard, *Frames of Mind: The Theory of Multiple Intelligences,* New York: Basic Books, 1985.

Garfein, A. J., Schaie, K. W., Willis, S. L., "Microcomputer Proficiency in Later-Middle-Aged and Older Adults: Teaching Old Dogs New Tricks," *Social Behavior* (1988), 3: 131-148.

Garrett, W. W., "Filial Responsibility Laws," *Journal of Family Law* (1980), 18: 793-818.

Gee, E. M., "Historical Change in the Family Life Course of Canadian Men and Women," in V. Marshall (ed.), *Aging in Canada* (2nd ed.), Markham, ON: Fitzhenry & Whiteside, 1987, pp. 265-287.

Gelfand, Donald, *Aging and Ethnicity: Knowledge and Services,* New York: Springer, 1994.

Gelfand, Donald, *The Aging Network: Programs and Services* (5th ed.), New York: Springer, 1999.

Gendell, Murray, "Trends in Retirement Age in Four Countries, 1965-95," *Monthly Labor Review* (August 1998), 121(8): 20-30.

George, Linda K., *Role Transitions in Later Life: A Social Stress Perspective,* Monterey, CA: Brooks/Cole, 1980.

George, Linda K., "Depressive Disorders and Symptoms in Later Life," *Generations* (Winter-Spring 1993), 17(1): 35-38.

Gibson, Rose C., "Reconceptualizing Retirement for Black Americans," *The Gerontologist* (1987), 27: 691-698.

Gibson, Rose C., "Work Patterns of Older Black and White and Male and Female Heads of Household," *Journal of Minority Aging* (1983), 8(1-2): 1-16.

Ginzberg, E., Balinsky, W., and Ostow, M., *Home Health Care,* Totowa, NJ: Rowman & Allanheld, 1984.

Giordano, J. A., and Giordano, N. H., "A Classification of Preretirement Programs: In Search of a New Model," *Educational Gerontology* (1983), 9: 123-137.

Gist, Yvonne, and Velkoff, Victoria, *Gender and Aging: Demographic Dimensions,* Washington, DC: U.S. Department of Commerce, Bureau of the Census, 1997.

Glaser, B. G., and Strauss, A. L., *Awareness of Dying,* Chicago: Aldine, 1965.

Glenn, N. D., and Hefner, T., "Further Evidence on Aging and Party Identification," *Public Opinion Quarterly* (1972), 36: 31-47.

Glick, Henry, *The Right to Die,* New York: Columbia University Press, 1992.

Glick, Paul C., "Updating the Life Cycle of the Family," *Journal of Marriage and the Family* (1977), 39: 5-13.

Gober, P., and Zonn, L., "Kin and Elderly Amenity Migration," *The Gerontologist* (June 1983), 23(3): 288-294.

Goffman, Erving, *Asylums,* Garden City, NY: Anchor, 1961.

Goleman, Daniel, *The Meditative Mind: The Varieties of Meditative Experience,* Los Angeles: Jeremy Tarcher, 1988.

Gomez, Carlos F., *Regulating Death: Euthanasia and the Case of the Netherlands,* New York: Free Press, 1991.

Gordon, Michael, Mitchell, Olivia, and Twinney, Marc (eds.), *Positioning Pensions for the Twenty-First Century,* Philadelphia: University of Pennsylvania, 1997.

Gorelick, P. B., "Stroke Prevention: An Opportunity for Efficient Utilization of Health Care Resources During the Coming Decade," *Stroke* (1994), 25: 220-224.

Grace Plaza of Great Neck, Inc. v. Elbaum, 623 N.E.2d, 513 (1993).

Graebner, William, *A History of Retirement: The Meaning and Function of an American Institution,* New Haven, CT: Yale University Press, 1980.

Granick, S., and Friedman, A. S., "Educational Experience and the Maintenance of Intellectual Functioning by the Aged: An Overview," in Lissy F. Jarvik, Carl Eisdorfer, and J. E. Blum (eds.), *Intellectual Functioning in Adults,* New York: Springer, 1973.

Gratton, Brian, "Familism Among the Black and Mexican-American Elderly: Myth or Reality?" *Journal of Aging Studies* (1987), 1(1): 19-32.

Gray, C. H. (ed.), *The Cyborg Handbook,* New York: Routledge, 1995.

Gresham, G. E., and Labi, M. L. C., "Functional Assessment Instruments Currently Available for Documenting Outcomes in Rehabilitation Medicine," in C. V. Granger and G. E. Greer (eds.), *Functional Assessment in Rehabilitation Medicine,* Baltimore: Williams and Wilkins, 1984.

Grijalva v. Shalala, 152 F.3d, 1115 (9th Cir. 1998).

Gruman, Gerald, "Modernization of the Life Cycle," in S. Spicker, K. Woodward, and D. Van Tassel (eds.), *Aging and the Elderly: Humanistic Perspectives on Gerontology,* Atlantic Highlands, NJ: Humanities Press, 1978, pp. 359-387.

Gubrium, Jaber F., *Living and Dying at Murray Manor,* New York: St. Martin's, 1975.

Gubrium, Jaber F., and Buckholdt, D. R., *Toward Maturity: The Social Processing of Human Development,* San Francisco: Jossey-Bass, 1977.

Gubrium, Jaber F., and Lynott, R. J., "Rethinking Life Satisfaction," *Human Organization* (1983), 42: 30-38.

Guttchen, David, and Pettigrew, Mary, "LTC Insurance: The Missing Link in Retirement Planning," *Employee Benefit Plan Review* (November 1998), 53(5): 38-40.

Haber, Carole, *Beyond Sixty-Five,* Cambridge, UK: Cambridge University Press, 1983.

Haber, David, *Health Promotion and Aging* (2nd ed.), New York: Springer, 1999.

Haber, E., and Short-DeGraff, M., "Intergenerational Programming for an Increasingly Age Segregated Society," *Activities, Adaptation, and Aging* (1990), 14(3): 35-49.

Haight, Barbara K., "Reminiscing: The State of the Art as a Basis for Practice," *International Journal of Aging and Human Development* (1991), 33(1): 1-32.

Halper, Thomas, *The Misfortunes of Other: End-Stage Renal Disease in the United Kingdom,* New York: Cambridge University Press, 1989.

Hamburg, David, *Today's Children: Creating a Future for a Generation in Crisis,* New York: Random House, 1992.

Harel, Z., Ehrlich, P., and Hubbard, R., *The Vulnerable Elderly: People, Services, and Policies,* New York: Springer, 1990.

Hareven, Tamara, and Adams, Kathleen (eds.), *Aging and Life Course Transitions,* New York: Guilford, 1982.

Harmon, Charles (ed.), *Using the Internet, Online Services, and CD-ROMs for Writing Research and Term Papers,* New York: Neal-Schuman, 1996.

Harrison, Harry, *Make Room! Make Room!* New York: Spectra, 1994.

Harrison, Stephen, and Hunter, David J., *Rationing Health Care,* London: Institute for Public Policy Research, 1994.

Hastings Center, *Guidelines on the Termination of Life-Sustaining Treatment and the Care of the Dying,* Bloomington: Indiana University Press, 1988.

Havighurst, Robert J., Neugarten, Bernice L., and Tobin, Sheldon S., "Disengagement and Patterns of Aging," in Bernice L. Neugarten (ed.), *Middle Age and Aging,* Chicago: University of Chicago Press, 1968, pp. 161-172.

Hayes-Bautista, David E., "Young Latinos, Older Anglos, and Public Policy: Lessons From California," *Generations* (Fall-Winter 1991), 15(4): 37-40.

Hayflick, Leonard, "The Limited in Vitro Lifetime of Human Diploid Cell Strains," *Experimental Cell Research* (1965), 37(3): 614-636.

Hays, Judith A., "Aging and Family Resources: Availability and Proximity of Kin," *The Gerontologist* (1984), 24: 149-153.

Heclo, H., "Generational Politics," in J. L. Palmer, T. Smeeding, and B. B. Torrey (eds.), *The Vulnerable,* Washington, DC: Urban Institute, 1988, pp. 381-442.

Heidrick, Margaret L., "Autoimmunity," in George L. Maddox (ed.), *The Encyclopedia of Aging,* New York: Springer, 1995, pp. 99-100.

Held, T., "Institutionalization and De-institutionalization of the Life Course," *Human Development* (1986), 29: 157-162.

Hellman, S., and Hellman, L. H., *Medicare and Medigap: A Guide to Retirement Health Insurance,* Newbury Park, CA: Sage, 1991.

Helson, R., Mitchell, V., and Moane, G., "Personality and Patterns of Adherence and Non-adherence to the Social Clock," *Journal of Personality and Social Psychology* (1984), 46: 1079-1096.

Hendricks, J., and Cutler, S. J., "Leisure and the Structure of Our Life Worlds," *Ageing and Society* (March 1990) 10: 85-94.

Hendricks, J., and Peters, C. B., "The Times of Our Lives: An Integrative Framework," *American Behavioral Scientist* (1986), 29(5): 662-676.

Henretta, J. C., and Campbell, R. T., "Status Attainment and Status Maintenance: A Study of Stratification in Old Age," *American Sociological Review* (1976), 41: 981-992.

Herzog, Regula A., Kahn, Robert L., Moergan, James N., Jackson, James S., and Antonucci, Toni C., "Age Differences in Productive Activities," *Journal of Gerontology: Social Sciences* (1989), 44: S129-S138.

Hess, Clinton, and Kerschner, P., *Silver Lobby,* Los Angeles: University of Southern California Press, 1978.

High, Dallas, "Why Are Elderly People Not Using Advance Directives?" *Journal of Aging and Health* (November 1993), 5(4): 497-515.

Hochschild, Arlie R., "Disengagement Theory: A Critique and Proposal," *American Sociological Review* (1975), 40: 553-569.

Hogan, D. P., and Astone, N. M., "The Transition to Adulthood," *Annual Review of Sociology* (1986), 12: 109-130.

Holden, K. C., Burkhauser, R. V., and Myers, Daniel A., "Income Transitions at Older Stages of Life: The Dynamics of Poverty," *The Gerontologist* (1986), 26: 292-297.

Holmes, Ellen, and Holmes, Lowell, *Other Cultures, Elder Years* (2nd ed.), Thousand Oaks, CA: Sage, 1995..

Holmes, T. H., and Rahe, R. H., "The Social Readjustment Rating Scale," *Journal of Psychosomatic Research* (1967), 11: 213-218.

Holstein, James A., "Discourse of Age in Involuntary Commitment Proceedings," *Journal of Aging Studies* (1990), 4(2): 111-130.

Holstein, Martha, "Productive Aging: A Feminist Critique," *Journal of Aging and Social Policy* (1992), 4(3-4): 17-34.

Holtzman, Abraham, *The Townsend Movement,* New York: Bookman Associates, 1963.

Honig, Marjorie, and Reimers, Cordelia, "Is It Worth Eliminating the Retirement Test?" *American Economic Review* (May 1989), 79: 103-107.

Horn, J. L., "The Theory of Fluid and Crystallized Intelligence in Relation to Concepts of Cognitive Psychology and Aging in Adulthood," in F. I. M. Craik and S. Trehub (eds.), *Aging and Cognitive Processes,* New York: Plenum, 1982, pp. 237-278.

Horn, J. L., and Donaldson, G., "Faith Is Not Enough: A Response to the Baltes-Schaie Claim That Intelligence Does Not Wane," *American Psychologist* (1977), 32: 369-373.

Hudson, Robert, "The 'Graying' of the Federal Budget and Its Consequences for Old-Age Policy," *The Gerontologist* (1978), 28: 428-440.

Hudson, Robert, "Tomorrow's Able Elders: Implications for the State," *The Gerontologist* (1987), 27(4): 405-409.

Humphry, Derek, *Final Exit: The Practicalities of Self-Deliverance and Assisted Suicide for the Dying,* Eugene, OR: Hemlock Society/Dell, 1992.

Hunnicutt, Benjamin K., "Aging and Leisure Politics," in Michael L. Teague, Richard D. MacNeil, and Gerald L. Hitzhusen (eds.), *Perspectives on Leisure and Aging in a Changing Society,* Columbia: University of Missouri Press, 1982, pp. 74-108.

Hunt, Michael E., et al. (eds.), *Retirement Communities: An American Original,* New York: Haworth, 1983.

Hunt, Michael E., Merrill, J. L., and Gilker, C. M., "Naturally Occurring Retirement Communities in Urban and Rural Settings," in W. Edward Folts and Dale E. Yeatts (eds.), *Housing and the Aging Population: Options for the New Century,* New York: Garland, 1994, pp. 107-120.

Ingram, D. K., et al., "Dietary Restriction and Aging: The Initiation of a Primate Study," *Journal of Gerontology* (1990), 45(5): B148-B163.

Inlander, C. B., and MacKay, C. K., *Medicare Made Easy* (rev. ed.), Reading, MA: Addison-Wesley, 1991.

In re Conroy, 98 N.J. 321 A.2d (1985).

In re Earle Spring 380 Mass. 629 (1980).

In re Guardianship of Estelle M. Browning, State of Florida v. Doris F. Herbert, 568 So.2d 4 (Fla. 1990).

In re Quackenbush, 156 N.J. 282, 353 A.2d 785 (1978).

In re Quinlan, 70 N.J. 10, 355 A.2d 647 (1976).

Isenberg, Sheldon, "Aging in Judaism: 'Crown of Glory' and 'Days of Sorrow,' " in Thomas Cole, David Van Tassel, and Robert Kastenbaum (eds.), *Handbook of the Humanities and Aging,* New York: Springer, 1992.

Iso, A. S. E., Jackson, E. L., and Dunn, E., "Starting, Ceasing, and Replacing Leisure Activities Over the Life-Span," *Journal of Leisure Research* (1994), 26(3): 227-249.

Jackson, J. S. (ed.), *The Black American Elderly,* New York: Springer, 1988.

Jacobs, Bruce, *Targeting Benefits for the Elderly: The Public Debate,* New York: Ford Foundation, 1990.

Jacobs, Ruth H., and Hess, Beth B., "Panther Power: Symbol and Substance," *Long Term Care and Health Services Administration Quarterly* (Fall 1978): 238-244.

Jacobson, Solomon G., "Equity in the Use of Public Benefits by Minority Elderly," in Ron C. Manuel (ed.), *Minority Aging: Sociological and Social Psychological Issues,* Westport, CT: Greenwood, 1982, pp. 161-170.

Jacques, Elliot, "Death and Midlife Crisis," *International Journal of Psychoanalysis* (1965), 46: 502-514.

James, D., Gibson, F., McAuley, G., and McAuley, J. "Adding New Life to Elders' Lives," *Ageing International* (March 1995), 22(1): 34-35.

Jerrome, Dorothy, " 'That's What It's All About': Old People's Organizations as a Context for Aging," in J. Gubrium and K. Charmaz (Eds.), *Aging, Self, and Community,* Greenwich, CT: JAI, 1992, pp. 225-235.

John, Randy A., *Social Integration of an Elderly Native American Population,* New York: Garland, 1995.

Johnson, Barbara B., "The Changing Role of Women and Social Security Reform," *Social Work* (1987), 32(4): 341-345.

Johnson, Colleen L., and Grant, Leslie A., *The Nursing Home in American Society,* Baltimore: Johns Hopkins University Press, 1986.

Johnson, Sandy, *Book of Elders: The Life Stories of Great American Indians,* San Francisco: Harper, 1994.

Johnson, T. E., "Increased Life-Span of Age-1 Mutants in Caenorhabditis Elegans and Lower Gompertz Rate of Aging," *Science* (1990), 249: 908.

Jones, Ian R., and Higgs, Paul, "Health Economists and Health Care Provision for the Elderly: Implicit Assumptions and Unstated Conclusions," in Kevin Morgan (ed.), *Gerontology: Responding to an Ageing Society,* London: J. Kingsley, 1992, pp. 118-135

Kahne, H., "Women and Social Security: Social Policy Adjusts to Social Change," *International Journal of Aging and Human Development* (1981), 13(3): 195-208.

Kaiser, Fran, Morley, John, and Coe, Rodney, *Cardiovascular Disease in Older People,* New York: Springer, 1997.

Kalish, Richard A., "The New Ageism and the Failure Models: A Polemic," *The Gerontologist* (1979), 19: 398-402.

Kane, Robert L., and Kane, Rosalie A., *A Will and a Way: What the U.S. Can Learn From Canada About Caring for the Elderly,* New York: Columbia University Press, 1985.

Kane, Rosalie A. (ed.), "Legacy" (special issue), *Generations* (1996), 20:3.

Kane, Rosalie A., and Kane, Robert L., *Assessing the Elderly: A Practical Guide to Measurement,* Lexington, MA: D. C. Heath, 1981.

Kane, Rosalie A., and Kane, Robert L., *Long-Term Care: Principles, Programs and Policies,* New York: Springer, 1987.

Kao, Rudolf Sing Kee, and Lam, Mary Leong, "Asian American Elderly" in Evelyn Lee (ed.), *Working With Asian Americans: A Guide for Clinicians,* New York: Guilford, 1997, pp. 208-223.

Kaplan, George, "Epidemiologic Observations on the Compression of Morbidity: Evidence From the Alameda County Study," *Journal of Aging and Health* (May 1991), 3(2): 155-171.

Kaplan, Max, *Leisure: Lifestyle and Lifespan,* Philadelphia: W. B. Saunders, 1979.

Kassner, Enid, "The Older Americans Act: Should Participants Share in the Cost of Services?" *Journal of Aging and Social Policy* (1992), 4(1-2): 51-71.

Kastenbaum, Robert, "Time Course and Time Perspective in Later Life," in C. Eisdorfer (ed.), *Annual Review of Gerontology and Geriatrics* (Vol. 3), New York: Springer, 1983, pp. 80-102.

Kastenbaum, Robert, "When Aging Begins: A Lifespan Developmental Approach," *Research on Aging* (March 1984), 6(1): 105-117.

Kastenbaum, Robert, and Candy, S. E., "The Four Percent Fallacy: A Methodological and Empirical Critique of Extended Care Facility Population Statistics," *International Journal of Aging and Human Development* (1973), 4: 15-21.

Katz, S., and Akpom, C. A., "A Measure of Primary Socio-biological Functions," *International Journal of Health Services* (1976), 6: 493-507.

Katz, S., et al., "Studies of Illness in the Aged: The Index of ADL: A Standardized Measure of Biological and Psychosocial Function," *Journal of the American Medical Association* (1963), 185: 914-919.

Kaufman, Sharon R., *The Ageless Self: Sources of Meaning in Later Life,* Madison: University of Wisconsin Press, 1986.

Kay, M. M. B., and Makinodan, T. (eds.), *Handbook of Immunology in Aging,* Boca Raton, FL: CRC Press, 1981.

Kaye, Richard, "Sexuality in the Later Years," *Aging and Society* (September 1993), 13(Pt. 3): 415-426.

Kearl, Michael C., "Dying Well: The Unspoken Dimension of Aging Well," *American Behavioral Scientist* (January 1996), 39(3): 336-360.

Kieffer, Jarold A., *Gaining the Dividends of Longer Life: New Roles for Older Workers,* Boulder, CO: Westview, 1983.

Kim, K. C., Kim, S., and Hurh, W. M., "Filial Piety and Intergenerational Relationship in Korean Immigrant Families," *International Journal of Aging and Human Development* (1991), 33: 233-245.

King, Nancy M. P., *Making Sense of Advance Directives,* Washington, DC: Georgetown University Press, 1996.

Kingson, E. R., and O'Grady, LeShane R., "Effects of Caregiving on Women's Social Security Benefits," *The Gerontologist* (April 1993), 33(2): 230-239.

Kleemeier, Robert W. (ed.), *Aging and Leisure,* New York: Columbia University Press, 1961.

Kleiler, Frank M., *Can We Afford Early Retirement?* Baltimore: Johns Hopkins University Press, 1978.

Klein, S. M., *In-Home Respite Care for Older Adults: A Guide for Program Planners, Administrators and Clinicians,* Springfield, IL: Charles C Thomas, 1986.

Koch, Susan, *Realizing the Benefits of New Computer and Telecommunication Technologies for Older Americans,* Washington, DC: National Association of Area Agencies on Aging, 1992.

Koenig, Harold G., *Aging and God: Spiritual Pathways to Mental Health in Midlife and Later Years,* Binghamton, NY: Haworth, 1994.

Koff, Theodore, *Long-Term Care: An Approach to Serving the Frail Elderly,* Boston: Little, Brown, 1982.

Koh, James, and Bell, William, "Korean Elders in the United States: Intergenerational Relations and Living Arrangements," *The Gerontologist* (1987), 27(1): 66-71.

Kohl, Marvin, *Beneficent Euthanasia,* Buffalo, NY: Prometheus, 1975.

Kohli, Martin, "The World We Forgot: An Historical Review of the Life Course," in Victor Marshall (ed.), *Later Life: The Social Psychology of Aging,* Beverly Hills, CA: Sage, 1986, pp. 207-303.

Kohli, Martin, "Retirement and the Moral Economy: An Historical Interpretation of the German Case," *Journal of Aging Studies* (1987), 1: 125-144.

Kolata, Gina, "New Views on Life Spans Alter Forecasts on Elderly," *New York Times* (November 16, 1992): A-1, A-15.

Kopac, C., "Bring Together the Young and Old With Intergenerational Day Care," *Pediatric Nursing* (1987), 13(4): 227-229.

Kotlikoff, Lawrence, *Generational Accounting,* New York: Basic Books, 1992.

Kotre, John, *Outliving the Self: Generativity and the Interpretation of Lives,* Baltimore: Johns Hopkins University Press, 1984.

Krain, Mark A., "Policy Implications for a Society Aging Well: Employment, Retirement, Education, and Leisure Policies for the 21st Century," *American Behavioral Scientist* (November-December 1995), 39(2): 131-151.

Krout, John, *Senior Centers in America,* New York: Greenwood, 1989.

Kubler-Ross, Elisabeth, *On Death and Dying,* New York: Macmillan, 1969.

Kuder, Linda, and Roeder, Phillip W., "Attitudes Toward Age-Based Health Care Rationing," *Journal of Aging and Health* (May 1995), 7(2): 301-327.

Kunitz, S. J., and Levy, J. E., *Navajo Aging,* Tucson: University of Arizona Press, 1991.

Lachs, Mark, et al., "Risk Factors for Reported Elder Abuse and Neglect: A Nine-Year Observational Cohort Study," *The Gerontologist* (August 1997), 37(4): 469-474.

Lamberts, S. W. J., van den Beld, A. W., and van der Lely, A.-J., "The Endocrinology of Aging," *Science* (1997), 278: 419-424.

Lamm, Richard D., "Intergenerational Equity in an Age of Limits: Confessions of a Prodigal Parent," in Gerald Winslow and James Walters (eds.), *Facing Limits: Ethics & Health Care for the Elderly,* Boulder, CO: Westview, 1993, 15-28.

Lammers, W., and Klingman, D. "Family Responsibility Laws and State Politics: Empirical Patterns and Policy Implications," *Journal of Applied Gerontology* (July 1986), 5: 5-25.

Langbein, John, "The Inheritance Revolution," *The Public Interest* (Winter 1991).

LaPuma, John, Orentlicher, David, and Moss, Robert J., "Advance Directives on Admission: Clinical Implications and Analysis of the Patient Self-Determination Act of 1990," *Journal of the American Medical Association* (July 17, 1991), 266: 404.

LaRock, S., "Neither Federal 'Carrot' nor 'Stick' Alters Early Retirement Patterns, 1979-1992," *Employee Benefit Plan Review* (July 1993), 48(1): 10-12.

Larson, R., "Thirty Years of Research on the Subjective Well-Being of Older Americans," *Journal of Gerontology* (1978), 33: 109-129.

Laslett, Peter, *The World We Have Lost,* New York: Scribner, 1971 (1965).

Laslett, Peter, *Household and Family in Past Time,* Cambridge, UK: Cambridge University Press, 1972.

Laslett, Peter, *The Emergence of the Third Age: A Fresh Map of Life,* Cambridge, MA: Harvard University Press, 1991.

Lawhon, T., Ennis, D., and Lawhon, D. C., "Senior Adults and Computers in the 1990s," *Educational Gerontology* (March 1996), 22(2): 193-201.

Lawton, M. Powell, *Environment and Aging,* Monterey, CA: Brooks/Cole, 1980.

Lee, Melinda A., and Ganzini, Linda, "Depression in the Elderly: Effect on Patient Attitudes Toward Life-Sustaining Therapy," *Journal of the American Geriatrics Society* (October 1992), 40(10): 983-988.

Leenaars, Antoon A., Maris, Ronald, McIntosh, John L., and Richman, Joseph (eds.), *Suicide and the Older Adult,* New York: Guilford, 1992.

Lehman, Harvey, *Age and Achievement,* Princeton, NJ: Princeton University Press, 1953.

Lehman, Harvey, "More About Age and Achievement," *The Gerontologist* (1962), 2: 141-148.

Leibold, K., "Employer-Sponsored On-Site Intergenerational Daycare," *Generations* (1989), 13(3): 33-34.

Levin, Jack, and Levin, William C., *Ageism: Prejudice and Discrimination Against the Elderly,* Belmont, CA: Wadsworth, 1980.

Levin, Jeffrey, "Age Differences in Mystical Experience," *The Gerontologist* (August 1993), 33(4): 507-513.

Levin, Jeffrey S., "Religious Research in Gerontology, 1980-1994: A Systematic Review," *Journal of Religious Gerontology* (1997), 10(3): 3-31.

Levine, Martin L., *Age Discrimination and the Mandatory Retirement Controversy,* Baltimore: Johns Hopkins University Press, 1989.

Levinson, Daniel J., *The Seasons of a Man's Life,* New York: Knopf, 1978.

Lewis, C. N., "Reminiscing and Self-Concept in Old Age," *Journal of Gerontology* (1971), 26: 240-243.

Lewis, Myrna, and Butler, Robert, "Why Is Women's Lib Ignoring the Older Women?" *International Journal of Aging and Human Development* (1972), 3(3): 223-231.

Lewis, P. A., and Charny, M., "Which of Two Individuals Do You Treat When Only Their Ages Are Different and You Can't Treat Both?" *Journal of Medical Ethics* (March 1989), 15(1): 28-32.

Light, Paul, *Artful Work: The Politics of Social Security Reform,* New York: Random House, 1985.

Litwak, Eugene, *Helping the Elderly: The Complementary Roles of Informal Networks and Formal Systems,* New York: Guilford, 1985.

Liu, Korbin, and Manton, Kenneth, "Nursing Home Length of Stay and Spenddown in Connecticut, 1977-1986," *The Gerontologist* (April 1991), 31(2): 165-173.

Locke, S. "Neurological Disorders of the Elderly," in William Reichel (ed.), *Clinical Aspects of Aging,* Baltimore: Williams and Wilkins, 1983.

London, William, and Morgan, John, "Living Long Enough to Die of Cancer," *Priorities* (1995), 7(4): 6-9.

Longino, Charles F., and Kart, C. S., "Explicating Activity Theory: A Formal Replication," *Journal of Gerontology* (1982), 37: 713-722.

Lopata, Helena, *Women as Widows: Support Systems,* New York: Elsevier, 1979.

Lopez, C., and Aguilera, E., *On the Sidelines: Hispanic Elderly and the Continuum of Care,* Washington, DC: National Council of La Raza, 1991.

Lowenthal, Marjorie F., and Chiriboga, David, "Transitions to the Empty Nest: Crisis, Change or Relief?" *Archives of General Psychiatry* (1972), 26: 8-14.

Lowy, Louis, "Major Issues of Age-Integrated Versus Age-Segregated Approaches to Serving the Elderly," *Journal of Gerontological Social Work* (1987), 10(3-4): 37-46.

Lubitz, J., and Prihoda, R., "The Use and Costs of Medicare Services in the Last Two Years of Life," *Health Care Financing Review* (1984), 5(3): 117-131.

Luce, Gay, *Your Second Life: Vitality and Growth in Maturity and Later Years From the Experiences of the SAGE Program,* New York: Dell, 1979.

Ludwig, Frederic, *Lifespan Extension: Consequences and Open Questions,* New York: Springer, 1991.

MacDonald, Martha, "Gender and Social Security Policy: Pitfalls and Possibilities," *Feminist Economics* (1998), 4(1): 1-25.

Mace, Nancy, and Rabins, Peter, *The 36-Hour Day,* Baltimore: Johns Hopkins University Press, 1981.

Mannheim, Karl, "The Problem of Generations," in Karl Mannheim, *Essays in the Sociology of Knowledge,* New York: Oxford University Press, 1952.

Manton, Kenneth G., Corder, L. S., and Stallard, E., "Chronic Disability Trends in Elderly United States Populations: 1982-1994," *Proceedings of the National Academy of Sciences* (March 1997), 94: 2593-2598.

Manton, Kenneth G., and Soldo, Beth J., "Dynamics of Health Changes in the Oldest Old: New Perspectives and Evidence," *Milbank Memorial Fund Quarterly* (1985), 63(2).

Margolis, Robin, "Will Funneling Seniors Into Managed Care Reduce Costs?" *Health Span* (March 1995), 12(3): 16-17.

Margulis, H. L., and Benson, V. M., "Age-Segregation and Discrimination Against Families With Children in Rental Housing," *The Gerontologist* (December 1982), 22(6): 505-512.

Markides, K. S., and Black, S. A., "Race, Ethnicity, and Aging: The Impact of Inequality," in R. H. Binstock and L. K. George (eds.), *The Handbook of Aging and the Social Sciences* (4th ed.), San Diego: Academic Press, 1996.

Marmor, Theodore R., *The Politics of Medicare,* Chicago: Aldine, 1973.

Marmor, Theodore R., "Fact, Fiction, and Faction: The Politics of Medical Care Reform in Canada as It Appears South of the Border," *Canadian Journal on Aging* (Summer 1995), 14(2): 426-436.

Marris, P., *Loss and Change,* Garden City, NY: Doubleday, 1975.

Martz, Sandra Haldeman (ed.), *When I Am an Old Woman, I Shall Wear Purple,* Watsonville, CA: Papier-Mache, 1987.

Masoro, E. J. (ed.), *Handbook of the Physiology of Aging,* Boca Raton, FL: CRC Press, 1981.

Masters, W., and Johnson, V., *Human Sexual Response,* Boston: Little, Brown, 1966.

McCabe, Kimberly A., and Gregory, Sharon S., "Elderly Victimization: An Examination Beyond the FBI's Index Crimes," *Research on Aging* (May 1998), 20(3): 363-372.

McConnell, Stephen R., and Usher, Carolyn E., *Intergenerational House Sharing: A Research Report and Resource Manual,* Lexington, MA: D. C. Heath, 1980.

McCrae, Robert R., Arenberg, David, and Costa, Paul T., "Declines in Divergent Thinking With Age: Cross-Sectional, Longitudinal, and Cross-Sequential Analyses," *Psychology and Aging* (June 1987), 2(2): 130-137.

McCrae, Robert R., and Costa, Paul T., *Personality in Adulthood,* New York: Guilford, 1990.

McGoldrick, Ann, and Copper, Cary, *Early Retirement,* Chichester, UK: Gower, 1989.

Mcgoon, Dwight C., *Parkinson's Handbook,* New York: Norton, 1990.

McIntosh, John, Santos, John, Hubbard, Richard, and Overholser, James, *Elder Suicide: Research, Theory and Treatment,* Washington, DC: American Psychological Association, 1994.

McKusick, David, "Demographic Issues in Medicare Reform," *Health Affairs* (January-February 1999), 18(1): 194-207.

McMahon, A. W., and Rhudick, P. J., "Reminiscing in the Aged: An Adaptational Response," in S. Levin and R. J. Kahana (eds.), *Psychodynamic Studies on Aging: Creativity, Reminiscing, and Dying,* New York: International Universities Press, 1967.

Meacham, J. A., "The Loss of Wisdom," in R. J. Sternberg (ed.), *Wisdom: Its Nature, Origin, and Development,* Cambridge, UK: Cambridge University Press, 1990, pp. 160-177.

Mechanic, David, "Cost Containment and the Quality of Medical Care: Rationing Strategies in an Era of Constrained Resources," *Milbank Memorial Fund Quarterly* (1985), 63: 453-475.

Medawar, Peter B., *Aging: An Unsolved Problem of Biology,* London: H. K. Lewis, 1952.

Medvedev, Z. A., "Repetition of Molecular-Genetic Information as a Possible Factor in Evolutionary Change of Life-Span," *Experimental Gerontology* (1972), 7: 227-234.

Melvin, C., and Ryder, K., "Among Friends: An Intergenerational Program for Alzheimer's Patients," *Caring* (1989), 8(8): 26-28.

Menzel, Paul T., *Strong Medicine: The Ethical Rationing of Health Care,* New York: Oxford University Press, 1990.

Meyrowitz, Joshua, *No Sense of Place: The Impact of Electronic Media on Social Behavior,* New York: Oxford University Press, 1985.

Mieskiel, S., "Inheritance," in L. Vitt and J. Siegenthalar (eds.), *Encyclopedia of Financial Gerontology,* Westport, CT: Greenwood, 1996, pp. 285-290.

Miller, Melvin E., and Cook-Greuter, Susanne R. (eds.), *Transcendence and Mature Thought in Adulthood: The Further Reaches of Adult Development,* Lanham, MD: Rowman & Littlefield, 1994.

Minkler, Meredith, and Estes, Carroll (eds.), *Readings in the Political Economy of Aging,* Farmingdale, NY: Baywood, 1984.

Minkler, Meredith, and Stone, R., "The Feminization of Poverty and Older Women," *The Gerontologist* (1985), 25: 351-357.

Minois, Georges, *History of Old Age: From Antiquity to the Renaissance* (trans. Sarah Hanbury Tenison), Chicago: University of Chicago Press, 1989.

Mieskiel, S. "Inheritance," in L. Vitt and J. Siegenthaler (eds.), *Encyclopedia of Financial Gerontology,* Westport, CT: Greenwood, 1996.

Montgomery, Rhonda J. V. (ed.) "The Age Discrimination in Employment Act (ADEA)" (special issue), *Research in Aging* (1991), 13(4): 411-486.

Montgomery, Rhonda J. V., "Respite Services for Family Caregivers," in M. D. Petersen and D. L. White, *Health Care of the Elderly: An Information Sourcebook,* Newbury Park, CA: Sage, 1989.

Moody, Harry R., *Abundance of Life: Human Development Policies for an Aging Society,* New York: Columbia University Press, 1988a.

Moody, Harry R., "Toward a Critical Gerontology: The Contribution of the Humanities to Theories of Aging," in James Birren and Vern Bengtson (eds.), *Emergent Theories of Aging,* New York: Springer, 1988b, pp. 19-40.

Moody, Harry R., "The Politics of Entitlement and the Politics of Productivity," in Scott A. Bass, Elizabeth A. Kutza, and Fernando Torres-Gil (eds.), *Diversity in Aging,* Glenview, IL: Scott, Foresman, 1990, pp. 129-149.

Moody, Harry R., and Carroll, David, *The Five Stages of the Soul: Charting the Spiritual Passages That Shape Our Lives,* New York: Doubleday Anchor Books, 1997.

Moore, Thomas, *The Care of the Soul: A Guide for Cultivating Depth and Sacredness in Everyday Life,* New York: HarperCollins, 1992.

Morgan, L. A., Eckert, J. K., and Lyon, S. M., *Small Board-and-Care Homes,* Baltimore: Johns Hopkins University Press, 1995.

Morgan, Nicole, *Nowhere to Go?* Chichester, UK: Gower, 1981.

Morrison, M., and Jedriewski, M. K., "Retirement Planning: Everybody Benefits," *Personnel Administrator* (January 1988), 74-80.

Morton, Jackson, "Census on the Internet," *American Demographics* (1995), 17(3): 52-54.

Moskowitz, Roland, and Haug, Marie, *Arthritis and the Elderly,* New York: Springer, 1985.

Moynihan, Daniel P., *Family and Nation,* San Diego: Harcourt Brace Jovanovich, 1986.

Muller, M. T., Van der Wal, G, van Eijk, J. Th. M., and Ribbe, M. W., *Journal of the American Geriatrics Society* (June 1994), 42(6): 624-629.

Munnell, Alicia H. (ed.), *Retirement and Public Policy,* Dubuque, IA: Kendall/Hunt, 1991.

Myers, Robert J., *Social Security* (3rd ed.), Homewood, IL: Irwin, 1985.

Nasar, Sylvia, "The Spend-Now, Tax-Later Orgy," *New York Times* (January 14, 1993): D-2.

National Center for Health Statistics, *Health—United States 1982,* Washington, DC: Government Printing Office, 1982.

National Center for Health Statistics, "Life Tables," Vital Statistics of the United States, 1987, Vol. 2, Section 6, Washington, DC: Government Printing Office, February, 1990.

National Center for Health Statistics, *Vital and Health Statistics,* Series 10, No. 189 ed. Washington, DC: Government Printing Office, 1994.

National Center for Health Statistics, *Health: United States 1994,* Hyattsville, MD: Author, 1995.

Naylor, C. D., "A Different View of Queues in Ontario," *Health Affairs* (1991), 10(3): 111-128.

Nelson, Gary M., "Social Class and Public Policy for the Elderly," *Social Service Review* (1982), 56: 85-107.

Nelson, Gary M., "Tax Expenditures for the Elderly," *The Gerontologist* (1983), 23: 471-478.

Neugarten, Bernice L., *Middle Age and Aging,* Chicago: University of Chicago Press, 1968.

Neugarten, Bernice L. (ed.), *Age or Need? Public Policies for Older People,* Beverly Hills, CA: Sage, 1983.

Neugarten, Bernice L., et al. (eds.), *Personality in Middle and Late Life,* New York: Atherton, 1964.

Newcomer, Robert J., Lawton, M. Powell, and Byerts, Thomas O. (eds.), *Housing an Aging Society,* New York: Van Nostrand Reinhold, 1986.

Newman, Katherine S., *Declining Fortunes: The Withering of the American Dream,* New York: Basic Books, 1993.

Newman, S., Lyons, C., and Onawola, R., "The Development of an Inter-generational Service-Learning Program at a Nursing Home," *The Gerontologist* (1984), 25(2): 130-133.

Nusselder, Wilma, and Mackenbach, Johan, "Rectangularization of the Survival Curve in the Netherlands, 1950-1992," *The Gerontologist* (December 1996), 36(6): 773-782.

O'Conner, Colleen, "Empirical Research on How the Elderly Handle Their Estates," *Generations* (1996), 20(3): 13-20.

O'Grady-LeShane, Regina, "Older Women and Poverty," *Social Work* (September 1990), 35: 422-424.

Okun, M., "The Relation Between Motives for Organizational Volunteering and Frequency of Volunteering by Elders," *Journal of Applied Gerontology* (1994), 13: 115-126.

Older Women's League, "Path to Poverty: An Analysis of Women's Retirement Income," in Carroll L. Estes and Meredith Minkler (eds.), *Critical Gerontol-*

ogy: Perspectives From Political and Moral Economy, Amityville, NY: Baywood, 1998, pp. 299-313.

Olsen, Kelly A., and Baylyff, Chris, "Keeping Track of Social Security Reform Proposals: An Update," *EBRI Notes* (April 1998), 19(4): 6-11.

Olshansky, S., Carnes, B., and Cassel, C., "In Search of Methuselah: Estimating the Upper Limits to Longevity," *Science* (1990), 250: 634-640.

Olshansky, S. J., Rudberg, M. A., Carnes, B. A., Cassel, C. K., Brody, J. A., "Trading Off Longer Life for Worsening Health: The Expansion of Morbidity Hypothesis," *Journal of Aging and Health* (May 1991), 3(2): 194-216.

Olson, Laura K., *The Political Economy of Aging,* New York: Columbia University Press, 1982.

O'Reilly, Patrick, and Caro, Francis G., "Productive Aging: An Overview of the Literature," *Journal of Aging & Social Policy* (1994), 6(3): 39-71.

Orwoll, L., and Perlmutter, M., "The Study of Wise Persons: Integrating a Personality Perspective," in R. J. Sternberg (ed.), *Wisdom: Its Nature, Origin, and Development,* Cambridge, UK: Cambridge University Press, 1990, pp. 181-211.

Osgood, Nancy J., *Senior Settlers: Social Integration in Retirement Communities,* New York: Praeger, 1982.

Osgood, Nancy J., *Suicide in Later Life: Recognizing the Warning Signs,* New York: Lexington Books, 1992.

Palmore, Erdman B., *The Honorable Elders,* Durham, NC: Duke University Press, 1975.

Palmore, Erdman B., *Social Patterns in Normal Aging,* Durham, NC: Duke University Press, 1981.

Palmore, Erdman B., *Ageism* (2nd ed.), New York: Springer, 1999.

Palmore, Erdman B., Burchett, B. M., Filenbaum, G. G., George, L. K., and Wallman, L. M., *Retirement: Causes and Consequences,* New York: Springer, 1985.

Palmore, Erdman B., and Manton, K., "Modernization and Status of the Aged: International Correlations," *Journal of Gerontology* (1974), 29: 205-210.

Panser, L. A., Rhodes, T., Girman, C. J., Guess, H. A., and Chute, C. G., "Sexual Function of Men Ages 40 to 79 Years: The Olmsted County Study of Urinary Symptoms and Health Status Among Men," *Journal of the American Geriatrics Society* (October 1995), 43(10): 1107-1111.

Parnes, Herbert S., et al., *Retirement Among American Men,* Lexington, MA: Lexington, 1985.

Peacock, W., and Talley, W., "Intergenerational Contact: A Way to Counteract Ageism," *Educational Gerontology* (1984), 10(1-2): 13-24.

Peck, M. Scott, *The Road Less Traveled: A New Psychology of Love, Traditional Values and Spiritual Growth.* New York: Simon & Schuster, 1993 (1980).

Peck, Robert C., "Psychological Development in the Second Half of Life," in Bernice L. Neugarten, *Middle Age and Aging,* Chicago: University of Chicago Press, 1968.

Peden, Ann, and Newman, Ann, "After Menopause," *Journal of Women and Aging* (1993), 5(3-4): 25-40.

Peters, R., Schmidt, W., and Miller, K., "Guardianship of the Elderly in Tallahassee, Florida," *The Gerontologist* (1985), 25(5): 532-538.

Peterson, Peter G., and Howe, Neil, *On Borrowed Time: How the Growth in Entitlement Spending Threatens America's Future,* San Francisco: ICS Press, 1988.

Pfeifer, Susan K., and Sussman, Marvin B. (eds.), *Families: Intergenerational and Generational Connections,* Binghamton, NY: Haworth, 1991.

Pifer, Alan, and Bronte, Lydia (eds.), *Our Aging Society: Paradox and Promise,* New York: Norton, 1986.

Pillemer, K., and Finkelhor, D., "The Prevalence of Elder Abuse: A Random Sample Survey," *The Gerontologist* (1988), 28(1): 51-57.

Portnow, Jay, *Home Care for the Elderly: A Complete Guide,* New York: McGraw-Hill, 1987.

Post, Joyce, "Internet Resources on Aging: Increasing Options and Human Factors," *The Gerontologist* (1997), 37(1): 125-129.

Post, Stephen, "Filial Morality in an Aging Society," *Journal of Religion & Aging* (1989), 5: 15-30.

Postman, Neil, *The Disappearance of Childhood,* New York: Delacorte, 1982.

Pratt, Henry J., *The Gray Lobby,* Chicago: University of Chicago Press, 1976.

Pratt, Henry J., "The 'Gray Lobby' Revisited," *National Forum* (1982), 62: 31-33.

Preston, Samuel H., "Children and the Elderly in the U.S.," *Scientific American* (1984), 251(6): 44-49.

Putnam, Jackson, *Old Age Politics in California: From Richardson to Reagan,* Stanford, CA: Stanford University Press, 1970.

Putnam, S. M., "Nature of the Medical Encounter," *Research on Aging* (March 1996), 18(1): 70-83.

Quadagno, Jill, *Aging in Early Industrial Society,* New York: Academic Press, 1982.

Quinn, Joseph F., "Retirement Income Rights as a Component of Wealth in the United States," *Review of Income and Wealth* (1985), 31: 223-236.

Quinn, Joseph F., "The Economic Status of the Elderly: Beware the Mean," *Review of Income and Wealth* (March 1987): 63-82.

Quinn, Joseph F., "Retirement Patterns and Bridge Jobs in the 1990s," *EBRI Issue Brief* (February 1999), No. 206: 1-22.

Quinn, Joseph F., et al., *Passing the Torch: The Influence of Economic Incentives on Work and Retirement,* Kalamazoo, MI: W. E. Upjohn, 1990.

Quinn, Joseph F., Segal, J., Raisz, H., and Johnson, C. (eds.), *Coordinating Community Services for the Elderly: The Triage Experience,* New York: Springer, 1982.

Quinn, M. J., and Tomita, S. K., *Elder Abuse and Neglect: Causes, Diagnosis and Intervention Strategies* (2nd ed.), New York: Springer, 1987.

Rabushka, A., and Jacobs, B., *Old Folks at Home,* New York: Free Press, 1980.

Rachels, James, *The End of Life: Euthanasia and Morality,* New York: Oxford University Press, 1986.

Radner, Daniel B., "Money Incomes of the Aged and Nonaged Family Units," *Social Security Bulletin* (1987), 50(8): 5-21.

Radner, Daniel B., "Economic Status of the Aged," *Social Security Bulletin* (Fall 1992), 55(3): 3-23.

Redburn, David E., "'Graying' of the World's Population," in David E. Redburn and Robert P. McNamara (eds.), *Social Gerontology,* Westport, CT: Auburn House, 1998, pp. 1-16.

Regan, John, "Protecting the Elderly: The New Paternalism," *Hastings Law Journal* (1981), 32(5): 1111-1132.

Rein, Jan Ellen, "Preserving Dignity and Self-Determination of the Elderly in the Face of Competing Interests and Grim Alternatives: A Proposal for Statutory Refocus and Reform," *George Washington Law Review* (1992), 60(6): 1818-1887.

Reisberg, Barry, *Alzheimer's Disease,* New York: Free Press (Macmillan), 1983.

Rejda, George E., "Reexamination of the Controversial Earnings Test Under the OASDI Program," *Benefits Quarterly* (1990), 6: 25-35.

Relman, Arnold S., "The Trouble With Rationing," *New England Journal of Medicine* (September 27, 1990), 323(13): 911-913.

Riggs, Karen E., *Mature Audiences: Television in the Lives of Elders,* New Brunswick, NJ: Rutgers University Press, 1998.

Riley, Matilda White, and Foner, Anne, *Aging and Society: Vol. 3, A Sociology of Age Stratification,* New York: Basic Books, 1972.

Riley, Matilda White, and Riley, John W., Jr. "Age Integration and the Lives of Older People," *The Gerontologist* (February 1994), 34(1): 110-115.

Rindfuss, R. R., Swicegood, C. G., and Rosenfeld, R. A., "Disorder in the Life Course: How Common and Does It Matter?" *American Sociological Review* (1987), 52: 785-801.

Ritter, K. P., "Preparation for Guardianship Cases Poses a Constant Challenge," *Journal of Long Term Care Administration* (1995), 23(3): 14-17.

Rivlin, Alice, and Wiener, Joshua, *Caring for the Disabled Elderly: Who Will Pay?* Washington, DC: Brookings Institution, 1988.

Robertson, Ann, "Beyond Apocalyptic Demography: Towards a Moral Economy of Interdependence," *Ageing and Society* (July 1997), 17(4): 425-446.

Robinson, John P., "Quitting Time," *American Demographics* (May 1991), 13(5): 34-36.

Rodin, J., and Langer, E., "Aging Labels: The Decline of Control and the Fall of Self-Esteem," *Journal of Social Issues* (1980), 36: 12-29.

Rodin, J., Timko, C., and Harris, S., "The Construct of Control: Biological and Psychosocial Correlates," in M. P. Lawton and G. Maddox (eds.), *Annual Review of Gerontology and Geriatrics* (Vol. 5), New York: Springer, 1985, pp. 3-55.

Rogers, Andrei, and Raymer, James, "Regional Demographics of the Elderly Foreign-Born and Native-Born Populations in the United States Since 1950," *Research on Aging* (January 1999), 21(1): 3-35.

Rosenbaum, Walter A., "Unquiet Future of Intergenerational Politics," *The Gerontologist* (August 1993), 33(4): 481-490.

Rosenbaum, Walter A., and Button, James W., "Is There a Gray Peril? Retirement Politics in Florida," *The Gerontologist* (1989), 29: 300-306.

Rosenbaum, Walter A., and Button, James W., "Perceptions of Intergenerational Conflict: The Politics of Young vs. Old in Florida," *Journal of Aging Studies* (Winter 1992), 6(4): 385-396.

Rosenmayr, L., *Die Spaete Freiheit* [The Late Freedom], Vienna: Severin, 1984.

Rosenthal, C. J., "Kinkeeping in the Familial Division of Labor," *Journal of Marriage and the Family* (1985), 47: 965-974.

Rosenthal, Carolyn, Matthews, Sarah, and Marshall, Victor, "Is Parent Care Normative? The Experiences of a Sample of Middle-Aged Women," *Research on Aging* (1989), 11(2): 244-260.

Rosenthal, Gary E., and Fortinsky, Richard H., "Differences in the Treatment of Patients With Acute Myocardial Infarction According to Patient Age," *Journal of the American Geriatrics Society* (August 1994), 42(8): 826-832.

Rosow, Irving, *Social Integration of the Aged,* New York: Free Press, 1967.

Rosow, Irving, *Socialization to Old Age,* Berkeley: University of California Press, 1974.

Rossi, Alice (ed.), *Gender and the Life Course,* New York: Aldine, 1985.

Roszak, Theodore, *America the Wise: The Longevity Revolution and the True Wealth of Nations,* Boston: Houghton Mifflin, 1998.

Roush, Wade, "Live Long and Prosper?" *Science* (July 5, 1996), 273(5271): 42-46.

Rowe, John W., and Kahn, R. L., *Successful Aging,* New York: Pantheon, 1997.

Ryder, Norman, "The Cohort as a Concept in the Study of Social Change," *American Sociological Review* (1965), 30: 843-861.

Ryff, Carol D., "Beyond Ponce de Leon and Life Satisfaction: New Directions in Quest of Successful Ageing," *International Journal of Behavioral Development* (1989), 12(1): 35-55.

Rudinger, Georg, and Thomae, Hans, "Bonn Longitudinal Study of Aging: Coping, Life Adjustment, and Life Satisfaction," in Paul B. Baltes and Margaret M. Baltes (eds.), *Successful Aging: Perspectives From the Behavioral Sciences,* New York: Cambridge University Press, 1990, pp. 265-295.

Ruiz, Dorothy Smith, "Demographic and Epidemiologic Profile of the Ethnic Elderly," in Deborah K. Padgett (ed.), *Handbook on Ethnicity, Aging, and Mental Health,* Westport, CT: Greenwood, 1995, pp. 3-21.

Sacher, George A., "Longevity, Aging and Death: An Evolutionary Perspective," *The Gerontologist* (1978), 18: 112-119.

Salthouse, T. A., "Effects of Age and Skill in Typing," *Journal of Experimental Psychology: General* (1984), 113: 345-371.

Salthouse, T. A., "Speed of Behavior and the Implications for Cognition," in James E. Birren and K. Warner Schaie (eds.), *Handbook of the Psychology of Aging* (2nd ed.), New York: Van Nostrand Reinhold, 1985a, pp. 400-426.

Salthouse, T. A., *A Theory of Cognitive Aging,* Amsterdam: North Holland, 1985b.

Sattler, J. M., "Age Effects on Wechsler Adult Intelligence Scale-Revised Tests," *Journal of Consulting and Clinical Psychology* (1982), 50: 785-786.

Sauvy, Alfred, *Zero Growth,* New York: Praeger, 1976.

Schachter-Shalomi, Zalman, and Miller, Ron, *From Age-ing to Sage-ing,* New York: Time Warner, 1995.

Schaie, K. Warner, "Midlife Influences Upon Intellectual Functioning in Old Age," *International Journal of Behavioral Development* (1984), 7: 463-478.

Schaie, K. Warner, *Intellectual Development in Adulthood: The Seattle Longitudinal Study,* Cambridge, UK: Cambridge University Press, 1996.

Schieber, Sylvester, and Shoven, John (eds.), *Public Policy Toward Pensions,* Cambridge, MA: MIT Press, 1997.

Schmahl, W. (ed.), *Redefining the Process of Retirement,* New York: Springer-Verlag, 1989.

Schneider, Edward L., and Guralnik, Jack, "The Aging of America: Impact on Health Care Costs," *Journal of the American Medical Association* (May 2, 1990), 263(17): 2335-2340.

Schnore, M., *Retirement: Bane or Blessing,* Atlantic Highlands, NJ: Humanities Press, 1985.

Scholen, K., and Chen, Y. P., *Unlocking Home Equity for the Elderly,* Cambridge, MA: Ballinger, 1980.

Schooler, C., and Schaie, K. W. (eds.), *Cognitive Functioning and Social Structure Over the Life Course,* Norwood, NJ: Ablex, 1987.

Schor, Juliet, *The Overworked American,* New York: Basic Books, 1991.

Schorr, Alvin L., *Filial Responsibility in the Modern American Family,* Washington, DC: Social Security Administration, 1961.

Schulz, James H., *The Economics of Aging* (6th ed.), Dover, MA: Auburn House, 1995.

Schurenberg, Eric, and Luciano, Lani, "The Empire Called AARP," *Money* (October 1988), 17: 120-146.

Schwarz, John, *America's Hidden Success,* New York: Norton, 1983.

Schwartz, William B., "Inevitable Failure of Current Cost-Containment Strategies: Why They Can Provide Only Temporary Relief," *Journal of the American Medical Association* (January 9, 1987), 257(2): 220-224.

Scitovsky, Anne A., "Medical Care in the Last Twelve Months of Life: The Relation Between Age, Functional Status, and Medical Care Expenditures," *Milbank Quarterly* (1988), 66(4): 640-660.

Seligman, Martin E. P., *Helplessness: On Depression, Development and Death,* San Francisco: Freeman, 1975.

Seltzer, Mildred M. (ed.), *Impact of Increased Life Expectancy: Beyond the Gray Horizon,* New York: Springer, 1995.

Seltzer, Mildred M., and Troll, Lilian E., "Conflicting Public Attitudes Toward Filial Responsibility," *Generations* (1982), 7(2): 26-27, 40.

Shanas, Ethel, "The Family as a Social Support System in Old Age," *The Gerontologist* (1979), 19: 169-174.

Shanas, Ethel, "Older People and Their Families: The New Pioneers," *Journal of Marriage and the Family* (1980), 42(9): 9- 15.

Shelanski, Vivien, "Assisted Suicide and the Courts: Spotlight on Palliative Care," *Journal of Long Term Home Health Care* (Winter 1998), 17(1): 17-28.

Sheppard, Harold, "The 'New' Early Retirement: Europe and the United States," in Irving Bluestone, Rhonda J. V. Montgomery, and John Owen (eds.), *The Aging of the American Work Force,* Detroit, MI: Wayne State University Press, 1990, pp. 158-178.

Sherwood, S., Morris, S. A., Ruchlin, H. S., and Sherwood, C. C., *Continuing-Care Retirement Communities,* Baltimore: Johns Hopkins University Press, 1997.

Shock, Nathan, "The Physiology of Aging," *Scientific American* (1962), 206: 100-110.

Shock, Nathan, Greulich, R. C., Cosa, P. T., Jr., Andres, R., Lakata, E. G., Arenberg, D., and Tobin, J. D., *Normal Human Aging: The Baltimore Longitudinal Study of Aging,* Washington, DC: Government Printing Office, 1984.

Silverman, Phyllis, *Widow-to-Widow,* New York: Springer, 1986.

Simmons, Leo W., *The Role of the Aged in Primitive Societies,* New Haven, CT: Yale University Press, 1945.

Simonton, Dean K., "Career Paths and Creative Lives: A Theoretical Perspective on Late Life Potential," in Carolyn E. Adams-Price (ed.), *Creativity and*

Successful Aging: Theoretical and Empirical Approaches, New York: Springer, 1998, pp. 3-18

Singleton, J. F., Forbes, W. F., and Agwani, N., "Stability of Activity Across the Lifespan," *Activities, Adaptation and Aging* (1993), 18(1): 19-27.

Sloane, Leonard, "Policies for Covering Cost of Long-Term Care," *New York Times* (January 2, 1992): 36.

Smeeding, Timothy M., "Children and Poverty: How U.S. Stands," *Forum for Applied Research and Public Policy* (Summer 1990), 5(2): 65-70.

Smith, Andrew H., "Age-Based Rationing: A Wrong Turn on the Road to Reform," *Ageing International* (September 1993), 20(3): 7-11.

Smith, Sheila, Freeland, Mark, Heffler, Stephen, and McKusick, David, "Next Ten Years of Health Spending: What Does the Future Hold?" *Health Affairs* (September-October 1998), 17(5): 128-140.

Smolensky, E., Danziger, S., and Gottschalk, P., "The Declining Significance of Age in the United States: Trends in the Well-Being of Children and the Elderly Since 1939," in J. L. Palmer, T. Smeeding, and B. Torrey (eds.), *The Vulnerable,* Washington, DC: Urban Institute Press, 1988, pp. 29-54.

Solomon, M., et al., "Decisions Near the End of Life: Professional Views on Life-Sustaining Treatments," *American Journal of Public Health* (January 1993): 14-23.

Somers, Anne R., and Spears, Nancy L., *Continuing Care Retirement Community: A Significant Option for Long-Term Care?* New York: Springer, 1992.

Sommers, K., "Generation Mix: Child Care in the Nursing Home," *Nursing Homes* (1985), 34(4): 27-30.

Spencer, Gregory, *Projections of the Population of the United States, by Age, Sex, and Race: 1988 to 2080,* U.S. Bureau of the Census, Current Population Reports Special Studies, P25-1018, Washington, DC: Government Printing Office, January 1989.

Spiegel, Allen D., *Medicaid Experience,* Rockville, MD: Aspen Systems, 1979.

Springer, D., and Brubaker, T. H., *Family Caregivers and Dependent Elderly: Managing Stress and Maximizing Independence,* Beverly Hills, CA: Sage, 1984.

Sprott, Richard L., and Roth, George S., "Biomarkers of Aging: Can We Predict Individual Life Span?" *Generations* (1992), 16(4): 11-14.

Stagner, R., "Aging in Industry," in James Birren and K. Warner Schaie (eds.), *Handbook of the Psychology of Aging* (2nd ed.), New York: Van Nostrand Reinhold, 1985, pp. 789-817.

Stanford, E. Percil, Happersett, Catherine, J., and Morton, Deborah, J., "Early Retirement and Functional Impairment From a Multi-ethnic Perspective," *Research on Aging* (March 1991), 13: 5-38.

Stanley, Jean F., Pye, David, and MacGregor, Andrew, "Comparison of Doubling Numbers Attained by Cultured Animal Cells With Life Span of Species," *Nature* (May 8, 1975).

Stearns, Peter N. (ed.), *Old Age in Pre-industrial Societies,* New York: Holmes and Meier, 1982.

Steckenrider, Janie, and Parrott, Tonya (eds.), *New Directions in Old-Age Policies,* Albany: State University of New York Press, 1998.

Stein, Bruno, "Pay-as-You-Go, Partial Prefunding, and Full Funding of American Social Security," *History of Political Economy* (Spring 1991), 23: 79-83.

Stephan, Paula E., and Levin, Sharon, G., *Striking the Mother Lode in Science: The Importance of Age, Place and Time,* New York: Oxford University Press, 1992.

Stephens, S., and Christianson, J., *Informal Care of the Elderly,* Lexington, MA: D. C. Heath, 1986.

Sterling, Bruce, *Holy Fire,* New York: Bantam, 1997.

Stewart, Alva W., *Social Security: Its Development From Roosevelt to Reagan,* Monticello, IL: Vance Bibliographies, 1982.

Stoller, Eleanor P., and Gibson, Rose C., *Worlds of Difference: Inequality in the Aging Experience,* Thousand Oaks, CA: Pine Forge, 1994.

Stone, Robyn I., "Familial Obligation: Issues for the Nineties," *Generations* (Summer-Fall 1991), 15(3): 47-50.

Stone, Robyn I., Cafferata, G., and Sangl, J., "Caregivers of the Frail Elderly: A National Profile," *The Gerontologist* (1987), 27: 616-626.

Stone, Robyn I., and Kemper, P., "Spouses and Children of Disabled Elders: How Large a Constituency for Long-Term Reform?" *Milbank Quarterly* (1989), 67: 485-506.

Streib, Gordon F., "Are the Aged a Minority Group?" in Alvin Gouldner and S. Miller (ed.), *Applied Sociology,* New York: Free Press, 1965.

Streib, Gordon F., "Socioeconomic Strata," in Erdman Palmore (ed.), *Handbook on the Aged in the United States,* Westport, CT: Greenwood, 1984, pp. 77-92.

Streib, Gordon F., "Social Stratification and Aging," in Robert H. Binstock and Ethel Shanas (eds.), *Handbook of Aging and the Social Sciences,* New York: Van Nostrand Reinhold, 1985, pp. 339-368.

Streib, Gordon F., and Bourg, C. F., "Age Stratification Theory, Inequality, and Social Change," in R. F. Thomason (ed.), *Comparative Social Research,* Greenwich, CT: JAI, 1984.

Streib, Gordon F., and Schneider, C., *Retirement in American Society,* Ithaca, NY: Cornell University Press, 1971.

Sullivan, D. A., "Informal Support Systems in a Planned Retirement Community: Availability, Proximity, and Willingness to Utilize," *Research on Aging* (June 1986), 8(2): 249-267.

Szilard, Leo, "On the Nature of the Aging Process," *Proceedings of the National Academy of Sciences USA* (1959), 45: 30.

Taeuber, Cynthia, "Diversity: The Dramatic Reality," in Scott A. Bass, Elizabeth A. Kutza, and Fernando Torres-Gil (eds.), *Diversity in Aging,* Glenview, IL: Scott, Foresman, 1990, pp. 1-45.

Teague, Michael L., and MacNeil, Richard D., *Aging and Leisure: Vitality in Later Life* (2nd ed.), Dubuque, IA: Brown and Benchmark, 1992.

Terkel, Studs, *Working,* New York: Ballantine, 1985.

Thernstrom, Stephan (ed.), *Harvard Encyclopedia of American Ethnic Groups,* Cambridge, MA: Belknap, 1980.

Thompson, Paul, " 'I Don't Feel Old': The Significance of the Search for Meaning in Later Life," *International Journal of Geriatric Psychiatry* (August 1993), 8(8): 685-692.

Thone, R. R., *Women and Aging: Celebrating Ourselves,* New York: Haworth, 1992.

Thursz, D., Liederman, D., and Shorr, L., "Generations Uniting," *Perspective on Aging* (1989), 18(1): 3-23.

Tierce, J., and Seelback, W., "Elders as School Volunteers," Educational Gerontology (1987), 13: 33-41.

Tilly, J., and Brunner, D., *Medicaid Eligibility and Its Effects on the Elderly,*
Washington, DC: American Association of Retired Persons, 1987.

Tornstam, Lars, "Quo Vadis of Gerontology: On the Scientific Paradigm of Gerontology," *The Gerontologist* (1992), 32(3): 318-326.

Tornstam, Lars, "Gero-transcendence: The Contemplative Dimension of
Aging," *Journal of Aging Studies* (Summer 1997), 11(2): 143-154.

Torres-Gil, Fernando M., "Retirement Issues That Affect Minorities," in
H. Dennis (ed.), *Retirement Preparation,* Lexington, MA: Lexington, 1984.

Torres-Gil, Fernando M., *The New Aging: Politics and Change in America,* New
York: Auburn House, 1992.

Torres-Gil, Fernando M., and Hyde, J. C., "The Impact of Minorities on Long
Term Care Policy in California," in P. Liebig and W. Lammers (eds.), *Cali-
fornia Policy Choices for Long-Term Care,* Los Angeles: University of
Southern California, 1990, pp. 31-52.

Treas, Judith, "Older Americans in the 1990s and Beyond," *Population Bulletin*
(1995), 50(2).

Uchitelle, Louis, "Stanching the Loss of Good Jobs," *New York Times* (January
31, 1993): 1-3.

Uhlenberg, Peter, Cooney, Teresa, and Boyd, Robert, "Divorce for Women After Midlife," *Journal of Gerontology* (1990), 45(1): S3-S11.

U.S. Bureau of the Census, "Estimates of the Population of the United States, by
Single Years of Age, Color, and Sex: 1900 to 1959," *Current Population Re-
ports,* Series P-25, No. 311, Washington, DC: Government Printing Office,
July 1965.

U.S. Bureau of the Census, "Educational Attainment in the United States: March
1981 and 1980," in *Current Population Reports,* Series P-20, No. 390, Washington, DC: Government Printing Office, August 1984.

U.S. Bureau of the Census, "Characteristics of the Population Below the Poverty
Level: 1984," in *Current Population Reports,* Series P-60, No. 152, Washington, DC: Government Printing Office, 1986.

U.S. Bureau of the Census, "America in Transition: An Aging Society," by
Cynthia Taeuber, *Current Population Reports,* Series P-23, No. 128, Washington, DC: Government Printing Office, September 1988.

U.S. Bureau of the Census, "Projections of the Population of the United States,
by Age, Sex, and Race: 1988 to 2080," by Gregory Spencer, *Current Population Reports,* Series P-25, No. 1018, Washington, DC: Government Printing
Office, January 1989.

U.S. Bureau of the Census, "Money Income and Poverty Status in the United
States: 1989," *Current Population Reports,* Series P-60, No. 168, Washington, DC: Government Printing Office, September, 1990.

U.S. Bureau of the Census, "Asset Ownership of Householders, 1993," by T. J.
Eller and Wallace Frances, in *Current Population Reports,* Series P-70, No.
47, Washington, DC: Government Printing Office, 1995.

U.S. Bureau of the Census, "65+ in the United States," by Frank B. Hobbs with
Bonnie L. Damon, in *Current Population Reports* (special issue), Series P-
23, No. 190, Washington, DC: Government Printing Office, 1996.

U.S. Bureau of the Census, "Aging in the United States: Past, Present, and Future" (wall chart), Washington, DC, 1997.

U.S. Congress, House Task Force on Social Security and Women, *Inequities Toward Women in the Social Security System,* Washington, DC: Government Printing Office, 1983.

U.S. Congress, House Task Force on Social Security and Women, *Earnings Sharing Implementation Plan,* Washington, DC: Government Printing Office, 1984.

U.S. Congressional Budget Office, *Older Americans Reports,* Washington, DC: Author, April 29, 1988.

U.S. Congressional Budget Office, *Long-Term Budgetary Pressures and Policy Options,* Washington, DC, May 1998.

U.S. Department of Labor, Bureau of Labor Statistics, *Handbook of Labor Statistics,* Bulletin 2217, Washington, DC: Author, June 1985.

U.S. Department of Labor, Bureau of Labor Statistics, "Worklife Estimates: Effects of Race and Education," Bulletin 2254, February, 1986.

U.S. General Accounting Office, *Social Security: Past Projections and Future Financing Concerns,* Washington, DC: Author, 1986.

U.S. General Accounting Office, *Long-Term Care Insurance: Risks to Insurance Should Be Reduced,* Washington, DC: Author, December 1991.

U.S. General Accounting Office, *Medicare: Increased HMO Oversight Could Improve Quality and Access to Care*, Washington, DC: Government Printing Office, August 1995.

U.S. House of Representatives, Committee on Ways and Means, *1998 Green Book: Background Material and Data on Programs Within the Jurisdiction of the Committee on Ways and Means,* Washington, DC: Government Printing Office, 1998.

U.S. Office of Technology Assessment, *Life Sustaining Technologies and the Elderly,* Washington, DC: Government Printing Office, 1987.

U.S. Senate, Special Committee on Aging, *Aging America: Trends and Projections,* Washington, DC: Author, 1991.

U.S. Social Security Administration, *Income of the Aged Chartbook,* 1994.

Vaco, Attorney General of New York, v. Quill, 117 S. Ct. 2293, 138 L.Ed.2d (1997).

Vaillant, George, *Adaptation to Life,* Boston: Little, Brown, 1977.

Van Gennep, A., *Rites of Passage,* Chicago: University of Chicago Press, 1960.

Van Tassel, David D., and Meyer, J. E. W., *U.S. Aging Policy Interest Groups,* Westport, CT: Greenwood, 1992.

Ventura-Merkel, C., and Doucette, D., "Community Colleges in an Aging Society," *Educational Gerontology* (March-April 1993), 19(2): 161-171.

Ventura-Merkel, C., and Friedman, M., "Helping At-Risk Youth Through Intergenerational Programming," *Children Today* (1988), 17(1): 10-13.

Verbrugge, L., Lepkowski, J., and Imanaka, Y., "Co-morbidity and Its Impact on Disability," *Milbank Quarterly* (1989), 67(3-4): 450-484.

Villers Foundation, *On the Other Side of Easy Street,* Washington, DC: Author, 1987.

Vitt, Lois A., "Home Equity Conversion Financing: A Recipe for Well- Being," *Innovations in Aging* (1998), 27(1): 10-12.

Vladeck, Bruce, *Unloving Care: The Nursing Home Tragedy,* New York: Basic Books, 1980.

Wagner, Lynn, "Alzheimer's Disease Tests Challenged," *Provider* (February 1996), 22(2): 65-66.

Walford, Roy, *Maximum Life Span,* New York: Norton, 1983.

Walford, Roy, *The 120 Year Diet: How to Double Your Vital Years,* New York: Pocket Books, 1986.

Walker, S. N., "Health Promotion and Prevention of Disease and Disability Among Older Adults: Who Is Responsible?" *Generations* (Spring 1994), 18(1): 45-50.

Walls, C. T., and Zarit, S. H., "Informal Support From Black Churches and the Well-Being of Elderly Blacks," *The Gerontologist* (1991), 31(4): 490-495.

Walsh, R., and Vaughan, Frances (eds.), *Paths Beyond Ego: The Transpersonal Vision,* Los Angeles: Tarcher, 1993.

Washington v. Glucksberg, 117 S. Ct. 2258, 138 L.Ed.2d (1997).

Watkins, S. C., Menken, J. A., and Bongaarts, J., "Demographic Foundations of Family Change," *American Sociological Review* (1987), 52: 346-358.

Watson, J. D., *Recombinant DNA* (2nd ed.), New York: Freeman, 1992.

Weibel-Orlando, Joan, "Grandparenting Styles: Native American Perspectives," in J. Sokolovsky (ed.), *The Cultural Context of Aging: Worldwide Perspectives,* New York: Bergin and Garvey, 1990.

Weindruch, R., and Walford, R. L., *The Retardation of Aging and Disease by Dietary Restriction,* Springfield, IL: Charles C Thomas, 1988.

Weinstein, M. H., "The Changing Picture in Retiree Economics" (Metropolitan Life Insurance), *Statistical Bulletin* (July-September 1988), 69:7.

Weitzman, Lenore, *The Divorce Revolution: The Unexpected Social and Economic Consequences for Women and Children in America,* New York: Free Press, 1985.

Welch, H. Gilbert, "Comparing Apples and Oranges: Does Cost-Effectiveness Analysis Deal Fairly With the Old and Young?" *The Gerontologist* (June 1991), 31(3): 332-336.

Wennberg, Robert, *Terminal Choices: Euthanasia, Suicide, and the Right to Die,* Grand Rapids, MI: Erdmans, 1989.

Whitbourne, Susan K., "Test Anxiety in Elderly and Young Adults," *International Journal of Aging and Human Development* (1976), 7: 201-210.

Whitbourne, S. K., "Sexuality in the Aging Male," *Generations* (Summer 1990), 14(3): 28-30.

White, L., et al., "Geriatric Epidemiology," in Carl Eisdorfer (ed.), *Annual Review of Gerontology and Geriatrics* (Vol. 6), New York: Springer, 1986.

Wiener, Joshua, "Long-Term Care Financing," *Nursing Homes Long Term Care Management* (February 1998), 47(2): 19-21.

Williams, G. C., "Pleitropy, Natural Selection, and the Evolution of Senescence," *Evolution* (1957), 11: 398-411.

Williams, Richard H., and Wirths, Claudine G., *Lives Through the Years,* New York: Atherton, 1965.

Williamson, John, "Should Women Support the Privatization of Social Security?" *Challenge* (July-August 1997), 40(4): 97-108.

Williamson, R. C., Rinehart, A. D., Blank, T. O., *Early Retirement: Promises and Pitfalls,* New York: Plenum, 1992.

Wilson, Janet, *Intergenerational Readings: 1980-1992,* Pittsburgh: Generations Together, 1992.

Wisensale, Steven K., "Grappling With the Generational Equity Debate: An Ongoing Challenge for the Public Administrator," *Public Integrity* (Winter 1999), 1(1): 1-19.

Wolf, R. S., and Pillemer, K., *Helping Elderly Victims: The Reality of Elder Abuse,* New York: Columbia University Press, 1989.

Wolfe, John R., *Coming Health Crisis: Who Will Pay for Care for the Aged in the Twenty-First century?,* Chicago: University of Chicago Press, 1993.

Wolff, Nancy, "Women and the Equity of the Social Security Program," *Journal of Aging Studies* (Winter 1988), 2: 357-377.

Work/Family Elder Directions, Inc., *Elder Care Handbook,* Watertown, MA: Work-Family Elder Directions, Inc., 1988.

Wu Ke Bin, *Income and Poverty in the United States in 1995: A Chart Book,* Washington, DC: American Association of Retired Persons, Public Policy Institute, 1998.

Yankelovich, Skelly, & White, *A 50 Year Report Card on the Social Security System: Attitudes of the American Public,* Washington, DC: American Association of Retired Persons, 1985.

Yee, Barbara W. K., "Elders in Southeast Asian Refugee Families," *Generations* (Summer 1992): 24-27.

Zarit, S., Orr, N. K., and Zarit, J. M., *The Hidden Victims of Alzheimer's Disease,* New York: New York University Press, 1985.

Zembek, B. A., and Singer, A., "The Problem of Defining Retirement Among Minorities: The Mexican Americans," *The Gerontologist* (1990), 30(6): 749-757.

Ziegler, S., and King, J., "Evaluating the Observable Effects of Foster Grandparents on Hospitalized Children," *Public Health Reports* (1982), 97(6): 550-557.

Zimny, George H., and Grossberg, George T. (eds.), *Guardianship of the Elderly: Psychiatric and Judicial Aspects,* New York: Springer, 1998.

Zweibel, N. R., Cassel, C. K., and Karrison, T., "Public Attitudes About the Use of Chronological Age as a Criterion for Allocating Health Care Resources," *The Gerontologist* (February 1993), 33(1): 74-80

Glossary/Index

Aaron, H., 45, 56-57, 239, 244-245

AARP. *See* American Association of Retired Persons

Abstracts, for research, 445

Abstracts in Social Gerontology, 442, 445

Abuse. *See* Elder abuse; Neglect

Accumulated advantage/disadvantage. *See* Cumulative advantage; Cumulative disadvantage

Accumulative waste theory of aging: the biological theory of aging that points to a buildup of cells of waste products that presumably interferes with metabolism, 342, 344

ACTION, 274, 275

Active euthanasia, 123-124. *See also* Euthanasia

Activities of daily living (ADLs): everyday tasks that are required for people to live on their own, such as the abilities to feed oneself, go to the toilet, take a bath, and get out of bed, 4

    home health care and, 24

    long-term care and, 19, 20, 22

    reserve capacity and, 327

Activity theory of aging: a view holding that the more active people are, the more likely they are to be satisfied with life, 318-320, 414, 419

Actualization, 299, 434

Acute health care, 20

Adaptation:

    capacity for, 30, 380

    recollection as, 423

    to the inevitable, 422

Adequacy: as applied to Social Security, the principle of maintaining a decent minimum income for everyone regardless of how much an individual contributed, 166, 237, 238, 250-251

ADLs. *See* Activities of daily living

Administration on Aging, U.S., 174

Adult children, 65-66, 69, 133. *See also* Family issues

Adult day care, 17, 24(exhibit)

Adult education, 405. *See also* Education; Training

Adult protective services: a local government agency that investigates allegations of elder abuse and intervenes where necessary to protect adults from harm, 117-118

Adults only movement, 224

Advance directive: a legal document authorizing decisions to be made, typically involving withholding lifesaving medical treatment, should circumstances arise in which a person has lost the capacity to make those decisions, 129, 131, 145-148

Adverse selection, 92

Advertising, 311

Advocates, 174, 175

AEI. *See* American Enterprise Institute

AFDC. *See* Aid to Families with Dependent Children

Affluence test: an approach designed to eliminate some benefit for those who are wealthy or above a specific income level, 197, 235. *See also* Means test

African Americans:

    as minority group, 155-156, 160

    crossover phenomenon and, 156

    economic well-being of, 161

    gender, aging, and, 158(exhibit)

    inter-ethnic equity and, 211, 212

    poverty rate for, 161

    retirement income of, 164-165

    self-esteem of, 154

    suicide rates of, 29

AGE. *See* Americans for Generational Equity

Age appropriateness, 309, 310
Age-based entitlements. *See* Entitlements, age versus
 need for
Age-based movements, 175-177
Age-based rationing. *See* Health care rationing
Age cohort. *See* Cohort
Age compression, 284. *See also* Compression of
 morbidity
Age differentiation: a process whereby people are
 socialized to act in different ways according to
 chronological age, 310
Age Discrimination in Employment Act, 174, 272,
 283. *See also* Ageism
Age grading: designation of people into categories
 based on chronological age; for example, in public school systems, 310
Age identification, 310-312
Age integration, 223, 225, 418
Ageism: prejudice or negative stereotypes about people based on chronological age, 153, 192, 288,
 320, 384
 compassionate, 185
 institutional, 279-280
AgeLine, 445
Age segregation: social or physical separation of
 groups of people according to chronological age,
 220, 222, 223-224, 225
Age stratification, 310
Age versus need. *See* Entitlements, age versus need for
Aging:
 as a disease, 46, 347
 as a gradual process, 310
 as an existential condition, 417
 biology of. *See* Biology of aging
 classic pattern of, 382
 conscious, 433-435
 cultural images of, 310-311
 denial of, 412
 diversity in, 152-163
 family and. *See* Family issues
 global, as transcendent issue, 195
 individual, xxvii-xxx, 152-153, 181
 inevitability of, 346-347
 journeys in, 417, 419
 meaning of. *See* Meaning, in old age
 normal, 4, 326, 339
 population, xxiii-xxx, 152-153, 157, 181
 primary, 4
 process of, 339-347. *See also* Aging theories
 productive, 273-275, 277-281, 305-306, 324, 417-418
 secondary, 4
 successful, 331

two worlds of, 153
vitality in, 353-360
Aging clock theory of aging: the idea that aging
 results from a preprogrammed sequence, as in a
 clock, built into the operation of the nervous or
 endocrine system of the body, 343-344
Aging interest groups: associations or other organizations that seek to influence government policies on behalf of the elderly, 175-177
Aging network: the national array of service programs helping older Americans, ranging from
 senior citizen centers and Area Agencies on
 Aging to programs offered by the federal Administration on Aging, 174
Aging policy. *See* Public policy
Aging society, America as, xxiii-xxx, 282-283
Aging theories:
 accumulative waste, 342, 344
 activity, 318-320, 414, 419
 aging clock, 343-344
 autoimmune, 343
 cellular, 345-346
 cognitive, 332
 continuity, 101, 102, 319, 414, 419
 cross-linkage, 344
 disengagement, 317-318, 322, 333, 414, 419, 432
 error accumulation, 342
 exchange, 65-66, 432
 free radical, 344-345
 implicit, 295
 interpretation, 319
 modernization, 316-317
 somatic mutation, 342
 wear-and-tear, 341-342
Aging work force, 283-284. *See also* Labor force
 participation
Aid to Families with Dependent Children (AFDC),
 187, 213
Aleut tribes, 40
Alimony, 165
Alternate-preferences hypothesis, 280
Altruistic suicide, 28
Alzheimer's Association, 67
Alzheimer's disease:
 burdens created by, 67
 compression of morbidity and, 364, 366
 death rates and, 6-7
 epidemiology of, 9-11
 genetics and, 10, 90-92, 350
 life expectancy and, 366
 projected trends in, 55
 survival prospects for, 5

AMA. *See* American Medical Association

Ambivalence, about old age, 316, 318, 334-335

American Association of Retired Persons (AARP), 176, 177, 222, 303, 304

American Bar Association, 76

American Enterprise Institute (AEI), 212, 213

American Indians. *See* Native Americans

American Medical Association (AMA), 14, 127, 131

Americans for Generational Equity (AGE), 207, 209, 213

American Society on Aging, 176

Animal life spans, 339-340, 357

Annuity: an investment vehicle permitting a lump sum of money to be paid out annually to projected life expectancy at a given age, 168, 243-244

Anomic suicide, 28

Antagonistic pleiotropy: the idea that some genetically determined trait can be beneficial early in life but harmful in later life, 327

Antioxidants: substances that destroy free radicals, thereby preventing damage to cell structures, 344, 345

Area Agencies on Aging, 174

Aristotle, 311, 342

Arthritis, 7-8, 19, 344

Artificial tissues and organs, 374-375

Artists, creativity of, 381, 387, 390, 401-402

Art of life, 428

Arts, participation in, 424

Asian Americans, 154, 155, 156-157, 160, 162

Assets:
  as retirement income, 163, 164, 165, 168-170
  diversity and, 154
  Medicaid eligibility and, 70, 71, 74-84

Assimilation, 157. *See also* Race and ethnicity

Assisted-living facilities: residential facilities for the elderly that provide limited supportive care and permit a high degree of independence, 17, 18

Assisted suicide, 44, 50, 124, 129-131, 139

Athletes, 392

Auerbach, A., 190

Austad, S. N., 350, 351-352

Australia, 236, 278

Autobiographical consciousness, 433. *See also* Life review

Autogenic training, 435

Autoimmune theory of aging: the idea that aging results from gradual decline in the body's auto-immune system, 343

Autonomy:
  balanced with best interests, 108-109

elder abuse and, 108-109, 110-111

end-of-life decisions and, 141

Baby boom generation: Americans born between 1946 and 1964, xxiv; xxiii
  economic status of, 170-171, 172
  generational equity and, 190, 195, 208
  generational interdependence and, 205
  public policy and, 178
  retirement and, 272, 284
  Social Security and, 229, 233

Backdoor rationing, 27-28, 37, 58-59

Bad choices, protection from. *See* Vulnerability

Baltes, P., 383, 403

Baltimore Longitudinal Study of Aging, 326

Bass, S. A., 276, 277-281

Bates, A., 73, 76-78

Belgium, 278

Bell, D., 298

Benefits, public. *See* Entitlements, age versus need for

Benevolence, and ethics, 140-142

Benson, H., 435

Bereavement, 321

Bergmann, B. R., 239, 247-250

Bernard, C., 358

Besdine, R. W., 44, 53-54

Best interest: the basis for making health care decisions for another person depending on what is thought will produce the most benefit for that person, 127
  autonomy balanced with, 108-109
  elder abuse and, 108-109
  termination of care and, 27, 127, 128

Binstock, R. H., 206

Bioengineering, 374-375

Biological clock, 343-344, 346, 348

Biology of aging, 325-330, 339-341
  chance versus fate in, 341
  genetics and, 327-328, 329, 340-342, 345, 352
  mechanisms of, 328-330
  mortality reduction and, 368-370
  prolonged life span and, 347-350
  theories of, 341-346. *See also* Aging theories

Biomarkers: specific physiological or functional processes that change with chronological age, 326

Biomedical advances. *See* Medical technology

Birth cohort. *See* Cohort

Birthrates, xxiv, xxv

Bismarck, O. von, 264

Blacks. *See* African Americans

Blaustein, A. I., 209

Blazer, D. G., 417

Board-and-care homes: small group homes that provide mainly custodial care for elderly people who do not need the intensive support of a nursing home, 17, 18, 24(exhibit)

Body image, 331

Body size, and biological aging, 340

Bonn Longitudinal Study of Aging, 332

Boomers. *See* Baby boom generation

Boren-Long amendment, 79

Borgatta, E. F., 282-289

Boxes of life, 316

Brain death, 127

Branch, L. G., 81

Brazil, 236

British health care system, 34, 42, 56-57. *See also* Great Britain

Brody, J., 351, 360-363

Brown, H. G., 319

Brown, R. N., 104, 105-107

Browning, E., 128

Bureaucratization of the life course, 316

Burnout, of caregivers, 67

Burtless, G., 239, 242-244

Busy ethic, 290-297, 319, 422

Butler, R., 44, 54-55, 431, 432

California Natural Death Act, 127

Callahan, D., 3, 44, 210, 211
    proposal by, 34, 36-39, 41-43, 45-51
    proposal by, criticism of, 51-54, 56

Caloric restriction, 347-348, 372

Campbell, R., 217

Canada, 102

Canadian health care system, 35

Cancer, 6, 8-9, 344, 345, 350

Canes versus kids, 214. *See also* Children

Cannon, W. B., 358

Capitalism, 301

Capitation: reimbursement of health care services on a per head basis rather than a per service basis, 59

Cardiovascular disease, 6, 9, 19, 372

Caregiving:
    burnout in, 67
    by families, 65-67, 68-69, 85-88, 203-204, 278, 284
    by women, 66, 85-88, 156, 166, 237, 238, 255-256
    elder abuse and, 109
    levels of, 66-67
    productive aging and, 278

Caro, F. G., 276, 277-281

Case management, 40

Cash balance plan: a retirement plan in which the employer makes annual contributions to an account in the employee's name, where the money increases at a guaranteed rate of return, 167

CCRC. *See* Continuing care retirement community

Cellular changes, and aging, 326, 327, 329-330, 341-342, 345-346

Cellular theory of aging: the view that aging can be explained largely by changes in structure and function taking place in the cells of an organism, 345-346

Century Village, 222

Cervantes, 401

Chateaubriand, F., 420-421

Chen, Y.-P., 276, 277-281

Chevreul, M., 402

Child care:
    dropout option, in Social Security, 238, 255-256
    in nursing homes, 221

Child dependency, 188, 189

Children:
    age segregation and, 224
    generational interdependence and, 198, 202
    intergenerational programs and, 221, 222
    poverty and, 187-188, 202, 207-208, 214
    rearing of, changes in, 323-324

Children's Defense League, 222

Chile, 236

China, 191, 381

Chinen, A., 434

Choices:
    end-of-life. *See* End-of-life decisions;
        Vulnerability

Chore service, 24(exhibit)

Chromosomes, 346. *See also* DNA; Genetics

Chronic conditions: sickness or disability that persists over an extended period of time, often interfering with activities of daily living, 7
    compression of morbidity and, 355-356, 361-363, 365, 368-369
    economic well-being and, 161
    long-term care for, 19-22
    preventive care for, 55
    See also specific conditions

Cicero, 324

Citizenship, 162

Civil commitment, 103, 104, 106, 107

Clark, B., 123

Class bias, 52. *See also* Social class

Classic aging pattern: a persistent pattern on IQ tests that shows relative stability in the verbal part but declines with age on the performance part of the IQ test, 382

Clinical depression: a psychiatric diagnosis involving symptoms such as loss of appetite, sleep disturbances, and deep sadness, 124-126. *See also* Depression

Clocks:
biological, 343-344, 346, 348
social, 310

Coaching, 324

Cocoon, 311, 325

Cognitive function, 333-334, 336
compensation in, 334, 384, 385, 386
creativity and, 380-387
flexibility in, 323, 334, 387
See also Intelligence

Cognitive reserve capacity: the degree of unused capacity for learning that exists at any given time, 385

Cognitive stability, 385-386

Cognitive theory of aging: a view of aging that emphasizes individual subjective perception, rather than actual objective change itself, as the factor that determines behavior associated with advanced age, 332

Cohort: a group of people born within a bounded period of years, such as the baby boomer generation (born 1946-1964), xxiv, 171, 184

Cohousing: an intergenerational residential arrangement in which planned communities offer self-sufficient housing units tied to shared common spaces, 225

COLA. *See* Cost-of-living adjustment

Collaborative cognition, 334

Collagen: a protein that makes up the connective tissue found in skin, bones, and tendons of the body, 344

Color, people of. *See* Race and ethnicity

Commitment, civil, 103, 104, 106, 107

Common sense, 383. *See also* Intelligence

Commonwealth Fund study, 274-275

Community service, 274, 306, 413

Compassion:
ageism and, 185
ethics and, 141-142

Compensation, in cognitive functioning, 334, 384, 385, 386

Competency, 104, 112-113

Competition, and conflict, 191, 199, 200

Compression, age, 284

Compression of morbidity: the postponement of illness until later and later into advanced age, 336, 337-370
biological aging process and, 339-341
biological constraints and, 368-370
biological theories of aging and, 341-346
chronic conditions and, 355-356, 361-363, 365, 368-369
differing views of, 353-371
inevitability of aging and, 346-347
life span prolongation and, 347-351
lifestyle and, 347-348, 355, 370
rectangular curve and, 356-360, 361-362, 368, 369
societal constraints and, 370

Computer technology, 406-407

Confidentiality, 99, 108

Conflict:
competition and, 191, 199, 200
economic rights and, 284
mediation of, 306

Conflict theory, 280, 281

Congregate housing: a residential arrangement in which nutrition, housekeeping, and supportive services are provided, 17, 19, 24(exhibit)

Congregate Housing Act, 174

Conroy, Claire, 127-128

Conscious aging, 433-435

Consensus approach, public, 384-385

Conservatorship, 103, 104, 106

Constitutional issues, 52, 104, 127, 128, 130, 131, 143. *See also* Legal issues; Rights

Consumer Price Index, 234. *See also* Inflation

Continuing care retirement community (CCRC): a type of residential facility that offers a combination of housing and health or supportive services to residents, 17, 18

Continuity theory of aging: the view that in aging people are inclined to maintain, as much as they can, the same habits, personalities, and styles of life they have developed in earlier years, 101, 102, 319, 414, 419

Continuum of care: a range of care options that are responsive to changing individual needs, from less intense to more intense, at home or in an institution, 23-25

Contract, physician-patient, 141

Cornell Study of Occupational Retirement, 265, 296

Cornman, J., 197-206

Cost-benefit analysis: examination of treatment costs in relation to the benefits created if a patient lives—for instance, greater productivity, 43, 204, 355

the plan and according to how successfully the funds are invested, 167, 243, 270

Degenerative joint disease, 8. *See also* Arthritis

Dehydroepiandrosterone (DHEA), 343

Deikman, A., 435

de León, P., 1, 372

Dementia:
   burdens of, 67
   epidemiology of, 9-11
   See also Alzheimer's disease

Demographic transition, xxv-xxvi, 151-152

Demographic transition theory: the idea that population aging can be explained by a decline in both birthrates and death rates following industrialization, xxiv

Denmark, 278

Dennis, W., 385, 387, 394-397

Dependency, 188, 189, 322, 355-356

Dependency ratio: a numerical measure of the economic burden on the working population caused by those not in the labor force, 188-189, 232, 283-284

Depression:
   clinical, 124-126
   continuum view of, 125
   end-of-life decisions and, 124-126
   meditation and, 435
   nursing homes and, 21
   stages of life and, 425
   suicide and, 29-30

DHEA. *See* Dehydroepiandrosterone

Diagnosis related groups (DRGs): distinct categories of diseases that are the basis for Medicare's financial reimbursements to hospitals, 14, 37

Dialysis, 34, 35

Diet, 347-348, 370, 371, 372. *See also* Meals-on-Wheels

Diogenes Syndrome, 115

Dirac, P., 398

Disability insurance, 230, 250-255, 288

Discovery:
   in training, 275. *See also* Training
   time of, 431

Discrimination, 153. *See also* Ageism; Stereotypes

Disease:
   discrete versus intrinsic causes of, 11
   longevity and, 4-5
   major, in old age, 6-11
   responses to, 11-12
   See also specific diseases

Disengagement theory of aging: the idea that separation of older people from active roles in soci-

ety is normal and appropriate, and benefits both society and older individuals, 317-318, 322, 333, 414, 419, 432

Displaced homemakers, 165

Distance learning, 408

Diversity, 152-163, 181
   economic well-being and, 158, 161-162
   gender and, 154, 157-160
   generational interdependence and, 198-199, 200, 202-203
   multiple jeopardy and, 160-161
   outlook for, 162-163
   race and, 153, 154, 155-157, 160-161, 208
   social class and, 153, 154-155

Divestment planning: a systematic approach to "spending down" accumulated assets in order to become eligible for Medicaid coverage in the future, 72

Divorce, 159, 160, 165, 238, 247, 255

DNA, 327, 329, 340, 342, 348, 349. *See also* Genetics

DNA testing, 91

Doctors. *See* Physicians

Domestic violence, 99. *See also* Elder abuse

Domiciliary care facilities: small facilities that provide mainly custodial care for elderly people who do not need the intensive support of a nursing home, 18

Dominant culture, 157. *See also* Race and ethnicity

Double-decker system, 239, 249, 253, 254-255

Double jeopardy: the state of being a member of two categories simultaneously for which old age brings special disadvantage, such as being female and a member of a racial minority, 160-161

Downsizing, 269, 304

Down's syndrome, 10

Downward mobility, 154

DRGs. *See* Diagnosis related groups

Driving Miss Daisy, 153-154, 312

Dubos, R., 358

Duke Longitudinal Study of Aging, 380, 416

Durable power of attorney for health care: a legal instrument in which one party names another individual to make health care decisions for him or her should the first party become incapacitated, 129, 146. *See also* Advance directive; Power of attorney

Durkheim, E., 28

Duty to die cheaply, 42

Dying well, 130. *See also* End-of-life decisions

Early retirement, 266, 271, 272, 304, 318. *See also* Retirement

Early retirement benefits: pension income and other benefits for which employees are eligible when they retire before some customary retirement age, 166, 168, 173, 180

Earnings, income from, 180. *See also* Income

Earnings sharing, 239, 248-249, 253, 254

Earnings test: the requirement that persons receiving Social Security must be to a substantial degree retired; that is, they may receive no more than a limited amount of income from employment (also known as the retirement test), 235, 268

Economics of health care, 12-16
   elderly's share of expenditures in, 12
   increasing costs in, 12, 13, 14, 15-16, 25, 33
   medical technology and, 15-16
   reimbursement systems in, 12-15. *See also* Medicaid; Medicare
   termination of treatment and, 27. *See also* Health care rationing
   See also Health care costs

Economic status, 163-172, 180-181
   gender and, 158, 161
   mean versus median measures of, 163
   of baby boomers, 170-171, 172
   outlook for, 170-172
   retirement income and, 163-170
   uncertainty and, 170-172
   See also Economic well-being; Financial matters; Generational equity; Socioeconomic status

Economic well-being, 151-152, 158, 161-162.
   See also Economic status; Financial matters; Generational equity

Economy:
   changes in, and retirement, 269-271, 298-299
   leisure and, 413-414
   moral, 209-211, 324-325

Edison, T. A., 389

Education:
   diversity and, 154
   life course and, 320, 321, 323
   older adult programs in, 405
   technology for, 406-408
   See also Learning; Training

Effectiveness. *See* Cost-effectiveness analysis

Egalitarianism, 162. *See also* Equity

Ego integrity, 417, 432

Egoistic suicide, 28

Ego transcendence, 318

Einstein, A., 379

Ekerdt, D. J., 276, 290-297

Elbaum, J., 27

Elder abuse, 67
   autonomy, and, 110-111
   autonomy, best interests, and, 108-109
   compared to child abuse, 98
   end-of-life decisions and, 128, 141, 143
   ethical issues and, 108-109, 110-113
   family issues and, 98, 109
   legal issues and, 99, 110-114
   protective services and, 117-118
   rate of, 98
   reporting of, 97, 99, 108-109
   risk factors for, 98-99
   vulnerability and, 96-99, 108-114

Elderhostel program, 405

Elderlaw: a specialized branch of law devoted to legal and regulatory issues affecting the elderly, 72

Electronic mail, 406, 407

Electronic media, 311

Employee Retirement Income Security Act (ERISA): a Federal law passed in 1974 that regulates private pension plans and offers protection against loss of benefits by retired workers, 167

Employment. *See* Labor force participation; Occupations; Work

Empty nest concept, 67

Encyclopedia of Aging, The, 442, 444

Encyclopedias, for research, 444

End-of-life decisions, 123-150
   advance directive and, 129, 131, 145-148
   depression and, 124-126
   euthanasia and, 123-124, 129, 130, 136-137, 139
   future of, 130-131, 148-149
   legal issues and, 126-131, 139, 143
   physicians and, 126, 129, 130, 131, 138-145
   quality of life and, 126, 132-139, 141-142
   right to die and, 26, 27, 126-130, 143
   suicide and, 124-126, 129-135, 139
   surrogates for, 306
   See also Death and dying

England. *See* British health care system; Great Britain

Entitlements, age versus need for, 183-220
   arguments for age in, 197-206
   arguments for need in, 195-197
   dependency ratio and, 188-189
   generational interdependence and, 197-206
   military budget and, 212-213
   moral economy and, 209-211
   poverty and, 185-188
   race, ethnicity, and, 208, 211-212, 216-219
   resentment hypothesis and, 211-212

scarce resources and, 191, 199-200, 201
social class and, 216-219
targets of benefits and, 191-220
taxes, accounting, and, 189-191, 204
victim blaming and, 206-215
Environmental approach, to prolonging the life span, 347-348. *See also* Diet; Metabolism
Epidemiology: the use of mathematical methods to study the distribution of disease in human populations, 6-12
Equal protection rights, 52, 143
Equity: as applied to Social Security, a fair return to beneficiaries depending on how much they contribute to the system, 166, 237, 247-257
adequacy and, 166, 237, 238
generational. *See* Generational equity
public policy and, 179
Equity, home. *See* Home equity
Erikson, E., 315, 335, 411, 417, 419, 422-425, 432
Erikson, J. M., 422-425
ERISA. *See* Employment Retirement Income Security Act
Error accumulation theory of aging: the idea that aging results from chance events that gradually damage the genetic code, 342
Eskimo tribes, 40
Estates:
guardianship of, 104
Medicaid eligibility and, 72, 76-78, 79-80
recovery programs and, 78, 79-80, 83
See also Inheritance
Ethics, and end-of-life decisions, 123-150
Ethnicity. *See* Race and ethnicity
Euthanasia, 44, 50
end-of-life decisions and, 123-124, 129, 130, 136-137, 139
types of, 123-124
Evolution, and longevity, 327-328
Exchange theory of aging: the idea that interaction in social groups is based on the reciprocal balancing of rewards depending on actions performed, 65-66, 432
Expert knowledge system, 383
Exploitation, 96, 97, 102-103, 117. *See also* Elder abuse
Extended care facilities, 20. *See also* Nursing homes
Extended family: the complete range of relatives, including grandparents, aunts and uncles, and cousins, as opposed to nuclear family, which consists of just parents and children, 68
Extrasensory perception, 433

Fabian, D. R., 105, 114-117
Failure model of old age, 179
Faith in Action Program, 415
Faith stages, 416-417. *See also* Religion; Spirituality
Family Friends program, 221
Family issues, 65-94
age-segregated housing, 224
caregiving, 65-67, 68-69, 85-88, 203-204, 278, 284
elder abuse, 98, 109
end-of-life decisions, 124, 133, 135, 136
generational interdependence, 202, 203-204, 209-210
living arrangements, 67-68, 85-86
Medicaid, 69-84, 88-90
race and ethnicity, 156, 157
structural changes, 237
vulnerability, 95-96, 97, 98, 99, 109
women as caregivers. *See* Women
Fear, 20-21, 57, 97, 98
Federation of Volunteer Interfaith Caregivers, 415
Feminist perspective, 160, 247-250
Feminization of poverty, 158
Fertility rates, xxvi, 195, 283
Filial responsibility: the obligation of adult children to provide care for aged parents, 69
Financial matters:
control of, 99, 104, 106
exploitation in, 96, 102-103
planning in, 71-73, 74-77, 119, 303-305
uncertainty in, 170-172
See also Economic status; Economic well-being; Generational equity; Income
Finland, 236
Florida-ization, xxiv
Fluid intelligence: the intellectual ability to solve novel tasks or problems, 380, 383, 385, 386
Food stamps, 187
Foster Grandparents Program, 221, 274
401(k) pension plan: an individual pension plan that permits individuals to set aside a portion of income on a tax-deferred basis, 168, 270-271
Four percent fallacy: the mistaken idea that nursing homes aren't important for older people because, at any single point in time, only 4% of those over 65 are likely to be living in a nursing home, 22
Fourteenth Amendment, 52, 143
Fowler, J., 416-417
France, 278
Freedom:
busy ethic and, 294
decision making and, 104, 105-107, 140
intellectual, 421

role loss and, 153
See also Autonomy

Free radicals: molecules of oxygen ionized because of an extra electron, 329-330, 344, 348

Free radical theory of aging: the idea that free radicals (unstable and highly reactive organic molecules) create damage that gives rise to symptoms we recognize as aging, 344-345

Friedan, Betty, 87

Friendly visitor support system, 24(exhibit)

Fries, J. F.:
comments on, 350, 351, 360-363, 368, 369, 370
readings by, 353-360, 364-367

Fulmer, Terry T., 105, 108-109

Functional age: age based on a measurement of performance abilities, such as strength, mobility, and mental capacity, that are distinct from chronological age, 327

Functional assessment, for long-term care, 22-23

Functionality:
biology of aging and, 326-328
disengagement theory and, 317, 318

Funded system: a pension system, public or private, in which future retirement benefits owed are paid out of money saved up in advance, 236

Futility, medical, 27

Galen, 312

GAO. *See* General Accounting Office

Gender issues:
aging experience, 158-160
biological aging, 339
caregiving, 66, 85-88
diversity, 154, 157-160
economic well-being, 158, 161
employment, 166
guardianship, 104
income, 158, 165
labor force participation, 264-265
Medicare coverage, 250, 251, 252, 253
multiple jeopardy, 160-161
pensions, 165-166
roles, 86-88, 158, 423
sex ratio, 157
sexuality, 101, 102
Social Security, 237-239, 247-257
stages of life, 425, 426-427
suicide rates, 29, 125, 134
See also Women

General Accounting Office (GAO), 79-80

Generation, meanings of, 184

Generational accounting: a comparative analysis of the impact of government tax and spending policies on differential historical cohorts, 190-191

Generational equity: the idea that differing cohorts should be treated similarly with respect to benefits over the life course, 179, 183-197, 206-213
age-based benefits and, 197-206
competition, conflict, and, 191, 199, 200
conscious aging and, 435
dependency ratio and, 188-189
generational accounting and, 190-191
military budget and, 212-213
moral economy and, 209-211
needs-based benefits and, 195-197
poverty, and, 185-187
poverty, children, and, 187-188, 202, 207-208, 214
race, ethnicity, and, 208, 211-212
scarce resources and, 191, 199-200, 201
targets of benefits and, 191-220
taxation and, 189-191
victim blaming and, 206-215
See also Intergenerational programs

Generational interdependence, 197-206. *See also* Generational equity; Intergenerational programs

Generational politics, 177

Generation in crisis, 187

Generations United, 222

Generativity, 315, 411, 425. *See also* Meaning, in old age

Genetics:
Alzheimer's disease and, 10, 90-92, 350
biology of aging and, 327-328, 329, 340-342, 345, 352
life span prolongation and, 349-350

Genetic screening, 90-92

Genocide, 61

Geriatrics: the medical specialty treating the diseases of old age, 6

Germany, xxiv

Gerontocracy, 191

Gerontological Abstracts, 445

Gerontological Society of America, 176

Gerontology, and meaning, 417-418

Gerontology term paper research, 439-449
abstracts for, 445
databases for, 445
encyclopedias for, 444
guides to, 446
handbooks for, 444
journals for, 448-449
periodicals for, 448-449
reference works for, 446-447

resources for, 444-449

search strategy in, 440-442

statistics for, 445-446

steps in, 442-443

textbooks for, 447

topic definition in, 440

See also Internet resources

Gerotranscendence, 333

Glycosylation: a process, commonly known as caramelization, in which proteins combine with sugar, as when food turns brown, 330

Goals, and meaning, 419, 422, 428, 430

Goethe, J. W. von, 381, 404, 420

Golden age, 68, 316

Gompertz law: the statistical tendency of mortality, or death rate, to double with every seven years of advancing age, 339

Gordon, H., 76

Government policy. *See* Public policy

Grace Plaza of Great Neck, Inc. v. Elbaum, 27

Graebner, W. A., 285

Graham, M., 387

Grandma Moses, 381

Graying of America, xxiii-xxx. *See also* Population aging

Gray lobby, 176

Gray market, 413

Gray Panthers, 176

Gray power, 177

Great Britain, 278. *See also* British health care system

Great Society legislation, 173

Greeks, ancient, 311, 312

Gruenberg, E. M., 368, 369, 370

Guardian at litem, 127

Guardianship: legal responsibility for another person's welfare, 103-104, 106, 111, 112

Gulliver's Travels, 1-2

Guns versus canes, 212-213

Habituation: the idea (from R. Kastenbaum) that aging can be understood as gradually becoming more and more mechanical in response to the environment, a process that can begin early in life, 435

Hagestad, G. O., 73, 85-88

Ham and Eggs Movement, 176

Handbooks, for research, 444

Handyman service, 24(exhibit)

Happiness, 125, 137. *See also* Life satisfaction; Quality of life

Hayes-Bautista, D., 211

Hayflick, L., 345

Hayflick limit: a maximum number of cell divisions that normal cells undergo, as typically measured in a laboratory dish, 345, 346, 350

Healing, as the essence of medicine, 144

Health care costs:

financing for, 69-71

for long-term care, 16, 25, 37. *See also* Medicaid

increases in, 12, 13, 14, 15-16, 25, 33

in last year of life, 39-40

termination of treatment and, 26-27

Health Care Financing Administration: that part of the U.S. Department of Health and Human Services charged with administering the Medicare and Medicaid programs, 12

Health care professionals:

elder abuse reporting by, 97, 99, 108-109

end-of-life decisions and, 131

See also Physicians

Health care rationing, 2-3, 14, 16, 33-63

alternatives to, 42-43

backdoor, 27-28, 37, 58-59

Callahan proposal on, 34, 36-39, 41-43, 45-51

cost versus age and, 41-42

criticism of, 36, 42, 51-57

economics and, 40

euthanasia, suicide, and, 44, 50

future of, scenarios on, 60-61

generational equity and, 185

justification for, 35-37

notch problem and, 43-44

precedents for, 34-35

savings based on, 37-38

Health insurance:

for hospitalization, 250, 251, 252, 253

for long-term care, 82, 84, 88-90, 91-92

Medigap, 14, 58

See also Medicaid; Medicare

Health Insurance Portability and Accountability Act of 1996, 89

Health maintenance organizations (HMOs), 57-60, 90

Health outcomes research, 43

Health promotion, 4, 15, 371-373

Health status. *See* Biology of aging; Chronic conditions; Compression of morbidity

Heart disease, 6, 9, 19, 344

Hebrews, ancient, 311

Heisler, C. J., 105, 110-114

HeLa cells, 345

Helplessness:

heroic, 429

learned, 322

Hemlock Society, 130

Henretta, J., 217
Henry, W. H., 295
Hentoff, N., 44, 51-54
Heroic helplessness, 429
Herzog, A. R., 277-278
Hewitt Associates, 168
Hidden victims, caregivers as, 67
Hilditch, T. P., 388
Hilton, J., 325
Hippocrates, 312
Hirschorn, B., 197-206
Hispanics, 154, 225
    as minority group, 155, 156, 160, 162
    gender, aging, and, 158(exhibit)
    inter-ethnic equity and, 211, 212
    poverty rate for, 161(exhibit)
Historical events, influence of, 320
History:
    of one's passage through life, 314-315, 320-321, 333
    of retirement, 264-268, 278-279, 285, 313
    of views on life course, 311, 312, 313, 316, 324
HMOs. *See* Health maintenance organizations
Holistic health care, 434
Holmes, O. W., 337, 361
Holy Fire, 60, 375
Home equity, 83-84, 169-170, 171, 172
Home health care, 25, 71
Homeless shelters, 221
Homemakers:
    displaced, 165
    Social Security and, 247-250, 253, 254, 255-256
    See also Social Security, and women
Homemaker service, 24(exhibit)
Homeostatis, 358
Homesharing, 17, 19
Hook, S., 132, 136-137
Hope, 422
Hormonal changes, 101, 102
Hospital insurance, 250, 251, 252, 253
Housewives. *See* Homemakers
Housing:
    family issues and, 67-68, 85-86
    long-term care and, 17-19
    subsidized, 19
    See also Living arrangements
Huber, E., 77
Hughes, L., 404
Human Genome Project, 92, 350, 352. *See also*
    Genetics
Humboldt, A. von, 402
Hyperborean theme, 325

Identity:
    meaning and, 417, 425, 432
    national, 162
Ill-derly and well-derly, 153. *See also* Diversity
Illness. *See* Disease
Immortal cells, 345
Immune system, 330, 343, 348
Implicit theory of aging, 295
Impoverishment:
    artificial, 76, 77
    fallacy of, 78-85
Income, 151, 180
    compared to wealth, 163
    diversity and, 154
    for retirement. *See* Retirement income
    gender and, 158, 165
    in economic status, 163-170
    of baby boomers, 171
    See also Economic status; Economic well-being;
        Financial matters
Income-related premiums, 37
Incompetency hearings, 104. *See also* Competency
Independence:
    compression of morbidity and, 355-356
    in living arrangements, 67-68. *See also* Housing
    technology and, 406
India, 381
Individual aging:
    diversity and, 152-153
    population aging and, xxvii-xxx, 181
Individual growth, 433. *See also* Meaning, in old age
Individual retirement account (IRA): a retirement
    savings plan that permits those qualified to set
    aside up to a maximum percentage of their
    income each year and that offers some tax shel-
    ter until the money is withdrawn, 168
    Social Security and, 232, 243, 288
    Super-, 232
Individuation, 332
Industrialization, xxv, 269, 316, 321. *See also*
    Postindustrial society
Inequality, patterns of, 160, 164. *See also* Diversity
Infant mortality, 359
Inflation, 168, 171, 180, 231, 234
Informal support systems, 154, 156-157. *See also*
    Family issues; Support systems
Inheritance, 72, 77, 118-119, 128. *See also* Estates
Inpatient hospital care, 24(exhibit)
In re Conroy, 127-128
In re Earle Spring, 127-128
In re Guardianship of Estelle M. Browning, 128
In re Quinlan, 127, 143

intervention procedures, 103-104, 106-107
See also specific legislation
Leguerrier, T., 126
Lehman, H.:
classic study of creativity by, 384-385, 387, 388-393
critiques of, 385, 394-397, 398-400
Leisure:
economics of, 413-414
history of, 298
legitimization of, 293
meaning and, 412-414
new age of, 299-302
participation patterns in, 413-414
productivity and, 180, 273
retirement and, 266-269, 273, 293, 295, 299-302, 413
Social Security and, 268
theories of aging and, 414
Leisure-oriented housing, 17, 19
Leisure Village, 222
Leisure World, 222, 408
Levin, J., 433
Levinson, D., 315, 335
Library research. *See* Gerontology term paper research
Life care communities, 18
Life course perspective: a perspective from which aging is viewed as part of the totality of human life, understood as a successive series of stages, from infancy through old age, 309-336
age identification and, 310-312
biology of aging and, 317, 325-330
bureaucratization of, 316
cognitive functioning and, 323, 333-334, 336
flexibility and, 323, 325
historical events and, 320-321
historical views on, 311, 312, 313, 316, 324
influences on life course, 320-322
life history and, 314-315, 320-321, 333
life transitions and, 314-315, 321
meaning and, 310, 315, 317, 324, 332, 418-419
moral economy and, 324-325
new map needed for, 335-336
postindustrial society and, 322-325
psychological functioning and, 331-334
religion and, 415
social class and, 310, 320-321
social institutions and, 321-322
social policies and, 321-322
stages of life and, 312-313, 335
theories of aging and, 316-320

time orientation and, 310, 322, 323-324, 336
unpredictable nature of, 322-323
Life cycle model of savings: an economic theoretical approach that predicts people will save more in later middle age, as they see retirement ahead, 171, 259
Life events: distinctive or memorable events that occur in an individual's life, xxiv
age identification and, 310-311
influence on life course of, 320-321
Life expectancy: the predicted length of life, usually from some specific point in time, such as birth:
Alzheimer's disease and, 366
increases in, xxiii-xxiv, xxix, 3, 198, 424
life span and, 3, 11, 338-340, 354, 360
retirement and, 266
Social Security eligibility and, 234
See also Compression of morbidity
Life history, 314-315, 320-321, 333
Lifelong learning, 405
Life review: a process of reminiscence that involves return of past memories so that individuals can work through conflicting feelings about the past, 431-433. *See also* Memories
Life satisfaction: a person's attitude of approval toward past and present life as a whole, 99, 310, 319, 331, 412. *See also* Meaning, in old age
Life Satisfaction Index, 100
Life span: the hypothetical maximum possible length of life, determined by observing the longest any member of a species has lived, 3, 11
across species, 339-340, 357
biology of aging and, 325-328
compression of morbidity and, 337-351, 360-361
diet and, 347-348
medical model and, 354
natural, 34, 36, 42, 47-48
prolongation of, approaches for, 347-351
transitions and, 314-315
See also Life expectancy
Life stages:
gender and, 425, 426-427
life course perspective on, 312-313, 335
meaning and, 416-421, 424, 425-428
Lifestyles:
compression of morbidity and, 347-348, 355, 370
health promotion and, 371-373
Life transitions, 314-315, 321
Literary creativity, 381, 391, 400
Living arrangements, 67-68, 85-86
age integration and, 223, 225
age segregation and, 220, 222, 223-224, 225

gender and, 159

quality of life and, 100

See also Housing

Living will: an individual's written statement specifying or limiting his or her medical treatment in a situation without hope of recovery, 128, 131, 146-147. *See also* Advance directive

Lobbying, 176. *See also* Aging interest groups

Locus of control: a range of subjectively perceived abilities to manage oneself in the environment, 322

Logan's Run, 60

Longevity:

biology of, 326-328. *See also* Biology of aging

challenges of, 1-5

disease and, 4-5

lifestyle and, 347-348, 355, 370, 371-373

See also Compression of morbidity; Life expectancy; Life span

Longitudinal research: research in which the same study individuals are followed over time, 22, 314, 317, 321, 326, 332, 380, 384, 414, 416

Long-term care, 3, 16-25

chronic care and, 19-22

compared to acute care, 20

continuum of care and, 23-25

costs of, 16, 25, 37

family issues, and, 68-84

financing of, 69-71

functional assessment for, 22-23

health care rationing and, 37

housing for, 17-19

insurance for, 82, 84, 88-90, 91-92

Medicaid and, 69-84, 88-90

risk sharing for, 82, 83-84

support systems in, 23-24

Losses, accumulation of, 134

Lost Horizon, 325

Loving charity, and ethics, 142

Luce, G., 434

Macmillan, D., 115

Malthus, T., 61

Managed care: a health service approach that combines insurance, care providers, and facilities within a single system designed to reduce costs, 40, 57-60

Mandatory reporting: a legal requirement that professionals observing signs of possible elder abuse must report such cases to authorities, 99

Mandatory retirement: a practice where people are forced to retire from work at a fixed, uniform age, 271-272, 283

Manton, K., 5, 351, 367-371

Marginal elderly, 217-219

Market risk, and Social Security, 241. *See also* Stocks

Maslow, A., 434

Mass media, 311

Masters, W., 100

Matisse, H., 381

Maximum length of life. *See* Life span

McIntosh, J. L., 132, 133

McKhann, C. F., 132, 138-139

Meals-on-Wheels, 24(exhibit)

Meaning, in old age, 411-437

active involvement and, 419, 422-425

activity theory of aging and, 414, 419

conscious aging and, 433-435

continuity theory of aging and, 414, 419

continuity with midlife activity and, 419, 420-422

disengagement theory of aging and, 414, 419

doubts and, 421

exchange theory of aging and, 432

gerontology and, 417-418

goals and, 419, 422, 428, 430

journal entries on, 429-431

journeys in, 417, 419

leisure and, 412-414

life course perspective and, 310, 315, 317, 324, 332, 418-419

memories and, 411, 423, 427, 431-433

power of, 411

psychology of, 417, 419, 424-428, 431, 432, 434-435

religion and, 413, 414-416, 427, 428, 433

roles and, 412, 423-425, 429

significance and, 47

spirituality and, 414-417, 430, 433-435

stages of life and, 416-421, 424, 425-428

transcendence and, 411, 434

wisdom and, 423, 424

Means test: a requirement that a person must fall below a certain level of income or assets in order to quality for a government benefit program, 37, 197

alternatives to, 193

Medicaid and, 70, 89, 217

Social Security and, 235

See also Entitlements, age versus need for

Medawar, P. B., 327

Median age: the age for which half the population is older and half the population is younger, xxiv

Media stereotypes, 311

Medicaid: a federal and state program that pays for health care expenses of people who fall below the poverty line, 12, 25
as public policy, 173
assets and, 70, 71, 74-84
class, race, and, 217-218
eligibility for, 70, 71-72, 74-84
limitations of, 46, 69
long-term care and, 69-84, 88-90
long-term care insurance and, 82, 84, 88-89
middle class and, 69-73, 76-78
planning for, 71-73, 74-77
ranking of coverage under, 35

Medicaid spenddown: the requirement that people divest themselves of assets down to a minimal level in order to quality for Medicaid coverage of nursing home care, 70, 119
fallacy of impoverishment and, 78, 81-82
middle class and, 72, 76-78
morality of, 72
need for planning of, 74-75

Medical futility, 27
Medical model of life and health, 353-354
Medical savings accounts, 36
Medical technology, 2, 5, 11-12
economics of health care and, 15-16
end-of-life decisions and, 25, 127, 132-133
expanded health span and, 54-55
health care rationing and, 37-40, 41
needs-based benefits and, 195

Medicare: the federal government program that pays for acute health care for older people:
aging interest groups and, 176
as public policy, 173
as scapegoat, 213
denial of coverage by, 59
equity and, 179
future scenarios for, 259, 260
gender issues and, 250, 251, 252, 253
growth of, 178
in last year of life, 39
limitations of, xxviii, 13-14, 15, 16
overview of, 12-15
Parts A and B, 13, 14
rationing and, 36-37, 39, 43-44
universality and, 163

Medicare Catastrophic Coverage Act, 82, 176, 177
Medicare HMOs, 57-60

Medigap insurance: an insurance policy that covers the difference between what Medicare pays for a service and what is actually charged for it, 14, 58

Meditation, 434, 435
MedLine, 445
Medvedev, Z., 341
Meek v. Martinez, 194
Memories:
meaning and, 411, 423, 427, 431-433
symbolic world of, 411
Memory loss, 333
Menopause, 102, 344
Mental health support services, 24(exhibit)
Mentoring, 324
Mercer, S. O., 134
Mercy killing, 123, 140, 142. *See also* Euthanasia
Merrill Lynch Baby Boom Retirement Index, 171
Metabolism, 340, 348
Michelangelo, 387, 421
Middle Ages, 312
Middle class, and Medicaid, 69-73, 76-78
Midlife transition, 315
Military budget, 212-213
Miller, S. J., 293
Millionaires, 155
Minkler, M., 194, 206-215
Minority groups:
diversity and, 155-157, 160-161
equity and, 179, 211-212
intergenerational issues and, 211-212, 225
part-time employment for, 287
preretirement planning for, 304
productivity and, 180
resentment hypothesis and, 211-212
retirement income of, 164-165
See also Race and ethnicity

Modernization theory of aging: the view that the status of the elderly has declined since industrialization and the spread of technology, 316-317
Molecular changes, and aging, 326, 327, 329
Molitor, G., 266
Monet, C., 381, 421
Montgomery, R. J. V., 276, 282-289
Moral continuity, between work and retirement, 290-297
Morale, 99-100, 412. *See also* Life satisfaction; Meaning, in old age; Quality of life
Moral economy, 209-211, 324-325
Morbidity: sickness or physical illness of some kind, 4, 5. *See also* Biology of aging; Chronic conditions; Compression of morbidity; Longevity
Morgan, J., 203
Mortality gap, 85-86

Mortality rates:
    biological aging process and, 340
    compression of mortality and, 359
    major diseases and, 6-7
    Medicare's future and, 36
    morbidity rates and, 4
    of infants, 359
    population aging and, xxiv, xxv, xxvi
    women as caregivers and, 85-86
    See also Death and dying; Suicide
Mortgage, reverse, 169-170
Moses, A. M. (Grandma), 381
Moses, S., 73, 78-85
Moynihan, D. P., 233
Multidimensional functional assessment: an exami-
    nation of an elderly person's physical, mental,
    and social condition, including the ability to per-
    form activities of daily living, 22-23
Multigenerational living arrangements, 68, 88
Multiple jeopardy, 160-161, 192
Musicians, creativity of, 391, 401
Mutual funds, 171. *See also* Savings
Mutual self-help groups, 67
Myers, R. J., 239, 246-247, 250-257
Mystical experiences, 433, 434
Myths of aging, 311. *See also* Stereotypes

Natanson v. Kline, 129
National Committee to Preserve Social Security and
    Medicare, 176, 177
National Council of Senior Citizens, 176
National Council on Aging, 176, 221, 222, 303
National Crime Victimization Surveys, 102
National health care, 40
National identity, 162
National Institute of Mental Health, 435
National Institute on Aging, 326, 348
National Nursing Home Survey, 126
National Retired Teachers Association, 176
National School Volunteers Program, 221
Native Americans, 157, 160
Natural death, 361. *See also* Death and dying
Natural life span, 34, 36, 42, 47-48. *See also* Life
    span
Naturally occurring retirement community
    (NORC): apartment buildings or neighborhoods
    that have evolved over time so that more than
    half their residents are over age 65, 17, 223
Near-poor, 186-187, 198. *See also* Poverty
Needs-based benefits: services, such as home health
    care, provided to people according to some

assessment of their individual requirements
    rather than according to age or some other cate-
    gorical basis, 179. *See also* Entitlements, age
    versus need for
Neglect, 98-99, 117
    self-, 99, 114-117
    See also Elder abuse
Nelson, G., 217, 218
Netherlands, 338
Net worth, 169, 170. *See also* Assets
Neugarten, B., 44, 184
Neurotic difficulties, 425-426
New Age phenomena, 433
New paternalism, 104
New Zealand, 278
No-fault divorce, 165
NORC. *See* Naturally occurring retirement
    community
Normal aging: the underlying time-dependent bio-
    logical process of aging in each species, which
    may involve functional loss or susceptibility to
    disease but is not in itself a disease, 4, 326, 339
Norway, 87
Notch problem, 43-44
Nuclear family: the minimally sized family structure
    needed for reproducing one generation from
    another: that is, mother, father, and children, 68
Nursing homes:
    child care and, 221
    costs, Medicaid, and, 70, 71
    costs, placement, and, 25
    fear of, 20-21
    four percent fallacy and, 22
    insurance for care in, 82, 84, 88-90
    percent of population in, 17, 21-22
    quality of, 21
    types of, 20, 24(exhibit)
    See also Long-term care
Nutrition. *See* Diet

OAA. *See* Older Americans Act
OARS. *See* Older American Resources and Services
    questionnaire
OASDI. *See* Old-Age, Survivors, and Disability
    Insurance
Occupations:
    creativity in. *See* Creativity
    diversity and, 154
    life course and, 310, 321, 323
O'Conner case, 128
O'Conner, J., 207

Oedipus cycle, 312
Office of Inspector General (OIG), 79-81, 82, 83
Office of Older American Volunteer Programs, 274
OIG. *See* Office of Inspector General
Old age, meaning in. *See* Meaning, in old age
Old-Age, Survivors, and Disability Insurance
(OASDI), 208, 250-255. *See also* Social
Security
Older adult education, 405. *See also* Education;
Training
Older American Resources and Services (OARS)
questionnaire, 22-23
Older Americans Act (OAA): federal law that
authorized and funds direct services such as
senior centers, nutrition programs, and informa-
tion and referral, 155
aging network and, 174
class, race, and, 218, 219
diversity and, 155, 162
equity and, 179, 192
productive aging and, 274
Older Women's League (OWL), 159-160
Oldest-old: people aged 85 and over, 16, 17, 40, 155,
208
Old-old: people aged 75 to 84, 208, 334, 414
"One-Hoss Shay," 337, 361
Online databases, for research, 445
Ontario Longitudinal Study of Aging, 414
Oral history projects, 306
Oregon, 35, 78, 129, 139
Orfshanksky, M., 209
Organ reserve, 357-358
Osgood, N. J., 133, 276, 298-303
Osteoporosis, 8, 55, 102
Out-of-pocket medical expenses: cost of health care
paid by the individual and not reimbursed or
covered by insurance, 13, 209
Outpatient medical care, 24(exhibit)
OWL. *See* Older Women's League

Pacific Islanders, 160. *See also* Asian Americans
Pain, treatment for, 130
Palliative care, 130
Parenthood, changes in, 323-324
Parkinson's disease, 8, 344, 350
Part-time employment, 287
Passage, rites of, 314-315
Passionate life, 429
Passive euthanasia, 124. *See also* Euthanasia
Patient dumping, 14
Patient Self-Determination Act (PSDA), 27, 131

Pay-as-you-go system: an approach to paying for
Social Security in which workers today contribute money used to pay benefits for those now
retired; that is, current workers pay current
expenses rather than saving up for future bene-
fits, 233, 236
Payroll tax, for Social Security, 230-231, 232-233.
See also Taxation
PBGC. *See* Pension Benefit Guaranty Corporation
Pension Benefit Guaranty Corporation (PBGC), 167,
271
Pensions, 163, 166-168
economy, changes in, and, 270-271
legislation on, 167, 173
portability of, 167
types of plans for, 167
women and, 165-166
Periodicals, for research, 448-449
Perlin, S., 133
Perlmutter case, 129
Permissive consensus, 179
Perry, D., 44, 54-55
Personal care support service, 24(exhibit)
Personality, 386, 424-425, 434
Personal relationships:
quality of life and, 100
sexuality and, 100-102
Personal Social Security accounts. *See* Social Secu-
rity, privatization of
Peterson, P. G., 194, 195-197
Phased retirement: a practice whereby older work-
ers nearing retirement gradually instead of
abruptly reduce their work schedules, 271
Philadelphia Geriatric Center Morale Scale, 100
Physician-assisted dying, 138-139
Physician-assisted suicide, 129, 130
Physicians:
contract with patient, 141
elder abuse reporting by, 97, 99, 108-109
end-of-life decisions and, 126, 129, 130, 131, 136,
138-145
trust and, 143-144
Picasso, P., 387
Plasticity: the potential for retraining and learning
new skills, 275
Plato, 311
Poets, creativity of, 381, 391, 400
Police power, 107. *See also* Legal issues
Policy, public. *See* Public policy
Politics:
attitudes and, 177
economic condition and, 180

federal program support and, 178
risk, Social Security, and, 241, 242, 243, 244

Population aging: a rise in the average age of the population; alternatively, an increase in the proportion of the population made up of people over age 65, xxiii
    causes of, xxiii-xxvii
    coping with, xxvii-xxx
    diversity and, 152
    economics and, 152-153
    individual aging and, xxvii-xxx, 181
    statistics on, xxiii-xxiv, 157
Population pyramid, xxvi
Portability of benefits, 89, 167
Postindustrial society, 322-325, 418-419. *See also* Industrialization
Postmodern culture, 419, 420
Postponement of chronic illness, 356, 369. *See also* Compression of morbidity
Poverty:
    children and, 187-188, 202, 207-208, 214
    class, race, and, 217-219
    equity and, 179, 185-188
    measurement problems in, 208-209
    rate of, 161, 163, 179, 185, 202, 209, 231
    women and, 158, 161, 165, 179, 237
Powell, D. H., 387, 403-404
Power of attorney, 111
    durable, for health care, 129, 146
Preprogramming. *See* Programming
Preretirement planning, 303-305
Presidents of American colleges and universities, 392
Preston, S., 188, 207, 213
Prevention, semantics of, 356
Preventive care, 15, 90, 354, 356, 362
Primary aging, 4
Privacy, 99, 127
Private accounts, and Social Security. *See* Social Security, privatization of
Privatization. *See* Social Security, privatization of
Probate court, 104
Problem solving, 383. *See also* Intelligence
Productive aging, 273-275, 277-281, 324
    future scenario on, 305-306
    meaning and, 417-418
    obstacles to, 279-281
    See also Creativity; Meaning, in old age
Productivity:
    computer technology and, 407
    creativity and, 381, 385, 391-393, 398-402
    public policy and, 180
    retirement and, 263, 268, 269, 273

Social Security and, 240
Programming, in biology of aging, 344, 345-346, 368
Progressive tax, 193
Prospective payment system: a form of prospective pricing in which it is determined in advance what reimbursement level is paid to a provider of health service for treating Medicare patients, 14
Protection from vulnerability. *See* Vulnerability
Protective proceedings, 106-107. *See also* Legal issues
Protective services, 117-118
Proxy decision making, 306
PSDA. *See* Patient Self-Determination Act
Psychological functioning, 331-334
Psychological tasks, series of, 315
Psychology:
    of creativity, 381
    of intelligence, 382-383, 385, 386-387
    of interiority, 318
    of life transitions, 314-315
    of meaning, 417, 419, 424-428, 431, 432, 434-435
Ptolemy, 312
Public consensus approach, 384-385
Public policy, 172-180
    aging interest groups in, 175-177
    aging network in, 174
    equity and, 179
    productivity and, 180
    trends in, 177-180
    See also Entitlements, age versus need for; Generational equity; Medicaid; Medicare; Social Security
Public service employment programs, 274. *See also* Community service

Quality-adjusted life years (QALYs): the number of years of life remaining according to some measure of the quality of life of those years, 43
Quality of life:
    compression of morbidity and, 338, 355
    control over, 309-310
    end-of-life decisions and, 126, 132-139, 141-142
    gender and, 158
    generational interdependence and, 198
    vulnerability and, 96-97, 98, 99-100
Quinlan, K. A., 127, 130, 143
Quinn, M. J., 105, 110-114

Race and ethnicity, 153, 154, 155-157
    age segregation and, 225

citizenship, national identity, and, 162
generational equity and, 208, 211-212
meaning of ethnicity in, 162
multiple jeopardy and, 160-161
productivity and, 180
retirement income and, 164-165
suicide rates and, 29, 130
Rate of living concept: the idea that the level of metabolism and average length of life are statistically related to one another, 340. *See also* Metabolism
Rathbone-McCuan, E., 105, 114-117
Rational suicide, 133
Rationing of health care. *See* Health care rationing
RBRVS. *See* Resource Based Relative Value Scale
Real estate, 171. *See also* Home equity
Recollection, as adaptation, 423. *See also* Reminiscence
Recovery programs, for estates, 78, 79-80, 83
Rectangular curve, and compression of morbidity, 356-360, 361-362, 368, 369
Reference works, for research, 446-447
Reformation, the, 312
Regressive tax: a tax for which the burden is proportionately greater for the poor than for the rich; the opposite of a progressive tax, 230
Reimbursement systems, 12-15. *See also* Medicaid; Medicare
Relaxation techniques, 434, 435
Religion, 154, 156, 311
  leisure and, 413
  meaning and, 413, 414-416, 427, 428, 433
  well-being and, 416
  See also Spirituality
Rembrandt, 381, 421
Reminiscence, 431-433. *See also* Memories
Renaissance, the, 312
Rental housing, 19
Replacement rate: the proportion of salary during working years that Social Security pays beneficiaries, 230, 244
Reporting, of elder abuse, 97, 99, 108-109
Research, term paper. *See* Gerontology term paper research
Resentment hypothesis, 211-212
Reserve capacity: the ability of the body to recover from assaults and to withstand peak-load demands on organic systems, 327
Reserve, organ, 357-358
Residential separation, by age, 220, 222, 223-224, 225
Resource Based Relative Value Scale (RBRVS), 15

Resources, competition for, 191, 199-200. *See also* Generational equity
Respite care: temporary care for dependent older people to allow the caregiver some time off, 17, 67
Restraints, freedom from, 105-107
Retired Senior Volunteer Program (RSVP), 275
Retirement, 263-308
  average age of, 272
  busy ethic and, 290-297
  early, 166, 168, 173, 180, 266, 271, 272, 304, 318
  economy, changes in, and, 269-271, 298-299
  employment and, 278-289, 298
  history of, 264-268, 278-279, 285, 313
  labor force trends and, 264-265, 266, 272, 299
  learning in, 405
  leisure and, 266-269, 273, 293, 295, 299-302, 413
  length of, 266
  life course perspective on, 313, 321, 325
  mandatory, 271-272, 283
  moral continuity with work, 290-297
  new view of, 271-275
  phased, 271
  planning for, 303-305. *See also* Financial matters; Retirement income
  productive aging and, 273-275, 277-281, 305-306
  productivity and, 180, 263, 268, 269, 273
  stereotype of, 265, 268
  voluntary activities in. *See* Volunteering
  work-life extension and, 272-273
Retirement Advisors, Inc., 303
Retirement communities:
  age segregation and, 222, 223
  continuing care (CCRC), 17, 18
  leisure oriented, 17, 19. *See also* Leisure
  naturally occurring (NORC), 17, 223
Retirement income:
  assets as, 163, 164, 165, 168-170
  earnings from employment and, 164
  ERISA and, 167
  investment decisions on, 257-259
  pensions as, 163, 164, 165, 166-168
  savings as, 163, 168, 169
  Social Security as, 163, 164, 165, 166, 168, 230
  sources of, 163-170
  three-legged stool of, 163
  See also Economic status; Economic well-being; Financial matters; Income
Retirement Survivors Disability Health Insurance, 288
Retraining, 275. *See also* Training

Reverse mortgage: a contract in which a bank guarantees a monthly income to a home owner for the remainder of life and then claims ownership of the home upon the owner's death, 169-170

Rheumatism, 7-8, 19. *See also* Arthritis

Rights:
  economic, 284
  to die, 26, 27, 126-130, 143. *See also* End-of-life decisions
  to equal protection, 52, 143
  vulnerability and, 104, 105-107
  See also Constitutional issues; Legal issues

Riley, M. W., xxix, xxviii

Risk:
  compression of morbidity and, 365, 368
  end-of-life decisions and, 126
  investment decisions and, 257, 258, 259
  of mortality, 326
  Social Security and, 240-244, 246-247
  vulnerability and, 95-96, 97, 98-99

Risk aversiveness, 257, 258

Rites of passage: rituals that mark major life events, thereby reinforcing shared norms about age grading, 314-315

Roleless role, 28-29, 153, 263, 332

Role loss: the process of giving up or losing previous roles, such as the role of spouse (with widowhood) or the role of worker (with retirement), 28-29, 153, 263, 332

Roles, social. *See* Social roles

Romans, ancient, 311, 312

Rose, M., 349

Rosow, I., 28-29

RSVP. *See* Retired Senior Volunteer Program

Rucinski, J., 115

Ryff, C., 332

Sacrifice, 411

Safety, 98, 102-103. *See also* Self-neglect

SAGE. *See* Senior Actualization and Growth Explorations

Sandwich generation: those people, usually women, who have obligations to care for children as well as elderly parents or in-laws, 66

Satisfaction. *See* Life satisfaction

Sauvy, A., 379

Savings:
  by baby boomers, 171
  life cycle model of, 171, 259
  retirement income and, 163, 168, 169
  Social Security and, 240, 243

See also Economic status; Economic well-being; Financial matters; Income

Scams, 102-103. *See also* Financial matters, exploitation in

Scandinavia, 34

Scarce resources, competition for, 191, 199-200, 201. *See also* Generational equity

Scarcity, in economics, 40

Schachter-Shalomi, Z., 434

Schneider, E. L., 351, 360-363

Schneider, I., 77

Schopenhauer, A., 421

Schwartz, W. B., 45, 56-57

Scientific creativity, 385, 388-389, 390-391, 400

SCORE. *See* Service Corps of Retired Executives

Scott-Maxwell, F., 419-420, 429-431

SCSEP. *See* Senior Community Service Employment Program

SDAT. *See* Senile dementia of the Alzheimer's type

Seattle Longitudinal Study, 384, 386

Seattle (WA), 35

Secondary aging, 4

Section 202 and Section 8 housing programs: federal laws providing subsidies for housing the elderly, 19

Selective optimization, 334

Self-actualization, 299, 434

Self-concept, 331-333, 432. *See also* Ego integrity

Self-determination, 129, 131. *See also* End-of-life decisions

Self-determined death:
  late-life suicide and, 28-30
  overview of, 3, 26-30
  See also End-of-life decisions; Suicide

Self-governance, 110-111. *See also* Autonomy

Self-help groups, 67

Self-image. *See* Ego integrity; Self-concept

Self-neglect, 99, 114-117

Semelparity, 343-344

Senescence, 354. *See also* Aging, process of; Biology of aging

Senile dementia of the Alzheimer's type (SDAT), 9. *See also* Alzheimer's disease

Senior Actualization and Growth Explorations (SAGE), 434

Senior centers, 24(exhibit), 174

Senior Community Service Employment Program (SCSEP), 274

Senior Companions Program, 274

SeniorNet, 407

Service Corps of Retired Executives (SCORE), 306

SES. *See* Socioeconomic status

"Seven Ages of Man," 312

Sex ratio, 157. *See also* Gender issues

Sexuality, 98, 100-102, 104

Shakespeare, 312, 313, 318

Shared housing: an alternative housing arrangement involving group residence with shared common areas or renting of unused rooms, 17, 19

Shaw, P., 115

Sheltering of assets, 80-81. *See also* Assets

Silver-Haired Legislatures, 176

Simonton, D. K., 387, 398-402

Singapore, 69

Skilled nursing facilities, 20, 24(exhibit). *See also* Nursing homes

Social breakdown syndrome, 115

Social class, 52, 153, 154-155, 216-219

    life course and, 310, 320-321

    See also Race and ethnicity

Social clock: the shared set of expectations about what behavior is proper or "on time" for any specific chronological age, 310

Social dimension, importance of, 23

Social gerontology, and meaning, 417-418

Social issues:

    diversity in. *See* Diversity

    economics and. *See* Economic status; Economic well-being; Socioeconomic status

    policy on. *See* Public policy

Social relationships, 331-333

Social roles:

    activity theory and, 319

    age identification and, 310-312

    employment and, 282-289, 412

    gender and, 158

    meaning and, 412, 423-425, 429

    productive aging and, 277-278, 324

    retirement and, 263, 273-275, 296

    self-concept and, 331, 332

    stages of life and, 313

    technological progress and, 316

Social Security:

    aging interest groups and, 176

    as public policy, 173

    as retirement income, 163, 164, 165, 166, 168, 230

    as scapegoat, 213

    average benefits from, 229

    baby boomers and, 229, 233

    changes in, 178-179

    disability insurance and, 230

    eligibility for, 166, 178, 229, 233, 234-235

    equity, adequacy, and, 166, 169, 237, 238, 250-251

    equity, gender, and, 247-257

    fairness of, 232-234

    future of, 229-262

    gender and, 237-239, 247-257

    generational equity and, 185, 190, 210

    generational interdependence and, 204-205

    growth of, 178

    inflation and, 168, 171, 180, 231, 234

    IRAs and, 232, 243, 288

    labor force participation and, 286-287

    limitations of, xxviii

    poverty rate and, 231

    privatization of. *See* Social Security, privatization of

    purpose of, 231-232, 268

    replacement rate and, 230-231

    risk and, 240-244, 246-247

    success of, 231, 260

    taxes for, 230-231, 232-233, 236

    trust funds for, 232-233, 244-247

    universality and, 163

    women and. *See* Social Security, and women

Social Security, and women:

    caregiving responsibilities and, 237, 238, 255-256

    child care dropout option in, 238, 255-256

    divorce and, 238, 247, 255

    double-decker system in, 238, 249, 253, 254-255

    dual entitlement in, 238

    earnings sharing in, 239, 248-249, 253, 254

    feminist perspective on, 247-250

    gender equity and, 250-257

    homemakers and, 247-250, 253, 254, 255-256

    married couples and, 238, 239, 247, 248-249, 253-254, 255

    one- versus two-earner families and, 247, 252-253

    spousal benefits and, 238, 247

Social Security, privatization of, 235-237

    equity, adequacy, and, 237

    individual private accounts and, 236-237, 240-244

    trust fund investments and, 244-247

Social Security Act, 173, 176, 230

    1939 expansion, 173

    1956 changes, 173

    1983 amendments, 178, 230, 232

    1993 revision, 231

Social Security surplus: the excess of Social Security payroll taxes collected over the amount paid out, including excess funds accumulated from prior years, 233

Social security systems, first, 278

Socioeconomic status (SES): the position of people within a system of stratification of social class, reflecting inequality of wealth, power, and prestige, 192-193, 320

Socrates, 380

Somatic mutation theory of aging: the biological theory that aging results from damage to the genetic integrity of the body's cells, 342

Sophocles, 312

Soylent Green, 61

Spenddown. *See* Medicaid spenddown

Spirituality, 414-417, 430, 433-435. *See also* Religion

Spiritual well-being: a measure of the role of religion in its positive impact on individual mental health, 417

Spousal benefits, 238, 247

Spousal impoverishment, 81-82

Spousal responsibility: a legal requirement that a spouse pay for the medical or long-term care expenses of a married partner, 65, 68

SSI. *See* Supplemental Security Income

Stages:
    in theory of dying, 30
    of faith, 416-417
    of life. *See* Life stages

Stagnation, and generativity, 315

Star Trek: First Contact, 374

Starvation, 126

State Agencies on Aging, 174

Statistics, for research, 445-446

Stereotypes:
    ageism as, 153
    of abandonment, 67
    of activities, 412-413
    of adaptation, 380
    of affluence, 172, 187, 206
    of age appropriateness, 309
    of age as great leveler, 152
    of age identification, 311
    of boredom, 380
    of creativity, 379-380, 398
    of fear of crime, 102
    of feeblemindedness, 334
    of frailty, 4, 331
    of isolation, 68
    of learning, 379
    of neuron loss, 333
    of retirement, 265, 268
    of self-neglect, 115
    of serenity, 421
    of sexuality, 100, 331
    of voting block, 206

Sterling, B., 60, 375

Stevens, L., 132, 134-135

Stocks:
    investment decisions and, 258, 259
    Social Security and, 235-236, 240-242, 243, 244-247

Stratification, 192, 310

Strauss, P. J., 73-75

Stress, coping with, 321, 416

Stroke, 6, 9, 344

Struldbruggs, 1-2

Subgroups. *See* Diversity

Subjective well-being, 99-100. *See also* Quality of life

Subsidized housing, 19. *See also* Housing

Subsidized jobs, 274. *See also* Labor force participation; Work

Substituted judgment: making health care decisions for an incapacitated other person based on an effort to determine what that person would want under the circumstances at hand, 127, 128

Successful aging, 331

Suicide:
    assisted, 44, 50, 129-131, 139. *See also* Physician-assisted dying
    end-of-life decisions and, 124-126, 129-135
    predictors of, 124
    rates of, 29, 125, 130, 132-134
    types of, 28-29, 133
    See also Self-determined death

Suicide clinics, 148-149

Sun City, Arizona, 222-223

Super IRA, 232

Superwoman squeeze, 87

Supplemental Security Income (SSI): a federal benefit program that provides at least a minimum income level to low-income people who are aged, blind, or disabled, 156, 187, 235

Support ratio. *See* Dependency ratio

Support systems, 23-24, 67
    aging network as, 174
    race, ethnicity, and, 156, 157

Survival curves, 356-360, 361-362, 368, 369

Sweden, 101, 278

Swift, J., 1-2, 51, 61

Switzerland, 34

Taft, L., 390

Tandy, J., 387

Targets of benefits, 191-220
    age as basis for, 197-210
    interdependence and, 197-210